The Use of Artificial Intelligence in the Public Sector in Shanghai

Diego Todaro

The Use of Artificial Intelligence in the Public Sector in Shanghai

Ambition, Capacity and Reality

palgrave
macmillan

Diego Todaro
Ca' Foscari University of Venice
Venice, Italy

ISBN 978-981-97-0596-2 ISBN 978-981-97-0597-9 (eBook)
https://doi.org/10.1007/978-981-97-0597-9

This Palgrave Macmillan imprint is published by the registered company Springer Nature Singapore Pte Ltd.
The registered company address is: 152 Beach Road, #21-01/04 Gateway East, Singapore 189721, Singapore

Paper in this product is recyclable.

For my wife, Wenjia, and our daughters, Emma and Lara.
You are the most beautiful "AI" (艾) in the world.

Acknowledgments

This book is the result of a Ph.D. research that would have not started without the encouragement and advice I received from Dr. Alessandro Arduino and Prof. Renzo Cavalieri, who supported me since the very beginning and continued to provide valuable comments until the final draft of this work, either as friends or Supervisors. I am also very grateful to Prof. Laura De Giorgi for her feedback and suggestions on the research proposal, and to Prof. Dr. Anja-Désirée Senz for guiding my work from Heidelberg.

My sister Martina Todaro had the patience and kindness to constantly offer useful suggestions to improve my writing, from the draft of the research proposal to the refinements of this book, and provided useful and timely inputs on specific chapters. I am also very grateful to my parents Giampaolo Todaro and Rosanna Lodi for their support during the months that led to the submission of this work.

Many friends and colleagues provided information, pointers, and comments that greatly helped me to improve this work. I am particularly thankful to five people. Dr. Gao Feng provided a wealth of insights into many aspects related to the use of AI in the public sector in Shanghai, and helped me to refine some considerations that I developed in this book. Director Lu Yong guided me through the regulations and initiatives for the promotion of public and private data sharing in Shanghai, improving my understanding of how data are used to enable public sector AI applications in the municipality. Director Qiu Tianle explained to me the intricacies of the Government Online-Offline Shanghai and the Single Platform for Urban Management. And Prof. Li Yihai and Dr. Fan Huihui provided valuable information to position this research in the context of Shanghai politics and society, and assisted me during the fieldwork. I am very grateful to all for your guidance and support.

Contents

Acronyms, Abbreviations, and Currencies

AI	Artificial Intelligence
AI Highland Plan	*Action Plan on Building Shanghai into an AI Highland and Creating a First-Class Innovation Ecosystem (2019–2021)*
AIDP	*New Generation Artificial Intelligence Development Plan*
AR	Augmented reality
CPC	Communist Party of China
DL	Deep learning
EUR	Euro
GOS	Government Online-Offline Shanghai
ML	Machine learning
NLP	Natural Language Processing
OCR	Optical character recognition
Opinions	*Implementation Opinions on Promoting the Development of a New Generation Artificial Intelligence in Shanghai*
RMB	Chinese yuan
SAIA	Shanghai Artificial Intelligence Industry Association
SBDC	Shanghai Municipal Big Data Center
SHEITC	Shanghai Municipal Commission of Economy and Informatization
SPM	Single Platform for Urban Management
SUOC	Shanghai Urban Operation Management Center
USD	US dollar
VR	Virtual reality

List of Figures

List of Boxes

List of Tables

CHAPTER 1

Approaching China's "Artificial Intelligence Development Highland"

Shanghai has set ambitious targets for the development of artificial intelligence (AI) in the municipality. In October 2017, the Shanghai government published the *Implementation Opinions on Promoting the Development of a New Generation Artificial Intelligence in Shanghai*. This programmatic document states that Shanghai will become a "national AI development highland" (国家人工智能发展高地), that is "China's leading source of AI innovation, demonstration site for applications, industry cluster and talent highland, reaching the world's most advanced levels in some fields[1]". In this context, Shanghai elevates the use of AI in the public sector to a priority of its AI plans, saying that it will "accelerate the in-depth application of AI in the key areas of […] urban governance and public services, improving […] public service capabilities and citizens' sense of gain[2]". To achieve these goals for AI in the public sector, the *Opinions* lay out a well-elaborated set of tasks that call for fostering the use of AI to improve city operations (e.g., public

[1] Shanghai Municipal Government, 2017. *Opinions* (cit. in Chapter 3.2), section 2, preamble. In original: "成为全国领先的人工智能创新策源地、应用示范地、产业集聚地和人才高地, 局部领域达到全球先进水平".

[2] Ibid., section 2, par. 2. In original: "加快人工智能在 […] 城市治理和公共服务重点领域的深度应用, 提升 […] 公共服务能力和市民获得感".

D. Todaro, *The Use of Artificial Intelligence in the Public Sector in Shanghai*, https://doi.org/10.1007/978-981-97-0597-9_1

security, environmental monitoring), public service delivery (e.g., administrative services, judiciary, education), transport and shipping (e.g., urban traffic), and medicine and healthcare (i.e., medical care, elderly care, public health prevention and control). In September 2019, Shanghai published another programmatic document for AI development, the *Action Plan on Building Shanghai into an AI Highland and Creating a First-Class Innovation Ecosystem (2019–2021)*. The *AI Highland Action Plan* reiterates the goals for AI in the public sector set by the *Opinions*, stating that Shanghai will encourage innovative AI applications aimed at ensuring high-quality life for its citizens and efficient urban operations.[3] Consistently, it requires that relevant government agencies and public institutions intensify the use of AI in medicine, education, urban management, government services, smart public security, and transportation, among others.

The determination of Shanghai to improve public service provision and the life of citizens by accelerating AI uptake in the public sector is best understood in light of the Chinese government's well-established approach that leverages technology to pursue national policy priorities. This approach is characterized by three intertwined features: (i) a techno-utilitarian vision that considers technology a valuable tool to promote national development in various policy areas; (ii) the use of quantitative techniques and technological tools to improve the management and control of society; and (iii) the digitalization of government activities to enhance the efficiency and effectiveness of public governance.[4] While these features are not specific to artificial intelligence, they provide useful insights to contextualize the approach of China and Shanghai to the use of AI in the public sector.

First is a **techno-utilitarian vision** that considers technology a useful tool to foster national development in various policy areas. In the first decades of the People's Republic of China, the focus on technological advancements was primarily aimed at fostering the modernization of the national defense industry. With the start of the reforms and opening-up

[3] SHEITC, 2019, *AI Highland Plan* (cit. in Chapter 3.2), section 3, subsection 4. In original: "充分发挥本市应用场景丰富优势, 鼓励全球人工智能最新成果在上海率先 "试水", 聚焦 [...] 市民高品质生活、城市高效率运行, 打造一批面向全球的创新应用".

[4] Defined here as "a government's ability to make and enforce rules, and to deliver services, regardless of whether that government is democratic or not" (Fukuyama, 2013, p. 350).

policies in the late 1970s, science and technology were officially integrated into the broader political discourse and masterplans of the Communist Party of China (CPC). This shift is condensed in Deng Xiaoping's landmark program of the "four modernizations" in agriculture, industry, science and technology, and defense.[5] Since then, the Chinese authorities have stressed the importance of science and technology to create economic growth and promote national development. In the first period of the reforms, technology was primarily considered a conduit to jump-start the productivity of the Chinese industrial sector and spur economic development. Today, economic growth arguably remains the primary driver for the Chinese government's adoption of advanced technologies like AI (Zeng, 2021). However, since the early 2000s, the negative externalities (e.g., environmental pollution, growing inequalities) generated by two decades of rapid industrial and economic progress have induced the Chinese leadership to leverage technology to address a wider range of socioeconomic issues.[6] Nowadays, technological innovation remains at the core of the Chinese government's efforts to restructure and transform the economy, and solve other grand challenges that China knows it faces.[7]

The breadth of the Chinese government's techno-utilitarian vision is documented by various national master plans and programmatic documents. In 2015, the plan *Made in China 2025* outlined a strategy for the digital and technological advancement of the Chinese industry. In the same year, the *"Internet Plus" Action Plan* vowed to integrate cloud computing, Big Data, and Internet of Things[8] in industry and the real

[5] The "four modernizations" (四个现代化) were introduced as early as 1954 by Premier Zhou Enlai. However, they were integrated into the activities of the CPC and the government only under the leadership of Deng. See: Government of the People's Republic of China, 2009. The Proposal of the Great Target of the Four Modernizations [四个现代化宏伟目标的提出]. *Government of the People's Republic of China* [中华人民共和国中央人民政府], 16 September, http://www.gov.cn/jrzg/2009-09/16/content_1418909.htm.

[6] Coisson, R., 2016. Development and Critical Factors in Chinese Research [Sviluppo e fattori di criticità della ricerca cinese]. *orizzonteCina*, 7(5), pp. 4–6.

[7] Xi, J., 2017. Build China into a World Leader in Science and Technology. In: Xi, J., 2017. *The Governance of China*. Beijing: Foreign Language Press, vol. 2, pp. 292–303.

[8] Cloud computing indicates systems that allow data to be processed and stored on the network on remote hardware. Big Data are datasets that require processing through databases and specialized technologies due to their volume and complexity. Internet of Things refers to devices connected to the Internet, and capable of communicating with

economy (Appendix III). The *"Internet Plus" Action Plan* is also at the center of various national initiatives that rely on digital technologies to promote advances in other policy areas. For instance, the Internet Plus healthcare initiative[9] has accelerated the efforts to use digital technologies to improve the quality of health services delivered across the country, and it is now considered an indispensable part of China's medical care system.[10] In education, various "Internet plus education" models aim at leveraging Internet, information technology, cloud platforms, and other digital technologies to share high-quality educational resources and ensure equitable access to education.[11] The importance of technology for China's socioeconomic development was reiterated by the *14th Five-Year Plan for Economic and Social Development* (2021–2025), which calls for leveraging technological innovation in order to "basically complete socialist modernization" by 2035. The 14th Five-Year Plan aims to foster applications of digital and smart solutions in the economy, governance, and the social sector. This focus is not new, but the contents and organization of the document indicate that increased priority is given to innovation and technology.[12]

The *New Generation Artificial Intelligence Development Plan*, China's national AI strategy, continues this longstanding techno-utilitarian tradition. It emphasizes that AI will be used to "promote the overall elevation of [China's] competitiveness and leapfrog development", and it articulates the Chinese government's intention to leverage AI to promote economic

the network and between each other (these definitions are expanded in Chapters 4.2 and 5.2).

[9] Yang, F., Shu, H. and Zhang, X., 2021. Understanding "Internet Plus Healthcare" in China: Policy Text Analysis. *Journal of Medical Internet Research*, 23(7), https://www.ncbi.nlm.nih.gov/pmc/articles/PMC8367124/.

[10] State Council News, 2018. Nation to promote Internet Plus healthcare. *State Council*, 12 April, http://english.www.gov.cn/premier/news/2018/04/12/content_281476109872514.htm; Xinhua, 2021. Over 1,600 internet hospitals established in China. *Xinhua Net*, 20 August, http://www.xinhuanet.com/english/2021-08/20/c_1310139614.htm.

[11] Xinhua, 2020. Short Story of Internet Education [“极简” 互联网教育史]. *Xinhua Net* [新华网], 4 August, http://www.xinhuanet.com/politics/2020-08/04/c_1126323902.htm.

[12] Grünberg, N. and Brussee, V., 2021. China's 14th Five-Year Plan—Strengthening the Domestic Base to Become a Superpower. *MERICS*, 9 April, https://merics.org/en/short-analysis/chinas-14th-five-year-plan-strengthening-domestic-base-become-superpower.

growth, enhance social governance and control, spur technological development in various fields, and improve national security (Chapter 3.1). Shanghai's municipal AI plans also indicate that Shanghai will use AI to foster advances in various areas. As noted, Shanghai states that it will leverage AI technologies to optimize city operations, improve the quality and efficiency of public services, improve transportation and shipping efficiency, and promote the accuracy and inclusiveness of medicine and healthcare. Shanghai will also leverage AI to promote the transformation and upgrading of the local manufacturing industry, spur financial and business innovation in the municipality,[13] and "enhance the city's capabilities and core competitiveness[14]" (Chapter 3.2).

A second feature of the Chinese government approach to technology is **the use of quantitative techniques and technological tools to enhance the management and control of society**. The idea that such techniques and tools are a valuable means to improve social governance[15] started to form in China in the 1970s, when the implementation of the economic reforms made it necessary to rebuild the State apparatus demolished during the turmoil of the Great Proletarian Cultural Revolution (1966–1976). In this reconstruction process, the Chinese leadership found useful support in the systems theory, an interdisciplinary research field initiated in the 1950s in Europe and the United States, which studies the common properties of physical and social systems with the aim of controlling their

[13] Shanghai Municipal Government, 2017. *Opinions* (cit.), section 2.

[14] SHEITC, 2019. *AI Highland Plan* (cit.), preamble. In original: "加快发展新一代人工智能 [...] 是上海面向全球、面向未来, 提升城市能级和核心竞争力的重要布局".

[15] In the current Chinese governance architecture, social governance (社会治理) is "a systematic project under the leadership of the CPC Central Committee to safeguard the social harmony and stability by coordinating with all parties in the society" (Liu, L., 2018. Social Governance in China: The Role of Government and Transformation of Government Functions. *Development Research Center of the State Council* [国务院发展研究中心], Research Report, No.85, 15 May, http://en.drc.gov.cn/2018-07/18/content_36598955.htm). It means that the government manages and regulates social affairs (社会事务), social organizations (社会组织), and social life (社会生活) to mitigate the threat of social conflicts and safeguarding social order and stability. The connotation of social governance is very broad, and it includes areas such as public security, social stability, social trust, the coordination of various social interests, food safety, emergency management, city management, and community governance (Yu, K., 2011. A Shift Towards Social Governance in China. *East Asia Forum Quarterly*, 3(2), pp. 28–29, https://www.eastasiaforum.org/2011/09/09/a-shift-towards-social-governance-in-china/).

behavior.[16] Systems theory was introduced in China by the aerospace engineer Qian Xuesen (1911–2009), one of the fathers of the Chinese nuclear and missile programs. In the view of Qian and his followers, society is a "gigantic open and complex system[17]" consisting of millions of interrelated subsystems (i.e., the individuals that make up society). This complex system is conditioned by objective laws (规律), in the same way as the natural world. These laws are intelligible, and they can be used to manipulate society by resorting to quantitative techniques and technological tools to obtain the desired results. In this regard, Qian proposed to apply engineering methods to social governance, so that order in the Chinese society could be predicted and controlled.

Consistently with this systemic approach, the Chinese government has often relied on technology and quantitative methods to manage various aspects of the life of its citizens. One famous example is China's one-child policy, introduced in 1980 also on the basis of demographic projections made by rocket engineer Song Jian, a protégé of Qian Xuesen.[18] A more recent example is the Social Credit System, which aims to create a cybernetic mechanism of awards and penalties that should steer the behavior of Chinese individuals, companies, and government agencies, in order to ensure the implementation, enforcement, and compliance of laws and regulations and enhance trust in society, economy, and public administration.[19] Systems theory continues to influence the Chinese government's approach to the management and control of society. For

[16] General systems theory formally originated in the 1940s in the work of the Austrian biologist Ludwig von Bertalanffy, although there are references to it as far back as the 1930s. This theory was furthered by various researchers and practitioners, and it found applications across many disciplines, from sociology to computer science, engineering, political science, cybernetics, etc. See: https://link.springer.com/referenceworkentry/10.1007%2F978-0-387-79061-9_941.

[17] Qian, X., Yu, J. and Dai, R, 1993. A New Discipline of Science—The Study of Open Complex Giant System and Its Methodology. *Chinese Journal of Systems Engineering and Electronics*, 4(2), pp. 2–12, https://ieeexplore.ieee.org/document/6073209.

[18] Greenhalgh, S., 2008. *Just One Child: Science and Policy in Deng's China*. Berkeley: University of California Press.

[19] Creemers, R., 2018. China's Social Credit System: An Evolving Practice of Control, http://dx.doi.org/10.2139/ssrn.3175792. See also: Drinhausen, K. and Brussee, V., 2021. China's Social Credit System in 2021. From fragmentation towards integration. *MERICS China Monitor*, https://merics.org/en/report/chinas-social-credit-system-2021-fragmentation-towards-integration.

instance, the fourth Plenum of the 19th Party Congress in 2019 reiterated the need to accelerate the modernization of social governance by leveraging artificial intelligence, Big Data, cloud computing, and other advanced technologies.[20]

The *New Generation Artificial Intelligence Development Plan* reflects this systemic approach, calling for the use of technological tools to improve social management and control. It aims to "promote the intelligentization of social governance[21]" by leveraging AI to enhance government's management capabilities in various areas, and increase the level of trust within the Chinese society.[22] This "systems-based view of AI development [...] not only reflects how society as a whole is seen as a complex system amenable to intervention, [...] it also clearly indicates the engineering-type solutions that AI technologies are envisaged to generate" (Creemers, 2020, p. 65). Shanghai's plans for AI development also emphasize the use of AI in social governance, stating that the municipality will deploy this technology to achieve the "refined governance of society[23]" (社会精细化治理). For instance, Shanghai will promote the comprehensive application of AI to monitor people's flows and provide early warnings to enhance its intelligent prevention and control capabilities,[24] and it will use AI to support public demand forecasting and public opinion analysis.[25] These and similar applications are examined in the analysis of the case studies (Chapters 5.2 and 5.3).

A third feature of the Chinese government approach to technology is the **digitalization of government activities to enhance the efficiency and effectiveness of public governance**. This feature is linked to China's

[20] Xinhua, 2020. Accelerate the promotion of modernization of social governance in urban areas [加快推进市域社会治理现代化]. *Xinhua Net* [新华网], 21 July, http://www.xinhuanet.com/politics/2020-07/21/c_1126264487.htm.

[21] State Council, 2017. *New Generation Artificial Intelligence Development Plan* (cit.), Section III, Focus Task 3, "Construct a safe and convenient intelligent society", par. 2 "Promote the intelligentization of social governance" (推进社会治理智能化). In original: "围绕 [...] 社会治理的热点难点问题, 促进人工智能技术应用".

[22] Ibid., Section III, Focus Task 3, "Construct a safe and convenient intelligent society", par. 4 "Promote social interaction and mutual trust" (促进社会交往共享互信).

[23] Shanghai Municipal Government, 2017. *Opinions* (cit.), section 2, preamble.

[24] Ibid., section 2, par. 2.3, "Strengthen intelligent perception and optimize comprehensive city operations" (强化智能感知优化城市综合运行).

[25] Ibid., Section 2, par. 2.4, "Strengthen decision-making assistance to improve the quality and efficiency of public services" (强化决策辅助促进公共服务提质增效).

techno-utilitarian vision and its systemic approach to social governance, and it focuses on areas where the Chinese authorities believe they can obtain their desired policy outcomes more efficiently and effectively with the aid of digital tools. Deep digital integration became possible following the diffusion of computers, the Internet, and other digital technologies in China. Examples of deep digital integration are found in urban management. Since the early 2010s, China's push to develop smart cities has led to the embedment of information and communication technologies in the urban texture, with the aim to improve the efficiency of urban operations (Han, 2020; Pan et al., 2016). In the judiciary, the launch of the "Internet courts" (互联网法院) project by the Supreme People's Court in 2017 has led to the progressive integration of digital technologies, including artificial intelligence, in the activities of Chinese tribunals. In public health, since the start of the Covid-19 pandemic in early 2020, various local versions of the healthcare QR code (健康码) were introduced nationwide to track the movement of the population and help contain the spread of the epidemic, and later became embedded in the life of Chinese citizens who had to show their QR codes to access public places or take public transport, among others. The aforementioned Social Credit System is an example of deep digital integration in social governance that aims to steer individuals, companies, and government agencies toward desirable behaviors identified by the relevant authorities. Well-known examples of digital integration in government activities can also be found in public security. For instance, the video surveillance system Skynet (天网), launched in 2005 and now present in most Chinese urban areas, allows real-time security monitoring through millions of security cameras.[26] Skynet is compounded by the rural surveillance program known as Sharp Eyes (雪亮), which serves to offload work from potentially understaffed police departments in remote and rural towns.[27]

[26] Shen, X., 2018. "Skynet", China's Massive Video Surveillance Network. *South China Morning Post*, 4 October, https://www.scmp.com/abacus/who-what/what/article/3028246/skynet-chinas-massive-video-surveillance-network. In 2015 the National Development and Reform Commission mandated that video surveillance covers 100% of China's public areas and key industries by 2020.

[27] Liu, C., 2018. Villages Gain Public Security Systems. *Global Times*, 2 April, https://www.globaltimes.cn/content/1096361.shtml. Information on the Sharp Eyes program

The penetration of digital technologies in government activities is expected to continue and further expand with the roll-out of China's AI strategy. In fact, the *New Generation Artificial Intelligence Development Plan* calls for "increasing the level of intelligentization of the whole society to form an all-encompassing and ubiquitous intelligent environment[28]". This message has been received by the Shanghai leadership, and the municipality provides ample evidence of the in-depth digitalization of government activities that is made possible by artificial intelligence and other advanced technologies like Big Data and Internet of Things. In particular, the analysis of the case studies shows that Shanghai is making extensive use of AI and advanced technologies in administrative service provision (Chapter 5.2.1), urban management services (Chapter 5.2.2), and public service delivery in various policy areas ranging from education to healthcare and the judiciary (Chapter 5.3).

The deployment of artificial intelligence in the public sector in Shanghai fits well with an established national approach that leverages technology to pursue government policy priorities. At the same time, the determination of Shanghai to improve public service provision and the life of citizens by accelerating AI uptake in the public sector can also be understood in light of the technological potential of artificial intelligence. Indeed, there are great expectations for what this technology can do for public organizations in terms of increasing efficiency and effectiveness, optimizing resource allocation, and enhancing decision-making capabilities (Chapter 2.2). This potential is very appealing to the leadership of one of the most populated and busiest cities in the world. In 2021, the municipality had a resident population of approximately 24,8 million people,[29] bigger than the majority of European countries (only Germany, the United Kingdom, France, Italy, Spain, and Poland have more citizens). With an extension of over 6,300 Km^2,

updated at March 2021 can be found in: Sohu, 2021. 2020 "Sharp Eyes Project" development situation and foundational features [2020年 "雪亮工程" 发展状况及建设特点]. *Sohu* [搜狐], 11 March, https://www.sohu.com/a/455282031_120058586.

28 State Council, 2017. *New Generation Artificial Intelligence Development Plan* (cit.), chapter III, Focus Task 3, "Establish a safe and convenient intelligent society". In original: "形成无时不有、无处不在的智能化环境, 全社会的智能化水平大幅提升".

29 Shanghai Municipal Bureau of Statistics, 2022. Shanghai Economic and Social Development Statistical Report 2021 [2021年上海市国民经济和社会发展统计公报]. *Shanghai Bureau of Statistics* [上海市统计局], 15 March, https://tjj.sh.gov.cn/tjgb/20220314/e0dcefec098c47a8b345c996081b5c94.html.

Shanghai is more than double the size of Luxembourg and seven times the size of Berlin. Shanghai is the largest urban economy in China, and in 2021 its GDP reached RMB 4.32 trillion[30] (approx. 617.35 billion Euro, greater than Austria), confirming Shanghai's economic leadership in the country.[31] Shanghai is also the major destination for foreign direct investment (FDI) and the most important financial center in terms of comprehensive competitiveness and market scale[32] in China, as well as the site of the earliest free trade zone in the country. In 2022 the municipality hosted the largest container port[33] and the third-busiest airport by cargo volumes[34] globally, and the longest operating subway system in the world.[35] The rising expectations of Shanghai's increasingly wealthy,[36] educated,[37] and elderly[38] population are likely to increase demand for

[30] Ibid.

[31] Tencent Net, 2022. The top 100 cities in mainland China by GDP in 2021 are released! [2021年中国内地GDP百强城市出炉!]. *Tencent Net* [腾讯网], 25 February, https://new.qq.com/omn/20220225/20220225A04Z2K00.html.

[32] SHFDI, 2021, p. 3. Shanghai is also home to China's largest, independently operated stock exchange ahead of the one in Shenzhen (European Chamber of Commerce in China, 2020. *European Business in China—Shanghai Position Paper 2020/2021*. Shanghai: European Chamber of Commerce in China, https://www.europeanchamber.com.cn/en/publications-local-position-paper).

[33] Statista, 2022. The largest container ports worldwide in 2021, based on throughput. *Statista*, 28 February, https://www.statista.com/statistics/264171/turnover-volume-of-the-largest-container-ports-worldwide/.

[34] Airports Council International, 2022. The top 10 busiest airports in the world revealed. *Airports Council International*, 11 April, https://aci.aero/2022/04/11/the-top-10-busiest-airports-in-the-world-revealed/.

[35] Shanghai Fabu, 2022. These rail transit lines in Shanghai run in the "air"! Is there anyone that you often take? [上海这些轨道交通线路行驶在"空中"!有你常乘坐的吗?]. *Shanghai Fabu* [上海发布], 15 August, https://mp.weixin.qq.com/s/EqKM4uE7n3NJcr2R4aTQAw.

[36] In 2021, the nominal GDP per capita was approximately 24,890 Euro. The per capita disposable income reached approximately 11,150 Euro, an 8% increase compared to the previous year (Shanghai Municipal Bureau of Statistics, 2022, cit.).

[37] In 2020, more than 33,870 people every 100,000 residents had a university degree or above, compared to 21,890 in 2010. See: The Paper, 2021. The main data of the seventh national census in Shanghai have been announced, understand them in one picture [上海市第七次全国人口普查主要数据情况公布, 一图读懂]. *The Paper* [澎湃新闻], 18 May, https://m.thepaper.cn/baijiahao_12735772.

[38] In 2021, average life expectancy in Shanghai was 84.1 years (Shanghai Municipal Bureau of Statistics, 2022). In 2020, 23.4% of the Shanghai residents was aged 60 or

public services. At the same time, the municipality is striving to "continuously improve its urban capacities, core competitiveness and governance as a modern socialist metropolis of international influence", as requested by Chinese President Xi Jinping[39] and reiterated by the local authorities.[40] In this context, it is perhaps not surprising that the Shanghai leadership considers AI—a general-purpose technology increasingly used to perform numerous tasks in many sectors (Palayes et al., 2020)—a valuable tool to improve its governance capabilities and provide better services to its citizens.

To contextualize the analysis developed in this book and especially the examination of the case studies, it is also useful to outline the administrative divisions of Shanghai and the organizational structure of the municipal government. Shanghai is a municipality directly under the central government (直辖市), meaning that it has the same political and jurisdictional rights as a province, the second-highest administrative level in China after the national government. The Shanghai municipality

above, compared to 15.1% in 2010 (The Paper, 2021. The main data of the seventh national census in Shanghai have been announced, cit.).

[39] CPC News, 2019. Xi Jinping: In-depth study and implementation of the spirit of the Fourth Plenary Session of the 19th CPC Central Committee to improve the governance capacity and level of a socialist, modern international metropolis [习近平: 深入学习贯彻党的十九届四中全会精神 提高社会主义现代化国际大都市治理能力和水平]. *CPC News* [中国共产党新闻网], 4 November, http://dangjian.people.com.cn/n1/2019/1104/c117092-31435292.html. In original: "着力提升城市能级和核心竞争力, 不断提高社会主义现代化国际大都市治理能力和治理水平".

[40] Yang, M., 2022. Party secretary outlines vision of city's future. *SHINE*, 25 June, https://www.shine.cn/news/metro/2206257193/. The vision of Shanghai as "a socialist, modern international metropolis with global influence" (具有世界影响力的社会主义现代化国际大都市) includes several components. Some are primarily economic, and overlap with initiatives like the "four major functions" (四大功能) that aim to make Shanghai an international hub for allocating global resources, nurturing sci-tech innovations, supporting high-end industries, and acting as a "gateway to the world". Other components of this vision focus on public services and governance. For instance, Shanghai aims to make the city more "people-oriented" and improve social governance, public services, people's livelihood, as well as a balanced development between urban and rural areas and between humans and nature. See for instance: Shanghai Observer, 2022. Building a socialist modern international metropolis with world influence requires the joint efforts of "a carriage drawn by three horses" [建设具有世界影响力的社会主义现代化国际大都市, 需要 "三驾马车" 共同发力]. *Shanghai Observer* [上观], 4 July, https://export.shobserver.com/baijiahao/html/503849.html.

is administratively subdivided into 16 districts.[41] Their extension varies widely: from more than 1,000 Km^2 (e.g., Pudong New Area and Chongming District) to less than 60 Km^2 (e.g., the districts of Putuo, Xuhui, Changning, Jing'an, or Huangpu). Their populations also display significant variations: from 5.6 million residents in Pudong New Area, to approximately 1.2 million in Putuo, Yangpu, and Qingpu districts, to less than 700,000 residents in Huangpu and Changning districts.[42] Below the districts, there are 215 township-level divisions (乡级行政区) that include 107 subdistricts (街道), 106 towns (镇), and two townships[43] (乡). The difference between these township-level units is that subdistricts are located in Shanghai's urban area, while towns and townships are often located in less urbanized, more rural parts of the municipality (e.g., both townships are located in Chongming Island, one of the less built-up areas of Shanghai). Like for districts, the extension of the township-level units and their populations vary widely: from the 20.9 Km^2 of the Huamu Subdistrict (花木街道) in Pudong New Area to the 1.6 Km^2 of the Jing'an Temple Subdistrict (静安寺街道) in Jing'an District; from the 125,000 residents of the Jiaxing Road Subdistrict (嘉兴路街道) in Hongkou District, to the 44,300 residents of Miaohang Town (庙行镇) in Baoshan District. Finally, below the township-level divisions there are 4563 residential communities (社区) and 1562 administrative villages (行政村), which are the basic administrative units of Shanghai.[44]

[41] The sixteen districts are: Baoshan (宝山), Changning (长宁), Chongming (崇明), Fengxian (奉贤), Hongkou (虹口), Huangpu (黄浦), Jiading (嘉定), Jing'an (静安), Jinshan (金山), Minhang (闵行), Pudong New Area (浦东新区), Putuo (普陀), Qingpu (青浦), Songjiang (松江), Xuhui (徐汇), and Yangpu (杨浦).

[42] The Paper, 2021. The main data of the seventh national census in Shanghai have been announced (cit.).

[43] The Paper, 2021. Shanghai's latest administrative division table announced, there are 107 subdistricts, 106 towns, and 2 townships [上海最新行政区划表公布，有107个街道106个镇和2个乡]. *The Paper* [澎湃新闻], 5 January, https://www.thepaper.cn/newsDetail_forward_10666130. For the sake of convenience, in the remainder of the book the three township-level divisions (i.e., subdistricts, towns, and townships) are collectively called "subdistricts" consistently with their hierarchical position within Shanghai's administrative system. The terminological distinction is only maintained when mentioning specific projects, for instance, the urban operation center of Kangqiao Town or the AI pilot application scenarios in the Xietu Road and Beixinjing Subdistricts.

[44] The Paper, 2021. Shanghai's latest administrative division table announced (cit.). These administrative units are often indicated by referring to their governing bodies: the neighborhood committees (社区居民委员会) and the villagers' committees (村民委员会).

At the vertex of this administrative architecture sits the Shanghai Municipal People's Government (上海市人民政府). The municipal government represents the executive power. It is guided by one Mayor and a number of Vice Mayors, who according to Chinese law are formally appointed by the Shanghai Municipal People's Congress[45] (上海市人民代表大会), the municipal legislature.[46] At the time of this writing, the Mayor of Shanghai Gong Zheng (龚正) is assisted by six Vice Mayors. Vice Mayors are responsible for specific areas of activity, such as urban transportation or market supervision, in cooperation with the relevant agencies of the municipal government. Municipal-level government agencies include the Shanghai General Office (市政府办公厅) and 24 "constituent departments" (组成部门). These consist of municipal commissions and bureaus[47] like the Municipal Commission of Commerce or the Municipal Bureau of Justice, and in some cases control operative agencies affiliated to them (e.g., the Urban Management and Law Enforcement Bureau under the Municipal Commission of Housing and Urban–Rural Development). Municipal-level government agencies also include: one "directly subordinated special institution" (直属特设机构), the Shanghai State-owned Assets Supervision and Administration Commission (SASAC, 上海市国有资产监督管理委员会); and nine "directly subordinated institutions" (直属特设机构), like the Landscaping and City Appearance Administrative Bureau (绿化和市容管理局), or the Municipal Civil Defense Office (民防办公室). This organizational structure is replicated in each of the 16 districts of Shanghai. These are guided by a district governor (区长) and a number of Vice governors,

[45] Government of the People's Republic of China, 2013. Introduction to the People's Congresses [人民代表大会简介]. *Government of the People's Republic of China*, http://www.gov.cn/guoqing/2013-03/01/content_5269663.htm. See also: National People's Congress, 2022. *Organic Law of the People's Republic of China on Local People's Congresses and Local People's Governments at All Levels* [中华人民共和国地方各级人民代表大会和地方各级人民政府组织法], 12 March, http://www.gov.cn/xinwen/2022-03/12/content_5678642.htm.

[46] The term of office of each legislature at any administrative level is five years. The Shanghai Municipal People's Congress usually holds one annual session. When the Municipal People's Congress is not in session, the legislative and other functions of the Congress are performed by its Standing Committee (上海市人民代表大会常务委员会).

[47] Shanghai Municipal Government, "Institutional responsibilities" [机构职责]. Shanghai Municipal Government website, https://www.shanghai.gov.cn/nw2405/index.html, last accessed on 6 November 2022.

who are formally appointed by district-level People's Congresses. District governments (e.g., 上海市静安区人民政府) carry out within their jurisdictions the executive functions of their municipal-level counterpart, and they control district-level commissions, bureaus, and institutions that are mostly identical to those at the municipal level (e.g., the Jing'an District Bureau of Justice, the Qingpu District SASAC, or the Songjiang District Civil Defense Office). At the township level, subdistricts, towns, and townships are guided by subdistrict offices (街道办事处), town governments (镇人民政府), and township governments (乡人民政府) respectively.[48] Below township-level divisions, residential communities and administrative villages are administered by neighborhood committees (社区居民委员会) and villagers' committees (村民委员会). These are not government bodies (政府机关), but "grassroots mass self-governing organizations" (基层群众性自治组织) that cooperate with government authorities in performing various activities.[49]

Finally, it bears to remind that Shanghai, like other government entities in mainland China, is structured as a parallel Party-government

[48] Township-level divisions have their People's Congresses. Government agencies at this level often include offices like Community Management Offices (社区管理办公室) responsible for urban management, Community Safety Offices (社区平安办公室) responsible for public security, Community Business Environment Offices (社区营商环境办公室)/Economic Development Offices (经济发展办公室) responsible for promoting business development and services, and Agriculture and Rural Development Offices (农业农村发展办公室), among others. See for instance: Pudong New Area People's Government, 2021. Huamu Subdistrict institutional setting [花木街道机构设置]. *Pudong New Area People's Government*, 27 December, https://www.pudong.gov.cn/14502.gkml_jgznl_jgsz/20220109/491437.html; Pudong New Area People's Government, 2021. Pudong New Area Wanxiang Town institutional setting [浦东新区万祥镇机构设置]. *Pudong New Area People's Government*, 27 December, https://www.pudong.gov.cn/14503.gkml_jgznl_jgsz/20220109/504901.html.

[49] See: *Organic Law of the People's Republic of China on the Urban Neighborhood Committees* [中华人民共和国城市居民委员会组织法], art. 2; and *Organic Law of the People's Republic of China on of Villagers' Committees* [中华人民共和国村民委员会组织法], art. 2. According to the Chinese Constitution (art. 111), grassroots mass self-governing organizations are "organizations of self-management, self-education and self-service of urban residents or rural villagers". They carry out a variety of tasks, from publicizing national laws and policies to mediating disputes between residents. They also cooperate with government and Party organizations in maintaining social order and performing other activities required by the authorities. See: Chinese Constitution, art. 111; Sohu, 2021. What is the relationship between residential communities, neighborhood committees and subdistrict offices?[社区、居委会、街道办之间到底是什么关系呢?]. *Sohu* [搜狐], 28 October, https://www.sohu.com/a/497700356_121198204.

system whereby the Communist Party of China (CPC) is de facto the highest authority. The Shanghai Mayor is appointed by the Organization Department of the CPC (中共中央组织部) via the municipal Party Committee,[50] and is then formally elected by the Shanghai Municipal People's Congress. In other words, the Shanghai Mayor is the highest-ranking official of the municipal government, has the same hierarchical level as provincial governors (because Shanghai is a municipality), and has a seat in the Central Committee of the CPC (中共中央委员会), the national political body that comprises the top leaders of the Party. However, the Mayor is hierarchically subordinated to the Party Secretary of the Shanghai Municipal Committee of the Communist Party of China[51] (中国共产党上海市委员会), Mr. Chen Jining (陈吉宁), and holds the position of Deputy Party Secretary of Shanghai.

Shanghai has embarked on an ambitious journey to promote AI in the public sector. This book examines whether the municipality is fulfilling its goal to improve public service provision by accelerating the integration of AI in public sector activities in various policy areas. This work asks the following questions: (1) does Shanghai have the capacity to use AI in the public sector? (2) How does this capacity translate into real-world policy initiatives, and what are their strengths and limitations in deploying AI in the public sector? (3) What are the implications of these

[50] See: Central Committee of the CPC, 2021. *Regulations on the Organizational Work of the Communist Party of China* [中国共产党组织工作条例]. China Central Government [中华人民共和国中央人民政府], 2 June, http://www.gov.cn/zhengce/2021-06/02/content_5615053.htm, art. 7: "Local Party Committees are primarily responsible for the organizational work in their areas. The main responsibilities are: [...] recommend key cadres to local State organs, CPPCC organizations, people's organizations, State-owned enterprises and institutions, etc." As explained by the Encyclopedia Britannica: "Even on the government side, all officials in these personnel departments are members of the CCP, and they follow rules and regulations that are not subject to control by the particular bodies of which they are formally a part. This system has been used to assure higher-level CCP control over the appointments to all key positions in the CCP, government, and other major organizations (enterprises, universities, and so forth)". See: Encyclopedia Britannica, *Encyclopædia Britannica online*. Entry: Administration of China, https://www.britannica.com/place/China/Administration, last accessed 10 Nov 2022.

[51] The Party Secretary is also appointed by the Organization Department of the CPC. See: Communist Party Member Network, 2022. Adjustments of the positions of leading comrades in the Shanghai Municipal Party Committee, Chen Jining also appointed as the Secretary of the Shanghai Municipal Party Committee [上海市委主要负责同志职务调整 陈吉宁兼任上海市委书记]. *Communist Party Member Network* [共产党员网], 28 October, https://www.12371.cn/2022/10/28/ARTI1666930647132795.shtml.

policy initiatives for public service provision in the municipality? While the municipal AI plans state that Shanghai will accelerate the use of AI also to improve citizens' lives, this book primarily focuses on public service provision for two main reasons. First, the results obtained by Shanghai in public service provision are measurable (e.g., improved efficiency of public service delivery; deeper integration of AI in public services; diffusion of AI-based public services across the municipality). On the other hand, there is still a lack of agreed-upon methods for measuring the social impacts of AI systems (Mishra et al., 2020; Crawford and Whittaker, 2016). Second, the correlation between enhanced efficiency in public service provision and improvements in citizens' lives is well established in many policy areas. For example, reduced time and bureaucracy to deliver administrative services, reduced traffic congestions, increased speed and accuracy of medical diagnoses have a positive effect on citizens' life. The same holds for improved public safety, well-maintained subway lines, or faster filing of judicial cases, among others. At the same time, other aspects beyond efficiency that may affect how public sector AI applications impact on the life of citizens are not neglected. The final section of this book discusses the shortcomings and unanswered questions of Shanghai's AI strategy, and how these may influence the ability of Shanghai to use AI and advanced technologies to enhance "citizens' sense of gain".

References

Crawford, K. and Whittaker, M., 2016. *The AI Now Report 2016: The Social and Economic Implications of Artificial Intelligence Technologies in the Near-Term*. New York: New York University, https://ainowinstitute.org/AI_Now_2016_Report.pdf.

Creemers, R., 2020. The Ideology Behind China's AI Strategy. In: Elliott, H. ed., 2020. *The AI Powered State: China's Approach to Public Sector Innovation*. Nesta, May 2020, pp. 63–69, https://www.nesta.org.uk/feature/ai-powered-state/.

Fukuyama, F., 2013. What Is Governance? *Governance*, 26(3), pp. 347–368, https://doi.org/10.1111/gove.12035.

Han, E., 2020. From Traffic Management to Smart Courts: China's Approach to Smart Cities. In: Elliott, H. ed., 2020. *The AI Powered State: China's Approach to Public Sector Innovation*. Nesta, May 2020, pp. 35–41, https://www.nesta.org.uk/feature/ai-powered-state/.

Mishra, S., Clark, J. and Perrault, C., 2020. *Measurement in AI Policy: Opportunities and Challenges*, 22 September, https://arxiv.org/abs/2009.09071.

Paleyes, A., Urma, R. and Lawrence, N., 2020. Challenges in Deploying Machine Learning: a Survey of Case Studies. *NeurIPS 2020 Workshop: ML Retrospectives, Surveys & Meta-Analyses (ML-RSA)*, https://doi.org/10.48550/arXiv.2011.09926.

Pan, Y., Tian, Y., Liu, X., Gu, D. and Hua, G., 2016. Urban Big Data and the Development of City Intelligence. *Engineering*, 2(2), pp. 171–178, https://doi.org/10.1016/J.ENG.2016.02.003.

Zeng, J., 2021. China's Artificial Intelligence Innovation: A Top-Down National Command Approach? *Global Policy*, 12(3), pp. 399–409, https://doi.org/10.1111/1758-5899.12914.

CHAPTER 2

Artificial Intelligence in the Public Sector in Shanghai: Conceptualization, Context, and Capacity

The study of artificial intelligence in the public sector is an emerging area of research. As AI evolved from pure academic investigation to an applied field, and AI technologies are increasingly being adopted in many industries, there are great expectations for what AI systems can do for improving public service efficiency and effectiveness, and producing other desirable outcomes in several policy areas (Dwivedi et al., 2021; Balakrishnan et al., 2020; Paleyes et al., 2020; Wirtz and Müller, 2019; Chui et al., 2018; Desouza, 2018; Eggers et al., 2017). Under these premises, there is a growing interest by public sector institutions to harness the potential benefits that AI can bring. An analysis of 34 national AI strategies[1] shows that modernizing the public sector through the deployment of AI is a key government priority for these nations (Fatima et al., 2020).

[1] "National AI strategy" indicates a public policy document that communicates the objective of supporting the development of AI, while also maximizing the benefits of AI for society (Stanford University, 2021, p. 155). As of December 2022, a total of 62 national AI strategies have been published, and 14 countries stated the intention to develop AI strategies (Stanford University, 2023, p. 285). Most national strategies indicate the intentions to use AI in the public sector (Fatima et al., 2020; Misuraca and van Noordt, 2020; OECD, 2019a, p. 122). The OECD AI Policy Observatory (https://www.oecd.ai/countries-and-initiatives) keeps track of the evolutions in national AI strategies and intergovernmental AI initiatives.

D. Todaro, *The Use of Artificial Intelligence in the Public Sector in Shanghai*, https://doi.org/10.1007/978-981-97-0597-9_2

The expanding list of AI implementations in public organizations[2] and other indicators[3] also confirm interest by public sector institutions to integrate AI in their activities. China is no exception. In July 2017, the State Council published one of the earliest and most comprehensive national strategies on the promotion of artificial intelligence, which establishes the use of AI in the public sector as a primary goal of China's plans for AI development. Since then, Chinese national and local authorities have intensified their efforts to promote AI in their jurisdictions (Zeng, 2021; Elliot, 2020; Ding, 2018; Lee and Sheehan, 2018). Shanghai is at the forefront of AI innovation in the public sector and other areas, and it is striving to become a leading international "AI highland".

In preparation to the study of AI in the public sector in Shanghai, this chapter establishes with greater precision what it means to use artificial intelligence in the activities of public organizations. It systematizes the prevalent research approaches of public sector AI scholarship, in order to derive a comprehensive analytical framework for examining the main sociotechnical factors affecting the use of AI in the public sector (2.1). Based on this framework, it offers a clear conceptualization of "AI in the public sector in China". This conceptualization encompasses a precise explanation of the key technical, social, and country-specific factors that influence the adoption and implementation of AI in the public sector in China (2.2). The chapter then introduces the policy capacity framework (2.3), which is used in the remainder of this book to assess the ability of Shanghai to use AI in the public sector, and gauge the strengths and limitations of the main policy initiatives that are fostering public sector AI applications in Shanghai. This chapter concludes by showing that the definition of "AI in the public sector in China" helps to bring into focus

[2] For instance, a survey in the European Union mapped 230 initiatives on the use of AI in public services promoted by the Member States (Misuraca and Van Noordt, 2020). The OECD Observatory of Public Sector Innovation maps 99 case studies of public sector AI implementations promoted by OECD countries in several policy areas, from public administration to transport and environmental protection (https://oecd-opsi.org/case_type/opsi/, last accessed on 24 November 2023). See also the examples of current public sector AI applications listed in Sect. 2.2.2.

[3] For instance, the number of mentions of artificial intelligence and machine learning in the proceedings of the U.S. Congress, the U.K. parliament and the Canadian parliament increased significantly between 2011 and 2020. There was also a significant increase in the mentions of AI in the communications of 16 central banks over the past 10 years (Stanford University, 2021, pp. 172–175).

a set of important elements to assess Shanghai's policy capacity to implement AI in the public sector, and the impacts of such capacity on public service provision (2.4).

2.1 Conceptualizing AI in the Public Sector

Gaining a clear conceptual understanding of artificial intelligence in the public sector is a necessary precondition to identify the complex aggregation of factors that affect the use of AI in this area, considering that academic research provides a growing but still limited view of AI applications and challenges for public organizations (Engstrom et al., 2020; Misuraca and Van Noordt, 2020; Pencheva et al., 2020; Sun and Medaglia, 2019; Wirtz and Müller, 2019; Wirtz et al., 2019). To establish with greater precision what it means to use AI in the public sector, next paragraphs introduce an analytical framework rooted in the sociotechnical approach used by previous studies on the integration of AI in social domains (Dobbe et al., 2021; Van del Poel, 2020; Cristianini and Scantamburlo, 2019; Selbst et al., 2019; Behymer and Flach, 2016; Dafoe, 2015; Jones et al., 2013). Building upon a larger research tradition[4] that has been exploring the relations between society, science and technology[5] for decades, these sociotechnical studies examine the technical, social, and institutional aspects that influence the use of AI systems in societal contexts. In this regard, **a clear conceptual understanding of AI in the public sector explicates the interactions of the technical**

[4] It is difficult to pinpoint sociotechnical approaches to a specific stream of research, as many scholars in the social studies of science and technology have explored the technical and social factors that affect the use of technology in society, from historians of technology (Hughes, 1987) to systems engineers (Franssen, 2015; Kroes et al., 2006) and researchers of AI systems in social domains (Cristianini and Scantamburlo, 2019; Selbst et al., 2019), among others. The sociotechnical approach of this book draws from the social construction of technology (SCOT), the research program initiated in the mid-1980s by Pinch and Bijker (1987), two scholars coming from the sociology and history of science and technology.

[5] This work acknowledges the existence of an ongoing debate in the literature on social and philosophical studies about the theoretical distinction between "science" and "technology", or lack thereof. See for instance: Niiniluoto, I., 2016. Science vs. Technology: Difference or Identity? In: Franssen, M., Vermaas, P., Kroes, P. and Meijers, A. eds., 2016. Philosophy of Technology after the Empirical Turn. *Philosophy of Engineering and Technology*, 23, pp. 93–106. This debate is beyond the scope of this book. When discussing AI technology, this work refers to the conceptual view of AI systems outlined in Sect. 2.2.1.

and social factors that shape the use of AI in the activities of public organizations. The validity of a sociotechnical approach is increasingly acknowledged by public sector AI scholars, who note that "[a]lthough the literature recognizes the complexity of AI projects [...], it does not explore in-depth the non-technical causes of such complexity and the related challenges" (Campion et al., 2020, p. 4). By examining how the interactions of technical and non-technical factors impact on the adoption and use of AI in this area, a sociotechnical approach offers a superior understanding of AI in the public sector, because it encompasses the several concurrent elements that are barely technological in essence, but are crucial for the success or failure of public sector AI implementations (Molinari et al., 2021).

Guided by this sociotechnical approach, this work started by surveying two types of sources that can help to establish a clear conceptual understanding of AI in the public sector. Namely: academic articles in English and Chinese language that examine the use of AI in the public sector; and documents on the AI technology that use an educated and technically precise language, while remaining mostly accessible to non-experts. These sources were retrieved following the methods outlined below.

The systematic literature review of *public sector AI scholarship in English and Chinese language* examined academic articles that discuss various aspects related to the use of AI in public sector activities. Following the principles indicated by Snyder (2019) and Bryman (2012, pp. 103–105), the review searched three online abstract and citation databases of peer-reviewed academic sources using a predefined research string. The databases are Taylor & Francis Online, Scopus, and—for Chinese-language sources—the China Knowledge Resources Online Database (CNKI), one of the largest online platforms for Chinese journals, dissertations, standards, and patents. The sources eligible for content analysis were selected by setting five inclusion criteria[6] and reading the

[6] The inclusion criteria are: (i) *time frame* (January 2015–January 2022), which provides an exhaustive view of the research approaches in public sector AI scholarship, while also keeping focus on studies that discuss AI technologies having capabilities similar to those of contemporary public sector AI applications; (ii) *disciplines* that are relevant to the scope of this investigation (e.g., "public administration and management"); (iii) proven *academic quality* (peer-reviewed articles, book chapters, and conference proceedings); (iv) an actual *research focus on "AI in the public sector"* (i.e., the focus on the AI technology and its applications in the public sector are central to the study); and (v) *appropriateness* for the purposes of establishing a clear understanding of AI in the public

abstract of each study. To complement the sources retrieved from the primary databases, a snowballing approach was then used to examine the references of the selected studies. Moreover, an additional search on the Google Scholar database was carried out at a later stage using the same research string and inclusion criteria. The final set of 54 studies in English language and 16 studies in Chinese language were fully read and summarized. The inclusion of Chinese-language sources in the literature review is motivated by three reasons. The first is the focus of this work on China in general and Shanghai in particular. As such, it seemed appropriate to gain a deeper understanding of how Chinese-language studies are exploring the use of AI in the public sector. Second, the analysis of Chinese-language sources complements and expands the knowledge of public sector AI research. This addition is important because China is considered a leading country in using AI for public sector innovation (Elliott, 2020; United Nations, 2020; UNESCAP, 2018). While Chinese authors writing in English are usually well represented in English-language scholarly databases, these contributions provide only a partial view of Chinese efforts in public sector AI research. Section 2.1.1 and Appendix I are a first attempt to narrow this knowledge gap. Finally, by expanding the basis of the literature review beyond English-language sources, Chinese scholarship corroborates the validity of the criteria underpinning the integrated analytical framework for the study of AI in the public sector proposed here (2.1.2), as well as the selection of drivers and barriers derived from previous research on AI in the public sector (2.2.2).

The review of *sources on the AI technology* focused on books, specialized articles, and blogs that discuss various aspects of AI research and the applications of AI technologies in economy and society. Considering the technical complexity of AI research and technologies, these sources were hand-searched and selected based on the following criteria: (i) they are technically precise at an abstraction level suitable for the purposes of this research, meaning that they are accurate but also understandable—in most of their parts—to non-technical experts (i.e., the great majority of policymakers, civil servants, and researchers that study AI in the public sector); (ii) they meet established criteria for the selection of documentary sources, meaning that they are credible, authentic, representative and

sector (i.e., sources contain insights on the research methods adopted by scholars to study the sociotechnical factors affecting the use of AI in the public sector, and/or provide lists or other classifications of these factors).

meaningful (Scott, 1990, p. 6; quoted in Bryman, 2012, p. 544); and (iii) they are not overly focused on mainstream AI technologies, but examine AI technologies that are applicable to both short- and long-term time horizons, without being speculative.

The importance to clarify the meaning of AI in the public sector is confirmed by extant public sector AI literature, which underlines the need to provide a better understanding of the use of AI in this area. Krafft et al. (2020, p. 72) argue that achieving consensus on a definition of AI in the public sector has proven particularly elusive, hampering the possibility of effective communication among different stakeholders. Misuraca and van Noordt (2020, p. 41) highlight the need to define what is "truly meant" by AI in the public sector, as researchers and practitioners struggle with the operationalization of the term. Johnson and Verdicchio (2017, p. 577) identify a serious semantic gap in the discussion of AI, which is misleading AI researchers and those in industry and public policy. Murdick et al. (2020, p. 2) state that policy analysts and policymakers should demand clarity about the boundaries of the scope of AI, and the methods or data used to identify it. Young et al. (2019, p. 1) argue that more precision in policy and legal discussions on AI would strengthen regulatory efforts by making underlying algorithmic components more legible. Cave et al. (2018, p. 5) and Dwivedi et al. (2021, p. 25) find a disconnect between fictional and non-fictional AI narratives and the reality of the technology, and argue that such a disconnect might have unintended consequences for policy analysis. Chinese-language sources like Jia and Jiang (2017) also emphasize "the necessity and urgency of in-depth discussions about the public policy issues of AI governance". Chen (2019) observes that the meaning of "intelligent governance" is still debated among the academic community. Li (2019) argues that the lack of a unified understanding of what AI is, and what benefits it may bring, is hampering in-depth discussions of AI regulation and governance. This increasing scholarly attention indicates that clarifying the meaning of AI in the public sector is a fundamental but understudied research issue. Establishing a common conceptual understanding of AI in this area is a prerequisite for examining applications and challenges of AI in the public sector (Wirtz et al., 2019), and it has significant downstream effects on the assessment of the factors that influence the use of AI in public organizations (Mishra et al., 2020; Misuraca and van Noordt, 2020). Hence, clarifying the meaning of AI in the public sector is a necessary precondition for the in-depth analysis of public sector AI applications in Shanghai.

To clarify the meaning of AI in the public sector, next sections review the main research approaches of public sector AI scholarship in English and Chinese language (2.1.1). By comparing these approaches, it is possible to derive a set of criteria to develop a comprehensive analytical framework for the study of the factors affecting the use of AI in the public sector (2.1.2). This framework is then applied in Chapter 2.2 to examine the complex aggregation of technical, social, and institutional elements that influence the use of AI in the public sector in China.

2.1.1 Research Approaches of Previous Studies on AI in the Public Sector

Guided by a sociotechnical approach, this book aims to clarify the meaning of AI in the public sector by examining the technical, social, and institutional factors that affect the use of AI in this area. In this regard, the literature review of public sector AI scholarship in English and Chinese language had two purposes. First, examine the main research approaches employed by the literature of AI in the public sector to study the variety of factors affecting the use of AI this area. These factors are defined here as "drivers" and "barriers" depending on whether they motivate or hinder AI uptake, as explained shortly. Understanding the main research approaches to study drivers and barriers of public sector AI applications serves to derive a set of criteria for the comprehensive examination of the sociotechnical factors affecting the use of AI in the public sector. The second purpose of the literature review was to compile a comprehensive list of the drivers and barriers of AI in the public sector identified by previous studies, in order to gain an inclusive and precise view of the vast range of technical, ethical, legal, and socioeconomic elements that influence the use of AI in public organizations. Both objectives aim to develop an accurate and updated understanding of the state of knowledge in this area of research, creating solid foundations to clarify the meaning of AI in the public sector. This and the following subsections focus on the first objective of the literature review. The categorization of drivers and barriers of AI in the public sector is discussed in Chapter 2.2 to offer a clear conceptualization of "AI in the public sector in China".

The term "research approach" here indicates how previous studies examine the sociotechnical factors that are motivating and hindering the use of AI in the public sector. These factors have been called by scholars with a variety of names: values, opportunities, benefits, driving forces, enabling factors, challenges, barriers, or risks, among others. For illustrative purposes, this terminology is condensed in "drivers" and "barriers". *Drivers* are the sociotechnical factors that motivate the adoption and implementation of AI in public organizations. On the contrary, *barriers* are the sociotechnical factors that hinder the adoption and implementation of AI in the public sector. The prevailing research approaches in public sector AI research were inductively classified in three categories: conceptual frameworks, maps of drivers and barriers, and organizational studies. Some overlapping may exist between these categories. For instance, some studies that map drivers and barriers sometimes develop conceptual frameworks to do so. Hence, the studies were classified by their main contents. These three categories are expounded here below with some illustrative examples:

Conceptual Frameworks: studies in this category examine the use of AI in the public sector by abstracting the drivers and barriers toward general, overarching frameworks. For instance, Chen et al. (2019) propose a four-stage model for AI in the public sector (i.e., relieve, assist, enhance, and transform), and integrate it with four aspects of AI benefits (i.e., relieving human resources, assisting in providing services, enhancing the capacity of decision-makers, and transforming public organizations). Chui et al. (2018) adopt a combination of "social-first" and "tech-first" approaches to assess the benefits that AI technologies are expected to bring in ten social domains. Fatima et al. (2021) use signaling theory to examine how existing national AI strategies define the drivers of AI in the public sector, like "effective government", "political participation", and "reform orientation", among others. Kankanhalli et al. (2019) examine the use of AI in the public sector by constructing a research framework for smart government that combines AI systems, policy areas, stakeholders, regulatory and ethical principles. Makasi et al. (2021) propose guiding principles and recommendations for creating and measuring public value in the use of AI in the public sector. Misuraca et al. (2020) examine three value drivers for AI in the public sector, namely performance, openness, and inclusion. Ojo et al. (2019) examine the value of the use of AI in the public sector in light of dominant public policy theories. Sousa et al. (2019)

outline a research framework for AI solutions for the public sector that focuses on the generation of value for the government. Toll et al. (2020) adopt an established e-government value framework to examine the values associated to the use of AI in the public sector, and code them into four value ideals (efficiency, service, professionalism, and engagement). Valle-Cruz et al. (2020) examine AI in the public sector by proposing a "Dynamic Public Policy-Cycle" model. Wirtz and Müller (2019) construct an integrated AI framework for identifying drivers and barriers of AI in public management, consisting of technological, functional, applicational, and policy layers. Zhang et al. (2021) elaborate a model that summarizes the drivers of government's uses of AI in the adoption and implementation stages. Among Chinese-language sources, Jia and Jiang (2017) propose a comprehensive public policy framework for the study of AI in the public sector AI. Li (2019) proposes a conceptual framework that examines the factors affecting the use of AI in the public sector in terms of AI as a knowledge form (知识形态), a product (产品形态), and the societal consequences of AI use (社会后果形态). Yu and Cui (2020) examine the drivers and barriers of AI in the public sector at the individual (human–machine cooperation), organizational (AI-enabled digital government and new intelligent platforms), and global levels (international competition in AI).

Maps of Drivers and Barriers: studies in this group examine the use of AI in the public sector by listing and appraising various types of drivers and barriers. In one of the earliest studies on AI in the public sector, Barth and Arnold (1999) discuss the potential benefits and dangers of AI in public administration in terms of the impacts of AI on administrative discretion. Dwivedi et al. (2021) present an extensive collection of analyses that assess opportunities and challenges of AI in the public sector and other domains. Engin and Treleaven (2019) identify opportunities and challenges for various types of government activities based on real-life applications in different countries. Engstrom et al. (2020) examine a set of cross-institutional, legal, and policy challenges raised by public sector uses of AI. Henman (2020) outlines four challenges to deploying artificial intelligence in public administration, and the technological and governance innovations that are being developed to address these challenges. Mikhaylov et al. (2018) discuss the opportunities and challenges for AI in the public sector in terms of cross-sectoral cooperation. Pencheva et al. (2020) offer an in-depth review of the literature on the role of Big Data and AI in the public sector to provide an overview of the benefits and challenges to their use and the resulting implications. Sun and Medaglia (2019) identify seven types of challenges of AI adoption and use in the public sector as perceived by different stakeholders. Wirtz et al. (2019) look at the main AI applications in public management and identify four dimensions of challenges of AI related to the public sector. Among Chinese-language sources, Tao (2020) identifies three main opportunities and four challenges of AI in public management. Li and Li (2021) examine the technical, governance, and ethical risks of AI in the public sector. Wu (2021) observes that while benefits like improved administrative efficiency and internal management capabilities are driving AI adoption in the public sector, there are several managerial, societal, and technological risks that should be considered. Zhang et al. (2019) examine the technical and institutional elements that are driving the use of AI in the construction of a smart society.

Organizational Studies: research in this group focuses on the integration of AI in public organizations, highlighting the managerial aspects that are driving and hindering the use of AI in the public sector. For instance, Campion et al. (2020) gather empirical evidence on the organizational challenges to AI adoption and implementation in the public sector, and the successful management strategies to address such challenges. Desouza (2021, 2018) elaborates a maturity model that examines the critical elements that need to be managed as AI projects are adopted and deployed in public organizations. Desouza et al. (2020) examine how public organizations can use AI to add value to their activities by looking at data, technology, organizational, and environmental domains. Eggers et al. (2017) examine how AI-enabled automation can potentially address resource constraints, paperwork burdens, and backlogs in the activities of public organizations. Mehr (2017) examines how the potential of AI to improve public service provision is driving AI adoption and use in public organizations in the United States. The Partnership for Public Service and IBM (2018) detail the practical experiences with AI of four public institutions in the United States to gain insights on the factors affecting AI use in the public sector.

The literature review did not identify Chinese-language studies in this category.

2.1.2 *Public Sector AI Research: Toward an Integrated Framework*

The literature review shows that scholars have adopted a variety of methods to scope and examine the multitude of elements affecting AI in the public sector. By comparing these research approaches, it is possible to highlight some commonalities that can be used as criteria for the comprehensive examination of the sociotechnical factors driving and hindering the use of AI in the public sector. In details:

Inclusiveness means that the analysis of the factors affecting AI in the public sector should consider the vast range of technical, policy, societal, legal, and economic elements that influence the use of AI in public organizations. Conceptual frameworks highlight the importance of inclusiveness. For instance, Kankanhalli et al. (2019) develop a comprehensive research framework for AI in the public sector that combines technical, policy, societal, and ethical elements. Wirtz and Müller (2019) propose a multi-layer framework for AI in public management into which they integrate the examination of technical, legal, and ethical aspects of individual AI solutions, in order to prevent analytical fragmentation. Chinese-language sources like Yang (2021) propose a model to examine the possible uses of AI in social governance consisting of five dimensions, which embrace technical, policy, and societal elements. Studies that map drivers and barriers of AI are those that most vividly highlight the need for inclusiveness, as they typically offer extensive lists of drivers and barriers of AI uptake. For instance, Pencheva et al. (2020) identify eight opportunities of AI in the public sector: legitimacy and collaboration; accountability and trust; cost savings and productivity gains; reduced fraud; better service and decision-making; improved policy analysis; continuous real-time evaluation; new business and performance models. Sun and Medaglia (2019) identify seven dimensions of challenges in the adoption and use of AI: social challenges; economic challenges; ethical challenges; political, legal, and policy-related challenges; organizational and managerial challenges; data challenges; and technological challenges. Zwiderwijk et al. (2021) identify nine categories of benefits and eight categories of challenges that drive and hinder AI uses in the public sector. Chinese-language sources like Li and Li (2019) examine a broad range of ethical, legal, and technical challenges of AI related to the public sector, such as security vulnerabilities, issues of fairness and accountability of AI systems, algorithm discrimination, and privacy violations. Finally, inclusiveness is important also when studying the organizational uses of AI. For instance, the maturity model for AI in public organizations by Desouza (2021) considers a variety of elements that need to be managed as AI projects are adopted and deployed in the public sector, from technological elements to the existence of an innovation climate, governance, and ethical frameworks, among others. Similarly, Campion et al. (2020) find manifold elements that affect AI adoption and implementation at the organizational level, from technological factors to the lack of leadership and partners, political will, and executive support.

Precision means that the analysis of the factors affecting AI in the public sector should account for how AI is actually used in the activities and operations of public organizations. Conceptual frameworks tend by design to address the use of AI in the public sector at an abstract level. Nonetheless, the importance of precision is documented by studies in this group that link their frameworks to prevailing classifications of government functions and sectors. For instance, the study by Misuraca et al. (2020) uses the COFOG categorization of functions of government[7] to identify the policy domains in which AI is currently in use, and identify the "value drivers" of AI in the public sector. Similarly, the framework proposed by Sousa et al. (2019) also adopts the COFOG classification to identify the areas of government that are using AI solutions and the benefits that are being generated in such areas. Chui et al. (2018) refer to the policy areas of the Sustainable Development Goals to develop their framework on the beneficial use of AI. Chinese-language sources like Meng and Jun (2021) develop an "AI-enabled technical framework of platform government" that precisely account for a wide range of administrative functions like smart Q&A, smart authentication, intelligent form filling, and intelligent file recognition. Precision is pursued also by the studies that map the opportunities and challenges of AI in the public sector. For instance, Engin and Treleaven (2019) base their analysis on a taxonomy

[7] The Classification of the Functions of Government (COFOG) classifies government expenditure into ten main categories (divisions known as the COFOG I level breakdown): general public services; defense; public order and safety; economic affairs; environmental protection; housing and community affairs; health; recreation, culture and religion; education; social protection (see also Chapter 2.2).

of public sector activities. Similarly, Engstrom et al. (2020) examine institutional, legal, and policy challenges of AI in the public sector based on a taxonomy of five types of government activities. Chinese-language sources like Tao (2020) look at the drivers and barriers of AI in public management by examining AI in relation to specific aspects, such as public service delivery, public decision-making, the costs of public administration, or the barriers of limited interoperability among different public organizations or within the same agency. Studies that focus on the organizational level also highlight the importance of considering how AI is actually used in public sector activities. Mehr (2017) bases the analysis of AI in public service delivery on five specific activities: answering questions, filling out and searching documents, routing requests, translation, and drafting documents. The Partnership for Public Service and IBM (2018) examine the use of AI in enforcement, task automation, and internal operations.

Contextualization means that the analysis of the factors affecting AI in the public sector should consider how different social and institutional contexts influence the use of AI in this area. The importance of contextualization can be deduced by looking at the conceptual frameworks. For instance, Chen et al. (2019) develop their model starting from a specific use case in a Chinese city. The value drivers of AI identified by Misuraca et al. (2020) are drawn from AI applications in the European Union. The values associated to the use of AI in the public sector identified by Toll et al. (2020) are extracted from the analysis of Swedish policy documents. Zhang et al. (2021) elaborate a model that summarizes the drivers for government's AI uptake that is specifically focused on China. Chinese-language sources like Yu and Cui (2020) argue that more emphasis should be placed on how organizational and institutional factors influence the development of AI and its social impacts. Contextualization is important also when mapping the drivers and barriers of AI in the public sector. In this group, the studies based on the analyses of use cases typically focus on the specific context of a single country. For instance, Engstrom et al. (2020) examine the use of AI in federal agencies in the United States. Mikhaylov et al. (2018) examine the opportunities and challenges in cross-sectoral cooperation in the United States. Schaefer et al. (2021) identify the perceived challenges of AI adoption from employee's perspective in twelve German municipalities. Similarly, Mikalef et al. (2019) look at the drivers and barriers of AI in Norwegian municipalities. Chinese-language sources like Wu (2021) highlight that the use of AI in governance should be defined according to China's current socioeconomic conditions. Finally, the importance of contextualization is documented by the studies of organizational adoption. Campion et al. (2020) base their study on the analysis of policy labs and offices of data analytics across the United States. Also, the studies of Mehr (2017) and the Partnership for Public Service and IBM (2018) are based on the analysis of public organizations in the United States. Even if the study by Desouza et al. (2020) is not explicitly based on organizations in a particular country, it recommends public organizations to "perform an environment scan" and to develop "a clear sense of environmental status".

The importance of inclusiveness, precision, and contextualization in the analysis of the use of AI in the public sector was derived empirically based on the literature review of scholarly sources. As just shown, these criteria can be found across all the research approaches examined. At the same time, the importance of inclusiveness, precision, and contextualization is also increasingly theorized among scholars. In terms of *inclusiveness*, Reis et al. (2019) lament the lack of a comprehensive overview of AI challenges for the public sector. Dwivedi et al. (2021) propose a research agenda based on multidisciplinary perspectives on the emerging challenges and opportunities for AI in the public sector. Wirtz et al. (2019) emphasize the importance of a conceptual framework that can offer a comprehensive overview of AI-based applications and challenges for the public sector. In terms of *precision*, Sousa et al. (2019) observe that "the construction of AI solutions in the public sector starts from demands generated in the functions of government". On a similar note, Misuraca and van Noordt (2020) posit that research on AI in the public sector should take into consideration the complexity of implementation within public administration. These observations are echoed by Engstrom et al. (2020), who observe that "we know precious little about how government agencies themselves use AI". Finally, in terms of *contextualization*, Campion et al. (2020) emphasize that "AI adoption is context specific and rooted in the dynamics of political embeddedness of the institutions enabling the project to occur". Pan et al. (2016) highlight that country-specific differences in administrative structures as well as levels of industrialization, informatization, and urbanization should be given proper consideration, as they bear direct implications on AI applications in the public sector. Hager et al. (2017) also observe that the use of AI in the public sector is influenced by the specific resources, capabilities, and characteristics of each location. As such, Zuiderwijk et al. (2021) call for public sector AI research that is "specific to certain [...] countries and at specific government levels in relation to AI".

Building upon the criteria of precision, inclusiveness, and contextualization, this work proposes a comprehensive analytical framework that clarifies the meaning of AI in the public sector by examining the key sociotechnical factors affecting the use of AI in public sector activities. This framework will be applied in Chapter 2.2 to offer a precise explanation of the key technological, social, and country-specific factors that influence the use of AI in the public sector in China:

- First, the framework outlines a conceptual view of AI systems that offers a technically precise explanation of the workings of contemporary AI systems, at a level suitable for public sector AI research (2.2.1). This helps to establish a solid basis for clarifying the meaning of AI in the public sector, as it provides a better understanding of the technology that public organizations are or could be using in their activities. In addition, this conceptual view underscores the relationship between public sector AI applications and the capabilities of contemporary AI systems. It captures the main elements that are relevant to understand the use of AI systems in the context of the public sector, bringing into focus the relationship between policy discussions about AI and key technical features of AI systems.
- Second, building upon a solid knowledge of AI systems, the framework presents a taxonomy that accurately identifies the activities where public organizations are currently applying AI, and it provides a comprehensive overview of the drivers and barriers that motivate and hinder the use of AI in such activities across different socioeconomic and political contexts (2.2.2). By grounding the analysis in the reality of current public sector AI applications, the framework provides a sound basis to understand the sociotechnical factors that affect the use of AI in this area, and it achieves greater explanatory power thanks to this combination of precision and inclusiveness.
- Third, the analysis is contextualized in the socio-institutional settings of interest. This stage identifies and examines two governance mechanisms in China's central-local relations and national innovation system that are contributing to fostering the fast and widespread applications of AI in the public sector in China. It also discusses the potential impacts on public sector AI applications resulting from the

emerging Chinese responses to the regulatory and ethical challenges of AI (2.2.3).

Scholars observe that "[t]he biggest challenge in creating an integrated AI framework model is therefore to weigh up the degree of clarity [...] and the degree of abstraction" (Wirtz and Müller, 2019, p. 1095). Based on the criteria of precision, inclusiveness, and contextualization, the proposed analytical framework is an attempt to address this challenge. This framework has the merit to address a set of priority research issues that emerged in the literature review. Such research issues were categorized in the technological and public sector domains (Table 2.1), and are interrelated. On one hand, efforts to clarify the meaning of AI in the public sector must consider how technology is used by public organizations, which need AI tools that are technically usable and at the same time meet the legal, ethical, and socioeconomic requirements linked to the unique institutional and social role of the public sector (ETAPAS, 2021; Engstrom et al., 2020; van Noordt and Misuraca, 2020; Desouza et al., 2020; Sousa et al., 2019). On the other hand, clarifying the meaning of AI in the public sector must also contend with the shortcomings of research in describing AI applications for public usage, resulting from the lack of a common definition of AI, and from the difficulties in developing an adequate comprehension of the technical underpinnings of AI applications (Mishra et al., 2020; Duan et al., 2019; Scantamburlo et al., 2018). By addressing priority research issues of extant public sector AI scholarship, the contribution of the analytical framework proposed by this book goes beyond the study of AI in the public sector in China.

2.2 Mapping the Field: Artificial Intelligence in the Public Sector in China

To examine the key factors affecting the use of AI in the public sector in China, next paragraphs proceed in three interrelated steps. First, they provide a clear definition of contemporary "AI systems" and a technically precise explanation of their workings, at a level suitable for public sector AI research. This offers a better understanding of the technology that public organizations are or could be using in their operations (2.2.1). Second, the analysis accurately indicates the main activities where public

Table 2.1 Priority research issues in the technological and public sector domains

Technological domain: clarifying the meaning of AI in the public sector requires first of all an understanding of what AI systems are, and what they can do based on the current status of technological development. Research issues in this dimension are related to defining 'artificial intelligence' and assessing the technical capabilities of contemporary AI systems, so that the multifaceted implications of the use of this technology (set of technologies) in the public sector can be better understood (Dwivedi et al., 2021; Zuiderwijk et al., 2021; Misuraca, et al., 2020; Mishra et al., 2020; Stanford University, 2016, 2021a; Duan et al., 2019; Marcus and Davis, 2019; Reis et al., 2019; Bibel, 2018; Cave et al., 2018; Scantamburlo et al., 2018; Russell and Norvig, 1995)	**Public sector domain: clarifying the meaning of AI in the public sector also requires the identification of the public sector-specific factors that affect the use of AI in this area, which has unique characteristics due to the needs and obligations that animate the use of this technology in the activities of public organizations. Research issues in this dimension are related to identifying and examining the complex aggregation of technical, non-technical and context-specific elements that influence AI adoption and implementation in the public sector** (ETAPAS, 2021; Makasi et al., 2021; Zuiderwijk et al., 2021; Desouza et al., 2020; Engstrom et al., 2020; Misuraca and Van Noordt, 2020; Campion et al., 2020; Chen, 2019; Li, 2019; Reis et al., 2019; Sousa et al., 2019; Wirtz et al., 2019; Zheng et al., 2018; Jia and Jiang, 2017; Mehr, 2017)

organizations are currently applying AI, and it provides a comprehensive and reasoned view of the drivers and barriers of AI in such activities derived from the literature (2.2.2). Finally, the analysis delves into the country-specific factors affecting the use of AI in the public sector in China. It focuses on the governance mechanisms in China's central-local relations and national innovation system, which are instrumental in fostering the use of AI in the Chinese public sector. It also reviews the main Chinese initiatives in AI ethics and AI regulations to draw preliminary conclusions on their expected impacts on public sector AI applications in China (2.2.3). By following the principles of precision, inclusiveness, and contextualization under an overarching sociotechnical approach, the analysis identifies the key elements that affect the use of AI in the public sector in China. In doing so, it outlines with greater precision the domain of investigation of this book, and it brings into focus a set of important elements to assess the policy capacity of Shanghai to implement AI in the public sector and the impacts of such capacity on the provision of public services in the municipality, as discussed in Chapter 2.4.

2.2.1 *Artificial Intelligence Systems*

Today, artificial intelligence still lacks an agreed-upon definition within the field of computer science. Some eminent AI scholars even question whether artificial intelligence can still be considered a discipline (Bibel, 2018). To ensure a consistent development of the study of AI in the public sector, it is therefore important to provide a clear and precise definition of "AI systems" that can be used as basis for a common language among researchers and practitioners who are interested to explore the use of AI in this area. As basis for a common language, this book adopts the definition of AI systems proposed by the OECD AI Experts Group. In the OECD definition, an AI system is:

> a machine-based system that can, for a given set of human-defined objectives, make predictions, recommendations or decisions influencing real or virtual environments. It uses machine and/or human-based inputs to perceive real and/or virtual environments; abstract such perceptions into models (in an automated manner e.g., with ML, or manually); and use model inference to formulate options for information or action. AI systems are designed to operate with varying levels of autonomy. (OECD, 2019a, p. 15)

This book adopts the OECD definition because it was conceived to be policy-oriented,[8] as it helps to highlight key policy questions, map the policy implications of AI technologies and applications, and support the analysis of policy options (OECD, 2019a, p. 3). This policy-oriented definition offers several advantages. First, it is technically precise at an abstraction level suitable for policy purposes, meaning that it is accurate but also understandable to non-technical experts (i.e., the great majority of policymakers, civil servants, and many researchers that study AI in the public sector). Second, it is technology-neutral (i.e., not overly focused on mainstream AI technologies), and future-proof (i.e., applicable to short-

[8] This concept is drawn from Krafft et al. (2020, p. 8), who argue that a "policy-facing definition" should meet the following criteria: (i) inclusivity of both currently deployed AI technologies and future applications, (ii) accessibility for non-expert audiences, and (iii) allowing for policy implementation of reporting and oversight procedures.

and long-term time horizons, without being speculative). Third, it is supported by a conceptual view of AI systems (see infra) that provides both definitional and analytical clarity, making the OECD definition not just descriptive, but also actionable for policy research because it captures the main elements of AI systems that are relevant to the examination of AI-related policy issues (Grobelnik, 2021; OECD, 2019a, pp 22–23). Fourth, this definition is authoritative (it was elaborated by an international panel of AI experts after 8-month consultations), and representative (it is adopted by the majority of the OECD countries and, with some minor adjustments, by the European Union).

Conceptual View of AI Systems

The OECD definition is centered upon the conceptual view of artificial intelligence systems detailed in the seminal work by Russel and Norvig (1995). In this view, AI systems are intelligent agents that interact with their environment. Environment is the space that AI systems can observe through perceptions and influence through actions.[9] The environment can be real (e.g., physical, social, mental), in which case it is usually only partially observable; or it can be virtual (e.g., board games), in which case it is generally fully observable (OECD, 2019b, p. 7). AI systems interact with the environment through sensors, operational logic, and actuators. **Sensors** (either machines or humans) collect raw data from the environment. **Actuators** (either machines or humans) act to change the state of the environment. The **operational logic** provides output for the actuators based on a given set of objectives and the input data it receives from sensors. These outputs take the form of recommendations, predictions,[10]

[9] Russell and Norvig (1995, p. 46) identify various types of environments in which intelligent agents operate: accessible vs. inaccessible; deterministic vs. non deterministic; episodic vs. non episodic; static vs. dynamic; discrete vs. continuous. Some environments are more demanding than others. Environments that are inaccessible, nondeterministic, non-episodic, dynamic, and continuous are the most challenging.

[10] "Prediction" indicates the process of using data to complete missing information. Risk assessment tools in criminal justice that use data on the offender (e.g., gender, age, years in jail) to estimate the likelihood that he/she will commit offense over a given period after the arrest; or autonomous driving systems that use data from sensors to distinguish between obstacles and instructions (e.g., traffic lights) are examples of AI systems making predictions (Scantamburlo, Charlesworth and Cristianini, 2018, pp. 8–9; OECD, 2019a, pp. 25, 36).

or decisions that can influence the state of the environment (OECD, 2019a, p. 23).

The operational logic is the core component of AI systems. It is based on a model (i.e., a set of rules or analytical functions) that describes the AI system's external environment, its structure and/or dynamics. It does so in a way that may be interpretable or not by humans (experts and non-experts). There are two main processes related to the modeling of AI systems (Marcus and Davis, 2019; OECD, 2019a; Russel and Norvig, 1995). The first is the **construction of the AI model**, which can be based on historical data and/or expert knowledge (e.g., the expert systems[11]). Model construction is designed by humans and/or automated tools (e.g., machine learning algorithms), and it is guided by objectives (e.g., output variables) and performance measures that are set by humans (e.g., accuracy, representativeness of the dataset, etc.). The second process is the **interpretation of the AI model** by humans and/or automated tools in order to make predictions, recommendations, and decisions that influence the environment. In some cases, a model can offer a single recommendation (e.g., deterministic rules). In other cases, a model can offer a variety of recommendations (e.g., probabilistic models). These recommendations are associated with different levels of performance measures like accuracy, confidence, robustness, or risk. In some cases, during the interpretation process, it is possible to explain why specific recommendations are made. In other cases, explanation is almost impossible, a phenomenon often referred to as "black box" (see Glossary).

A conceptual view of AI systems that distinguishes between sensors, actuators, and operational logic highlights how different components of the AI system bear different relevance for the analysis of the opportunities and challenges of using AI in the public sector. This view brings into

[11] Expert systems use hand-coded knowledge and rules to perform extremely specific tasks, and are based on a software that can automate the decision-making of human experts. Very popular in the 1980s, they were designed to solve complex problems in a particular domain by reasoning through bodies of knowledge that contain the data, information, and past experiences about the domain of interest acquired from extensive interviewing of experts (Russell and Norvig, 1995, pp. 22–24). Expert systems belong to symbolic AI (see Glossary), more specifically to the category of knowledge-based systems. In such systems, knowledge is explicitly represented as ontologies or rules, rather than implicitly via code. Knowledge-based systems can be subdivided into systems that base decision-making on prior case experience; and rule-based systems where the domain knowledge is coded in the form of event-condition-action, such as using IF–THEN or IF–THEN–ELSE rules (Engin and Treleaven, 2019, p. 450).

focus the components of the AI system that are most important to understand the policy implications linked to the use of AI in each specific case. As such, it helps to establish a clearer relationship between policy and academic discussions about public sector AI applications, and the technical underpinnings of the technology. The expediency of this conceptual view can be appreciated by looking at two illustrative examples about autonomy and fairness, two topics that are often mentioned in the use of AI in social domains.

Contemporary AI systems are designed to operate with varying levels of autonomy. From autonomous vehicles and smart robots to the automatization of tasks and decision-making, the potential loss of human control and the transfer of human activities and prerogatives to AI give rise to concerns that relate to policy, legal, and ethical issues (Johnson and Verdicchio, 2017; see Sect. 2.2.2.3). Understanding the meaning of autonomy is crucial to support discussions of such issues. In computer science, autonomy refers to artifacts in which the course of action is established at run time, without human intervention, on the basis of computational processes that give the machine instructions and the inputs that the artifact draws from the environment. As such, the autonomy of AI systems is determined by the boundaries of their program and hardware. For instance, sanitation robots are programmed to clean floors and nothing else, and will not perform unrelated activities since they don't necessarily have the necessary mechanical parts and are not programmed to do so. The general connotation of the term autonomy, however, suggests the human characteristics of having the capacity to make decisions and act freely, including machines' own interests that would come into play in decision-making. By providing a technically precise yet understandable description of AI system, this conceptual view shows that autonomy is constrained by the human objectives embedded in the operational logic of AI systems and the features of their actuators. As such, this conceptual view of AI systems supports the analysis of benefits and risks of public sector AI applications by helping to critically approach the many descriptions on machine autonomy that "hide how computational artefacts actually work and how the workings of the hypothetical artefacts of the future are [...], in fact, impossible with the kind of computing available today and for the foreseeable future" (Johnson and Verdicchio, 2017, p. 586).

Contemporary AI systems can also make recommendations or decisions that affect humans (e.g., AI in law enforcement, allocation of policy benefits, etc.; see Sect. 2.2.2.1). Therefore, ethical issues potentially related to the use of AI have garnered great attention in recent years. Among these, fairness is discussed in most AI ethics principles worldwide,[12] including most Chinese AI ethics initiatives (Appendix II). While it is hard to dispute the importance of fairness in AI, understanding its meaning in relation to this technology is crucial to support discussions about AI fairness in the public sector. This requires to discern that there are different *types* of bias, that this bias can occur in different *parts* of the AI systems, and that they can have different *origins* (OECD, 2019b, pp. 9–10, 16). For instance, perception bias can happen when the data collected over-represent (or under-represent) one population, making the AI system operate better (or worse) for that population. Perception bias may also arise from constraints of the technology itself, like algorithms that work better or worse with a different set of variables and features (e.g., in 2016 the computer vision-based vehicle detection system of a Tesla Model S did not notice the white side of the tractor trailer in daylight, and the car in autopilot did not brake). Modeling bias can happen when a human, manually designing all or part of a model, does not take into account some aspects of the environment, consciously or unconsciously (e.g., risk assessment tools used in criminal justice that do not take into account the offender's age or gender, for instance because the designer of the AI model only worked with male or young offenders in the past, would include this modeling bias). Moreover, bias can also occur in the outputs of AI systems, either as a result of the embedded model, or introduced by the external environment (e.g., Microsoft chatbot Tay, developed largely by learning from user interactions, started to generate sexist and hate speech under the attack of malicious users; see Marcus and Davis, 2019).

This conceptual view of AI systems can also support the analysis of other ethical issues that are expected to influence the adoption of AI in the public sector (2.2.2.3). For instance, when discussing the *accountability* of AI systems, this conceptual view helps to focus the analysis

[12] See, for instance, the online databases of the Linking Artificial Intelligence Principles and AI Ethics Lab, https://www.linking-ai-principles.org/ (table on content analysis), or the toolbox Dynamics of AI principles (https://aiethicslab.com/big-picture/). In addition, since 2019 the Fairness, Accountability, and Transparency Conference became part of the activities of the prestigious Association for Computing Machinery (https://facctconference.org/index.html).

on the performance measures that determine the level of accountability of such systems. These performance measures are embedded in model building and model inference (i.e., operational logic). When discussing the ***alignment with human values***, this conceptual view helps to focus the analysis on the human-defined objectives that underpin the construction and interpretation of the model (i.e., operational logic). When exploring issues of ***transparency***, this conceptual view helps to focus the analysis on how the model is constructed and interpreted, such as if model building is automated or not, and if the resulting model is interpretable or not by humans. As for ***risk management***, this conceptual view helps to look not only at the operational logic of the AI system, but also at how the actuators of the AI system actually impact on the environment.

Systematizing AI-related Terminology

Besides defining AI systems, to ensure clarity and consistency of language it is also useful to systematize some general terms and concepts that frequently appear in the study of AI in the public sector. These terms and concepts can be classified into three categories that are often used to define the AI industry value chain[13] (Deloitte China, 2019; Ding, 2018; Tencent and CAICT, 2017):

> **Foundational Layer**: it refers to all the elements that support the development of AI technologies and their applications (see next two layers). The foundational layer includes elements such as: AI research areas (e.g., symbolic AI, statistical AI) and their subsets (e.g., machine learning, neural networks); the availability of digital data; hardware and other technological infrastructure that support and enable AI technologies and applications, like computing power, high-speed Internet connection (broadband and mobile), Internet

[13] There are various possible classifications of AI value chain, which serve different purposes and consider different dimensions of AI. Possible purposes and AI dimensions that could inform the classification of AI value chain include: the vision of what AI should be (e.g., autonomous agents or support systems for human decision); AI as a discipline (e.g., theoretical innovation); or AI technology and applications (similar to the technology and application layers used in this book). See: Rossi (2021) and Stanton et al. (2019) and Corea, F., 2018. AI Knowledge Map: How To Classify AI Technologies. *Forbes*, 22 August, https://www.forbes.com/sites/cognitiveworld/2018/08/22/ai-knowledge-map-how-to-classify-ai-technologies/?sh=666c8e357773.

of Things, etc.; and "AI frameworks" that include standard interfaces, libraries, and toolkits for designing, training, and verifying AI algorithms, such as the open-sourced deep learning frameworks like PyTorch or TensorFlow[14];

Technology Layer: it refers to computer vision, Natural Language Processing, predictive analytics, cognitive robotics, and other machine-based capabilities that allow AI systems to perform tasks that are usually associated with human intelligence, such as: translate or analyze text; detect and classify objects based on images or videos; recognize and interpret human speech; or automating manual tasks that are largely rule-based, structured, and repetitive using software robots (e.g., Robotic Process Automation);

Application Layer: it consists of the integration of AI technologies into products and services, from virtual agents ("AI chatbots") that interact with the users by means of speech recognition and computer vision, to applications that leverage computer vision for medical diagnosis, or risk assessment tools based on predictive analytics that are used in criminal justice. The application layer is usually the most visible, although not all AI-enabled products and services are recognized by users and regulators as belonging to artificial intelligence.[15]

The definition of AI systems, its supporting conceptual view, and the systematization of AI-related terminology provide a better understanding of the working of this technology. This is a necessary preliminary step

[14] AI frameworks are a set of programming shortcuts that make it simpler for researchers and engineers to design, train, and experiment with AI models. They make it possible to use common deep learning concepts such as certain types of hidden layers or activation functions, without directly implementing the relevant math (Webster, 2019, pp. 3–4). Despite the global dominance of PyTorch and TensorFlow, recently in China there has been a growth in the use of locally developed frameworks like Baidu's Paddle Paddle and Huawei's Mindspore (Jeffrey Ding, ChinAI Newsletter #176, 14 March 2022, https://chinai.substack.com/archive).

[15] This is the so-called "AI effect" or "odd paradox", whereby people become accustomed to AI technologies that are widely used in products and services (e.g., speech recognition used in smartphones), and stop to consider these technologies of AI (Stanford University, 2016, p. 12). An illustrative example is the Automated License Plate Readers (ALPR) often used by police forces for the identification of car plates. Despite relying on computer vision, ALPR systems are often not recognized as AI neither by their users nor by the lawmakers (Young et al., 2019).

to clarify the meaning of AI in the public sector, because the study of AI in public organizations requires first of all to explain what AI systems are, and what they can do in the current status of technological development. Based upon this sound understanding of contemporary AI systems, next section examines the technical and social factors that are affecting the uptake and implementation of artificial intelligence in the activities of public organizations, in order to provide a precise conceptualization of "AI in the public sector".

2.2.2 AI in the Public Sector: Activities, Drivers, and Barriers

To clarify and operationalize the meaning of AI in the public sector, this section provides a taxonomy of classes of activities where public organizations are currently applying AI (2.2.2.1). Then it examines the drivers (2.2.2.2) and barriers (2.2.2.3) of AI in the public sector identified by the literature in light of the needs and obligations that motivate and hinder the use of AI in public organizations, thus offering a deeper understanding of the factors affecting the deployment of AI in such activities. Public organizations are defined here as entities that are owned or controlled by the national or local governments, subject to administrative law, and financed by public money to provide public services. Public services indicate services of general interest[16] supplied by public organizations in order to benefit all the people in a particular society or community[17] in economic affairs, health, education, social protection, general public services, and other areas included in the Classification of the Functions of Government (COFOG).[18]

[16] European Economic and Social Committee, "Services of general interest". *European Economic and Social Committee*, https://www.eesc.europa.eu/en/policies/policy-areas/services-general-interest.

[17] Collins English Dictionary, https://www.collinsdictionary.com/dictionary/english/public-service.

[18] These are the areas of activity contained in the OECD's Classification of the Functions of Government (COFOG). The COFOG classification identifies ten first-level groups of expenditures by their socioeconomic objectives (i.e., it classifies government expenditure data from the System of National Accounts by the purpose for which the funds are used which mostly correspond to a specific policy area). The ten first-level groups are: general public services; defense; public order and safety; economic affairs; environmental protection; housing and community affairs; health; recreation, culture and religion; education; and social protection. It further splits each first-level group into nine sub-groups (e.g.,

The COFOG classification is a widely accepted frame to categorize public services. It is the standard classification adopted by OECD countries, the European Union, and the International Monetary Fund, and it offers a comprehensive view of government functions. At the same time, the need for a taxonomy based on specific classes of public sector AI activities was motivated in Chapter 2.1. The analysis explained that academic research on AI in the public sector still provides limited empirical evidence on the use of AI in this area, offering only a partial view of public sector AI applications. Hence, as a basis to clarify the meaning of AI in the public sector, it is paramount to adopt an inclusive yet precise approach that grounds the analysis in empirical evidence, and shows what public organizations are actually doing with AI in their activities.

The examination of drivers and barriers of AI in the public sector serves not only to provide a comprehensive view of the vast range of technical, ethical, legal, and economic elements that influence the use of AI in public organizations. It is also motivated by the existence of contrasting narratives about the benefits and risks that AI can bring to the public sector and other domains, ranging from overly optimistic views to catastrophic ones (Marcus and Davis, 2019; Cave et al., 2018; Calo, 2017). In this regard, scholars of AI in the public sector call for a balanced approach that considers both the benefits and challenges of AI (Wirtz et al., 2019, p. 609). By examining drivers and barriers of AI in the public sector in light of the needs and obligations of public organizations using this technology, this chapter provides a nuanced view of the key sociotechnical factors affecting the implementation of AI in this area, further clarifying the scope of "AI in the public sector".

There are a number of analytical advantages in looking at specific classes of public sector activities, and examining drivers and barriers of AI in light of the needs and obligations that shape the use of this technology in public organizations. First, at the most fundamental level, this approach presents a multidimensional perspective that is empirically grounded (i.e., the taxonomy looks at what public organizations are actually doing with AI now), but also dynamic (i.e., it brings into focus the needs and obligations that are likely to determine how public organizations will adjust AI applications to meet their requirements).

"economic affairs" include transport, communication, etc.) See: OECD, 2021. *Government at a Glance 2021*, Paris: OECD Publishing, https://doi.org/10.1787/1c258f55-en, pp. 258–259.

Second, compared to other widely used classifications based on abstract government functions (e.g., COFOG[19]) or single AI use cases,[20] the taxonomy proposed here provides a comprehensive yet precise understanding of the activities where public organizations are currently applying AI. This taxonomy highlights the main tasks that public organizations accomplish with the support of AI technologies, grounding the analysis in the reality of prevailing public sector AI applications. In doing so, it outlines with greater precision what it means to use artificial intelligence in this area.

Third, examining drivers and barriers of AI in the public sector in light of needs and obligations of public organizations deepens our knowledge of the factors that motivate and hinder the use of AI in public sector activities. It provides valuable criteria to assess the theoretical validity of identifying certain benefits and challenges of AI as drivers and barriers of AI in the public sector. By emphasizing that public organizations are animated by some established needs and obligations when using AI in their activities, it is logical to postulate that the benefits of AI that help public organizations to achieve their needs are drivers of AI in the public sector; on the contrary, challenges of AI that hinder public organizations from fulfilling their obligations are barriers to AI in the public sector. Next paragraphs develop and implement this approach.

Fourth, because of the unified nature of the AI technology and the similarities of the activities performed by public organizations worldwide

[19] The COFOG categories of public services (see above) are sometimes used as basis for the taxonomy of AI in the public sector (Misuraca, van Noordt and Boukli, 2020; Sousa et al., 2019). Each COFOG function (e.g., environmental protection) is very abstract, and includes different classes of activities (e.g., public service delivery, enforcement, and compliance, etc.). This classification offers little insights on what public organizations are doing with artificial intelligence in practice. Indeed, even a study that uses both the COFOG function-based taxonomy and the task-based classification by Engstrom et al. (2020) observes: "Considering the governmental tasks in association with the COFOG taxonomy [...] helps keep some distance from the often too abstract COFOG functions in relation with the need to reduce the level of ambiguity regarding certain policy sectors" (Misuracá and van Noordt, 2020, p. 26).

[20] A classification based on single activities would not allow to gain a comprehensive view about the use of AI in the public sector. For instance, "filling out and searching documents" is an activity that can be used in various classes of public sector tasks: help citizens search documents (public service delivery); assist civil servants to find documents needed for their work (internal management); or identify users that are eligible for a certain service or benefit (adjudication), among others.

(Gal, 2020), which are especially true in the case of AI applications in cities,[21] the drivers and barriers discussed here are expected to be relevant globally. This assumption is corroborated by showing that these drivers and barriers are discussed both in international and Chinese-language sources. Notably, the existence of some universal drivers and barriers of AI in the public sector does not invalidate the argument made earlier about the importance of context-specific research, but it rather complements it. In fact, it is widely agreed that conducting in-depth investigation on the adoption of AI in the public sector must also consider the economic, political, and social factors of different countries (Zhang et al., 2021; Zuiderwijk et al., 2021). Therefore, consistently with research framework developed earlier, Sect. 2.2.3 integrates the analysis of universal drivers and barriers of AI in the public sector by examining context-specific factors of AI uptake and implementation in the public sector in China.

AI in the Public Sector: Classes of Activities

To gain a comprehensive view of the main tasks that public organizations currently accomplish with the support of AI technologies, this section adopts a taxonomy based on classes of public sector activities. This taxonomy builds upon the classification proposed by Engstrom et al. (2020) in studying the use of AI in United States government agencies, and it is integrated with a class of activities ("public infrastructure management") drawn from an earlier study by Engin and Treleaven (2019). The classes of activities in this taxonomy aren't necessarily discrete conceptual units,[22] and the use cases were assigned to each class based on their main function. The use cases were collected from academic studies, policy reports, websites of public agencies and international organizations, news articles, and other open sources.

[21] Previous studies observed that "[s]ince the scope of activities of municipalities is to a large extent similar world-wide, areas of using AI, as well as challenges faced during adoption, or even barriers to adoption are likely to be the same also in other countries" (Mikalef et al., 2019, p. 10).

[22] For instance, the Seoul Night Bus—an AI-based service that uses mobile phone and geospatial data to provide public transport services—contributes to improving public service delivery as well as the operation of public infrastructure. See: Seoul Solution, 2017. Night Bus (called Owl Bus): Route Design Using Big Data https://seoulsolution.kr/en/content/night-bus-called-owl-bus-route-design-using-big-data.

Public Service Delivery and Engagement indicates the use of AI systems to support the direct provision of services to the public, or facilitate communications with the public for regulatory or other purposes. Many activities in this class currently fall into five types, which use AI to support the interactions with citizens and their access to public services: answering questions, filling out and searching documents, routing requests, translation, and drafting documents (Mehr, 2017). There is, however, also a growing use of AI systems to empower public employees and organizations by augmenting their capabilities to perform their functions (Desouza, 2021, pp. 6–8; Duan et al., 2019). Examples of AI applications in this class include:

- Emma, a computer-generated virtual assistant (chatbot) that can answer in writing to frequently asked questions about citizenship and immigration services in the United States[23];
- the chatbot UNA used by the Register of Enterprises of the Republic of Latvia to answer in writing frequently asked questions regarding the process of registering a company[24];
- the use of AI systems to improve the speed and accuracy of medical diagnosis and screening for diseases[25];
- China's Internet Courts that use AI and other digital technologies to facilitate users' engagement with the tribunals.[26]

[23] U.S. Citizenship and Immigration Services (USCIS), 2018. *Meet Emma, Our Virtual Assistant*. https://www.uscis.gov/tools/meet-emma-our-virtual-assistant (last accessed on 27 November 2023). To answer a question, Emma searches through the USCIS website and provides short answers and links to contents. If Emma is unable to offer a reply, she directs the customer to a live agent. Emma can type answers in English and Spanish and speak in English. See also: https://www.dhs.gov/sites/default/files/publications/privacy-pia-uscis-livechat-may2017.pdf.

[24] OECD Observatory of Public Sector Innovation, *UNA—The First Virtual Assistant of Public Administration in Latvia*. https://oecd-opsi.org/innovations/una-the-first-virtual-assistant-of-public-administration-in-latvia/. Chatbot website: https://www.ur.gov.lv/en/about-us/una/ (last accessed on 27 November 2023).

[25] World Health Organization, 2021. WHO Issues First Global Report on Artificial Intelligence (AI) in Health and Six Guiding Principles for Its Design and Use. *WHO Website*, 28 June, https://www.who.int/news/item/28-06-2021-who-issues-first-global-report-on-ai-in-health-and-six-guiding-principles-for-its-design-and-use.

[26] CGTN, 2021. How China's 'Internet Courts' Are Adapting to a New Era. *CTGN News*, 7 March, https://news.cgtn.com/news/2021-03-07/How-China-s-Internet-Courts-are-adapting-to-a-new-era-YqTdsiEcVy/index.html/

Internal Management indicates the use of AI systems to support a wide range of activities related to public organizations' internal operations. Activities in this class include: the use of AI to reduce administrative burdens and backlogs (e.g., automating some aspects of the call centers work, or deploying Robotic Process Automation systems to access multiple databases accurately and rapidly); the use of AI to support internal operations related to human resources management (e.g., hiring new staff), IT services (e.g., updating passwords), or public procurement (e.g., ensuring compliance with existing regulations), among others. Examples of AI applications in this class include:

- the U.S. Air Force trialing the use of AI to make sense of complex acquisition regulations, so it can speed up the process of buying goods and services (Partnership for Public Service and IBM, 2018);
- the use of Tengai, an interviewer robot adopted by the recruitment agency of a Swedish municipality to make the hiring process faster and less biased than traditional interview practices (Misuraca and van Noordt, 2020);
- the Hong Kong Immigration Department algorithmic system for sorting passport applications and transferring them to a visa officer for revision and final evaluation (Desouza, 2018).

Adjudication indicates the use of AI systems to assist or conduct the granting of benefits or the entitlement of rights to citizens. This class of activities often includes the management of public records (i.e., archives, databases) and correspondence (i.e., forms and submissions, communications). Activities in this class use AI to: collect and process data in public records (e.g., automated systems for the digitalization of documents, big data analytics for extracting information from digital databases); classify user-generated data and assign them to the relevant archive/database; or support decision-making in granting benefits and other entitlements, among others. Examples of AI applications in this class include:

- the use of AI systems to determine welfare benefits eligibility in areas like public housing, health, or education in the United States,[27]

[27] AI Now, 2018. *Algorithmic Accountability Policy Toolkit*. AI Now Institute, https://ainowinstitute.org/aap-toolkit.pdf.

or the U.S. Patent and Trademark Office's use of AI tools for adjudicating patent and trademark applications (Engstrom et al., 2020);

- a nursery child-recruitment system in Warsaw (Poland) that uses an AI model to examine the data provided by parents and automatically assigns children into individual nurseries (Misuraca and van Noordt, 2020);
- the Mirsal service developed in the United Arab Emirates to enhance the correspondence system of official letters among public organizations, and between public organizations and businesses.[28]

Public Infrastructure Management indicates the use of AI systems to maintain and operate public physical assets (e.g., public roads, transport systems, power and water supply networks, waste management, etc.). Activities in this class include the use of AI to control and optimize traffic flows, or manage and maintain public infrastructure (e.g., through Building Information Modeling, that is the digital model of a facility used to support construction, refurbishment, or management), among others. Examples of AI applications in this class include:

- ActiveRemediation, an AI model that predicts lead contamination of water from pipes used in Michigan[29];
- the use of AI for a faster detection of energy saving potential in public buildings adopted in Belgium[30];
- the use of AI systems to assist in planning road maintenance, deployed in some Chinese highways[31];

[28] OECD Observatory of Public Sector Innovation, *Mirsal*. https://oecd-opsi.org/innovations/mirsal/ (last accessed on 27 November 2023).

[29] Abernethy, J. et al., 2018. ActiveRemediation: The Search for Lead Pipes in Flint, Michigan. *Cornell University Library*, August 17, https://arxiv.org/abs/1806.10692.

[30] Flanders Department of Economy, Science and Innovation. *Innovative Functionalities and Artificial Intelligence for Energy Saving in the Public Sector*, https://www.innovatieveoverheidsopdrachten.be/en/projects/innovative-functionalities-and-artificial-intelligence-energy-saving-public-sector (last accessed on 27 November 2023).

[31] OECD Observatory of Public Sector Innovation, *SenseTraffic ICV Maint for Improving Highway and Road Maintenance Operations*, https://oecd-opsi.org/innovations/sensetraffic-icv-maint/ (last accessed on 27 November 2023).

- real-time traffic flow management systems like the Alibaba City Brain adopted in several cities in China and other countries,[32] or the analogous Surtrac (Scalable URban TRAffic Control) adaptive signal control system used in Pittsburg, United States (Desouza, 2018; Hager et al., 2017), among others.

Enforcement indicates the use of AI systems to identify and/or prioritize targets of enforcement action, and to promote compliance with existing laws and regulations. Activities in this class include the use of AI to support public security, the work of the judiciary, enforcement agencies, and other public organizations (e.g., tackle welfare fraud, false declarations or the misuse of public funding). Examples of AI applications in this class include:

- the Coast Guard using AI to randomize its boat patrol routes in cities like New York and Los Angeles, making their day-to-day security-related activities less predictable for criminals[33];
- the USA Securities and Exchange Commission using AI to identify financial reporting fraud and detect suspicious share trading (Engstrom et al., 2020);
- various police forces in Spain using VeriPol AI systems that leverage Natural Language Processing to detect false reports[34];
- the Protection Assistant for Wildlife Security (PAWS) project that applies AI algorithms to predict poaching attacks and optimize the patrol routes of game wardens in Uganda[35];

[32] Alibaba City Brain for real-time traffic flow management, developed in Hangzhou, is now used in more than 20 Chinese cities. Alibaba Cloud, 2019. *City Brain Now in 23 Cities in Asia*, 28 October, https://www.alibabacloud.com/blog/city-brain-now-in-23-cities-in-asia_595479.

[33] Savitz, S., Davenport, A. and Ziegler, M., 2020. The Marine Transportation System, Autonomous Technology, and Implications for the U.S. Coast Guard. *RAND Corporation*, https://doi.org/10.7249/PE359.

[34] Mega, E., 2019. An Algorithm That Can Spot When People Lie to the Police. *Scientific American*, 1 February, https://www.scientificamerican.com/article/an-algorithm-that-can-spot-when-people-lie-to-the-police/.

[35] Snow, J., 2016. Rangers Use Artificial Intelligence to Fight Poachers. *National Geographic*, 12 June, https://www.nationalgeographic.com/animals/article/paws-artificial-intelligence-fights-poaching-ranger-patrols-wildlife-conservation#:~:text=PAWS%2C%20which%20stands%20for%20Protection,poachers%20from%20learning%20patrol%20patterns. The PAWS project continues to study the use of AI to prevent poaching and protect wildlife in several countries. See: https://teamcore.seas.harvard.edu/news/news/paws (last accessed on 27 November 2023).

- the smart case-handling system named System 206 adopted by the Shanghai High People's Court for assisting the judiciary and enforcement agencies in criminal trials.[36]

Public Policy Research, Analysis, and Monitoring indicate the use of AI systems to collect or analyze information that supports decision-making in the public sector. Activities in this class include: the use of AI for modeling proposed policies before they are implemented; developing forecasting models to monitor the efficacy of policy interventions and recommend corrections when needed; or facilitating community participation in policy development, among others. Examples of AI applications in this class include:

- the nEmesis system, which uses Natural Language Processing to identify social media posts of restaurant customers that report symptoms of foodborne illness over the next 72 hours, in order to help health departments in Las Vegas to optimize the inspections of local restaurants (Hager et al., 2017);
- the Dublin Beat, an AI system that collects and analyzes public social media posts in order to give a regular overview of citizen's most pressing concerns in the Dublin Area.[37]

Box 2.1 AI technologies in public sector activities
Computer vision and Natural Language Processing (NLP) are two of the most widely used AI technologies in both the private and public sectors. In a study of public sector AI applications, the McKinsey Global Institute (Chui et al., 2018) identified 18 "AI capabilities" that lend themselves to public sector usages. Among these, 14 "AI capabilities" belong to computer vision and NLP. Later studies based on a survey of public sector

[36] Cui, Y., 2020. *Artificial Intelligence and Judicial Modernization*. Shanghai: Shanghai People's Publishing House.

[37] Pellegrin, J., Colnot, L. and Delponte, L., 2021. *Research for REGI Committee—Artificial Intelligence and Urban Development*. European Parliament, Policy Department for Structural and Cohesion Policies, Brussels, https://www.europarl.europa.eu/RegData/etudes/STUD/2021/690882/IPOL_STU(2021)690882_EN.pdf, p. 20.

AI applications in the European Union and the United States corroborate this finding, showing the prevalent use of NLP and computer vision among AI technologies deployed in the public sector (Engstrom et al., 2020; Misuraca et al., 2020). Some examples of public sector applications involving these AI technologies are presented below in relation to the classes of activities just examined.

Computer vision: computer vision is applied in public sector activities that require to perform tasks that are most easily accomplished through the analysis of images and videos. For instance: managing public infrastructure (the AI system used for supporting road maintenance in some Chinese highways); managing public records and adjudication (SATIKAS analyses satellite images to automatically detect whether mowing has taken place on the Estonian grasslands[38]); conduct enforcement and compliance (e.g., China's Internet courts that use AI to support online trials); or real-time decision-making (assist in parsing satellite images to find flooded and unusable roads across a large area after a hurricane, Chui et al., 2018, pp. 28–29).

Some computer vision applications consist of tasks a human being could potentially accomplish on an individual level, but the required number of instances is so large that it exceeds human capacity (e.g., identify criminal suspects in video recordings). In other cases, AI systems can be more accurate than humans, often by processing more information faster (e.g., the IP Australia's Australian Trade Mark Search is a service that enables users to upload a logo and search instantaneously IP Australia's database of 400,000 images, which then return trademark results based on visual similarity through image recognition).

Natural Language Processing: NLP is applied in classes of public sector activities that require to access and use information stored in unstructured textual form, such as user queries, incident reports, health records, or SMS messages and social media posts. For instance: delivering public services

[38] The mowing of the grasslands is one of the most mentioned obligations for all the various agricultural subsidies offered by the Estonian government, and has one of the highest amounts of non-compliances in the country (Misuraca and van Noordt, 2020, p. 42).

(the chatbots Emma and UNA that answer in writing to frequently asked questions), enforcement and compliance (the VeriPol system used in Spain to detecting false police reports), or public policy development (e.g., the nEmesis system and Dublin Beat that scan websites and social media posts to identify discussions on certain topics). NLP and computer vision can be used together, for instance to analyze text from scanned documents (e.g., the criminal case-handling System 206), or text embedded in images and videos.

As with methods based on computer vision, in some cases a human could probably perform a task with greater accuracy than a trained machine-learning model can. Nonetheless, Chui et al. (2018) observe that the speed of "good enough" AI systems can enable meaningful scale efficiencies (e.g., providing automated answers to questions that citizens may ask through emails). In other cases, especially those that require processing and analyzing vast amounts of information quickly, AI models can outperform humans (e.g., monitoring the outbreak of disease by analyzing social media posts[39]).

There are of course other AI technologies and solutions that have been adopted in the public sector: from AI models that parse large datasets to identify patterns in the data that are shared with experts for further analysis, to service robots in medicine or public security and the use of AI-enabled autonomous equipment in transport and other areas. At the same time, various studies of extant public sector AI applications confirm that computer vision and NLP are the dominant technologies now in use in public organizations (Desouza, 2021; Engstrom et al., 2020; Chui et al., 2018; Wirtz et al., 2019; Misuraca and van Noordt, 2020, pp. 22–23; CCC, 2017; OPSI's Case Study Platform[40]; OECD AI Policy Observatory[41]).

Drivers: Benefits of Using AI in the Public Sector

The use of AI in the activities of public organizations is driven by a fundamental need to improve the efficiency and effectiveness of public

[39] Lin, L., and Hou, Z., 2020. Combat COVID-19 with Artificial Intelligence and Big Data. *Journal of Travel Medicine*, 27(5), https://doi.org/10.1093/jtm/taaa080.

[40] Observatory of Public Sector Innovation (OPSI), OECD, https://oecd-opsi.org/case_type/opsi/.

[41] OECD AI Policy Observatory, https://oecd.ai/en/policy-areas.

sector operations and public service provision. This need is exemplified by the applications described in the taxonomy of public sector AI activities (2.2.2.1). For instance, in "public service delivery and engagement", the chatbot UNA in Latvia makes the communications with users more accessible and friendly, and it also saves citizens' time and money as they don't have to attend the service centers in presence. By replying automatically to standard questions, the chatbot UNA also enables civil servants to delegate routine work and focus on higher value tasks. In "internal management", the Tengai robot in Sweden makes the selection and hiring processes faster and cheaper, freeing up crucial resources to be spent on other tasks. The adoption of AI systems at the Hong Kong Immigration Department increases the speed with which transactions are processed, reprioritizing the assignment of tasks between humans and machines.[42] In "adjudication", the use of deep learning models for adjudicating patent and trademark applications at the U.S. Patent and Trademark Office improves the efficiency and reduces the search costs in patent examination (Engstrom et al., 2020). In "public infrastructure management", real-time traffic flow management systems like the Alibaba City Brain in China are used to automatically reduce traffic congestion and assist in routing emergency vehicles,[43] allowing the public sector to save resources and provide better services. In "enforcement", the use of Natural Language Processing in the VeriPol system in Spain is helping police forces to save time and human resources by detecting false police reports with higher accuracy than humans, so that police don't misallocate its assets to investigate cases that had never occurred.[44] In "public policy research, analysis and monitoring", the nEmesis system allows public organizations to focus their limited resources on problematic cases. This led to significant improvements to the efficacy of the inspections, resulting in 9,000 fewer food poisoning incidents in Las Vegas during the course of the study.[45] Earlier empirical studies confirm that improving the efficiency

[42] Chun, H., n.d. AI Success Stories, https://www.cs.cityu.edu.hk/~hwchun/AIProjects/stories/km/ebrain/ (last accessed on 29 September 2022).

[43] MacroPolo, ChinAI, Select AI-Related Government Projects at the Local Level. MacroPolo Website, https://macropolo.org/digital-projects/chinai/the-plan/ (last accessed on 10 October 2022).

[44] Mega, 2019 (cit.).

[45] National Science Foundation, 2016. Fighting Food Poisoning in Las Vegas with Machine Learning, https://www.nsf.gov/news/news_summ.jsp?cntn_id=137848.

and effectiveness of public sector operations and public service provision is a crucial need that motivates AI adoption in public organizations. A survey of 85 public sector AI applications in the European Union concluded that "most of the AI-technologies are implemented with efficiency gains in mind", while values like "openness" and "inclusion" only constitute secondary drivers (Misuraca et al., 2020, p. 96). Similarly, a survey of AI uses at 142 federal department, agencies, and sub-agencies in the United States revealed that the great majority of AI applications have been developed to improve the accuracy and efficiency of government operations (Engstrom et al., 2020).

The operational benefits of AI identified by the literature are expected to help public organizations to meet their need for improved efficiency and effectiveness in performing their activities, therefore they are postulated to be drivers of AI in the public sector and are examined accordingly. To organize the analysis of these drivers, this section builds on two widely cited studies that focus on the analysis of the benefits of AI in the public sector[46] (Chen et al., 2019; Eggers et al., 2017). By combining the classifications of these studies with the insights derived from the review of public sector activities, this research deduced three general categories of drivers of AI in the public sector: improving public service provision, optimizing resource allocation, and enhancing decision-making capabilities. The analysis conducted here expands on earlier studies: it is based upon a more precise understanding of the activities that AI technologies are expected to improve (i.e., the taxonomy developed in 2.2.2.1); and it makes explicit the link between these drivers and a fundamental need of public organizations using AI in their activities, thus providing deeper insights into the factors motivating AI applications in the public sector.

[46] In their study discussing the motivations for the public sector to adopt AI, Chen et al. (2019) summarize four categories of benefits, namely: relieving human resources; assisting in providing services; enhancing the capacity of decision-makers; and promoting the transformation of public sector. Based on their analysis of the potential benefits of AI for government, Eggers et al. (2017) propose four automation choices: relieve (i.e., freeing workers for more valuable work); split up (i.e., breaking a job into steps and automating as many as possible, leaving humans to do the remainder); replace (i.e., technology is used to do an entire job once performed by a human); and augment and extend (i.e., humans and computers combining their strengths to achieve faster and better results, often doing what humans couldn't do before). The category "promoting the transformation of public sector" proposed by Chen et al. (2019) was discarded because only two of the studies reviewed identify the transformation of the public sector as a driver of AI adoption and application (the same Chen et al., 2019; Pencheva et al., 2020).

1. **Improving Public Service Provision**. Scholars agree that AI can increase the efficiency, effectiveness, accuracy, and speed of process of the public sector. Wirtz and Müller (2019) indicate that AI can improve public sector operations by enhancing the magnitude, scope, and speed of information processing, which yields an efficient and sustainable allocation of public resources so that public management tasks can be performed better. AI can also accelerate the provision of services (e.g., AI-guided completion of application forms) by improving submission and forwarding of requests, achieving an improved standard of quality, and a decreasing error rate due to deep learning algorithms. Pencheva et al. (2020) state that AI can improve efficiency and effectiveness in the delivery of public services by supporting public managers in aggregating and analyzing citizens' policy preferences and needs, in order to better understand which incentives will work and under what circumstances. Other scholars agree that AI is bringing improvements to the existing practices of public organizations (Engstrom et al., 2020), offers benefits in the provision of public services (Sousa et al., 2019), and is expected to improve the quality and efficiency of service provision (Toll et al., 2020). Chen et al. (2019) argue that AI can improve public service delivery, ease the internal administrative burden of public organizations by reducing the number of administrative backlogs, and better respond to public demands, thus making public organizations more effective. Misuraca, van Noordt, and Boukli (2020) observe that Natural Language Processing can support efficiency and effectiveness by automatically translating government information, providing interactions through chatbots, or conducting sentiment analysis of textual data. In addition, the profiling capabilities of AI systems allow the government to provide more tailored public services, or personal recommendations based upon the citizen's profile and those with similar needs. The use of AI to provide personalized public services is reiterated by Dwivedi et al. (2021), who state that AI-based advanced analytics can extract relevant details from government databases and generate tailored forms (e.g., income tax return forms) for every user based on age, gender, literacy level, special needs, and eligibility, and autofill most of the fields, making the service more efficient. Going a step further, the authors suggest AI-based advanced analytics can help governments to provide "predictive services", whereby public services or

the benefits get delivered to eligible citizens automatically when they need them (e.g., pensions, financial allowances, etc.). Tinholt et al. (2017) also emphasize that AI solutions can improve public service quality through service personalization. Quality improvements are also expected in terms a better understanding of the needs of citizens based on advanced analytics (e.g., predictive healthcare, optimizing the maintenance of public areas), more accurate and reliable public services, and shorter waiting lists due to AI systems full-service availability that outperforms human employees. The use of automated algorithms is also expected to significantly reduce fraud and errors in service processing, as AI can help in detecting anomalies within big datasets to help organizations focus on specific cases which, according to the algorithm, stand out from the rest (Misuraca et al., 2020). Scholars also emphasize that AI can increase efficiency and effectiveness by promoting the communications between the public sector and citizens, both in terms of answering inquiries and facilitating engagement (Pencheva et al., 2020; Chen et al., 2019; Mehr, 2017). Androutsopoulou et al. (2019) observe that chatbots and other types of AI solutions (e.g., machine learning algorithms, process automation, and image recognition software) can significantly reduce the administrative burden of public organizations and advance the communication between government and citizens for the provision of public services, which has been problematic for a long time. Similarly, Eggers et al. (2017) argue that cognitive automation and engagement systems (i.e., AI chatbots) can be used as interactive virtual assistants to answer questions, check users' qualifications, and refer them to human staff, if necessary, thus improving the efficiency of public service delivery. Such systems can also be deployed by public organizations for internal operations to improve the efficiency of several internal applications. Zheng et al. (2018) also observe that virtual agents can improve efficiency by allocating tasks to areas of responsibility. At a more general level, Kankanhalli et al. (2019) observe that AI technologies can be applied in areas such as transportation, healthcare, public safety to improve the efficiency of governance and the quality of life of citizens. Other studies also argue that AI can make public service delivery more effective, more targeted, and more personal (Zuiderwijk et al., 2021; Ojo et al., 2019). Chinese-language sources also state that AI can enhance the quality of public service delivery and the level of administrative efficiency (Kang and Tang, 2021; Wu, 2021; Tao 2020; Chen, 2019; Wang and Wang, 2019; Mei, 2018), arguing that AI has become an indispensable technological tool for the modernization of national governance (Xu and Xu, 2020) and for improving China's public management capacity (Yu, 2020).

2. **Optimizing Resource Allocation**. Scholars note that AI can help governments to optimize the allocation of scarce resources. Berryhill et al. (2019) indicate that some of the most immediate impacts of AI in the public sector involve automating simple tasks, changing the way that public servants themselves do their jobs, helping government shift from low-value to high-value work, and better focus on core responsibilities by reducing or eliminating repetitive tasks. Similarly, Dwivedi et al. (2021) argue that AI chatbots, rule-based systems, speech recognition, machine translation, computer vision, machine learning, robotics, and Natural Language Processing have the potential to free up precious cognitive resources of public workers, who can then be allocated to tasks of higher added value. Other scholars agree that one significant benefit that AI technologies bring to public organizations is relieving public employees from straightforward but repetitive tasks that are highly time-consuming, freeing their employees for more valuable work (Chen et al., 2019). Eggers et al. (2017) observe that robotics and cognitive automation (i.e., AI) allow machines to replicate human actions and judgment, freeing people from manual tasks in order to do work that requires uniquely human abilities. This is expected to address three common pain points for the public sector: resource constraints (through both resource redistribution and workforce optimization); paperwork burdens; and backlogs (e.g., AI can sift through large amount of data and take appropriate action, leaving difficult cases to human experts, while robotic process automation can reduce backlogs by performing tasks with little human interaction). By better allocating their resources, public organizations can address the shortage of experts (Mehr, 2017). Wirtz and Müller (2019) agree that AI can automate routine tasks that require a low level of expert knowledge, assigning to human staff some special cases requiring high-skilled decision-makers. As such, AI improves the efficiency and effectivity of human labor so that human expert skills are deployed where and when they are actually needed. In addition, by automating at least some parts of the working process,

AI is expected to reduce costs while at the same time improving efficiency (Dwivedi et al., 2021; Zuiderwijk et al., 2021; Pencheva et al., 2020; Wirtz et al., 2019). Chinese-language sources discuss the optimization of resources mostly in terms of improved data sharing across different public agencies, arguing that AI will reduce the costs of government operations and effectively control the scale of government (Tao, 2020; Chen, 2019; Zhang, 2019; Zhang et al., 2019).

3. **Enhancing Decision-Making Capabilities**. Scholars observe that AI can provide useful tools to help public organizations make accurate decisions. Chen et al. (2019) argue that Big Data, AI, and other advanced technologies are expected to improve the quality of public decision-making. The high velocity of AI systems in processing and analyzing data enables policymakers to quickly react to and incorporate information from a variety of sources, including channels outside the formal policy realm such as social media or online consultations. As such, AI can help to design policies and services that closely match the demands of the citizens (Pencheva et al., 2020; Chen et al., 2019; Zheng et al., 2018). In particular, Pencheva et al. (2020) observe that AI can improve policy analysis in two ways: first, advanced analytics can observe variables at the aggregate (e.g., neighborhood, city, etc.) as well as the individual level, thus providing a greater degree of granularity; second, AI's capacity to handle time-series data from multiple, diverse sources supports the holistic measurement of policy outcomes. These two advantages enable public managers to understand the long-term effects of interventions in policy areas that have an impact throughout one's life, such as healthcare and education. Mehr (2017) notes that AI is expected to enhance public decision-making due to its capability to support the aggregation and summarization of diverse data, and make accurate predictions of different projected scenarios and their outcomes. Zuiderwijk et al. (2021) also argue that machine learning can lead to better and more accurate decisions, identifying potential areas for action. Eggers et al. (2017) observe that AI can enhance decision-making capacities in three ways. First, AI systems that employ neural networks can understand complex scenarios and identify pertinent patterns in data. Second, AI technologies embedded with sensors and cameras allow public organizations to track and report important information in real time, improving

decision-making in various classes of activities (e.g., public infrastructure maintenance, enforcement, policy research, analysis, and monitoring). Third, AI can improve prediction. Machine learning and Natural Language Processing can reveal patterns and guide effective responses to problems. Similarly, Misuraca et al. (2020) observe that AI is expected to make predictions that are far more comprehensive and accurate than human predictions, as machine predictions are based on huge data volumes. In their analysis of AI applications for the public sector, Wirtz et al. (2019) observe that AI-based predictive analytics, data visualization, and other techniques based on statistical analysis of data can improve public decision-making. Chinese-language sources also emphasize that AI can improve public decision-making in several ways: expand the channels for collecting data and improving data analytics (Chen, 2019; Mei, 2018; Wu, 2021); improve policy formulation, policy implementation, and policy evaluation (Wu, 2021; Zhang, 2019); effectively analyze data collected from citizens to better understand their needs (Mei, 2018, Xu and Xu, 2020, Wu, 2021); and effectively predict and monitor various social risks (Yang, 2021).

Barriers: Challenges of Using AI in the Public Sector
The use of AI in the activities of public organizations is also shaped by a set of fundamental obligations. These obligations are due to the unique institutional and social role of the public sector, and they imply that public organizations are subjected to more complex and often more stringent requirements than the private sector when using AI in their activities. The public sector must ensure that the outcomes of its activities are beneficial to the society as a whole, beyond the expected impacts on the intended recipients (ETAPAS, 2021; Makasi et al., 2021; Desouza et al., 2020; Henman, 2020; Mikhaylov et al., 2018; Crawford and Whittaker, 2016). Similarly, the role of the public sector as regulator of AI implies that it must keep the technology oriented toward improving the lives of citizens, ensuring that AI usages are benign and inclusive (Dwivedi et al., 2021; Misuraca and van Noordt, 2020). Public organizations must also fulfill a high level of transparency, fairness, and accountability in decision-making and operations, as citizens have the statutory right to equitable treatment (Makasi et al., 2021; Engstrom et al., 2020; Tinholt et al., 2017). Public

organizations must also satisfy ethical concerns, building a broad understanding and acceptance of AI in society, as well as creating a sense of security (Wirtz et al., 2019). Finally, given that public sector AI activities are taxpayer-funded, they face regular scrutiny and oversight that are generally not seen in the private sector use of AI (Desouza et al., 2020).

The technological, ethical, legal, and socioeconomic challenges of AI identified by the literature are expected to hinder public organizations from fulfilling their established obligations to ensure the beneficial, inclusive, fair, transparent, and accountable use of AI in the public sector; hence, they are postulated to be barriers of AI in the public sector and will be examined accordingly. The following categories build upon the classification of Wirtz et al. (2019), who identified "AI technology", "AI laws and regulations", "AI ethics", and "AI society" as the main challenges of the use of AI in the public sector. These four categories accurately capture the manifold factors that scholars believe are hindering AI uptake and implementation in public organizations, providing a good basis for a systematic and comprehensive review of the barriers to AI in the public sector identified by other studies.

1. **AI Technology, Infrastructure, and Operations**. While AI technologies are the same in the public and private sectors, scholars identified a number of features that specifically complicate the use of AI in public organizations: an operational logic that is often incompatible with human cognitive capabilities; learning capacity from both data and human interactions, which can happen without human supervision; the ability to profile individuals and groups based on environmental characteristics (e.g., user profiles) and previous interactions; and the limitations of AI systems to properly account for or understand the interactions between technical systems and social contexts (Misuraca and van Noordt, 2020; Desouza et al., 2020). These features are not unique to the public sector. However, they are especially important in this area because they present a special range of opportunities and challenges in public decision-making, which has to deal with the constantly changing variables and complexities of the human environment (Dwivedi et al., 2021; Mikhaylov et al., 2018). In addition, there are other general technological challenges that can undermine public sector AI applications.

Data availability, quality, and integration are expected to pose fundamental barriers to AI uptake and implementation in public organizations (Dwivedi et al., 2021; Zuiderwijk et al., 2021; Desouza, Dawson and Chenok, 2020; Engstrom et al., 2020; Pencheva et al., 2020; Chen et al., 2019; Engin and Treleaven 2019; Sun and Medaglia, 2019; Tinholt et al., 2017; Chui et al., 2018; Mehr, 2017). Using big volumes of data and AI platforms also requires that public organizations replace, modify, or retire their often-outdated IT infrastructure, break data silos, and address the misalignments in data governance protocols that limit the interoperability and integration of multiple databases across different public agencies, among others (Desouza, 2021; Engstrom et al., 2020; Sun and Medaglia, 2019; Mehr, 2017). There is also a lack of specialization and expertise due to the scarcity of human capital with relevant skillsets to design, manage, and execute AI projects in the public sector (Dwivedi et al., 2021; Zuiderwijk et al., 2021; Pencheva et al., 2020; Chen et al., 2019; Mikalef et al., 2019; Sun and Medaglia, 2019; Tinholt et al., 2017; Wirtz et al., 2019). One specific challenge in terms of skills is that public organizations must ensure that AI tools are both usable and compliant to legal obligations (Engstrom et al., 2020; Berryhill et al., 2019); in turn, this requires a combination of expertise (e.g., ethical and privacy issues, data science, engineering knowledge) that hardly occur together, and almost never in the public sector (Hager et al., 2017). In addition, due to a general shortage of qualified AI experts, the financial compensation for technical AI expertise is very high in the commercial sector, straining the ability of public sector organizations to recruit (Engstrom et al., 2020; Chui et al., 2018). Scarce supply is further complicated by the fact that the interests and working practices of computing and policy domains tend to be very different, and require professionals who can understand both the functional elements of the organizations' processes as well as appreciate the technical elements of AI (Engin and Treleaven 2019; Hager et al., 2017). Other challenges in this dimension are related to financial feasibility and economic sustainability. Scholars agree that AI adoption has significant upfront costs, as it requires sophisticated technological infrastructure to store and process data, to hire highly skilled personnel, and the costs of operation and maintenance. As such, limited financial resources can hinder AI use in the public sector (Desouza, 2021; Dwivedi et al., 2021; Sun and Medaglia, 2019). Financial feasibility challenges are also due to budgetary constraints and the manner in which programs are funded in the public sector, which often makes it easier to secure funding for existing programs than to propose new efforts (Engstrom et al., 2020). In addition, as public sector projects are taxpayer-funded, they face regular scrutiny and oversight that is generally not seen in the private sector (Desouza et al., 2020). Chinese-language sources highlight the limited interoperability among the datasets and platforms of different organizations (Wu, 2021; Chen, 2019; Wang and Wang, 2019); issues related to information security (Li and Li, 2021; Wu, 2021; Tao, 2020; Zhang et al., 2019); the bureaucratic inertia that can hinder AI adoption (Chen, 2019; Wang and Wang, 2019; Jia and Jiang, 2017); and the difficulties in training and recruiting adequate human resources (Tao, 2020).

2. **AI Laws and Regulations**. Challenges in this dimension include issues of political principles, legal regulations, and public policy affecting the use of AI in the public sector (Sun and Medaglia, 2019). Scholars highlight the challenges related to the governance of autonomous intelligence systems, which requires that regulators comprehend and control the decisions and actions of AI systems that in some cases operate as "black boxes" (Pencheva et al., 2020). The difficulties in interpreting the decision of AI systems pose questions of legal responsibility and accountability (Dwivedi et al., 2021; Zuiderwijk et al., 2021; Kankanhalli et al., 2019; Tinholt et al., 2017; Wirtz et al., 2019). These difficulties also imply choosing suitable regulatory mechanisms that ensure legal and political accountability when using AI in public organizations (Engstrom et al., 2020). Scholars also identify the impact of automated decision-making on the political accountability of public governance as a challenge of AI adoption (Dwivedi et al., 2021; Duan et al., 2019). Similar to considerations about AI safety (see below), data privacy is deemed especially important in the public sector because public organizations by mandate collect sensitive information on citizens that, if used together, could significantly undermine privacy (Dwivedi et al., 2021; Zuiderwijk et al., 2021; Engstrom et al., 2020; Pencheva et al., 2020; Kankanhalli et al., 2019; Wirtz and Müller, 2019). In this respect, there is a challenge to reconcile data sharing needs with data privacy obligations

(Engstrom et al, 2020). In addition, AI applications also give rise to challenges in administrative law and procedural fairness.: judgments based on probabilistic calculations, the reduction of human discretion in administrative decision making, and the opaqueness of machine learning algorithms all pose challenges to AI adoption (Zuiderwijk et al., 2021; Engstrom et al., 2020; Henman, 2020). Furthermore, AI-based predictions might allow administrative judges to readily compare their inclination to that of others, threatening notions of decisional independence (Engstrom et al., 2020). Legal and regulatory challenges are complicated by the lack of agreement on how to address them. Some call for new laws and institutions, arguing that the existing regulatory framework is insufficient (Turner, 2017). Others recommend that policymakers should see the regulation of AI as an extension of existing legislation (e.g., privacy and data protection laws), arguing that existing regulations are often adequate to limit the unintended and unwanted consequences of AI deployment (Misuraca and van Noordt, 2020). Others again observe that great effort has gone into generating regulatory frameworks that are unnecessary or irrelevant (since most essentially argue that AI should obey the law or be "good"), while also pointing to the difficulties of applying existing laws to AI systems that differ from other ICT technologies in use in public organizations and society (Chesterman, 2021). At present, legislative frameworks that specifically regulate AI may be nascent or non-existent (Makasi et al., 2021), and most AI regulatory efforts focus either on some specific aspects such as data privacy, or on broad issues that often overlap with AI ethics and are difficult to operationalize into policy actions (Calo, 2017). Chinese-language sources emphasize the importance of the legal uses of AI and the need to establish legal norms for AI (Li and Li, 2021; Wu, 2021), the need to define the legal personality of AI systems (Li, 2019), and the legal problems that may be generated by the use of AI (Xu and Xu, 2020; Mei, 2018).

3. **AI Ethics**. The ethical dimension is a central focus of AI governance efforts worldwide (Misuraca and Van Noordt, 2020; Calo, 2017). Challenges in this dimension are related to considerations whether the use of certain AI applications and their expected consequences are ethical and morally justifiable. Scholars argue that AI adoption entails issues of explainability and transparency, which include the

consequences for citizens resulting from AI-based decision-making and potential misjudgments (e.g., due to biased or unrepresentative data), or the fact that the process that led to AI-based decisions may not be interpreted by humans (Engstrom et al., 2020; Henman, 2020; Kankanhalli et al., 2019; Sun and Medaglia, 2019; Chui et al., 2018). Ensuring AI safety is also considered a challenge for public organizations, as they typically collect sensitive and personal information about citizens (Dwivedi et al., 2021; Engstrom et al., 2020; Kankanhalli et al., 2019; Sun and Medaglia, 2019; Chui et al., 2018). In relation to AI safety, scholars note that the entrenched risk-averse mentality that characterizes public organizations and a broader bureaucratic inertia may impede AI adoption (Desouza, 2021, 2018; Pencheva, Esteve and Mikhaylov, 2020; Mikalef et al., 2019). Creating ethical consistency among AI systems and humans is also considered a challenge of AI in the public sector, due to the fact that human decision-making is based not only on rational principles (like AI systems), but also on factors like emotions and consciousness (Dwivedi et al., 2021; Wirtz et al., 2019). The possibility of moral dilemmas—situations in which AI systems need to choose between conflicting alternatives both having undesirable moral consequences—can be a barrier to AI applications (Kankanhalli, Charalabidis and Mellouli, 2019; Wirtz et al., 2019). Scholars also note challenges related to AI discrimination, which refers to inequality and lack of fairness that might be caused by AI systems. Issues include the discrimination arising from the profiling capabilities of AI systems, the absorption of human prejudices through the design of AI algorithms, or the use of datasets that include biases (Dwivedi et al., 2021; Henman, 2020; Chen et al., 2019; Tinholt et al., 2017; Chui et al., 2018). Chen et al. (2019) raise questions of administrative ethics, asking whether machines can have the same legitimacy of civil servants. Sun and Medaglia (2019) argue that the unethical use of data sharing is a main barrier to AI adoption in the public sector. Others also emphasize the challenge of evaluating the ethical costs and benefits of using AI in public organizations (Desouza, 2021; Hager et al., 2017). Chinese-language sources also agree that the use of AI in public organizations can create several ethical challenges, such as: algorithm discrimination, privacy violations, and trust crisis (Li and Li, 2021); the complexity of improving ethical awareness in order to prevent data and privacy abuses (Wu,

2021); the moral dilemmas generated by AI (Xu and Xu, 2020); or the creation of new social biases (Kang and Tang, 2021).

4. **AI in Society**. Challenges in this dimension are related to the wider social and economic implications of using AI in public organizations and society. Workforce substitution and transformation are among the most discussed societal challenges related to the introduction of AI,[47] and refer to the automation of work tasks currently performed by humans (Zuiderwijk et al., 2021; Tinholt et al., 2017; Wirtz et al., 2019). In efforts to quantify the magnitude of this issue, in 2017 McKinsey Global Institute estimated that 51.2% of work activities in China could be automated, affecting the equivalent of 394 million full-time employees.[48] While AI-induced job displacement is not limited to public organizations, Tinholt et al. (2017) highlight "the special employment status of public sector employees", noting that the legal protections in place for civil servants might prevent the public workforce from becoming "AI-driven". Social acceptance, that is the trust in AI systems and the social concerns about the expected impacts of AI on society (Makasi et al., 2021), is another barrier. Sun and Medaglia (2019) argue that the lack of trust in AI-based decision-making can deter AI adoption. Similarly, Androutsopoulou et al. (2019) argue that social barriers that impede the adoption of AI technologies in the public sector are

[47] Some widely cited studies on this topic include: Barton, D., Woetzel, J., Seong, J. and Tian, Q., 2017. *Artificial Intelligence: Implications for China*. McKinsey Global Institute, Discussion Paper, https://www.mckinsey.com/featured-insights/china/artificial-intelligence-implications-for-china; Arntz, M., Gregory, T. and Zierahn, U., 2016. *The Risk of Automation for Jobs in OECD Countries: A Comparative Analysis*. OECD Social, Employment and Migration Working Papers, No. 189, Paris: OECD Publishing, https://doi.org/10.1787/5jlz9h56dvq7-en; Hawksworth, J., Berriman, R. and Goel, S., 2017. *Will Robots Really Steal Our Jobs? An International Analysis of the Potential Long-Term Impact of Automation*. PricewaterhouseCoopers, https://www.pwc.com/hu/hu/kiadvanyok/assets/pdf/impact_of_automation_on_jobs.pdf; and Frey, C. and Osborne, M., 2013. *The Future of Employment: How Susceptible Are Jobs to Computerisation?* Oxford: University of Oxford, https://www.oxfordmartin.ox.ac.uk/downloads/academic/The_Future_of_Employment.pdf.

[48] Barton et al., 2017 (cit.), pp. 9–10. An earlier study by a Chinese scholar provides even higher estimates, projecting the percentage of jobs being replaced by AI in China in the coming 20 years to approximately 76% of the working force, or 65% if only the non-agricultural working force is considered (Chen, Y., 2013. How AI Will Impact Employment. *Journal of Northeast University of Finance and Economics*, No. 3/2013; quoted in Tsinghua, 2018, p. 93).

mainly rooted in the opposition to the replacement of employees by machines, and the lack of citizens' trust in machine intelligence. Wirtz, Weyerer, and Geyer (2019) observe that social acceptance is also connected with, and dependent on, the resolution of other challenges in the socioeconomic and other dimensions, such as AI safety, privacy, discrimination, and workforce substitution that may negatively affect citizens in a direct way. Others note that the challenges of translating social and policy problems in a way that can be tractable for AI systems (Hager et al., 2017) can inhibit the use of AI in public organizations. Chinese-language sources also discuss the socioeconomic disruptions that may be generated by AI (Li, 2019; Mei, 2018), with particular attention to issues related to employment (Yu and Cui, 2020; Xu and Xu, 2020), and to a widening digital divide in citizens' access to smart technology and governance due to differences in gender, age, education, occupation, and income, which may lead to the polarization of society (Wu, 2021; Xu and Xu, 2020; Zhang et al., 2019).

2.2.3 *Factors Affecting the Use of AI in the Public Sector in China*

To complete the outline of the field of investigation of this book, this section examines key country-specific factors that are influencing the use of AI in the public sector in China. First, it looks at two established governance mechanisms that are instrumental in promoting the adoption and implementation of AI. These mechanisms are: the evaluation system for the promotion of local officials (2.2.3.1), and the platforms for guiding the development of government-prioritized technologies in concert with private sector enterprises (2.2.3.2). While these mechanisms were not specifically designed to promote the use of AI, they are important because they mobilize local administrations and engage private companies, which are crucial actors for promoting AI applications in China (Zeng, 2021; Roberts et al., 2020; Ding, 2018; Lee and Sheehan, 2018; Triolo and Goodrich, 2018). By explaining the importance of local governments and private companies in China's AI policy in general and public sector AI applications in particular, and elucidating the mechanisms that mobilize and engage these actors, the analysis offers a deeper understanding of some fundamental factors that affect the adoption and use of AI in China.

Second, this section explores possible ethical and legal challenges of AI related to the public sector by reviewing the main Chinese initiatives in AI ethics and AI regulations (2.2.3.3). These are two areas where China has been very active in recent years: between 2019 and 2022, the country promulgated two main AI-specific regulations and announced a third one; between 2017 and 2022, China issued 10 AI ethics initiatives, half of which were elaborated by government agencies. In China like other countries, the responses to the legal and ethical challenges of AI are expected to be highly context-specific. On one hand, experts about AI in social domains observe that the ethical challenges in the use of technology may have different importance in different societies (Wirtz et al., 2019). For instance, Scantamburlo et al. (2018, p. 3) note that "obligations such as transparency and accountability may be more highly valued in some countries, or in decision-making systems, than in others"; hence, the nature and degree of observance of the normative principles that should regulate AI systems may vary according to cultural and disciplinary expectations. On the other hand, it is generally accepted that differences in political and social contexts may impact on how AI is regulated in different countries. Scantamburlo et al. (2018) again observe that the nature of the decision-making system impacts on the type of legal principles that AI systems should comply with. Similarly, Turner (2019) notes that rights are collective fictions whose form can be shaped to any given context, thus affecting how the regulations of AI are designed in different countries. Therefore, while in certain countries a high number of initiatives in AI ethics and regulations might suggest that public organizations are subjected to several ethical and legal constraints (e.g., the emerging regulatory framework in the European Union), it is useful to examine how such initiatives are actually impacting on AI adoption and use in the public sector in China.

Mobilizing Local Governments: the Evaluation System for Promotion
There is a sizable literature that discusses the distinctive characteristics of China's decentralized administrative system and its implications for the relations between central and local governments[49] (Zhou et al., 2017;

[49] See also: Lieberthal, K. and Lampton, D. eds., 1992. *Bureaucracy, Politics, and Decision Making in Post-Mao China*. Berkeley: University of California Press; Lieberthal, K. and Oksenberg, M., 1988. *Policy Making in China: Leaders, Structures, and Processes*. Princeton: Princeton University Press.

Xu, 2011; Kipnis et al., 2009; Saich, 2008). With different nuances, scholars generally agree that the rapid economic changes ignited by the economic reforms since the end of the 1970s have resulted in a de facto division of authority[50] between the central government and local administrations[51] (i.e., any administrative levels below the national government) in various policy areas. The result of this pragmatic division of authority can be understood as a system where political control is centralized, but socioeconomic management is decentralized to local governments:

> On the one hand, the national government's control is substantial in that the Chinese political and personnel governance structure has been highly centralized. Sub-national government officials are appointed from above, and the appointment and promotion of sub-national government officials serve as powerful instruments for the national government to induce regional officials to follow the central government's policies. [...] On the other hand, the governance of the national economy is delegated to sub-national governments. Regional economies (provinces, municipalities, and counties) are relatively self-contained, and sub-national governments have overall responsibility for initiating and coordinating reforms, providing public services, and making and enforcing laws within their jurisdictions. (Xu, 2011, p. 1078)

This combination of centralized political control and decentralized socioeconomic management creates a classic principal-agent problem, whereby there is a potential conflict in priorities between local governments (the "agents") and the central government (the "principal"). The Chinese central government has been trying to solve this principal-agent problem by creating incentives for officials at all levels of government

[50] Xu (2011) notes that the Chinese Constitution stipulates local administrations have no inherent power, and their authority is granted by the central government, which can delegate power to local administrations as well as rescind it. The central government preserves its discretionary power over local administrations, and this power has been repeatedly exercised during the reform era, both de jure (e.g., the recentralization of tax-collection) and de facto (e.g., sanctioning the "success" of bottom-up policy experiments).

[51] Relaxation of political control from national authorities happened also before the economic reforms promoted by Deng Xiaoping, but it was mainly due to pragmatic considerations, such as contingent situations that weakened the national government's capacity for central planning of (Knight, 2014, p. 1336; Zhou, 2020, p. 482). In the reform and opening-up era started in the late 1970s, shifts between concentration and relaxation of political control have also happened periodically, without altering the basic division of authority widely acknowledged in the literature (Zeng, 2021, p. 2).

to pursue national policy priorities (Knight, 2014, p. 1338). These **incentives have been institutionalized into an evaluation system for promotion** that ties career advancements for Chinese officials across the bureaucracy to the achievements of targets set by the higher authorities. This evaluation system is known as Target Management Responsibility System (岗位目标管理责任制), and it is based on performance targets for officials cascaded down from the top leadership to lower levels of governments. Under this system, Chinese subnational governments not only compete against quantifiable targets (e.g., GDP growth), but they also often compete in initiating or testing new policies that may fulfill the goals of the central government.[52] In doing so, local governments are given considerable responsibility for local coordination as a way of overcoming resistance to reform and reducing the risks of policy innovation (Xu, 2011). This incentive system is effective because it leverages China's centralized political and personnel governance structure, in which officials are evaluated, rewarded, and allocated through a top-down process. This governance structure is designed for the implementation of top-down directives from higher authorities who, through their delegated officials, exercise power in personnel control and resource mobilization at all levels of government. In this upward accountability system, officials are responsive to political signals, directives, and evaluation coming from higher authorities, which the State uses to encourage local administrations to pursue national policy priorities and promote policy experiments in State-endorsed priority areas (Zhou, 2020, p. 479; Zhou et al., 2013; Teets and Hasmath, 2020; Xu, 2011).

The Target Management Responsibility System is the result of China's experimenting with performance management in various sectors since the mid-1980s (Burns and Zhou, 2010). Its current configuration is rooted in the civil service reforms started in 1993 and later codified in the 2005 *Civil Servants Law*, which ties the careers of public officials to their performance.[53] Local officials usually sign target responsibility

[52] As neatly stated by Heilmann (2008, pp. 2–3), the policy experiments practiced in China are focused on "finding innovative *policy instruments*, rather than defining *policy objectives*, which remains the prerogative of Party leadership" (emphasis in original). See also: Zhang and Zhu, 2019.

[53] The 2005 *Civil Servants Law of the People's Republic of China* (中华人民共和国公务员法, last amended in 2018) contains several features of direct relevance to the current configuration of the Target Management Responsibility System, including: competitive

contracts with the superior level of government, and they are evaluated on the degree of fulfillment of these targets. There are different categories of performance targets, some of which are explicitly linked to personnel decisions.[54] Performance targets also differ according to the level of government, usually being broader at the top, and more specific and quantifiable at lower levels of government[55] (e.g., townships). In addition to the individual performance of each single official, the career advancements linked to the Target Management Responsibility System also depend on relative performance compared to other officials among the same level of government (Xu, 2011; Teets and Hasmath, 2020; Zhang and Zhu, 2019). This horizontal competition between provinces, municipalities, counties, and townships for performance rankings and promotion—sometimes called "tournament competition" (Xu, 2011; Zhou and Lian, 2011)—reinforces the top-down system of incentives by stimulating efforts to initiate activities conducive to national policy goals, because there is evidence that officials from relatively better-performing localities have more chances of being promoted.

promotion based on performance; the performance appraisal of civil servants focused on individual evaluations of officials on their work performance; and performance-based rewards at the individual level, which add up to those introduced in 1980s that were more focused on the organization rather than on individual work achievements (Burns and Zhou, 2010, pp. 7–9; 13).

54 "Core targets" (核心指标) typically focus on economic objectives such as GDP growth, industrial production, or use of foreign investment. "Common targets" (共性指标) focus on political objectives such as Party building, social security, or family planning. Fulfilling core targets is usually linked to bonuses and political rewards, whereas completion of common targets usually affects personnel decisions (Xu, 2011, p. 1093). In fact, common targets may include targets "with veto power" (or "one-item veto", 一票否决) explicitly linked to personnel decisions. This means that a local government's failure to meet one of such targets would cause the negation of all achievements in its administrative jurisdiction, consequently denying any promotion opportunity to local officials (Zhou and Lian, 2011, pp. 5–6; Burns and Zhou, 2010, p. 15). Core and common targets are ultimately linked to the central government's programmatic documents. For instance, the national goals for economic growth in the Five-Year Plans or the annual targets for tax collection approved by the National People's Congress are distributed to all provinces, and followed by a process of target specification and cascading that imposes targets for GDP growth and tax collection on the lower-level authorities.

55 "Functional targets" (职能指标) are often more job-specific, and they tend to be linked to the activities of lower levels of governments, such as income targets for township enterprises, or various types of revenue targets.

Local officials, whether concerned about career advancement or job security, are theorized to be incentivized to implement policies or design experimental pilots that might score points on the evaluation system (Teets et al., 2017). Moreover, since 2016 the Target Management Responsibility System has incorporated the Ideological Responsibility System (意识形态责任制), introduced the previous year to improve the ideological unification and loyalty of the bureaucracy.[56] The addition of "ideological targets" has likely reinforced and expanded the reach of the promotion system as a tool to align local administrations to national policy priorities, especially for policy goals that the national government publicly supports (Zhang and Zhu, 2019). Certainly, the decision-making process of local officials is more complex than a linear response to an evaluation system, and there are various factors beyond performance that affect promotion decisions (e.g., factional connections, political influence, position buying, collusion among local governments at different levels in the bureaucratic hierarchy, among others; Knight 2014, p. 1340). Nonetheless, the importance of the incentives created by China's personnel control system to promote the national government's policy objectives remains central in the literature on Chinese bureaucratic behaviors, and alternative analytical models that later emerged complement rather than invalidate this explanation.[57]

[56] The General Office of the CPC Central Committee in 2015 issued the *Implementation Measures of the Ideological Responsibility System of the Party Committee (Party Groups)* [党委(党组)意识形态工作责任制实施办法]. Since 2016, this inner-party regulation has been integrated into the Target Responsibility System. As a result, "ideological responsibility" (i.e., ideological commitment of local cadres to the Party and the central authority) has the same, or even more, weight as economic development, political construction, Party building, or other performance targets. See: Chen, X., 2018. Remaking the loyal cadres: the Ideological Responsibility System in China's new era. *Journal of Chinese Governance*, 3(3), pp. 292–306, https://doi.org/10.1080/23812346.2018.1493023. The importance of the Ideological Responsibility System for the evaluation of local officials was confirmed in a conversation of the author with the Director of the Security Crisis Management International Center of the Shanghai Academy of Social Sciences (20 December 2021).

[57] The importance of institutionalized incentives in governing central-local relations is theorized in explanatory models such as the "regionally decentralized authoritarian regime" (Xu, 2011), or the "tournament-competition" model by Zhou Li'an (2008; 2007; 2004), and are consistent with the prevailing "experimentation under hierarchy" model proposed by Heilmann (2008, cit.). Later analytical models integrate this explanation of bureaucratic behavior based on incentives by examining additional sources of variation that result in distinct behavioral patterns in the Chinese bureaucracy at the local level, such as administrative mechanisms (e.g., "control-right theory" by Zhou and Lian 2011; the

This evaluation system for promotion offers an effective instrument to foster AI adoption and implementation in China. By elevating artificial intelligence to a national strategic priority, **the national government can make AI development another metric on which local officials are evaluated**, actively incentivizing local administrators to accelerate the adoption of AI as they seek to score points on the evaluation system for promotion (Lee and Sheehan, 2018; Sheehan, 2018). In this perspective, the State Council's *New Generation Artificial Intelligence Development Plan* (AIDP, Chapter 3.1) is best understood as a "symbolic mandate" (Liu, 2020), a signal of the strategic importance of AI that drives the Chinese bureaucracy to view the promotion of AI development as politically important (Triolo and Goodrich, 2018). By imbuing AI with a stamp of approval from the central government and the Chinese Communist Party, the AIDP indicates to local officials that the success in fostering AI will be rewarded under the incentive structure of the Target Management Responsibility System, actively encouraging local officials to experiment with AI in their jurisdictions. This signal is reinforced by the attention to AI that the top leadership officially expressed in numerous occasions,[58] and by the publication of several national policy documents on AI that swiftly followed the AIDP (Chapter 3, Appendix IV). Previous studies provide statistical evidence that top-down policy signals of the national government have a strong stimulating effect on subnational governments (Zhang and Zhu, 2019; Xu, 2011). Clearly, in AI policy these signals have been received throughout the Chinese bureaucracy, as demonstrated by the flurry of local AI plans that followed the publication of China's

"muddling through" model by Zhou et al., 2013), or individual preferences and cohort effect (Teets et al., 2017; Hasmath et al., 2019). However, these studies do not contest the importance of the incentives created by the personnel control system; rather, they build upon them: "These explanations are not rival hypotheses, but actually interact with each other to explain the complex motivation of local policy experimenters" (Teets and Hasmath, 2020, pp. 53–54).

[58] For instance, President Xi Jinping referenced AI in his work report to the 19th Party Congress in October 2017, and one year later stated that China must "make sure that critical and core AI technologies are grasped firmly in its own hands". See: Speech during the ninth group study session of the Politburo of the Central Committee of the Chinese Communist Party on 31 October 2018. Xinhua, 2018. Promote the healthy development of China's New Generation Artificial Intelligence Development Plan [习近平: 推动我国新一代人工智能健康发展]. *Xinhua*, 31 October, http://www.xinhuanet.com/politics/2018-10/31/c_1123643321.htm. The attention of the top leadership for AI development has been regularly reiterated in various occasions.

national AI strategy.[59] Looking at all the local AI plans that outline specific figures, the aggregated benchmark for the core AI industry is 429 billion RMB by 2020, which far exceeds the AIDP's target of 150 billion RMB (Ding, 2020).

Incentivizing local governments is crucial to promote AI applications because AI is a general-purpose technology that has virtually unlimited usages across countless of tasks. As such, no command-and-control structure or single blueprint could efficiently direct State resources toward exploiting all the manifold applications of AI (Lee and Sheehan, 2018). The active contribution of local governments is thus necessary to find AI applications suitable to local conditions and expand the impact of AI across economy and society, as advocated by China's AI strategy (Sheehan, 2018). For instance, densely populated urban areas may find it useful to adopt AI-enabled traffic control systems or chatbots for public service delivery, while rural areas may want to promote AI-enabled telemedicine or distant learning, etc. In addition, the active contribution of local governments is necessary because the deployment of AI often requires the adaptation of local infrastructure, from the creation of an adequate technological architecture that supports AI applications (e.g., data centers, fast Internet connection, etc.), to the construction of physical infrastructure like testing areas for autonomous vehicles or other AI applications (Lee and Sheehan, 2018; Lewis, 2019). In this perspective, Zeng (2021) observes that China's AI strategy is a loose slogan that is kept deliberately vague and broad to accommodate the interests of domestic stakeholders. This decentralized approach suits well the omni-use nature of AI, possibly unlocking AI applications that could hardly be accounted for in a top-down blueprint. Indeed, the importance of local experimentation in AI policy is explicitly emphasized by China's AI strategy, which requires all localities and relevant departments to "launch trials and demonstrations for the implementation of major AI tasks and key policies", and to "disseminate replicable experiences and methods[60]".

[59] Forward Looking Industry Research Institute [前瞻产业研究院], 2018. An article takes you through the latest policies for the AI industry in the whole country in 2018 [一文带你了解2018年全国各地人工智能行业最新政策]. *Sohu* (搜狐), 30 March, https://www.sohu.com/a/226831586_297710.

[60] State Council, 2017. Section 6, Organization and Implementation (组织实施), par. 2.3. In original: "对人工智能重大任务和重点政策措施，要制定具体方案，开展试点示范。

The evaluation system for promotion incentivizes local officials to foster progress in all the priority areas indicated by China's national AI strategy, from theoretical and applied AI research to the development of the local AI industry. Among these priorities (Chapter 3.1), the incentive system is particularly important for spurring the use of AI in the public sector, given that this is an area where local governments in China play an outsized role, being the main providers of services in education, healthcare, and other areas[61] where the *New Generation Artificial Intelligence Development Plan* wants to leverage AI to "greatly improve the level of precision in public services". As emphasized by previous studies on public service delivery in China: "Most public goods and services are provided by subnational levels of government and consequently they have expenditure responsibilities that are quite out of line with international practices [...]. The central authorities in China have transferred a much greater percentage of expenditure responsibilities to local governments than is normally the case" (Saich, 2008, pp. 58–59). In addition, the incentive system is important for spurring public sector AI applications because the adoption of AI in public service delivery is an innovation that carries a variety of complexities and uncertainties (see discussions in 2.4). As such, the existence of an incentive-based mechanism that de-risks and actively supports public sector AI projects is crucial to encourage local governments to try the use of AI in the public sector activities, and explore which AI applications are most suitable for them (Ma et al., 2021; Roberts et al., 2020; Lee and Sheehan, 2018).

Engaging AI Companies: The State as a Partner

In China, the national innovation system—that is "the network of institutions in the public and private sectors whose activities and interactions initiate, import, modify and diffuse new technologies" (Freeman, 1987, quoted in Bazavan, 2019)—has been evolving over time (Bazavan, 2019; UNESCAP, 2018; Schmid and Wang, 2016). This evolution generated

加强对各部门、各地方试点示范的统筹指导, 及时总结推广可复制的经验和做法。通过试点先行、示范引领, 推进人工智能健康有序发展".

[61] The study of Stepan and Duckett on digital innovation in China's social development agenda (2018, p. 14) shows that local-government public expenditure on education, healthcare, social safety, and employment greatly and consistently exceeds central-government public expenditure on these areas in the period 2004–2016.

new governance mechanisms that increasingly rely on private companies to develop and deploy government-prioritized technologies. Acknowledging the existence of these mechanisms and understanding their functioning is important, because they are instrumental in fostering the use of AI in the public sector. However, several misconceptions rooted in past practices and incomplete reconstructions of China's innovation policy hamper the analysis of these governance mechanisms.

Common accounts in the literature emphasize State dirigisme, centrally sponsored megaprojects, or the concentration of subsidies on large State-owned enterprises. These accounts are often based on the analysis of large-scale, fiscally expensive science and technology (S&T) programs initiated by the national government since the 1980s,[62] including the more recent "megaprojects" of the *National Outline for Medium- and Long-Term Science and Technology Development Plan (2006–2020)*.[63]

[62] Prominent large-scale S&T programs initiated by the Chinese State in the period 1980–2000 include: the National Key Technologies R&D Program (国家科技攻关计划) in 1982, which aims at making breakthroughs in technologies expected to support the Chinese economy; the Spark Program (星火计划), officially named National Program for the Use of Science and Technology to Promote Rural Economic Development (中国依靠科学技术促进农村经济发展的计划), which was launched in 1986 for the technological upgrade of small and medium enterprises in rural areas; the 863 Program (officially: the National High-Tech Research and Development Program, 国家高技术研究发展计划) for high-technology R&D, aimed at reducing the gap between China and the developed world (since 1987); the Torch Program (火炬计划) that provided the legal and organizational frameworks for the creation of high-tech industrial development zones (since 1988); and the 973 Program (officially: National Key Basic Research Program, 国家重点基础研究发展规划) for basic research (since 1997). As a result of these initiatives, by 2012 China became the third largest global investor in R&D behind the United States and Japan (Fu et al., 2016, pp. 4–5; Heilmann et al., 2013). In 2014, China created a funding mechanism for National Key R&D Program (NKP), a cluster of R&D projects that target key technologies aimed at social welfare and improving people's livelihoods, to consolidate previously independent funding mechanisms like the 863 Program, the 973 Program. New NKPs are announced each year, and they generally expire after 5 years (Colvin et al., 2020, p. 17).

[63] Published in February 2006 by the State Council, the Plan 2006–2020 [国家中长期科学和技术发展规划要纲 (2006–2020 年)] aims at expanding R&D, increasing the role of the market in S&T innovation, and building a top-quality research system. The plan launched sixteen national megaprojects (重大专项/ 目项) to accelerate innovation in selected strategic industries, including civil aviation, integrated circuits, and large advanced nuclear reactors. Reported megaproject funding has been variable in recent years, as the past batch of megaprojects reached completion in 2020, and the new batch of 2030 innovation megaprojects (科技新创 2030 重大目项), such as the New Generation of Artificial Intelligence (新一代人工智能) Megaproject, is underway (these megaprojects

These accounts tend to overstate the role of the government in China's national innovation system. In reality, statistics show that Chinese private R&D spending has risen steadily since the 1990s: in 2016, China's private R&D expenditures reached 76.1% of the national total, second only to Japan (78.1%) among the world's largest R&D spenders.[64] Tax incentives and other forms of public support for private R&D expenditures are also relatively low (Bazavan, 2019, pp. 3–4; Schmid and Wang, 2016, p. 4; Sun and Cao, 2014, p. 1008). Even in the case of State-initiated technology plans, the share of government funding has been steeply declining, from a 96% share in the 973 Program, to just 5% in the Spark Program and 1% in the Torch Program (Heilmann et al., 2013, p. 7). Although limited in volume, the Chinese government R&D expenditures often concentrate extensive funding toward a selected number of priority areas (e.g., the target industries of the *Made in China 2025*, see Appendix III), thus possibly contributing to the misconceptions about the locus of the Chinese government in innovation policy (Bazavan, 2019).

Similar misconceptions about the role of the government in China's national innovation system also exist in relation to artificial intelligence (Zeng, 2021; Ding, 2018). For instance, reports that China is outspending other countries in public investment in AI research most likely overstate the Chinese government expenditures in AI R&D[65]

were initiated by the *13th 5-Year Plan for National Science and Technology Innovation*, implementation period 2020–2030). The Plan 2006–2020 also contained the target to strengthen "indigenous innovation" (自主创新), aiming to decrease reliance on imported technology to 30% by 2020. The focus on indigenous innovation has been reiterated by later initiatives like the 2015 *Made in China 2025* (Colvin et al., 2020; Acharya and Arnold, 2019; Ding, 2018; Schmid and Wang, 2016).

[64] The rising share of R&D spending by private enterprises is also due to the transformation of applied research institutes into business entities. For instance, the PC company Lenovo was founded in 1984 by engineers from the Institute of Computing Technology of the Chinese Academy of Science (CAS), and initially funded by the CAS itself. In 1995, Lenovo took over the direction of the Institute of Computing Technology (Fu et al., 2016, p. 5).

[65] Deriving estimates of Chinese public investment in AI-related research and development is challenging for several reasons: publicly available information on Chinese government spending (e.g., Ministry of Finance annual reports) is often aggregated and does not specifically call out AI-related spending; identifying AI-related spending requires a level of detail that is usually not found in publicly available budgetary documentation, and is even rarer in publicly available Chinese documents; and even when a line of spending can be associated with AI, identifying the R&D portion of that spending is challenging (e.g., spending on an AI-enabled surveillance system likely includes development

(Acharya and Arnold, 2019). And despite common narratives, there is also scarce evidence that China is pursuing a unified, top-down approach to AI development (Zeng, 2021; Ernst, 2020). Possible explanations of such misconceptions in China's AI innovation policy could be: the fact that since 2015 the Chinese government has regularly issued major policy documents that reiterate the importance of artificial intelligence to support the advancement of the Chinese industry, society, and other sectors (Appendix III); the publication in July 2017 of the *New Generation Artificial Intelligence Development Plan*, one of the most comprehensive AI strategies worldwide that states China's intentions to "lead the world in new trends of AI development [...], spur the overall elevation of national competitiveness[66]" (Chapter 3.1); the sizable number of Chinese ministries and top bureaucratic agencies that are claiming their stakes in AI policy (Chapter 3.1); or the aforementioned list of S&T programs characterized by a strong degree of government support and intervention, which explains the tendency to position AI innovation policy within China's longstanding tradition of central planning in science and technology (Sheehan, 2018).

These misconceptions overlook the fact that China has a track record of using its private technology sector to power public service innovations[67] (UNESCAP, 2018). They also discount the fact that governance mechanisms in China's national innovation system have been evolving over time. The overarching paradigm change is that **the government increasingly aims to become a platform creator, facilitator, and strategy-setter for innovation**, rather than a principal actor or sponsor itself. "While

and acquisition of hardware, spending on associated equipment, and pay for personnel and/or contractor support; the portion of spending that is AI-related research and development is rarely identified). For these and other methodological challenges, see: Colvin et al., 2020.

[66] State Council, 2017 (cit.), Sect. 2.1, the Strategic Situation (战略态势), par. 8. In original: "引领世界人工智能发展新潮流，服务经济社会发展和支撑国家安全，带动国家竞争力整体跃升".

[67] Recent examples include: Alibaba's Alipay City Services (online services that enable the payment of utility bills for gas, water, and electricity, traffic fines and taxes via the superapp Alipay), replacing the face-to-face system operated by government authorities; or Tencent's WeChat superapp that is accepted on public transport systems in numerous cities across China instead of traditional tickets or rechargeable swipe cards. Alipay and WeChat also support the mobile version of the Government Online-Offline Shanghai (Chapter 5.2.1).

in some industries, the state follows the classical approach of central-led investments and heavy protectionism, in others, it acts more as a business-partner and multiplier for private investment. There are also those industries where the government stimulates emerging technology by completely refraining from any action or regulation" (Bazavan, 2019).

This more sophisticated innovation policy is proving particularly useful in the field of artificial intelligence, which is dominated by private companies, not by State-owned enterprises or other government-affiliated institutions. Private companies are the main suppliers of the AI technologies that the Chinese government wants to see implemented across the economy and society, and Chinese policymakers have realized that rapidly evolving AI capabilities are developed outside the immediate scope of traditional State-owned enterprises; hence, AI development must move in lockstep with the advancements of leading AI companies (Sheehan, 2019; Larsen, 2019). In addition, public–private agreements for AI need to be more collaborative than traditional sourcing projects, in which the public sector specifies what is required, the private sector responds with bids, and a vendor is chosen to work on the project. In fact, it is unlikely that public organizations will be able to specify AI-related requirements in as much detail as traditional procurement, and the implementation of AI systems also requires to build long-term collaborations to keep refining their technological capability and sophistication (Desouza, 2018). Hence, promoting AI applications in the public sector requires to actively engage private companies, nudging them closer to the State priorities in AI and the activities of public organizations. Doing so requires methods that go beyond the classical approach based on financial incentives and other subsides. On one hand, the major AI players are already internationally successful in their respective fields, independently of State support (Roberts et al., 2020). On the other, the general-purpose nature of AI implies that the number of companies is much wider than in other technologies (Shanghai alone hosts more than 1,000 AI companies, see Chapter 4.4); as such, sponsoring every AI company across the economy would be wildly inefficient and ultimately unfeasible (Lee and Sheehan, 2018).

To engage AI firms, the Chinese government is leveraging mechanisms for guiding AI development in greater concert with private sector enterprises that advance key AI technologies and applications (Larsen, 2019, p. 16). Next paragraphs examine two main initiatives where the State acts as a "platform creator" to promote the use of AI in the public sector.

Namely: the National New Generation Artificial Intelligence Open Innovation Platforms, a State-led initiative that opens various policy areas to private companies in order to spearhead innovation in these domains; and China's Artificial Intelligence Industry Development Alliance, a platform for cooperation between private sector, government, and academia that serves to promote the Chinese government's goals for AI development in industrial development and the public sector.

National New Generation Artificial Intelligence Open Innovation Platforms (AIOIPs)

Since 2017, the Ministry of Science and Technology (MOST) has started to recruit private companies to build AI open platforms in areas that the Chinese government considers strategic, including in the public sector.[68] These platforms are called "National New Generation Artificial Intelligence Open Innovation Platforms" (AIOIPs, 国家新一代人工智能开放创新平台). The establishment of these open platforms is formally top-down: the government indicates the areas where it wants to create AIOIPs, and companies apply to develop the platforms. Applicants are selected by the MOST based on the assessment of their technological capabilities and the expected results of the AIOIP.[69] In November 2017, the MOST selected the first batch of private companies, colloquially known as the "national AI team" (人工智能国家队): Internet giants Baidu (autonomous driving AIOIP), Alibaba (smart city AIOIP), and Tencent (medical imaging AIOIP), and the leading Natural Language Processing company iFlyTek (smart audio AIOIP).[70] In September 2018, computer vision company SenseTime was added to the national team

[68] State Council General Office, 2017. 15 Ministries and Agencies Together Establish the First Four National Innovation Platforms—Focus on the National New Generation Artificial Intelligence Development Plan [15个部委合力 首批4家国家创新平台确立——聚焦我国新一代人工智能发展规划]. *China Central Government*, 23 November, http://www.gov.cn/guowuyuan/2017-11/23/content_5241718.htm.

[69] MOST, 2019. Understanding "China's New Generation Artificial Intelligence Open Innovation Platform Construction Guidelines [图解《国家新一代人工智能开放创新平台建设工作指引》], 6 August, http://www.most.gov.cn/xxgk/xinxifenlei/fdzdgknr/fgzc/zcjd/202106/t20210625_175388.html.

[70] Forward Economist, 2018. Ten Pictures to Understand China's Four Big Artificial Intelligence Open Innovation Platforms—The BATI Layout [十张图了解中国四大人工智能开放创新平台—BATI的布局]. *Forward Economist* [前瞻经济学人], 11 September, https://www.qianzhan.com/analyst/detail/220/180910-bc57e6cb.html.

to create a smart vision AIOIP.[71] In August 2019, the initiative was expanded to include 10 more companies and related AIOIPs, namely: MiningLamp (smart marketing), Huawei (software/hardware), JD.com (smart supply chain), Xiaomi (smart home), Yitu (computer vision), China Ping'an (inclusive finance), HIKvision (video perception), Megvii (image perception), 360 Qihoo (cybersecurity), and TAL (smart education).[72] Later, other AIOIPs were announced: the smart network AIOIP in 2022, and the public computing power (公共算力) AIOIPs in 2023.[73]

The AIOIP mechanism is spurring AI applications in the public sector by actively engaging private companies to provide AI solutions that optimize public sector operations and the provision of public services: "These platforms are actively supported by the MOST and provincial-level S&T management departments by promoting application of the relevant technologies. This implies, for instance, providing space for testing autonomous vehicles (Baidu), access to city infrastructure for monitoring and upgrade (Alibaba), access to public medical data (Tencent), access to the judicial system (iFlyTek), and access to surveillance systems (SenseTime), among other public areas that are being opened to private-sector development" (Larsen, 2019, p. 17). In doing so, the government grants private companies a large space to experiment in the public sector, selectively opening public domains and associated data repositories, as long as this is conducive to spur AI development in the areas prioritized by the government. The AIOIPs don't include only public sector applications, but these are a key component of the mechanism, and there is

[71] Xinhua News, 2018. The first National New Generation Artificial Intelligence Open Innovation Platform in Smart Vision Makes Its Official Debut [智能视觉国家新一代人工智能开放创新平台正式亮相]. *Xinhua News*, 20 September, http://www.xinhuanet.com/politics/2018-09/20/c_1123461737.htm.

[72] Yicai, 2019. National New Generation Artificial Intelligence Open Innovation Platforms Announced, these 10 Platforms Are Selected [国家新一代人工智能开放创新平台发布, 这10大平台入选]. *Yicai* [第一财经], 29 August, https://www.yicai.com/news/100312280.html.

[73] China Mobile, 2022. The Smart Network National New Generation Artificial Intelligence Open Innovation Platform Is Unveiled [智慧网络国家新一代人工智能开放创新平台揭牌]. *China Mobile* [中国移动], 11 December, https://www.10086.cn/aboutus/news/groupnews/index_detail_43757.html; Tianjin Commercial Bureau, 2023. The First National Batch! This Innovation Platform of Tianjin Enters the "National Team" [全国首批!天津这个创新平台入列 "国家队"]. *Tianjin Commercial Bureau* [天津市商务局], 12 September, https://shangwuju.tj.gov.cn/tjsswjzz/zwdt/wmdt/zmsyq/202309/t20230912_6404425.html.

evidence of continuous cooperation of AIOIP companies in public sector projects.[74] Indeed, an engagement approach that leverages government-led AI projects is attractive for both government and companies. The government can promote its AI policy goals, both in terms of industrial development and public sector applications, while also bringing the expertise and resources of private companies closer to the needs of the State apparatus (Ding, 2018; Lewis, 2019). On their part, private companies gain commercial, technical (e.g., access to government data), and policy benefits by cooperating in government-led projects (Han, 2020; Sheehan, 2019), as further explained later in the case of Shanghai (Chapter 4.4).

While the AIOIPs is formally a top-down approach whereby the State picks winners in the AI industry, it differs from previous State-sponsored national champions in that the members of the "national team" are private companies[75] invested by foreign firms.[76] These companies are already internationally successful in their respective fields independently of State support. Therefore, they are less dependent on government financial handouts. In addition, the members of the national AI team are not shielded from domestic competition[77] (Han, 2020; Roberts et al., 2020;

[74] For instance, on the same day that the Yitu computer vision AIOIP was unveiled, the company signed agreements with the National Industrial Information Security Development Research Center (国家工业信息安全发展研究中心), the Third Research Institute of the Ministry of Public Security (公安部第三研究所), and the Institute of Traffic Management Science of the Ministry of Public Security (公安部交通管理科学研究所). See: China Daily, 2019. Yitu Starts the Plan to Open an Innovation Platform for AI Chip Computer Vision, the Layered Decoupling of the Platform Empowers the Industry [依图启动AI芯片视觉计算创新平台开放计划, 平台分层解耦赋能行业], 31 October, https://tech.chinadaily.com.cn/a/201910/31/WS5dba962da31099ab995e91c0.html.

[75] A possible exception is iFlytek. The company's largest shareholder is the State-owned telecom giant China Mobile. Also, government subsidies comprise 20–25% of its annual net income (Ding, 2019).

[76] In 2021, Alibaba's top shareholder was the Japanese multinational holding Softbank, with a share around 25%. Other large foreign stockowners are leading asset managers from the US and the United Kingdom (e.g., Vanguard Group, BlackRock) that together owned 10% of Alibaba's shares. Tencent's largest shareholder is the South African multinational Naspers (31%), while three US-based asset managers also own shares of the company (Vanguard, 2%; BlackRock, 1%; and Capital Research, 1%). Source: Lundvall, B, and Rikap, C., 2022. China's catching-up in artificial intelligence seen as a co-evolution of corporate and national innovation systems. *Research Policy*, 51(1), 2022, p. 11, https://doi.org/10.1016/j.respol.2021.104395.

[77] For instance, Baidu, Alibaba and Tencent are actively working to develop their own speech and facial recognition capabilities so as to reduce reliance on the services

Ding, 2018). As such, to make participation to the AIOIPs' initiative attractive to private companies and increase its impacts, the government offers various forms of support, from preferential contract bidding to the selective opening of public sector areas relevant to the construction of the AIOIPs, as just described. In exchange for government support, private companies are required to deliver on four key tasks: promote R&D, foster ecosystem participation, share data and open-source software, and support small and medium enterprises, thus also contributing to development of the national AI ecosystem (Larsen, 2019).

The Artificial Intelligence Industry Alliance (AIIA)

Established in October 2017, China's Artificial Intelligence Industry Alliance (AIIA, 中国人工智能产业发展联盟) operates under the supervision of the National Development and Reform Commission (NDRC), the MOST, the Ministry of Industry and Information Technology (MIIT), and the Cyberspace Administration of China (CAC). First established at the national level, it has been replicated in several local AI alliances across China, including in Shanghai. In 2022, AIIA included 783 entities, organized in three tiers[78]: vice-chairs of the board (副理事长单位, 30 entities); board members (理事单位, 205 entities); and ordinary members (普通会员单位, 548 entities). While the majority of the AIIA members are private companies, the Alliance is heavily influenced by government entities and government-affiliated members. Apart from the steering role played by the NDRC, MOST, MIIT, and the CAC, nearly half of the entities in the top-ranking "vice-chair" tier (14 out of 30) are State-owned enterprises (SOEs) or government-affiliated institutions such as universities and research institutes. In addition, 9 of the 16 private companies in the "vice-chair" are members of the "national AI team", whose link with the government in AI policy was explained in illustrating the AIOIPs.

of other national team members iFlytek and Sensetime (Ding, 2019; Ruehl, M. et al., 2021. Can SenseTime become a Chinese AI champion? *Financial Times* [online], 29 September, https://www.ft.com/content/c735e0f3-5704-47b5-a76f-7a02d53a1525). The same is true in other areas, like Baidu and Alibaba developing their own AI chips as an alternative to those produced by another national team member Huawei.

[78] Artificial Intelligence Industry Alliance (AIIA, 中国人工智能产业发展联盟) website: http://www.aiiaorg.cn/index.php?m=alliance&c=index&a=structure. Literally, the name of the Association is "Artificial Intelligence Industry Development Alliance". However, the official website translates it as Artificial Intelligence Industry Alliance. Last accessed on 24 January 2022.

The tight ties between the State and the Alliance demonstrated by its government-dominated leadership structure, coupled by its role as a channel to distribute government subsidies to AI companies, suggest that AIIA activities reflect the central government's priorities rather than the interests of private companies (Luong and Arnold, 2021, pp. 7–9). As such, AIIA is best understood not just as an industry alliance, but as a platform for cooperation between government, enterprises, universities, research institutes, and end users[79] (政产学研用), which aims at guiding AI development in greater concert with the private sector. This interpretation is corroborated by major AI policy documents that anticipate the creation of the Alliance. In July 2017, the *New Generation Artificial Intelligence Development Plan* stated that China would encourage "government, enterprises, universities, research institutes, and end-users to co-creation and share innovation[80]". A few months later, the MIIT's *Promoting AI Industry 3-Year Action Plan 2018–2020* reiterated that China would "promote the coordination of government, enterprises, universities, research institutes, and end-users[81]". The use of industry alliances to promote national policy goals in the field of AI replicates what the Chinese government is already doing in other areas. For instance, the Smart Manufacturing Industry Alliance (智能制造产业联盟) or the Smart Manufacturing Promotion Alliance (智能制造推进联盟) support the implementation of the *Made in China 2025*, the ambitious industrial masterplan for the digital and technological advancement of the Chinese manufacturing sector.

In promoting the Chinese government's goals for AI development, the Alliance is not limited to advancing the national agenda in industrial and technologic development, or in national security, but also in the public sector. This is confirmed by looking at the AIIA committees

[79] An explanation of this concept, which originates from the 产学研 notion introduced in the 1990s, can be found in: People.cn, 2013. Government, enterprises, universities, research institutes, and end users, ultimately it is about applications [政产学研用, 最终在于用]. *People.cn* [人民网], 5 July, http://scitech.people.com.cn/n/2013/0705/c1057-22084717.html. The aim to "establish an innovation platform that integrates the efforts of government, enterprises, universities, research institutes, and end-users [政产学研用平台]" was announced in XIII Five-Year Plan 2016–2020 (Luong and Arnold, 2021).

[80] State Council, 2017. Section 2.2, General Obligations (总体要求), par. 2.2, Basic principles (基本原则). In original: 促进产学研用各创新主体共创共享.

[81] MIIT, 2017 (cit. in Chapter 3, Appendix IV). Section 2.1, General Obligations (总体要求), par. 2.2 Basic principles (基本原则). In original: 促进产学研用相结合.

(委员会), whose activities reflect the priority areas of the Alliance.[82] In January 2022, half of the six committees focused on public sector applications, namely: urban governance (lit., "new smart cities", 新型智慧城市), medicine (医学人工智能), and transport (交通 + 人工智能深度融合). Shanghai confirms that AI industry alliances play a key role to foster the policy priorities of the government, including the use of AI in the public sector. Consistently with the municipal AI plans that state the intention to integrate AI in various areas of the public sector, the Shanghai Artificial Intelligence Industry Association[83] (上海人工智能行业协会) is actively coordinating and supporting the activities of AI companies in urban governance, healthcare, transport, smart community management, and other AI policy priorities of the Shanghai municipal government.[84]

While there are other initiatives in China's national innovation system that engages private companies to promote AI development (Box 2.2), the AIOIPs and the AIIA are two platforms that purportedly stimulate the uptake and use of AI in the public sector. The AIOIPs directly pick private companies to apply AI solutions that optimize public sector operations and public service provision in urban governance, public security, medicine, transport, and the judiciary, among others. The AIIA adopts a more indirect approach. It acts as a platform that coordinates, supports, and steers the work of private companies to achieve the goals of China's AI strategy, including the promotion of public sector AI applications. The importance of these governance mechanisms is amplified by the fact that they create models that can be replicated and adapted to local conditions

[82] The working groups (工作组) focus on horizontal topics such as standardization, property rights, safety, etc. The steering groups (推进组) focus on aspects in the AI foundation layer (2.1), namely AI open source (AI开源开放推进组) and AI computing framework and chips (AI计算架构与芯片推进组). The committees (委员会) are more sector-specific.

[83] The Shanghai Artificial Intelligence Industry Association was established in July 2019 as the Shanghai AI Development Alliance (SAIA, 上海人工智能发展联盟). It works under the supervision of the Shanghai Municipal Commission of Economy and Informatization. In July 2020, SAIA formally became an association (协会). Since then, SAIA has introduced stricter admission obligations (interview with SAIA Secretariat, 21 April 2021). At the time of this writing, SAIA has approximately 300 members.

[84] In an interview with the author at the SAIA office in Shanghai (3 February 2021), representatives of the Secretariat stated the Association is tasked with developing the Shanghai AI ecosystem in five priority areas: smart city, healthcare, transportation, smart community, and smart finance (AI + 智慧城市、AI + 健康、AI + 交通、AI + 金融及AI + 智慧社区).

by cities and provinces. Shanghai is a case in point. The Shanghai Artificial Intelligence Association supports private companies that develop AI solutions for the public sector and other areas prioritized by the municipal AI plans, as it was just explained. Similarly, the approach of the AIOIPs is replicated in the Shanghai "AI pilot application scenarios" (人工智能试点应用场景). This is a policy initiative that pairs public organizations (e.g., schools, hospitals) that want to use AI technologies in their activities with private companies that can supply such technologies and the related expertise (detailed analysis in Chapter 5.3).

Box 2.2 China's government guidance funds

Government guidance funds (GGFs, 政府引导基金) are public–private investment funds with a dual mandate to produce financial returns and further government policy goals. They raise money from public and private sources and make equity investments in companies in government-prioritized sectors. They are another mechanism used by the Chinese authorities at the national and local levels to stimulate technology innovation by engaging private companies, including in AI. "The fund itself is an entity formed by or at the behest of a central, provincial, or local government agency. Typically, the governmental sponsor creates the fund, selects the recipient sector, sets a fundraising target, allocates capital to part of that target directly from budget outlays, and tries to raise the rest (typically 70–80% of the target) from other investors, whose contributions are called 'social capital'[85]" (Luong et al., 2021). For private investors, the advantages of the GGFs include: ample financial support (i.e., as a co-investor, the government participates with part of the capital and often

[85] The term social capital (社会资本), and its synonyms social fund (社会资金) and social investment (社会投资), refer to any source of funding outside of government budget. These terms encompass not only investments by private individuals and private institutions, but also investments from State-funded entities such as State-owned enterprises, including State-run banks. One noteworthy example comes from the AI industry. The National Integrated Circuit Industry Investment Fund Co. (国家集成电路产业投资基金股份有限公司) is primarily invested by the Ministry of Finance (25.95%) and China Development Bank Capital Corporation (23.07%). Other State-owned enterprises such as China National Tobacco Corporation (14.42%), Beijing E-Town International Investment and Development Co., Ltd. (7.21%), and China Mobile (7.21%) all own shares in this GGF. No private capital participated in the first financing phase of the fund (Luong et al., 2021, p. 23).

takes a greater share of the risk); policy support (i.e., the government's sizable capital contributions also signal the government's commitment to the relevant industries, making participation more attractive); and, in some cases, the GGFs guarantee a minimum return for the partner investors (Luong et al., 2021; Bazavan, 2019; Ding, 2018).

Differently from AIOIPs and AIIA, the GGFs were not specifically designed for AI promotion. They started as an experiment by the Beijing Municipal government in 2002, the Zhongguancun Venture Capital Guiding Fund. The method was later granted official recognition by the NDRC in 2008. Since then, the number of GGFs has proliferated, with a large wave of GGFs established in 2015 to jump-start innovation-led growth, and shift away from manufacturing-led growth (Colvin et al., 2020, p. 25; Lewis, 2019, p.14). Estimating the amount of investment from GGFs in the AI industry is problematic.[86] However, there is evidence that GGFs are increasingly used to finance AI companies (Luong et al., 2021, pp. 15, 27; Ding, 2018, pp. 21–22). Indeed, Shanghai has been widely using GGFs as a tool to support the local AI industry (Chapter 4.4). In addition, the use of GGFs to finance AI activities is consistent with the indications of the *New Generation Artificial Intelligence Development Plan*, which explicitly encourages to "use existing government investment funds to support eligible AI projects, and encourage leading enterprises and industrial innovation alliances to lead the establishment of market-oriented AI development funds[87]".

GGFs are important because they confirm the shift in China's approach to innovation policy, whereby the government is trying to engage private companies in promoting government-prioritized technologies, including artificial intelligence. Through the GGFs, the government acts as a facilitator and multiplier for private investments, rather than the principal sponsor. The GGFs share with the AIOIPs and the AIIA the double

[86] Colvin et al. (2020, p. 26) observe: "To determine the amount of AI-focused expenditures through GGFs would require information on each recipient of investment to assess the degree to which they are AI-focused. Public reporting of these investments is only partial [...], so it would not be possible to use this approach to comprehensively estimate the amount of investments in AI companies".

[87] State Council, 2017. Section 2.4, Resource Allocation (资源配置). In original: 利用现有政府投资基金支持符合条件的人工智能项目，鼓励龙头骨干企业、产业创新联盟牵头成立市场化的人工智能发展基金.

benefits of accelerating the growth of the AI industry and involving the expertise of private companies in promoting AI development. At the same time, there is less evidence that they are stimulating public sector AI applications. Nonetheless, their existence confirms that in China's AI policy is emerging a close-knitted link between central planning, decentralized experimentation, and active private sector participation, further discussed in the conclusions of this chapter (2.4).

Chinese Initiatives in AI Regulation and AI Ethics

The Chinese government has shown great attention to issues related to AI ethics and AI regulation. In 2017, the *New Generation Artificial Intelligence Development Plan* stated that China would establish AI laws and regulations, ethical norms, and security assessment and control capabilities by 2025. It also stated that the country will construct a comprehensive system of AI laws and regulations, ethical norms, and policies by 2030.[88] Next paragraphs provide an overview of the main Chinese initiatives in AI regulation and AI ethics to draw conclusions on their expected impacts on AI adoption in China, building on the assumption that regulatory and ethical issues are expected to be two major challenges of AI uptake in the public sector (2.2.2.3). This review cannot do justice to the growing body of specialized literature on these topics. Nonetheless, the analysis conducted here has the merit to offer deeper insights on whether and how regulatory and ethical issues are affecting AI adoption and implementation in China.

Chinese Initiatives in AI Regulation

Between 2019 and 2022, China has published three main documents that specifically regulate some aspects of AI. This subsection examines the main contents of these AI regulations to draw insights on their possible impacts on the use of AI in the public sector in China. In addition, since 2017 China started a major overhaul of its laws and standards on data

[88] The creation of ethical norms (伦理规范) for AI is mentioned among the strategic objectives of the AIDP (Sect. 2.2, The Overall Obligations/总体要求, par. 2.3, Strategic Objectives/战略目标). Section 5, Guarantee measures (保障措施), par. 2.1 articulates the need to "develop laws, regulations, and ethical norms that promote the development of AI" (制定促进人工智能发展的法律法规和伦理规范).

protection, which are relevant for contemporary AI applications that are mostly based on machine learning techniques that use big volumes of digital data. These privacy regulations are reviewed in Chapter 4.1 to assess their impacts on Shanghai's capacity to access and use data for public sector AI applications.

In December 2019, the Cyberspace Administration of China (CAC, 国家互联网信息办公室) published the ***Provisions on the Governance of the Online Information Content Ecosystem***,[89] which cover a wide range of "online content service platforms" such as websites, Apps, and online forums. This document regulates the use of "personalized algorithmic recommendations technologies" (性化算法推荐技术) in these platforms. The regulations (art. 6) stipulate personalized algorithmic recommendations that are subject to content restrictions. Such algorithmic recommendations should not include contents that jeopardize national security (危害国家安全), damage the reputation or interests of the State (损害国家荣誉和利益), or disseminate rumors that disturb economic and social order (散布谣言, 扰乱经济秩序和社会秩序). Instead, the document (art. 5) requires that personalized algorithmic recommendations create a "positive and healthy environment". This means promoting contents that publicize the Xi Jinping Thought on Socialism with Chinese Characteristics for a New Era (习近平新时代中国特色社会主义思想) and the Party's principles and policies (党的理论路线方针政策), showcasing the successes of economic and social development (展示经济社会发展亮点), reflecting the great struggle and enthusiastic life of the people (反映人民群众伟大奋斗和火热生活), or carrying forward the core socialist values (弘扬社会主义核心价值观). To ensure the promotion of State-desired contents, online platforms are required to parse posts and comments, and carry out real-time inspections (art. 9).

[89] Cyberspace Administration of China, 2019. *Provisions on the Governance of the Online Information Content Ecosystem* [网络信息内容生态治理规定], Order of the Cyberspace Administration of China (No. 5) [国家互联网信息办公室令第5号], 20 December, http://www.cac.gov.cn/2019-12/20/c_1578375159509309.htm. English translation: Zhang, B. and Barata, J., 2020. Provisions on the Governance of the Online Information Content Ecosystem, The Center for Internet and Society. *Stanford Law School*, 1 March, https://wilmap.stanford.edu/entries/provisions-governance-online-information-content-ecosystem.

In March 2022, the ***Internet Information Service Algorithmic Recommendation Management Provisions***[90] came into effect. Jointly issued by the CAC, the Ministry of Industry and Informatization (MIIT), the Ministry of Public Security (MPS), and the State Administration for Market Regulation (SAMR), these regulations attracted global attention because they are considered the most extensive set of rules for the implementation of algorithmic recommendations in the world. They demand transparency about the functioning of algorithms, and afford users more control over which data can be used to feed algorithmic recommendations. The regulations prohibit algorithmic recommendation service providers from generating fake news or disseminating information from unauthorized sources, and from using algorithms to influence online public opinion or evade supervision and management, among others. Like the aforementioned CAC regulations on managing the online information content ecosystem, these new regulations (art. 6) encourage algorithmic recommendation service providers to "uphold mainstream value orientations"(坚持主流价值导向), and "actively disseminate positive energy" (积极传播正能量). The regulations specify a licensing requirement for algorithmic recommendation service providers operating in online news, and they prohibit algorithmic generation of fake news (art. 13). The regulations state that CAC and other relevant ministries and departments will establish a "graded and categorized algorithmic security management system" (算法分级分类安全管理制度) for algorithmic recommendation service providers. This security management system is based on criteria like: the "public opinion properties or the social mobilization capabilities of algorithmic recommendation services" (根据算法推荐服务的舆论属性或者社会动员能力); content categories; or the degree of importance of data handled by algorithmic recommendations, among others (art. 23). Providers of algorithmic recommendation services with "public opinion properties" or having social mobilization capabilities shall register with

90 CAC, MIIT, MPS and SAMR, 2021. *Internet Information Service Algorithm Recommendation Management Provisions* [互联网信息服务算法推荐管理规定], 31 December, http://www.cac.gov.cn/2022-01/04/c_1642894606364259.htm. English translation: Creemers, R., Webster, G. and Toner, H., 2022. Translation: Internet Information Service Algorithmic Recommendation Management Provisions—Effective March 1, 2022. *DigiChina, Stanford University*, https://digichina.stanford.edu/work/translation-internet-information-service-algorithmic-recommendation-management-provisions-effective-march-1-2022/.

relevant authorities (art. 24). The new regulations confirm the attention of Chinese regulators to issues like opaque recommendation models, which had been partly addressed in the *Personal Information Protection Law* (Chapter 4.1).

One month before the *Internet Information Service Algorithm Recommendation Management Provisions* became effective, CAC presented a separate but related draft proposal on the regulation of deep synthesis technology and services, called the ***Internet Information Service Deep Synthesis Management Provisions***.[91] Entered into force on 10 January 2023, these regulations address "synthetic content", an umbrella term encompassing fake news, synthetic audio, and deepfake images and videos (i.e., audio and video contents where a person's face is stitched onto someone else using AI). This document stipulates that producers of deepfake software are required to verify the real names of creators, and "conspicuously label" any deep-faked content (which in practice is often done using digital watermarks). Like the other two regulations just examined, the document (art. 4) requires deep synthesis service providers and deep synthesis service users to adhere to the "correct political direction" (正确政治方向). Moreover, the document (art. 6) states that deep synthesis service providers should not engage in activities harming national security (危害国家安全), disrupting social stability (破坏社会稳定), or upsetting social order (扰乱社会秩序). In addition, deep synthesis service providers should not produce, publish, or disseminate information inciting subversion of State power (煽动颠覆国家政权), or harming national security and social stability (危害国家安全和社会稳定).

By requesting that the use of AI promotes "a positive and healthy environment", "contents that publicize Xi Jinping Thought", "socialist core values", or a "correct political direction", while at the same time strictly prohibiting any reference to contents that may question the Party leadership, Chinese AI regulations appear to be designed to support State action and promote State-endorsed values. This pattern has been confirmed

[91] Cyberspace Administration of China, 2022. *Internet Information Service Deep Synthesis Management Provisions (Draft for comment)* [互联网信息服务深度合成管理规定 (征求意见稿)], 28 January, http://www.cac.gov.cn/2022-01/28/c_1644970458520968.htm. English translation: Creemers, R. and Webster, G., 2022. Translation: Internet Information Service Deep Synthesis Management Provisions (Draft for Comment)—Jan. 2022. *DigiChina, Stanford University*, https://digichina.stanford.edu/work/translation-internet-information-service-deep-synthesis-management-provisions-draft-for-comment-jan-2022/.

by the *Interim Measures for the Management of Generative Artificial Intelligence Services*[92] effective from August 2023, which require that generative AI services "preserve national security" and "uphold core socialist values". As noted by Russell Wald of Stanford University in relation to the *Internet Information Service Algorithmic Recommendation Management Provisions*, Chinese regulations do not apply to the government's use of algorithms or data, and some new rules such as those promoting particular values are about maintaining government control and benefiting the regime.[93] More generally, other scholars observe that in the field of AI China is adopting an "experiment first and regulate later" approach that allows the country to make swift progress in AI applications (Elliot, 2020). The current regulatory focus is on speeding up technology development, data collection, and implementing pilots: "issues like risk management, data privacy and accountability are coded in policy, but appear to be secondary to the development imperative" (Han, 2020, p. 39). Experts also observe that, despite some similarities between the Chinese AI regulations and the European Commission's *Proposal for a Regulation on Artificial Intelligence*[94] on topics like grading AI systems in terms of risks to society, China diverges in regulatory targets, as Chinese regulations focus on what companies—not government organizations—should or should not do (Lee, 2022). Overall, these considerations suggest that at present Chinese AI regulations are not constraining AI adoption and use by the public sector. The overview of China's data privacy system (Chapter 4.1) and evidence collected during the fieldwork in Shanghai (Chapter 5) corroborate these conclusions.

[92] CAC, National Development and Reform Commission, Ministry of Education, MOST, MIIT, MPS, and State Administration of Radio and Television, 2023. *Interim Measures for the Management of Generative Artificial Intelligence Services* [生成式人工智能服务管理暂行办法], 13 July, http://www.cac.gov.cn/2023-07/13/c_1690898327029107.htm. English translation: China Law Translate, 2023. Interim Measures for the Management of Generative Artificial Intelligence Services. *China Law Translate*, https://www.chinalawtranslate.com/en/generative-ai-interim/.

[93] Russell Wald, director of policy for Stanford's Institute for Human-Centered Artificial Intelligence. Quoted in: Konrad, J. and Knight, W., 2022. China is about to regulate AI—and the world is watching. *Wired*, 22 February, https://www.wired.com/story/china-regulate-ai-world-watching/.

[94] European Commission, 2021. *Proposal for a Regulation on Artificial Intelligence*, https://digital-strategy.ec.europa.eu/en/library/proposal-regulation-laying-down-harmonised-rules-artificial-intelligence.

Chinese Initiatives in AI Ethics

China has also been particularly active in the realm of AI ethics. Between 2017 and 2022, all the main Chinese AI policy actors have issued AI ethics principles. Here the analysis focuses on government-endorsed efforts, that is, AI ethics initiatives produced by government institutions independently or in cooperation with private companies and research institutes (which are usually public, government-controlled entities). These initiatives constitute half of Chinese AI ethics principles and guidelines published so far. The remainder are AI ethics guidelines published by leading AI companies like Baidu, Tencent, and Megvii, which often are also involved in drafting State-led collaborative AI ethics guidelines (the full list of Chinese initiatives in AI ethics and their main contents are summarized in Appendix II the end of the chapter).

In May 2019, the first set of government-endorsed AI principles was published by the Beijing Academy of Artificial Intelligence (BAAI, 北京智源人工智能研究院), an institution under the guidance of the Ministry of Science and Technology. The ***Beijing AI Principles***[95] were drafted by the BAAI in a multi-stakeholder consultative process that includes Peking University, Tsinghua University, the Chinese Academy of Sciences' Institute of Automation and Institute of Computing Technology, and a group of technology firms like Baidu, Alibaba, and Tencent. The BAAI ethics document consists of 15 principles categorized in three groups: (i) Research and Development (研发), such as "AI should conform to human values and interests" or "improve the transparency, explainability, and predictability of AI, reducing biases"; (ii) use (使用), such as "ensure that users of AI systems understand the impact of such systems on their rights and interests"; and (iii) governance (治理), such as adaptation and moderation (适应与适度) in adjusting AI principles, policies, and regulations to the development of AI, not only to avoid hindering its proper utilization, but also to ensure that it is beneficial to society and the natural environment.

In May 2019, another government-endorsed AI ethics initiative was published as the result of a multi-stakeholder consultative process led by the aforementioned Artificial Intelligence Industry Alliance. The ***Joint Pledge on Artificial Intelligence Industry Self-Discipline (Draft for***

95 Beijing Academy of Artificial Intelligence, 2019. *Beijing AI principles* [人工智能北京共识], https://www-pre.baai.ac.cn/news/beijing-ai-principles-en.html.

Comment),[96] effective from June 2019, consists of 18 articles that include principles such as: AI development should be beneficial to humans and enhance their well-being; AI systems should operate safely, securely, reliably, and controllably; responsibilities should be clarified at each stage of AI development, from research to manufacturing and implementation; and AI development should consider current and future workforce challenges. The Joint Pledge was drafted under the guidance of the China Academy of Information and Communications Technology affiliated to the Ministry of Industry and Information Technology, and it is specifically targeted to companies in the AI industry (and no other organizations).

The first AI ethics guidelines independently issued by a government institution are the ***Governance Principles for the New Generation Artificial Intelligence—Developing Responsible Artificial Intelligence***,[97] published in June 2019 by the National New Generation Artificial Intelligence Governance Expert Committee (国家新一代人工智能治理专业委员会). The Expert Committee was established in March 2019 as another AI policy agency affiliated to the Ministry of Science and Technology, like the New Generation AI Strategic Advisory Committee (Chapter 3.1). The Expert Committee is composed of seven members, including five public research entities (Tsinghua University, Peking University, Shanghai University, East China University of Political Science and Law, and the Chinese Academy of Sciences), and two private companies (JD.com and

[96] Artificial Intelligence Industry Alliance, 2019. *Joint Pledge on Artificial Intelligence Industry Self-Discipline (Draft for Comments)* [人工智能行业自律公约 (征求意见稿)]. China Information Security [中国信息安全], WeChat account, 2 June, https://mp.weixin.qq.com/s/x7HTx4AR6oNBWwWxUpnSuQ. English translation: Webster, G., 2019. Translation: Chinese AI Alliance Drafts Self-Discipline "Joint Pledge". *New America*, 17 June, https://www.newamerica.org/cybersecurity-initiative/digichina/blog/translation-chinese-ai-alliance-drafts-self-discipline-joint-pledge/?from=timeline&isappinstalled=0. Articles 1–14 contain AI ethics principles, while articles 15–18 list a set of general provisions.

[97] National New Generation Artificial Intelligence Governance Expert Committee, 2019. *Governance Principles for the New Generation Artificial Intelligence—Developing Responsible Artificial Intelligence* [新一代人工智能治理原则—发展负责任的人工智能]. *China Information Security* [中国信息安全], WeChat account, 17 June, https://mp.weixin.qq.com/s/JWRehPFXJJz_mu80hlO2kQ; English translation: Laskai, L., and Webster, G., 2019. Translation: Chinese Expert Group Offers "Governance Principles" for "Responsible AI". *New America*, 17 June, https://www.newamerica.org/cybersecurity-initiative/digichina/blog/translation-chinese-expert-group-offers-governance-principles-responsible-ai/.

Megvii Technology, the latter releasing its own guidelines on AI governance soon after; see Appendix II). This document contains eight very general principles like "harmony and friendliness" (和谐友好), "fairness and justice" (公平公正), and "open collaboration" (开放协作).

On 2 July 2019, the Shanghai Artificial Intelligence Industry Security Expert Advisory Committee (上海人工智能产业安全专家咨询委员会) was officially announced. It includes experts from universities, research institutes, and enterprises, and it operates under the coordination of the Shanghai municipal government. On the same day, the Advisory Committee presented its ***Initiative for the Safe Development of Artificial Intelligence in Shanghai***,[98] which consists of eight principles whose contents are largely aligned with previous multi-stakeholder efforts like those of BAAI and AIIA. For instance, the document calls for upholding privacy protection (隐私保护), ensuring algorithmic justice (算法公正), or promoting open cooperation (开放合作), among others.

Finally, in September 2021 the National New Generation Artificial Intelligence Governance Expert Committee issued another set of AI ethics principles, the ***Ethical Norms for New Generation Artificial Intelligence***.[99] This document consists of 25 articles that spell out ethical guidelines for responsible AI research and development. The document aims to integrate ethics into the entire lifecycle of AI systems. It provides ethical guidelines for natural persons, legal persons, and organizations engaged in AI-related activities. It includes six "fundamental ethical norms" (基本伦理规范), from enhancing the well-being of humankind (增进人类福祉) to ensuring controllability and trustworthiness (确保可控可信), which reiterate the eight AI ethics principles that the Committee published in June 2019. These fundamental ethical norms are compounded by "norms of management" (管理规范), "norms of research and development" (研发规范), "norms of supply" (供应规

[98] Shanghai Artificial Intelligence Industry Security Expert Advisory Committee, 2019. *Initiative for the Safe Development of Artificial Intelligence in Shanghai* [人工智能安全发展上海倡议]. *CINN.cn* [中国工业新闻网], 3 July, http://www.cinn.cn/dfgy/201907/t20190703_214884.html. See also: http://english.sheitc.sh.gov.cn/news/683036.htm.

[99] MOST, 2021. *Ethical Norms for New Generation Artificial Intelligence* [新一代人工智能伦理规范]. Ministry of Science and Technology, 26 September, http://www.most.gov.cn/kjbgz/202109/t20210926_177063.html. English translation: Murphy, B. ed., 2021. Ethical Norms for New Generation Artificial Intelligence Released. *Center for Security and Emerging Technologies*, https://cset.georgetown.edu/wp-content/uploads/t0400_AI_ethical_norms_EN.pdf.

范), and "norms of use" (使用规范) that should be followed in the corresponding AI-related activities.

The attention of the Chinese government to AI ethics is confirmed by continuous developments in this area, such as the ***Opinions on Strengthening the Ethical Governance of Science and Technology***[100] published in March 2022 by the Central Committee of the Communist Party of China and the State Council. The document (II) outlines five general principles of technology ethics (科技伦理) that, as elaborated in its following sections, primarily apply to artificial intelligence, life sciences, and medicine. These principles largely overlap with previous government-led initiatives in AI ethics, and include: enhancing the well-being of humankind (增进人类福祉); respect the right to life (尊重生命权利); uphold fairness and justice (坚持公平公正); reasonably control risks (合理控制风险); and maintain openness and transparency (保持公开透明). The document (III, 2) requires that entities engaged in AI, life sciences, and medicine establish ethical committees (科技伦理 (审查) 委员会). It (IV, 1) calls for formulating technology ethics norms and guidelines in these disciplines, and for improving related technology ethics standards (制定生命科学、医学、人工智能等重点领域的科技伦理规范、指南等, 完善科技伦理相关标准). The document also requires that relevant institutions and policy actors improve legislation and governance of technology ethics in AI, life sciences, and medicine (IV, 3), and strengthen research on the ethical issues related to technological innovation (IV, 4). Finally, the document calls for strict control and supervision in technology ethics (V), and for improving the training of personnel and dissemination of information in relation to the ethical governance of science and technology (VI).

The number of Chinese initiatives in AI ethics dispels misconceptions that China lacks debate around the ethical use of AI. Similar to AI regulations, however, it is difficult to find evidence that China's AI ethics initiatives are creating any barriers of AI adoption and use in

[100] General Office of the Central Committee of the Communist Party of China, General Office of the State Council, 2022. *Opinions on Strengthening the Ethical Governance of Science and Technology* [关于加强科技伦理治理的意见]. China Central Government, 20 March, http://www.gov.cn/zhengce/2022-03/20/content_5680105.htm. English translation: Zeng, Y., 2022. Opinion on Strengthening the Ethics and Governance in Science and Technology [China]. *International Research Center for AI Ethics and Governance*, https://ai-ethics-and-governance.institute/2022/03/22/china-released-opinion-on-strengthening-the-ethics-and-governance-in-science-and-technology/.

the public sector. First, Chinese AI ethics initiatives are scarcely actionable and not embedded in the processes and institutions that shape decision-making within government, like most other AI ethics initiatives worldwide (Arcesati, 2021; Stanford University, 2021b; Berryhill et al., 2019; Calo, 2017). Even the *Ethical Norms for New Generation Artificial Intelligence*—which to date are the most structured collection of Chinese ethical principles for AI—are very general. They state broad principles like "promote agile governance" (art. 5), "strengthen self-discipline and consciousness" (art. 10), "respect market rules" (art. 14), or "avoid misuse" (art. 19), and do not indicate any enforcement mechanism. Second, the Chinese government remains the final judge of the ethical values that should regulate the AI technology, meaning that the Party-State is the arbitrator of how and to whom these values should apply (Lee, 2022). This is consistent with the broader ideological discourse of the current leadership, which rediscovered the use of selected Confucian principles to legitimize the government approach to digital governance: by presenting technology as an instrument to promote the common good, social order, and harmony, a hierarchy is established whereby the State—the highest expression of morality—leverages technology to strengthen its abilities to act in the interest of the whole society (Kirk et al., 2020). Third, despite these AI ethics initiatives, there is evidence that the State is making an extensive use of technology for social control. Even scholars arguing that Chinese AI principles largely align with global ones note that some AI applications in China have established "a culture of pervasive monitoring of citizens" (Gal, 2020). This observation is corroborated by the discussions made in Chapter 1, which highlighted the extensive reach of technological penetration in Chinese society. Finally, some scholars observe that, despite some signs of change, Chinese AI ethics guidelines have an "opaque nature" and a low level of engagement with international initiatives (Arcesati, 2021; Ding, 2018).

Defining "AI in the Public Sector in China"

Scholars agree that establishing a common conceptual understanding of AI in the public sector is a prerequisite for examining opportunities and challenges of AI in this area, and it has significant downstream effects on the assessment of the factors that influence the use of AI in the activities of public organizations (2.1). To fill a gap in research and practice, and support the analysis of public sector AI applications in Shanghai, the analysis conducted so far provided a precise definition of AI systems (2.2.1), an integrated analysis of technical and non-technical factors affecting the use of AI in the public sector that can be generalized to different socioeconomic and political contexts (2.2.2), and examined country-specific dynamics that shape public sector AI applications in China (2.2.3). This analysis underpins the proposed definition of "AI in the public sector in China", which will be used as a guidance for studying public sector AI implementations in Shanghai:

> AI in the public sector indicates the use of AI systems to support public organizations in performing a broad range of activities that currently include: communicating with the public about its rights and obligations; managing internal resources and public infrastructure; enforcing regulatory mandates; adjudicating government benefits and rights; and monitoring and analyzing public policies. The use of AI in the public sector is driven by the need to improve the efficiency and effectiveness of public service provision, optimize resource allocation, and enhance decision-making capabilities. At the same time, the use of AI is hindered by a complex aggregation of technical, legal, ethical and socioeconomic challenges that reflect the multiple obligations of public organizations. In addition, in-depth research on the use of AI in the public sector in China must consider the governance mechanisms in central-local relations and in the national innovation system that promote the implementation of AI in public organizations in the country, as well as the emerging Chinese responses to the regulatory and ethical challenges of AI in the public sector.

The aforementioned definition also serves to bring into focus key cross-cutting and country-specific factors that characterize public sector AI applications in the Chinese context. These factors are important to gain a deeper understanding of the ability of Shanghai to implement AI in the public sector, which in this book is assessed through the lens of the policy capacity framework presented in Chapter 2.3. The implications of these cross-cutting and country-specific factors for the assessment of Shanghai's policy capacity to use AI in the public sector are explained in detail in Chapter 2.4.

2.3 Using AI in the Public Sector in Shanghai: The Policy Capacity Framework

Policy capacity remains an elusive concept in public policy and political sciences (Brenton, Baekkeskov and Hannah, 2022; Gleeson et al., 2009). While they provide different definitions, scholars agree that policy capacity is vital to achieve the desired policy outputs and outcomes, and capacity deficits are considered a major cause of policy failure and sub-optimal outcomes (Brenton et al., 2022; Woo, 2021; Mukherjee and Bali, 2019; Wu et al., 2015; Howlett and Ramesh, 2015, 2014; Fukuyama, 2013). As such, assessing the policy capacity of Shanghai to implement AI in the public sector is a necessary step to examine whether the municipality is fulfilling its goal to improve public service provision by accelerating AI integration in public sector activities, because without adequate policy capacity Shanghai would not be able to develop, access, and mobilize the resources necessary to foster the use of AI in the public sector efficiently and effectively.

To examine the policy capacity of Shanghai to implement AI in the public sector, this book adopts the policy capacity framework of Wu et al. (2015). This framework builds upon the strategic triangle of Mark Moore, which identifies public value, organizational capacity, and legitimacy and support as crucial for the functioning of public organizations[101]

[101] The strategic triangle is part of Moore's work on Public Value Management (PVM). This is a normative theory of public administration arguing that public organizations must contribute to increasing the overall well-being of the community, an outcome that PVM calls the creation of public value. To ensure that public organizations can create public value, Moore recommends that public managers consider both the external demands and the internal capabilities of their organizations, in order to check whether public organizations are efficiently producing what their political overseers and the citizens are demanding. In this perspective, the strategic triangle forms the basis for "strategic planning" in public organizations (Moore, 1995, pp. 70–73). Strategic planning was later developed in the concept of strategic public management, which introduces additional analytical techniques to help public managers obtain political legitimacy and support (monitoring the political environment and keeping the organization responsive to public aspirations), and improve operational capacity of their organizations (searching for productivity gains in value creation), in order to sustain or create greater public value (Moore, 2013, p. 110). In addition to the research developed by Moore (1995, 2013), Benington (2007), and Moore and Benington (2011), which primarily focuses on public administration, there are other streams of research on public value. A review of the scholarship on public value can be found in Van der Wal, Z., Nabatchi, T., and de Graaf, G., 2015. From Galaxies to Universe: A Cross-Disciplinary Review and Analysis of Public Values

(Moore, 1995). Chapter 2.3 presents the key tenets of the policy capacity framework (2.3.1), and it explains how the conceptual tools of this framework will be used to gauge the ability of Shanghai to implement AI in the public sector (2.3.2).

2.3.1 Assessing Policy Capacity

The policy capacity framework of Wu, Ramesh, and Howlett defines and assesses policy capacity as the combination of analytical, operational, and political skills and resources at the systemic, organizational, and individual levels, which are necessary to perform policy functions[102] (Wu et al., 2015, p. 166).

Consistently with this framework, this book examines the policy capacity of Shanghai to implement AI in the public sector by assessing its ability to develop, access, and mobilize the analytical, operational, and political skills and resources necessary to use AI in public sector activities. It also uses this framework to examine how such capacity translates into real-world policy initiatives by highlighting the analytical, operational, and political capabilities that determine their strengths and limitations in deploying AI in the public sector in Shanghai.

The policy capacity framework defines analytical, operational, and political capacities as follows:

- **Analytical Capacity** is the ability to "ensure policy actions are *technically sound* in the sense they can contribute to the attainment of policy goals if carried out" (Wu et al., 2015, pp. 167–168; emphasis in original). Analytical capacity is required to make accurate and effective policies (Woo, 2021, p. 33).
- **Political Capacity** is the ability to "obtain and sustain *political support* for policy actions" (Wu et al., 2015, p. 168; emphasis in original). Political capacity is required to ensure that policies possess the necessary endorsement and legitimacy for success (Woo, 2021, p. 36).

Publications from 1969 to 2012. *American Review of Public Administration*, 45, pp. 13–28; and Williams, I. and Shearer, H., 2011. Appraising Public Value: Past, Present and Futures. *Public Administration*, 89, pp. 1367–1384.

102 The concept of policy capacity is outlined also in other articles published by the authors (Howlett and Ramesh, 2015, 2014), and in a dedicated book (Wu et al., 2018).

- **Operational Capacity** is the ability to "[align] resources with policy actions so that they can be implemented *in practice*" (Wu et al., 2015, p. 168; emphasis in original). Operational capacity is required to translate the available resources into actionable policies and implementing these policies (Woo, 2021, p. 34).

Each type of capacity involves skills and resources at three different levels—individual, organizational, and systemic—generating nine types of policy-relevant capacities, exemplified in Table 2.2.

The policy capacity framework provides a multidimensional heuristic to identify the types of capabilities at different levels that are crucial to perform the desired policy actions. It has the advantage to offer a comprehensive set of criteria to examine the core components of policy capacity, while avoiding the overly abstract levels of conception of previous studies on this topic (Woo, 2021). This framework also underscores that the components of policy capacity are interrelated and affect each other at and across different levels, as explained by the **nested model of policy capacity** (Wu et al., 2015, p. 168). Next section explains how this nested model and other conceptual tools of the policy capacity framework are applied to examine the ability of Shanghai to implement AI in the public sector.

2.3.2 *Assessing Shanghai's Policy Capacity to Use AI in the Public Sector*

The nested model of policy capacity offers a systemic view of policy capacity that brings into focus the components of such capacity and their interactions, allowing to exercise more precision in the assessment of the ability of governments to make good policy choices and implement them effectively (Wu et al., 2015, p. 170). It offers three main analytical advantages to examine the ability of Shanghai to use AI in the public sector.

First, this model emphasizes that **policy capacity is what results from the combination of analytical, operational, and political capabilities**, all of which are important to perform the desired policy actions (Wu et al., 2015, pp. 167–168). Building upon this consideration, this research highlights how each of the three components of policy capacity contributes to the integration of AI in the public sector in Shanghai. Documentary

Table 2.2 Types and levels of policy capacities, examples (Woo, 2021; Mukherjee and Bali, 2019; Wu et al., 2018; Wu et al., 2015)

	Analytical capacity	*Operational capacity*	*Political capacity*
Individual	The ability of individuals (policymakers, civil servants, policy analysts within government) to access and develop the technical and scientific knowledge, analytical skills, data, and information necessary to devise and implement policies in an efficient and effective way	The ability of policymakers and civil servants to perform key managerial functions to support the operations of the public organization they direct or work for. It includes a broad set of functional skillsets, depending on the role of the individual in the organization. These include: financial management, strategic planning, organizational staffing, budgeting, among others	The political knowledge and experience that allow policymakers and civil servants to identify other key actors, understand their interests and ideologies, and the relationships among them. It involves skillsets such as political communication and public relations, among others

	Analytical capacity	*Operational capacity*	*Political capacity*
Organizational	The availability within an organization of skills and resources needed to make accurate and effective policies, such as: individuals with analytical skills; equipment and processes for collecting and analyzing data as inputs into the policy and decision-making process; and organizational commitment to evidence-based policymaking	It includes the organizational structures and processes affecting how well public organizations perform their activities and deliver public services. For instance: clarity of mission, systems of performance measurement and human resource management, inter-agency division of labor, or an organizational culture that emphasizes discipline and cohesiveness. It also involves the relations with the political-institutional environment in which the organization works	It consists of developing learning relationships between the public organization, its governance partners, and the general public in order to obtain and sustain political support for the activities of the public organization
Systemic	The general state of scientific, statistical, and educational facilities in a society or a country, which influences the ability of policymakers and civil servants to gain access to high-quality information needed to carry on their analytical and managerial functions	Generally defined in terms of coordination of governmental and non-governmental efforts to address collective problems in a society	It indicates the general level of socio-political trust that policymakers and civil servants are able to build up with their citizens across the political, economic, social, and security spheres

research on Shanghai's AI policy environment and AI ecosystem (Chapters 3 and 4), and the interviews with experts of Shanghai AI policy (Chapter 5.1) look for evidence that Shanghai has developed solid capabilities in all three dimensions of policy capacity. The analysis of the case studies then examines how such capacity translates into practice by assessing the analytical, political, and operational capabilities that determine the strengths and limitations in deploying AI in the public sector of the main policy initiatives through which Shanghai is fostering the use of AI in this area. While the policy capacity framework postulates that these capacities do not need to be present in equal measure or all at the same time, their adequate combination is theorized to be more likely to lead to policy success. The analysis of the case studies delves into this point. It provides empirical evidence demonstrating that the combination of analytical, political, and operational capacities is facilitating the integration of AI in the public sector in Shanghai via the Government Online-Offline Shanghai (Chapter 5.2.1), the Single Platform for Urban Management (Chapter 5.2.2), and the AI pilot application scenarios (Chapter 5.3).

Second, the nested model of policy capacity highlights that **policy skills and resources are interconnected across different levels**, and affect each other both "upwards" and "downwards". The policy capacity framework underscores that "system level resources affect organizational ones and vice versa, just as organizational and individual level resources interact in the same fashion" (Wu et al., 2015, p. 167). Building upon this consideration, this research discusses how capabilities at different levels concur to determine the capacity of Shanghai to implement AI in the public sector. The analysis of Shanghai's AI policy environment explains how political capacity at the national level empowers political capacity at the municipal level, and it underscores the related implications for the assessment of Shanghai's AI policy capacity. The analysis of the case studies examines how policy capacities at different levels interact with each other in practice, and how they determine the strengths and limitations in deploying AI in the public sector of key policy initiatives in Shanghai. It shows that the level of policy capacities that primarily drives the deployment of AI in the public sector in Shanghai varies, depending on the design of each policy initiative: some policy initiatives primarily rely on municipal-level capacities (the Government Online-Offline Shanghai, the Single Platform for Urban Management), while others primarily rely on organizational-level capacities, under a municipal program (the AI pilot application scenarios). The analysis also demonstrates that Shanghai is leveraging municipal-level capacities to support policy capabilities at the organizational level in various ways.

Third, the nested model **extends beyond government to assess the skills and resources that constitute policy capacity**. It acknowledges that other stakeholders outside the government, including a range of non-governmental organizations, universities, and private companies also contribute to policy capacity. That is, the skills and resources of these actors are also involved in policy processes, affect the government's own ability to perform, and thus form an important aspect of policy capacity (Wu et al., 2015). Building upon this consideration, this research focuses on the role of private AI companies due to their importance in affecting Shanghai's policy capacity. As discussed earlier (2.2.3.2), private sector enterprises are a fundamental resource for implementing AI in the public sector in China, and public sector AI scholarship agrees that harnessing private sector skills and resources in AI is crucial to improve the ways in which public services are delivered to citizens (Chapter 6). Documentary research and the expert interviews examine the contribution of private companies to the policy capacity of Shanghai, and underscore what the municipality is doing to engage private companies in public sector AI projects. The analysis of the case studies shows how the participation of AI companies in public sector AI initiatives contributes to determining the strengths and limitations of such initiatives in deploying AI in the public sector, and it underscores that cooperation with private firms can support analytical and operational capacities to implement AI in the public sector at the municipal as well as the organizational level.

While it adopts the types of policy capabilities in their original form, this book adjusts the levels of analysis compared to the nested model of policy capacity of Wu et al. (2015). Instead of looking at systemic, organizational, and individual capabilities, this work gauges policy capacity at the following levels: **national** (analogous to, but arguably more precise than, the "systemic level" of the original framework); **municipal** (the level of Shanghai as a whole unit of analysis); and **organizational** (public organizations or jurisdictions below the municipal level). Before operationalizing these concepts, it useful to explain two key reasons that motivated such adjustments.

The first reason is to account for *the importance of local governments in implementing AI in the public sector in China*. As noted earlier (2.2.3.1), AI is a general-purpose technology. Its applications can hardly be included in a rigid top-down national blueprint. On the contrary, it is necessary that local administrations find AI applications suitable to local conditions. Indeed, the Chinese national government is incentivizing cities and provinces to play a more active and direct role in AI implementation compared to previous State-driven efforts to promote emerging technologies. Moreover, in China most public goods and services are provided by local administrations, which consequently play a key role in public sector AI applications. By placing municipal-level capacities at the center of the policy capacity framework, the analysis accounts for the fact that these capacities are crucial for the success of public sector AI applications in Shanghai, and are the most important capabilities in determining the current developments of AI in the public sector in the municipality. At the same time, by incorporating national-level capacities into the analysis, the framework accounts for the fact that the Chinese national government maintains its traditional guiding role also in AI policy. It defines strategic policy objectives (e.g., China's national AI strategy), and steers local governments and private companies toward national AI priorities (e.g., the incentive system for the promotion of local officials, State-led projects and platforms for the engagement of AI firms). In this regard, the analysis underscores the most relevant aspects of national-level policy capacity that affect municipal-level policy capacity, as explained shortly.

The second reason is to acknowledge the findings of a growing body of literature that emphasizes the *importance of organizational capacities in the use of AI in the public sector* (2.1.2). There is an increasing consensus among scholars that adequate organizational capabilities are important to ensure the successful integration of AI in the public sector, transitioning from AI pilots to established applications (Chapter 5.3.2). While it maintains municipal-level capacities at the center of the analysis for the reasons just explained, this research also highlights that there is a relationship between capabilities at the municipal and organizational levels, which can add or detract from each other. This approach is consistent with the aforementioned nested model of policy capacity, which postulates that policy skills and resources are interconnected across different levels, and affect each other both "upwards" and "downwards". As just noted, the analysis of the case studies examines the interactions of municipal-level and organizational-level capacities in practice, and their implications for the strengths and limitations in deploying AI in the public sector of key policy initiatives in Shanghai. In particular, the analysis demonstrates that Shanghai is leveraging municipal-level capacities to support policy capabilities at the organizational level in various ways.

Based upon these adjustments, the policy capacity of Shanghai to implement AI in the public sector is examined by looking at the interactions of analytical, political, and operational capacities at the national, municipal, and organizational levels. These types and levels of public sector AI policy capacity are defined as follows:

National-level policy capacity consists of: the *analytical capacity* of the Chinese national government to devise public sector AI applications that can contribute to achieving national goals in this area, if carried out; the *political capacity* to create and sustain support and legitimacy for such public sector AI applications; and the *operational capacity* to implement public sector AI applications in practice. National-level policy capacity depends on the skills and resources of the central government and the State agencies involved in AI policy (e.g., the Ministry of Science and Technology, the Cybersecurity Administration of China). It also depends on the ability of the national government to mobilize and orchestrate the policy resources available in the whole nation in order to promote public sector AI applications (e.g., the AIOIPs that leverage government data and corporate know-how). Consistently with the nested model of policy capacity and the focus of this research, the analysis will underscore the facets of national-level capacity that most directly affect the municipal-level capacity of Shanghai to implement AI in the public sector. The analysis of Shanghai's AI policy environment shows that promoting the use of AI in the public sector is a national priority, and the goals and the tasks for AI in the public sector outlined by the Shanghai municipal AI plans are aligned with those indicated by China's national AI strategy. This alignment supports the political capacity of Shanghai to drive forward with public sector AI applications. On the other hand, the high-profile political endorsement of AI development from the national leadership can generate vested interests for Shanghai officials to set over-ambitious AI plans, due to institutionalized incentives to comply with the policy priorities of superior authorities. The existence of these vested interests is accounted for in the analysis of Shanghai's analytical and political capacities. The analysis of the AI ecosystem of Shanghai discusses the general state of operational capacity at the national level in order to contextualize the relative strengths of Shanghai's operational capacity, and it identifies additional operational resources that Shanghai may gain access to.

Municipal-level policy capacity consists of: the *analytical capacity* of the Shanghai government to devise public sector AI applications that can contribute to achieving municipal goals in this area, if carried out; the *political capacity* to create and sustain support and legitimacy for such public sector AI applications, including cases where this endorsement is indirect (i.e., AI applications are part of broader policy initiatives for public sector digital innovation, like the Government Online-Offline Shanghai); and the *operational capacity* to implement public sector AI applications in practice. Municipal-level policy capacity depends on the skills and resources of the Shanghai government and its agencies, as well as on the ability of the municipal government to access and put to use the policy skills and resources available in the whole municipality. More specifically, municipal-level capacity includes skills and resources of *municipal agencies and organizations* (e.g., the analytical capacity of the Shanghai Government General Office to devise policy actions that can effectively integrate AI in administrative services and urban governance; the operational capacity of the Shanghai Municipal Big Data Center to translate policy actions into practice). Municipal-level capacity also consists of the ability of the Shanghai government to *mobilize and orchestrate* the policy resources and capabilities available in the whole municipality—including resources outside government agencies—in order to promote public sector AI applications (e.g., the capacity of the Shanghai government to aggregate and coordinate operational resources such as digital infrastructure and private AI companies, in order to promote the creation of AI-enabled platforms for administrative services and urban governance). Municipal-level policy capacity is examined from multiple perspectives. The analysis of the AI policy environment and AI ecosystem appraises the analytical capacity of Shanghai to devise policy actions that can contribute to the attainment of the municipal goals for the use of AI in the public sector, its political capacity to obtain and sustain political support for implementing these policy actions, and its operational capacity to orchestrate and deploy the resources of the AI ecosystem in order to implement AI in the public sector in practice. The expert interviews refine and validate the findings of desk research, providing empirical evidence regarding how Shanghai's municipal-level policy capacity is promoting the use of AI in the public sector in the municipality. The analysis of the case studies examines how municipal-level policy capacity translates into real-world policy initiatives that foster AI integration in the public sector in Shanghai. It delves into the analytical, operational, and political capabilities that determine the strengths and limitations of these policy initiatives in deploying AI in the public sector, and discusses the interactions of municipal-level capabilities with those of the organizations participating in such initiatives.

Organizational-level policy capacity consists of: the *analytical capacity* of government agencies and public institutions below the municipal level to devise public sector AI applications that, if carried out, can contribute to achieving the goals for AI set in their organizations or jurisdictions—which, in turn, are expected to contribute to the goals set by the municipal government, as discussed at length in this book[103]; the *political capacity* to create and sustain support and legitimacy for such public sector AI applications; and the *operational capacity* to implement these policy actions in practice. Organizational-level policy capacity depends on resources and skills of *government agencies in districts and subdistricts* that promote public sector AI applications in their jurisdictions (e.g., district governments, neighborhood committees, district-level Big Data Centers, subdistrict Urban Operation Centers). It also depends on the skills and resources of *public institutions* that are implementing AI in their activities (schools, hospitals, courts). As noted, organizational-level policy capacities can add to or detract from municipal-level policy capacities. However, they do not directly affect the deployment of AI in the public sector beyond a specific organization or jurisdiction, and they remain subordinated to municipal-level capacities (e.g., district governments can devise AI applications for citizen services in their jurisdictions, as long as they contribute to the goals set by the municipal government; district-level Big Data Centers are built and operated according to the standards set by the Shanghai Municipal Big Data Center, are operationally subordinated to it, and directly control only the data within their jurisdictions). Nonetheless, this does not diminish the importance of organizational-level capacities. These capacities are theorized to be important for the successful integration of AI in the public sector, and all the main policy initiatives for the integration of AI in the public sector in Shanghai entail some combination of municipal- and organizational-level capacities. Therefore, the analysis of the case studies examines how organizational-level policy capacity contributes to the strengths and limitations of the main policy initiatives that are fostering public sector AI

[103] In addition to the analysis of the upward accountability system of the Chinese bureaucracy (2.2.3.1), see also the examination of the case studies (Chapters 5.2 and 5.3) and the considerations developed in the conclusions (Chapter 6.1.1).

applications in Shanghai, highlighting the interactions of organizational-level and municipal-level capabilities in such policy initiatives.

In examining the policy capacity of Shanghai to implement AI in the public sector, this book responds to earlier studies that call for assessing not only the availability of resources and skills that can increase or decrease policy capacity, but also the actual contributions of such capacity to making effective policies and efficiently implement them (Brenton et al., 2022, pp. 5–6). As neatly expressed by Painter and Pierre (2005, p. 3): "evidence of policy capacity can be gathered both from the analysis of the quality and quantity of institutional resources and from the success of specific outputs and outcomes". Consistently, this research examines the availability of policy-relevant resources and skills in Shanghai, as well as their actual implementations and the resulting implications for the provision of public services. This work provides a detailed documentary assessment of the ability of Shanghai to implement AI in the public sector by gauging the availability of the skills and resources necessary to use AI in this area in the municipality, and it refines these findings with primary data derived from interviews with key stakeholders of Shanghai's AI policy. Then, it focuses on the output and outcomes resulting from such capacity. It examines the different types and levels of policy capacity that determine the strengths and limitations of the main policy initiatives that foster AI integration in the public sector in Shanghai, creating a sound basis for gauging their implications for public service provision. This analytical approach has two merits. First, it addresses the aforementioned theoretical stances that call for assessing policy capacity in terms of skills, resources, outputs, and outcomes. Second, it offers a deeper understanding of public sector AI applications in Shanghai. By looking at real-world policy initiatives, it provides empirical evidence to assess whether the municipality is fulfilling its goal to improve public service provision by accelerating AI integration in public sector activities, the research objective of this book.

As the use of AI in public sector activities is becoming increasingly common worldwide, a small but growing number of studies have started to pay attention to the capacity of governments and public organizations to use AI in the public sector. While they often provide useful indicators of the resources and skills needed to use AI in the public sector, these studies seldom offer a comprehensive view that considers the interactions of different types of capacities at different levels. On one hand, some studies focus on skills and resources at the macro level, such as the whole government or the country, and primarily look at operational capabilities (Castro and McLaughlin, 2021; Oxford Insights, 2020; Castro et al., 2019; Ding, 2019, 2018; Lee and Sheehan, 2018). On the other hand, some studies examine broader types of capabilities, but almost exclusively focus on skills and resources at the organizational level, such as the managerial aspects of integrating AI in public sector activities (Mikalef and Gupta, 2021; Desouza, 2021; Campion et al., 2020; Engstrom et al., 2020; Berryhill et al., 2019; Desouza, 2018). Against this background, the policy capacity framework—while it originally does not directly account for the use of advanced technologies in the public sector—has the advantage to offer a comprehensive yet precise view of policy capacity, which not only encompasses different types and levels of skills and resources that determine policy capacity, but also examines their interactions. As such, the policy capacity framework provides a superior operationalization of the concept of policy capacity, and offers a valuable lens to assess the ability of Shanghai to implement AI in the public sector and its implications for public service delivery.

2.4 Implications for Studying AI in the Public Sector in Shanghai

By clarifying the meaning of AI in the public sector in China, this chapter brought into focus and explained some cross-cutting and country-specific factors that characterize the use of AI in this area in the Chinese context. These factors are important to assess the policy capacity of Shanghai to implement AI in the public sector and the impacts of such capacity on public service provision. Understanding these factors serves as a starting point for the analysis of Shanghai's AI policy environment and AI ecosystem (Chapters 3 and 4), it offers indications on some aspects that will need to be integrated with findings from empirical research (Chapter 5.1), and it provides a roadmap to guide the in-depth analysis of the case studies (Chapters 5.2 and 5.3). The importance of these cross-cutting and country-specific factors for the assessment of Shanghai's policy capacity to use AI in the public sector is explained below.

Regarding **cross-cutting factors**, this chapter highlighted the **complexity of using AI in the public sector**. This complexity is related to the technical features of contemporary AI systems, their sophisticated operational logic that allows to perform a wide range of tasks, the manifold ways in which such systems interact with the environment, and the resulting policy implications. Public sector AI researchers observe that "being a family of emergent, numerous and diversified technologies (not to speak about the proliferation of custom solutions) AI also holds traits of uncertainty and ambiguity [that] make the adoption and implementation of AI more complex and different from the adoption and implementation of 'conventional' Information and Communication Technology (ICT)" (Molinari et al., 2021, p. 5). This chapter showed that the technical complexity of AI combines with the difficulties of using this technology in social domains, and emphasized that the use of AI in the public sector is characterized by a unique aggregation of technical, ethical, legal, and social factors (Desouza et al., 2020). This sociotechnical complexity is further exacerbated by the paucity of case studies of AI in the public sector, which makes it difficult for policymakers to know what is possible when thinking about the uses of AI in their work (Hager et al., 2017); and by the lack of agreed-upon methods for measuring the social and economic impacts of AI systems (Mishra et al., 2020; Crawford and Whittaker, 2016). The findings of previous research on AI in the public sector suggest that this sociotechnical complexity could affect the ability of public organizations to use AI in their work in all three dimensions of policy capacity:

- First, sociotechnical complexity makes it difficult to assess the feasibility, viability, effects, and consequences of the use of AI solutions in the public sector, among others (Berryhill et al., 2019; Mehr, 2017; Crawford and Whittaker, 2016); these analytical difficulties could affect the ability of public organizations to devise applications and initiatives that can contribute to achieving the desired policy goals for AI in the public sector (analytical capacity);
- Second, these analytical difficulties, combined with the scarce evidence on whether AI solutions are obtaining the intended results, imply that the adoption and use of AI technologies entail an element of risk, ambiguity, and uncertainty (Molinari et al., 2021; Fatima et al., 2020). This makes it difficult to make a compelling case for AI being a viable solution to improve public service delivery, and it could affect the ability to obtain and sustain the political support necessary to implement public sector AI applications (political capacity);
- Third, the deployment of AI in the public sector is characterized by a combination of technical, ethical, legal, and social elements.

Successful AI applications in the public sector require that significant progress is made in all these sociotechnical aspects, not only in technology (Misuraca et al., 2020; Wirtz and Müller, 2019). This is a complex endeavor that could affect the ability to develop the resources and skills needed to implement public sector AI applications in practice (operational capacity).

To account for the possible influences of these sociotechnical complexities on Shanghai's policy capacity to implement AI in the public sector, the findings derived from the study of documentary sources are integrated by primary data gathered from in-depth interviews with persons who are directly involved in or have first-hand knowledge of Shanghai's AI policy and public sector AI applications. The interviews offer valuable insights not only into the availability of AI policy skills and resources in Shanghai, but also into how such skills and resources are mobilized and put to use to implement public sector AI applications in the municipality. As noted in the conclusions of the previous section (2.3.2), an approach that looks at the actual manifestations of policy capacity allows to get a precise, evidence-based evaluation of Shanghai's analytical, political, and operational capabilities, their implications for public service provision, and it is consistent with previous studies that postulate that policy capacity is better understood not only in terms of resources, but also in terms of outputs (Woo, 2021; Painter and Pierre, 2005). By combining documentary research and fieldwork investigation, the analysis thus provides a comprehensive assessment of Shanghai's policy capacity that serves to support the examination of the case studies.

Another set of cross-cutting factors is specifically related to the **barriers to the use of AI in the public sector and their expected impacts during the lifecycle of AI projects**. The analysis of the drivers of AI in the public sector showed that this technology has the potential to bring benefits to the activities of public organizations, hence the attention it has been receiving from policymakers. But AI applications in the public sector are also associated with several technological, legal, ethical, and socioeconomic challenges that are expected to hinder the use of AI in this area. While these barriers characterize both the adoption and implementation phases,[104] scholars argue that their impacts mostly

[104] Adoption is the stage where AI is tested and evaluated ex ante, and the decision to use the technology is taken. Implementation comes after the adoption phase and describes

emerge during implementation. Available evidence indicates that many AI projects successfully completed the adoption phase before finding some unexpected, yet critical issues in the phase of implementation, which led to a partial or total dismantling of the initial technology deployment (Molinari et al., 2021; Engstrom et al., 2020; Campion et al., 2020). Indeed, scholars observe the existence of "last mile" implementation challenges in deploying and sustaining AI systems. This means that public organizations need continued access to some level of AI-related skills to be able to integrate AI solutions, including engineers who can maintain or improve on the systems, or data scientists who can extract meaningful output from AI, among others (Chui et al., 2018, pp. 33–34). Recognizing the technical, political, ethical, legal, and other "contextual factors" that affect the use of AI systems even after their successful adoption is important to assess the impacts of AI applications on the delivery of public services (Molinari et al., 2021). A strong capacity to implement AI in the public sector is expected to result in a sizable number of projects that promote the use of AI in this area, and Shanghai confirms this correlation. To understand whether these projects are improving public service provision by means of AI, the analysis of the case studies examines the strengths and limitations in deploying AI in the public sector of the main policy initiatives that are fostering public sector AI integration in Shanghai. By explaining the policy capacities that determine these strengths and limitations, the analysis creates a solid basis to gauge the impacts of these initiatives on public service provision in the municipality.

Regarding **country-specific factors**, this chapter elucidated the roles of local administrations, national government, and private companies in implementing AI policy in China. Previous studies observed that public sector innovation in China is traditionally characterized by a combination of central planning, decentralized experimentation, and active private sector participation (UNESCAP, 2018, p. 73). This pattern is continuing with artificial intelligence, whereby China's ambitious AI strategy is set by the central government, but the actual innovation is expected

the integration and impacts of the technology on the activities of public organizations (Molinari et al., 2021; Campion et al., 2020). These two phases are correlated, and recent studies have developed the concept of "AI appropriation" to indicate the union of adoption and implementation phases, defined as a sequence of two logically distinct (and sometimes recurring or alternating, rather than linearly consecutive) phases (Molinari et al., 2021, pp. 3–4).

to be driven by the private sector and local governments (Zeng, 2021; Roberts et al., 2020; Lee and Sheehan, 2018). This chapter examined the governance mechanisms that support and coordinate this tripartite relationship, offering an improved understanding of the roles of the key actors in implementing AI policy. In doing so, it brought into focus and explained some country-specific factors that are important to examine the policy capacity of Shanghai to implement AI in the public sector and the impacts of municipal AI policy initiatives on the provision of public services.

First, **Chinese local administrations are the main policy actors in the application of artificial intelligence**. As neatly put by earlier studies, China's AI policy is local (Ding, 2020). While the role of cities and provinces in policy implementation in China is well known, the importance of local governments is greatly increased by the general-purpose nature of the AI technology, whose applications can hardly be included in a rigid top-down blueprint. Implementing AI requires the proactive contribution of local governments to adopt AI solutions, adapt local infrastructures and organizational processes, and find applications that can unlock the manifold potential uses of this technology. In addition, most public goods and services are provided by local administrations in China, which consequently play a key role in public sector AI applications. As the national government incentivizes local administrations to play a more active and direct role compared to previous State-driven efforts to promote emerging technologies—which were often designed by national authorities and implemented via State-owned enterprises (e.g., high-speed railway, 5G)—the capacities of Shanghai are crucial for the success of public sector AI applications in the municipality. Therefore, the analysis in the next chapters focuses on policy resources and skills at the municipal level because these are the most relevant capabilities to examine the current developments of AI in the public sector in Shanghai. At the same time, consistently with the nested model of the policy capacity framework, these capacities are contextualized in relation to national-level capacities (see next paragraph) and organizational-level capacities (the analysis of the case studies delves into the interactions between municipal-level and organizational-level capabilities, and their implications for the deployment of AI in key public sector AI initiatives in Shanghai).

Second, **the Chinese national government maintains its traditional guiding role also in AI policy**, meaning that defining strategic policy objectives remains the prerogative of the Party-State (Heilmann, 2008).

The governance mechanisms in central-local relations and the national innovation system are helping the Chinese State to steer cities, provinces, and private companies toward national AI priorities; AI regulations are directing entrepreneurs toward uses of the technology that reinforce the authority and control capabilities of the Party-State; and AI ethics initiatives are oftentimes State-led collaborative efforts that further cement the cooperation between private companies and the government in the field of AI. Understanding the role of the national government in China's AI policy is important for assessing Shanghai's AI policy capacity. On one hand, AI in the public sector is a priority of the national government, and this creates a favorable policy environment that supports the political capacity of Shanghai to drive forward with public sector AI applications. On the other, this high-profile endorsement can generate vested interests for Shanghai officials to overstate the scale of local AI initiatives due to institutionalized incentives to comply with the policy priorities of superior authorities. Because the assessment of Shanghai's analytical and political capacities starts from the analysis of the municipal AI plans, these potential distortions need to be considered. In addition, this incentive structure works at all levels of governments, meaning that policy actors in Shanghai subordinated to the municipal government (e.g., district governments, schools, hospitals, etc.) are also incentivized to bandwagon with the municipal initiatives for AI development, in spite of having an actual interest or sufficient capabilities to promote public sector AI applications. Hence, empirical research must assess the incidence of projects that make only superficial uses of AI, and exclude them from the analysis of the case studies (see exclusions in Chapter 5.3).

Third, **private AI firms are key partners in the deployment of public sector AI projects in China** (Larsen, 2019), not only suppliers of technology. The governance mechanisms in China's national innovation system clearly show that private companies are a fundamental resource for implementing AI in the public sector. Hence, understanding what Shanghai is doing to engage private companies in public projects is important to assess the operational capacity of Shanghai to bring public sector AI applications to fruition. At the same time, Chinese researchers (Appendix I) observe that the cooperation between government and companies in AI can be problematic in China, despite the fact that public sector AI applications often represent beneficial solutions for both government and companies (Chapter 4.4). Some of the main issues include: the risks of overdependence on large enterprises that master Big Data and AI technology (Chen, 2019); the existence of "data monopoly enterprises" (数据垄断企业) deeply involved in public administration and government services (Tao, 2020) and other forms of "platform monopoly" (平台垄断; Li, 2019); or the risks related to information disclosure due to government reliance on technologies developed by the private sector (Wu, 2021). As such, the analysis of the case studies and the conclusions will examine how the complex dynamics between government and companies are affecting the provision of public services in the municipality.

Building upon the considerations developed so far, the remainder of this book examines whether Shanghai is fulfilling its goal to improve public service provision by accelerating the integration of AI in public sector activities. To do so, the analysis is structured into two parts. First, it scopes Shanghai's AI policy environment (Chapter 3) and AI ecosystem (Chapter 4) in order to assess the capacity of Shanghai to develop, access, and mobilize the analytical, operational, and political skills and resources necessary to use AI in public sector activities. Policy capacity is vital to achieve the desired policy outputs and outcomes. Thus, assessing Shanghai's policy capacity to implement AI in the public sector is the first, necessary step to examine whether the municipality is improving public service provision by accelerating AI integration in the public sector, because without adequate policy capacity Shanghai would not be able to develop, access, and mobilize the resources necessary to foster the use of AI in the public sector efficiently and effectively.

Second, the analysis explores how Shanghai's policy capacity to implement AI in the public sector translates into practice. To do so, Chapter 5 refines and validates the findings of documentary research (5.1), carries out an in-depth analysis of case studies of public sector AI initiatives in Shanghai that highlights the analytical, operational, and political capabilities that determine their strengths and limitations in deploying AI in the public sector, and it examines how these policy initiatives are impacting on public service provision in the municipality (5.2 and 5.3). Based on this analysis, the conclusions in Chapter 6 summarize the main findings of this book, and discuss possible development trajectories of AI in the public sector in Shanghai.

Appendix I: Chinese-Language Public Sector AI Research

In order to create a literature basis of Chinese-language scholarly papers on AI in the public sector, a title and abstract search was conducted on the China Knowledge Resources Online Database (CNKI), one of the largest online platforms for Chinese journals, dissertations, standards, and patents. The search resulted in a total of 16 suitable articles. This sample size is consistent with similar literature reviews of English-language scholarly sources.[105] The length of the articles varies. Nearly half of the sources consist of 3–5 pages (approximately 9,500 Chinese characters), others are longer. Chinese-language sources are mostly found in academic journals of public administration and management, such as *E-Government* (电子政务, 6 articles) and *Chinese Public Administration* (国行政管理, 2 articles), and in academic journals of social sciences (4 articles).

The analysis in Chapter 2.1 showed that there are many similarities among Chinese-language sources and English-language sources in terms of the research approaches for examining drivers and barriers of AI in the public sector. Apart from these approaches, the research findings are also not dissimilar. Like the drivers of AI identified by the English-language literature, Chinese scholars agree that AI can bring a wide range of benefits to public sector activities. AI can enhance the efficiency of public service delivery, the quality of decision-making, the level of administrative efficiency, and the internal management capabilities of public organizations (Kang and Tang, 2021; Wu, 2021; Tao 2020; Yu, 2020; Chen, 2019; Mei, 2018). As such, AI has become an indispensable technological tool for the modernization of national governance (Xu and Xu, 2020), for improving China's public management capacity (Yu, 2020), for promoting the refinement of government governance (政府治理精细化, Chen, 2019), and for improving urban governance capacity and innovation (Kang and Tang, 2021). AI makes social governance intelligent and can improve State capacity to solve social problems and provide public services (Wang and Wang, 2019).

[105] Using different methodologies and combinations of search terms, Zuiderwijk et al. (2021) retrieved 26 articles for the period 2010–2020. Wirtz et al. (2019) identified 30 suitable studies for the period 2003–2017. Pencheva et al. (2020) identified 83 sources up to April 2018, using a broader range of search terms that include "Big Data", "Data Analytics", and "Data Science".

In terms of barriers to AI adoption in the public sector, the analysis of Chinese scholars also does not significantly differ from the analysis carried out in the English-language literature. Chinese-language studies agree that the use of AI in government can create several legal, ethical, and societal challenges, such as information security, personal privacy violations and abuses, the creation of new social bias, the lack of transparency and accountability, social fragmentation, the polarization of society, and ethical and legal issues that stem from the technical characteristics of contemporary AI systems that rely on huge volumes of data (Kang and Tang, 2021; Li and Li, 2021; Wu, 2021; Xu and Xu, 2020; Li, 2019; Wang and Wang, 2019; Zhang et al., 2019; Mei, 2018).

Although the drivers and barriers of AI identified by scholars writing in Chinese language do not substantially differ from the English-language literature, there are some context-specific topics that recur in the Chinese-language papers examined in this review. First, the use of AI in the public sector is meant first of all to "improve the efficiency of State power and extend its scope" (提高国家权力能效和延伸权力范围; Wang and Wang, 2019, p. 88). In this perspective, AI is presented as a valuable tool to improve State control of both society and local governments:

> The view of AI as a useful tool to control local governments is related to China's political-administrative structure, whereby decentralized socioeconomic management under centralized political control creates a classical principal-agent problem, which the national government is addressing through bureaucratic mechanisms that incentivize local governments to fulfill national policy aims (Roberts et al., 2020; Xu, 2011). In this context, with the support of AI "[t]he central government can directly obtain the information required for national governance in a more intelligent way, reduce the information advantage of local governments and increase central-local information symmetry, so as to restrict the space for opportunistic actions of local governments[106]" (Mei, 2018). In addition, AI is described as a tool to control the official acts (公务行为) of hierarchically subordinated public officials, including work efficiency and corruption (Xu and Xu, 2020, p. 62).

106 Mei (2018, p. 25). In original: "中央可以通过更加智能的方式直接获取国家治理所需的社会信息, 压缩地方的信息优势, 增加央地信息对称性, 从而约束地方机会主义行动的空间".

The view of AI as a useful tool to control society is related to China's vision of social governance. As stated by Mei (2018): "In the Chinese context, national governance is essentially a process in which the ruling governance team and State institutions—with the Communist Party of China at the core—realize the national will and goals. Assuming a broader dichotomy between State and society, the actual goal of State governance is the whole society[107]". In this context, AI technologies can help the government to efficiently and effectively analyze data collected from citizens in order to better understand their needs and views on several public issues (Xu and Xu, 2020; Wu, 2021). As such, when formulating and implementing public policies, "the government will be able to more accurately judge the best interests of the public in different situations [and] it will also have an unprecedented ability to choose the way it can best protect and promote the public interest[108]" (Zhang, 2019). The government can use AI platforms that capture the needs and opinions of the citizens, in order to monitor and supervise public sentiment in society and in the cyberspace, so that government responsiveness and scientific decision-making can be greatly enhanced[109] (Chen, 2019). In other words, "[w]hen administrative organs formulate and implement public policies, Big Data and algorithms can also help them reflect the opinions of the people and promote the democratization of public policies[110]" (Xu and Xu, 2020). In this context, Yang (2021) recommends to use AI technologies like Natural Language Processing to comprehensively monitor the risk of public opinion in social media, and effectively evaluate it to prevent social risks.

[107] Mei (2018, p. 22). In original: "在中国语境下，国家治理归根到底是以中国共产党为核心的执政施政团队和国家机构实现国家意志与目标的过程．如果遵从宽泛的国家与社会二分法，国家治理的实际对象就是广阔的社会".

[108] Zhang (2019, p. 120). In original: "政府也将有能力更准确地判断公众在不同处境中的最佳利益，同时也将有前所未有的能力选择最能保护与促进公共利益的方式".

[109] Chen (2019, p. 30). In original: "日常的政府与民众互动、信息的收集和分类、社会舆情的监控、网络空间舆情的监管等工作可以由政府建立的人工智能平台来应对，民众的意愿和诉求可以准确有效地被政府关注到，政府的回应性能够得到很大程度的增强".

[110] Xu and Xu (2020). In original: "行政机关在制定和执行诸多公共政策时，大数据和算法也能够帮助其体现民众的意见，促进公共政策的民主化".

A second context-specific topic that recurs in the Chinese-language papers is the importance of the efficient cooperation between government and companies for the adoption and use of AI in the public sector. This focus is related to the central role played by private companies in China's public sector innovation (UNESCAP, 2018). In this context, scholars point to the risks of government dependence on large enterprises that master the advantages of Big Data and AI technology (Chen, 2019). The government should safeguard its leading position in public management and public decision-making, strengthen public data security management, and regulate the "data monopoly enterprises" (数据垄断企业) that are deeply involved in public administration and government services (Tao, 2020). The government should consider the existing forms of "algorithmic coercion" (算法强制) and inducement based on specific commercial interests, as well as the problem of "platform monopoly" (平台垄断), which means that only software development in line with the corporate strategy of the platform developer will be accepted by the platform (Li, 2019). Government reliance on technologies developed by the private sector (lit., capitalists, 资本家) can create risks such as information disclosure, and blurs the boundary between the public and private spheres to the point that all kinds of intelligent platforms can collect personal information, creating a contradiction between the benefits of information disclosure and the need to protect personal privacy (Wu, 2021). At the same time, the government should also ensure the steady development of the AI industry, and establish an effective cooperation mechanism (效的合作机制) with the enterprises to transfer technological developments in the private sector to public governance (Wu, 2021). The government should cooperate with AI developers and companies to promote the organic implementation of AI in social governance, combining "top-level design and bottom-level deployment" (顶层设计和底层布局), strengthen the planning of smart application platforms, and promote the coordinated construction of relevant infrastructure, among others (Kang and Tang, 2021). The government should also coordinate the cooperation between State, companies, and society in the use of AI in social governance, clarifying the respective duties of government, market, and society so that AI can better address social needs and reduce the risks brought forward by the use of this technology (Wang and Wang, 2019). In general, the government should strike a balance between regulating AI companies and reserving space for the development of this new technology (Li, 2019).

These context-specific topics point to some peculiarities of China's approach to AI development, which are examined from different angles in various parts of this book. The distinctive characteristics of China's decentralized administrative system, its implications for the relations between central and local governments, and the related impacts on Chinese AI policy were examined in Sect. 2.2.3.1. The view of AI as a useful tool for improving both the provision of public services and the capacity of the government to exert a more effective social control was discussed in the Introduction in Chapter 1, while its practical implications for public sector AI applications in Shanghai are examined in the case studies in Chapters 5.2 and 5.3. The importance of cooperation mechanisms between government and private companies to foster the adoption and use of AI in the public sector in China was examined in Sect. 2.2.3.2. The analysis of the AI ecosystem in Chapter 4 explains the contribution of private enterprises to the capacity of Shanghai to bring public sector AI projects to fruition, and the case studies in Chapters 5.2 and 5.3 examine the practical implications of public–private cooperation for public sector AI applications in Shanghai.

Appendix II: Main Contents of Chinese AI Ethics Principles

Table 2.3 summarizes the contents of the Chinese AI ethics initiatives published by March 2022, providing a brief introduction for each initiative (excluding those examined in the Sect. 2.2.3.3). The essence of each principle is condensed in one or two sentences to provide an agile yet complete understanding of the contents of each initiative, offering a useful reference for the discussions developed in the chapter. Links to the original Chinese documents and English translations (where available) are provided.

Table 2.3 Main contents of Chinese AI ethics principles

Title	*Principles*
(1) ***Baidu Four Principles of AI Ethics*** Baidu[111] Private company May 2018	These principles were announced in May 2018 by the co-founder and CEO of Internet giant Baidu, Robin Li Yanhong, at the Guizhou Digital Fair in Guiyang. They were reiterated in September 2018 at the first edition of the Shanghai World Artificial Intelligence Conference. Baidu plays an important role in the use of AI in the public sector. The company is a "national AI champion" involved in the AIOIPs (3.3.2), is one of the council vice-chairs of the Artificial Intelligence Industry Alliance (3.3.2; document 4), and it was involved in the drafting of the Beijing AI Principles (document 3) 1. The highest principle of AI is safety and controllability (AI的最高原则是安全可控) 2. AI's innovative vision is to promote more equal access to technology and capabilities (AI的创新愿景是促进人类更平等地获取技术和能力) 3. The existential value of AI is to teach people to learn and make people grow, instead of surpassing humans and replacing people (AI的存在价值是教人学习, 让人成长, 而非超越、替代人); and 4. The ultimate ideal of AI is to bring more freedom and possibility to mankind (AI的终极理想是为人类带来更多自由与可能)
(2) ***ARCC: An Ethical Framework for Artificial Intelligence*** Tencent[112] Private company September 2018	These principles were published by the Tencent Research Institute, established in 2007 to develop Tencent's core technologies and nurture Chinese talents in the hi-tech industry. As the other Chinese hi-tech juggernaut Baidu, Tencent also plays an important role in China's public sector AI applications, it is a "national AI champion" involved in the AIOIPs (3.3.2), it plays a leading member of the Artificial Intelligence Industry Alliance (3.3.2; document 4), and it was involved in the drafting of the *Beijing AI Principles* (document 3)

(continued)

[111] Robin Li Yanhong, 2018. AI伦理四原则, https://baijiahao.baidu.com/s?id=1601519015320714350&wfr=spider&for=pc. English version: https://www.firstxw.com/view/208592.html. The principles also have a dedicated entry in Baike, Baidu's online encyclopedia, where they are ambitiously named "AI ethics" (AI伦理), https://baike.baidu.com/item/AI%E4%BC%A6%E7%90%86/22885688?fr=aladdin.

[112] Si, X., 2018. Si Xiao: Building an Ethical "Ark", Make AI Comprehensible, Controllable, Available and Reliable [司晓: 打造伦理"方舟", 让人工智能可知、可控、可用、可靠], *Tencent Research Institute*, https://mp.weixin.qq.com/s/_CbBsrjrTbRkKjUNdmhuqQ.

Table 2.3 (continued)

Title	*Principles*
	1. Availability (可用): AI should be an inclusive, unbiased and widely-shared technology that aims to promote the well-being of mankind 2. Reliability (可靠): AI applications need to be safe, reliable, and secure, and the data used to train AI systems should be treated in compliance with privacy requirements 3. Controllability (可控): humans should always be in charge; and 4. Comprehensibility (可知): the way in which AI systems reach certain decisions should be more transparent and comprehensible
(3) ***Beijing AI Principles*** Beijing Academy of Artificial **Intelligence**[113] Multi-stakeholder May 2019	The BAAI principles are organized into three sections: Research and Development/研发: 1. Do good (造福): AI should promote the progress and well-being of society and ecology 2. For humanity (服务于人): AI should conform to human values and interests 3. Be responsible (负责): AI research and development should consider the potential ethical, legal and social impacts and risks brought in by the technology 4. Control risks (控制风险) to ensure the security of data, AI systems and the external environment where AI systems are deployed 5. Be ethical (合乎伦理) and improve the transparency, explainability, and predictability of AI, reducing biases 6. Be diverse and inclusive (多样与包容) to benefit as many people as possible 7. Open and share (开放共享) to disseminate the benefits of AI development Use/使用: 8. Use wisely and properly (善用与慎用), and have sufficient understanding of the potential impacts to avoid possible misuse and abuse 9. Informed-consent (知情与同意) to ensure that users of AI systems understand the impact of such systems on their rights and interests, introducing data and service revocation mechanisms to protect users' rights;

113 Beijing Academy of Artificial Intelligence, 2019. *Beijing AI principles* [人工智能北京共识], https://www-pre.baai.ac.cn/news/beijing-ai-principles-en.html.

Title	*Principles*
	10. Education and training (教育与培训) to help users to adapt to the psychological, emotional and technical impact of AI Governance/治理: 11. Optimizing employment (优化就业) to encourage new forms of work that would give full play to human advantages 12. Harmony and cooperation (和谐与合作) in AI governance across disciplines, sectors and regions 13. Adaptation and moderation (适应与适度) in adjusting AI principles, policies and regulations to the development of AI, not only to avoid hindering its proper utilization, but also to ensure that it is beneficial to society and nature 14. Subdivision and implementation (细化与落实): consider possible scenarios of AI applications for further formulating more specific and detailed guidelines 15. Long-term planning (长远规划), encouraging research on the potential risks of Artificial General Intelligence
(4) *Joint Pledge on Artificial Intelligence Industry Self-Discipline (Draft for Comment)* Artificial Intelligence Industry Alliance[114] Multi-stakeholder May 2019	The AIIA principles consist of 18 articles: 1. Human-centered (以人为本): AI development should be beneficial to humans and uphold basic rights such as human freedom and dignity 2. Enhance well-being (增进福祉): AI development should enhance people's well-being 3. Fairness and justice (公平公正): ensure fairness and justice, avoid bias or discrimination against specific groups or individuals, and avoid placing disadvantaged people (弱势人群) in an even more unfavorable position

(continued)

114 Artificial Intelligence Industry Alliance, 2019. *Joint Pledge on Artificial Intelligence Industry Self-Discipline (Draft for Comment)* [人工智能行业自律公约 (征求意见稿)] China Information Security [中国信息安全], WeChat account, 2 June, https://mp.weixin.qq.com/s/x7HTx4AR6oNBWwWxUpnSuQ. English: https://www.newamerica.org/cybersecurity-initiative/digichina/blog/translation-chinese-ai-alliance-drafts-self-discipline-joint-pledge/?from=timeline&isappinstalled=0.

Table 2.3 (continued)

Title	*Principles*
	4. Avoid harm (避免伤害): avoid harming the interests of society and the public 5. Safety and controllability (安全可控): Ensure that AI systems operate safely, securely, reliably, and controllably 6. Transparency and explainability (透明可释): ensure predictability and verifiability for algorithmic logic, system decisions, and action outcomes 7. Privacy protection (保护隐私): adhere to the principles of legality, legitimacy, and necessity (合法、正当、必要的原则) when collecting and using personal information. Strengthen privacy protection for special data subjects such as minors 8. Clarify responsibilities (明确责任) at each stage of AI R&D, manufacturing, operations, etc 9. Diversity and inclusivity (多元包容): ensure that algorithms don't discriminate against users 10. Self-discipline and self-governance (自律自治) for industry and practitioners, strengthening industry supervision mechanisms 11. Standards' formulation (制定标准): enhance the measurability of ethical principles such as transparency, privacy protection, and inclusiveness 12. Promote sharing (促进共享): share the dividends of AI research and governance experience 13. Universal education (普及教育): AI development should consider current and future workforce challenges 14. Continually push forward (持续推动): strengthen research on the potential risks of AI development (Articles 15–18 list a set of general provisions)

Title	*Principles*
(5) ***Governance Principles for the New Generation Artificial Intelligence: Developing Responsible Artificial Intelligence*** National New Generation Artificial Intelligence Governance Expert Committee[115] Government June 2019	1. Harmony and friendliness (和谐友好): AI development should conform to human values, ethics, and morality 2. Fairness and justice (公平公正): AI development should promote fairness and justice, eliminate bias and discrimination in the whole process (from data collection to AI applications) 3. Inclusivity and sharing (包容共享): AI should promote green development, narrow regional disparities, improve the adaptability of disadvantaged groups, eliminate the digital divide, avoid data and platform monopolies 4. Respect privacy (尊重隐私): respect and protect personal privacy and fully protect the individual's rights to know and rights to choose (知情权和选择权) 5. Safety and controllability (安全可控): continuously improve transparency, explainability, reliability, and controllability, and gradually achieve auditability, supervisability, traceability, and trustworthiness 6. Shared responsibility (共担责任): AI stakeholders should possess a strong sense of social responsibility and self-discipline (社会责任感和自律意识), and strictly abide by laws, regulations, ethics, morals, standards, and norms 7. Open collaboration (开放协作): promote multidisciplinary cooperation and international dialogue 8. Agile governance (敏捷治理): Respect the laws of AI development (人工智能发展规律) and promote the innovative and orderly development of AI, anticipating possible risks These principles form the basis for the "general norms" of *Ethical Norms for the New Generation Artificial Intelligence* published by the Expert Committee in September 2021 (document 10)

(continued)

115 National New Generation Artificial Intelligence Governance Expert Committee, 2019. *Governance Principles for the New Generation Artificial Intelligence: Developing Responsible Artificial Intelligence* [新一代人工智能治理原则——发展负责任的人工智能], China Information Security [中国信息安全], WeChat account, 17 June, https://mp.weixin.qq.com/s/JWRehPFXJJz_mu80hlO2kQ; English translation: https://www.newamerica.org/cybersecurity-initiative/digichina/blog/translation-chinese-expert-group-offers-governance-principles-responsible-ai/.

Table 2.3 (continued)

Title	*Principles*
(6) ***Artificial Intelligence Application Criteria*** Megvii Artificial Intelligence Ethics Committee[116] Private company July 2019	Established in 2011 in Beijing by three former students of Tsinghua University, Megvii is a global leader in computer vision that specializes in facial recognition and deep learning solutions that include algorithms and AI-enabled IoT devices. In October 2019, the Unites States placed Megvii on a banned trade list for its alleged involvement in human rights violations against the Muslim minorities in the Xinjiang Autonomous Region 1. Legitimacy (正当性): comply with applicable laws and generally accepted ethical principles to enhance social well-being 2. Human Supervision (人的监督) of AI technology and systems 3. Technical reliability and security (技术可靠性和安全性) 4. Fairness and diversity (公平和多样性): minimize the systemic bias of AI solutions 5. Accountability and timely correction (问责和及时修正): AI solutions should be auditable and accountable. Errors, defects, biases should be immediately recognized and actively dealt with 6. Data security and privacy protection (数据安全与隐私保护): it is necessary to strictly protect users' personal privacy and ensure data security when developing and using AI solutions

116 Tencent Net, 2019. Megvii's "Artificial Intelligence Application Criteria" Full Text Announced, Advocates the Beneficial Use of AI Technology [旷视《人工智能应用准则》全文公布 提倡善用AI技术], 17 July, https://new.qq.com/omn/20190717/20190717A0NAZV00.html.

Title	*Principles*
(7) ***Shanghai Initiative for the Safe Development of Artificial Intelligence*** Shanghai Artificial Intelligence Industry Security Expert Advisory Committee[117] Multi-stakeholder July 2019	1. Future oriented (面向未来): ensure coordination between innovation, safety, and security 2. People oriented (以人为本): ensure that AI serves human well-being 3. Clear responsibility (责任明晰): the responsibilities of the actors involved in AI development should be clearly assigned 4. Privacy protection (隐私保护): strengthen data protection legislation and the protection of users' privacy in AI applications 5. Algorithmic justice (算法公正): ensure the interpretability of AI systems and avoid bias 6. Transparent supervision (透明监管): ensure that the operations of AI systems are reviewable and traceable 7. Peaceful use (和平利用): prudently use AI in the military field 8. Open cooperation (开放合作): establish international norms and standards for the safe development of AI to avoid security risks caused by incompatible technologies and policies

(continued)

[117] China Industry News Network, 2019. Shanghai released the "Shanghai Initiative for the Safe Development of Artificial Intelligence", and the Shanghai Artificial Intelligence Industry Security Expert Advisory Committee was established [上海发布《人工智能安全发展上海倡议》人工智能产业安全专委会成立], China Industry News Network [中国工业新闻网], 3 July, http://www.cinn.cn/dfgy/201907/t20190703_214884.html.

Table 2.3 (continued)

Title	*Principles*
(8) *Chinese Young Scientists' 2019 Shanghai Declaration on the Innovative Governance of Artificial Intelligence* Chinese Young Scientists Association[118] Academy August 2019	This initiative by the Chinese Young Scientists Association is a follow up to the *Governance Principles for the New Generation Artificial Intelligence* issued in June 2019 (document 5), and to the call for creating sound regulations, ethical standards, and governance system as part of the establishment in May 2019 of the Shanghai National New Generation Artificial Intelligence Innovative Development Pilot Area (上海国家新一代人工智能创新发展试验区; Chapter 5). These principles are organized into four sections: Ethical responsibility/伦理责任: 1. Privacy (隐私保护): strengthen the awareness of privacy protection, and lawfully collect and use data 2. Diversity and fairness (多样公平): AI systems should be based on diverse data and unbiased algorithms 3. Ethics (道德规范): ensure that AI complies with human values and interests Safety responsibility/安全责任: 4. Technology robustness (技术稳健): ensure that AI is safe, secure and reliable 5. Algorithmic transparency (算法透明): ensure that AI is transparent and interpretable Legal responsibility/法律责任: 6. Legal accountability (法治问责) to ensure that AI is auditable and traceable 7. Humanistic approach (人类作用) to allow users to monitor or involve in the decision-making process Social responsibility/社会责任: 8. Eco-friendliness (环境友好): ensure that AI research and development is environmentally sustainable 9. Beneficial uses (应用益民): prioritize human well-being

[118] Jinri Toutiao, 2019. "Chinese Young Scientists 2019 Shanghai Declaration on the Innovative Governance of Artificial Intelligence" announced in Shanghai [《中国青年科学家2019人工智能创新治理上海宣言》在沪发布], 29 August, Jinri Toutiao [今日头条], https://www.toutiao.com/i6730580493214941703/.

Title	*Principles*
(9) ***Six AI principles by the Center for International Strategy and Security*** Center for International Strategy and Security of the Tsinghua University[119] Academy August 2019	These principles were presented at the 2019 Shanghai World AI Conference in August 2019 by Ms. Fu Ying, director of the Center for International Strategy and Security of the Tsinghua University. The CISS AI ethics principles focus on the geopolitical implications of AI adoption 1. Principle of well-being (福祉原则) to serve the common interests of humankind and respect human dignity and rights 2. Principle of security (安全原则), AI systems shall not harm human beings, must be secure and controllable, and need to protect privacy, prevent data breaches and abuses, and avoid algorithm discrimination 3. Principle of sharing (共享原则) to enable people to benefit from AI development of AI and prevent the digital divide 4. Principle of peace (和平原则) to improve transparency and establish confidence building measures 5. Principle of the rule of law (法治原则) to align AI applications to the purposes of the UN Charter and the basic principles of modern international law 6. Principle of cooperation (合作原则) to promote international exchanges of AI technologies and talents

(continued)

119 These principles were later included in an essay written by the CISS Director Ms. Fu Ying (傅莹). Fu, Y., 2019. Preliminary Analysis of the Impact of Artificial Intelligence on International Relations [人工智能对国际关系的影响初析]. *International Political Science* [国际政治科学], 4(1) (13), pp. 1–18.

Table 2.3 (continued)

Title	*Principles*
(10) ***Ethical Norms for the New Generation Artificial Intelligence*** National New Generation Artificial Intelligence Governance Expert Committee,[120] Government September 2021	General provisions Article 3: It states that all types of AI activities shall comply with the following basic ethical norms (基本伦理规范), which form the basis of the more specific management, R&D, supply and use norms outlined in the next sections: (i) advance human welfare (增进人类福祉): abide by shared human values, respect human rights and appeals to fundamental human interests; (ii) promote fairness and justice (促进公平公正): promote fair sharing of AI benefits by all of society, respect and help vulnerable groups and special groups (弱势群体、特殊群体); (iii) protect privacy and security (保护隐私安全): Fully respect everyone's right to know the extent of the use of, and to consent to the use of, their personal information (iv) assure controllability and trustworthiness (确保可控可信): ensure that AI is always under human control; (v) strengthen accountability (强化责任担当): humans are the ultimately responsible entities (人类是最终责任主体) for AI activities, and AI accountability mechanisms should be established to define responsibilities (vi) improve the cultivation of ethics (提升伦理素养): Objectively understand ethical issues, and do not underestimate or exaggerate ethical risks These basic ethical norms reiterate those included in the *Governance Principles for the New Generation Artificial Intelligence* that the Committee published in June 2021 (see document 5) Management norms (管理规范)

[120] MOST, 2021. *Ethical Norms for the New Generation Artificial Intelligence* [新一代人工智能伦理规范]. 26 September, http://www.most.gov.cn/kjbgz/202109/t20210926_177063.html. English translation: Murphy, B. (ed.), 2021. Ethical Norms for New Generation Artificial Intelligence Released. Center for Security and Emerging Technologies (CSET), https://cset.georgetown.edu/wp-content/uploads/t0400_AI_ethical_norms_EN.pdf.

Title	*Principles*
	Article 5: Promote agile governance (推动敏捷治理). Understand AI's potential and limitations, optimize governance mechanisms, promote the healthy and sustainable development of AI in an orderly manner
	Article 6: Actively practice demonstrations (积极实践示范). Comply with AI-related regulations, policies, and standards, and actively incorporate AI ethics throughout the management process
	Article 7: Correctly exercise authority (正确行权用权). Clearly define the official duties and authority boundaries of AI-related management activities;
	Article 8: Strengthen risk prevention (加强风险防范). Strengthen risk awareness and research on and assessment of potential risks in AI development,
	Article 9: Promote tolerance and openness (促进包容开放). Encourage the application of diverse AI technologies to solve the actual problems of economic and social development. Encourage exchanges and cooperation across academic disciplines
	<u>R&D Norms</u> (研发规范)
	Article 10: Strengthen self-discipline consciousness (强化自律意识). Strengthen self-restraint in AI R&D-related activities
	Article 11: Improve data quality (提升数据质量). Strictly comply with data-related laws, standards, and norms
	Article 12: Enhance security and transparency (增强安全透明). Improve transparency, explainability, comprehensibility, reliability, and controllability
	Article 13: Avoid bias and discrimination (避免偏见歧视). Prevent any data bias and algorithmic bias issues that may emerge, and strive to achieve AI system inclusivity, fairness, and non-discrimination
	<u>Supply Norms</u> (供应规范)
	Article 14: Respect market rules (尊重市场规则). Strictly comply with the various rules and regulations governing market entry, competition, transactions, and other such activities

(continued)

Table 2.3 (continued)

Title	*Principles*
	Article 15: Strengthen quality control (加强质量管控). Strengthen quality monitoring and use assessment of AI products and services Article 16: Safeguard user rights and interests (保障用户权益). Users should be clearly informed of the use of AI technology in products and services. Guarantee users' rights to be informed and to consent (保障用户知情、同意等权利) Article 17: Strengthen emergency support (强化应急保障). Timely monitor AI systems, and guard against systemic failures Use Norms (使用规范) Article 18: Promote well-intentioned use (提倡善意使用). Strengthen pre-use demonstrations and assessments of AI products and services. Gain a full understanding of the benefits of AI products and services Article 19: Avoid misuse (避免误用滥用). Avoid improper use and abuse of AI products and services Article 20: Prohibit violations and malicious use (禁止违规恶用). Prohibit the use of AI products and services that fail to comply with laws and regulations, ethics, standards, or norms Article 21: Actively provide prompt feedback (及时主动反馈). Promptly report to the relevant entities concerning such problems as technical security vulnerabilities, policy or regulatory vacuums, and regulatory lags Article 22: Improve use abilities (提高使用能力). Ensure the safe and efficient use of AI products and services

References

Acharya, A. and Arnold, Z., 2019. *Chinese Public AI R&D Spending: Provisional Findings*. Center for Security and Emerging Technology, CSET Issue Brief, https://cset.georgetown.edu/publication/chinese-public-ai-rd-spending-provisional-findings/.

Androutsopoulou, A., Karacapilidis, N., Loukis, E. and Charalabidis, Y., 2019. Transforming the Communication Between Citizens and Government Through AI-Guided Chatbots. *Government Information Quarterly*, 36(2), pp. 358–367, https://doi.org/10.1016/j.giq.2018.10.001.

Arcesati, R., 2021. *Lofty Principles, Conflicting Incentives: AI Ethics and Governance in China*. Mercator Institute for China Studies, https://merics.org/en/report/lofty-principles-conflicting-incentives-ai-ethics-and-governance-china.

Balakrishnan, T., Chui, M., Hall, B. and Henke, N., 2020. *The State of AI in 2020*. McKinsey and Company, https://www.mckinsey.com/Business-Functions/McKinsey-Analytics/Our-Insights/Global-survey-The-state-of-AI-in-2020.

Barth, T. and Arnold, E., 1999. Artificial Intelligence and Administrative Discretion: Implications for Public Administration. *The American Review of Public Administration*, 29(4), pp. 332–351, https://doi.org/10.1177/02750749922064463.

Barton, D., Woetzel, J., Seong, J. and Tian, Q., 2017. *Artificial Intelligence: Implications for China*. McKinsey & Company, https://www.mckinsey.com/featured-insights/china/artificial-intelligenceimplications-for-china.

Baxter, G. and Sommerville, I., 2011. Socio-Technical Systems: From Design Methods to Systems Engineering. *Interacting with Computers*, 23(1), pp. 4–17, https://doi.org/10.1016/j.intcom.2010.07.003.

Bazavan, A., 2019. Chinese Government's Shifting Role in the National Innovation System. *Technological Forecasting & Social Change*, 148, pp. 1–11, https://doi.org/10.1016/j.techfore.2019.119738.

Behymer, K. and Flach, J., 2016. From Autonomous Systems to Sociotechnical Systems: Designing Effective Collaborations. *She Ji: The Journal of Design, Economics, and Innovation*, 2(2), pp. 105–114, https://doi.org/10.1016/j.sheji.2016.09.001.

Benington, J. and Moore, M. eds., 2011. *Public Value Theory and Practice*. Basingstoke: Palgrave Macmillan.

Benington, J., 2005. From Private Choice to Public Value. Institute of Governance and Public Management (IGPM), Warwick Business School, pp. 1–36, https://www.researchgate.net/publication/252055942.

Berryhill, J., Kok Heang, K., Clogher, R. and McBride, K., 2019. Hello, World: Artificial Intelligence and its Use in the Public Sector. *OECD Working Papers on Public Governance*, No. 36, https://doi.org/10.1787/726fd39d-en.

Bibel, W., 2018. On a Scientific Discipline (Once) Named AI. *Proceedings of the Twenty-Seventh International Joint Conference on Artificial Intelligence* (IJCAI-18), pp. 5143–5149, https://www.ijcai.org/proceedings/2018/0713.pdf.

Bijker, W., 1987. The Social Construction of Bakelite: Toward a Theory of Invention. In: Bijker, W., Hughes, T. and Pinch, T. eds., 1987. *The Social Construction of Technological Systems: New Directions in the Sociology and History of Technology*. Cambridge: MIT Press, pp. 159–187.

Bijker, W., Hughes, T. and Pinch, T. eds., 1987. *The Social Construction of Technological Systems: New Directions in the Sociology and History of Technology*. Cambridge: MIT Press.

Brenton, S., Baekkeskov, E. and Hannah, A., 2022. Policy Capacity: Evolving Theory and Missing Links. *Policy Studies*, pp. 1–19, https://doi.org/10.1080/01442872.2022.2043266.

Brooks, R., 2017. Machine Learning Explained. *The Future of Robotics and Artificial Intelligence*, http://rodneybrooks.com/forai-machine-learning-explained/.

Bryman, A., 2012. *Social Research Methods*. 4th ed. New York: Oxford University Press.

Burns, J. and Zhou, Z., 2010. Performance Management in the Government of the People's Republic of China: Accountability and Control in the Implementation of Public Policy. *OECD Journal on Budgeting*, Volume 2010/2, https://doi.org/10.1787/16812336.

Cai, Z., 2016. Forty Years of Chinese AI [中国人工智能40年]. *Science & Technology Review* [科技导报], 34(15), pp. 12–32, http://www.kjdb.org/CN/abstract/abstract13768.shtml.

Calo, R., 2017. Artificial Intelligence Policy: A Primer and Roadmap, https://doi.org/10.2139/ssrn.3015350.

Campion, A., Gasco-Hernandez, M., Mikhaylov, S. and Esteve, M., 2020. Managing Artificial Intelligence Deployment in the Public Sector. *Computer*, 53, pp. 28–37, https://www.computer.org/csdl/magazine/co/2020/10/09206418/1npxF00DQru.

Castro, D., McLaughlin, M. and Chivot, E., 2019. *Who Is Winning the AI Race: China, the EU or the United States?* Center for Data Innovation, https://www.datainnovation.org/2019/08/who-is-winning-the-ai-race-china-the-eu-or-the-united-states/.

Cath, C., 2018. Governing Artificial Intelligence: Ethical, Legal and Technical Opportunities and Challenges. *Philosophical Transactions of the Royal Society A: Mathematical, Physical and Engineering Sciences*, 376(2133), https://doi.org/10.1098/rsta.2018.0080.

Cave, S., Dihal, K. and Singler, B., 2018. *Portrayals and Perceptions of AI and Why They Matter*. London: The Royal Society, https://royalsociety.org/-/media/policy/projects/ai-narratives/AI-narratives-workshop-findings.pdf.

Chen, P., 2019. Governance in the Era of Artificial Intelligence: Adaptation and Transformation [人工智能时代的政府治理: 适应与转变]. *E-Government* [电子政务], 3(195), pp. 27–34.

Chen, T., Ran, L. and Gao, X., 2019. AI Innovation for Advancing Public Service: The Case of China's First Administrative Approval Bureau. *Proceedings of dg.o 2019: 20th Annual International Conference on Digital Government Research*, June 18–20, Dubai, United Arab Emirates. ACM, New York: USA, https://doi.org/10.1145/3325112.3325243.

Chesterman, S., 2021. *We, the Robots? Regulating Artificial Intelligence and the Limits of the Law*. Cambridge: Cambridge University Press.

Chui, M., Harryson, M., Manyika, J., Roberts, R., Chung, R., van Heteren, A. and Nel, P., 2018. *Notes from the AI Frontier: Applying AI for Social Good*. McKinsey Global Institute, https://www.mckinsey.com/featured-insights/artificialintelligence/applying-artificial-intelligence-for-social-good.

Chun, A. 2020. Breaking the Iron Triangle: AI in China's Healthcare System. In: Elliot, H. ed., 2020. *The AI Powered State: China's Approach to Public Sector Innovation*. Nesta, May 2020, pp. 19–25, https://www.nesta.org.uk/feature/ai-powered-state/.

Colvin, T., Liu, I., Babou, T. and Wong, G., 2020. *A Brief Examination of Chinese Government Expenditures on Artificial Intelligence R&D*. Institute for Defense Analysis, IDA Document D-12068, https://www.jstor.org/stable/resrep22826.1.

Crawford, K. and Whittaker, M., 2016. *The AI Now Report 2016: The Social and Economic Implications of Artificial Intelligence Technologies in the Near-Term*. New York: New York University, https://ainowinstitute.org/AI_Now_2016_Report.pdf.

Creemers, R., 2018. China's Social Credit System: An Evolving Practice of Control, https://doi.org/10.2139/ssrn.3175792.

Cristianini, N. and Scantamburlo, T., 2019. On Social Machines for Algorithmic Regulation. *AI & Society*, 35, pp. 645–662, https://link.springer.com/article/10.1007/s00146-019-00917-8.

Dafoe, A., 2015. On Technological Determinism: A Typology, Scope Conditions, and a Mechanism. *Science, Technology, & Human Values*, 40(6), pp. 1047–1076, https://doi.org/10.1177/0162243915579283.

Desouza, K., Dawson, G. and Chenok, D., 2020. Designing, Developing, and Deploying Artificial Intelligence Systems: Lessons from and for the Public Sector. *Business Horizons*, 63(2), pp. 205–213. https://doi.org/10.1016/j.bushor.2019.11.004.

Desouza, K., 2018. Delivering Artificial Intelligence in Government: Challenges and Opportunities. *IBM Center for the Business of Government*, Washington, DC: USA, http://www.businessofgovernment.org/report/delivering-artificial-intelligence-government-challenges-and-opportunities.

Desouza, K., 2021. Artificial Intelligence in the Public Sector: A Maturity Model. *IBM Center for the Business of Government*, Washington, DC: USA, https://www.businessofgovernment.org/report/artificial-intelligence-public-sector-maturity-model.

Ding, J., 2018. *Deciphering China's AI Dream*. Oxford: University of Oxford, https://www.fhi.ox.ac.uk/deciphering-chinas-ai-dream.

Ding, J., 2019. *China's Current Capabilities, Policies, and Industrial Ecosystem in AI*. Testimony before the U.S.-China Economic and Security Review Commission Hearing on Technology, Trade, and Military-Civil Fusion: China's Pursuit of Artificial Intelligence, New Materials, and New Energy, 7 June, https://www.uscc.gov/sites/default/files/June%207%20Hearing_Panel%201_Jeffrey%20Ding_China%27s%20Current%20Capabilities%2C%20Policies%2C%20and%20Indu.

Ding, J., 2020. Promoting Nationally, Acting Locally: China's Next Generation AI Approach. In: Elliott, H. ed., 2020. *The AI Powered State: China's Approach to Public Sector Innovation*. Nesta, May 2020, pp. 11–16, https://www.nesta.org.uk/feature/ai-powered-state/.

Dobbe, R., Krendl Gilbert, T. and Mintz, Y., 2021. Hard Choices in Artificial Intelligence. *Artificial Intelligence*, 300 (2021) 103555, pp. 1–17, https://doi.org/10.1016/j.artint.2021.103555.

Duan, Y., Edwards, J. and Dwivedi, Y., 2019. Artificial Intelligence for Decision Making in the Era of Big Data—Evolution, Challenges and Research Agenda. *International Journal of Information Management*, 48, pp. 63–71, https://www.sciencedirect.com/science/article/abs/pii/S0268401219300581.

Dwivedi, Y.K., Hughes, L., Ismagilova, E., Aarts, G., Coombs, C., Crick, T., Duan, Y., Dwivedi, R., Edwards, J., Eirug, A., Galanos, V., Ilavarasan, P.V., Janssen, M., Jones, P., Kar, A.K., Kizgin, H., Kronemann, B., Lal, B., Lucini, B., Medaglia, R., Le Meunier-FitzHugh, K., Le Meunier-FitzHugh, L.C., Misra, S., Mogaji, E., Sharma, S.K., Singh, J.B., Raghavan, V., Raman, R., Rana, N.P., Samothrakis, S., Spencer, J., Tamilmani, K., Tubadji, A., Walton, P. and Williams, M.D., 2021. Artificial Intelligence (AI): Multidisciplinary Perspectives on Emerging Challenges, Opportunities, and Agenda for Research, Practice and Policy. *International Journal of Information Management*, 57, https://doi.org/10.1016/j.ijinfomgt.2019.08.002.

Eggers, W., Schatsky, D. and Viechnicki, P., 2017. *AI Augmented Government: Using Cognitive Technologies to Redesign Public Sector Work*. Deloitte Center for Government Insights, https://scholar.google.com/scholar_lookup?title=AI%20augmented%20government%3A%20using%20cognitive%20technologies%20to%20redesign%20public%20sector%20work&author=W.D.%20Eggers&publication_year=2017.

Engin, Z. and Treleaven, P., 2019. Algorithmic Government: Automating Public Services and Supporting Civil Servants in using Data Science Technologies. *The Computer Journal*, 62(3), pp. 448–460, https://doi.org/10.1093/comjnl/bxy082.

Engstrom, F., Ho, D., Sharkey, C., and Cuéllar, M., 2020. *Government by Algorithm: Artificial Intelligence in Federal Administrative Agencies*. Report Submitted to the Administrative Conference of the United States, https://ssrn.com/abstract=3551505.

Ernst, D., 2020. *Competing in Artificial Intelligence Chips: China's Challenge amid Technology War*. Waterloo: Centre for International Governance Innovation, https://www.cigionline.org/publications/competing-artificial-intelligence-chips-chinas-challenge-amid-technology-war.

ETAPAS (Ethical Technology Adoption in Public Administration Services), 2021. *The Social Impacts of Disruptive Technologies in the Public Sector*. ETAPAS, 8 July, https://www.etapasproject.eu/news/?slug=the-social-impacts-of-disruptive-technologies-in-the-public-sector.

Fatima, S., Desouza, K. and Dawson, G., 2020. National Strategic Artificial Intelligence Plans: A Multi-dimensional Analysis. *Economic Analysis and Policy*, 67, pp. 178–194, https://doi.org/10.1016/j.eap.2020.07.008.

Fatima, S., Desouza, K., Denford, J. and Dawson, G., 2021. What Explains Governments Interest in artificial intelligence? A Signaling Theory Approach. *Economic Analysis and Policy*, 71, pp. 238–254, https://doi.org/10.1016/j.eap.2021.05.001.

Franssen, M., 2015. Design for Values and Operator Roles in Sociotechnical Systems. In: van den Hoven, J., Vermaas, P. and van de Poel, I. eds., 2015. *Handbook of Ethics, Values, and Technological Design. Sources, Theory, Values and Application Domains*. Dordrecht: Springer, pp. 117–149.

Fu, X., Woo, W. and Hou, J., 2016. Technological Innovation Policy in China: The Lessons, and the Necessary Changes Ahead. *Economic Change and Restructuring*, 49, pp. 139–157, https://doi.org/10.1007/s10644-016-9186-x.

Fukuyama, F., 2013. What Is Governance? *Governance*, 26(3), pp. 347–368, https://doi.org/10.1111/gove.12035.

Gal, D., 2019. Perspectives and Approaches in AI Ethics: East Asia. In: Dubber, M., Pasquale, F. and Das, S. eds., 2019. *Oxford Handbook of Ethics of Artificial Intelligence*. Oxford University Press.

Gal, D., 2020. China's Approach to AI Ethics. In: Elliot, H. ed., 2020. *The AI Powered State: China's Approach to Public Sector Innovation*. Nesta, May 2020, pp. 53–61, https://www.nesta.org.uk/feature/ai-powered-state/.

Galanos, V., 2021. Science and Technology Studies. In: Dwivedi, Y.K., Hughes, L., Ismagilova, E., Aarts, G., Coombs, C., Crick, T., Duan, Y., Dwivedi, R., Edwards, J., Eirug, A., Galanos, V., Ilavarasan, P.V., Janssen, M., Jones, P.,

Kar, A.K., Kizgin, H., Kronemann, B., Lal, B., Lucini, B., Medaglia, R., Le Meunier-FitzHugh, K., Le Meunier-FitzHugh, L.C., Misra, S., Mogaji, E., Sharma, S.K., Singh, J.B., Raghavan, V., Raman, R., Rana, N.P., Samothrakis, S., Spencer, J., Tamilmani, K., Tubadji, A., Walton, P. and Williams, M.D., 2021. Artificial Intelligence (AI): Multidisciplinary Perspectives on Emerging Challenges, Opportunities, and Agenda for Research, Practice and Policy. *International Journal of Information Management*, 57, pp. 23–26, https://doi.org/10.1016/j.ijinfomgt.2019.08.002.

Gleeson, D., Legge, D. and O'Neill, D., 2009. Evaluating Health Policy Capacity: Learning from International and Australian Experience. *Australia and New Zealand Health Policy*, 6(3), pp. 1–15, https://doi.org/10.1186/1743-8462-6-3.

Grobelnik, M., 2021. There Won't Be Any Perfect Definition of AI, But We Urgently Needed a 'Good Enough' One Yesterday. Presentation at the Online Seminar *Regulation: What We Need to Talk About When We Talk About AI*, Humane AI Net, 3 June, https://www.humane-ai.eu/event/regulation/.

Haenlein, M. and Kaplan, A., 2019. A Brief History of Artificial Intelligence: On the Past, Present, and Future of Artificial Intelligence. *California Management Review*, 61(4), pp. 5–14, https://journals.sagepub.com/doi/10.1177/0008125619864925.

Hager, G., Drobnis, A., Fang, F., Ghani, R., Greenwald, A., Lyons, T., Parkes, D., Schultz, J., Saria, S., Smith, S. and Tambe, M., 2017. *Artificial Intelligence for Social Good*. Computing Community Consortium, https://cra.org/ccc/events/ai-social-good/.

Han, E., 2020. From Traffic Management to Smart Courts: China's Approach to Smart Cities. In: Elliott, H. ed., 2020. *The AI Powered State: China's Approach to Public Sector Innovation*. Nesta, May 2020, pp. 35–41, https://www.nesta.org.uk/feature/ai-powered-state/.

Hasmath, R., Teets, J. and Lewis, O., 2019. The Innovative Personality? Policy Making and Experimentation in an Authoritarian Bureaucracy. *Public Administration and Development*, 39(2), pp. 514–562, https://doi.org/10.1002/pad.1854.

Heilmann, S., Shih, L. and Hofem, A., 2013. National Planning and Local Technology Zones: Experimental Governance in China's Torch Programme. *The China Quarterly*, 216, pp. 896–919, https://doi.org/10.1017/S0305741013001057.

Heilmann, S., 2008. From Local Experiments to National Policy: The Origins of China's Distinctive Policy Process. *The China Journal*, 59, pp. 1–30, https://www.jstor.org/stable/20066378.

Elliott, H. ed., 2020. *The AI Powered State: China's Approach to Public Sector Innovation*. Nesta, May 2020, https://www.nesta.org.uk/feature/ai-powered-state/.

Henman, P., 2020. Improving Public Services Using Artificial Intelligence: Possibilities, Pitfalls, Governance. *Asia Pacific Journal of Public Administration*, 42(4), pp. 209–221, https://doi.org/10.1080/23276665.2020.1816188.

Howlett, M. and Ramesh, M., 2014. The Two Orders of Governance Failure: Design Mismatches and Policy Capacity Issues in Modern Governance. *Policy and Society*, 33, pp. 317–327, https://doi.org/10.1016/j.polsoc.2014.10.002.

Howlett, M. and Ramesh, M., 2015. Achilles' Heels of Governance: Critical Capacity Deficits and Their Role in Governance Failures. *Regulation & Governance*, 10(4), pp. 301–313, https://doi.org/10.1111/rego.12091.

Hughes, T., 1987. The Evolution of Large Technological Systems. In: Bijker, W., Hughes, T. and Pinch, T. eds., 1987. *The Social Construction of Technological Systems: New Directions in the Sociology and History of Technology*. Cambridge: MIT Press, pp. 51–82.

Jia, K. and Jiang, Y., 2017. Three Fundamental Issues of Artificial Intelligence Governance: Principle, Challenge and Public Policy [人工智能治理的三个基本问题: 技术逻辑、风险挑战与公共政策选择]. *Chinese Public Administration* [中国行政管理], 10(388), pp. 40–45.

Johnson, D. and Verdicchio, M., 2017. Reframing AI Discourse. *Minds & Machines*, 27, pp. 575–590, https://doi.org/10.1007/s11023-017-9417-6.

Jones, A., Artikis, A. and Pitt, J., 2013. The Design of Intelligent Socio-Technical Systems. *Artificial Intelligence Review*, 39, pp. 5–20, https://doi.org/10.1007/s10462-012-9387-2.

Kang, L. and Tang, Q., 2021. Innovation of Municipal Social Governance in the Era of Artificial Intelligence: Power, Challenges and Approaches [人工智能时代的市域社会治理创新: 动力、挑战及进路]. *Jiangnan Forum* [江南论坛], 2021 (1), pp. 27–29.

Kankanhalli, A., Charalabidis, Y. and Mellouli, S., 2019. IoT and AI for Smart Government: A Research Agenda. *Government Information Quarterly*, 36(2), pp. 304–309, https://doi.org/10.1016/j.giq.2019.02.003.

Kipnis, A., Tomba, L. and Unger, J., 2009. *Contemporary Chinese Society and Politics*. London and New York: Routledge.

Kirk, H., Lee, K. and Micallef, C., 2020. The Nuances of Confucianism in Technology Policy: An Inquiry into the Interaction Between Cultural and Political Systems in Chinese Digital Ethics. *International Journal of Politics, Culture, and Society*, 35, pp. 129–152, https://doi.org/10.1007/s10767-020-09370-8.

Klein, H. and Kleinman, D., 2002. The Social Construction of Technology: Structural Considerations. *Science, Technology, & Human Values*, 27(1), pp. 28–52, https://doi.org/10.1177/016224390202700102.

Knight, J., 2014. China as a Developmental State. *The World Economy*, 37(10), pp. 1335–1347, https://doi.org/10.1111/twec.12215.

Krafft, P., Young, M., Katell, M., Huang, K. and Bugingo, G., 2020. Defining AI in Policy versus Practice. *Proceedings of the 2020 AAAI/ACM Conference on AI, Ethics, and Society (AIES '20)*, February 7–8, 2020, New York: USA, pp. 72–78, https://doi.org/10.1145/3375627.3375835.

Kroes, P., Franssen, M., van de Poel, I. and Ottens, M., 2006. Treating Socio-Technical Systems as Engineering Systems: Some Conceptual Problems. *Systems Research and Behavioral Science*, 23, pp. 803–814, https://doi.org/10.1002/sres.703.

Kroes, P. and Mejiers, A., 2002. The Dual Nature of Technical Artifacts—Presentation of a New Research Programme. *Techné*, 6(2), https://scholar.lib.vt.edu/ejournals/SPT/v6n2/pdf/kroes_meijers.pdf.

Larsen, C., 2019. China's National AI Team. The Role of National AI Open Innovation Platform. In: Webster, G. ed., 2019. AI Policy and China: Realities of State-Led Development. *Stanford-New America DigiChina Project*, 29 October, pp. 16–20, https://www.newamerica.org/cybersecurity-initiative/digichina/blog/special-report-ai-policy-and-china-realities-of-state-led-development/.

Lee, K. and Sheehan, M., 2018. *China's Rise in Artificial Intelligence: Ingredients and Economic Implications*. China in an Emerging World, Hoover Institution, Fall Series, Issue 218, https://www.hoover.org/research/chinas-rise-artificial-intelligence-ingredients-and-economic-implications.

Lee, C., 2022. *Artificial Intelligence in China: Players, Regulations, Prospects*. Webinar for the EU Delegation to China, 25 March 2022.

Lewis, D., 2019. China's Techno-Utilitarian Experiments with Artificial Intelligence. *Digital Asia Hub*, 16 March, https://www.digitalasiahub.org/2019/03/16/chinas-techno-utilitarian-experiments-with-artificial-intelligence/.

Li, X., 2019. A Redefinition of the Concept of AI and the Government's Governance: An Analysis from the Perspectives of Technology, Market and Politics [人工智能概念的再界定与政府的治理回应: 基于技术、市场和政治视角的分析]. *E-Government* [电子政务], 3(195), pp. 2–8.

Li, L. and Li, Y., 2021. Risks in AI-Embedded Government Governance and Their Avoidance [人工智能嵌入政府治理的风险及其规避]. *Journal of South China University of Technology (Social Science Edition)* [华南理工大学学报(社会科学版)], 23(5), pp. 1–13.

Luong, N. and Arnold, Z., 2021. *China's Artificial Intelligence Industry Alliance. Understanding China's AI Strategy Through Industry Alliances*. Center for Security and Emerging Technology, CSET Data Brief, https://cset.georgetown.edu/publication/chinas-artificial-intelligence-industry-alliance/.

Luong, N., Arnold, Z. and Murphy, B., 2021. *Understanding Chinese Government Guidance Funds. An Analysis of Chinese-Language Sources*. Center for Security and Emerging Technology, CSET Issue Brief, https://cset.georgetown.edu/publication/understanding-chinese-government-guidance-funds/.

Ma, L., Christensen, T. and Zheng, Y., 2023. Government Technological Capacity and Public-Private Partnerships Regarding Digital Service Delivery: Evidence from Chinese Cities. International Review of Administrative Sciences, Vol. 89(1), pp. 95-111. https://doi.org/10.1177/00208523211018849.

Makasi, T., Tate, M., Desouza, K. and Nili, A., 2021. Value-Based Guiding Principles for Managing Cognitive Computing Systems in the Public Sector. *Public Performance & Management Review*, 44(4), pp. 929–959, https://doi.org/10.1080/15309576.2021.1879883.

Marcus, G. and Davis, E., 2019. *Rebooting AI: Building Artificial Intelligence We Can Trust*. New York: Pantheon Books.

Mehr, H., 2017. Artificial Intelligence for Citizen Services and Government. *Harvard Kennedy School Ash Center for Democratic Governance and Innovation*, August 2017, https://ash.harvard.edu/files/ash/files/artificial_intelligence_for_citizen_services.pdf.

Mei, L., 2018. How AI Affects National Governance: A Predictive Analysis [人工智能如何影响国家治理: 一项预判性分析]. *Hubei Social Sciences* [湖北社会科学], 2018 (8), pp. 20–28.

Meng, Q. and Jun, J., 2021. AI-Enabled Platform Government: A Technical Framework and a Practical Path [人工智能支撑的平台型政府: 技术框架与实践路径]. *E-Government* [电子政务], 09(225), pp. 37–46.

Mikalef, P., Fjørtoft, S. and Torvatn, H., 2019. Artificial Intelligence in the Public Sector: A Study of Challenges and Opportunities for Norwegian Municipalities. *Proceedings of the 18th IFIP WG 6.11 Conference on e-Business, e-Services and e-Society*, 18–20 September, 2019, Trondheim: Norway, pp. 267–277, https://doi.org/10.1007/978-3-030-29374-1.

Mikalef, P. and Gupta, M., 2021. Artificial Intelligence Capability: Conceptualization, Measurement Calibration, and Empirical Study on Its Impact on Organizational Creativity and Firm Performance. *Information & Management*, 58(3), pp. 1–20, https://doi.org/10.1016/j.im.2021.103434.

Mikhaylov, S., Esteve, M. and Campion, A., 2018. Artificial Intelligence for the Public Sector: Opportunities and Challenges of Cross-Sector Collaboration. *Philosophical Transactions of the Royal Society A: Mathematical, Physical and Engineering Sciences*, 376 (2128), https://doi.org/10.1098/rsta.2017.0357.

Mishra, S., Clark, J. and Perrault, C., 2020. *Measurement in AI Policy: Opportunities and Challenges*, 22 September, https://arxiv.org/abs/2009.09071.

Misuraca, G., van Noordt, C. and Boukli, A., 2020. The Use of AI in Public Services: Results from a Preliminary Mapping Across the EU. *Proceedings of the 13th International Conference on Theory and Practice of Electronic Governance (ICEGOV 2020)*, 23–25 September 2020, Athens: Greece, pp. 90–99, https://doi.org/10.1145/3428502.3428513.

Misuraca, G. and van Noordt, C., 2020. *Overview of the Use and Impact of AI in Public Services in the EU*. Luxembourg: Publications Office of the European Union, https://doi.org/10.2760/039619.

Misuraca, G. and Viscusi, G., 2015. Shaping Public Sector Innovation Theory: An Interpretative Framework for ICT-Enabled Governance Innovation. *Electronic Commerce Research*, 15, pp. 303–322, https://doi.org/10.1007/s10660-015-9184-5.

Molinari, F., van Noordt, C., Vaccari, L., Pignatelli, F. and Tangi, L., 2021. *AI Watch. Beyond Pilots: Sustainable Implementation of AI in Public Services*. Luxembourg: Publications Office of the European Union, https://publications.jrc.ec.europa.eu/repository/handle/JRC126665.

Moore, M., 1995. *Creating Public Value: Strategic Management in Government*. Cambridge: Harvard University Press.

Moore, M., 2013. *Recognizing Public Value*. Cambridge: Harvard University Press.

Mukherjee, I. and Bali, A., 2019. Policy Effectiveness and Capacity: Two Sides of the Design Coin. *Policy Design and Practice*, 2(2), pp. 103–114, https://ink.library.smu.edu.sg/soss_research/3036.

Murdick, D., Dunham, J. and Melot, J., 2020. *AI Definitions Affect Policymaking*. Center for Security and Emerging Technology, https://cset.georgetown.edu/research/ai-definitions-affect-policymaking/.

Van Noordt, C. and Misuraca, G., 2020. Evaluating the Impact of Artificial Intelligence Technologies in Public Services: Towards an Assessment Framework. *Proceedings of the 13th International Conference on Theory and Practice of Electronic Governance (ICEGOV 2020)*, 23–25 September 2020, Athens: Greece, pp. 8–16, https://doi.org/10.1145/3428502.3428504.

OECD, 2019b. *Scoping the OECD AI Principles: Deliberations of the Expert Group on Artificial Intelligence at the OECD (AIGO)*. OECD Digital Economy Papers, November 2019, No. 291, https://www.oecd-ilibrary.org/science-and-technology/scoping-the-oecd-ai-principles_d62f618a-en.

Ojo, A., Mellouli, S. and Ahmadi Zeleti, F., 2019. A Realist Perspective on AI-Era Public Management. *dg.o 2019: Proceedings of the 20th Annual International Conference on Digital Government Research*, pp. 159–170, https://doi.org/10.1145/3325112.3325261.

Oxford Insights and IDRC (International Research Development Centre), 2020. *Government AI Readiness Index 2020*. Oxford Insights and IDRC, on file with the author.

Painter, M. and Pierre, J., 2005. Unpacking Policy Capacity: Issues and Themes. In: Painter M. and Pierre, J. eds., 2005. *Challenges to State Policy Capacity: Global Trends and Comparative Perspectives*. Basingstoke: Palgrave Macmillan, pp. 1–18.

Paleyes, A., Urma, R. and Lawrence, N., 2020. Challenges in Deploying Machine Learning: A Survey of Case Studies. *NeurIPS 2020 Workshop: ML Retrospectives, Surveys & Meta-Analyses (ML-RSA)*, https://doi.org/10.48550/arXiv.2011.09926.

Pan, Y., Tian, Y., Liu, X., Gu, D. and Hua, G., 2016. Urban Big Data and the Development of City Intelligence. *Engineering*, 2(2), pp. 171–178, https://doi.org/10.1016/J.ENG.2016.02.003.

Panagiotopoulos, P., Klievink, B. and Cordella, A., 2019. Public Value Creation in Digital Government. *Government Information Quarterly*, 36(4), pp. 1–8, https://doi.org/10.1016/j.giq.2019.101421.

Partnership for Public Service and IBM (IBM Center for the Business of Government), 2018. *The Future Has Begun: Using Artificial Intelligence to Transform Government*. IBM Center for the Business of Government, 8 January, http://www.businessofgovernment.org/sites/default/files/Using%20Artificial%20Intelligence%20to%20Transform%20Government.pdf.

Pencheva, I., Esteve, M. and Mikhaylov, S., 2020. Big Data and AI—A Transformational Shift for Government: So, What's Next for Research? *Public Policy and Administration*, 35(1), pp. 24–44, https://doi.org/10.1177/0952076718780537.

Pinch, T. and Bijker, W., 1987. The Social Construction of Facts and Artifacts: Or How the Sociology of Science and the Sociology of Technology Might Benefit Each Other. In: Bijker, W., Hughes, T. and Pinch, T. eds., 1987. *The Social Construction of Technological Systems: New Directions in the Sociology and History of Technology*, Cambridge: MIT Press, pp. 17–50.

Reis, J., Santo, P. and Melão, N., 2019. Artificial Intelligence in Government Services: A Systematic Literature Review. In: Rocha Á., Adeli H., Reis L., Costanzo S. eds., 2019. New Knowledge in Information Systems and Technologies. *WorldCIST'19 2019. Advances in Intelligent Systems and Computing*, 930, pp. 241–252, https://doi.org/10.1007/978-3-030-16181-1_23.

Roberts, H., Cowls, J., Morley, J., Taddeo, M., Wang, V. and Floridi, L., 2020. The Chinese Approach to Artificial Intelligence: An Analysis of Policy, Ethics, and Regulation. *AI & Society*, 36, pp. 59–77, https://doi.org/10.1007/s00146-020-00992-2.

Rossi, F., 2021. Can We Really Define AI? Presentation at the Online Seminar *Regulation: What We Need to Talk About When We Talk About AI*, Humane AI Net, 3 June, https://www.humane-ai.eu/event/regulation/.

Russell, S. and Norvig, P., 1995. *Artificial Intelligence: A Modern Approach*. Englewood Cliffs: Prentice Hall.

Saich, T., 2008. *Providing Public Goods in Transitional China*. New York: Palgrave Macmillan.

Scantamburlo, T., Charlesworth, A. and Cristianini, N., 2018. *Machine Decisions and Human Consequences*. On file with the author.

Deloitte China, 2019. *Scenarios and Potentials of AI's Commercial Applications in China*. Deloitte Digital Difference, https://www2.deloitte.com/cn/en/pages/innovation/articles/china-ai-industry-whitepaper-intelligence-driven-by-innovation.html.

Schaefer, C., Lemmer, K., Kret, K., Ylinen, M., Mikalef, P. and Niehaves, B., 2021. Truth or Dare?—How Can We Influence the Adoption of Artificial Intelligence in Municipalities? *Proceedings of the 54th Hawaii International Conference on System Sciences*, pp. 2347–2356, http://hdl.handle.net/10125/70899.

Schmid, J. and Wang, F., 2016. Beyond National Innovation Systems: Incentives and China's Innovation Performance. *Journal of Contemporary China*, 26(104), pp. 280–296, https://doi.org/10.1080/10670564.2016.1223108.

Selbst, A., Boyd, D., Friedler, S., Venkatasubramanian, S. and Vertesi, J., 2019. Fairness and Abstraction in Sociotechnical Systems. *FAT* '19: Proceedings of the Conference on Fairness, Accountability, and Transparency*, pp. 59–68, https://doi.org/10.1145/3287560.3287598.

Stepan, M. and Duckett, J. eds., 2018. *Serve the People: Innovation and IT in China's Social Development Agenda*. Mercator Institute for China Studies, https://merics.org/en/report/serve-people.

Sheehan, M., 2018. How China's Massive AI Plan Actually Works. *MacroPolo*, 13 February, https://macropolo.org/chinas-massive-ai-plan-actually-works/.

Sheehan, M., 2019. *The Transpacific Experiment: How China and California Collaborate and Compete for Our Future*. Counter Point Press.

SHFDI (Shanghai Foreign Investment Development Board), 2020. *Shanghai Foreign Investment Guide 2020* [2020上海外商投资指南], https://www.investsh.org.cn/upload/index/2020%20Shanghai%20Foreign%20Investment%20Guide.pdf.

SHFDI, 2021. *Shanghai Foreign Investment Guide 2021* [2021上海外商投资指南], https://www.investsh.org.cn/upload/upload/channel/file/2021_2/4_30/04koko3pi67s.pdf.

Snyder, H., 2019. Literature Review as a Research Methodology: An Overview and Guidelines. *Journal of Business Research*, 104, pp. 333–339, https://doi.org/10.1016/j.jbusres.2019.07.039.

Sousa, W., Melo, E., Bermejo, P., Farias, R. and Gomes, A., 2019. How and Where Is Artificial Intelligence in the Public Sector Going? A Literature Review and Research Agenda (Review). *Government Information Quarterly*, 36(4), pp. 1–14, https://doi.org/10.1016/j.giq.2019.07.004.

Stanford University, 2016. *Artificial Intelligence and Life in 2030: One Hundred Year Study on Artificial Intelligence*, Stanford: Stanford University, https://ai100.stanford.edu/2016-report.

Stanford University, 2019. *The AI Index 2019 Annual Report*. AI Index Steering Committee, Human-Centered AI Institute, Stanford: Stanford

University, December 2019, https://hai.stanford.edu/sites/default/files/ai_index_2019_report.pdf.

Stanford University, 2021a. *The AI Index 2021 Annual Report*. AI Index Steering Committee, Human-Centered AI Institute, Stanford: Stanford University, March 2021, https://aiindex.stanford.edu/report/.

Stanford University, 2021b. *Gathering Strength, Gathering Storms: The One Hundred Year Study on Artificial Intelligence (AI100) 2021 Study Panel Report*. Stanford: Stanford University, September 2021, http://ai100.stanford.edu/2021-report.

Stanford University, 2023. *The AI Index 2023 Annual Report*. AI Index Steering Committee, Institute for Human-Centered AI, Stanford: Stanford University, April 2023, https://aiindex.stanford.edu/wp-content/uploads/2023/04/HAI_AI-Index-Report_2023.pdf.

Stanton, C., Lung, V., Zhang, N., Ito, M., Weber, S. and Charlet, K., 2019. What the Machine Learning Value Chain Means for Geopolitics. *Communications of the Association for Computing Machinery*, https://cacm.acm.org/news/238651-what-the-machine-learning-value-chain-means-for-geopolitics/fulltext.

Sun, Y. and Cao, C., 2014. Demystifying Central Government R&D Spending in China. *Science*, 345(6200), pp. 1006–1008, https://www.science.org/doi/10.1126/science.1253479?cookieSet=1.

Sun, T. and Medaglia, R., 2019. Mapping the Challenges of Artificial Intelligence in the Public Sector: Evidence from Public Healthcare. *Government Information Quarterly*, 36 (2), pp. 368–383, https://www.sciencedirect.com/science/article/abs/pii/S0740624X17304781.

Tao, Y., 2020. The Modernization of Public Management in the Era of Artificial Intelligence [人工智能时代公共管理现代化发展之路]. *Audit Observation* [审计观察], 2020 (8), pp. 64–67.

Teets, J. and Hasmath, R., 2020. The Evolution of Policy Experimentation in China. *Journal of Asian Public Policy*, 13(1), pp. 49–59, https://doi.org/10.1080/17516234.2020.1711491.

Teets, J., Hasmath, R. and Lewis, O., 2017. The Incentive to Innovate? The Behavior of Local Policymakers in China. *Journal of Chinese Political Science*, 22, pp. 505–517, https://doi.org/10.1007/s11366-017-9512-9.

Tencent and CAICT (Tencent Research Institute, Tencent AI Lab and China Academy of Information and Communications Technology), 2017. *Artificial Intelligence: A National Strategic Initiative for Artificial Intelligence* [人工智能: 国家人工智能战略行动抓手]. Beijing: China Renmin University Press.

Tinholt, D., Carrara, W. and van der Linden, N., 2017. Unleashing the Potential of Artificial Intelligence in the Public Sector. *Capgemini Consulting*, pp. 1–10, https://www.capgemini.com/consulting/wp-content/uploads/sites/30/2017/10/ai-in-public-sector.pdf.

Toll, D., Lindgren, I., Melin, U. and Madsen, C., 2020. Values, Benefits, Considerations and Risks of AI in Government: A Study of AI Policy Documents in Sweden. *JeDEM—EJournal of EDemocracy and Open Government*, 12(1), pp. 40–60, https://doi.org/10.29379/jedem.v12i1.593.

Triolo, P. and Goodrich, J. 2018. From Riding a Wave to Full Steam Ahead: As China's Government Mobilizes for AI Leadership, Some Challenges Will Be Tougher Than Others. *New America DigiChina Project*, 28 February, https://www.newamerica.org/cybersecurity-initiative/digichina/blog/riding-wave-full-steam-ahead/.

Turner, J., 2019. *Robot Rules. Regulating Artificial Intelligence*. London: Palgrave Macmillan.

Twizeyimana, J. and Andersson, A., 2019. The Public Value of E-Government—A Literature Review. *Government Information Quarterly*, 36(2), pp. 167–178, https://doi.org/10.1016/j.giq.2019.01.001.

UNESCAP (United Nations, Economic and Social Commission for Asia and the Pacific), 2018. *Evolution of Science, Technology and Innovation Policies for Sustainable Development: The Experiences of China, Japan, the Republic of Korea and Singapore*, UNESCAP, https://www.unescap.org/sites/default/files/publications/UN_STI_Policy_Report_2018.pdf.

United Nations, 2020. *E-Government Survey 2020*. Digital Government in the Decade of Action for Sustainable Development. New York: United Nations, https://publicadministration.un.org/en/Research/UN-e-Government-Surveys.

Valle-Cruz, D., Criado, J., Sandoval-Almazán, R. and Ruvalcaba-Gomez, E., 2020. Assessing the Public Policy-Cycle Framework in the Age of Artificial Intelligence: From Agenda-Setting to Policy Evaluation. *Government Information Quarterly*, 37(4), pp. 1–12, https://doi.org/10.1016/j.giq.2020.101509.

Van de Poel, I., 2020. Embedding Values in Artificial Intelligence (AI) Systems. *Minds and Machines*, 30, pp. 385–409, https://doi.org/10.1007/s11023-020-09537-4.

OECD (Organisation for Economic Co-operation and Development), 2019a. *Artificial Intelligence in Society*. Revised version, August 2019. Paris: OECD Publishing, https://doi.org/10.1787/eedfee77-en.

Wang, X. and Wang, X., 2019. "Technological Leviathan": Potential Risks of Artificial Intelligence Embedded in Social Governance and Government Response [“技术利维坦”: 人工智能嵌入社会治理的潜在风险与政府应对]. E-*Government* [电子政务], 5(197), pp. 86–93.

Webster, G. ed., 2019. AI Policy and China. Realities of State-Led Development. *Stanford-New America DigiChina Project*, Special Report No. 1, 29 October, https://d1y8sb8igg2f8e.cloudfront.net/documents/DigiChina-AI-report-20191029.pdf.

Wirtz B., Weyerer J. and Geyer, C., 2019. Artificial Intelligence in the Public Sector—Applications and Challenges. *International Journal of Public Administration*, 42(7), pp. 596–615, https://www.tandfonline.com/doi/abs/10.1080/01900692.2018.1498103?journalCode=lpad20.

Wirtz, B. and Müller, W., 2019. An Integrated Artificial Intelligence Framework for Public Management. *Public Management Review*, 21(7), pp. 1076–1100, https://doi.org/10.1080/14719037.2018.1549268.

Woo, J., 2021. *Capacity-Building and Pandemics*. Singapore's Response to Covid-19. Singapore: Palgrave Macmillan.

Wu, X., 2021. Application Dilemmas and Policy Suggestions for AI in Government Governance [人工智能在政府治理中的应用困境与政策建议]. *China National Conditions and Strength* [中国国情国力], 8(343), pp. 51–53.

Wu, X., Howlett, M. and Ramesh, M. eds., 2018. *Policy Capacity and Governance: Assessing Governmental Competences and Capabilities in Theory and Practice*. Cham: Palgrave Macmillan.

Wu, X., Ramesh, M. and Howlett, M., 2015. Policy Capacity: A Conceptual Framework for Understanding Policy Competences and Capabilities. *Policy and Society*, 34, pp. 165–171, https://www.tandfonline.com/doi/full/10.1016/j.polsoc.2015.09.001.

Xu, L. and Xu, C., 2020. Double Orientations of Political Power in the Era of AI [人工智能时代政治权力的双重面相]. *Journal of Lanzhou University (Social Sciences Edition)* [兰州大学学报 (社会科学版)], 48(221), pp. 56–63.

Xu, C., 2011. The Fundamental Institutions of China's Reforms and Development. *Journal of Economic Literature*, 49(4), pp. 1076–1151, https://www.jstor.org/stable/23071664?seq=1.

Xue, L., 1997. A Historical Perspective of China's Innovation System Reform: A Case Study. *Journal of Engineering and Technology Management*, 14(1), pp. 67–81, https://doi.org/10.1016/S0923-4748(97)00002-7.

Yang, K., 2021. Innovative Thinking and Analysis of Social Risk Management in the Era of Artificial Intelligence [人工智能时代的社会风险治理创新思考分析]. *Digital Technology & Application* [数字技术与应用], 39(9), pp. 162–164.

Young, M., Katell, M. and Krafft, P., 2019. Municipal Surveillance Regulation and Algorithmic Accountability. *Big Data & Society*, 6(2), pp. 1–14, https://doi.org/10.1177/2053951719868492.

Yu, X. and Cui, Z., 2020. Research on AI and Public Management: Technological Possibility, Issue Reconstruction and Governance Innovation [人工智能与公共管理研究: 技术可能性、议题重构和治理创新]. *Chinese Public Administration* [国行政管理], 2020 (3), pp. 6–11.

Yu, W., 2020. AI and Public Management: Opportunities and Challenges [人工智能与公共管理: 机遇与挑战]. *Journal of Beijing University of Aeronautics and Astronautics (Social Sciences Edition)* [北京航空航天大学学报 (社会科学版)], 33(4), pp. 50–54.

Zeng, J., 2021. China's Artificial Intelligence Innovation: A Top-Down National Command Approach? *Global Policy*, 12(3), pp. 399–409, https://doi.org/10.1111/1758-5899.12914.

Zeng, Y., Lu, E. and Huangfu, C., 2019. Linking Artificial Intelligence Principles. *Proceedings of the AAAI Workshop on Artificial Intelligence Safety*, https://arxiv.org/abs/1812.04814.

Zhang, Q., 2019. Artificial Intelligence and the Normative Prospects of Public Services [人工智能与公共服务的规范前景]. *Administrative Tribune* [行政论坛], 2019 (6), pp. 115–120.

Zhang, Y. and Zhu, X., 2019. Multiple Mechanisms of Policy Diffusion in China. *Public Management Review*, 21(4), pp. 495–514, https://doi.org/10.1080/14719037.2018.1497695.

Zhang, L., Feng, X. and Tang, Z., 2019. The Realistic Basis and Path Choice of Building a Smart Society in China—an Analytical Dimension Based on Technology and System [中国建设智慧社会的现实基础与路径选择—基于技术与制度的分析维度]. *E-Government* [电子政务], 04(196), pp. 18–26.

Zhang, W., Zuo, N., He, W., Li, S. and Yu, L., 2021. Factors Influencing the Use of Artificial Intelligence in Government: Evidence from China. *Technology in Society*, 66, pp. 1–16, https://doi.org/10.1016/j.techsoc.2021.101675.

Zheng, Y., Yu, H., Cui, L., Miao, C., Leung, C. and Yang, Q., 2018. SmartHS: An AI Platform for Improving Government Service Provision. *Proceedings of the AAAI Conference on Artificial Intelligence*, 32(1), pp. 7704–7711, https://doi.org/10.1609/aaai.v32i1.11382.

Zhou, X., 2020. Organizational Response to COVID-19 Crisis: Reflections on the Chinese Bureaucracy and Its Resilience. *Management and Organization Review*, 16(3), pp. 473–484, https://doi.org/10.1017/mor.2020.29.

Zhou, X., Lian, H., Ortolano, L. and Ye, Y., 2013. A Behavioral Model of "Muddling-Through" in the Chinese Bureaucracy: The Case of Environmental Protection. *The China Journal*, 70, pp. 120–147, https://doi.org/10.1086/671335.

Zhou, X. and Lian, H., 2011. *Modes of Governance of Chinese Bureaucracy: A "Control-Rights" Theory*. On file with the author.

Zhu, X., 2014. Mandate vs. Championship: Vertical Government Intervention and Diffusion of Innovation in Public Services in Authoritarian China. *Public Management Review*, 16(1), pp. 117–139, https://www.tandfonline.com/doi/abs/10.1080/14719037.2013.798028.

Zuiderwijk, A., Chen, Y. and Salem, F., 2021. Implications of the Use of Artificial Intelligence in Public Governance: A Systematic Literature Review and a Research Agenda. *Government Information Quarterly*, 38(3), pp. 1–19, https://doi.org/10.1016/j.giq.2021.101577.

CHAPTER 3

The AI Policy Environment of Shanghai

In October 2017, the Shanghai municipal government issued the *Implementation Opinions on Promoting the Development of a New Generation Artificial Intelligence in Shanghai*. This programmatic document states that Shanghai will become a "national AI development highland (国家人工智能发展高地), China's leading source of AI innovation, demonstration site for applications, industry cluster and talent highland, reaching the world's most advanced levels in some fields".[1] In this context, Shanghai elevates the use of AI in the public sector to a priority of its AI development strategy, saying that the municipality will improve "public service capacity and citizens' sense of gain" by accelerating the in-depth application of AI in urban governance and public services. To achieve these goals, the *Opinions* lay out a well-elaborated set of tasks that call for fostering the use of AI in various policy areas, from the provision of administrative services to medicine and healthcare. The *Opinions* have soon been propped up with the release of several supporting and actionable policy documents as well as concrete initiatives. These paved the way to the publication in September 2019 of the *Action Plan on*

[1] Shanghai Municipal Government, 2017. *Opinions* (cit. in Chapter 3.2), section 1, par. 2, Development Goals (发展目标). In original: "基本建成国家人工智能发展高地，成为全国领先的人工智能创新策源地、应用示范地、产业集聚地和人才高地，局部领域达到全球先进水平".

D. Todaro, *The Use of Artificial Intelligence in the Public Sector in Shanghai*, https://doi.org/10.1007/978-981-97-0597-9_3

Building Shanghai into an AI Highland and Creating a First-Class Innovation Ecosystem (2019–2021). This is a comprehensive operational plan for fostering AI development that reiterates the goals for AI in the public sector set by the *Opinions*. It states that Shanghai will encourage innovative AI applications aimed at ensuring a high-quality life for its citizens and efficient urban operations[2] and requires that relevant government agencies and public institutions intensify the use of AI in medicine, education, urban management, government services, smart public security, transportation, smart courts, and garbage sorting.

Starting from the analysis of these two main municipal plans for AI development, this chapter examines Shanghai's analytical and political capacities to implement AI in the public sector. Analytical capacity indicates the ability of the Shanghai government to devise public sector AI applications that can contribute to achieving municipal goals in this area, if carried out. Political capacity indicates the ability of Shanghai to create and sustain support and legitimacy for such public sector AI applications. To measure analytical capacity, this chapter examines the tasks for accelerating the use of AI in the public sector listed in Shanghai's municipal AI plans. It gauges the consistency of these tasks with the goal of using AI to improve public service provision and citizens' sense of gain set forth by such municipal plans. To measure political capacity, this chapter assesses the importance that Shanghai's municipal AI plans assign to the use of AI in the public sector. If using AI to improve public service provision and citizens' sense of gain is a political priority, public sector AI applications aimed at achieving these goals are expected to enjoy political support. The existence of goals for AI in the public sector is itself indication that the use of AI in this area is high on the agenda of the Shanghai leadership. However, comparing them to other policy priorities included in the AI plans helps gauge the actual level of political support for AI in the public sector. The chapter also examines the political support that Shanghai's plans are expected to receive from the national government. Finally, the findings about Shanghai's analytical and political capacity are corroborated by looking at real-world policy initiatives that resulted from the municipal AI plans, and by identifying other digital initiatives that show

[2] SHEITC, 2019, *AI Highland Plan* (cit. in Chapter 3.2), section 3, subsection 4. In original: "充分发挥本市应用场景丰富优势, 鼓励全球人工智能最新成果在上海率先 "试水", 聚焦 […] 市民高品质生活、城市高效率运行, 打造一批面向全球的创新应用".

the capacity of Shanghai to leverage AI and other advanced technologies to improve government operations and public service delivery.

Shanghai's analytical and political capacities do not exist in a vacuum. The goals and tasks for AI in the public sector set forth by the municipality are aligned with China's ambitious AI strategy published by the State Council in July 2017. The national AI strategy also emphasizes that artificial intelligence can "greatly improve the level of precision in public services, comprehensively enhancing the people's quality of life", and it sets the use of AI in the public sector among the national policy priorities for AI development. Hence, the chapter starts by providing a thorough overview of China's national AI strategy. It discusses how political capacity at the national level empowers political capacity at the municipal level and delves into the related implications for the assessment of Shanghai's AI policy capacity.

3.1 China's AI Strategy: The New Generation Artificial Intelligence Development Plan

Since the publication of the *Made in China 2025* and the *"Internet Plus" Action Plan* in 2015, the Chinese government has regularly issued major policy documents that reiterate the importance of technology to support the advancement of the Chinese industry, society, and other sectors. These policy documents constitute a programmatic core in China's AI policy system (Tsinghua 2018, p. 78), and they influenced the formulation of China's earlier policies for the promotion of AI that started to appear in 2016. These policies culminated in China's national strategy for AI development published in the summer of 2017: the *New Generation Artificial Intelligence Development Plan*. The review of these earlier policy documents is useful to contextualize the analysis of China's AI strategy, and it is presented in Appendix III at the end of this chapter. Next paragraphs delve into the main contents of the *New Generation Artificial Intelligence Development Plan*. The analysis lifts important aspects that affect the capacity of Shanghai to implement AI in the public sector and highlights the related implications for the assessment of such capacity.

Published by the State Council in July 2017, the *New Generation Artificial Intelligence Development Plan*[3] (hereinafter: AIDP, or the Plan) is one of the most comprehensive and well-funded national AI strategies worldwide (Stanford University 2021a). It outlines the current situation of Chinese AI and sets the policy goals for China's AI development (Section 1); it states the overarching principles and guidelines for the promotion of AI in the country (Section 2); it identifies six major tasks that indicate the path toward achieving the goals set by the Plan (Section 3); it outlines the resources (Section 4) and measures (Section 5) needed to successfully perform these tasks; finally, it provides indications for the efficient implementation of the Plan (Section 6) (Table 3.1). Previous Chinese policy documents had already highlighted the importance of AI for national development. However, it is the AIPD that officially elevates artificial intelligence to a national strategic priority[4] and states the intentions to build China's first-mover advantage in the development of AI, making the country a global power in science and technology.[5] The AIDP emphasizes the value of AI to foster China's advancements in economy, technology, society, and national security, saying that China must "lead the world in new trends of AI development, serve economic and social development, and support national security, spurring the overall elevation of national competitiveness".[6]

[3] State Council, 2017. *New Generation Artificial Intelligence Development Plan* [新一代人工智能发展规划]. Guo Fa (2017) 35, 8 July, http://www.gov.cn/zhengce/content/2017-07/20/content_5211996.htm.

[4] "国务院印发 "新一代人工智能发展计划", 这是本世纪以来中国发布的第一个人工智能系统性战略规划", quoted from: Shanghai Association for Science and Technology, 2021. From basics to applications, AI research fully blossoms—Explaining the 2021 World Artificial Intelligence Conference youth outstanding essay award [从基础到应用, 人工智能研究全面开花—解读2021世界人工智能大会青年优秀论文奖]. *WeChat Post*, 9 July, https://mp.weixin.qq.com/s/GRl-8l8UOBcfblxND1KguA. See also: Triolo and Goodrich (2018, p. 16) and Tencent and CAICT (2017, p. 179).

[5] State Council, 2017. In original: "为抢抓人工智能发展的重大战略机遇, 构筑我国人工智能发展的先发优势, 加快建设创新型国家和世界科技强国, […], 制定本规划".

[6] Ibid., Section 1, the Strategic Situation (战略态势), par. 8. In original: "引领世界人工智能发展新潮流, 服务经济社会发展和支撑国家安全, 带动国家竞争力整体跃升".

There is no public information on the process that led to the release of the AIDP,[7] but there is evidence that China's top bureaucratic agencies (Box 3.1) have started an intense competition to assert their claims on AI policy (Ding 2018, pp. 14–15). In May 2016, the *"Internet Plus" and AI Three-Year Implementation Plan* (Appendix III) had given the mandate to advance the AI industry to four agencies: the National Development and Reform Commission (NDRC), the Ministry of Science and Technology (MOST), the Ministry of Industry and Information Technology (MIIT), and the Cyberspace Administration of China (CAC). In July 2017, however, the AIDP assigned the formal lead in AI policy solely to the MOST, which is tasked by the State Council to establish and coordinate the New Generation Artificial Intelligence Development Plan Implementation Office (新一代人工智能发展规划推进办公室). In addition, none of the other three agencies involved with the *"Internet Plus" and AI Three-Year Implementation Plan* is mentioned in the AIDP, a notable exclusion given how comprehensive the document is in other respects. While the MOST was entrusted with coordinating the Chinese national AI strategy, other agencies are shoving for asserting their authority in AI policy. In December 2017, the MIIT issued its own three-year action plan for AI (Appendix IV), which focuses on implementing a set of tasks related to the AIDP and the *Made in China 2025*. And when the New Generation Artificial Intelligence Development Plan Implementation Office was officially created in November 2017, the number of agencies involved had risen to 15 offices.[8] This jostling for influence in AI policy among the main bureaucratic players further confirms the strategic importance of artificial intelligence for the Chinese government.

The AIDP is a long document consisting of more than 19,800 Chinese characters (approximately 11,400 English words). Next subsection focuses on the goals set forth in the AIDP in order to understand what the Chinese priorities for the use of AI in the public sector are and their relative importance in China's AI strategy. The ambitious targets

[7] Some observers argue that Chinese government efforts to drive AI development are riding a wave of private sector development already under way (Zeng 2021; Triolo and Goodrich 2018).

[8] State Council General Office, 2017. MOST convenes the starting meeting for the New Generation Artificial Intelligence Development Plan and science and technology megaprojects [科技部召开新一代人工智能发展规划暨重大科技项目启动会]. *China Central Government*, 20 November, http://www.gov.cn/xinwen/2017-11/20/content_5241019.htm.

set by the Plan have attracted the attention of scholars and observers, especially in terms of technological development (China aims to become the global leader in AI innovation by 2030) and economic growth (the scale of the core AI industry shall reach 150 billion RMB by 2020, which would represent a tenfold increase in three years[9]). At the same time, the AIDP also indicates that the Chinese leadership strongly prioritizes the use of AI in the public sector (i.e., AI for "social construction"), which is positioned among the major goals of China's AI strategy. Understanding the national goals for AI in the public sector and the political support they enjoy is important to contextualize the AI plans of Shanghai and examine the municipal capacity to implement AI in the public sector.

3.1.1 The Goals of the AIDP: Technology, Economy, Society, and Security

The AIDP states that China will improve its research and development capabilities in artificial intelligence and make use of AI to foster advances in China's economy, society and national security[10]: "By making the acceleration of the deep integration of AI with the economy, society and national defense as the primary line, and by making the elevation of the scientific and technological innovation capacity in the new generation of AI as the main direction of attack, [the Plan aims to] develop a smart economy, build a smart society, protect national security, [...] inclusively enhance society's productive forces, comprehensive national power and national competitiveness, in order to accelerate the construction of an innovative country and a global science and technology power".[11] The scope and scale of these goals is described as follows:

[9] According to iMedia Research Group's "2017 Special Report on China's Artificial Intelligence Industry", China's AI industry had a gross output of RMB 10 billion in 2016, and it was expected to grow to around RMB 15 billion in 2017 (Ding 2018, pp. 10–11).

[10] Chinese commentators write: "《新一代人工智能发展规划》[...] 支撑科技、经济、社会发展和国家安全四项任务". Quoted from: China Association of Science and Technology, 2020. Academician Pan Yunhe: AI must take aim at the interdisciplinary frontier [潘云鹤院士: 人工智能要瞄准学科交叉前沿]. *China Science and Technology Journal* [中国科学报], 30 August, retrieved from: https://tech.sina.cn/2020-08-30/detail-iivhuipp1474735.d.html.

[11] Ibid., Section 2, The Overall Requirements, par. Guiding Ideology. In original: "以加快人工智能与经济、社会、国防深度融合为主线, 以提升新一代人工智能科技创新能

- **AI Technological Progress**: "[China must] organically combine the accelerated accumulation of technical capabilities with massive data resources, huge application requirements, and an open market environment, forming a unique advantage in the development of artificial intelligence in China".[12] The AIDP sets benchmarks for China's overall technological progress in AI: by 2020, China will achieve important progress in AI foundational theories and core technologies, and AI applications will become a new way to improve people's livelihoods; by 2025, China will achieve global leadership in some AI theories, technologies and applications, and AI will be widely used in intelligent manufacturing, medicine, urbanization, agriculture, national defense and other fields; by 2030, China will become the world's primary AI innovation center, and AI will be extensively used in industry, social governance, and national defense.
- **Economic Development**: "AI has become a new engine of economic development. AI has become the core driving force for a new round of industrial transformation [...]. China must accelerate the rapid application of AI, cultivating and expanding AI industries to inject new kinetic energy into China's economic development".[13] The AIDP sets specific benchmarks for China's AI industry: by 2020, the scale of AI's core industry[14] will reach 150

力为主攻方向, 发展智能经济, 建设智能社会, 维护国家安全, [...] 全面提升社会生产力、综合国力和国家竞争力, 为加快建设创新型国家和世界科技强国 [...]".

[12] Ibid., Section 1, the Strategic Situation, par. 6. In original: "加速积累的技术能力与海量的数据资源、巨大的应用需求、开放的市场环境有机结合, 形成了我国人工智能发展的独特优势".

[13] Ibid., Section 1, the Strategic Situation, par. 3. In original: "人工智能成为经济发展的新引擎。人工智能作为新一轮产业变革的核心驱动力 [...]. 我国[...]必须加快人工智能深度应用, 培育壮大人工智能产业, 为我国经济发展注入新动能".

[14] The line between "core AI industry" (人工智能核心企业) and "AI-related industries" (相关产业) is blurred. Perhaps the clearest distinction in the Chinese context is offered by the NDRC *"Internet Plus" and AI Three-Year Implementation Plan*. This plan outlines nine major "core AI technologies" and eight other technology types. The "core AI technologies" include basic research in deep learning, the development of basic software and hardware such as chips and sensors, and applied research in areas like computer vision and cybersecurity. The eight technology types include smart vehicles, smart wearable devices, and smart robots, among others (Ding 2018, p. 11). This definition of "core AI" fits with that of leading market research firms like CB Insights and Roland Berger, which define "core AI companies" as those focused on general-purpose AI applicable across a variety of industries (Castro et al. 2019; Ding 2018; Tsinghua 2018).

billion RMB, exceeding 1 trillion RMB including the related industries. By 2025, the scale of AI's core industry will surpass 400 billion RMB, exceeding 5 trillion RMB including the related industries. By 2030, the scale of the AI core industry will surpass 1 trillion RMB, exceeding 10 trillion RMB including the related industries.[15]

- **National Security**: "The world's main developed countries are taking the promotion of AI as a major strategy to enhance national competitiveness and protect national security [...]. China [...] must look at the world, and take the development of AI to the national strategic level with systemic layout, [...] to create new competitive advantage [and] effectively protect national security".[16]
- **Social Construction**: "AI brings new opportunities for social construction. [...] Population aging, environmental constraints and other challenges remain serious. The widespread use of AI in education, medical care, elderly care, environmental protection, urban operations, judicial services and other fields will greatly improve the level of precision in public services, comprehensively enhancing the people's quality of life. AI technologies can accurately sense, forecast and provide early warning of major situations for infrastructure facilities and social security operations; grasp group cognition and psychological changes in a timely manner; and actively provide policy responses, which will significantly elevate the capability and level of social governance, playing an irreplaceable role in effectively maintaining social stability".[17]

[15] Ibid., Section 2 "Overall Requirements" (总体要求), par. 3 "Strategic Objectives" (战略目标).

[16] Ibid., Section 1, the Strategic Situation, par. 2. In original: "世界主要发达国家把发展人工智能作为提升国家竞争力、维护国家安全的重大战略。我国 [...] 必须放眼全球, 把人工智能发展放在国家战略层面系统布局 [...], 打造竞争新优势 [...], 有效保障国家安全".

[17] Ibid., Section 1, the Strategic Situation, par. 4. In original: "人工智能带来社会建设的新机遇。[...] 人口老龄化、资源环境约束等挑战依然严峻, 人工智能在教育、医疗、养老、环境保护、城市运行、司法服务等领域广泛应用, 将极大提高公共服务精准化水平, 全面提升人民生活品质。人工智能技术可准确感知、预测、预警基础设施和社会安全运行的重大态势, 及时把握群体认知及心理变化, 主动决策反应, 将显著提高社会治理的能力和水平, 对有效维护社会稳定具有不可替代的作用".

3.1.2 AI in the Public Sector: Build an Intelligent Society

To achieve these goals, the AIDP lays out six "focus tasks" (重点任务). These tasks are often characterized by a high level of detail and intricacy, and they form the core part of the Plan, occupying nearly 60% of the whole document. The third focus task is dedicated to the use of AI in the public sector. In order to improve people's living standards and quality of life (提高人民生活水平和质量的目标), the AIDP requires to "establish a safe and convenient intelligent society" and "greatly increase the level of 'intelligentization' of the whole society by accelerating the deep application of AI and forming a ubiquitous intelligent environment".[18] This focus task consists of four sub-tasks that indicate in further detail how China aims to use AI for social construction. Namely:

1. **Develop Convenient and Efficient Intelligent Services** (发展便捷高效的智能服务). This subtask calls for accelerating the application of AI to provide personalized, diversified, and high-quality public services in the following areas:
   - *Intelligent education* (智能教育): use technology to accelerate the reform of personnel training models and teaching methods and create a new education system that includes smart and interactive learning. Carry out the establishment of smart campuses and promote the application of AI in the whole process of teaching, management and resource building. Develop online learning and education platforms based on Big Data intelligence. Develop intelligent education assistants and establish an intelligent, fast and comprehensive education analysis system. Establish a learner-centered education environment, provide accurate education services, and personalize daily education and lifelong education.
   - *Intelligent medical care* (智能医疗): promote the application of new models and methods of AI-based treatment and establish a fast and accurate intelligent medical system. Explore the

[18] Ibid., Section 3, Focus Task 3, Establish a safe and convenient intelligent society (建设安全便捷的智能社会). In original: "加快人工智能深度应用, 形成无时不有、无处不在的智能化环境, 全社会的智能化水平大幅提升".

construction of smart hospitals, develop man–machine collaborative surgical robots, intelligent diagnosis and treatment assistants, develop flexible wearable devices, biocompatible physiological monitoring systems, develop man–machine collaborative clinical intelligent diagnosis and treatment programs, and realize intelligent image recognition, pathological classification, and intelligent multi-disciplinary consultation. Leverage artificial intelligence to carry out large-scale genome recognition, proteomics, metabolomics and other research and foster new drug research and development as well as the intelligentization of pharmaceutical supervision. Strengthen the intelligent surveillance, prevention and control of epidemics.

– *Intelligent healthcare and elderly care* (智能健康和养老): strengthen the overall intelligent health management, achieve breakthroughs in key technologies such as Big Data analysis and the Internet of Things for health, research and develop health management wearable devices and home smart health detection and monitoring equipment, and promote the evolution of health management "from point monitoring to continuous monitoring" (从点状监测向连续监测), from short-process management to long-process management. Build smart elderly care communities and institutions and create a safe and convenient intelligent elderly care infrastructure system. Strengthen the intelligentization of products for the elderly as well as the adaptation of smart products to the needs of the elderly. Develop audio-visual aids, physical aids, and other smart home elderly care equipment. Develop mobile social and service platforms for the elderly, and "emotional caregiving assistants" (情感陪护助手) to improve the quality of life of the elderly.

2. **Promote the Intelligentization of Social Governance** (推进社会治理智能化). This subtask calls for promoting the modernization of social governance and fostering the application of AI in public administration, judiciary, urban management, environmental protection, and other hot and difficult issues in social governance[19]:

[19] In original: "围绕行政管理、司法管理、城市管理、环境保护等社会治理的热点难点问题, 促进人工智能技术应用, 推动社会治理现代化".

- *Intelligent government services* (智能政务): Develop artificial intelligence platforms suitable for government services and decision-making, build an open-environment decision-making engine (面向开放环境的决策引擎), and apply it to major strategic decisions such as research and evaluation of complex social issues, policy evaluation, risk forecast, and emergency response. Strengthen the consolidation of government information resources and the accurate prediction of public demand, smoothen the interaction channels between the government and the public.
- *Smart courts* (智慧法庭): Build data platforms for smart courts that integrate trials, personnel, data applications, judicial disclosure, and dynamic monitoring. Promote the application of artificial intelligence in evidence collection, case analysis, legal document reading and assessment. Achieve the intelligentization of trial system and trial capabilities of the courts.
- *Smart cities* (智慧城市): create intelligent urban infrastructure and intelligent buildings, and promote the intelligent transformation and upgrading of municipal infrastructure such as underground pipe corridors. Establish urban Big Data platforms and create urban operation management systems that integrate multiple and heterogeneous data. Realize a comprehensive perception of the urban infrastructure and the city's natural ecosystem (green areas, wetlands, etc.) and achieve an in-depth understanding of the operations of complex urban systems. Promote the R&D and construction of public service information systems in residential communities, and foster the collaboration between these community service systems (社区服务系统) and residential smart home systems (居民智能家庭系统); promote the intelligentization of the whole lifecycle of urban administration, including planning, construction, management, and operations.
- *Intelligent transportation* (智能交通): research and establish systems for autonomous driving commercial vehicles and for smart traffic infrastructures. Develop a comprehensive Big Data application platform for multidimensional traffic information in complex scenarios. Establish smart transportation command-and-control centers. Build an intelligent system for the control, management and service of road transportation,

railway transportation, low-altitude air traffic, and maritime traffic.
- *Intelligent environmental protection* (智能环保): establish a Big Data platform for the intelligent monitoring of air, water, and soil. Build intelligent and integrated environmental monitoring networks and service platforms. Develop forecasting models and early warning solutions for resource and energy consumption, and for pollutant emissions. Strengthen the construction of intelligent prevention and control systems for environmental protection and emergency response in major national strategic areas such as the Beijing-Tianjin-Hebei region and the Yangtze River Economic Belt.

3. **Leverage AI to Improve Public Security Capabilities** (利用人工智能提升公共安全保障能力): this subtask calls for deepening the application of artificial intelligence in public security. It involves several activities: fostering the construction of intelligent monitoring, early warning and control systems; developing smart security and police products that integrate detection and sensing technologies, video image information analysis and recognition technologies, and biometric identification technologies; establishing an intelligent monitoring platform that focuses on the urgent needs of social governance, criminal investigations and anti-terrorism; strengthening the intelligent transformation and upgrading of security equipment in key public areas; supporting qualified communities or cities to carry out demonstrations of public security areas that deploy AI technologies; and strengthening the use of AI for food safety and for the early warning, monitoring and response to natural disasters.
4. **Promote Social Interaction and Mutual Trust** (促进社会交往共享互信): this subtask calls for giving full play to the role of AI in enhancing social interaction and promoting credible communication. It includes several activities: strengthening the research and development of next-generation social networks; accelerating the application of augmented reality, virtual reality, and mixed-reality technologies; developing technologies that can be used in different scenarios such as work, study, life, and entertainment to improve the need of real-time information; developing intelligent products that can accurately understand emotional interactions and improve the interpersonal communication needs, thus "realizing a virtuous circle

of emotional communication and demand satisfaction" (实现情感交流和需求满足的良性循环); promoting the integration of blockchain technology and AI; establishing a new social credit system; and minimizing the cost and risks of interpersonal communications.

The AIDP sets clear policy goals for the use of AI in the public sector ("social construction"): improve the provision of public services and enhance people's quality of life, and at the same time maintain social and political stability. In other words, China's leadership identifies AI both as a useful tool for improving the provision of public services and a channel for more effective domestic control (Creemers 2020). This vision is perhaps not surprising in light of the Chinese government's approach to technology, which values its use to enhance State's governance capacity and favors the integration of technology in society (Chapter 1). The AIPD also indicates how China intends to achieve its goals for AI in the public sector, articulating a broad but well-elaborated set of policy actions (i.e., the "focus tasks") that cover virtually every area of public service provision, like education, medicine and healthcare, administrative services, urban governance, judiciary, transportation, environmental protection and public security. If carried out, these tasks would help China to build a "safe and convenient intelligent society", an indicator of analytical capacity. Finally, the goal of leveraging AI to promote social construction is enshrined among the four main priorities of China's AI strategy, suggesting that policy initiatives aimed at promoting the use of AI in the public sector will enjoy political support from the Chinese leadership. The AIDP outlines a clear vision for AI in the public sector and states a high-profile political endorsement for it, thus empowering Shanghai and other Chinese cities and provinces to drive forward with AI implementations in the public sector: the national government is indicating what it wants to achieve, and it is telling local administrations that this policy goal is politically important. At the same time, the incentive structure that mediates this combination of central signaling and local implementation in the Chinese policymaking process can create distortions that complicate a realistic assessment of Shanghai's AI plans (Chapter 2.4). Next section explains such distortions and proposes some remedies to ensure a sound analysis of Shanghai's analytical and political capacities.

Table 3.1 Main contents of the New Generation Artificial Intelligence Development Plan (July 2017)

Section 1, The Strategic situation (战略态势)	AI has become a new focus of ***international competition***. China's situation in national security and international competition is more complex. China must firmly seize the strategic initiative in the new stage of international competition in AI development, to create new competitive advantage, and effectively protect national security AI has become a new engine of ***economic development***. As China's economic development enters a new normal, deepening the supply side of structural reform task is very arduous, [and China] must accelerate the rapid application of AI, cultivating and expanding AI industries to inject new kinetic energy into China's economic development AI brings new opportunities for ***social construction***. The widespread use of AI in education, medical care, pensions, environmental protection, urban operations, judicial services, and other fields will greatly improve the level of precision in public services, comprehensively enhancing the people's quality of life. AI technologies will significantly elevate the capability and level of social governance, playing an irreplaceable role in effectively maintaining social stability The uncertainties in the development of AI create ***new challenges***. While vigorously developing AI, China must attach great importance to the potential safety risks and challenges, and ensure the safe, reliable, and controllable development of AI China possesses a favorable ***foundation for the development of AI***. China released a series of policy initiatives to foster science and technology R&D, promoted applications and industrial development, and other aspects. As a result of many years of continuous accumulation, China has achieved important progress in the field of AI (e.g., voice and visual recognition). The accumulation of technological capabilities and massive data resources together constitute China's unique advantage in AI development At the same time, there is still ***a gap between China's overall AI development relative to that of developed countries***. China lacks major original results in the basic theory, high-end chips, AI software and other areas. Moreover, adapting to the development of AI requires the urgent improvement of basic infrastructure, policies and regulations, and standards systems China must lead the world in new trends in the development of AI, serve economic and social development, and support national security, promoting the overall elevation of the nation's competitiveness and leapfrog development

Section 2, Overall Requirements (总体要求)	2.1. Guiding ideology: accelerate the deep integration of AI with the economy, society and national defense as a primary line, enhance scientific and technological innovation capacity for a new generation of AI as the main direction of attack; develop a smart economy, build a smart society, protect national security; build knowledge clusters, technology clusters, and industry clusters mutually integrated with talent, system, and culture. Inclusively enhance society's productive forces, comprehensive national power and national competitiveness, in order to accelerate the construction of an innovative country and a global science and technology power, achieving the two centennial goals and the great rejuvenation of the Chinese nation 2.2. Basic principles: China's AI development shall be ***technology-led*** (enhance China's original innovation capability in AI, and accelerate the construction of a first-mover advantage); ***systemic*** (including foundational research, technological R&D, industrial development and commercial applications), ***market-oriented*** (accelerate the commercialization of AI technology and results, while the government firmly maintains the lead in planning and guidance) and ***open*** (based on cooperation between industry, research and government, including civil-military integration) 2.3. Strategic objectives: the AIDP sets specific benchmarks for China's AI and AI-related industries, including a gross output of RMB 1 trillion for the core AI industry and RMB 10 trillion for related industries by 2030. In the same period, China will make substantial progress in AI research, technology and applications 2.4. Overall deployment: China shall pursue a healthy and sustainable development of AI. The country will tackle its weaknesses in AI development (e.g., basic theories and others listed in section 1), predict AI's challenges and maximize risk prevention through reasonable regulation, foster industrial development, and fully support science and technology, the economy, social development, and national security
Section 3, Focus Task 1: "Build an open and coordinated science and technology innovation system for AI" (构建开放协同的人工智能科技创新体系)	3.1.1. Establish basic theory systems for a new generation AI: promote advances in basic AI research, focusing on the areas that may trigger "paradigmatic change in AI" and support AI applications, such as Big Data intelligence, cross-media sensing and computing, human–machine blended intelligence, mass intelligence, autonomous cooperation and decision-making 3.1.2. Build a key general technology system for a new generation AI: Raise China's international competitiveness in AI by creating a mature technological system across a number of "key general technologies" (关键共性技术) such as knowledge computing engines, swarm intelligence, autonomous unmanned systems, etc. 3.1.3. Coordinate the layout of AI innovation platforms: strengthen the foundations of R&D and applications in AI by building basic, open-source support platforms in various areas that overlap with the theories and technologies listed in the aforementioned paragraphs 3.1.1 and 3.1.2 3.1.4. Create pools of high-end AI talents who have not only 'vertical skills' in basic and applied AI research, operations and maintenance, but who can also master the use of AI in economy, society, management, law and other areas; attract top AI talents, and establish AI majors in universities

(continued)

Table 3.1 (continued)

Section 3, Focus Task 2: "Nurture a high-end, highly efficient smart economy" (培育高端高效的智能经济)	AI will contribute to a substantial increase in productivity and the quality and efficiency of economic development. It includes four sub-tasks: 3.2.1. Forcefully develop new AI industries: develop new AI industries by accelerating the application of key AI technologies, stimulating the integration of AI technologies into business models, and promoting the development of smart products like smart software and hardware, smart robot, smart delivery tools, etc. 3.2.2. Promote the upgrade of industrial intelligentization by fostering the use of AI in all sectors, especially in manufacturing, agriculture, logistics, finance, commerce and smart household goods 3.2.3. Forcefully develop smart enterprises by supporting companies to use AI technologies in their core operations, promoting the diffusion of smart factories that leverage Big Data and automation, and supporting the creation of global leading AI enterprises in unmanned aircrafts, smart robots, smart cars, etc. 3.2.4. Create AI innovation heights: promote the innovation of the AI industry by creating regional AI industry and innovation hubs, launching pilot demonstrations for AI applications, and establishing innovation clusters for the AI industry that also involve colleges, universities and scientific research institutes
Section 3, Focus Task 3: "Construct a safe and convenient intelligent society" (建设安全便捷的智能社会)	See analysis in Sect. 3.1.2
Section 3, Focus Task 4: "Strengthen military-civilian integration in the AI domain" (加强人工智能领域军民融合)	It states the need to establish mechanisms to standardize communication and coordination among scientific research institutes, universities, enterprises and the military industry. Integration is presented as a two-way transformation process, whereby civilian AI should be guided toward national defense applications, and military AI should be guided toward civilian applications
Section 3, Focus Task 5: "Build a safe and efficient smart infrastructure system" (构建泛在安全高效的智能化基础设施体系)	It indicates that the construction of a smart infrastructure system is based on three pillars: – *network infrastructure* (e.g., accelerate the deployment of 5G communication technology and related infrastructure, promote the construction of high-precision navigation and positioning systems, improve the Internet of Things infrastructure); – *Big Data infrastructure* (e.g., building upon national data-sharing exchange platforms, open data platforms and other public infrastructure, provide massive data support for AI research and development and extensive applications, while also strengthening data security and privacy protection); and – *high-performance computing infrastructure* (e.g., enhance the service support capabilities of supercomputing centers for AI applications, while also reducing the environmental impacts of supercomputers)

Section 3, Focus Task 6: "Plan ahead for new generation artificial intelligence major science and technology projects" (前瞻布局新一代人工智能重大科技项目)	It links AI development to other national science and technology megaprojects (国家科技重大专项), such as the "Hegaoji" (核高基) megaproject[20] and the "Technological Innovation 2030—Mega-Projects[21]" (科技创新2030—重大项目). It also requires the National Key Research and Development Plans[22] (国家重点研发计划) and the National Natural Science Fund[23] (国家自然科学基金) to increase support for AI development

(continued)

20 HeGaoJi is one of the 16 State-backed major technology projects (megaprojects) announced in 2006. It was allocated more than 100 billion yuan (15 billion USD) in funding by 2020 to develop core electric components (核心电子器件), high-end chips for general applications (高端通用芯片) and basic computing software (基础软件). Led by the Ministry of Science and Technology and organized by Ministry of Industry and Information Technology, HeGaoJi is under the ***National Medium-and Long-Term (2006–2020) Program Outline for Scientific and Technological Development*** (国家中长期科学和技术发展规划纲要(2006–2020年)) issued by the State Council in 2006 (chapter 3.3.2). In 2009, the Ministry of Science and Technology issued the ***Notice of 2009 Application for the Megaproject of "Core Electronics Components, High-end Chips and Basic Software Products"*** ("核心电子器件、高端通用芯片及基础软件产品" 科技重大专项2009年课题申报的通知).

21 The ***13th Five-year Plan for Science, Technology and Innovation***, published by the State Council in August 2016, stated that the 16 megaprojects announced in 2006 will gradually be replaced by a new category of Megaprojects in the period 2016–2020, reflecting and incorporating new developments in national and international science and technology priorities. As a result, 15 new "2030 Innovation Megaprojects" (科技创新2030—重大项目) were listed in the ***13th Five-year Plan for Science, Technology and Innovation***, with the implementation period ending in 2030. The New Generation Artificial Intelligence megaproject presented here has become the sixteenth program of the "2030 Innovation Megaprojects" originally approved in 2016.

22 These plans were created after the 2014 reform of the national science and technology innovation funding system. They have incorporated numerous previously-existing programs, such as the Ministry of Science and Technology's "863 Program" for R&D and the "973 Program" for basic research (Chapter 2.2.3). See: Chinainnovationfunding.eu, 2022. National Key R&D Programmes, http://chinainnovationfunding.eu/national-key-rd-programmes/.

23 The National Natural Science Fund is a national fund to support basic research, identify and foster scientific talents, and promote progress in science and technology. The fund is administered by the National Natural Science Foundation of China, which was established in 1986 directly under the jurisdiction of the State Council.

Table 3.1 (continued)

Section 4 **Resource allocation** (资源配置)	It calls for establishing financial mechanisms to support AI development, guided by the government and dominated by the market [see the box on Government Guidance Funds in Chapter 2.2.3]. It also calls for building AI technological and industrial innovation bases, led by enterprises in cooperation with academic and research institutions. Finally, it encourages domestic AI enterprises to "go out", and says that the State will support powerful AI enterprises conducting foreign mergers, acquisitions and other activities abroad
Section 5 **Guarantee measures** (保障措施)	China will develop laws, regulations, and ethical norms that promote the development of AI; improve key policies for the support of AI development (e.g., tax incentives, adaptation of the existing policy system in education, medical care, social insurance); create technology standards and intellectual property system for AI; establish an AI security supervision and evaluation system with a near-term focus on the AI impacts on employment, and a long-term focus on the impacts on social ethics; strengthen the training of an AI labor force; and popularize AI among Chinese citizens, comprehensively improve the level of the whole society on the application of AI
Section 6 **Organization and implementation** (组织实施)	Under the leadership of the Party and the State Council, the National Science and Technology Structural Reform and Innovation System Construction Leading Small Group (国家科技体制改革和创新体系建设领导小组) will take the lead in comprehensive planning and coordination, it will deliberate major tasks, major policies, major questions, and major work arrangements Under the leadership of the Ministry of Science and Technology, the AI Planning Implementation Office (人工智能规划推进办公室) will be concretely responsible for the implementation of the AIDP China will launch AI trial applications and demonstrations in all departments and all localities, quickly disseminating replicable experiences and methods. This trial-based approach will contribute to fostering the healthy and orderly development of AI in the country China shall fully use all kinds of traditional and new media to disseminate new progress and achievements in AI, to let the healthy development of AI become a consensus in all Chinese society

3.1.3 *The AIDP: Implications for the Study of Shanghai's AI Plans*

The AIDP sets forth ambitious goals to promote AI technological progress and use this technology to foster advances in Chinese economy, society national security. It indicates that artificial intelligence has been elevated to a national strategic priority, and unambiguously signals China's political support for AI development across all the areas indicated in the Plan. The publication of the AIDP has been followed by a number of national policy documents issued by the top bureaucratic agencies of China's AI policy. These documents are formally linked to the AIDP and provide more specific indications on how to achieve the goals of the Plan in different policy areas (Appendix IV). This powerful institutional backing confirms the political prioritization of AI development and indicates that the implementation of the Plan will be guided by the national government. The Ministry of Science and Technology has the formal lead, but the Ministry of Industry and Information Technology (China's administration for industrial policy), the National Development and Reform Commission (the Chinese government's central economic planning ministry and major macroeconomic coordinator) and other national agencies are also actively involved in the implementation of China's AI policy (Box 3.1; Ding 2018; Triolo and Goodrich 2018).

Although these bodies provide guidance and supervision, the Plan is not meant to work as a centrally enacted directive. As noted, the multipurpose nature of AI and the mostly private ownership of this technology imply that a rigid top-down masterplan is not suitable to promote AI development. In this perspective, Zeng (2021) observes that China's AI strategy is a loose slogan rather than a concrete policy plan; this slogan is kept deliberately vague and broad to accommodate the interests of domestic stakeholders. "Recognising this point is important: the AIDP is an ambitious strategy set by the central government, but the actual innovation and transformation is expected to be driven by the private sector and local governments. In other words, it is more appropriate to view the AIDP as a highly incentivised 'wish list', to nudge, and coordinate other relevant stakeholders, rather than a central directive" (Roberts et al. 2020, p. 61). To universities and research institutes, the AIDP tells that their efforts to introduce AI majors, promote AI research and other tasks outlined by the Plan will be rewarded by government fundings (e.g., AIDP section 3, focus task 1, subtask 4). To AI companies, the AIDP tells that the enterprises that contribute to China's AI development will receive various forms of government support (e.g., AIDP section 5), a message reinforced by initiatives in national innovation policy that engage private AI firms, like the AIOIPs and AIIA mentioned earlier.

To local officials, the AIDP signals that the success in promoting AI in their jurisdictions will likely benefit their careers (Zeng 2021; Webster 2019; Sheehan 2018). The incentive structure for local administrations is best understood in light of the evaluation system for promotion that encourages Chinese officials to pursue the policy priorities set by higher-level authorities (Chapter 2.2.3). By imbuing AI with a stamp of approval from the central government and the Chinese Communist Party, the AIDP signals to local administrators that AI is a metric for evaluating their performance, encouraging them to promote local projects that make use of AI in some way (Lee and Sheehan 2018). Incentivizing local governments is crucial to spur AI adoption and explore the manifold potential applications of the technology, fostering local policy experiments that promote AI development and help to achieve the goals set forth in the national AI strategy. Through public procurement, pilot projects, infrastructure adaptations, subsidies, regulatory accommodation or other policy instruments, the intervention of local administrations is essential to make use of AI in a way that suits local conditions and capabilities, expanding the impact of AI across economy and society as advocated by China's AI strategy (Ding 2019; Lee and Sheehan 2018). Local participation is especially important for the use of AI in the provision of public services, an area where subnational governments traditionally play a primary role in China.

Understanding that the AIDP works as a coordinating mechanism under which local administrations are incentivized to promote AI in their jurisdictions is important to contextualize the analysis of Shanghai's AI plans. Between October 2017 and December 2020, Shanghai issued two major policy documents and various supporting and actionable measures for AI development, positioning itself at the forefront of an extensive wave of subnational activity spurred by the publication of the AIDP. While this combination of central government signaling and local government implementation is particularly suited to accelerating the implementation of an "omni-use technology" like AI (Lee and Sheehan, 2018), the incentive structure that encourages local AI experiments also complicates the assessment of the actual scale and intentions of the Shanghai AI plans. By linking AI promotion to career advancements, such incentive structure creates vested interests for local officials to overstate the scale of local AI initiatives in order to show compliance with national AI policies (Ding 2020). This is well exemplified by the industrial benchmarks contained in the Shanghai AI plans, which set the target for the municipal AI industry to a scale of 110 billion RMB by 2020, which alone would account for nearly 3/4 of the AIDP's target of 150 billion RMB by 2020. This incentive structure could also result in the pursuit of "achievement projects" (政绩工程) aimed at scoring points in the evaluation system for promotion, without actually contributing to AI development.

These considerations do not imply that Shanghai's AI plans—or those of other Chinese cities and provinces—are necessarily a mere "political performance, reflecting the art of political correctness" (Zeng 2021, p. 4). In fact, there is evidence that some local AI initiatives predate the AIDP, including the first set of provincial-level AI policies in 2009 (Tsinghua 2018, p. 78); China Speech Valley (中国声谷) created in Hefei in 2012; or the Hangzhou AI Town (杭州人工智能小镇) inaugurated in July 2017. Shanghai has also developed a consistent vision for AI development that links it to other policy priorities of the municipality, as discussed shortly. At the same time, historical evidence from other sectors,[24] previous studies,[25] the flurry of local initiatives "following the steps of the central government" (Tsinghua 2018, p. 106) since the publication of the AIDP, and the overstated industrial benchmarks often contained in Shanghai's and other local AI plans indicate that the tendency to show compliance is real. The analysis of the Shanghai AI policy environment needs to account for this tendency. Examining Shanghai's analytical and political capacities solely based on the contents of the municipal AI plans without any additional benchmarks may result in erroneous assessments, since these plans could be only an act of symbolic compliance or political

[24] In 2017, the municipality of Tianjin, the Liaoning Province and other provincial-level administrative units "admitted" to faking their economic data. Financial Times, 2018. China fake data mask economic rebound. *Financial Times*, 16 January, https://www.ft.com/content/a9889330-f51c-11e7-88f7-5465a6ce1a00. There is also emerging evidence of pursuing "achievement projects" in some AI-related industries, such as the semiconductor industry, a component of the basic layer of the AI value chain. See: Yu, D., 2020. The birth of 5 ten-billion-yuan giants marks the change of the semiconductor industry [5只百亿巨兽诞生, 半导体产业彻底变天]. *HuxiuApp*, 9 September, https://mp.weixin.qq.com/s/FqRRfEbKp-UJ60wihRjyDg.

[25] Earlier research observed that "the logic of meeting targets often induces coping behaviors (both legitimate and illicit) such as selective implementation, distortion or fabrication of records which would induce a decoupling of symbolic compliance from substantive compliance" (Zhou et al. 2013, p. 125).

performance (Zeng 2021; Zhou et al. 2013). Therefore, next sections will also look for additional evidence that corroborates the assessments based on documentary analysis, thus addressing the potential distortions introduced by this latent tendency to show compliance to national policy priorities.

Box 3.1 Ministries and top bureaucratic agencies leading China's AI policy

The State Council, China's highest executive body, exercises unified leadership over the work of ministries and agencies involved in the making of China's AI policy. The main bureaucratic players are presented here, integrating the analysis conducted in earlier studies (Triolo and Goodrich 2018; UNESCAP 2018). The list excludes institutions that don't have a direct involvement in the making of China's AI policy, such as technical bodies (e.g., the National Information Security Standardization Technical Committee/全国信息安全标准化技术委员会, or the China Electronics Standardization Institute/中国电子技术标准化研究所), or institutions with a peripheral role in civilian AI policy (e.g., the People's Liberation Army, who is represented in the New Generation Artificial Intelligence Development Plan Implementation Office discussed here, but primarily focuses on assimilating civilian AI innovations in the Chinese military[26]).

Ministry of Science and Technology (MOST)

The MOST has the nominal lead of China's AI policy. The State Council formalized roles and responsibilities for AI development through the establishment of the New Generation Artificial Intelligence Development Plan Implementation Office (新一代人工智能发展规划推进办公室), led by the MOST with 15 other agencies participating, which held its first meeting in November 2017. The responsibility of the MOST-led office is to coordinate inter-ministry implementation of China's AI strategy

[26] A review of the advances in the Chinese military and defense industry to date, including the potential adoption of AI-enabled autonomous weapons, can be found in: Kania, E., 2020. "AI weapons" in China's military innovation. *Brookings Institution*, 20 April, https://www.brookings.edu/wp-content/uploads/2020/04/FP_20200427_ai_weapons_kania_v2.pdf.

, including large-scale AI-related megaprojects, and to lead interaction with major private sector players.[27]

MOST was designated the lead on China's AI strategy given its role in earlier S&T programs such as the already mentioned 863 and 973 Programs, which have produced progress on some of the technologies underlying AI. MOST also controls the majority of central government's S&T expenditures (Sun and Cao 2014), and has asserted itself in the AI policy arena. One of MOST's subordinate organizations responsible for basic research funding, the Natural Science Foundation of China (国家自然科学基金委员会), is also re-directing resources towards basic S&T research in AI (Acharya and Arnold 2019).

In November 2017, MOST also announced the establishment of the New Generation AI Strategic Advisory Committee (新一代人工智能战略咨询委员会), headed by Pan Yunhe, academician at the Chinese Academy of Engineering (CAE) and deputy chairman of the China Association for Artificial Intelligence (CAAI). The committee originally consisted of 27 members and was heavy on academicians.[28] It also included specialists in civilian-military integration, and representatives from the first four AI "national team" companies named by MOST in 2017 (i.e., Alibaba, Baidu, Tencent, and iFlytek), and one from Horizon Robotics (a developer of AI

[27] CAC, 2017. The MIIT holds meeting for starting the New Generation Artificial Intelligence Development Plan and megaprojects [科技部召开新一代人工智能发展规划暨重大科技项目启动会]. *CAC website*, 16 November, http://www.cac.gov.cn/2017-11/16/c_1121964697.htm.

[28] CAS Institute of Automation, 2017. New Generation AI Strategic Advisory Committee established, Director of the Institute of Automation Xu Bo appointed as member [新一代人工智能战略咨询委员会成立 自动化所所长徐波担任专家委员]. *CAS website*, 21 November, http://www.ia.cas.cn/xwzx/ttxw/201711/t20171121_4896939.html.

chips for autonomous vehicles and other applications, later included in the "national team").

National Development and Reform Commission (NDRC)
The NDRC has broad administrative and planning authority over the economy that includes drafting five-year plans, and supervising the implementation of the plans through performance management systems. With the Ministry of Finance, the NDRC is responsible for long-range planning and overall investment levels in key high-tech sectors. Most importantly, it has broad discretionary spending authority, allowing it to quickly provide subsidies in the form of grants to domestic AI-related firms. It also has a hand in foreign investment decisions in the high-tech sector, both inbound and outbound, and retains clout within China's cyberspace and high-tech interagency processes. In October 2017, the NDRC announced the establishment of China's Artificial Intelligence Industry Development Alliance (中国人工智能产业发展联盟), under the leadership and supervision of NDRC, MOST, the Ministry for Industry and Information Technology (MIIT), and the Cyberspace Administration of China (CAC).

Ministry of Industry and Information Technology (MIIT)
The MIIT is responsible for industrial policy for both new and traditional industries such as manufacturing, telecoms, and electronics. The MIIT has also historically overseen parts of the semiconductor and software industries, both of which are important component of the foundational layer of the AI value chain. Following the publication of the AIDP in July 2017, the MIIT issued two main national AI policy documents, the *Three-Year Action Plan for Promoting the Development of a New Generation Artificial Intelligence Industry (2018–2020)* in December 2017, and the *Work plan for unveiling the focus tasks of the New Generation Artificial Intelligence Industry Innovation* in November 2018 (Appendix IV).

Cyberspace Administration of China (CAC, 国家互联网信息办公室)
Compared to the three major ministry-level players (i.e., MOST, NDRC and MIIT), the CAC has lower influence on the general AI policy. Operating under the Office of the Central Cyberspace Affairs Commission (中共中央网络安全和信息化委员会办公室), the CAC focuses primarily on the legal, regulatory, and standards issues surrounding AI and Big Data. In addition, CAC maintains its traditional lead in cyberspace security and Internet content regulation, and in increasingly important areas related to AI such as data privacy, data protection, and transfers of data across borders.

If the integration of AI technology across industry and society auspicated by the *New Generation Artificial Intelligence Development Plan* materializes, the number of Ministries and national agencies involved in AI policy will likely further expand. Indications of this trend can be inferred by looking at the AI policy documents issued by the Ministry of Education in 2018 and 2020 (Appendix IV).

3.2 The Municipal Plans for AI Development in Shanghai

Following the publication of the AIDP in July 2017, Shanghai has been quick to issue its own municipal plans for promoting AI development. In October 2017, the Shanghai municipal government published a programmatic policy document, the *Implementation Opinions on Promoting the Development of a New Generation Artificial Intelligence in Shanghai*[29] (hereinafter: *Opinions*). This document sets four main goals for AI development in Shanghai, namely: (i) promote AI applications, with particular attention to public sector AI implementations; (ii) foster research and technological innovation; (iii) spur industrial and economic advancements; and (iv) build a municipal AI ecosystem. The *Opinions* were soon propped up with the release of several actionable policy documents and supporting initiatives. These paved the way to the publication in September 2019 of the *Action Plan on Building Shanghai into an AI Highland and Creating a First-Class Innovation Ecosystem (2019–2021)*[30] (hereinafter: the *AI Highland Plan*), another comprehensive policy document that reiterates the *Opinions*' goals and tasks for AI development. This section examines the main contents of the *Opinions* and the *AI*

[29] Shanghai Municipal Government, 2017. *Implementation Opinions on Promoting the Development of a New Generation Artificial Intelligence in Shanghai* [关于本市推动新一代人工智能发展的实施意见]. Hufu Banfa (2017) 66, 26 October, http://www.sheitc.sh.gov.cn/cyfz/20171113/0020-675566.html.

[30] Shanghai Municipal Commission of Economy and Informatization (SHEITC), 2019. *Action Plan on Building Shanghai into an AI Highland and Creating a First-Class Innovation Ecosystem (2019–2021)* [关于建设人工智能上海高地构建一流创新生态的行动方案(2019–2021年)]. Hujingxinzhi (2019) 707, 13 September, http://www.sheitc.sh.gov.cn/xxfw/20190923/0020-683713.html.

Highland Plan as a starting point to assess Shanghai's analytical and political capacity to implement AI in the public sector, and then provides additional evidence to corroborate the findings of the analysis.

3.2.1 *The Opinions on Promoting a New Generation AI in Shanghai*

In October 2017, the General Office of the Shanghai Municipal People's Government published the *Implementation Opinions on Promoting the Development of a New Generation Artificial Intelligence in Shanghai*. The *Opinions* were explicitly issued "in order to carry out and implement the national *New Generation Artificial Intelligence Development Plan*".[31] Just like the AIDP indicates China's lofty aspirations in AI, the *Opinions* set ambitious goals for Shanghai's AI development. By 2020, Shanghai will become a "national AI development highland (国家人工智能发展高地), China's leading source of AI innovation, demonstration site for applications, industry cluster and talent highland, reaching the world's most advanced levels in some fields".[32] The municipality will "give full play to Shanghai's advantages in rich data resources, wide application areas, and complete range of industries, [will] fully implement the 'smart Shanghai (AI@SH)' action, and form a new generation of AI development system driven by application, technology leadership, industry collaboration, ecosystem cultivation, and talent gathering".[33] Like the AIDP, the time horizon of the *Opinions* stretches to 2030. By that time, the overall development of AI in Shanghai will have reached international advanced levels, and the city will have established solid foundations to become an "AI development highland" and an "excellent global city" (Table 3.2).

The goals (发展目标) and related benchmarks for Shanghai's AI development are outlined in the "smart Shanghai (AI@SH)" action ("智能上

[31] Shanghai Municipal Government, 2017, preamble.

[32] Ibid., Section 1, par. 2, Development Goals (发展目标). In original: "基本建成国家人工智能发展高地，成为全国领先的人工智能创新策源地、应用示范地、产业集聚地和人才高地, 局部领域达到全球先进水平".

[33] Ibid., Section 1 "Clarify the overall requirements" (明确总体要求), par. 1 "Guiding ideology" (指导思想). In original: "发挥上海数据资源丰富、应用领域广泛、产业门类齐全的优势 [...], 全面实施 "智能上海 (AI@SH)" 行动, 形成应用驱动、科技引领、产业协同、生态培育、人才集聚的新一代人工智能发展体系".

海 (AI@SH)" 行动), which focuses on Application, Innovation, Superior industry and Harmonious ecosystem[34]:

- *Application*: Shanghai will pursue AI applications that are "compatible with the operations of a super large city". By 2020, the municipality will create approximately six "AI innovation application demonstration areas" (人工智能创新应用示范区), 60 "AI in-depth application scenarios" (人工智能深度应用场景), and more than 100 "AI application demonstration projects" (人工智能应用示范项目).
- *Innovation*: Shanghai will develop AI technology innovation capabilities that are in line with the international mainstream level. By 2020, Shanghai will significantly improve the municipality's R&D capabilities in cutting-edge theories and key technologies, reach global advanced level in some key areas, and build around ten "AI innovation platforms" (人工智能创新平台).
- *Superior Industry*: Shanghai will form a cluster of "core AI industries" (人工智能重点产业) able to compete at the international level. By 2020, the municipality will foster the emergence of new artificial intelligence industries, business forms and models. The municipality will build approximately five AI industry clusters, cultivate around ten "AI innovation benchmark enterprises (人工智能创新标杆企业), and the scale of Shanghai core AI industries will exceed 100 billion yuan (see earlier discussions about this aspirational target).
- *Harmonious Ecosystem*: Shanghai will build an AI ecosystem characterized by "active innovation and open collaboration". By 2020, Shanghai will become a cluster of AI talents and leverage artificial intelligence to foster innovation and entrepreneurship. The collection and circulation of data in the city will reach international advanced levels, intelligent infrastructures will significantly improve, and Shanghai will create an "East–West interaction and multi-point linkage".[35]

[34] Ibid., Section 1, par. 2, Development Goals (发展目标). In original: 人工智能深度应用 (Application) 格局; 人工智能科技创新 (Innovation) 能力; 人工智能重点产业 (Superior Industry) 集群; and 人工智能融合生态 (Harmonious Ecosystem). The English words appear in the original Chinese document.

[35] The "East–West interaction and multi-point linkage" (东西互动、多点联动) indicates the creation of industrial clusters of AI leading companies and unicorns on the East–West axis of Shanghai, namely: Pudong Zhangjiang AIsland (浦东张江人工智能岛, see

The goals for the use of AI in the public sector and the tasks to achieve them are listed as part of the broader objective to promote "AI applications that are compatible with the operations of a super large city" (Section 1, par. 2). In this context, the *Opinions* require that government agencies, public institutions and other stakeholders "accelerate the in-depth application of AI in key areas of economic development, urban governance and public services, improving labor productivity, public service capabilities, and citizens' sense of gain".[36] Unpacking these goals and focusing on the contents of interest, the *Opinions* articulate that Shanghai wants to accelerate the integration of AI in public services and urban governance in order to improve public service provision (lit. "capabilities") as well as citizens' sense of gain. Consistently, the *Opinions* lay out a well-elaborated set of tasks that are technically sound in that they can contribute to achieving these goals if carried out, an indicator of analytical capacity to implement AI in the public sector. These tasks include:

1. **Optimize City Operations**. AI will be integrated in public security, environmental management and urban infrastructure. To enhance the city's intelligent prevention and control capabilities, Shanghai will promote the comprehensive application of AI in social governance, monitoring people's flows and providing early warnings. To improve the intelligent management of the city's environment, Shanghai will deploy AI in public safety monitoring, natural disaster prediction, environmental monitoring, food safety traceability and other areas. To ensure the intelligent and orderly operations of urban infrastructure, the municipality will implement AI for the intelligent monitoring and maintenance of electricity, water,

chapter 5), the West Bund International AI Center in Xuhui (徐汇西岸国际人工智能中心); the multipoint linkage indicates the Shanghai Maqiao AI Innovation Pilot Area (上海马桥人工智能创新试验区) and other AI-related industrial clusters in Yangpu, Changning, Jing'an, Songjiang, Baoshan, Qingpu and other districts of Shanghai.

36 Shanghai Municipal Government, 2017. Section 2, Expand the application scenarios of AI integration (拓展人工智能融合应用场景), preamble. In original: "加快人工智能在经济发展、城市治理和公共服务重点领域的深度应用，提升全员劳动生产率、公共服务能力和市民获得感".

gas, transportation infrastructure, and for monitoring the energy consumptions and safe operations of urban buildings.[37]

2. **Improve the Quality and Efficiency of Public Services**. AI will be leveraged to improve government decision-making and enhance service quality. To support government scientific decision-making (政府科学化决策), Shanghai will deploy AI for public demand forecasting (公共需求预测) and public opinion analysis. To improve the efficiency of government services, the municipality will use AI and service robots in government hotlines, online portals, and administrative service centers. To promote the construction of smart courts, Shanghai will integrate AI technologies in various aspects of the judiciary. To improve educational and cultural services, the municipality will promote intelligent interactive learning, digital cultural performances (数字文化展演), and other AI applications.[38]
3. **Improve Transportation and Shipping Efficiency**. AI will improve the overall management of urban traffic and the efficiency of shipping services in the municipality. To improve the intelligentization of traffic management, Shanghai will deploy AI in urban traffic planning, monitoring traffic flows and driving behavior, promoting driverless car applications and other smart applications. To improve efficiency of shipping and port operations, the municipality will promote the intelligentization of port supervision and

[37] Ibid., Section 2, par. 2.3, "Strengthen intelligent perception and optimize comprehensive city operations" (强化智能感知优化城市综合运行). In original: "完善智能感知和数据采集机制, 提高城市安防、环境、基础设施等管理能力。推动图像识别、生物特征识别等技术在社会综合治理、大人流监测预警等领域深度应用, 增强城市智能防控能力。推动动态感知网络在公共安全监控、自然灾害预测、环境监测、河道监管、食品安全追溯等领域的应用, 提高城市综合环境智能化管理水平。推动物联传感、智能预测在电力、给排水、燃气等管网, 建筑能耗监控和安全运行监测, 交通基础设施运行维护等领域的应用, 保障城市基础设施智能有序运行".

[38] Ibid., Section 2, par. 2.4 "Strengthen decision-making assistance to improve the quality and efficiency of public services" (强化决策辅助促进公共服务提质增效). In original: 建设人工智能为辅助的公共服务支持平台, 改善政府决策与服务质量。推动多维度数据分析、感情识别等在公共需求预测、社会舆情分析中的应用, 支撑政府科学化决策。推动自然语言处理、服务机器人在政府热线、门户网站、服务窗口的应用, 提升政府公共服务效能。推动司法业务智能化记录、核查、评价, 推动执法管理智能化联动, 促进智慧法庭建设。推动智能交互学习、数字文化展演等应用, 提高教育文化服务体验感.

logistics and will use AI for the analysis of shipping supervision, transaction arbitration, and other data.[39]

4. **Promote the Accuracy and Inclusiveness of Medicine and Healthcare**. Shanghai will integrate AI technologies in various aspects of medicine and healthcare. The city will use AI to improve diagnosis and treatment assistance, health management, elderly care and other services. AI, intelligent medical robots and equipment will also be used to improve the accuracy of medical services. To enhance the universality of public health (公共卫生普惠性), Shanghai will leverage Big Data mining and analysis for epidemic prevention and control, health monitoring, disease screening and other applications. To improve elderly care services, Shanghai will promote the widespread application of intelligent nursing robots (智能陪护机器人) and intelligent health equipment.[40]

The *Opinions* set the goals for the use of AI in the public sector in Shanghai. They call for accelerating the implementation of AI in urban governance and public services in order to improve public service capabilities and citizens' sense of gain. Consistently with these goals, the *Opinions* outline four main tasks that call for the integration of AI in city operations (security, environment, basic infrastructures), public services (administrative services, judiciary, education, culture), transportation (urban traffic, maritime logistics) and public health (treatment assistance, elderly care, disease prevention and control). If carried out, these tasks will lead to the deep and extensive integration of AI in urban governance and public services that is instrumental in achieving the goals for AI in the public

[39] Ibid., Section 2, par. 2.5 "Focus on intelligent recognition to improve transportation and shipping efficiency" (聚焦智能识别提升交通航运效率). In original: 利用图像识别和机器学习技术, 提升城市交通综合管理和航运服务效率。推动实时数据分析、计算机视觉等在城市交通规划、路网客流监控疏导、驾驶行为监测等领域应用, 发展智能化停车场, 探索建设无人驾驶汽车应用、城市交通非现场执法等场景, 提升交通智能化组织和管理能力。加强航运监管、交易仲裁等数据动态分析, 推动口岸监管、海事管理、港口物流等业务流程智能化, 发展智能化海空枢纽港, 提升港口运行效率和监管水平.

[40] Ibid., Section 2, par. 2.6 "Focus on cognitive computing to promote the accuracy and inclusiveness of medicine and healthcare" (聚焦认知计算推进医疗健康精准普惠). In original: 利用认知计算和深度学习技术, 提升诊疗辅助、健康管理和养老照护等服务能力。加强自主智能医疗机器人和医疗设备等在辅助病症诊断、影像分析、手术诊疗、精准医疗中的推广应用, 促进医疗服务精准化。基于大数据挖掘和分析, 加强流行病预测与防控、体质监测、慢病管理和疾病筛查, 增强公共卫生普惠性。推动智能陪护机器人、智能健康设备等广泛应用, 提升养老服务感受度.

sector set by the municipality, indicating Shanghai's analytical capacity to implement AI in this area. In terms of political capacity, the goals of the *Opinions* are almost identical to those of the AIDP ("improve the level of precision in public services, comprehensively enhancing the people's quality of life"). Moreover, virtually all the tasks indicated by the *Opinions* correspond to the AIDP's tasks for using AI for social construction (section 3, focus task 3). For instance: AI for public security (*Opinions*' "Optimize city operations", AIDP 3.3); AI in the judiciary (*Opinions*' "Improve the quality and efficiency of public services", AIDP 3.2); AI in education (*Opinions*' "Improve the quality and efficiency of public services", AIDP 3.1); or AI in medicine (*Opinions*' "Promote the accuracy and inclusiveness of medicine and healthcare", AIDP 3.1). Under a bureaucratic system that is structured to transmit top-down directives (Chapter 2.2.3), this alignment of goals and tasks between the *Opinions* and the AIDP indicates that the municipal blueprint to foster AI in the public sector enjoys the political support from the national government. This means that Shanghai has the political endorsement and legitimacy needed to implement public sector AI applications. Looking within Shanghai, the goals of improving public service provision and citizens' sense of gains by means of AI are positioned among the policy priorities set forth by the *Opinions*, and they are a key component of the "smart Shanghai" (AI@SH) action. This indicates that promoting the use of AI in the public sector is high on the agenda of the Shanghai leadership. If using AI to improve public service provision and citizens' sense of gain is a political priority, public sector AI applications aimed at achieving these goals are expected to enjoy political support from the Shanghai government. Moreover, the *Opinions* also state that the municipality will "push forward government departments at all levels to take the lead in using artificial intelligence to improve operational efficiency and management service levels",[41] reiterating the political determination of the Shanghai government to promote public sector AI applications.

A further indicator of Shanghai's political capacity to obtain and create support for public sector AI applications is the mobilization of three key municipal agencies, which have sprung into action following the publication of the *Opinions*, and since then have been actively involved in

41 Ibid., Section 5, par. 5.2 "Increase government guidance and support" (加大政府引导支持力度). In original: "推动各级政府部门率先运用人工智能提升业务效率和管理服务水平, 依托政务云引入和开发人工智能应用模块".

Table 3.2 Main contents of the Implementation Opinions on Promoting the Development of a New Generation Artificial Intelligence in Shanghai (October 2017)

Section 1, Clarify the overall requirements (明确总体要求)	1.1. Guiding ideology: give full play to Shanghai's advantages in rich data resources, wide application areas, and complete range of industries, fully implement the 'Smart Shanghai (AI@SH)' action, and form a new generation of artificial intelligence development system driven by application, technology leadership, industry collaboration, ecological cultivation, and talent gathering 1.2. Development goals: By 2020, the efficiency of artificial intelligence in driving Shanghai's innovation-driven development, economic transformation and upgrading, and refined social governance will be significantly improved. Shanghai will become a national AI development highland, China's leading artificial intelligence innovation source, demonstration site for AI applications, and industrial cluster and a talent highland, reaching global advanced level in some areas – *Application*: form an in-depth application pattern of artificial intelligence that is compatible with the operation of super large cities – *Innovation*: form artificial intelligence technology innovation capabilities that reaches the international mainstream level – *Superior industry*: form an internationally competitive artificial intelligence key industry cluster – *Harmonious ecosystem*: form an innovative, active, open and collaborative artificial intelligence integrated ecosystem
Section 2, APPLICATIONS: Expand the application scenarios of AI integration (拓展人工智能融合应用场景)	2.1. Strengthen human–machine collaboration to promote the transformation and upgrading of the ***manufacturing industry***: leverage AI to improve the level of intelligent manufacturing. Promote the application of intelligent equipment such as intelligent robots, promote the construction of 'unmanned factories' (无人工厂), accelerate the application of technologies like Big Data and machine learning in supply chain management 2.2. Strengthen data analysis to drive ***financial and business innovation***: deploy Big Data analysis to improve financial supervision, risk prevention and service innovation capabilities. Expand collection and use of Big Data in business to improve intelligent analysis, the efficiency of cross-border trade, and promote precision marketing and other business services 2.3. Strengthen intelligent perception and optimize comprehensive ***city operations***: AI will be integrated in urban security, environment, and infrastructure 2.4. Strengthen decision-making assistance to improve the quality and efficiency of ***public services***: AI will be leveraged to improve government decision-making and service quality 2.5. Focus on intelligent recognition to improve ***transportation and shipping efficiency***: AI will improve the overall management of urban traffic and the efficiency of shipping services in the municipality 2.6. Focus on cognitive computing to promote the accuracy and inclusiveness of ***medicine and healthcare***: Shanghai will integrate AI technologies in various aspects of medicine and healthcare

Section 3, INNOVATION: Strengthen the forward-looking layout of AI research **(加强人工智能科研前瞻布局)**	3.1. Strengthen research in frontier areas: enhance the basic capabilities of scientific and technological innovation. Promote breakthroughs in the theory of brain intelligence, strengthen research on human–computer hybrid enhanced intelligence. Establish a new intelligent algorithm library, carry out parallel distributed intelligent computing paradigm research, and construct neuromorphic simulation and self-learning intelligent computing models 3.2. Strengthen research in key common technology: promote advances in intelligent perception technology (智能感知技术), cognitive technology (认知技术) and computing processing technology (计算处理技术), including chips. Strengthen the research on intelligent execution technology, focusing on autonomous unmanned systems 3.3. Promote the construction of functional platforms: such platforms include basic innovation (基础创新平台), general innovation (通用创新平台) and application innovation platforms (应用创新平台). The basic innovation platform is focused on the construction of the Shanghai brain-inspired intelligent scientific research base (上海类脑智能科学研究基地). The general innovation platform is centered upon brain-like chips and intelligent systems on a chip. The application innovation platforms target applications in key areas such as smart manufacturing, smart cars, smart medicine, robotics, Beidou navigation [China's satellite system], industrial Internet of Things, and industrial control security
Section 4, SUPERIOR INDUSTRY: Promote the clustering and development of the AI industry **(推动人工智能产业集聚发展)**	4.1. Smart driving industry: Shanghai will promote the industrialization of intelligent driving tools and advances in the intelligent networked automobile industry (智能网联汽车产业), including the development of a National Intelligent Networked Automobile Industry Measurement and Test Center (国家智能网联汽车产业计量测试中心). The city will also promote unmanned urban rail transit system and related industries. By 2020, the scale of the smart driving industry will reach 30 billion yuan 4.2. Smart robot industry: the municipality will promote the use of industrial robots, and the industrialization of intelligent service robots for specific applications such as education and entertainment, medical rehabilitation, elderly care and security rescue. By 2020, the scale of the intelligent robot industry will reach 20 billion yuan 4.3. Smart hardware industry: Shanghai will promote the development of the smart hardware industry, including smart home products, smart surveillance cameras and security products; intelligent medical devices, intelligent unmanned systems and other products [that largely overlap with the AIDP]. By 2020, the scale of the smart hardware industry will reach 20 billion yuan 4.4. AI software industry: the municipality will support software solutions for the development of artificial intelligence, and promote the coordinated development of software and hardware. By 2020, the scale of the intelligent software industry will reach 20 billion yuan 4.5. AI chip industry: Shanghai will foster the R&D and production of central processing units (CPU), graphic processing units (GPU), field programmable gate arrays (FPGA), neural network processing units (NPU) and other chips for AI applications. By 2020, the scale of the smart chip industry will reach 20 billion yuan 4.6. Smart sensor industry: Shanghai will promote smart industrial sensors (e.g., for intelligent manufacturing and unmanned systems), and smart consumer electronics sensors. By 2020, high-end smart sensors used in industrial and consumer electronics will achieve breakthroughs in industrialization and fill the gaps in the country Note: the target set by the *Opinions* for the Shanghai AI industry is to reach a scale of 110 billion RMB by 2020. As discussed earlier, local authorities tend to set overambitious targets in order to signal compliance with central government policies. Shanghai AI industry's targets alone account for nearly 3/4 of the AIDP's target of 150 billion RMB by 2020

(continued)

Table 3.2 (continued)

Section 5, HARMONIOUS ECOSYSTEM: Build a diversified AI innovation ecosystem (营造人工智能多元创新生态)	5.1. Accelerate the sharing and opening of data resources: Shanghai will take the lead in advancing the orderly opening of government data resources, focusing on key areas such as education, transportation, environment, medical care and commerce, improve the open policy for sharing government data resources. The municipality will encourage and guide public service organizations (公共服务机构) to open data in the fields of meteorology, electricity, gas and communications. Shanghai will build a Shanghai Big Data Application Innovation Center (上海大数据应用创新中心) to promote the sharing and exchange of social data resources 5.2. Increase government guidance and support: the municipality will provide special support to create a supportive market and policy environment for AI development. Shanghai will encourage all levels of government departments to use AI to improve business efficiency and management service levels, improve the government's special support policies for AI development, and will use government investment funds to foster the local AI industry 5.3. Establish an AI talents' highland: attract a large number of Chinese and foreign top AI talents, and formulate special policies and open green channels for attracting them to the municipality. Introduce AI majors in selected universities, and support the cooperation between academia, research institutes, industry alliances and key enterprises in the construction of AI talent bases for key industry applications. Create the Shanghai AI Strategic Expert Advisory Group (上海人工智能战略专家咨询组) to carry out research on strategic issues and major decision-making consultations [the group was created in with the name of Shanghai Artificial Intelligence Strategic Advisory Expert Committee, 上海市人工智能战略咨询专家委员会] 5.4. Stimulate the innovation vitality of the market: help AI enterprises to become bigger and stronger (做大做强), promote the establishment of regional headquarters, innovation centers, incubators and "double innovation" platforms by leading global AI companies. Reduce the costs for AI enterprises and provide specialized public services to support innovation and entrepreneurship (e.g., the public supply of supercomputing and intelligent cloud services). Form an artificial intelligence innovation alliance [the Shanghai Artificial Intelligence Industry Association, 上海市人工智能行业协会was created in July 2019]. Hold global artificial intelligence high-end conferences [i.e., the World Artificial Intelligence Conference, held in Shanghai since 2018] 5.5. Strengthen the planning of industrial space layout: optimize the industrial layout for AI development, build a national AI industry cluster, create an AI research highland and industrialization core base (打造人工智能科研高地和产业化核心基地) 5.6. Improve basic service support system: increase the supply of basic services to support the development of artificial intelligence, including the creation of technical standards, the protection of intellectual property rights for new AI technologies, the establishment of high-performance computing facilities and the acceleration of the construction of network infrastructure such as next-generation mobile communications and IoT technologies

promoting initiatives to roll out this programmatic document (Box 3.2). In less than two years, these municipal agencies published two actionable documents aimed at supporting AI development in the municipality. These policy documents display a primary focus on AI usages in the industry and the economy, consistently with *Opinions*' call for in-depth AI applications in the economy and the development of the local AI industry. In December 2017, the Shanghai Municipal Commission of Economy and Informatization (SHEITC) and the Shanghai Municipal Finance Bureau jointly published the *Detailed Rules for Supporting the Implementation of Shanghai Special Projects for AI Innovation and Development*[42] (hereinafter: the *Rules*). This document aims to promote the development of the city's AI industry and accelerate the application of AI products. The main provision of the *Rules* is the creation of "special support funds" (专项支持资金) for AI development, valid until 31 December 2021. These special funds, which were mentioned in the *Opinions*, are dedicated to "expanding integrated applications" (e.g., remote inspection, predictive maintenance, logistics) and "developing core industries" (e.g., smart vehicles, smart robots, smart security, chips for deep learning and industrial applications).

In September 2018, SHEITC and four other government agencies published the *Implementation Measures for Accelerating the High-Quality Development of Artificial Intelligence in Shanghai*[43] (hereinafter: the *Measures*). The *Measures* aim to boost the development of Shanghai as a global AI hub by leveraging AI talent, open data, industrial innovation and agglomeration and government guidance and financial support.[44]

[42] SHEITC, Shanghai Financial Affairs Bureau, 2017. *Shanghai Artificial Intelligence Innovation and Development Special Support Implementation Detailed Rules* [上海市人工智能创新发展专项支持实施细则]. Hujingxinfa (2017) 896, 12 December, http://app.sheitc.sh.gov.cn/zxzjzcwj/685847.htm.

[43] Shanghai Municipal Commission of Economy and Informatization, Shanghai Development and Reform Commission, Shanghai Science and Technology Commission, Shanghai Human Resources and Social Security Bureau, 2018. *Implementation measures for accelerating the high-quality development of Artificial Intelligence in Shanghai* [加快推进上海人工智能高质量发展的实施办法]. Hujingxinji (2018) 569, 17 September, http://app.sheitc.sh.gov.cn/sswgh/679122.htm.

[44] Ibid., Section 1 "Speed up the construction of an AI talent team" (加快人工智能人才队伍建设); Section 2 "Deepen the openness and application of data resources" (深化数据资源开放和应用); Section 3 "Deepen collaborative innovation in the AI industry" (深化人工智能产业协同创新); Section 4 "Promote industrial layout and agglomeration"

The *Measures* consist of a list of 22 tasks to be implemented by the municipal authorities by the end of 2020. Like the *Opinions* and the *Rules*, the *Measures* have a strong focus on applications: Shanghai will establish "AI application demonstration projects", "towns with AI characteristics", and "demonstration parks with AI characteristics" to support the application of technologies and products by local AI companies and promote industrial agglomeration in Shanghai.[45] The *Measures* also encourage AI firms to participate in the *Opinions*' "Smart Shanghai" action[46] and pledge various forms of financial support for spurring AI applications: they state that Shanghai will use the special support funds for AI companies introduced by the *Rules* to contribute to investments in AI and announce the establishment of a government guidance fund of the scale of a 100 billion RMB.[47]

The *Rules* and the *Measures* do not contain explicit reference to public sector AI applications. Nonetheless, they are important because they demonstrate that the *Opinions* have immediately had actionable follow-ups. This steadfast mobilization of top bureaucratic actors provides further indications that AI development is a political priority of the Shanghai municipal government, which has set specific tasks and timelines (i.e., 2021 for the *Rules* and 2020 for the *Measures*) for promoting AI applications in Shanghai.

(推动产业布局和集聚); and Section 5 "Increase government guidance, investment and financing support" (加大政府引导和投融资支持力度).

[45] Ibid., measure no. 8. In original: "支持本土人工智能企业新技术、新产品、新模式的应用推广, 形成60个左右人工智能深度应用场景, 建设100个以上人工智能应用示范项目"; and Section 4 "Promote industrial layout and agglomeration", measure no. 15. In original: "推动本市相关集聚区政策覆盖人工智能领域, 打造华泾北杨等3–4个人工智能特色小镇, 建设5个人工智能特色示范园区". The 60 'AI in-depth application scenarios' and 100 'AI application demonstration projects repeat the wording of the Opinions.

[46] Ibid., Section 2 "Deepen the openness and application of data resources", measure no. 9. In original: 支持人工智能企业参与 '智能上海' 行动建设".

[47] Ibid., Section 3 "Deepen collaborative innovation in the artificial intelligence industry", measure no. 11, in original: "按照本市人工智能创新发展专项支持实施细则 [*the Rules, NdT*], 给予总投资最高30%, 总额最高2000万元的支持"; Section 5 "Increase government guidance and investment and financing support", measure no. 20, in original: "发挥政府投资基金撬动作用, 引导社会资本设立千亿规模人工智能产业发展基金".

Box 3.2 Main government agencies of Shanghai's AI policy

The *Opinions*, in their section 5.6, list the main bureaucratic players involved in the making of AI policy in Shanghai. These include two municipal agencies and the local office of the National Development and Reform Commission.

Shanghai Municipal Commission of Economy and Informatization (SHEITC)

The Municipal Commission of Economy and Informatization (上海市经济和信息化委员会) promotes the integration of informatization and industrialization in Shanghai, supporting the use of advanced technologies in industry to foster industrial upgrading. It implements the industrial and informatization aspects of national and municipal projects in science and technology, and promotes the cooperation between industry, university and research institutions in order to foster the industrialization of scientific research achievements.

SHEITC has been tasked with coordinating the implementation of several AI projects and operational policies in Shanghai. Following the publication of the *Opinions*, the Commission issued two documents (the *Rules* and the *Measures* described above) that contain operative measures for supporting the development of the AI industry in Shanghai. Since December 2018, the Commission oversees the implementation of the Shanghai municipal AI pilot application scenarios, a major effort to spur AI applications in the municipality, with a focus on public sector implementations (see infra and Chapter 5.3). In September 2019, the Commission published the *Action Plan on Building Shanghai into an AI Highland and Creating First-Class Innovation Ecosystem (2019–2021)*, a main policy document for the promotion of AI in the municipality.

SHEITC is also responsible for the supervision of the Shanghai (Pudong New Area) Artificial Intelligence Innovation Application Pilot Zone (上海 (浦东新区) 人工智能创新应用先导区), launched in May 2019 under the supervision of the MIIT, the ministerial counterpart of the Commission. The pilot zone focuses on various legal, policy, and operational issues related to the promotion of AI applications, and on enhancing the international competitiveness of China's and Shanghai's smart industry, among others (Chapter 4.2).

In addition, SHEITC established an Artificial Intelligence Development Office (人工智能发展处) that formulates and organizes the implementation of AI development plans and policies, promotes the development and application of major AI projects, and organizes international exchanges and cooperation in the field of AI. The Commission also coordinates the activities of the Shanghai Artificial Intelligence Strategy Advisory Expert Committee (上海市人工智能战略咨询专家委员会), an advisory body of AI experts that reports to the municipal leadership on strategic issues related to AI development. The Commission also supervises the activities of the Shanghai Artificial Intelligence Association (上海人工智能行业协会; the official English name does not include "industry", 行业), the Shanghai branch of China's Artificial Intelligence Industry Alliance (Chapter 2.2.3).

Shanghai Municipal Science and Technology Commission (STCSM)
The Science and Technology Commission of Shanghai (上海市科学技术委员会) is the municipal agency in charge of scientific and technological affairs and innovation development. It is mainly responsible for the compilation and implementation of science and technology development plans, and for the formulation, implementation and evaluation of policies and measures to support the development of scientific and technological innovation in Shanghai.

The STCSM drafted the 2018 *Measures* together with the SHEITC and the Shanghai Development and Reform Commission. In addition, the STCSM is responsible for the management of the Shanghai National New Generation Artificial Intelligence Innovation Development Trial Zone (上海国家新一代人工智能创新发展试验区), launched in May 2019 under the supervision of the MOST, the ministerial counterpart of STCSM (Chapter 4.2). This trial zone focuses on the application of AI in healthcare, smart transportation, and smart neighborhoods, aiming to make Shanghai a leading national and global testing area for AI applications that can be replicated in other Chinese cities. The STCSM also coordinates various scientific research projects in the field of AI.

Shanghai Municipal Development and Reform Commission (Shanghai DRC)
The Shanghai Municipal Development and Reform Commission (上海市发展和改革委员会) is the municipal branch of the National Development and Reform Commission. It drafted the 2018 *Measures* with the SHEITC and STCSM. Similar to its ministerial counterpart, the Shanghai DRC focuses on economic and industrial development policy, including key high-tech sectors such as AI. It has broad discretionary spending authority and budgetary resources to support the development of the AI industry as well as other projects that promote AI development.

3.2.2 *Action Plan for Building Shanghai into an AI Highland (2019–2021)*

In September 2019, SHEITC published a comprehensive document for the promotion of AI in the municipality, the *Action Plan for Building Shanghai into an AI Highland and Creating a First-Class Innovation Ecosystem (2019–2021).*[48] Like the *Opinions*, the *AI Highland Plan* sets the promotion of AI ecosystem, applications, innovation and industry as its main "action goals" (行动目标):

> By 2021, fully launch the iconic brand of Shanghai artificial intelligence 'first-class *innovation ecosystem*'. Stimulate the innovation vitality of all parties [...] and deploy ten world-leading innovative *application scenarios*. Strengthen the original *innovation power*, promote the opening of five hub innovation platforms, and cultivate a group of top international innovation teams. [B]uild ten leading *innovative enterprises*, one hundred innovative benchmarking enterprises, and form *core industries* with an output value on the scale of 100 billion.[49] (emphasis added)

To achieve these goals, the *AI Highland Plan* sets forth 18 tasks and seven "special actions". The plan organizes these tasks into five groups: (i) "build integrated innovation carriers" is about developing the AI industry, products and industry clusters (tasks 1–3, special action 1); (ii) "create common innovation platforms" focuses on innovation in AI research and technology (tasks 4–8, special action 2–3); (iii) "gather world-class innovation teams" calls for gathering and nurturing AI talents as a core component of Shanghai's AI ecosystem (tasks 9–11, special action 4); (iv) "create world-class application scenarios" focuses on expanding AI applications in various sectors (tasks 12–14, special action 5); and (v) "institutional settings" (tasks 15–18, special actions 6–7) requires to optimize the municipal AI ecosystem by providing various forms of financial and policy support, and creating a regulatory and governance framework for AI (Table 3.3). To facilitate the analysis, these tasks are grouped

[48] SHEITC, 2019 (cit.).

[49] Ibid., Section 2 Action goals (行动目标). In original: "到2021年, 全力打响上海人工智能 "一流创新生态" 标志性品牌. 激发各方创新活力 [...] 部署十大全球领先创新应用场景。强化原始创新动力, 推进开放五大枢纽创新平台, 培育一批国际顶尖创新团队。提升支撑创新能力, 打造十家创新龙头企业, 百家创新标杆企业, 形成重点产业千亿产值规模".

here below according to their relevant "action goal" (i.e., ecosystem, applications, innovation and industry):

- *Application scenarios*: like the *Opinions*, the *AI Highland Plan* outlines the goals for the use of AI in the public sector and the tasks to achieve them as part of the broader goal to promote innovative AI applications in the municipality. The *AI Highland Plan* states that Shanghai "will give full play to the city's advantages in application scenarios, encourage the latest achievements of global artificial intelligence to take the lead in 'testing the water' in Shanghai, focusing on high-quality economic development, high-quality life for the citizens, and efficient urban operations".[50] In doing so, the *AI Highland Plan* reiterates the goals for AI in the public sector set forth by the *Opinions*, namely: improve public service provision and citizens' sense of gain by accelerating the integration of AI in urban governance and public services. The *AI Highland Plan* outlines a number of tasks to achieve high-quality life for the citizens and efficient urban operations by means of AI: it calls for the creation of demonstrative AI projects in public services (公共服务"示范项目", task 14); it encourages government departments at all levels to take the lead in using AI to improve efficiency and service levels, and states that Shanghai will include AI products into the "Shanghai Innovative Product Recommendation Catalogue" (上海市创新产品推荐目录) supporting the government's first purchase of AI technologies[51] (task 13); and it requires to intensify the use of AI in medicine, education, urban management, government services, smart public

[50] Ibid., Section 3, subsection 4, Create world-class application scenarios (深入打造世界级的场景应用). In original: "充分发挥本市应用场景丰富优势, 鼓励全球人工智能最新成果在上海率先 "试水", 聚焦经济高质量发展、市民高品质生活、城市高效率运行, 打造一批面向全球的创新应用".

[51] The Shanghai Innovative Product Recommendation Catalogue is periodically published by SHEITC. The 2021 edition includes products and solutions in integrated circuits, artificial intelligence, biomedicine and medical equipment, digital economy transition (经济数字化转型) environmental protection, software and IT services and high-end equipment. Companies submit their applications, and the products included in the Catalogue are both approved and recommended for purchase by government agencies. It also serves as a basis for granting funds and other forms of public support at the district level. At the time of writing, the latest edition of the Catalogue was published in June 2021. See: http://www.sheitc.sh.gov.cn/jsjb/20210618/b2d7f6a66d5f42c29f224952bcd15ae7.html.

security, transportation, smart courts and garbage sorting (tasks 12 and 14).

- *Innovation*: Shanghai will promote innovation in basic theories, algorithms, computing power, data and application technologies. As anticipated in the *Opinions* (section 3.3), the municipality will create various innovation platforms (i.e., platforms for frontier theoretical research/前沿理论研究平台; open-source platforms/ 开源开放社区平台; innovation platforms for industrial applications/行业应用创新平台; computing service platforms/重大算力服务平台; and data exchange platforms/数据有序开放交换平台). Shanghai will increase support to overcome the algorithmic and technological bottlenecks in areas such as autonomous driving, human–computer interaction, industrial manufacturing, finance, commerce, medical diagnosis, chips, and software frameworks. The city will also create "Big Data joint innovation laboratories" in medicine, transportation, finance, urban management, education and other areas.[52]
- *Industry*: Shanghai will build ten leading innovative enterprises, one hundred innovative benchmarking enterprises, and form core industries with an output value on the scale of 100 billion.[53] The municipality will establish internationally competitive industrial clusters in chips, intelligent connected cars, intelligent robots and intelligent hardware, and support the industry by promoting AI applications in manufacturing, medicine, transportation, finance and other fields.[54]
- *Ecosystem*: Shanghai will "vigorously build an open, inclusive and diversified innovation ecosystem, fully stimulate the innovation vitality of market players, establish an institutional environment

[52] Ibid., Section 3, subsection 2, Create open and cutting-edge common innovation platforms (打造开放前沿共性的创新平台); Special Action 2, Build a hub-style innovation platform (专项行动2: 建设枢纽型创新平台); and Special Action 3, Establish Big Data joint innovation laboratories (专项行动3: 建设大数据联合创新实验室).

[53] Ibid., Section 3, subsection 1, Special Action 6, Establish and operate the city's AI industry investment fund (专项行动6: 建立运作市人工智能产业投资基金): "Incubate and nurture ten leading innovative enterprises, one hundred innovative benchmarking enterprises, and form a scale of 100 billion output value of key industries" (孵化培育十家创新龙头企业, 百家创新标杆企业, 形成重点产业千亿产值规模). These are the same benchmarks listed in Section 2, Action goals.

[54] Ibid., Section 3, subsection 1, Focus on building integrated innovation carriers (着力建设复合融合的创新载体); Special Action 1: Build a 4 + X integrated innovation carriers.

> based on market competition and efficient resource flows, and promote the sustainable and healthy development of AI".[55] This AI ecosystem will rely on a high-quality "investment ecosystem" (投资生态) and on the innovation capacity of AI companies. The municipality will create a "Shanghai model" (上海模式) of AI governance in healthcare, finance, transportation and other areas.[56] Shanghai will also gather "world-class innovation teams" (国际一流的创新团队), attracting a pool of international AI talents, nurture outstanding local young talents, cultivate cross-industry professionals, and build a talent team that meets the needs of industry development.[57]

Two years after the *Opinions*, the *AI Highland Plan* confirms that promoting AI applications is a key objective of the municipal plans for AI development. Among these applications, the *AI Highland Plan* reiterates that the use of AI in the public sector is a priority of the Shanghai government. The goals for the use of AI in the public sector are almost identical between the two municipal AI plans: the *Opinions* call for improving public service capabilities and citizens' sense of gain by accelerating the in-depth application of AI in urban governance and public services; the *AI Highland Plan* calls for using AI to ensure high-quality life for the Shanghai citizens and efficient urban operations. In this regard, the *AI Highland Plan* confirms that improving the outputs and outcomes of public services by means of AI remains high on the agenda of the Shanghai government, thus indicating that public sector AI applications aimed at achieving these goals will enjoy political support. In terms of analytical capacity, the *AI Highland Plan* lays out a concise but well-articulated set of tasks that can contribute to achieving the municipal goals for AI in the public sector. These tasks cover the same policy areas

[55] Ibid., Section 3, Tasks arrangements (任务安排), subsection 5, Accelerate the creation of a vibrant institutional environment (加快创造活力迸发的制度环境). In original: "大力建设开放、包容、多元的创新生态, 充分激发市场主体的创新活力, 建立市场充分竞争、资源高效流动的制度环境, 促进人工智能持续健康发展".

[56] Ibid., Section 3, subsection 5; Special Action 6, Establish and operate the city's AI industry investment fund (专项行动6: 建立运作市人工智能产业投资基金); and Special Action 7, Take the lead in building an institutional system for AI governance (专项行动7: 率先构建人工智能治理的制度体系).

[57] Ibid., Section 3, subsection 3, Vigorously gather a world-class innovation team (大力汇聚国际一流的创新团队); and special action 4, Build a talent team that meets the needs of industrial development (专项行动4: 建设符合产业发展需求的人才队伍).

that were prioritized by the *Opinions*: education, administrative services, smart courts (i.e., the *Opinions*' 'public services'), urban management, public security and garbage classification (i.e., the *Opinions*' 'city operations'), transportation (ibid.) and medicine (i.e., the *Opinions*' 'public health'). The similarities between the *AI Highland Plan* and the *Opinions* highlight Shanghai's consistent ability to devise public sector AI applications that can contribute to achieving municipal goals in this area and the continued political prioritization of such applications, thus corroborating the assumptions that Shanghai has developed solid analytical and political capacities to implement AI in the public sector.

3.2.3 Goals and Actions: Substantiating the AI Plans of Shanghai

Assessing analytical and political capacity based on indicators contained in the Shanghai policy documents suits the characteristics of China's policymaking process, whereby the national government sets the strategic objectives and provide general policy guidelines, while local administrations usually retain autonomy in deciding which policy instruments are most suitable to achieve these goals (Xu 2011; Heilmann 2008). This well-known pattern has not changed in AI policy: the national government provides guidance, but implementation is devolved to local administrations, which are the primary actors in the implementation of China's AI policy (Zeng 2021; Ding 2020; Roberts et al. 2020; Chapter 2.4). In this context, the Shanghai AI plans are an essential source to gather precise and reliable information on the policy goals for AI in the public sector, how Shanghai will pursue them, and the political importance of AI in the public sector for Shanghai policymakers. Hence, policy documents provide a valid starting point to assess analytical and political capacities. Indeed, previous studies demonstrated that AI plans offer a rich source of evidence to understand how governments prepare to use AI to modernize the public sector (Fatima et al. 2020). At the same time, as noted earlier, an assessment based on the contents of the municipal AI plans must consider that in the Chinese political and bureaucratic system there is a tendency to comply with national policy priorities, which may result in erroneous conclusions due to the fact that such AI plans could be only an act of symbolic compliance or political performance (Zeng, 2021; Zhou et al., 2013).

To address the potential analytical distortions introduced by this latent tendency to show compliance to national policy priorities, next paragraphs

Table 3.3 Main contents of the Action Plan for Building Shanghai into an AI Highland and Creating a First-Class Innovation Ecosystem (2019–2021) (September 2019)

Section 1, Guiding ideology (指导思想)	Based on the in-depth study and implementation of General Secretary Xi Jinping's important instructions on the development of a new generation of artificial intelligence and the spirit of his important speech during the inspection of Shanghai, give full play to Shanghai's basic advantages in rich scientific and educational resources, massive data, infrastructure and application scenarios. Focus on the core roles of talents and enterprises as the main resources for innovation
Section 2, Action goals (行动目标)	By 2021, fully launch the iconic brand of Shanghai artificial intelligence 'first-class innovation ecosystem' Stimulate the innovation vitality of all parties, lay out the construction of 4 + X integrated innovation carriers, and deploy ten world-leading innovative application scenarios Strengthen the original innovation power, promote the opening of five hub innovation platforms, and cultivate a group of top international innovation teams Improve the ability to support innovation, build ten leading innovative enterprises, one hundred innovative benchmarking enterprises, and form core industries with an output value on the scale of 100 billion
Section 3, Tasks arrangements (任务安排)	This section outlines the tasks to achieve each of the "action goals" (1) **Build integrated "innovation carriers"** (创新载体) 1. ***Optimize the deployment of innovation basis***: strengthen leadership by demonstration, accelerate the construction of the Shanghai National New Generation Artificial Intelligence Innovation Development Trial Zone (上海国家新一代人工智能创新发展试验区), the Shanghai (Pudong New Area) Artificial Intelligence Innovation Application Pilot Zone (上海 (浦东新区) 人工智能创新应用先导区), be the first to implement and try out, and establish a well-oiled method (机制路径) that can be replicated and promoted. Create key industrial innovation clusters, cultivate and introduce leading companies, and build industrial clusters with international competitiveness 2. ***Develop new innovation space***: encourage large enterprises in Shanghai to take the lead in opening-up resources and exploring innovative cooperation models for AI applications. Provide comprehensive innovation services such as R&D and design, data training, pilot applications, technology and finance, etc. Encourage all districts to build industrial joint innovation bases with industry leaders as the core 3. ***Reduce the innovation costs***: give priority to guaranteeing municipal-level AI innovation platforms and industrial projects. Support the construction of public supporting facilities for innovative services. Coordinate the construction and operation of a new generation of information infrastructure (e.g., 5G, Internet of Things, cloud computing, supercomputing) to support the development of AI enterprises. Support districts to provide enterprises with different forms of innovation funding, encourage qualified districts to actively attract innovative leading enterprises to settle in --- --- --- ***Special Action 1: Build 4 + X integrated innovation carriers***. Promote AI applications in manufacturing, medicine, transportation, finance and other leading fields. Create key industrial clusters in chips, intelligent connected cars, intelligent robots and intelligent hardware. Promote industrial clusters that can leverage the advantages of areas such as Zhangjiang, Lingang New Area, and Jinqiao [all located in the Pudong New Area]. Form an "AI gathering growth space" (人工智能集聚成长空间) that integrates headquarters office, international exchanges, demonstration applications and experiences, and incubation. Based on the characteristics of districts like Yangpu, Jing'an, Putuo, Changning, Baoshan and the corresponding industries, gather and develop intelligent life, Big Data, intelligent robots, autonomous driving and other AI applications

(2) Create open and cutting-edge common innovation platforms

4. *Establish scientific and the theoretical research platforms*: support the construction of AI algorithm research institutes, accelerate research on cutting-edge algorithms and theories (e.g., swarm intelligence, brain theory), encourage enterprises to cooperate with universities and research institutes to establish AI laboratories, and achieve breakthroughs in technical bottlenecks
5. *Create open platforms*: support the establishment of "open-source AI research institutes" (人工智能开源开放研究院), promote the development of open-source AI software frameworks, interconnect with well-known open-source communities at home and abroad, establish the key nodes of an international AI ecosystem
6. *Build industry applications innovation platforms*: support the construction of an innovation center for the AI industry, led by leading companies or research institutions. Build technology supply platforms for AI applications in finance, manufacturing, transportation, medicine and other industries. Provide support for the 'intelligentization' of traditional industries
7. *Establish computing service platforms*: support the construction of the world's leading AI high-performance open computing platform. Serve the common computing power needs of research institutes and small and medium-sized enterprises. Support applications in security, transportation, finance and other industries, and reduce the R&D and use costs of artificial intelligence. Support enterprises to independently build computing power platforms, and encourage chip companies to participate in the construction of computing platforms
8. *Establish an orderly and open data exchange platform*: establish a public data open platform in Shanghai, and vigorously promote the sharing of public data. Promote the integration of multi-source data, provide high-quality, large-capacity resource libraries and training sets for the AI industry in order to support innovative AI applications

--- --- ---

Special Action 2: Build a hub-style innovation platform. Increase support to overcome the algorithm bottlenecks in the application of artificial intelligence in areas such as autonomous driving, human–computer interaction, industrial manufacturing, finance and commerce, and medical diagnosis, as well as key basic technologies such as chips and software frameworks. Promote the cooperation of Fudan University, Jiaotong University, Tongji University and other universities and research institutes with enterprises in order to establish 10 key joint laboratories. Accelerate the intelligent transformation of enterprises. Relying on industry leaders, build 10 municipal-level AI innovation centers to demonstrate and popularize AI applications

Special Action 3: Establish Big Data joint innovation laboratories. Focus on medical, transportation, tourism, energy, finance, urban management, steel, high-end equipment, education and scientific research, social credit services, new retail and other fields, build 15 Big Data joint innovation labs. Provide the AI industry with a training ground characterized by "data resources + industry experts + application scenarios". Give special funds and key support to outstanding projects linked to the Big Data joint innovation labs

(3) Gather world-class innovation teams

9. *Gather international top talents*: establish an international talent pool in AI core algorithms, deep learning, smart chips, human–computer interaction and other core theories and technologies
10. *Introduce outstanding young talents*: focus on cultivating a hundred outstanding young talents. Give full play to Shanghai's various talent policies to attract top-level young overseas talents
11. *Cultivate cross-industry professionals*: promote the construction of application-oriented disciplines in the field of AI. Support the training of technical and high-skilled personnel urgently needed in the field of artificial intelligence. Encourage school-enterprise cooperation. Build a public service platform for artificial intelligence education that focuses on the improvement of practical job capabilities

(continued)

Table 3.3 (continued)

--- --- ---

Special Action 4: Build a talent team that meets the needs of industry development. Focusing on the development needs of the AI industry, intensify the introduction and training of talents, and strive to double the scale of Shanghai's AI talents to 200,000 people in three years. Establish a team of AI talents with international influence in the fields of brain-like intelligence, computer vision, and unmanned systems. Implement support actions for young talents, focusing on outstanding young talents (青年卓越人才, 青年优秀人才). Support the establishment of AI disciplines in universities and build a public service platform for AI education. Develop AI training institutions and continuing education training bases. Support the development of international exchanges and technical cooperation in AI

(4) Create world-class application scenarios

12. *Continue to carry out application scenarios*: intensify the opening of Shanghai's AI application scenarios, establish a "dynamic publishing system" for AI application scenarios in medical care, education, urban management, and manufacturing. Promote the gradual establishment of AI joint application test platforms in various scenarios to provide a real test environment for innovative products and services
13. *Support and encourage innovative products*: guide and encourage all kinds of new artificial intelligence technologies and products to "first show" in Shanghai, and support the establishment of AI products' display and experience centers in landmark areas. Give priority to the inclusion of marketable AI products in the "Shanghai Innovative Product Recommendation Catalogue (上海市创新产品推荐目录), support the government's first purchase and order of AI products, and recommend these products to the units and institutions involved in the application scenarios
14. *Deepen the construction of public service "demonstration projects"* (示范项目): support government departments at all levels to take the lead in using artificial intelligence to improve efficiency and management service levels. Build AI public demonstration projects (人工智能公共示范项目) in government cloud, the Government Online-Offline Shanghai (一网通办), smart public security, smart courts, garbage sorting and other key areas, providing demonstrative applications for companies to expand to domestic and foreign markets

--- --- ---

Special Action 5: Strive to build world-class AI application scenarios. Create 10 "demonstration areas for AI innovative applications" (人工智能创新应用示范区) and form 100 "in-depth application scenarios of artificial intelligence" (人工智能深度应用场景) in 10 categories [not specified in the document]. For major special projects listed in the government-endorsed AI pilots [e.g., the Shanghai Artificial Intelligence Pilot Application Scenarios, 上海市人工智能试点应用场景], 30% of the project investment will be supported up to a maximum amount of 20 million yuan. For innovative products that are included in application scenario solutions, priority is given to being included in the "Shanghai Innovative Product Recommendation Catalogue"

(5) Institutional settings

15. *Accelerate the formation and circulation of "innovative capital"* (创新资本): establish a regular communication mechanism between the government, enterprises, and investment institutions, and give priority to investing in high-quality small and medium-sized AI enterprises in Shanghai to form a high-quality "investment ecosystem" (投资生态). Establish Shanghai's artificial intelligence industry investment fund (人工智能产业投资基金), and encourage State-owned enterprises and industry-leading enterprises to establish sub-funds under the framework of the fund
16. *Enhance the innovation power of market players*: provide various forms of financial and policy support to promote the innovation capacity of companies (e.g., expand the coverage of the "Science and Technology Innovation Coupons"/ 科技创新券and the "Four New Coupons"/ 四新券, provide subsidies for innovation expenditures up to 2 million RMB, lower the rates of corporate income tax for high-tech companies, etc.)

	17. *Promote the circulation of innovative ideas and results*: promote the exchanges of scientific research personnel between enterprises and public institutions. Allow the personnel of scientific research institutions who left to pursue AI entrepreneurship to retain the original position for 3–5 years. Hire corporate scientists as part-time experts in scientific research institutions. Encourage foreign companies to set up R&D centers in Shanghai, and support local companies to set up global R&D centers overseas. Strengthen the protection of intellectual property rights in the field of AI 18. *Promote for rule of law standards* (法治标准): encourage relevant parties to carry out research on information security, privacy protection, ethics, laws and regulations in the field of AI. Carry out pilot trials in healthcare, finance, and transportation. Promote institutional innovations in industry applications and data circulation, and explore the formation of industry rules and standards for AI. Form the "Shanghai model" (上海模式) of AI governance --- --- --- *Special Action 6: establish the AI industry investment fund*. The first phase of the investment fund will have a scale of 10 billion RMB, and it will be expanded to 100 billion RMB through social capital investments and other market mechanisms. The investment fund will focus on AI chips, sensors, AI algorithms, intelligent industries (e.g., intelligent driving, intelligent hardware, intelligent robots, "AI+" vertical applications, Big Data, cloud computing, Internet of Things, etc.). Leverage the investment fund to build ten leading innovative enterprises, 100 innovative benchmarking enterprises, and reach an output of 100 billion RMB for key industries [as stated in the major goals of the plan in Section 2] *Special Action 7: take the lead in building an institutional system for AI governance*. Establish an expert working group to carry out research on AI governance in areas such as information security, privacy protection, intellectual property, Big Data, etc. Combining with the city's AI application scenarios, relying on industry organizations and social institutions to formulate guidelines for AI applications in healthcare, finance, transportation, and other areas. Promote the formation of a number of corporate standards or industry standards. Research and propose general AI governance guidelines
Section 4, Guarantee Measures (保障措施)	Strengthen the communications between the leadership of the Shanghai municipality and key enterprises and expert groups such as the Shanghai AI Industry Leadership Working Group (人工智能产业工作领导小组) or the Shanghai AI Strategic Advisory Expert Committee (人工智能战略咨询专家委员会). Build a municipal high-speed intelligent network. Achieve the "dual gigabit" city-wide coverage for mobile networks and fixed broadband, and take the lead in 5G communications and other technologies that support the construction of an information highway for in-depth and extensive AI applications

provide evidence that corroborate the assessments made about Shanghai's analytical and political capacities. First, they show that two major tasks related to the use of AI in the public sector indicated by the *Opinions* and the *AI Highland Plan* have translated into real-world policy initiatives, namely the Shanghai Data Innovation Center and the "AI pilot application scenarios". These initiatives demonstrate that Shanghai is actually drawing from its analytical and political capacities to promote projects that contribute to the integration of AI in the public sector, consistently with the goals set by the municipality. Second, next paragraphs identify other policy initiatives that show the capacity of Shanghai to leverage AI and other advanced technologies to improve government operations and public service delivery. These digitalization efforts—not formally related to the municipal AI plans—have been promoted by the Shanghai government in recent years, and they are now progressively integrating AI technologies.

The Shanghai Big Data Application Innovation Center, the "AI pilot application scenarios", and other digital innovation efforts offer concrete examples of the ability of Shanghai to design applications that leverage AI to enhance the provision of public services, as required by the municipal AI plans (analytical capacity). Moreover, these projects involve multiple government agencies, private actors, and extend over time (usually four years or longer), showing the ability of Shanghai to create and sustain political support for public sector AI applications that can contribute to achieving related municipal goals (political capacity). As such, these projects confirm the findings on Shanghai's analytical and political capacity that were derived from the content analysis of the municipal plans for AI development.

Shanghai Data Innovation Center

In October 2017, the *Opinions* stated that the municipality would "build the Shanghai Big Data Application Innovation Center (上海大数据应用创新中心) to promote the sharing and exchange of social data resources".[58] In April 2018, the Shanghai Data Innovation Center (SDIC) was jointly established by a coalition of prominent Shanghai companies and public organizations (事业单位), under the guidance

[58] Shanghai Municipal Government, 2017, Section 5, par. 5.1, cit. "Social data" (社会数据) indicates data from non-public institutions, including private and State-owned enterprises.

of the Shanghai Municipal Commission of Economy and Informatization.[59] In September 2018, the SDIC was officially presented to the public.[60] The SDIC is "the first national Big Data professional supporting institution dedicated to serve AI development".[61]

The mission of the SDIC is to "promote the fusion of government and private sector data" (推动政企数据融合). It also supports R&D in algorithms used for Big Data analysis, carries out research on standardization, nurtures professional talents, and works as an incubator for industrial applications.[62] The sharing of public data—both between public organizations and between the public and the private or non-profit sectors—is considered a major driver of innovation in the public sector, and an effective way to foster the promotion of AI technologies and applications. Contemporary AI systems are often based on machine learning models that require vast amounts of data to fine-tune their functions, and the public sector is one of the most data-intensive sectors. Hence, government data sharing becomes a critical asset for the development of AI solutions that can be used to enhance the delivery of public services and improve outcomes for citizens. In addition, by modernizing its data governance policies and practices in a way that facilitates interoperability

[59] The literal English translation would be "Shanghai Big Data Application and Innovation Center" (上海大数据应用创新中心). However, the official English translation adopted by the SDIC itself is shortened in Shanghai Data Innovation Center.

[60] CRI Online, 2018. Shanghai Data Innovation Center unveiled in Jing'an [上海大数据应用创新中心静安揭牌成立]. *CRI Online*, 19 September, http://sh.cri.cn/20180918/1ff84a4f-211c-cfec-31d5-5193586287e1.html.

[61] Tencent Open Content Platform, 2018. Focus on the World Artificial Intelligence Conference—Shanghai Data Innovation Center established [聚焦世界人工智能大会|上海大数据应用创新中心成立]. *Tencent Open Content Platform*, 19 September, https://page.om.qq.com/page/OZF64I_tq2dgA7yqb1w8EDsw0. In original: 国内首家服务人工智能发展的大数据专业支撑机构.

[62] SDIC, 2019. Shanghai Data Innovation Center (SDIC) Presentation [上海大数据应用创新中心 (SDIC) 介绍]. SDIC WeChat official account, 23 April, https://mp.weixin.qq.com/s?__biz=MzU5ODc5MjUyNQ==&mid=100000094&idx=1&sn=0584fc8888aae5b98d4d4951b2305ad1&chksm=7ebf817c49c8086a8ca8b8ad08eaddc53c53d84e125dcbb2e3db29fb7ee8c168d19fb45bbc42&mpshare=1&scene=1&srcid=1015qFDq1XFVDAjBXzjTROlO&sharer_sharetime=1634306389311&sharer_shareid=0eff9b0dfc3ad5b6a3f1957365a92ab7&exportkey=AUDja%2BbUYETumQuP1fTY5j8%3D&pass_ticket=UES%2BBZ70BF7nicqvuWk7d%2BW1bMLizBgV7hYARpL9DQbi8LxLJQg7avww0QV%2BXOmG&wx_header=0#rd.

and connectivity of data repositories, the public sector can take advantage of data-intensive AI applications (Desouza 2018).

The SDIC is a core component of Shanghai's strategy to promote public data sharing and AI applications in areas such as public services, smart transportation, environmental protection, medicine and healthcare, as well as to expand the commercial and industrial use of data advocated by the Shanghai municipal AI plans. In July 2018, two months before its official unveiling, the SDIC was included in the list of the Shanghai Big Data Joint Innovation Labs (上海市大数据联合创新实验室), a key component of the municipality's efforts to foster the sharing and utilization of public data (see further discussions in Chapter 4.1). Under this framework, the SDIC has been tasked with focusing on urban management,[63] one of the priority areas for the use of AI in the public sector indicated by Shanghai AI plans, confirming the importance of SDIC in promoting public sector AI applications and in the data-sharing regime established by the municipality.

The SDIC is a public service platform (公共服务平台) that relies upon the cooperation between various public and private actors, including: local universities and research institutes (Shanghai Jiaotong University, Fudan University, Shanghai University, the Shanghai Polytechnic University, the Shanghai Industrial Technology Research Institute, etc.); public institutions (the Third Bureau of the Public Security Department, various district governments); and a number of private and State-owned companies (Shanghai Information Investment Company, Shibei Hi-Tech Park Company, Shanghai Data Exchange Center, Huawei, Trip.com, SIPG, Wanda Information Technologies, Transwarp Technologies, Zamplas Technologies, etc.), among others.[64] In this perspective, the SDIC also offers a concrete example of the industry engagement approach that Shanghai is pursuing to develop the municipal AI ecosystem (Chapters 4.4, 5.2, 5.3 and 6).

[63] Sohu.com, 2018. Shanghai Big Data Joint Innovation Laboratory—Officially Established in the Field of Urban Management [上海市大数据联合创新实验室—城市管理领域正式授牌成立]. *Sohu* [搜狐], 18 July, https://www.sohu.com/a/241925372_622773. More information on the members of the SDIC can be found in articles released before the official launch of the SDIC. See for instance: https://dzb.sjtu.edu.cn/Data/View/2201.

[64] Sohu.com, 2018 (cit.).

The AI Pilot Application Scenarios

In October 2017, the *Opinions* stated that Shanghai would create 60 "AI in-depth application scenarios" (人工智能深度应用场景) and more than 100 "AI application demonstration projects" (人工智能应用示范项目). In September 2019, the *AI Highland Plan* reiterated this commitment by stating that Shanghai will build 100 "AI in-depth application scenarios of artificial intelligence" (人工智能深度应用场景) in 10 categories (not specified in the document), and 10 "demonstration areas for AI innovative applications" (人工智能创新应用示范区).

In between the two policy documents, action already started. In December 2018, the Shanghai government initiated a concerted effort to spur AI applications in the municipality that by December 2020 led to the approval of 40 government-endorsed "AI pilot application scenarios" (人工智能试点应用场景). Examined in detail in Chapter 5.3, these AI pilots[65] pair public entities (schools, hospitals, museums, government service centers, utility providers, industrial parks) with private companies that provide the AI technologies used in the pilot applications. Through the SHEITC, public entities publish a description of the "application scenario" they want to apply AI to, and companies apply to supply the AI technologies for the desired applications. The projects are subject to the review and evaluation by the relevant municipal authorities, eligible projects receive government funds, and the most valuable application scenarios are awarded the title of "municipal-level AI demonstration application scenarios" (市级人工智能示范应用场景).

The AI pilot application scenarios have a prevalent focus on public sector implementations. In December 2020, nearly two thirds of the total AI pilots projects (i.e., 25 out of 40) were designed to use AI to optimize the operations of public organizations and the provision of public goods and services. Moreover, all four "municipal-level AI demonstration application scenarios" selected as best practices of AI applications in the municipality—announced in December 2020 after the completion of the 12-month trial period of the first batch of AI pilots (April 2019)—consist

[65] The term试点 literally means "experimental point". It is translated here as "pilot project" consistently with the analysis made by Heilmann et al. (2013, p. 5), who observe that pilot projects (shidian 试点) deal with a single policy domain in important ways, and differ from experimental zones (shiyanqu 试验区) where an entire jurisdiction is authorized by the central government to conduct reorganization measures and promotional programs that may cut across diverse policy domains. This is confirmed by the analysis of Shanghai's AI experimental zones (Chapter 4.2).

of public sector AI implementations in education, healthcare, community management and urban management.[66]

Digital Initiatives for Public Sector Innovation

In addition to the Shanghai Data Innovation Center and the "AI pilot application scenarios", in recent years Shanghai has been promoting other policy initiatives—not formally related to the municipal AI plans—that aim to spur digital innovation in the public sector. These initiatives have been progressively integrating AI technologies in their activities. Like the goals set by the municipal AI plans, these initiatives aim to leverage digital technologies to improve government operations and public service delivery in urban management, public services, and public health. They mostly started before the introduction of the *Opinions* and the *AI Highland Plan*, and since then they have been a consistent policy priority of the Shanghai government. For instance:

- in urban management, Shanghai has been promoting various smart city initiatives since as early as 2010.[67] The smart city plan published in 2020 states that by 2022 Shanghai will be a global leading smart city, which makes extensive use of the Internet, Big Data, artificial intelligence and other information technologies to promote urban governance and "improve the level of scientification, precision and intelligentization of urban management[68]";

[66] SHEITC Notice, 2020c. *Notice of the Shanghai Municipal Commission of Economy and Informatization on the announcement of the city's first batch of AI demonstration application scenarios* [上海市经济信息化委关于公布本市首批人工智能示范应用场景的通知]. Hujingxintui (2020) 1085, 14 December, http://www.sheitc.sh.gov.cn/xxfw/20201216/259fd0aedd5049c29c73631164654014.html.

[67] The 2016 municipal government plan on smart cities write: "Since 2010, Shanghai has been comprehensively promoting the construction of the future smart city, and the level of urban digitalization, network connection and intelligence have been clearly enhanced" [2010年以来，本市全面推进面向未来的智慧城市建设，城市数字化、网络化、智能化水平显著提升]. Shanghai Municipal Government, 2016. *Thirteen Five-Year Plan for Promoting the Construction of a Smart City in Shanghai* [上海市推进智慧城市建设"十三五"规划], Hufufa [2016] 80, 19 September, https://www.shanghai.gov.cn/nw12344/20200814/0001-12344_50147.html.

[68] Shanghai Municipal Government, 2020a. *Several Opinions on Further Accelerating the Construction of a Smart City* [关于进一步加快智慧城市建设的若干意见], 10 February, https://www.shanghai.gov.cn/nw44142/20200824/0001-44142_63566.html. In original: "到2022年，将上海建设成为全球新型智慧城市的排头兵，[...] 更多运用互

– in public services, since 2017 the municipality has been implementing the Government Online-Offline Shanghai (一网通办), which is later mentioned also by the *AI Highland Plan* (task 14). This is an e-government platform that leverages Big Data and AI to provide Chinese and foreign individuals and enterprises with paperless and "user-centric, personalized, precise, autonomous and smart services".[69] Together with its mobile version called the "Suishenban" (随申办),[70] the Government Online-Offline Shanghai is the center of an expanding network of applications that leverage AI and other advanced technologies to support the provision of administrative services.[71] The importance of this digital platform for the integration of AI in the public sector in Shanghai is examined in detail in Chapter 5.2.1;
– in public health, since 2014 Shanghai has been promoting the integration of Internet and digital technologies in healthcare management, elderly care, vaccination records and other areas.[72] Over the years, the municipality has introduced several digital initiatives in various areas of public health. These have made Shanghai a pioneering city in this field in China. These initiatives encourage the

联网、大数据、人工智能等信息技术手段，推进城市治理制度创新、模式创新、手段创新，提高城市科学化、精细化、智能化管理水平".

[69] Shanghai Municipal Government, 2020b. *In 2020 Shanghai will deepen the reform of the "Government Online-Offline Shanghai"* [2020年上海市深化"一网通办"改革工作要点], 24 February, https://www.shanghai.gov.cn/nw12344/20200813/0001-12344_64071.html. In original: "以用户为中心，全面提升个性化、精准化、主动化、智能化服务水平".

[70] As examined in Chapter 5.2.1, the "Suishenban" is a mobile application (App) for administrative service provision linked to the Government Online-Offline Shanghai (sui shen 随申 "follow Shanghai" has the same pronunciation of sui shen 随身 "take along").

[71] See for instance: Shanghai Municipal Government, 2021. *Work plan for comprehensively deepen the reform of the "Government Online-Offline Shanghai" in 2021* [2021年上海市全面深化"一网通办"改革工作要点], 12 March, https://www.shanghai.gov.cn/nw12344/20210312/4652749fb81d4e9c9ab4029322ff58c4.html, articles 14 and 16.

[72] SHEITC, Municipal Health Commission, Municipal Human Resources Bureau, Municipal Civil Affairs Bureau and Municipal Food and Drugs Administration, 2014. *Shanghai Working Solution for the Promotion of Internet Healthcare* [上海市健康物联网推进工作方案], https://www.zhihuichengshi.cn/XinWenZiXun/ChengShiZhuanLan/21432.html.

use of AI products in "Internet hospitals[73]" (互联网医院), and state that AI, 5G, and Big Data are the three pillars of the comprehensive digital transformation of Shanghai's medical and health service system.[74]

Besides public sector AI applications, it seems logical that an omni-use, enabling technology like AI can be appealing to the Shanghai leadership as a valuable tool that is instrumental in achieving the goals of the municipal government in various policy areas. This is particularly evident in economic development, where Shanghai has assigned AI a central role in the plans to upgrade the local industrial sector. AI has been identified by the municipality as one of the three "strategic emerging industries" (战略性新兴产业), together with integrated circuits and the biopharmaceutical industry. It is also one the six core areas (六大核心领域)—also including integrated circuits, the biopharmaceutical industry, aerospace, new materials, and intelligent manufacturing—where the municipality is applying the "park economy" (园区经济) approach, which aims to create industrial zones dedicated to support the development of high-end and high-tech industries (SHFDI, 2020, p. 12). Artificial intelligence features prominently also in initiatives such as the *Shanghai Action Plan for the Promotion of the Digital Economy (2020–2022)*,[75] which employs an array of technologies like AI and Big Data to upgrade traditional industries; and the *Shanghai Action Plan for Promoting the Construction of New Infrastructure (2020–2022)*,[76] where AI is a pillar of the new infrastructures that will help Shanghai to "cultivate new drivers of economic development".

[73] Shanghai Municipal Health Commission, 2019. *Shanghai Internet Hospitals Management Guidelines* [上海市互联网医院管理办法]. Huweigui (2019) 004, 16 July, http://wsjkw.sh.gov.cn/yzgl3/20190812/0012-64913.html.

[74] Shanghai Municipal Health Commission, Shanghai Development and Reform Commission, SHEITC, Shanghai Shenkang Hospital Development Center, Shanghai Data Exchange Center, Shanghai Finance Bureau, 2021. *Shanghai "Convenient Medical Service" Digital Transformation Work Plan* [上海市 "便捷就医服务" 数字化转型工作方案]. Huwei Xinxi (2021) 5, 4 June, http://wsjkw.sh.gov.cn/zhgl2/20210607/6cab5f1b39f44211a60c1fcb2a5f1d06.html.

[75] Shanghai Municipal Government, 2020. *Shanghai Action Plan for the Promotion of the Digital Economy (2020–2022)* [上海市促进在线新经济发展行动方案 (2020–2022年)]. Hufubanfa (2020) 1, 14 April, http://app.sheitc.sh.gov.cn/bsxgzcwj/685498.htm.

[76] Shanghai Development and Reform Commission, 2020. *Shanghai Action Plan for Promoting the Construction of New Infrastructure (2020–2022)* [上海市推进新型基础设施

3.3 Main Findings

This chapter showed that the use of AI in the public sector is one of the four main goals of China's national strategy for AI development. The AIDP requires to "greatly increase the level of intelligentization of the whole society by accelerating the deep application of AI and forming a ubiquitous intelligent environment", in order to "improve the level of precision in public services, comprehensively enhancing the people's quality of life". In practice, this means that China's leadership is encouraging the integrated use of AI in a wide range of public sector activities, including education, medicine and healthcare, judicial services, government affairs, smart cities, transportation, public security and other areas indicated by the AIDP. This high-profile political support has been replicated in Shanghai. In less than two years, the municipality issued two main policy documents for promoting AI development, accompanied by supporting and actionable policy documents and concrete initiatives.

The analysis of the *Opinions* and the *AI Highland Plan* indicates that Shanghai has developed a consistent vision for the use of AI in the public sector, and this vision enjoys stable political support. The *Opinions* and the *AI Highland Plan* require that government agencies and public institutions improve public service capabilities and citizens' sense of gain by accelerating the integration of AI in the public sector. They outline a well-elaborated set of tasks aimed at achieving these goals, and these tasks cover the same policy areas: city operations (security, environment, basic infrastructures), public services (administrative services, judiciary, education, culture), transportation (urban traffic, maritime logistics), and public health (treatment assistance, elderly care, prevention and control). This consistency within and between the municipal AI plans suggests that Shanghai has the analytical ability to devise public sector AI applications (i.e., the "tasks" of the municipal AI plans) that can contribute to achieving municipal goals in this area, if carried out. The analysis also shows that using AI to improve public service provision and citizens' sense of gain is a policy priority that remained unchanged in the two main municipal AI plans, indicating that public sector AI applications aimed at achieving these goals enjoy stable political support of the Shanghai leadership. In addition, the goals and tasks for AI in the public sector

建设行动方案 (2020–2022年)]. Hufu (2020) 27, 12 May, https://fgw.sh.gov.cn/zgjjl/20200512/63f3630e9d824e07976d6c552ed364e7.html.

outlined by the *Opinions* and the *AI Highland Plan* are also aligned with those of the national AI strategy, indicating that Shanghai's blueprint for AI in the public sector enjoy the support from the national government. Altogether, these indicators suggest that Shanghai has the analytical and political skills and resources necessary to use AI in the public sector. The examination of the municipal AI plans was integrated by looking at policy initiatives that stemmed from these plans and other digital innovation efforts in the public sector, further corroborating the findings about the analytical and political capabilities of Shanghai.

This chapter provides solid documentary evidence about the analytical and political capacities of Shanghai to implement AI in the public sector. To account for the possible impacts of the sociotechnical complexities of AI on Shanghai's capacity to implement AI in the public sector (Chapter 2.4), the findings of the analysis of Shanghai's AI policy environment will be integrated with primary data gathered from key informant interviews (Chapter 5.1). By verifying and expanding the findings of documentary research, it is possible to gain a deeper understanding of how analytical and political capacities are actually affecting public sector AI implementations in Shanghai. The refined results on analytical and political capacities will serve as a starting point to examine the main policy initiatives through which the Shanghai government is promoting the use of AI in the public sector (Chapters 5.2 and 5.3).

Appendix III: Toward China's National AI Strategy (2015–2016)

Since the publication of *Made in China 2025* and the *"Internet Plus" Action Plan* in 2015, the Chinese government has regularly issued major policy documents that reiterate the importance of technology to support the advancement of the Chinese industry, society, and other sectors. These policy documents constitute a programmatic core in China's AI policy system and influence the formulation of China's policies for the promotion of AI (Tsinghua 2018, p. 78), which culminated in the State Council's *New Generation Artificial Intelligence Development Plan* of July 2017.

In May 2015, the State Council published ***Made in China 2025***[77] (MIC25), an ambitious industrial masterplan for the digital and technological advancement of the Chinese manufacturing sector. MIC25 designates the efforts to accelerate the integration of information technology and industrial production in ten production areas. Namely: new generation information technology, high-end computerized machines and robots, space and aviation, maritime equipment and high-tech ships, advanced railway transportation equipment, new energy and energy-saving vehicles, energy equipment, agricultural machines, new materials, and biopharma and high-tech medical devices. MIC25 refers to developing intelligent equipment and smart devices, advancing production automation, and promoting smart applications in smart homes, smart devices, smart cars, and robotics, all topics that will appear in the subsequent policy documents on AI. MIC25 does not contain direct reference to artificial intelligence, a term that does not appear in the document. However, its focus on topics such as automation, robotics, and smart device places MIC25 in close relation to the field of AI. This link is confirmed by the *Three-Year Action Plan for Promoting the Development of a New Generation Artificial Intelligence Industry (2018–2020)*, which in its introduction makes explicit reference to the MIC25.

In July 2015, the State Council issued the ***"Internet Plus" Action Plan***,[78] which aims to promote the integration of the Internet across eleven key sectors that the Chinese government hopes can establish new industrial modes and contribute to national development, including artificial intelligence.[79] The section on artificial intelligence ("互联网+" 人工智能) articulates the need to foster AI backbone enterprises (骨干企业), and to leverage AI to create new services, products and applications in the automotive industry, robotics, manufacturing, public security, smart households, and other sectors. It also identifies other areas of intervention for fostering AI development, including breakthroughs in AI core technologies (核心技术, a recurring term in all the main subsequent AI plans); the creation of databases for training AI systems; and the R&D and commercialization of key technologies (关键技术) such

[77] State Council, 2015a. *Made in China 2025* [中国制造2025]. Guofa (2015) 28, 8 May, http://www.gov.cn/zhengce/content/2015-05/19/content_9784.htm.

[78] State Council, 2015b. *"Internet Plus" Action Plan* ["互联网+" 行动]. Guofa (2015) 40, 4 July, http://www.gov.cn/zhengce/content/2015-07/04/content_10002.htm.

[79] The sectors are: entrepreneurial innovation, collaborative manufacturing, modern agriculture, smart energy, inclusive finance, people-first services, efficient logistics, e-commerce, convenient transportation, green ecology and artificial intelligence.

as speech processing, computer vision, Natural Language Processing, among others. In addition, other sections of the *Internet Plus* contain supporting measures for developing the AI value chain. For instance, the document states the need to accelerate the R&D and production of advanced hardware such as chips and high-end servers, or promoting software infrastructures such as cloud computing and Big Data services.

The first major policy document specifically dedicated to the promotion of artificial intelligence is the ***"Internet Plus" AI Three-Year Implementation Plan***.[80] Published in May 2016 by the National and Development Reform Commission, the Ministry of Science and Technology, the Ministry of Industry and Information Technology and the Cybersecurity Administration of China, this document connects AI development to the *"Internet Plus" Action Plan* published a year earlier. The main goal of the Implementation Plan is to increase the level of "intelligentization" (智能化) of Chinese economy and society by promoting the industrialization of AI technologies and their application in a variety of areas. The document also sets a target for the development of China's AI industry, which should reach a market size of hundreds of billions RMB by 2018.[81] To achieve its goals, the document puts forward nine "focus programs[82]" that include AI applications that in China are typically provided by the public sector, such as healthcare, medicine, education, public security, and environment control (section 3, par. 1, 2 and 3; section 4, par. 1, 2 and 3).

In August 2016, the State Council published the ***13th National Five-Year Plan for Science and Technology Innovation***,[83] which identifies a set of advanced technologies as near-term priorities for research and

[80] NDRC, MOST, MIIT and CAC, 2016. *"Internet Plus" AI Three-Year Implementation Plan* ["互联网+" 人工智能三年行动实施方案]. Fagai Gaoji (2016) 1078, 18 May, http://www.gov.cn/xinwen/2016-05/23/content_5075944.htm.

[81] In original: "到2018年 [...] 形成千亿级的人工智能市场应用规模".

[82] The nine "focus programs" (重点工程) are: (i) R&D and industrialization of core technologies (核心技术研发与产业化工程); (ii) open service platforms of basic resources (基础资源公共服务平台工程); (iii) smart home demonstration (智能家居示范工程); (iv) R&D and industrialization of smart cars (智能汽车研发与产业化工程); (v) applications of smart unmanned systems (智能无人系统应用工程); (vi) promotion of smart security (智能安防推广工程); (vii) enhancing the capacity of smart end-use applications (智能终端应用能力提升工程); (viii) developing smart wearable devices (智能可穿戴设备发展工程); and (ix) R&D and application of smart robots (智能机器人研发与应用工程).

[83] State Council, 2016a. *National 13th Five-Year Plan for Science and Technology Innovation* ["十三五" 国家科技创新规划]. Guo Fa (2016) 43, 8 August, http://www.gov.cn/zhengce/content/2016-08/08/content_5098072.htm.

investment. The main goals of the plan are to achieve outstanding results in innovation-driven development, improve the country's comprehensive innovation capacity so that it will rank among the top 15 countries in the world, bring China into the ranks of innovative countries (创新型国家), and provide strong support to form "a well-off society in an all-round way". The plan mentions several AI technologies: intelligent perception and cognition, Big Data-driven human-like intelligence, human-like vision, hearing, speech, and thinking to support AI-driven industrial development, and demonstrative applications in key sectors such as education, office work, and healthcare. It indicates that AI is expected to contribute to building China into a "global science and technology power" (世界科技强国).

In November 2016, the State Council issued the ***XIII Five-Year Plan for Developing National Strategic Emerging Industries***.[84] This document links AI development to the top-level socioeconomic planning of the Five-Year Plans, confirming that AI has become a strategic priority in the policy agenda of the national government. The document positions AI at the sixth place among a total of 69 "focus tasks" (重点任务) that the government has to pursue in developing the "strategic emerging industries" (战略性新兴产业) in the period 2016–2020. These industries are expected to contribute to 15% of China's gross domestic product by 2020 and to become a leading force for China's sustained and healthy economic development by 2030. In the section on artificial intelligence (section 2, par. 5), the plan requires to "cultivate an AI industry ecosystem, promote the use and application of AI in key economic and social fields, and build a leading international technology system". To do so, it identifies two key tasks. One is to accelerate the construction of an "AI support system" (人工智能支撑体系建设), which includes research on AI theories and technologies, the R&D and commercialization of AI technologies, the construction of computing clusters that support large-scale deep learning, and the know-how of leading companies. The other task is to foster AI applications in various areas (推动人工智能技术在各领域应用), building pilot demonstrations in education, healthcare, environmental protection, commerce, manufacturing, cybersecurity, transportation, and social governance, in order to promote the progressive application of artificial intelligence.

[84] State Council, 2016b. *13th Five-Year Plan for Developing National Strategic and Emerging Industries* ["十三五" 国家战略性新兴产业发展规划的通知]. Guo Fa (2016) 67, 29 November, http://www.gov.cn/zhengce/content/2016-12/19/content_5150090.htm.

Overall, the policy documents issued in 2015–2016 have a strong focus on the industrialization of AI technologies and applications, indicating that economic growth is a major goal of China's AI plans. Indeed, the view of AI as a "core driving force for a new round of industrial transformation" will later be codified into the 2017 *New Generation Artificial Intelligence Development Plan*, which sets economic development among the main targets of China's AI strategy: "As China's previous growth model of export-led, low-added value manufacturing has run out of steam and its economy is entering a 'new normal' of lower annual GDP growth, AI promises new sources of productivity growth, as well as potential new markets for China's increasingly sophisticated digital goods and services" (Creemers 2020, p. 64; see also Zeng 2021; Ding 2018).

Another common topic of these earlier policy documents is the emphasis on the "intelligentization" (智能化) of Chinese society, identifying AI as a promising conduit for the better provision of public services. In particular, the *XIII Five-Year Plan for Developing National Strategic Emerging Industries* articulates the need to "promote intelligentization of services such as healthcare, education, social insurance, employment, transportation, and tourism. Expand the application of new smart cities, promote the innovation of Internet-based public service models, promote the construction of public platforms for cloud-based information services, and enhance the supply of public goods" (section 2, par. 2 "Promote the 'Internet Plus' initiative"). The "intelligentization" of society is a theme that will be resumed and expanded in the *New Generation Artificial Intelligence Development Plan* as part of the government intentions to use AI technologies for "social construction" (社会建设), one of the main goals of China's AI strategy.

Appendix IV: Main National AI Policy Documents published After the AIDP

See Table 3.4.

Table 3.4 Main national AI policy documents published after the New Generation Artificial Intelligence Development Plan, which make explicit reference to the AIDP

Issuer and Date	*Document name*	*Main contents*
National Development and Reform Commission (NDRC), October 2017	*The National Development and Reform Commission organization and implementation of the major projects of "Internet+", Artificial Intelligence Innovation Development and digital economy pilot projects*[85]	It contains a part dedicated to accelerating the implementation of the AIDP
Ministry of Industry and Information Technology (MIIT), December 2017	*Three-Year Action Plan for Promoting the Development of a New Generation Artificial Intelligence Industry (2018–2020)*[86]	It aims to "implement the *New Generation Artificial Intelligence Development Plan* and carry out the plan ***Made in China** 2025* in an in-depth manner". It sets out specific benchmarks in many AI products and services through 2020, including some concrete metrics that can be applied to measure progress in the integration of AI and industry. It states that AI will be a new engine for building China into a manufacturing and cyber-superpower (制造强国和网络强国). It calls for the development of a new generation AI industry (新一代人工智能产业) through the implementation of four key tasks: scale-up the development of key AI products, enhance core competencies in AI, deepen the development of smart manufacturing, and establish the foundation for an AI industry support system

(continued)

[85] National Development and Reform Commission, 2017. *The National Development and Reform Commission organization and implementation of the major projects of "Internet+", Artificial Intelligence Innovation Development and digital economy pilot projects* [发展改革委组织实施2018年"互联网+"、人工智能创新发展和数字经济试点重大工程]. Fagaiban Gaoji (2017) 1668, 11 October, http://www.gov.cn/xinwen/2017-10/29/content_5235181.htm.

[86] Ministry of Industry and Information Technology, 2017. *Three-Year Action Plan for Promoting the Development of a New Generation Artificial Intelligence Industry (2018–2020)* [促进新一代人工智能产业发展三年行动计划 (2018–2020年)]. Gongxinbuke (2017) 315, 13 December, http://www.cac.gov.cn/2017-12/15/c_1122114520.htm.

Table 3.4 (continued)

Issuer and Date	*Document name*	*Main contents*
Ministry of Education (MoE), April 2018	*Artificial Intelligence Action Plan for Institutions of Higher Education*[87]	Referring to the AIDP in its preamble, this plan encourages universities to bolster foundational and cutting-edge AI research, and further improve the ability of Chinese universities to innovate and train talented people in the field of AI
Ministry of Science and Technology (MOST), October 2018	*Science and Technology Innovation 2030—"New Generation Artificial Intelligence" Major Project, 2018 Project Application Guidelines*[88]	It focuses on Big Data intelligence, cross-media intelligence, swarm intelligence, hybrid enhanced intelligence, and autonomous intelligence systems, research areas that were mentioned in the AIDP (Section 3, Focus Task 1). It calls for building an AI ecosystem including knowledge clusters, technology clusters, and product clusters consisting of four levels: basic theory, support systems, key technologies, and innovative applications
Ministry of Industry and Information Technology (MIIT), November 2018	*Work plan for unveiling the focus tasks of the New Generation Artificial Intelligence Industry Innovation*[89]	It aims to accelerate the innovation and development of the "New Generation Artificial Intelligence industry" and implement the *Three-year Action Plan for Promoting the Development of the New Generation of Artificial Intelligence Industry (2018–2020)* issued by the MIIT in December 2017

[87] Ministry of Education, 2018. *Artificial Intelligence Action Plan for Institutions of Higher Education* [高等学校人工智能创新行动计划]. Jiaoji (2018) 3, 2 April, http://www.moe.gov.cn/srcsite/A16/s7062/201804/t20180410_332722.html.

[88] Ministry of Science and Technology, 2018. *Science and Technology Innovation 2030—"New Generation Artificial Intelligence" Major Project 2018 Project Application Guidelines* [科技创新2030—"新一代人工智能" 重大项目2018年度项目申报指南]. Guoke Fazi (2018) 208, 12 October, http://www.gov.cn/zhengce/zhengceku/2018-12/31/content_5446330.htm.

[89] Ministry of Industry and Information Technology, 2018. *Work plan for unveiling the focus tasks of the New Generation Artificial Intelligence Industry Innovation* [新一代人工智能产业创新重点任务揭榜工作方案]. Gongxin Tingke (2018) 80, 8 November, http://www.gov.cn/zhengce/zhengceku/2018-12/31/content_5443931.htm.

Issuer and Date	*Document name*	*Main contents*
MoE, NDRC and Ministry of Finance, January 2020	*Certain Opinions on Promoting Curricula Merging at "Double World-Class" Institutes of Higher Education and on Accelerating the Cultivation of Graduate Students in the AI Field*[90]	It recommends a number of measures to improve China's system for cultivating AI talent that address the disconnect between academic training of AI graduate students and the work being done in industry, as well as the difficulty of designing curricula for an interdisciplinary field as AI. It mentions the AIDP in its preamble, and it also refers to the need to develop "AI + X interdisciplinary talents" ("人工智能+X" 复合型人才) advocated by the AIDP (focus task 1)
Ministry of Science and Technology (MOST), July 2021	*Science and Technology Innovation 2030—"New Generation Artificial Intelligence" Major Project, 2021 Project Application Guidelines*[91]	It focuses on areas such as foundational AI theories, software, hardware and other supporting systems; machine learning and reinforcement learning; autonomous intelligent systems; semiconductors; Big Data security; and the use of AI in medicine, epidemic control, agriculture, etc.

90 Ministry of Education, National Development and Reform Commission, and Ministry of Finance, 2020. *Certain Opinions on Promoting Curricula Merging at "Double World-Class" Institutes of Higher Education and on Accelerating the Cultivation of Graduate Students in the AI Field* [关于"双一流"建设高校促进学科融合 加快人工智能领域研究生培养的若干意见]. Jiao Yan (2020), 4, 21 January, https://www.gov.cn/zhengce/zhengceku/2020-03/03/content_5486326.htm.

91 Ministry of Science and Technology, 2021. *Science and Technology Innovation 2030—"New Generation Artificial Intelligence" Major Project 2021 Project Application Guidelines* [科技创新2030—"新一代人工智能"重大项目2021年度项目申报指南]. Guoke Fazi (2021) 191, 1 July, http://www.ncsti.gov.cn/kjdt/tzgg/202107/t20210707_36198.html.

References

Acharya, A. and Arnold, Z., 2019. *Chinese Public AI R&D Spending: Provisional Findings*. Center for Security and Emerging Technology, CSET Issue Brief, https://cset.georgetown.edu/publication/chinese-public-ai-rd-spending-provisional-findings/.

Castro, D., McLaughlin, M. and Chivot, E., 2019. *Who Is Winning the AI Race: China, the EU or the United States?* Center for Data Innovation, https://www.datainnovation.org/2019/08/who-is-winning-the-ai-race-china-the-eu-or-the-united-states/.

Creemers, R., 2020. The Ideology Behind China's AI Strategy. In: Elliott, H. ed., 2020. *The AI Powered State: China's approach to public sector innovation*. Nesta, May 2020, pp. 63–69, https://www.nesta.org.uk/feature/ai-powered-state/.

Desouza, K., 2018. Delivering Artificial Intelligence in Government: Challenges and Opportunities. *IBM Center for the Business of Government*, Washington D.C.: USA, http://www.businessofgovernment.org/report/delivering-artificial-intelligence-government-challenges-and-opportunities.

Ding, J., 2018. *Deciphering China's AI Dream*. Oxford: University of Oxford, https://www.fhi.ox.ac.uk/deciphering-chinas-ai-dream.

Ding, J., 2019. *China's Current Capabilities, Policies, and Industrial Ecosystem in AI*. Testimony before the U.S.-China Economic and Security Review Commission Hearing on Technology, Trade, and Military-Civil Fusion: China's Pursuit of Artificial Intelligence, New Materials, and New Energy, 7 June, https://www.uscc.gov/sites/default/files/June%207%20Hearing_Panel%201_Jeffrey%20Ding_China%27s%20Current%20Capabilities%2C%20Policies%2C%20and%20Indu.

Ding, J., 2020. Promoting Nationally, Acting Locally: China's Next Generation AI Approach. In: Elliott, H. ed., 2020. *The AI Powered State: China's Approach To Public Sector Innovation*. Nesta, May 2020, pp. 11–16, https://www.nesta.org.uk/feature/ai-powered-state/.

Fatima, S., Desouza, K. and Dawson, G., 2020. National Strategic Artificial Intelligence Plans: A Multi-Dimensional Analysis. *Economic Analysis and Policy*, 67, pp. 178–194, https://doi.org/10.1016/j.eap.2020.07.008.

Heilmann, S., 2008. From Local Experiments to National Policy: The Origins of China's Distinctive Policy Process. *The China Journal*, 59, pp. 1–30, https://www.jstor.org/stable/20066378.

Heilmann, S., Shih, L. and Hofem, A., 2013. National Planning and Local Technology Zones: Experimental Governance in China's Torch Programme. *The China Quarterly*, 216, pp. 896–919, https://doi.org/10.1017/S0305741013001057.

Lee, K. and Sheehan, M., 2018. *China's Rise in Artificial Intelligence: Ingredients and Economic Implications*. China in an Emerging World, Hoover

Institution, Fall Series, Issue 218, https://www.hoover.org/research/chinas-rise-artificial-intelligence-ingredients-and-economic-implications.

Roberts, H., Cowls, J., Morley, J., Taddeo, M., Wang, V. and Floridi, L., 2020. The Chinese Approach to Artificial Intelligence: An Analysis of Policy, Ethics, and Regulation. *AI & Society*, 36, pp. 59–77, https://doi.org/10.1007/s00146-020-00992-2.

Sheehan, M., 2018. How China's Massive AI Plan Actually Works. *MacroPolo*, 13 February, https://macropolo.org/chinas-massive-ai-plan-actually-works/.

SHFDI (Shanghai Foreign Investment Development Board), 2020. *Shanghai Foreign Investment Guide 2020* [2020上海外商投资指南], https://www.investsh.org.cn/upload/index/2020%20Shanghai%20Foreign%20Investment%20Guide.pdf.

Stanford University, 2021a. *The AI Index 2021 Annual Report*. AI Index Steering Committee, Institute for Human-Centered AI, Stanford: Stanford University, March 2021, https://aiindex.stanford.edu/report/.

Sun, Y. and Cao, C., 2014. Demystifying Central Government R&D Spending in China. *Science*, 345(6200), pp. 1006–1008, https://www.science.org/doi/10.1126/science.1253479?cookieSet=1.

Tencent and CAICT (Tencent Research Institute, Tencent AI Lab and China Academy of Information and Communications Technology), 2017. *Artificial Intelligence: A National Strategic Initiative for Artificial Intelligence* [人工智能: 国家人工智能战略行动抓手]. Beijing: China Renmin University Press.

Triolo, P. and Goodrich, J. 2018. From Riding a Wave to Full Steam Ahead: As China's Government Mobilizes for AI Leadership, Some Challenges Will Be Tougher Than Others. *New America DigiChina Project*, 28 February, https://www.newamerica.org/cybersecurity-initiative/digichina/blog/riding-wave-full-steam-ahead/.

Tsinghua University, 2018. *China AI Development Report 2018*. Beijing: China Institute for Science and Technology Policy at Tsinghua University, on file with the author.

UNESCAP (United Nations, Economic and Social Commission for Asia and the Pacific), 2018. *Evolution of Science, Technology and Innovation Policies for Sustainable Development: The Experiences of China, Japan, the Republic of Korea and Singapore*. UNESCAP, https://www.unescap.org/sites/default/files/publications/UN_STI_Policy_Report_2018.pdf.

Webster, G. ed., 2019. AI Policy and China. Realities of State-Led Development. *Stanford-New America DigiChina Project*, Special Report No. 1, 29 October, https://d1y8sb8igg2f8e.cloudfront.net/documents/DigiChina-AI-report-20191029.pdf.

Xu, C., 2011. The Fundamental Institutions of China's Reforms and Development. *Journal of Economic Literature*, 49(4), pp. 1076–1151, https://www.jstor.org/stable/23071664?seq=1.

Zeng, J., 2021. China's Artificial Intelligence Innovation: A Top-Down National Command Approach? *Global Policy*, 12(3), pp. 399–409, https://doi.org/10.1111/1758-5899.12914.

Zhou, X., Lian, H., Ortolano, L. and Ye, Y., 2013. A Behavioral Model of "Muddling-Through" in the Chinese Bureaucracy: The Case of Environmental Protection. *The China Journal*, 70, pp. 120–147, https://doi.org/10.1086/671335.

CHAPTER 4

The AI Ecosystem of Shanghai

The analysis of the Shanghai municipal plans for AI development shows that improving public service provision and citizens' sense of gain by fast-tracking AI integration in the public sector are political priorities of the Shanghai government. Hence, public sector AI applications aimed at achieving these goals are expected to enjoy political support from the municipal leadership. The *Opinions* and the *AI Highland Plan* also demonstrate the ability of the Shanghai government to devise such public sector AI applications, as both AI plans consistently outline a well-elaborated set of tasks that can contribute to improving public service provision and citizens' sense of gain, if carried out. In addition, the goals and tasks for AI in the public sector outlined by the *Opinions* and the *AI Highland Plan* are aligned with those of China's national AI strategy, indicating that Shanghai's blueprint for AI in the public sector is supported by the central government. While these analytical and political capabilities are crucial for using AI in the public sector, Shanghai also needs the operational capacity to implement public sector AI applications in practice. To assess this capacity, this chapter examines the status of Shanghai's AI ecosystem, which is defined here as the aggregation of skills and resources needed to make AI applications possible. It looks at what Shanghai is doing to expand such resources and orchestrate them to bring public sector AI projects to fruition.

D. Todaro, *The Use of Artificial Intelligence in the Public Sector in Shanghai*, https://doi.org/10.1007/978-981-97-0597-9_4

There are no standard classifications to measure AI ecosystems (Castro et al., 2019). The metrics most commonly found in the literature are often used to compare AI development among nations.[1] In addition, there is a paucity of sources that specifically examine the capacity of the public sector to implement AI in its activities (Oxford Insights and IDRC, 2020; Misuraca and van Noordt, 2020). Building on previous research on AI ecosystems, this chapter examines five indicators to assess the resources for AI implementation available in Shanghai and draw conclusions on the operational capacity of the municipality to deploy AI in the public sector. First, many of today's AI systems use large amounts of **data** to train their models accurately, so the access and usability of data is necessary for AI applications, in the public sector like in other areas. Second, the use of AI in the public sector requires that adequate **technological and physical infrastructure** are in place to support the deployment of AI technologies and applications. Third, public sector AI applications also rely on the availability of **AI talents**, skilled human capital who is able to apply AI technologies to real-world problems. Fourth, the technologies needed for public sector AI implementations are mostly provided by **AI companies**, which are leading players in China's and Shanghai's AI policy, as emphasized in Chapter 2.2.3. Fifth, the analysis looks at the public perception of AI in China to gauge the level of **social acceptance** of AI-enabled public services. Each indicator consists of a number of quantitative and qualitative metrics that are assessed based on secondary data primarily collected from Chinese-language sources that had largely been unexplored. At the same time, the analysis is not limited to determining the quantity and quality of Shanghai's resources for AI implementation. Previous studies observe that the availability of resources is not sufficient to assess operational capacity, which also entails the ability to deploy such resources in public sector AI applications (Mikalef and Gupta, 2021). Hence, this chapter also investigates the capability of Shanghai to orchestrate the resources of the AI ecosystem to promote implementations in the public sector.

[1] Some works that assess China's AI ecosystem in the context of the country's international competitiveness by using all or part of the metrics adopted in this chapter include: Castro and McLaughlin (2021), Ernst (2020), Oxford Insights and IDRC (2020), Castro et al. (2019), SJTU et al. (2019), Tsinghua (2018), Ding, 2018, Tencent and CAICT (2017), and the ChinAI website by the Paulson Institute (https://macropolo.org/digital-projects/chinai/chinai-intro/).

The use of metrics to assess Shanghai's AI ecosystem present some caveats. First, these metrics gauge resources and skills that are not exclusively linked to AI applications in the public sector. Second, some aspects of these metrics are difficult to quantify (e.g., the output of human capital), and there are some methodological issues that will be identified for each metric when relevant. Third, as for other research areas in China, statistics may not be available, or they can be incomplete and/or inconsistent, especially when contextualizing municipal-level and national-level data. Nonetheless, structuring the analysis by metrics is valuable for the purposes of this book. This approach helps to unpack the components of the Shanghai AI ecosystem, the relationships between them, and their relative impact on public sector AI implementations. It also allows to identify with greater precision what Shanghai is doing to develop and utilize the resources of the municipal AI ecosystem, offering insights on the development trajectory of the Shanghai AI ecosystem in the near term.

Contextualizing the AI Ecosystem: Shanghai's Ability to Innovate

The AI ecosystem contains the most relevant set of indicators for assessing the operational resources and skills needed of Shanghai to implement public sector AI applications in practice. At the same time, operational capacity at a fundamental level also involves possessing the necessary capabilities and expertise in various organizational functions, which public management and administration literature commonly groups under leadership, strategic planning and management, and other broad managerial functions (Woo, 2021, p. 34). These types of managerial capabilities and expertise are accounted for in the analysis. As just explained, this chapter delves into the ability of Shanghai to orchestrate the resources of the AI ecosystem and put them to use in public sector AI applications. Nonetheless, to contextualize the capacity of Shanghai to manage its AI ecosystem, it is useful to look at three indicators showing that the municipal government has already demonstrated strategic planning and management capabilities in the promotion of digital and technological innovation.

First, since the 13th Five-Year Plan (FYP) period (2016–2020), Shanghai has pursued a concerted strategy to become an international center of economy, finance, trade, shipping, and sci-tech innovation. A key component of this strategy is the improvement of Shanghai's public governance capabilities. These efforts led to progress in a landmark program in public sector innovation, which was mentioned in Chapter 3 and is examined as a case study for the integration of AI in the public sector in Shanghai (Chapter 5.2.1). Namely: the Government Online-Offline Shanghai (一网通办). This is an e-government platform that has significantly increased the efficiency in the provision of administrative services by leveraging Big Data, artificial intelligence, and other digital technologies. This platform is paired by the Single Platform for Urban Management (一网统管), which uses AI and other advanced technologies to improve urban governance operations (Chapter 5.2.2). These efforts to create a city-wide intelligent system are also an integral part of the 14th FYP's goal to further improve digital governance by 2025, an area where Shanghai is already recognized as a global leader by the United Nations based on a comprehensive index that considers technology, content provision, service provision, and participation and engagement (United Nations, 2020, p.157).

Second, nurturing science and technology innovation is one of the "four major functions" (四大功能) to upgrade urban capacities, which the Shanghai government is developing as part of the strategy to enhance the competitiveness of the municipality (the other three functions are allocating global resources, supporting high-end industries, and further promoting opening-up and reform; see Chapter 1). Like the initiatives in public administration, these efforts are part of a long-term strategy initiated by the 13th Five-Year Plan and now extended to 2025, the time horizon of the 14th FYP. A main initiative to bolster sci-tech innovation in Shanghai has been the creation of the Science and Technology Innovation Board (the STAR market) of the Shanghai Stock Exchange, which allows the public listing of loss-making firms to facilitate the initial public offering (IPO) for companies operating in artificial intelligence, biotech, and other technology-intensive sectors. Other initiatives that show Shanghai's planning and managerial capacities to promote science and technology innovation include: the execution of a total of 854 National Science and Technology Major Projects (国家重点研发计划项目) as part of the national 2030 Innovation Megaprojects Initiative (Chapters 2.2.3 and 3.1), for which Shanghai ranks first in China and received RMB 31.62 billion by the central government (SHFDI, 2020, p. 5); and the establishment of several institutes for advanced research in science and technology, including the Shanghai Research Center for

Quantum Sciences, 44 national-level key laboratories, and 21 National Engineering Technology Research Centers (SHFDI, 2021, p. 8).

Third, Shanghai has established a well-developed ecosystem for science and technology innovation that goes beyond artificial intelligence. According to the *Global Innovation Hubs Index 2021* by Tsinghua University, which measures the science and technology innovation capabilities of 50 cities worldwide, Shanghai ranks 14th globally and first in China.[2] The index consists of three dimensions: "scientific center" (科学中心), "innovation highland" (创新高地), and "innovation ecosystem" (创新生态). The first dimension measures the presence of scientific research institutions, research infrastructure (科学基础设施), and human resources. The second dimension measures the number of patents registered in the locality, the number of hi-tech companies, and the local level of economic development, among others. The third dimension is where Shanghai has the highest relative score, ranking 10th globally. Importantly, this dimension is closely related to government resources and managerial capabilities. It considers indicators including public infrastructure and services like government data centers, cloud platforms, e-government, but also broadband connection and speed, and the general level of education and cultural facilities.

These three indicators suggest that Shanghai has strategic planning and management capabilities to promote digital and technological innovation. These capacities are not surprising considering the pivotal role traditionally played by Shanghai in China's economic reforms and opening-up policies: from the creation of the Pudong Special Economic Zone in 1990, to the establishment of China's first pilot free trade zone in 2013 that served as a testing ground for the regulations of the other 20 Chinese free trade zones (at October 2023), to the decision (June 2021) of the Standing Committee of the National People's Congress to grant Shanghai legislature's the authority to adapt within the Pudong New Area the provisions of statutes, administrative regulations, and departmental rules issued by State Council agencies. These managerial abilities

[2] Tsinghua University, 2021. *Global Innovation Hubs Index 2021* [国际科技创新中心指数2021], Center for Industrial Development and Environmental Governance (CIDEG, 清华大学产业发展与环境治理研究中心), http://www.cideg.tsinghua.edu.cn/upload_files/file/20210925/1632566301884089089.pdf. *Global Innovation Hubs Index 2021* is the official English translation of the report, which literally translates "Global Scientific and Technological Innovation Centers Index 2021".

are reflected in the capacity of Shanghai to orchestrate the resources of the AI ecosystem and put them to use in public sector AI applications, examined in the next paragraphs.

4.1 Access and Use of Data

Contemporary AI systems based on statistical techniques usually rely on vast quantities of data for accurately training their models to perform tasks (Glossary). As AI algorithms are fed more training data—past examples of the phenomenon the AI systems are designed to understand—they gain greater accuracy. Chinese and international observers generally agree that the availability of huge data volumes is a key strength of China's AI ecosystem (Ding, 2018; Tsinghua, 2018; Tencent and CAICT, 2017). In 2017, the President of the Chinese Academy of Sciences, Bai Chunli, estimated that "[b]y 2020, China will hold 20% of the global data, which is expected to reach 44 trillion gigabytes".[3] Shanghai also claims to have access to vast troves of data. Both the *Opinions* and the *AI Highland Plan* state that abundant data resources are a competitive advantage of the municipality,[4] and local authorities often emphasize the strength of Shanghai in this metric.

4.1.1 Data Metrics for Shanghai

Despite these claims, there are no straightforward metrics for measuring the amount of digital data in a particular place. Some studies use statistics on the population engagement in digital activities as a proxy to estimate the relative amount of data available in a given location, based on the consideration that individuals produce a significant amount of data when using the Internet (Castro and McLaughlin, 2021; Oxford Insights and IDRC, 2020). To assess Shanghai's position in the data metric, this

[3] Chinese Academy of Sciences. China's AI Business Ready to Lead the World. *Chinese Academy of Sciences*, 2 June 2017, http://english.cas.cn/newsroom/news/201706/t20170602_177674.shtml.

[4] "Give full play to Shanghai's advantages in rich data resources" (the *Opinions*, section 1, guiding ideology). "Give full play to Shanghai's basic advantages in [...] massive data" (*AI Highland Plan*, section 1, guiding ideology).

section examines the amount of public data[5] that Shanghai accumulated on the municipal databases. This choice was made for two reasons. First, metrics on Shanghai's population engagement in digital activities are not entirely available. Second, compared to the population engagement in digital activities, metrics based on government databases provide a more accurate estimate of the data that can actually be utilized by Shanghai public organizations, because (i) such data are already accessible for government use (i.e., they are already stored in Shanghai's databases), and (ii) they include data sources (e.g., surveillance cameras, traffic monitoring, etc.) that other methodologies fail to capture (Oxford Insights and IDRC, 2020, p. 118).

Useful indicators on the volumes of public data available in Shanghai are offered by the digital platform Government Online-Offline Shanghai for the provision of administrative services. In December 2020, this e-government platform gave the Shanghai government access to 1.4 billion data points from more than 16,000 data sources in 50 organizations (CAICT and CMG, 2020, pp. 18–19). In the same period, this platform already cumulatively processed more than 60 million documents (办件量), collecting information on more than 29 million individuals and 2 million legal entities. By March 2023, the number of registered users of the platform surpassed 79 million individuals and 3 million legal entities, while the cumulative number of documents processed by the platform exceeded the figure of 330 million items.[6] This accumulation of data is spurred by the municipal policies on public data sharing, discussed in the next subsection. In May 2020, Shanghai municipal data lakes (i.e., repositories that allow to store structured and unstructured data) had already collected 34 billion items of data. By May 2020, Shanghai municipal databases had also completed 3.15 billion data transfers to various

[5] Shanghai defines public data as "all types of data collected or produced by the city's State organs, public institutions (事业单位), organizations authorized to have public affairs functions in accordance with the law, as well organizations providing public services such as water, electricity, and public transportation (hereinafter collectively referred to as public management and service bodies) in the performance of public management and service duties". See: *Shanghai Municipal Data Regulations (draft)* [上海市数据条例 (草案)], art. 2, par. 4 (examined in the next paragraphs of this section).

[6] The Paper, 2023. Shanghai's "Government Online-Offline Shanghai" has more than 80 million users, and a cumulative handling volume of 336 million items [上海 "一网通办" 用户已超八千万，累计办件量达3.36亿件]. *The Paper* [澎湃新闻], 11 May, https://baijiahao.baidu.com/s?id=1765579216636993694&wfr=spider&for=pc.

districts of the municipality, and public institutions in the city had made a total of 73.16 million transfers of national data. In the same period, Shanghai public data open platforms shared 2,086 government datasets from 64 departments.[7] By the end of 2020, Shanghai had more than 4,000 municipal open datasets in eleven core sectors, including smart transportation and other industries.[8] The municipality has also completed the creation of databases on legal persons, actual population, and spatial geographic information.[9] Importantly, Shanghai government databases are continuously expanding. Municipal policy initiatives like the Government Online-Offline Shanghai are driving the growth of municipal open datasets, which reached nearly 5,400 by October 2023.[10] In addition, various projects at the district level are also contributing. For instance, the Jing'an District Big Data City Management Innovation Project (静安区大数据城市管理创新工程), launched in 2017, has already deployed 200,000 sensors and initiated the construction of two city brains in the district[11] (Chapter 5.3). In addition, other indicators confirm that Shanghai public organizations have access to big volumes of data. For

[7] NDRC, 2020. Shanghai Builds a Big Data Innovation Ecosystem and Promotes the Development of Industrial Agglomeration [上海打造大数据创新生态, 促进产业集聚发展]. *NDRC Website*, 3 July, https://www.ndrc.gov.cn/xwdt/ztzl/szhzxhbxd/zxal/202007/t20200703_1233045.html?code=&state=123. In original: "截至2020年5月, 上海已 [...] 形成 "数据湖", 累计归集入湖的公共数据达340亿条. [...] 截至2020年5月, 上海已经建成全市统一的电子证照库, 已归集345类高频证照, 总数突破9256万张. 截至2020年5月[...] 向各区数据落地交换31.5亿条, 全市各单位累计调用国家数据7316万次 [...]。截至2020年5月, 公共数据开放平台已开放64个数据部门2086项政府数据集, 实现各市级部门的主要业务领域的全覆盖".

[8] Shanghai Government General Office, 2021b. *Shanghai Comprehensively Promotes the 14th Five-Year Plan of Urban Digital Transformation* [上海市全面推进城市数字化转型 "十四五" 规划], Hufubanfa (2021) 29, 24 October, https://www.shanghai.gov.cn/nw12344/20211027/6517c7fd7b804553a37c1165f0ff6ee4.html. In original: "截至2020年底, 累计开放数据集超过4000项, 推动普惠金融、商业服务、智能交通等多个产业共11个公共数据开放应用试点项目建设" (section 1.2).

[9] Shanghai World AI Conference, 2021. Shanghai Academy of Social Sciences "Report": Shanghai Has Entered a Period of AI Development [上海社科院《报告》: 上海进入AI发展发力期]. *WeChat Blogpost*, 17 March, https://mp.weixin.qq.com/s/qZwcCYdIGXHcVIA87m8Qkg.

[10] Shanghai Public Data Open Platform (上海市公共数据开放平台), https://data.sh.gov.cn/index.html (accessed on 21 October 2023).

[11] NDRC, 2020 (cit.); Jing'an District Government, 2018. Jing'an District Big Data Urban Management Application Innovation "151 Project" Street and Town Work Briefing Conference was held [静安区大数据城市管理应用创新 "151项目" 街镇工作说明会举行].

instance, in 2019 the flow of data on urban traffic increased by 30 GB daily, while the shared database of Shanghai medical institutions already included 25 billion data items.[12] The number of medical data collected by the Shanghai government skyrocketed in April 2022, when the municipal healthcare cloud became the focal point for sharing information on the mass testing of virtually all 25 million citizens during the Covid-19 pandemic.[13]

To contextualize Shanghai's position in the data volume metric, it is also useful to look at national statistics that consider the Chinese population's digital engagement. In 2022, China had more than 589 million fixed broadband subscriptions,[14] that is 41.35 subscriptions per 100 people,[15] and 76% of the Chinese population used the Internet via a computer, mobile phone, personal digital assistant, digital TV, or other means.[16] In 2022, China had 1.78 billion mobile cellular subscriptions,[17] and as early as 2019 over 577 million Chinese individuals already made mobile payments (i.e., payments made by using a mobile device to scan, tap, swipe, or check an order to make a point-of-sale transaction, excluding purchases such as those of digital goods on mobile devices;

Jing'an District Government Website, 20 March, https://www.jingan.gov.cn/rmtzx/003008/003008002/20170705/0b6021a0-edd5-474f-8db9-a491d5b4b374.html.

[12] Yang, F., 2019. The Shanghai (Pudong) AI Innovation Application Pilot Zone Has Started Construction, with Three Major Targets [上海 (浦东) 人工智能创新应用先导区已启动建设, 有三大定位]. *The Paper* [澎湃新闻], 18 June, https://www.thepaper.cn/newsDetail_forward_3707858.

[13] IT Times, 2022. For the Health of 25 Million People, "Two Hearts" Are Beating at the Same Time [为了2500万人的健康, "两颗心脏" 在同时跳动]. *IT Times* [IT时报], 27 December, https://baijiahao.baidu.com/s?id=1753367219624875382&wfr=spider&for=pc.

[14] World Bank, 2022. "Fixed Broadband Subscriptions" Indicator, World Bank Open Data [online], https://data.worldbank.org/indicator/IT.NET.BBND?view=chart&locations=CN (accessed on 21 October 2023).

[15] World Bank, 2022. "Fixed Broadband Subscriptions (per 100 People)" Indicator, World Bank Open Data [online], https://data.worldbank.org/indicator/IT.NET.BBND.P2?locations=CN (accessed on 21 October 2023).

[16] World Bank, 2022. "Individuals Using the Internet (% of Population)" Indicator, World Bank Open Data [online], https://data.worldbank.org/indicator/IT.NET.USER.ZS?locations=CN (accessed on 21 October 2023).

[17] World Bank, 2022. "Mobile Cellular Subscriptions" Indicator, World Bank Open Data [online], https://data.worldbank.org/indicator/IT.CEL.SETS?locations=CN (accessed on 21 October 2023).

Castro and McLaughlin 2021, p. 19). In data generated by Internet of Things devices, China collected approximately 152 million terabytes in 2018.[18] In the same year, China collected 684 million TB of productivity data (i.e., data generated by private and public organizations in their activities; Castro et al., 2019, p. 39). China fares better than the United States—which outperform other countries across most metrics of the AI ecosystem—in the majority of these digital engagement indicators,[19] with the exception of population using the Internet (76% in China in 2022, compared to 92% in the United States in 2021) and productivity data (684 million TB versus 966 million TB in the United States in 2018). Considering that China's national-level statistics on digital engagement are driven by regional technology hubs like Shanghai, which compensate for a still significant urban–rural technological divide,[20] China's overall good performance in digital engagement indirectly corroborates the strong position of Shanghai in data volumes.

Volumes alone, however, offer only a partial view of the data indicator. A more in-depth analysis of how data can affect AI applications also requires to consider the multidimensionality of data, which can be expressed in terms of breadth, quality, and depth (Lee and Sheehan, 2018; MacroPolo):

[18] Reinsel, D., Wu, L., Gantz, J. and Rydning, J., 2019. The China Datasphere: Primed to Be the Largest Datasphere by 2025, *International Data Corporation*, January 2019, https://usermanual.wiki/m/acd018d74c4827ee4310fe8aec0f9069b07e06977de2cceb9fa24290c8c82cc8.pdf.

[19] Fixed broadband subscriptions: China 589 million subscriptions, US 127 million subscriptions; China has 41.35 subscriptions per 100 people, the US 37.58 subscriptions per 100 people. Mobile cellular subscriptions: China 1.78 billion, US 372.68 million subscriptions. In 2019, 577 million Chinese people made mobile payments, compared to 64 million in the United States. In 2018, the data generated by Internet of Things devices amounted to 152 million terabytes in China, more than double the 69 million terabytes in the United States. Sources: World Bank, 2022 (cit.), Castro et al., 2019 (cit.). The World Economic Forum's *Global Competitiveness Report 2019* also notes that China outperforms 25 OECD countries on the ICT adoption pillar, which measures similar indicators of digital engagement (pp. 15, 156). See: https://www3.weforum.org/docs/WEF_TheGlobalCompetitivenessReport2019.pdf.

[20] In 2020, only 201 million rural citizens had Internet access in China, compared to 680 million in urban areas. In the same period, 309 million rural citizens still had no Internet access. See: China Internet Network Information Center (CNNIC), 2021. The 47th "China Statistical Report on Internet Development" [第47次 "中国互联网络发展状况统计报告"]. *CNNIC Website*, 3 February, http://www.cnnic.cn/hlwfzyj/hlwxzbg/hlwtjbg/202102/t20210203_71361.htm.

- *Breadth* refers to the number of users of a given service, the population whose actions are captured in data. In this dimension, Shanghai appears very strong because it can draw from a large urban population (nearly 25 million permanent residents in 2022) that benefits from one of the most advanced technological infrastructures in China (see infra 4.2), thus generating large volumes of data.
- *Quality* refers to the structuring and labeling of digital data (e.g., data that contain correct information and are already formatted into machine-readable formats like Excel, so that they can be used by AI systems). This dimension is likely a weak point of Shanghai, considering that Chinese public organizations have a legacy of weak standards on data collection,[21] and a low level of data interoperability.[22] However, in recent years China made notable progress in this dimension, due also to national plans for improving the utilization of data. Shanghai is part of these national pilot programs,[23]

[21] "According to the *Economic Information Daily* report, 80% of China's information data resources are currently controlled by government departments at various levels. Since the development of China's big data is still in its nascent stage, a lot of fundamental data is neglected by government agencies and very few of these data resources are openly available. [...] According to a report on open data by Chinese local governments jointly issued by Fudan University and Xinhuanet.com, of the 8,398 open pieces of data on 19 local government open data platforms in China, about 25 percent were unable to be read by computers as of April 2017". Wang, J., 2018. The Bigger Picture. Challenges Lie Ahead as China Is Set to Become the World's Biggest Source of Data by 2020. *Beijing Review*, 22 February, http://www.bjreview.com/Business/201802/t20180211_800117684.html.

[22] For instance, in 2012 a survey found that 48% of Chinese hospitals had basic forms of Electronic Health Record (HER) systems. Since then, the number of Chinese hospitals using electronic records may have grown to more than 90%. However, qualitative evidence suggests interoperability is very low, and Chinese hospitals frequently use EHR systems that are not interoperable, forcing patients to bring printed health records when seeing doctors in different hospitals. See: Lei, J., Sockolow, P., Guan, P., Meng, Q. and Zhang, J., 2013. A Comparison of Electronic Health Records at Two Major Peking University Hospitals in China to United States Meaningful Use Objectives. *BMC Medical Informatics and Decision Making*, 13, 28 August, https://www.ncbi.nlm.nih.gov/pmc/articles/PMC3847100/; Zhang, L., Li, Q., Zhao, M. and Zhan, Q., 2018. Big Data and Medical Research in China. *BMJ*, 360, 5 February, https://doi.org/10.1136/bmj.j5910.

[23] Following the publication of the *Action Plan for the Promotion of Big Data Development* [促进大数据发展行动纲要, Guofa (2015) 50] in August 2015, China has established eight data-sharing pilot programs in Guizhou, Shanghai, Shenyang, Chongqing, Henan, Inner Mongolia, the Pearl River Delta and the Jing-Jin-Ji cluster (including Beijing, Tianjin and Hebei). These pilot programs are collectively known as "National Big Data

and the city has been very active in promoting data collection, standardization, and sharing, as discussed in the next subsection.

- *Depth* refers to the different data points generated about the activities of each user (i.e., how many different activities of a given user are captured in digital form). In this dimension, Shanghai is strong because the municipality has started to collect a large portion of data of its citizens within the framework of initiatives like the Social Credit System or the individual healthcare QR code[24] (Chapter 1). In addition, Shanghai has promoted its own digital government initiatives, like the already mentioned Government Online-Offline Shanghai, that combine several data sources on individual users and has advanced profiling capabilities.

4.1.2 Public Data Sharing

Metrics on volumes, breadth, quality and depth suggest that Shanghai enjoys a solid position in the data indicator. This strength is amplified by the attention that Shanghai has been attaching to public data sharing, that is the sharing of government and other public sector data in accordance with guidelines, policies or other instruments that govern data formats and dictate data management, retention, security, and privacy rules (United Nations, 2020, p. 156). Even before the Chinese government included data among the "factors of production[25]" indicating their

General Pilot Zones (国家大数据综合试验区), and have been jointly promoted by the Cyberspace Administration of China (CAC), the National Development and Reform Commission (NDRC) and the Ministry of Industry and Information Technology (MIIT). According to the scheme, these provinces and municipalities must establish their respective pilot programs in 3–5 years. See: Sohu, 2017. Taking Stock of the Eight Big National Big Data General Pilot Zones, How Many Do You Know? [盘点八大国家大数据综合试验区, 你知道几个?]. *Sohu* [搜狐], 25 May, https://www.sohu.com/a/143337087_820654.

[24] In October 2017 Shanghai introduced the *Shanghai Municipal Social Credit Provisions* (上海市社会信用条例) to regulate the Social Credit System in the municipality (http://www.spcsc.sh.cn/n1939/n1948/n1949/n1986/u1ai152106.html). By May 2019, the Shanghai social credit database accumulated 320 million data points on companies and individuals, https://www.creditchina.gov.cn/biaozhunguifan/difangbiaozhunguifan/201905/t20190523_156374.html.

[25] State Council, 2020. *Opinions of the Central Committee of the Communist Party of China and the State Council on Building a More Complete System and Mechanism for Market-Oriented Allocation of Factors of Production* [中共中央国务院关于构建更加完善

strategic importance for national development, Shanghai municipal AI plans already showed a consistent focus on public data sharing.[26] In Shanghai, shared data are accessible internally within and between public organizations, and externally to commercial actors that participate in the municipal data sharing initiative. As explained earlier in relation to the Shanghai Data Innovation Center (Chapter 3.2.3), the sharing of public data—both between public organizations and between the public and the private or non-profit sectors—is considered a major driver of innovation in the public sector, and an effective way to foster the promotion of AI technologies and applications. As contemporary AI systems usually require the processing of vast amounts of high-quality data and the public sector is one of the most data-intensive sectors, data sharing becomes a critical asset for the development of AI solutions that can be used to enhance the delivery of public services and improve outcomes for citizens. In addition, by modernizing its data governance policies and practices in a way that facilitates interoperability and connectivity of data repositories, the public sector can take advantage of data-intensive AI applications (United Nations, 2020, p. 150; Engin and Treleaven, 2019, p. 450; Desouza, 2018).

Shanghai has introduced several guidelines for managing and using public data in the municipality. In 2018, it issued the *Management*

的要素市场化配置体制机制的意见], 9 April, http://www.gov.cn/zhengce/2020-04/09/content_5500622.htm. This document added "data" to land, labor, capital and technology as a new factor of production.

26 The *Opinions* state that Shanghai wants to "take the lead in advancing the orderly opening of government data resources, focusing on key areas such as education, transportation, environment, medical care and commerce", and "establish a supervision and management system for safely sharing and exchanging data". The *Measures* require to standardize the collection and sharing of public data, to draw up an open list of public data resources to be shared with AI companies in areas such as education, medical care and tourism, and to accelerate the construction of data centers (Section 2 "Deepen the openness and application of data resources", measure no. 7. In original: "制定公共数据资源开放清单, 依法有序向人工智能企业开放教育、医疗、旅游等重点领域数据信息"; and section 5, measure no. 22, in original: 加快 [...] 数据中心 [...] 等新一代信息基础设施建设). The *AI Highland Plan* states that Shanghai will vigorously spur the sharing of public data by establishing "public data open platforms" (公共数据开放平台) and fifteen "Big Data joint innovation laboratories" (大数据联合创新实验室) in three years, focusing on medicine, transportation, tourism, energy, finance, urban management, education and other fields (Task 8, special action 3).

Measures on Public Data and the Government Online-Offline Shanghai,[27] and three guidelines for electronic certificates, electronic seals, and electronic files to accelerate the centralized management of public data.[28] In August 2019, Shanghai published China's first local government regulations specifically aimed at the sharing of public data, the *Interim Measures of Shanghai Municipality on Public Data Opening*.[29] Since then, Shanghai has regularly issued policy documents on the promotion of public data sharing, including the *Shanghai 2021 Public Data Governance and Application Key Work Plan*,[30] which lays out the general requirements for Shanghai public data governance and applications, stipulates data sources and collection must be expanded, and calls for improving data quality and governance, among others.

These guidelines on public data sharing have been followed up by several related initiatives. In 2016, the Shanghai Data Exchange Center (SDEC, 上海数据交易中心) was jointly created by SHEITC and the Shanghai Municipal Commission of Commerce.[31] The SDEC is a State-owned company that coordinates a coalition of national and municipal private and government-owned enterprises. It is in charge of the "integrated use of government and commercial data" (政府数据与商业数据融合应用), and it focuses on the opening and sharing of data on urban management, transportation, public safety, commerce, finance, marketing, and other areas.[32] The SDEC cooperates with other local

[27] Shanghai Municipal Government, 2018. *Management Measures on Public Data and the Government Online-Offline Shanghai* [上海市公共数据与一网通办管理办法], Decree no. 9, 30 September, http://jtw.sh.gov.cn/2018nszfgz/20190226/0010-29087.html.

[28] NDRC, 2020 (cit.).

[29] Shanghai Municipal Government, 2019. *Interim Measures of Shanghai Municipality on Public Data Opening* [上海市公共数据开放暂行办法], Hufuling 21, 29 August, https://www.shanghai.gov.cn/nw45024/20200824/0001-45024_62638.html.

[30] Shanghai Government General Office, 2021a. *Shanghai 2021 Public Data Governance and Application Key Work Plan* [2021年上海市公共数据治理与应用重点工作计划], Hufuban (2021) 18, 5 March, https://www.shanghai.gov.cn/nw12344/20210331/f378a8ba5f96452cb5644f5d1626cb37.html.

[31] Shanghai Data Exchange Center, Introduction to the Shanghai Data Exchange Center [上海数据交易中心介绍], https://www.chinadep.com/about.html (last accessed on 25 October 2023).

[32] Among the various services offered by the Shanghai Data Exchange Center, the one specifically dedicated to government users is the ChinaDOP (China Data Open Platform, 中国数据开放平台). In original: "是面向政府用户的公共数据开放管理套件，由数据开放

governments in China (it receives public data from more than 15 Chinese provinces) and abroad (it collects approximately 1000 global AI datasets). It also contributes to national programs on Big Data, such as the National Engineering Laboratory for Big Data Circulation and Transaction Technology (大数据流通与交易技术国家工程实验室), and the National Natural Science Foundation Big Data Sample Database Platform (国家自然科学基金会大数据样本库平台). Besides the SDEC, other notable projects on public data sharing in Shanghai include: the aforementioned Shanghai Data Innovation Center, which is recognized as a best practice by the 2020 e-government survey carried out by the United Nations (UN, 2020, p. 157); the National Big Data (Shanghai) General Trial Zone (国家大数据（上海）综合试验区), unveiled in Shanghai in 2016 as part of a national program for data sharing (see footnote 23); the creation of eight municipal data centers (城市数据中心) that carry out data analysis and storage to support Shanghai's economic, social, and digital development[33]; and the establishment of eleven Big Data Joint Innovation Labs (大数据联合创新实验室) in finance, healthcare, tourism, transportation, energy, urban management, social credit, data sharing, academic research, and other areas.[34]

门户、开放管理系统、开放数据网关三个核心组件构成", https://www.chinadep.com/system.html#3; https://mp.weixin.qq.com/s/owWS1OkbGIMLK-Ssr36ZBw.

[33] SHEITC and SHDRC, 2021. Notice on Relevant Issues for the Overall Construction of Data Centers in Shanghai in 2021[关于做好2021年本市数据中心统筹建设有关事项的通知]. *SHEITC Website*, 7 April, http://sheitc.sh.gov.cn/xxfw/20210407/3774163f0b3f4bb399e15ad592f7c2f8.html; CESI (2021, p. 27).

[34] In 2018, Shanghai established seven Big Data Joint Innovation Labs in the aforementioned areas, https://cloud.tencent.com/developer/news/278946. In October 2021, there were 11 Big Data Joint Innovation Labs that expanded their coverage to academic research and other areas (author WeChat conversation with the Director of the Shanghai Data Exchange Center, 20 October 2021). In the same month, SHEITC and CAICT published another call for proposal for the creation of further Big Data Joint Innovation Labs (https://www.shanghai.gov.cn/gwk/search/content/faf4005be3904ce997c34eaf2c5bfc8c).

4.1.3 Data Privacy Regulations

In recent years, China has initiated a major overhaul of its data privacy system.[35] Since the publication of the *Cybersecurity Law* in 2017, the country started to put in place a new regulatory framework on data protection, which includes both legally-binding regulations and non-compulsory standards (Box 4.1). Against this background, in September 2021 Shanghai issued the *Shanghai Municipal Data Regulations (draft)*.[36] The draft consists of 91 articles that aim to "promote the orderly and free flow of data in accordance with the law, ensure data security, accelerate the cultivation of the market of data as a 'production factor' and the development of the digital economy" (art. 1). The draft indicates the duties of government agencies at each administrative level, relevant departments, and data expert committees with regard to the development, use, and protection of data (art. 4–6). The draft aims to optimize Shanghai's system for public data's collection and aggregation (art. 25–31), management (art. 32–35), sharing (art. 36–40), and development and use (art. 41–43), including pricing mechanisms for products and services that use municipal data (art. 44–45). Finally, articles 76–83 outline a municipal system for data security within the framework of national laws (e.g., the *Data Security Law*). While systematizing municipal data privacy regulations, the *Shanghai Municipal Data Regulations (draft)* also confirm the enduring focus of Shanghai on the sharing of public data, stating that "[t]he sharing of public data between public management and service agencies shall be the rule, and not the exception".[37]

Like the national regulatory framework on data protection, Shanghai's data regulations can be "understood to exist in reference to the private

[35] Sacks, S., 2018. China's Emerging Data Privacy System and GDPR. *Center for Strategic & International Studies*, March 9, https://www.csis.org/analysis/chinas-emerging-data-privacy-system-and-gdpr.

[36] Shanghai Municipal People's Congress, 2021. *Shanghai Municipal Data Regulations (draft)* [上海市数据条例 (草案)], 30 September, http://www.spcsc.sh.cn/n8347/n8481/n9119/index.html.

[37] Ibid., article 36 (Principles and Mechanisms for Data Sharing). In original: "公共管理和服务机构之间共享公共数据, 应当以共享为原则, 不共享为例外". This became article 38 in the final version effective from 1 January 2022.

sector, not the State".[38] Indeed, according to some observers, "[t]he 'privacy strategy' within China appears to aim to protect the privacy of a specific type of consumer, rather than that of citizens as a whole, allowing the government to collect personal data whenever it may be necessary or merely useful for its policies[39]" (Roberts et al., 2020, p. 14). It is also observed that "[China's] legal and regulatory framework reflects the Party-State's view of data as a freely accessible governance resource and a commodity aiding economic development. Laws and regulations focus on facilitating data aggregation and on sharing between stakeholders rather than privacy rights".[40] In practice, laws and standards on data privacy appear to have limited impacts on the activity of the government and public organizations. The *Shanghai Municipal Data Regulations* became effective in January 2022.[41] Conversations with the leadership of the Shanghai Data Exchange Center—the biggest platform for public data sharing in China—confirmed that the regulations do not restrict its operations: they promote data uses in general, like government open data and data exchanges with the private sector.[42] This is consistent with a general trend indicating that public organizations in Shanghai at present do not face significant restrictions to the access and use of data, as it emerged from the analysis of the case studies and other evidence collected during the fieldwork for this book (see relevant discussions in Chapter 5).

[38] Gorman, L., 2021. China's Data Ambitions. Strategy, Emerging Technologies, and Implications for Democracies. *The National Bureau of Asian Research*, 14 August, https://www.nbr.org/publication/chinas-data-ambitions-strategy-emerging-technologies-and-implications-for-democracies/.

[39] On a similar note, commenting on the 2021 *Personal Information Protection Law* (PIPL), another scholar wrote: "[T] he PIPL and its attendant regulations serve to primarily regulate the relationship between large technology companies and consumers, as well as prevent cybercrime. It does not create meaningful constraints on data collection and use by the state". Creemers, R., 2021. *China's Emerging Data Protection Framework*, 16 November, http://doi.org/10.2139/ssrn.3964684.

[40] Von Carnap, K., Drinhausen, K. and Shi-Kupfer, K., 2020. Tracing. Testing. Tweaking. Approaches to Data-Driven Covid-19 Management in China. *MERICS*, 24 June, https://merics.org/en/report/tracing-testing-tweaking, p. 10.

[41] National Laws and Regulations Database [国家法律法规数据库], https://flk.npc.gov.cn/detail2.html?ZmY4MDgxODE3ZjQyMGFjODAxN2Y0Zjc5OTY0ZDA2N2Q (accessed on 21 October 2023). The final version of the *Shanghai Municipal Data Regulations* modified the order of some articles, but the contents remained unchanged.

[42] Author WeChat conversation with the director of the Shanghai Data Exchange Center, 29 April 2022.

Box 4.1 China's regulatory framework for personal data protection
China's regulatory framework for personal data protection includes a number of laws and standards, which were introduced or revised in recent years:

- the *Cybersecurity Law*[43] (CSL, 网络安全法), in force since June 2017, features a section on data privacy, defining principles of legality, proportionality and necessity for the collection and use of personal data. This law, however, does not stipulate enforcement mechanisms for the regulations.
- the main benchmarks for personal data protection in China are found in the *Personal Information Security Specifications*[44] (个人信息安全规范) a non-binding standard issued by the National Information Security Standardization Technical Committee, effective from May 2018. Its revised version is effective from October 2020. This standard requires explicit consent and encryption to collect sensitive information like biometric data, travel history or health information.
- the new *Civil Code*[45] adopted in May 2020 strengthens privacy protection by more clearly defining under what circumstances personal information can be gathered and used (art. 111), and by expanding civil liability for infringement of privacy rights (title 4, section 6). The *Civil Code*, however, only states the fundamental legal principles of personal data protection, without any details on implementation.

[43] National People's Congress, 2016. *Cybersecurity Law of the People's Republic of China* [中华人民共和国网络安全法], http://www.npc.gov.cn/npc/c30834/201611/270b43e8b35e4f7ea98502b6f0e26f8a.shtml.

[44] National Information Security Standardization Technical Committee, 2020. *Personal Information Security Specifications* [个人信息安全规范], http://openstd.samr.gov.cn/bzgk/gb/newGbInfo?hcno=4568F276E0F8346EB0FBA097AA0CE05E.

[45] National People's Congress, 2020. *Civil Code of the People's Republic of China* [中华人民共和国民法典], http://www.npc.gov.cn/npc/c30834/202006/75ba6483b8344591abd07917e1d25cc8.shtml.

- the *Data Security Law*[46] (DSL, 数据安全法), effective from 1 September 2021, establishes a hierarchical data categorization system. Key categories include: "national core data" (i.e., related to national security, important public interests, etc.), for which mishandling could carry penalties or criminal charges; and "important data" (introduced by the CSL). The definition of what constitutes "important data" is still evolving. The DSL states that a consortium of national-level agencies will develop catalogues of "important data", while local governments and regulatory agencies are required to develop more detailed catalogues to identify the scope of "important data" based on their region and sectors. At the same time, the DSL focuses on the general principles regarding data security, without specific reference to personal information; and previous sector-specific laws don't provide clear indications on what constitutes personal information (e.g., the *Basic Healthcare and Health Promotion Law* of 2019 prohibits illegal collection, use and sale of personal data, but it does not clearly define "personal health data").
- the *Personal Information Protection Law*[47] (PIPL, 个人信息保护法), effective from 1 November 2021, marks China's first comprehensive legal attempt to define personal information and regulate the storing, transferring, and processing of personal data. Like the European Union's *General Data Protection Regulation*, the PIPL states that personal information gathered by a company must be limited to the minimum amount necessitated by the purpose of data usage (art. 6). The law also defines the concept and scope of personal information, and introduces the principle of minimization (art. 28–30).

[46] National People's Congress, 2021a. *Data Security Law of the People's Republic of China* [中华人民共和国数据安全法], http://www.npc.gov.cn/npc/c30834/202106/7c9af12f51334a73b56d7938f99a788a.shtml.

[47] National People's Congress, 2021b. *Personal Information Protection Law of the People's Republic of China* [个人信息保护法], http://www.npc.gov.cn/npc/c30834/202108/a8c4e3672c74491a80b53a172bb753fe.shtml.

In general, it is also observed that these laws and standards have different implications in terms of the amount of data that are made available to public and private organizations. For instance, requirements for reporting data breaches have little effect on the availability of data, while the requirements to minimize data collection or retain data for limited periods of time (like those, not compulsory, of the *Personal Information Security Specification*) can have significant impacts on data availability (Castro et al., 2019).

Besides official laws and standards, there is an emerging debate about data privacy in China. This debate includes a spectrum that ranges from those advocating for greater data privacy protection, to those calling for increased data liberalization to benefit AI development (Ding, 2018). The "liberal faction" is mostly represented by companies. For instance, Internet giant Tencent argues that data liberalization could spur further innovation: "It can be said that the issue of data liberalization is a pain point in the development of AI in China, and it needs to be elaborated upon in a more comprehensive and in-depth manner in the [China's national AI] strategy" (Tencent and CAICT, 2017, p. 181). Data privacy is also a major topic discussed by private companies and government bodies in the Chinese AI ethics initiatives (Appendix II), which usually show attention to the privacy rights of the final users, in line with many other countries (Gal, 2020). At the more "conservative" end of the privacy spectrum, there is a faction advocating for greater data privacy protection and more comprehensive safeguards to personal information. This group is more variegate, and it includes scholars, experts and the general public, who often express their views on social media and other non-official channels.[48] At present, however, there is no evidence that these public debates are constraining the government use of data (see also 4.5)

[48] Some examples collected by the author include: Leiphone, 2018. Is Your Personal Information Safe? MIIT Arrange Talks with Baidu, Ant Financial and Jinri Toutiao [你的个人信息安全吗?工信部约谈百度蚂蚁金服今日头条], *Sina Tech* [新浪科技], 12 January,http://tech.sina.com.cn/roll/2018-01-12/doc-ifyqqciz5880474.shtml; Hong, Y., 2018. Personal Information Security Specification: 5 Deeply Felt Questions and Answers [对《个人信息安全规范》五大重点关切的回应和解释], 5 February, https://mp.weixin.qq.com/s/rSW-Ayu6zNXw87itYHcPYA; Lao, D., 2019. The Hidden Worries of Facial Recognition Technology [人脸识别技术的隐忧], https://mp.weixin.qq.com/s/7eo7AqcPJ6qiaTTh2o25zA?fbclid=IwAR0ZxckmxEGmD2rgZIloKYF3DiaAjvHpdki6oqwgH8EubR2I-Eb1y8_ySKQ (this case is mentioned also in the study presented in 5.5); Liu, W., 2021. Focus on Front-End Governance: Prospects for Face Data Protection

4.1.4 *Conclusions on the Data Indicator*

The metrics examined in this section indicate that Shanghai has a strong position in the data indicator. Shanghai has accumulated a great amount of data on its municipal data platforms, and it has shown great attention to data collection and use. In particular, Shanghai has been very active in promoting the sharing of public data, which is a critical resource for the development of public sector AI implementations. Shanghai is officially recognized as a national best practice in this area. In March 2021, the average daily data transaction volume of the Shanghai Data Exchange Center accounted for 50% of the national total.[49] By July 2021, Shanghai had established the largest number (50) of open data libraries in China (CESI, 2021, p. 39). And in the period 2018–2020, the city ranked first in government data sharing among all Chinese provinces and municipalities for three consecutive years,[50] confirming its position in 2021 and remaining in the top 3 also in 2022.[51] Shanghai public data sharing is part of a strategy to position the municipality as the major Big Data center in China and an international data hub, as documented by the several high-profile initiatives recently adopted by the municipality.[52] As such, it is likely that the Shanghai government will continue to promote

Legislation [重在前端治理: 人脸数据保护立法展望]. *Caijing E-Law*, 4 November, https://mp.weixin.qq.com/s/BQBBJc0mCGS9_tOvHIwh2g?fbclid=IwAR2d9KWuY-ESd5DXj3vpalYsCAi3QB1jnjQWrS1B6p9BZS52iMBd00q_oO0.

[49] Shanghai World AI Conference, 2021 (cit.).

[50] NDRC, 2020 (cit.). In original: "截至2020年5月，上海已连续三年在第三方测评的《中国地方政府数据开放报告》排名中位列省级第一".

[51] Fudan University DMG Lab [复旦大学数字与移动治理实验室], Open Data Index [开放数林指数] Website, http://ifopendata.fudan.edu.cn/report (last accessed on 21 October 2023).

[52] Shanghai Data Innovation Center, 2021. Ten Big Developments in Big Data in 2020 [2020年大数据发展十大事件], *WeChat Blogpost*, 5 January, https://mp.weixin.qq.com/s/3P89gv6-wKR0-gI6BTV1pQ; Shanghai Data Exchange Center, 2021. Shanghai Data Exchange Established, Global Data Ecosystem Conference 2021 Held in Shanghai [上海数据交易所揭牌成立 2021全球数商大会在沪召开], 25 November, https://mp.weixin.qq.com/s/PemYGovwrh23wH6iL2BgVg. The Shanghai Data Exchange (上海数据交易所) is a data trade platform that includes organizations servicing data transaction, data asset evaluation, data security and other sectors. According to the exchange, no transaction will be conducted if the data purchaser cannot explain the exact scenario in which the data will be used.

the sharing of public data, further consolidating this important resource for public sector AI applications.

China's evolving data protection regime and the debates over data privacy combat common misperceptions that the country pays scarce attention to how data is managed and shared, but they are yet to have any visible impact on the capacity of Chinese and Shanghai public organizations to collect and use data. While the fieldwork conducted for this book suggests that data privacy receives significant attention by Shanghai policymakers and public organizations, the interviewees also confirm that they face few restrictions in data collection and use (Chapter 5.1). This finding is consistent with the breadth and depth of data collected on Shanghai's government databases, the partnerships between public organizations and tech companies discussed in the analysis of the case studies, and evidence suggesting that Chinese public organizations in general face lesser limitations to the collection and use of personal data.[53]

4.2 Technological and Physical Infrastructure

The use of AI in the public sector, like in other areas of activity, requires that adequate infrastructure is in place to support the deployment of AI technologies and applications. Such infrastructure is technological, as data-intensive AI systems generally need continuous data collection (e.g., smart sensors) and related storage capabilities (e.g., data lakes), sufficient computing power to process the information collected (e.g., computing centers and platforms), and a network for the fast and reliable transmission of data (e.g., 5G, high-speed broadband), among others. Such infrastructure is also physical, because real-world implementations of AI systems often need the adaptation or creation of infrastructure such as roads for autonomous and connected smart driving, pilot zones to test AI applications before they can be adopted on large-scale, and structural adjustments to schools, hospitals, government administrative centers, or any other physical asset that must accommodate AI systems.

This section examines two sets of metrics to assess the status of the technological and physical infrastructure that enable AI implementations

[53] Simonite, T., 2019. How Health Care Data and Lax Rules Help China Prosper in AI. *Wired*, January 8, https://www.wired.com/story/health-care-data-lax-rules-help-china-prosper-ai/; Sheehan, M., 2019. Much Ado About Data: How America and China Stack Up. *MacroPolo*, July 16, https://macropolo.org/ai-data-us-china/.

in Shanghai. For physical infrastructure, it tracks the advancements of the municipal-level AI clusters of Shanghai, which have significant physical footprints and are the main foci of AI activity in the municipality. For technological infrastructure, it looks at metrics that measure fast mobile and broadband connections, Internet of Things, and computing power.

4.2.1 Physical Infrastructure

To support real-world applications of AI technologies, Shanghai has created two municipal experimental areas: the Shanghai National New Generation Artificial Intelligence Innovation Development Trial Area (Shanghai AI Trial Area, 上海国家新一代人工智能创新发展试验区), and the Shanghai (Pudong New Area) Artificial Intelligence Innovation Application Pilot Zone (Pudong AI Pilot Zone, 上海 (浦东新区) 人工智能创新应用先导区). Both launched in May 2019, these two experimental areas are hallmark projects in the creation of physical infrastructure for AI development. They were designed and developed to support AI implementations in Shanghai, consistently with the focus on AI applications highlighted in the municipal AI plans. More specifically:

- the **Shanghai AI Trial Area** is China's second National New Generation AI Innovation Development Trial Area after the one established in Beijing in February 2019 (at the time of this writing, China has 18 national AI trial areas). Announced by the Ministry of Science and Technology (MOST), the Shanghai Trial Area is managed by the Shanghai Municipal Commission for Science and Technology. It focuses on the application of AI in healthcare, smart transportation, and smart neighborhoods. It aims to make Shanghai a leading national and global pilot area for AI applications that can be replicated in other Chinese cities[54];
- the **Pudong AI Pilot Zone** is China's first pilot zone entirely dedicated to AI applications. It was announced by the Ministry of Industry and Information Technology (MIIT), and it is managed by SHEITC. The zone has three official tasks: address the legal,

[54] Xinhua, 2019. Construction of the Shanghai National New Generation Artificial Intelligence Innovation Development Trial Area Has Started [上海国家新一代人工智能创新发展试验区建设启动]. *Xinhua News*, 25 May, http://www.xinhuanet.com/2019-05/25/c_1124541193.htm.

policy, and institutional obstacles faced by AI applications; explore new working methods that make good use of policies, standards, and financial supervision; and leverage technology, talents, applications, and companies to enhance the international competitiveness of China's smart industry.[55]

A few months after the launch of these two AI experimental areas, in September 2019 the *AI Highland Plan* announced the creation of four **AI innovation clusters** in Shanghai, called "carrier spaces" (载体空间). These are located in the areas of Pudong Zhangjiang, Xuhui West Bund, Lingang New Area, and Minhang Maqiao.[56] Also known as "4 + X" carrier spaces,[57] the AI innovation clusters are located within the Shanghai AI Trial Area and the Pudong AI Pilot Zone. Having a specific physical location, they allow to track with greater precision the progress of Shanghai's major physical infrastructure for AI development. During the fieldwork, the author could visit three of these four municipal AI clusters.

The main center of AI activity in **Pudong Zhangjiang** is the Zhangjiang AIsland (张江人工智能岛), one of the AI pilot application scenarios approved by Shanghai in April 2019 (Chapter 5.3). Established in 2018, the AIsland is a demonstration park dedicated to the integrated application of AI, IoT, and 5G technologies. It covers an area of 100,000 square meters, and by 2025 it is planned to expand to 3.5 million square meters. The AIsland aims to create replicable and scalable models for AI applications that can be extended to other parks in the Zhangjiang area and in Pudong (SJTU et al., 2019). When the author visited the AIsland in January 2021, the first phase of the project was completed. The AIsland is a testbed for various AI applications in public security (smart surveillance, fire prevention), environment management and supervision (smart buildings, smart lampposts smart irrigation, smart

[55] SHEITC News, 2019. The Construction of the Shanghai Pudong AI Innovation Application Pilot Zone Steadily Advances [上海浦东人工智能创新应用先导区建设稳步推进]. *SHEITC Website*, 17 July, http://sheitc.sh.gov.cn/zxxx/20190717/0020-683111.html; Yang, 2019 (cit.).

[56] SHEITC, 2019 (cit.), *AI Highland Plan*, section 3, subsection 1, task 1. In original: "推动优势集聚, 布局浦东张江、临港新片区、徐汇滨江、闵行马桥等产业创新重点集聚区, 培育引进领军企业, 建设具有国际竞争力的产业集群".

[57] Sohu, 2021. The Development Status of Shanghai's AI Industry and the Next Steps [上海人工智能产业发展情况和下一步规划], *Sohu* [搜狐], 9 July, https://www.sohu.com/a/476548734_120056153.

dustbins for automatic garbage sorting), service robots (security robots), and autonomous driving (driverless street-sweeping cars, vehicles that sell food and beverage inside the park). The AIsland also hosts numerous AI and hi-tech companies, two major AI research institutes (the Tongji University's Research Institute for Intelligent Autonomous Systems and the Microsoft AI & IoT Insider Lab), and financial investors (Sequoia Capital).

The AI Space on West Bund (西岸智慧谷) is the main AI cluster situated in **Xuhui West Bund**. Announced at the end of 2019, the AI Space on West Bund is concentrated in an area of 0.5 km^2, but it has a strong vertical development with a total floor area of 1.2 million m^2. Its landmark project is the 200-meter-high West Bund AI Tower (西岸国际人工智能中心). A self-proclaimed "vertical Silicon Valley", the AI Tower consists of two twin buildings that integrate government, industry, education, research, and applications, aiming to facilitate academic exchanges and business cooperation. For companies that contribute to city operations in AI (对城市运营有帮助的企业), the AI Tower provides tailor-made policies and services, making the location attractive for many AI players.[58] Visited by the author in September 2021, the AI Tower is a major hub of leading AI companies (Alibaba, Huawei, Mininglamp, Shanghai INESA, Yitu and others), fast-growing startups, and municipal-level research facilities that host nearly 160 PhD researchers (Microsoft Research Asia; Shanghai AI Lab, see infra; Shanghai Qi Zhi Institute; Conflux Blockchain Research Center). This cluster is becoming a driver for the integration of AI research and business development in Shanghai.

The **Lingang New Area**, part of the National (Shanghai) Pilot Free Trade Zone, has also been designated as a hub for AI development.[59]

[58] Shanghai Xuhui District Government, 2020. What Are the Implications of Xuhui Building an AI Ecosystem in the West Bund for Shanghai's Industrial Innovation and Upgrading? [徐汇打造西岸智慧谷人工智能生态圈, 对上海产业创新升级有哪些启示?], *Xuhui District Government*, 10 September, http://www.xuhui.gov.cn/xwzx_bmlf/20200910/273072.html.

[59] China (Shanghai) Pilot Free Trade Zone Lingang New Area Management Committee, 2019. *China (Shanghai) Pilot Free Trade Zone Lingang New Area Several Policies and Measures for the Promotion of Industrial Development and the Agglomeration of Integrated Circuits, Artificial Intelligence, Biomedicine, and Aerospace Industries* [中国（上海）自由贸易试验区临港新片区促进产业发展若干政策和集聚发展集成电路、人工智能、生物医药、航空航天产业若干措施], 20 October, https://www.sh-keji.cn/kjcx/1116.html.

The area hosts several AI companies and an important project of Shanghai's technological infrastructure (i.e., SenseTime AI computing platform; see infra, 4.2.2). One landmark project with extensive physical footprint is the Shanghai Lingang Intelligent Connected Vehicles Comprehensive Demonstration Zone (上海临港智能网联汽车综合测试示范区), an AI pilot application scenario like Zhangjiang AIsland. Established in August 2019, the Lingang demonstration zone focuses on priority application areas set forth in the Shanghai AI plans: autonomous driving applications for public transport, smart logistics, and AI-powered urban management (infrastructure maintenance like street cleaning[60]). The demonstration zone covers a bounded area of 3.2 km^2 (physically separated from the surrounding public roads), which includes 4.7 km of roads for testing autonomous vehicles. Visited by the author in September 2020, the demonstration zone was fully operational, entirely covered by 5G signal, and equipped with traffic lights and other equipment that simulate real-life driving conditions, including urban scenarios (e.g., parked vehicles, dummies of pedestrians and cyclists), a tunnel, and water pipes to simulate raining conditions. The control center of the zone showed real-time information on vehicles, drivers, and activities in the zone, collecting images from over 70 cameras. Autonomous vehicles that receive a certificate from the certification body of the demonstration zone, the Shanghai Lingang Intelligent Connected Vehicle Innovation Center, are allowed to conduct tests on authorized public roads surrounding the demonstration zone, with a total length of over 26 km.

The fourth municipal AI cluster is located in **Minhang Maqiao**. The landmark project in this cluster is the Maqiao AI Innovation Experimental Zone (上海马桥人工智能创新试验区), an area of 15.7 km^2 established in July 2019 that entered the first stage of development in December 2020. The Maqiao AI Zone was designed to promote AI applications for "intelligent production, intelligent life, and intelligent ecosystem". It includes an "application comprehensive practice area" (应用综合实践区) of 4.9 km^2 dedicated to AI applications in "urban management, social governance, and people's livelihood services", which focuses on the use of AI

[60] Shanghai Fabu, 2020. "Driverless" Sweepers, Passenger Cars and Mining Cards... You Can See Them in the Lingang Demonstration Area ["无人" 驾驶的清扫车、乘用车、矿卡……临港这个示范区就能看到!]. *WeChat Post*, 4 July, https://mp.weixin.qq.com/s/0Ow1EvrYBAV67Yr6f-gSPw.

in government services, public transportation, medicine and healthcare, among others.[61]

4.2.2 Technological Infrastructure

In addition to the infrastructure for storing and sharing data (4.1), Shanghai has also been very active in creating the technological infrastructure necessary to transfer, process, and use the big amounts of digital information required by contemporary AI systems. Such infrastructure relies upon fast mobile and broadband connections, Internet of Things, and computing power as its main pillars.[62]

5G connections represent the current state-of-the-art in mobile connectivity, and their speed and low latency is considered a prerequisite for supporting several AI applications.[63] Shanghai has the most developed 5G network in China. In March 2019, Shanghai became the first city in the world to complete the 5G coverage of an entire district (Hongkou

61 Shanghai Government General Office, 2019. *Notice of the Shanghai Government General Office on the Publication of the "Work Plan for Promoting the Construction of Shanghai Maqiao Artificial Intelligence Innovation Experimental Zone"* [推进上海马桥人工智能创新试验区建设工作方案], Hufu Banfa (2019) 19, https://www.shanghai.gov.cn/nw44388/20200824/0001-44388_61289.html.

62 The *Opinions* call for the establishment of high-performance computing facilities and the acceleration of the construction of network infrastructure such as next-generation mobile communications and Internet of Things technologies (section 5, par. 5.6). The *AI Highland Plan* calls for: coordinating the construction and operation of 5G, Internet of Things, cloud computing, supercomputing (section 3, 1.3); building high-performance AI open computing platforms that serve the computing power needs of research institutes and small and medium-sized enterprises, and supporting applications in security, transportation, finance and other industries (section 3, 2.7); and establishing a municipal high-speed intelligent network that consists of "dual gigabit" high-speed city coverage for mobile networks and fixed broadband, taking the lead in 5G communications and other technologies that support the construction of an information highway for in-depth and extensive AI applications (section 4, Guarantee Measures).

63 The 5G networks usually support 20 gigabits per second per cell, with an average per user of at least 1 gigabit. They also have a very low latency (i.e., the waiting time for the connection between devices), about 1 millisecond from current rates of 20 milliseconds. These features are expected to enable instantaneous communication between smart cars, the remote control of surgical robots, the deployment of drones and several other AI applications. See: https://www.gruppotim.it/en/innovation/infrastructure/5g/the-full-potential-of-5G.html.

district), and started trial applications in it.[64] Since then, Shanghai has maintained a leading position in 5G networks in China (CAICT and BDA, 2020), which in 2020 was already the country with the widest 5G coverage in the world with a total of 718,000 5G stations (CESI, 2021, p. 28). In August 2021, Shanghai had built and activated 31,190 5G stations,[65] approximately 4.3% of the national total, and the average 5G download speed was around 300Mps outdoor.[66] In 2021, the Shanghai government announced that by 2025 the total number of 5G stations in the municipality would more than double to reach 70,000.[67] This target was already surpassed in October 2023, when Shanghai had installed approximately 88,000 5G stations, further cementing its leadership in China.[68]

The availability of **high-speed broadband** is also an enabling factor of AI implementations because it supports the fast and steady transmission of data necessary to support manifold AI applications, including all the applications that rely on quick and stable access to databases (e.g., facial recognition, or Big Data analytics in general). At the end of 2020, Shanghai basically achieved full coverage of gigabit fixed broadband connections,[69] and the average available download for fixed broadband

[64] People.cn, 2019. Shanghai Makes the First 5G Mobile Call [上海拨通首个5G手机通话]. *People.cn* [人民网], 31 March, http://scitech.people.com.cn/n1/2019/0331/c1007-31004919.html.

[65] Yu, K., 2021. Shanghai Has Built More Than 30,000 5G Base Stations, Will Reach 70,000 by 2025 [上海已建成5G基站超3万个，到2025年这一数据将达7万]. *The Paper* [澎湃], 16 August, https://www.thepaper.cn/newsDetail_forward_14066108.

[66] SHEITC, 2021. Notice on the Implementation of "Free Upgrade of 100M Broadband for Families in Difficulty" [为困难家庭免费升级百兆宽带"实施工作的通知], Hujingxinji (2021) 139, 18 February, http://www.sheitc.sh.gov.cn/xxfw/20210218/7514587f8d2741d9930f2a21d3828984.html.

[67] Ibid.

[68] Shanghai Security News, 2023. A Total of 88,000 5G Stations Have Been Built and Opened in Shanghai, and Its Computing Power Ranks Among the Top in the Country. [上海累计建成并开通8.8万个5G基站 算力水平位居全国前列]. *Shanghai Security News* [上海证券报], 19 October, https://news.cnstock.com/news,bwkx-202310-5136884.htm.

[69] Gigabit broadband is an Internet connection that offers a speed of 1 gigabit per second (1Gbps/1 Gb) or more, compared to average download rates that are currently in the range of 10 Mb and 600 Mb, depending on the provider. See: https://www.broadbandgenie.co.uk/broadband/help/what-is-gigabit-broadband.

was slightly above 50Mbps according to government sources.[70] This made Shanghai the first city in China to surpass the 50Mbps threshold.[71] In the same period, the municipality also strengthened its status as an international information and communication hub, and the capacity of submarine optical cable communication reached 22Tbps.[72] Since then, Shanghai has consolidated its leadership in average available download for fixed broadband, reaching 60.06Mbps in December 2022.[73]

Internet of Things (IoT) is an important source for the collection of digital data. While this indicator was not used in the data metric (4.1) due to the lack of statistics on the amount data of collected in Shanghai from IoT sources, IoT is also a useful indicator to assess the level of development of Shanghai's technological infrastructure. At the end of 2020, Shanghai had installed nearly 600,000 smart sensors, covering more than 30 types of sensors.[74] Another proxy to assess the status of Shanghai's IoT is the diffusion of Internet Protocol Version 6 (IPv6[75]), which is a prerequisite to accommodate and support the integration and diffusion of IoT. In 2020, Shanghai had an average of 54.73 IPv6 addresses per million

[70] Shanghai Government General Office, 2021. *Shanghai Comprehensively Promotes the 14th Five-Year Plan of Urban Digital Transformation* (cit.). In original: "截至2020年底, 本市基本实现千兆固定宽带家庭全覆盖, 平均可用下载速率超过50Mbps".

[71] SHEITC, 2021. Notice on the Implementation of "Free Upgrade of 100M Broadband for Families in Difficulty" (cit.).

[72] Shanghai Government General Office, 2021. *Shanghai Comprehensively Promotes the 14th Five-Year Plan of Urban Digital Transformation* (cit.). In original: "国际信息通信枢纽地位增强, 通信海光缆容量达到22Tbps" (section 1.1).

[73] IT Times, 2022. Where in China Is There the Fastest Internet Speed (Which Locality Has the Fastest Internet Speed?) [中国哪里的网速最快(中国什么地方网速最快?)]. *IT Times* [IT时报], 5 December, https://www.rdhyw.com/news/show-17088.html.

[74] Shanghai Government General Office, 2021b. *Shanghai Comprehensively Promotes the 14th Five-Year Plan of Urban Digital Transformation* (cit.). In original: "建设30余种智能传感终端近60万个" (section 1.1). Smart sensors measure a physical phenomenon like temperature or movement, and convert it into digital data. Commercially available smart sensors include motion sensors, temperature sensors, light sensors, leak sensors (for water), air quality sensors, weather sensors, among others.

[75] The IPv is a communication protocol that assigns a unique IP address for identification and location definition to devices connected to the Internet, which is necessary for the device to communicate with the network. The protocol specifies how communications take place between one device and another through an addressing system. Compared to its predecessor IPv4 that works on 32 bits, IPv6 works on 128 bits and thus allows far more IP addresses (2^{128} against 2^{32}) to connect devices to the Internet, including smart sensors and various other IoT devices.

citizens, in line with other major Chinese cities (CESI, 2021, p. 29). In April 2023, 71.5% of Shanghai's active Internet users had an IPv6 address, confirming the leading position of Shanghai in this indicator.[76]

Finally, adequate **computing power** is needed to process massive amounts of data and support other features of contemporary AI systems. In this indicator Shanghai is also a recognized leader among Chinese cities and provinces. In terms of total capacity, in 2020 Shanghai ranked in the top three cities and provinces in China with Beijing and Guangdong province, with an average of more than 15 EFlops[77] each. Shanghai computing power grew by more than 50% in 2020, and the municipality led nationally in various dimensions of computing power, including "basic computing" (基础算力, i.e., traditional servers) and smart computing (智能算力, i.e., computing for AI training models; CAICT, 2021, pp. 30–31). Since then, Shanghai has maintained its leading position in China. In 2022, Shanghai was ranked as the second "strongest city" (强市) for computing power after Beijing (CAICT, 2023, p. 44), confirming the strengths of Shanghai in various dimensions of computing power (CAICT, 2023, pp. 32, 38–39). Shanghai also hosts one of China's leading smart computing centers,[78] the SenseTime Technology Shanghai New Generation AI Computing and Empowerment Platform (商汤科技上海新一代人工智能计算与赋能平台). Initiated

[76] Shanghai Observer, 2023. IPv6 Internet active users account for 71.51%, and Shanghai ranks among the top in the country in terms of development level in this field [IPv6互联网活跃用户占比71.51%, 这一领域的发展水平上海居全国前列]. *Shanghai Observer* [上观], 26 April, https://export.shobserver.com/baijiahao/html/606738.html.

[77] Flops stands for "floating point operations per second". One ExaFlop is equivalent to 10^{18} Flops. In 2020, China's computing power reached 135 exaFlops (EFlops), accounting for about 31% of the global share, maintaining a high growth rate of 55% year-on-year, which is about 16% higher than the global average (CAICT, 2021).

[78] "Smart computing centers" (智能计算中心) focus on AI training models. "[They] use advanced AI chips and the latest AI theories to provide shared computing power, mathematical and algorithmic services for the computing needs of processing massive amounts of data, intelligent algorithm acceleration, and high-speed training and inference in diverse scenarios of AI. The new type of computing power infrastructure is receiving extensive attention from governments, enterprises and research institutions. In April 2020, for the first time the National Development and Reform Commission incorporated smart computing centers into the computing power infrastructure category (算力基础设施范畴), and it proposed to deploy about 10 regional data center clusters and smart computing centers across the country". The CAICT report estimated that the proportion of smart computing power in China's overall compute stock would increase to 70% by 2023 (CAICT, 2021, p. 15).

in July 2020,[79] it started operations in January 2022.[80] The SenseTime Shanghai platform, now called AIDC, focuses on computer vision, the core business of SenseTime. The platform "can meet the needs of 4 ultra-large-scale cities [*i.e., cities with more than 20 million citizens*] at the same time, and provides the capabilities to access 8.5 million video channels" (CAICT, 2021, p. 16). The CAICT report highlights that the SenseTime Shanghai platform is an example of government-enterprise cooperation (政企合作), similar to other smart computing centers implemented by Huawei and other technology companies in collaboration with local governments of other cities and provinces (e.g., Shenzhen, Wuhan).

4.2.3 *Conclusions on the Infrastructure Indicator*

The indicators examined in this section suggest that Shanghai has a solid position in the infrastructure metric. In physical infrastructure, the construction of the municipal-level AI clusters is proceeding steadily. Three of the four AI clusters (Maqiao, Zhangjiang and Lingang) serve as "physical sandboxes" that allow for proof-of-concept and small-scale trials for AI applications that are highly relevant to the activities of the public sector. As emphasized earlier, Zhangjiang AIsland is testing various applications related to smart city operations, including public security, environment supervision, autonomous driving, and other applications that integrate AI, IoT, and 5G technologies; Lingang hosts the demonstration zone for Connected Vehicles, and it is actively promoting the creation of public infrastructure to support autonomous vehicles and public transport; Maqiao is designed to be a testbed for AI applications in urban management, social governance, and the use of AI in government services, public transportation, medicine, and healthcare. The fact that these demonstration zones are owned and operated by the municipal government allows Shanghai to steer AI applications toward areas that

[79] SenseTime, 2020. SenseTime Technology "New Generation AI Computing and Empowerment Platform" Major Project Officially Kicked-Off [商汤科技 "新一代人工智能计算与赋能平台" 重点项目正式启动]. *SenseTime Website*, 7 July, https://www.sensetime.com/cn/news-detail/54512?categoryId=72.

[80] Lingang Group, 2022. SenseTime Artificial Intelligence Computing Center AIDC Is Put into Use Today, Dongfang Xingang Helps the Ecosystem Innovation and Development of AI Computing Power! [商汤科技人工智能计算中心AIDC今日投用, 东方芯港助力人工智能算力生态创新发展!], *Lingang Group Website*, 24 January, https://www.shlingang.com/lg1/lingangjituan/xwzx/focusnewarea/202201/t20220125_24516.shtml.

are useful to the government, consistently with other pilot zones in the country.[81] Besides supporting trial applications of technologies that are expected to feed into public sector applications, these AI clusters have created hubs of AI companies that bring tax revenues, employment, and other benefits to the municipality; hence, it is reasonable to infer that Shanghai will continue to provide infrastructural support to sustain the development of these AI clusters.

In technological infrastructure, Shanghai is a national leader in 5G networks, fast broadband connection, Internet of Things, and computing power. These are universal enablers of AI applications and are necessary for applications in the public sector like other areas. It could be objected that being a national leader does not imply that Shanghai has an advanced technological infrastructure, given that China lags behind many developed nations in this indicator (e.g., uneven broadband coverage). At the same time, it is widely acknowledged that the methodology used to calculate aggregate scores for China is often deceptive, because the stark digital divide between urban and rural areas tends to underrate the more developed areas like Shanghai, where the infrastructure is far more advanced (see earlier discussions in the data metric). In addition, recent municipal documents indicate that Shanghai will continue to expand its technological infrastructure. The *14th Five-year Plan for Urban Digital Transformation* published in October 2021 states that by 2025 the average speed of 5G mobile connection in Shanghai will reach approximately 500 Mbps, while the average available download rate for broadband connection will surpass 120 Mbps, more than doubling the 50 Mbps of 2020. While these are statements about the future, Shanghai has a proven track of meeting targets in AI-related infrastructure, as demonstrated for instance by the rapid construction of data centers (4.1) and clusters of AI development. Particularly ambitious is the target set for the Internet of Things, where Shanghai aims to accelerate the transition to the so-called Artificial Intelligence of Things, that is the use of data for optimizing and personalizing products and services. By 2025, the number of smart sensors in the municipality will exceed 100 million,[82] a nearly 16.700% increase compared to the 600,000 smart sensors installed

[81] China Daily, 2020. China Promotes Local AI Pilot Zones. *China Daily*, 9 May, https://www.chinadaily.com.cn/a/202005/09/WS5eb6723fa310a8b241154837.html.

[82] Shanghai Government General Office, 2021. *14th Five-Year Plan for Urban Digital Transformation* (cit.), section 2.3, table of indicators.

at the end of 2020. While this target may be overambitious, this political determination is consistent with the municipality's focus on "new infrastructures" outlined in the *Shanghai Action Plan for Promoting the Construction of New Infrastructure (2020–2022)* and the subsequent *Shanghai Action Plan for the Further Promoting the Construction of New Infrastructure (2023–2026)*.[83] This political commitment is expected to drive Shanghai to consolidate position in technological infrastructure.

4.3 AI TALENTS

Studies on AI ecosystems usually define AI-skilled human capital in terms of AI talents. These are experts who are active in the field of AI, hold advanced degrees in computer science/artificial intelligence or related quantitative fields, and can claim AI-related patents and/or publications to their names (Castro et al., 2019; Ding, 2019; Tsinghua, 2018). AI talents are important for implementing this technology in practice because contemporary AI systems often display high levels of complexity, requiring that experts "fine-tune" such systems to work for a given domain and dataset (Marcus and Davis, 2019). Capable AI researchers, practitioners, and engineers are crucial to apply artificial intelligence to specific problem sets, including in the public sector; hence, their availability is used here as a proxy to measure the human capital needed to make AI implementation possible in the public sector, as done by previous research on AI readiness in government (Oxford Insights and IDRC, 2020.

This section adopts a multidimensional approach to assess the AI talent indicator in Shanghai. It examines three metrics: (i) the size and sources of Shanghai's AI talent pool, as a baseline indicator of the availability of the human resources needed to promote AI implementations; (ii) the output produced by these talents (i.e., AI publications and patents), as a proxy of the quality and impacts of the municipal talent pool; and (iii) the

[83] Shanghai Municipal People's Government, 2023. *Shanghai Action Plan for Further Promoting the Construction of New Infrastructure (2023–2026)* [上海市进一步推进新型基础设施建设行动方案(2023–2026年)]. Hufu (2023) 51, 15 September, https://www.shanghai.gov.cn/nw12344/20231018/8050cb446990454fb932136c0b20ba4d.html. The *Shanghai Action Plan for Promoting the Construction of New Infrastructure (2020–2022)* was quoted in Chapter 3.2.

initiatives that Shanghai is promoting in AI education and talent attraction policies, two primary sources of inputs to expand the municipal AI talent base. Assessing both inputs and outputs is essential: inputs may take time to eventually materialize into measurable outputs, while outputs do not reflect all the innovative potential of the inputs (Ding, 2018). Statistics for AI talents are mainly drawn from Tsinghua University's *China AI Development Report 2018* (Tsinghua, 2018), an authoritative source that covers most of the metrics considered in this section, allowing to contextualize Shanghai's position in this indicator. Statistical discrepancies with other, more recent sources are highlighted when relevant to the analysis.

4.3.1 *The AI Talent Pool of Shanghai*

Shanghai is a leading city for the **concentration of AI talents** in China. In 2017, Shanghai hosted 10,592 Chinese AI talents, defined as researchers having Chinese AI-related patents or AI-related academic papers in Chinese or English over the last ten years. In relative terms, in 2017 Shanghai hosted 5.25% of the total 201,281 Chinese AI talents (Tsinghua, 2018, p. 42), ranking fourth nationwide. Shanghai closely trailed Nanjing (third) and Xi'an (second), while Beijing maintained a clear edge in the size of its talent pool, ranking first in China with 27,355 AI talents, or 13.5% of the national total. The relative gap of Shanghai in the size of the AI talent pool reduces when looking at top AI talents in terms of H-index score.[84] In this indicator, in 2017 Shanghai was second in China with an average score of 8, trailing only Beijing with an average H-index of 9, and ahead of the other "second echelon" cities like Xi'an, Nanjing or Wuhan.

[84] A person or entity can be said to have an h-index of *h* when producing *h* papers each of which receives at least *h* forward citations. See: University of Michigan Library, Research Impact Metrics: Citation Analysis, https://guides.lib.umich.edu/c.php?g=282982&p=1887449.

Shanghai's AI talent pool benefits from the presence of three elite[85] **universities**—Shanghai Jiaotong University, Fudan University, and Tongji University—that offer AI undergraduate majors and carry out important AI research projects:

- Shanghai Jiaotong University ranked third nationally for the size of its AI talent pool, with 2,211 AI talents in 2017 (Tsinghua, 2018, p. 43). Since 2005, it hosts the national-level AI lab Intelligent Computing and Intelligent Systems Laboratory (智能计算与智能系统重点实验室) co-developed with Microsoft Research Asia (Tsinghua, 2018, p. 96). In January 2018, it also established its Artificial Intelligence Institute (上海交通大学人工智能研究院), which coordinates eleven research centers that work on AI-related topics (robotics, computer vision, language processing, among others).
- Fudan University also hosts a national-level AI research center, the Institute of Science and Technology for Brain-Inspired Intelligence (复旦大学类脑人工智能科学与技术研究院), established in 2015 (Tsinghua, 2018, p. 96). In addition, in 2020 Fudan University and Shanghai Jiaotong University jointly founded the Shanghai National Applied Mathematics Center (上海国家应用数学中心), one of 13 such centers nationwide, which carries out applied research in AI and other fields[86];
- Tongji University also has an Artificial Intelligence Institute (同济大学人工智能研究), created in May 2017 to coordinate the university's several AI-related research centers, including the Robotics and Artificial Intelligence Lab (机器人与人工智能实验室), the Design AI Lab

[85] China's elite universities are often ranked according to the so-called Project 985 (985工程). This is a project aimed at promoting the Chinese higher education system announced by President Jiang Zemin at the 100th anniversary of Peking University on 4 May 1998. The objective is to develop, in cooperation with local governments, several top universities to be world-leading. In 2022, Fudan University, Shanghai Jiaotong University, and Tongji University were ranked in the top 10. Another Shanghai university, the East China Normal University, was ranked 20 on a total of 39 institutions. See: Daxuesheng Bibei Net, 2022. 2022 National 985 University Ranking List (39) [2022全国985大学排名名单一览表 (39所)]. *Daxuesheng Bibei Net* [大学生必备网], 14 September, https://www.dxsbb.com/news/1591.html.

[86] World AI Conference, 2021. Breakthroughs 2021: 6 Big Expectations in Scientific Innovation in Shanghai [突破2021: 上海科创6大期待]. *WeChat Post*, 4 January, https://mp.weixin.qq.com/s/zscPh01Xt_z2d2QyKEHbGQ.

(设计人工智能实验室), the AI and Blockchain Intelligence Lab (同济大学人工智能与区块链智能实验室), and the Research Institute for Intelligent Autonomous Systems (上海自主智能无人系统科学中心).

Most researchers having Chinese AI-related patents or AI-related academic papers are affiliated to universities. At the same time, AI and technology **companies** are also an important source of skilled human capital and offer another indicator to assess the strength of Shanghai's AI talent pool. Shanghai is the city with the second highest concentration of AI companies in China (see infra, 4.4). Recent statistics on human resources employed in the AI industry confirm that Shanghai's AI talent pool is expanding. Data released at a press meeting before the 2022 World AI Conference indicate that the AI talent pool of Shanghai grew from approximately 100,000 AI practitioners in 2018 to 180,000 in 2021.[87] The *White Paper on the Shanghai Artificial Intelligence Industry Talent Development* (上海人工智能产业人才发展白皮书) confirms this trend, reporting that the pool of Shanghai AI human capital reached 232,000 in the first part of 2022.[88] While it is difficult to confirm these figures, they steadily indicate an upward trend in the size of Shanghai's AI talent pool. Moreover, they provide a rough sense of the importance of AI companies in the AI talent landscape of Shanghai. This is consistent with the role of China's AI companies in nurturing AI talents that is emphasized by other authoritative sources, which highlight the contribution of companies in the formation of AI human capital in China (CAICT and AIIA, 2021, p. 32).[89]

[87] The Paper, 2022. The Number of AI Talents in Shanghai Reached 180,000 Last Year, and Global Top Resource Links Have Been Launched [上海AI人才去年达到18万人, 全球顶级资源链接落地]. *The Paper* [澎湃], 26 August, https://baijiahao.baidu.com/s?id=1742195102188078890&wfr=spider&for=pc.

[88] NetEase, 2022. Shanghai Has More Than 232,000 Talents in the Field of AI, with Algorithms, Intelligent Driving and Other Areas Most in Short Supply [上海人工智能领域人才超过23.2万人, 算法、智能驾驶等方面最紧缺]. *NetEase* [网易], 2 September, https://www.163.com/dy/article/HG8G8V3O0534A4SC.html.

[89] In addition to the CAICT and AIIA (2021) report, the China Science and Technology Development Strategy Research Center and the Ministry of Science and Technology's New Generation Artificial Intelligence Development Research Center state that government, institutes of higher education, research institutions and companies all actively contribute to nurturing [AI] talents [政府、高校、科研院所、企业等积极参与人

Finally, one qualitative indicator to assess Shanghai's talent pool is the municipality's position at the center of **the AI talent cluster of the Jiang-Zhe-Hu** (Jiangsu, Zhejiang and Shanghai). The Jiang-Zhe-Hu area is one of the two main AI talent clusters in China's eastern region alongside the Beijing area. These Eastern AI clusters accounted for 62.7% of China's total AI talents in 2017, and Jiangsu province alone hosted 19,293 AI talents, or 9.6% of the national total (Tsinghua, 2018, p. 41). The Jiang-Zhe-Hu, which covers a good part of the Yangtze River Delta,[90] hosts some leading AI universities like Zhejiang University and the Nanjing University of Aeronautics and Astronautics, as well as the talents and resources gravitating around major AI and technology companies like Alibaba and HIKvision. Considering the already excellent transportation network in this region and the national plan for continuing to improve the connectivity of the Yangtze River delta, including a further integration of the technology ecosystem of the area,[91] it is reasonable to assume that AI talents located in this area are an important feed to Shanghai's AI talent pool.

4.3.2 *Shanghai's AI Talent Outputs*

The output produced by Shanghai AI talents offers insights about the quality of the local talent pool, and the impacts that Shanghai AI talent can generate in the municipality. Two commonly used indicators to assess AI research outputs are publications and patents (Castro and McLaughlin, 2021; Stanford, 2021; Tsinghua, 2018). Approximately 95.4% of China's

才培养]. See: World Internet Conference, 2020. China New Generation Artificial Intelligence Development Report 2020 [中国新一代人工智能发展报告2020: 中国人工智能产业结构逐渐完善]. *WIC Website*, 23 October, http://2020.wicwuzhen.cn/web20/news/report/202010/t20201023_21564232.shtml.

[90] Centered around Shanghai, the Yangtze River Delta extends across the provinces of Zhejiang, Jiangsu and Anhui. It includes 27 cities, covers 225,065 square kilometers, and represents a total population of over 163 million people. EY Greater China, https://www.ey.com/en_cn/china-opportunities/how-is-yangtze-river-delta-driving-china-economic-development.

[91] Central Committee of the Communist Party of China, State Council, 2019. *Outline of the Regional Integration Development Plan of the Yangtze River Delta* [长江三角洲区域一体化发展规划纲要], 1 December, http://www.gov.cn/zhengce/2019-12/01/content_5457442.htm. Technological integration is mentioned in section 4, "Strengthen the construction of collaborative and innovative industrial system (加强协同创新产业体系建设).

AI scientific publications were associated with the academic field in 2019, with government institutions being the second largest contributor and companies a distant third (affiliations are not mutually exclusive; Stanford, 2021, pp. 21). Shanghai Jiaotong University is the fourth major Chinese research institution by the number of AI publications in the period 1997–2017 (Tsinghua, 2018, p. 18), and the fifteenth Chinese research institution (thirteenth in Mainland China) with the greatest output of "highly cited" and "hot" AI papers—an indicator of research quality[92]—in the period 2007–2017 (Tsinghua, 2018, p. 24). In addition, in the period 1997–2017 Shanghai Jiaotong University (third position) and Fudan University (eighteenth position) are among the Chinese institutions with the highest output of articles citing top AI papers, another indicator of research quality that considers AI articles doing further research on the technologies, data, and theories put forward by the top papers (Tsinghua, 2018, p. 26).

The quality of Shanghai AI publications can be contextualized by looking at studies that compare China's AI research to that of other countries[93] (Castro and McLaughlin, 2021; Stanford, 2021; Castro et al., 2019). In 2019, China had a Field-Weighted Citation Impact of 0.8, which means researchers cited Chinese authors 20% less than the global average. In comparison, the United States had an FWCI of 1.4. However, China's FWCI had steadily increased from 2012 (0.6) to 2017 (0.9) before a decline in 2018 (Castro and McLaughlin, 2021, p. 11). In addition, the Allen Institute for Artificial Intelligence found that China's

[92] Tsinghua (2018) defines "highly cited papers" as papers that perform in the top 1% based on the number of citations received when compared to other papers in the same subject category in the same year. "Hot papers" are papers published in the last two years that have been cited enough times in the most recent bimonthly period to place them in the top 0.1%.

[93] These studies use different sources from the Tsinghua report. As databases for AI papers, Stanford (2021) and Castro et al. (2019, 2021) present data from the Scopus database. Tsinghua (2018) instead presents data from the Web of Science database by Clarivate Analytics. As indicators for assessing publications' quality, Stanford (World Bank) and Castro et al. (2019, 2021) use the Field-Weighted Citation Impact (FWCI), which is the average number of citations received by publications originating from a country or region divided by the average number of citations by all publications worldwide in the same publication year, subject area, and document type (1.0 represents the world average; more than or less than 1 means publications are cited more or less than expected, according to the world average). As previously clarified, Tsinghua (2018) instead considers "highly cited papers" and "hot papers".

share of the 10% most cited AI papers has steadily grown from almost 0% in 1982 to 26.5% in 2018.[94] While China's number of citations may be inflated by self-citation (when an article cites another article in the same journal), these and other indicators show that the quality of Chinese AI publications—including those affiliated to Shanghai institutions—has increased both in absolute and relative terms (Stanford, 2021, pp. 185–186, 188–189).

In **AI patents**, the share of contributions between universities and other actors is more balanced. In the period 2013–2017, Chinese research institutions and universities filed 52% of AI-related patents, while companies accounted for 48%. Shanghai Jiaotong University ranks twelfth among Chinese universities and research institutions in AI patents, with 441 AI-related patents assigned in that period, ahead of leading tech companies like Huawei, Alibaba, and Tencent (Tsinghua, 2018, p. 32). The AI patent indicator shows that performance varies greatly among Chinese companies, with the government-owned State Grid Corporation of China alone accounting for nearly 53% of China's total enterprise AI patents in the period 2013–2017.[95] At the same time, the patent indicator can only partially capture the contribution of AI companies to the AI talents' output in Shanghai, because it is challenging to assign an enterprise patent to a specific location (e.g., Baidu, Tencent and other major AI and tech companies have R&D centers in Shanghai and other

[94] Schoenick, C., 2019. China May Overtake US in AI Research. *Allen Institute for Artificial Intelligence*, March 13, https://medium.com/ai2-blog/china-to-overtake-us-in-ai-research-8b6b1fe30595. The Allen Institute suggests that China will surpass the United States in producing papers ranked in the top 10% and 1% of all AI research papers by 2020 and 2025, respectively.

[95] If the top and bottom contributors in both categories are not considered, the share of AI patents assigned to research institutions and academia increases to 65.4% (calculations by the author) in the period 2013–2017. Total AI patents by enterprises: 8154 patents. Top contributor enterprises: 4246 patents (State Grid Corporation of China). Bottom contributor enterprises: 167 patents (GREE). Total AI patents by academia: 8349 patents. Top contributor academia: 897 patents (Chinese Academy of Sciences Systems). Bottom contributor academia: 386 patents (Zhejiang University of Technology). Calculations: (8154 − 4246 − 167) = 3741 company AI patents; (8349 − 897 − 386) = 7066 academia AI patents. 3741 + 7066 = 10.807. (7066/10.807)*100 = 65.38%. Data source: Tsinghua (2018, p. 32).

Chinese cities, but the location patent filing—even if available—would not necessarily represent the "origin" of the patented technology[96]).

As for AI publications, the comparison with other countries helps contextualize the quality of Shanghai's AI patents in light of China's global positioning. Because standards for granting patents differ between countries, Castro et al. (2019) consider AI patents filed under the international Patent Cooperation Treaty (PCT) and the highly cited patent families (i.e., patents filed for the same invention in numerous jurisdictions). These indicators suggest that China trails the United States and other countries in the quality of AI patents. Indeed, a 2019 report by the World Intellectual Property Organization[97] found that only 4% of patent applications first filed in China are then filed in other jurisdictions, compared to 32% of the U.S and 40% of Japan (Castro et al., 2019, pp. 28–29). Stanford University's analysis of AI patents citations also indicates that the quality of Chinese patents is on average lower than other countries (Stanford, 2021, pp. 183, 191).

4.3.3 *Shanghai's AI Talent Inputs*

Looking at the policies that Shanghai is promoting in AI education and talent attraction is important to understand what the municipality is doing to expand its AI talent base. Shanghai municipal AI plans indicate the determination to strengthen the city's standing in **AI education**. The *Opinions* (in their section 5.4) and the *AI Highland Plan* (measure 11, special action 4) both call for supporting the establishment of AI disciplines in local universities and building a public service platform for AI education. In 2019, the number of enrolments in AI-related disciplines was 11,490, bringing the total number of AI students to 35,492, indicating that Shanghai is nurturing large reserve of future AI talents. In July 2020, 11 institutes of higher education in Shanghai established AI research institutes, 9 institutes established undergraduate AI majors,

[96] It is well known that methodological challenges raise questions about the reliability of data on the share of AI patents by geographic area. One reason is that applications published by patent offices often identify the inventors by their residencies, not affiliations. While patent applications often have the information about the "assignees" of a patent, they do not necessarily mean the underlying inventions originate from the assignee institutions. Therefore, detected affiliations may be inaccurate (Stanford, 2021, p. 182).

[97] World Intellectual Property Organization, 2019. *WIPO Technology Trends 2019: Artificial Intelligence*, https://www.wipo.int/edocs/pubdocs/en/wipo_pub_1055.pdf.

and 38 institutes opened 104 artificial intelligence-related disciplines.[98] Shanghai's focus on AI education is continuing. By 2022, the number of institutes of higher education that established AI majors in the municipality had risen to 15.[99] In addition, Shanghai has rolled out some prominent AI education initiatives. One of the most highly touted is the *Global AI Academic Alliance* (GAIAA, 全球高校人工智能学术联盟) jointly initiated in Shanghai in July 2018 by Shanghai Jiaotong University, Fudan University, Shanghai University, ShanghaiTech University, SenseTime and prestigious research institutions like the Massachusetts Institute of Technology, Tsinghua University, and others, with the aim to build the world's top AI academic exchange and cooperation platform.

Shanghai municipal AI plans also show great attention to **talent attraction policies** as a way to expand the pool of skilled human resources in AI.[100] Two of the local AI clusters, Lingang New Area and the Zhangjiang AIsland, have significantly strengthened their talent policies in recent years. Lingang has introduced preferential housing policies, medical insurance, fiscal incentives and subsidies, and visa and working permit facilitations to attract domestic and foreign talents in AI and

98 Sohu, 2021. The Development Status of Shanghai's AI Industry and the Next Steps [上海人工智能产业发展情况和下一步规划] (cit.).

99 Sohu, 2022. 438 Universities Have Been Approved to Set up Artificial Intelligence Undergraduate Majors, and the First Batch of Students Are About to Enter the Job Market [438所高校获批设立人工智能本科专业, 首批学生即将走向就业市场]. *Sohu* [搜狐], 13 April 2022, https://www.sohu.com/a/537514082_104992.

100 The *Opinions* state that by 2020 Shanghai will build "a highland of AI talents" (人工智能人才高地) by introducing top international talents and gathering a large number of national and international high-level talents (section 1.1). To do so, Shanghai will explore and formulate personalized policies and open green channels to facilitate the settlement of top AI talents (section 5.3, in original: "实施人工智能人才高峰建设行动, 着力引进国际顶尖人才及团队, 集聚一大批海内外高层次人才。针对人工智能领域高峰人才, 探索制定个性化政策, 开通落户绿色通道"). The *AI Highland Plan* contains a section dedicated to "vigorously gathering a world-class innovation team", and states that Shanghai will strengthen services for international talents, implement measures such as facilitation of entry and exit, and issuance of short-term work residence permits to gather international top talents in AI theories and technologies. Shanghai will attract top-level young overseas talents by giving full play to Shanghai's various talent policies. The municipal government also encourages foreign companies to set up R&D centers in Shanghai, and support local companies to set up global R&D centers overseas (section 3.3, Vigorously gather a world-class innovation team [大力汇聚国际一流的创新团队]; measure 9, Gather international top talent [集聚国际高端人才]; measure 10, Introduce and form outstanding young talent [引育青年卓越人才]).

other three major focus industries of Lingang (i.e., integrated circuits, biomedicine, and aerospace[101]). The Zhangjiang High-Tech Park, which manages the Zhangjiang AIsland, has also strengthened its preferential policies to attract domestic and international high-tech talents, including China's first permanent residence service center, visa facilitations (e.g., two-year visa, one-stop service) for foreign talents and China-born talents that specialized abroad,[102] as well as various fiscal and policy incentives. Xuhui and Minhang districts, which host the two other municipal-level AI clusters, have also in place various forms of policy support to attract talents, including cash rewards, dedicated housing allowances (e.g., prioritized access to housing subsidy and low-rent housing), or administrative support for children education and employment assistance for next of kin.

Shanghai's policies for promoting AI education and talent attraction are expected to continue in the mid-term, as building world-class AI human capital is an integral part of China's national AI strategy. In acknowledging that "there is still a gap between China's overall level of development of AI relative to that of developed countries", the AIDP calls for recruiting top international scientists through programs like the "Ten Thousand Talents", originally launched in 2007 with substantial political and financial backing.[103] In education, the AIDP requires to establish AI majors and pilot AI colleges in universities, increase the quotas of doctoral and master's candidates in AI, among others. These indications have been

[101] China (Shanghai) Pilot Free Trade Zone Lingang New Area Management Committee, 2019 (cit.); Shanghai Chronicles Office, 2021. *Shanghai Almanac 2021, Lin-gang Special Area Special Edition*. Shanghai Almanac Editorial Department, p. 109; SHFDI, 2020 (cit.), p. 58.

[102] Ma, Y., 2021. Ten Years in Zhangjiang, Shanghai Zhangjiang Has Become a "Dream Workshop" for Scientific Innovation of 2 Million Young Talents [张江十年, 上海张江 200万青年人才的科创 "梦工场"]. *Xinmin Evening Post*, 1 April, http://stcsm.sh.gov.cn/xwzx/mtjj/20210401/f0df5e38266346ef9f6d7ff5fae69d3a.html; author interview with Zhangjiang Group, 26 January 2021.

[103] In general, China's talent attraction programs achieved mixed results. But national and local level talent programs in AI, together with the recruiting efforts by Chinese tech companies that established their own overseas research institutes abroad, appear to have successfully lured a number of talented AI researchers to work in China or for Chinese tech companies (Ding, 2018, pp. 5, 19–21). Still, research shows that between 1998 and 2017 the United States attracted 22 times more AI talents from other nations than China (Castro et al., 2019, p. 18).

operationalized by two major plans on AI education,[104] resulting in a significant increase in the number of AI majors at Chinese universities.[105] The first batch of AI undergraduate majors was officially introduced at 35 universities in September 2019.[106] In 2020, the Ministry of Education approved applications for 180 more universities to offer AI majors, which became the fastest expanding discipline at Chinese universities. In March 2021, 130 universities and higher-learning institutions have added AI majors to their undergraduate disciplines.[107] University enrolments in such majors have continued to surge, with over 380,000 students enrolling in 2022, an 8% rise from the previous year.[108]

Box 4.2 China and the United States in the AI talent metric
Tsinghua University (2018) estimates that China ranks second globally with a size of more than 18,200 international AI talents (i.e., researchers with AI-related patents and/or publications in English language over the last ten years). With 8.9% of the global total, China trails only the approximately 28,500 AI talents of the United States (13.9% of the global

[104] The *Artificial Intelligence Action Plan for Institutions of Higher Education* issued by the Ministry of Education (MoE) in April 2018, and the *Certain Opinions on Promoting Curricula Merging at 'Double World-Class' Institutes of Higher Education and on Accelerating the Cultivation of Graduate Students in the AI Field* issued in January 2020 by MoE, NDRC and Ministry of Finance (Chapter 3, Appendix IV).

[105] Yu, H., 2018. Nankai and Tianjin University Inaugurated the School of Artificial Intelligence on the Same Day, Each Focusing on Robotics and Brain Cognition [南开和天津大学同日揭牌人工智能学院, 各侧重机器人与脑认知]. *The Paper* [澎湃新闻], 16 May, https://www.thepaper.cn/newsDetail_forward_2133192.

[106] Xinhua, 2019. Chinese Colleges Start Offering AI Major for Undergraduates. *Xinhua News*, 23 April, http://www.xinhuanet.com/english/2019-04/23/c_138001636.htm. Before that date there were already 36 universities approved by the Ministry of Education to offer "Intelligent Science and Technology" undergraduate programs, in addition to 79 programs related to AI (Tsinghua, 2018, p. 95).

[107] Liao, S., 2021. AI Is Among 37 Undergrad Majors Added by China's Universities. *Yicai Global*, 3 March, https://www.yicaiglobal.com/news/ai-is-among-37-undergrad-majors-added-by-china-universities; Dai, S., 2020. AI Is the Fastest Expanding Discipline in China's Universities, with 180 More Approved to Offer It as a Major. *South China Morning Post*, 4 March, https://www.scmp.com/tech/policy/article/3064956/ai-fastest-expanding-discipline-chinas-universities-180-more-approved.

[108] Ye, Z., 2023. AI Is Booming in China, But Its Grads Are Trapped in a Talent Gap. *Sixth Tone*, 5 August, https://www.sixthtone.com/news/1013462.

total). This gap, however, becomes much wider in "top AI talents", which Tsinghua defines as international AI talents whose H-index score ranks among the top 10% of AI researchers. In this category, China has 977 top AI talents, or just 17.7% of the 5,518 top AI talent pool of the United States. It also means that top AI talent is a small portion (5.4%) of China's total AI talent pool (Tsinghua, 2018, pp. 35–36). Some scholars link China's deficit of top AI talents to the fact that only 25% of Chinese AI researchers have more than ten years of experience, compared with nearly 50% of U.S. AI researchers (Castro et al., 2019, p. 19).

Other reports support the conclusion that China is second only to the United States in the size of its AI talent pool, but it lags behind in the number of top AI talents. Using a broader definition of AI talents, the Tencent Research Institute found that in 2017 China had an AI talent pool of 39,200 individuals (13% of the global total), compared to the United States' 78,700 AI talents (26% of the global total). Adopting a view of AI talent pool that includes both fundamental and applied researchers, in 2020 ElementAI counted 6,401 Chinese AI authors on arXiv (11.42% of the global total, second worldwide), compared to 26,818 AI authors from the United States (47.9% of the global total, first worldwide). In the broader indicator of "specialized AI technical talents" (e.g., people holding advanced degrees in machine learning, computer science, artificial intelligence or related quantitative fields), ElementAI counted 22,191 AI talents from China (4.6% of the global total, fourth worldwide), compared to 188,300 AI talents from the US (39.4% of the global total, first worldwide).[109]

[109] See: Tencent Research Institute, 2017. White Paper on Global AI Talent 2017 [2017全球人工智能人才白皮书], https://www.tisi.org/Public/Uploads/file/20171201/20171201151555_24517.pdf; Gagne, J. et al., 2020. Global AI Talent Report 2020, *Element AI*, https://jfgagne.ai/global-ai-talent-report-2020/, who use the AI/ML repositories on arXiv as a proxy.

In terms of outputs produced by Chinese AI talents, Stanford University reports that in 2019 China led the world in the share of peer-reviewed AI publications, making up 22.4% of the number of AI papers globally. China published 3.5 times more peer-reviewed AI papers in 2019 than it did in 2014, a faster increased than both the European Union (2 times more peer-reviewed AI papers) and the United States (2.75 times more peer-reviewed AI papers) over the same period (Stanford, 2021, p. 20). Other reports confirm that China leads globally in the number of AI papers since 2018, when for the first time in nearly a decade it published more AI papers than the European Union, accounting for around 28% of the world total (Castro and McLaughlin, 2021, p. 9). Similar relative figures are provided by Tsinghua University, which reports that China's AI publications in 2017 (including Hong Kong and Macao) accounted for 27.68% of the world total[110] (Tsinghua, 2018, p. 14). China leads the world also in the quantity of AI-related patent filings. Tsinghua University estimates that China ranks first ahead of the United States and Japan (Tsinghua, 2018, p. 30). Other sources confirm that since 2014 the Chinese Patent Office accepts the most first patent filings in AI, followed by the U.S. Patent and Trademark Office (Ding, 2019).

Overall, the quality of China's AI related publications and patents still trails other countries, but the significant increase in China's share of the 10% most cited AI papers suggests that the country may reduce the quality gap in the near future. In addition, some experts believe that the role of top AI talents in AI applications is likely less important than in research, because AI technologies applied to real-life implementations often require highly-skilled AI researchers and practitioners, but not necessarily "best-of-best" AI talents (Lee and Sheehan, 2018).

4.3.4 *Conclusions on the AI Talent Indicator*

Beijing holds the national leadership in AI talents and hosts the majority of China's most prestigious universities and research institutes in the field

[110] Like Stanford (2021), Castro and McLaughlin (2021) and Castro et al. (2019) present data from the Scopus database. The two studies, however, use different methodologies for indexing publications, resulting in different percentages on total global. On the other hand, Tsinghua (2018) presents data from the Web of Science database by Clarivate Analytics. In absolute numbers, Castro and McLaughlin (2021) attribute 24,929 AI papers to China, while Tsinghua attributes to China more than 37,000 publications.

of artificial intelligence. At the same time, the metrics examined in this section indicate the abundance and variety of Shanghai AI talents.[111] The analysis serves to put in perspective the accounts that state that the shortage of AI talents in China is a major weakness of the national AI ecosystem[112]: while this gap arguably exists at the aggregate national level, there is no evidence that it affects Shanghai capacity to implement AI in the public sector, especially if AI talents in private companies are considered. In addition, Shanghai has been very active in promoting AI research in recent years, another factor that is likely to develop and attract AI talents to the municipality. Some notable AI institutes created in Shanghai include: the Key Laboratory of Artificial Intelligence, Ministry of Education (人工智能教育部重点实验), jointly established by the Ministry of Education and Shanghai Jiaotong University in 2017 to conduct high-level applied research and promote the link between academia and industry[113]; and the Shanghai Artificial Intelligence Laboratory (上海人工智能实验室), created in July 2020 and located in the Xuhui West Bund AI cluster, which cooperates with Shanghai Jiaotong University, Fudan University, Tongji University, East China Normal University, Shanghai University, and other major academic institutions in mainland China and Hong Kong to produce original AI research and technologies.[114]

[111] For the size of the talent pool, the Shanghai government provides greater figures than the 10,000 AI talents counted by the Tsinghua report. The September 2019 *AI Highland Plan* (cit.) estimated the scale of Shanghai's AI talents at 100,000 individuals (special action 4). The Shanghai Foreign Investment Development Board states that Shanghai hosts 1/3 of China's AI talents (SHFDI, 2020, p. 22). These figures are difficult to confirm because the sources do not explain how "AI talents" are defined. As for variety, Shanghai claims to have formed a "ladder-type AI talent highland advantage" (梯度人才高地优势) that includes scientific research experts (科研专家), technical talents (技术人才) and 'subject talents' (学科人才). Shanghai World AI Conference, 2021. Shanghai Academy of Social Sciences "Report": Shanghai enters the AI development full-force period (cit.).

[112] Fan, F., 2022. Deep Learning Rising in Importance Within Booming AI Sector. *China Daily*, 22 April, https://global.chinadaily.com.cn/a/202204/06/WS624cef90a310fd2b29e553b1.html; Jarvis, D., 2020. The AI Talent Shortage Isn't over Yet. *Deloitte*, 30 September, https://www2.deloitte.com/us/en/insights/industry/technology/ai-talent-challenges-shortage.html.

[113] Key Laboratory of Artificial Intelligence, Ministry of Education website: https://ailab-moe.sjtu.edu.cn/.

[114] Shanghai Artificial Intelligence Laboratory website: https://www.shlab.org.cn/.

The impact of AI talents on public sector AI applications in Shanghai will also depend on how this human capital is engaged in public sector activities. In this regard, there are signs that Shanghai is making good use of its AI human resources to support government-led AI projects. The use of talents and expertise of private companies was discussed in the analysis of the governance mechanisms of China's innovation system (Chapter 2.2.3), and it is further explained when examining the engagement of private companies in Shanghai (see infra, 4.4). The municipality has also been promoting the involvement of AI talents from academia. For instance, Fudan University contributes to the Big Data Joint Innovation Labs,[115] projects that are instrumental to spur innovation in the public sector and an effective way to foster the promotion of AI technologies and applications; Tongji University is involved in the design and operations of the Maqiao AI Innovation Experimental Zone, which is a testbed for AI application in government service, public transportation, and medicine and healthcare; Shanghai Jiaotong University in July 2020 founded the Shanghai Baiyulan Open AI Research Center (上海白玉兰开源开放研究院), an initiative sponsored by the Shanghai CPC Standing Committee and the Pudong New Area to promote AI applications that support economic and social development. Furthermore, academic and industry experts form an integral part of the Shanghai Artificial Intelligence Strategic Advisory Expert Committee (上海市人工智能战略咨询专家委员会) created in 2019, which holds regular consultations with the municipal leadership on various AI policy issues.[116] Moreover, the Shanghai Data Exchange Center (4.1) also functions as a training base for the China Pudong Cadre Academy (中国浦东干部学院) and the Party School of the Shanghai Committee of the Communist Party of China (中共上海市委党校), suggesting the existence of channels for sharing knowledge between the municipal leadership and AI experts that was corroborated during the interviews with stakeholders of Shanghai's AI policy (Chapter 5.1).

115 Fudan University manages a lab on big data in finance. See: https://cloud.tencent.com/developer/news/278946.

116 Author interview with a foreign professor member of the Shanghai Artificial Intelligence Strategic Advisory Expert Committee, 15 December 2020; author interview with the Shanghai Association of Artificial Intelligence, 21 April 2021.

4.4 AI Companies

AI companies own the technologies and expertise needed for public sector AI implementations and are an important repository of AI talents. Private firms play a key role in implementing AI in the public sector in China and Shanghai. This point was already highlighted from different angles, examining the governance mechanisms to engage private firms in China's innovation policy (Chapter 2.2.3), and introducing the AI pilot application scenarios of Shanghai (Chapter 3.3.3; detailed analysis in Chapter 5.3). Building upon these discussions, next paragraphs assess the position of Shanghai in the AI companies' indicator. The metrics adopted are the number of AI companies located in the municipality, and their level of funding. The AI technologies that Shanghai can access are of course not limited to those provided by the AI firms based in the municipality. However, Shanghai has been deploying various tools to attract AI enterprises and foster the development of the local AI industry, a major goal set by the Shanghai AI plans. Part of this attraction strategy consists of offering AI firms the opportunity to participate in AI projects and applications sponsored by the municipal government, for which companies are de facto required to have a legal presence in Shanghai. Therefore, the pool of AI companies in Shanghai offers a good proxy of the size and type of companies that are most likely to partner with the Shanghai government in public sector AI implementations.

4.4.1 AI Companies in Shanghai

In China like in other countries, the statistics about AI enterprises may overstate the number of "real" AI companies. For instance, one analysis of European AI firms in CrunchBase found that AI was material to a company's value proposition for only 60% of the firms, while the remaining 40% of the companies desired to be known as an "AI firm" for commercial and other reasons (Castro et al., 2019, p. 84). In China, the inflation of statistics on the AI industry was mentioned when discussing the tendency of local governments to show compliance to national policy priorities (Chapter 3.1). Besides political opportunism, there are other motivations that concur to produce inflated Chinese statistics on AI companies. On the one hand, the line between "core AI industry" and "AI-related industry" is blurred, leaving flexibility for different interpretations—as it was mentioned in the analysis of the AIDP, and further elaborated by some

Chinese commentators.[117] On the other hand, some market actors have manipulated the ambiguous definition of "AI company" to deceive the government and obtain subsidies earmarked for the AI industry (Zeng, 2021).

To ensure analytical consistency in light of these statistical discrepancies, this section examines the presence of AI companies in Shanghai by referring to the information provided by the China Academy of Information and Communications Technology (CAICT) Data Research Center (中国信息通信研究院数据研究中心). The CAICT, subordinate to the Ministry of Industry and Information Technology, provides policy input on various technical issues such as standards and emerging technology sectors like artificial intelligence. CAICT is an authoritative and reliable source of data that is used by many Chinese-language reports on China's AI development, including the Tsinghua University's *China AI Development Report 2018* and the Shanghai Jiatong University's *AI@SH Action Report* (SJTU et al., 2019), the main sources for this section. In addition, other independent reports confirm the estimates of the CAICT Data Research Center, corroborating the validity of this government source.[118]

In July 2019, **Shanghai hosted 244 AI companies** (SJTU et al., 2019, p. 20). These are companies having AI technologies, products, services, and related solutions as their core business.[119] According to these figures, in 2019 Shanghai was the second city for concentration

117 Wang, X., 2018. Pseudo-Concepts Proliferate, and Cognition Is Fuzzy, AI Marketing May Need a Re-education [伪概念泛滥, 认知模糊, AI营销或需一场再教育]. *Sohu* [搜狐], 5 September, https://www.sohu.com/a/251909149_117917. See also Zeng, 2021.

118 Data from the CAICT report presented in these paragraphs are also used in: Liu, L., 2020. How Far Is the Gap in the AI Industry Between China and the United States? An Article to Understand the Layout and Latest Trends of the Chinese and US AI Industries, an In-Depth Report on the Chinese and US AI Industries [中美AI 产业的差距究竟有多远?一文看懂中美 AI 产业布局及最新趋势, 中美 AI 产业深度报告], *Leiphone* [雷峰网], 16 April, https://www.leiphone.com/category/industrynews/Hegr5IfY9Z21CoVN.html; Forward Industry Research Institute, 2019. Forward Industry Research Institute: 2019 Report on the Status and Development Trend of the Artificial Intelligence Industry [前瞻产业研究院: 2019年人工智能行业现状与发展趋势报告]. Forward Industry Research Institute [前瞻产业研究院], https://img4.qianzhan.com/report/file/19/1910081709070618/1910081709070618_catalog.pdf.

119 The CAICT methodology defines AI enterprises as those having AI technologies, products, services and related solutions as their core business (Tsinghua, 2018, p. 11). The *AI@SH Action Report* (SJTU et al., 2019) is based on CAICT data, so it is reasonable to deduce that it adopts this taxonomy to count the 244 "AI companies" in Shanghai.

of AI companies in China, with approximately 20% of China's total AI firms (SJTU et al., 2019, p. 10). Shanghai was also estimated to be the fourth city globally by number of AI enterprises (Tsinghua, 2018, p. 47). This assessment about the global standing of Shanghai's commercial AI ecosystem is consistent with various international studies that estimate that China ranks second in the world after the United States by number of AI companies (Castro et al., 2019; Stanford, 2019; Ding, 2018).

Extending the definition of AI companies to include enterprises that have a "strong relevance to AI technology", Shanghai was home to **1,107 core AI companies**[120] (人工智能核心企业) in July 2019. Among these "core AI companies": 194 firms (17.5%) are active in the AI foundational layer (e.g., hardware, computing power, toolkits for training AI models, etc.); 109 companies (9.8%) are active in the technology layer[121]; and 804 (72.6%) are active in the application layer, mostly operating in sectors such as finance (107), medicine and healthcare (81), and manufacturing (68). The *AI@SH Action Report* states that this "application dominance" is a distinctive feature of Shanghai's AI industry, and it is due to the fact that Shanghai is a megacity with rich application scenarios and mature industrial sectors that can provide manifold applications for AI technologies (SJTU et al., 2019, p. 24).

In terms of **territorial distribution** within the municipality, one-third of Shanghai's core AI companies (375) are located in the Pudong New Area (SJTU et al., 2019, p. 23). This is consistent with the fact that Pudong hosts the two AI clusters of Zhangjiang and Lingang (4.2.1), and it confirms that the municipal strategy of creating hubs of AI companies

[120] The *AI@SH Action Report* distinguishes between 2,423 "AI-related companies" (泛人工智能企业) and 1,107 "core AI companies" (人工智能核心企业), based on their strong of weak "relevance to AI technology" (与人工智能技术的关联度). These figures are confirmed by later data that place the number of Shanghai's "core AI companies" in 2020 between 1,149 (Sohu, 2021, cit.) and 1,200 (Yu, C., 2021. Decoding the AI "National Team": 15 Pilot Areas Were "Deposited" in 13 Provinces, and Urban "Wisdom Governance" Scenarios Drive Industrial Innovation [解码人工智能"国家队": 15个试验区 "落子" 13省份, 城市 "智治" 场景牵动产业创新]. *21st Century Business Herald*, 10 July, https://m.21jingji.com/article/20210710/945d6ef5f6d29bc6854d8413b1412b30.html).

[121] The technology layer mainly includes computer vision (biometric recognition, image recognition, video recognition), Natural Language Processing (machine translation, reading comprehension), and speech recognition. This was also the largest segment of China's AI industry in 2017, representing nearly 35% of the market (Tsinghua, 2018, p. 53).

is bearing fruits. Other Shanghai districts with high concentration of AI companies are Xuhui (130 AI companies), which also hosts a municipal AI cluster, the West Bund AI Space; and Yangpu District (93 companies), which hosts the campuses of various Shanghai universities and some government-backed AI incubators like AI Space (similar name, but different from the Xuhui project). In addition, each district has specialized in different AI applications: Pudong has the most complete range of sectors, from finance to healthcare, smart manufacturing and services; Xuhui has a higher concentration of AI companies specialized in medical applications; Yangpu is specialized in education-related AI applications. While these categorizations are a bit crude, they further confirm that Shanghai is pursuing a policy of "AI clustering".

In terms of **types of AI enterprises**, Shanghai hosts a variegate spectrum of companies. It ranges from Internet and technology giants that leverage data from their extensive user bases to optimize algorithms for AI applications, to emerging AI startups that are trying to push the technological edge. For instance, Shanghai hosts industry leaders like Baidu, Alibaba, SenseTime, Tencent, and iFlytek, all members of the "AI national team" (Chapter 2.2.3). It also hosts numerous Chinese unicorns[122]—i.e., startup companies valued at 1 billion USD—like Bytedance (字节跳动), SenseTime (商汤科技), Cambricon (寒武纪), Cloudwalk (云从), Horizon Robotics (地平线), Unisound (云知声), CloudMinds (达闼), and Yitu (依图), among others. The municipality is also home to fast-growing Shanghai local AI companies like Xiao i (智臻智能), UCloud (优刻得), DeepBlue (深兰), Pateo (博泰悦臻), 51 YXedu (乂学), Liulishuo (流利说), or Leyan Technology (乐言科技). Finally, a number of rapidly growing startups such as Videojj (极链), Tunicorn (图麟), Westwell Lab (西井), Enflame Tech (燧原), CraiditX (氪信), or Tigerobo (虎博) have also established their presence in Shanghai (SJTU et al., 2019, p. 20).

Recent statistics confirm that Shanghai has maintained its strong position in the AI industry. A report by independent consultancy Forward Economist (前瞻经济学人) showed that in August 2023 Shanghai hosted

122 For context, in 2018 CBInsights counted 32 AI unicorns worldwide, of which 10 are Chinese firms (CBInsights, 2019. The Increasingly Crowded AI Unicorn Club. *CBInsights*, 14 February, https://www.cbinsights.com/research/ai-unicorn-club/). In 2021, a report by Analytics Insight confirmed the presence of 3 Chinese companies in the top 10 AI unicorns worldwide (Dialani, P., 2021. Top 10 AI Unicorns That Are Setting the Stage on Fire. *Analytics Insight*, 21 April, https://www.analyticsinsight.net/top-10-ai-unicorns-that-are-setting-the-stage-on-fire/).

more than 2,000 AI firms.[123] This report does not indicate the methodology used for classifying "AI companies". Hence, it is not possible to compare this figure with either the 1,107 core AI companies (人工智能核心企业) or the 2,423 "AI-related companies" (泛人工智能企业) mapped by the *AI@SH Action Report* in 2019. Nonetheless, these recent statistics confirm the growing trend of the Shanghai AI industry. They show that while the number of newly registered AI companies has steadily declined since 2018, the output of Shanghai's AI industry has increased by 30.43% between 2020 and 2022.

The number, types, and output of AI firms offer valid metrics to gauge the size and variety of the Shanghai AI industry. The **amount of financing** raised by AI firms helps to complete the picture of the local AI company landscape. In 2018, Shanghai AI companies—including the core AI companies and the 2,423 "AI-related companies"—received 62.2 billion RMB in funding, greatly exceeding the 52.4 billion RMB obtained in 2017, and more than doubling the 26.3 billion RMB accrued in 2015 (SJTU et al., 2019, p. 25). These figures closely reflect the trend of financing for Chinese AI companies nationwide in the same period (Stanford, 2021, p. 96). In terms of funding rounds received by Shanghai's "core AI companies", the *AI@SH Report* interprets the downward trend from 98 funding rounds in 2017 to 92 rounds in 2018 as an indicator that the AI industry has started to mature and stabilize (SJTU et al., 2019, p. 25). This interpretation is corroborated by looking at the funding received by Chinese AI companies nationwide. Between 2013 and 2017, China received 60% of global investments in AI. From 2015, early-phase financing (e.g., seed, angel and series A funding) started to decrease as a percentage of the total AI financing, indicating the increasing maturity of the industry (Tsinghua, 2018, p. 52). Data for later years confirm this trend: after 2018, investments in China's AI progressively declined both in number of transactions and total investment amounts. The proportion of Series C (average amount raised: 25 million USD) and D funding rounds (venture capital, variable amount raised) has continuously declined

[123] Forward Economist, 2023. Important! The Map of Shanghai's AI Industry Chain in 2023 (with Industrial Policies, Map of the Status of the Industrial Chain, Industrial Resources Spatial Layout, and Industrial Chain Development Plans) [重磅!2023年上海市人工智能产业链全景图谱(附产业政策、产业链现状图谱、产业资源空间布局、产业链发展规划)]. *Forward Economist* [前瞻经济学人], 19 October, https://baijiahao.baidu.com/s?id=1780162679387223435&wfr=spider&for=pc.

until the third quarter of 2020, and there has not been a new batch of Chinese AI unicorns in the market between 2018 and the end of 2020.[124] In 2023, China added ten new AI unicorns, partly due to a surge of investments in large language models that followed the global sensation caused by OpenAI's ChatGPT. However, the underlying trend didn't change. By November 2023, the number of financing events in China's AI sector in the primary market recorded a 26% decrease compared to the same period in 2022, and the total financing transaction amount decreased by 38% in the same period.[125]

Finally, by comparing the financings received by Shanghai AI companies with those in other Chinese cities, it emerges that **Shanghai AI companies are on average well-funded**. In terms of financing amount and number of transactions, Shanghai was second only to Beijing in 2017. The Chinese capital city leads by a distance, with more than 250 billion RMB in funding (compared to Shanghai's 52.4 billion RMB in 2017), and more than 450 transactions (compared to less than 200 in Shanghai). However, Shanghai is ahead of other industrial and technological powerhouses like Zhejiang province (third), Jiangsu province (fourth) and Guangdong province (fifth), among others (Tsinghua, 2018, p. 51). At the same time, while breakout data for Shanghai are incomplete, it is reasonable to suppose that financing in Shanghai AI companies is highly concentrated on few firms, similarly to what happens for Chinese AI companies at the national level.[126]

[124] iResearch [艾瑞研究院], 2020. China Artificial Intelligence Industry Research Report 2020 [2020年中国人工智能产业研究报告], retrieved from Sohu [搜狐], 28 December, https://www.sohu.com/a/440974489_445326.

[125] China Money Network, 2023. Despite Dip in VC Funding, China Adds Ten New AI Unicorns in 2023. *China Money Newtork*, 14 December, https://www.chinamoneynetwork.com/2023/12/14/despite-dip-in-vc-funding-china-adds-ten-new-ai-unicorns-in-2023#:~:text=Here%20are%20some%20of%20the,venture%20capitalist%20Kai%2DFu%20Lee.

[126] China's total private financing for AI firms between January 2018 and October 2019 reached approximately USD 25 billion, second only to the United States. Of the total Chinese private investment in AI, USD 16.6 billion went to 486 startup companies in the period July 2018–July 2019, a relatively small number of companies compared to the 1,749 American and 993 European AI startups that received investments in the same period. This means that Chinese AI startups receive on average much higher rates of investment (USD 34 million for each startup) than their Western counterparts (Stanford, 2019, pp. 89, 92–93). As for the distinction between "core AI" and "AI-related industries", statistics on the scale of AI financing vary widely between sources. In addition,

4.4.2 *Supporting and Engaging AI Companies*

The development of the AI industry is a main goal of Shanghai's AI plans. The *Opinions* set a target for the scale of Shanghai core AI industries to exceed 100 billion yuan by 2020, with a focus on autonomous driving, smart robotics, intelligent software and hardware, AI chips, and smart sensors.[127] The *AI Highland Plan* reiterates that Shanghai will create several leading and innovative AI enterprises and form a 100 billion AI industry focused on AI chips, smart cars, robots, and hardware. Shanghai will support the AI industry by promoting applications in manufacturing, medicine, transportation, finance, and other fields, and the municipality will become the first landing pad for AI technologies.[128] To achieve these goals, Shanghai is supporting and guiding AI industrial development by using three main policy instruments, one of which bears direct impact on the use of AI in the public sector.

The first policy instrument is **direct financial handouts**. In 2017, Shanghai introduced "special support funds" (专项支持资金) for AI development.[129] These funds are dedicated to "developing core AI industries" (e.g., smart vehicles, smart robots, smart security, chips for deep learning and industrial applications). In October 2019, Shanghai had disbursed more than 600 million RMB of such special support

global data on private financing seldom capture government funding, which plays a very important role in China's AI enterprise development, mostly through government guidance funds like the already mentioned "Big Fund" or the China Internet Investment Fund (Chapter 2.2.3). The role of public financing in Shanghai's AI commercial ecosystem is discussed in the next section.

127 Shanghai Municipal People's Government, 2017. *Opinions* (cit.). Section 1, par. 2, Development Goals (发展目标); section 4, Promote the clustering and development of the AI industry (推动人工智能产业集聚发展).

128 SHEITC, 2019. *AI Highland Action Plan* (cit.). Section 3.1, Focus on building integrated innovation carriers (着力建设复合融合的创新载体); Special Action 1: Build a 4 + X integrated innovation carriers.

129 Shanghai Economy and Informatization Commission, Shanghai Financial Affairs Bureau, 2017 (cit., Chapter 2.2). For projects with a total investment below 15 million RMB, the maximum support amount for single project is 3 million yuan; for projects with a total investment above 15 million, the maximum support cannot exceed 30% of the total investment or 20 million RMB.

funds, distributed among 106 projects.[130] In addition, in 2019 Shanghai created the *Shanghai AI Industry Investment Fund* (上海人工智能产业投资基金). This is a government guidance fund initiated by the China (Shanghai) Pilot Free Trade Zone Lingang New Area Management Committee, Guosheng Group, Lingang Group, and other entities. The fund started with a total scale of 10 billion and completed the first round of fundraising (Sohu, 2021). In August 2021, the fund had invested in 8 AI-related projects that ranged from AI technologies such as robotics, to AI foundations like integrated circuits and software platforms, disbursing a total amount of several hundred million USD.[131] As of September 2022, its investments had quickly risen to nearly 200 local AI companies, and the fund announced a new project worth 1 billion RMB in AI-enabled finance, focusing on metaverse, digital economy and smart terminals[132] (智能终端). Other major municipal government funds that invest in AI include: the *G60 Science & Technology Innovation Corridor AI Industry Fund* (G60 科创走廊AI产业基金); the *Yangpu District AI Venture Capital Fund* (杨浦人工智能创业投资母基金); the *Zhangjiang Hi-Tech Innovation Fund* (张江高科科创基金); the *Shanghai Integrated Circuits Industry Investment Fund* (上海集成电路产业投资基金, a 50-billion-yuan investment fund created in 2017); and the *Shanghai Integrated Circuits Equipment and Materials Fund* (上海集成电路装备材料基金, created in 2018).

A second policy instrument used by Shanghai to spur the local AI industry consists of various **preferential policies**. The municipal government offers a wide range of incentives to high-tech companies in general and AI enterprises in particular. These include: lower rates of corporate income tax, tax exemptions for a certain number of years, subsidies for

130 Sohu, 2019. Shanghai Announces 600 Million AI Special Funds to Support Companies: 106 Firms Are on the List [上海 6 亿 AI 专项资金拟支持单位公示: 106 家上榜]. *Sohu* [搜狐], 17 October, https://www.sohu.com/a/347785593_465914.

131 Qichacha, Entry: Shanghai AI Industry Fund (上海人工智能产业资基金), https://www.qcc.com/investor/2b94ea9dbd69376606630920e89815a2.html (accessed 18 November 2021).

132 Lingang Group, 2022. "AI Travels with Company", the Shanghai Artificial Intelligence Industry Investment Fund Held the Launch Ceremony of "New Track to Support the Financial Ecosystem" ["AI行而有伴", 上海人工智能产业投资基金举行 "金融生态圈助力新赛道" 启动仪式]. *Lingang Group* [临港集团], 22 September, https://www.shlingang.com/lg1/lingangjituan/xwzx/jtdt/202209/t20220905_26730.shtml.

innovation expenditures, easier access to capital, favorable land use policies, talent attraction policies, and various other forms of policy support. As for government funds supporting the AI industry, the districts of Shanghai often replicate and expand the preferential policies of the municipal government. The proliferation of supporting measures for the AI industry makes it difficult to keep an updated account of all preferential policies, but at least eight of Shanghai's 16 districts introduced supporting measures specifically targeted to AI development. For instance, Yangpu District introduced a one-time reward of up to 5 million RMB for newly established AI companies that have received venture capital investments. Minhang District offered AI companies subsidies equivalent to 10–30% of their R&D spending capped at 5 million RMB, and subsidies equivalent to 10–20% of their new equipment investment capped at 10 million RMB, for a cumulative total of maximum 10 million RMB. Jinshan District offered a subsidy of up to 10 million RMB for property purchase and construction, or 1.2 million RMB yearly rental subsidies for five years for companies in the unmanned aerial vehicle (drone) industry (SHFDI, 2020, pp. 48, 50, 52). The Lingang Special Area has introduced the most complete set of supporting policies for AI companies, including financial subsidies, incentives, and tax rebates, as well as land, talent, housing, social insurance, and other preferential policies.[133]

In addition to these two traditional policy instruments, Shanghai offers companies the opportunity to test their technologies in **real-world application scenarios** as a way to promote AI industrial development and attract AI firms to the municipality. This engagement approach has two intertwined components that are both relevant for public sector AI applications. One is creating **trial and demonstration zones** where AI companies can test their products and technologies in controlled environments that resemble real-life applications. As examined in Sect. 4.2.1, trial and demonstration zones are often used to promote AI applications that can be transferred to the public sector (e.g., the Zhangjiang AIsland, Maqiao AI Town, the Lingang test zone for smart vehicles). Being an effective instrument to promote industrial development as well as AI technologies that the government considers beneficial to its use,

[133] Lingang Special Area, 2020. Several Measures for the Development of the AI Industry in the Lingang New Area of China (Shanghai) Pilot Free Trade Zone [中国(上海) 自由贸易试验区临港新片区集聚发展人工智能产业若干措施]. *Shanghai Invest*, 10 January, http://www.shanghaiinvest.com/cn/viewfile.php?id=14190.

demonstration zones have become a key component of Shanghai's AI policy, and they are expanding. The plans for enlarging the Zhangjiang AIsland are a case in point (Chapter 5.3). Autonomous driving offers another illustrative example. In June 2016, Shanghai established the Intelligent Connected Vehicle Comprehensive Test Zone in Jiading district, the first such zone in China. This was followed up by the launch of the "AI + transportation scenario program" in January 2019 (AI + 交通场景计划; SJTU et al., 2019), which in November 2021 resulted in Shanghai having 615 public roads with a total length of nearly 1,290 km dedicated to testing autonomous vehicles.[134] At the end of 2023, the municipality confirmed its position as the national leader in AI-enabled autonomous driving, with nearly 1,800 km of test roads for autonomous driving vehicles.[135]

The second component of this engagement approach consists of actively **involving companies in AI projects in the public sector**. This direct engagement usually results in some form of public–private cooperation (政企合作), whereby AI companies provide the core technology that enables government-led AI projects, and fine-tune it to the specific needs of those projects. Such cooperation with private AI companies goes beyond traditional public procurement of ICT products and is crucial for

[134] These test roads are mainly located in Jiading District (616.40 km) and Lingang New Area (539.40 km), followed by Fengxian District and other parts of the Pudong New Area. In November 2021, the Municipal Transportation Commission also announced that Shanghai would add more than 720 km of public roads for testing autonomous driving in the Jiading New City and Lingang New Area. See: Tencent Net, 2021. Shanghai Expands Open Test Roads for Intelligent Connected Vehicles, Adding More Than 7,000 Test Scenarios [上海拓展智能网联汽车开放测试道路, 新增七千余个测试场景]. *Tencent Net* [腾讯网], 7 November, https://new.qq.com/omn/20211107/20211107A04N8Z00.html.

[135] Gasgoo, 2023. Shanghai so far Opens 926 Autonomous Driving Test Roads Spanning 1,800 km. *Gasgoo*, 13 October, https://autonews.gasgoo.com/m/70028912.html#:~:text=In%20the%20realm%20of%20autonomous,the%20forefront%20of%20national%20development. For autonomous driving specifically on Shanghai's expressways, see: Zhu, Y., 2022. Shanghai Unveils First Batch of Autonomous Driving Roads. *SHINE*, 7 November, https://www.shine.cn/news/metro/2211072487/.

many public sector AI applications, as explained earlier.[136] An illustrative example of the complexity and importance of this direct engagement is offered by an AI project implemented in the judiciary in Shanghai. In February 2017, the Shanghai High People's Court was tasked by the Supreme People's Court to create and test a case-handling system for criminal trials, called System 206 (206系统). The system was developed by an ad-hoc working group jointly created by the Shanghai High People's Court, Shanghai People's Procuratorate, Shanghai Municipal Bureau of Public Security, Shanghai Bureau of Justice and the AI company iFlytek. The AI company assigned more than 300 of its technicians to work on the project throughout the R&D, trial, test, and implementation phases, starting from May 2017 to the first implementation in December 2018, and continuing since then.[137]

Involvement of private companies in public sector AI projects is applied at scale in Shanghai through the AI pilot application scenarios (Chapter 5.3). Later, it was also embedded in Shanghai municipal AI plans.[138] Besides the pilot application scenarios, another mechanism adopted by Shanghai to engage private firms is the "reveal the rankings" initiative (揭榜挂帅), which relies on competitive methods to select the most capable companies to work on important government projects in technology and research. Introduced by the Ministry of Industry and Information Technology in 2018,[139] this working method was first

[136] "Partnership agreements for AI will need to be more collaborative than traditional information system sourcing projects, in which the [public] agency specifies in detail what is required, the private sector responds with bids, and a vendor is chosen to work on the project. It is unlikely that the agency will be able to specify AI requirements in as much detail as traditional systems. Moreover, given that an agency is looking for partners to work with after the initial system is deployed, the focus should be on building long-term collaborations [and] keep refining the system to increase its capability and sophistication" (Desouza, 2018, p. 30).

[137] Cui, Y., 2020. *Artificial Intelligence and Judicial Modernization*, Shanghai: Springer, pp. xvi–xvii, 64.

[138] The *AI Highland Plan* encourages AI companies to cooperate in various government-led projects like the creation of "key joint laboratories" (重点联合实验室; task 4, special action 2), innovation centres for the AI industry that focus on AI applications in finance, manufacturing, transportation, medicine and other industries (task 6), or the construction of municipal computing platforms (task 7), among others.

[139] The MIIT document that introduced the "reveal the rankings" mechanism is the 2018 *Work Method on Revealing the Rankings for the New Generation Artificial Intelligence Industry Innovation Key Tasks* [新一代人工智能产业创新重点任务揭榜工作方案].

adopted in Shanghai in a project on AI medical imaging analysis in Pudong.[140] Since then, the Shanghai Municipal Commission for Science and Technology has been very active in implementing the "reveal the rankings" scheme,[141] with some of the most recent initiatives announced in July 2023.[142] Finally, the engagement of private firms in government-led AI projects can also happen in ad-hoc projects, like the already mentioned Shanghai Data Innovation Center, Shanghai Data Exchange Center, SenseTime Technology Shanghai New Generation AI Computing and Empowerment Platform, or the System 206, among others. The implications of involving private companies in public sector AI projects are further discussed in Chapters 5 and 6.

An engagement approach that leverages public sector AI projects and public infrastructure (i.e., the trial and demonstration zones) is attractive for both government and companies, to the point that some scholars call this form of engagement a "symbiotic relationship" (Han, 2020, p. 40). For the Shanghai government, this relationship is valuable because it helps to achieve two main goals of the municipal AI plans at once.[143] First, engaging private companies serves to spur the development of the

The document focuses on four major areas (i.e., smart products, core foundations, key technologies and equipment for smart manufacturing, and support systems) and related products and technologies. See: http://www.gov.cn/xinwen/2021-04/13/content_5599203.htm.

140 Author WeChat conversation with a senior consultant of the Shanghai government on AI policy, who is also open data consultant of the Baiyulan Open AI Institute (see 4.3), and technical director of the government-sponsored incubator AI Space in Yangpu District, 19 November 2021.

141 San Si Pai, 2021. The Domestic and International Practice and Revelation of the 'Revealing the Ranking System' for Scientific Research Projects [科研计划项目 "揭榜制" 国内外做法与启示]. *NetEase* [网易], 15 March, https://www.163.com/dy/article/G559QE8B0511D98B.html. In August 2021, the Shanghai Municipal Commission for Science and Technology issued the *Notice on the issuance of the 2021 Shanghai Municipal Science and Technology "Reveal the Rankings" Project Guide* [关于发布2021年度上海市科技攻关 "揭榜挂帅"项目指南的通知], http://stcsm.sh.gov.cn/zwgk/kyjhxm/xmsb/20210812/cb6dbd895d5742f49bc01c8d358c5039.html.

142 The Paper, 2023. Shanghai Launches the "Reveal the Rankings" Work for Major Application Scenarios of Metaverse in 2023 [上海启动2023年元宇宙重大应用场景 "揭榜挂帅" 工作]. *The Paper* [澎湃新闻], 9 July, https://baijiahao.baidu.com/s?id=1770910124808777522&wfr=spider&for=pc.

143 The relation between AI applications and industrial development is also emphasized by Yu (2021, cit.), who comments: "In fact, the expansion of AI application scenarios and the development of industrial innovation are complementary to each other [事实上,

local AI industry. It gives AI firms the opportunity to deploy business products and technical solutions that can be marketed and adopted elsewhere. Second, this engagement helps Shanghai to steer and guide private companies toward AI applications prioritized by the municipal government such as city management, public services, and public health (Lee, 2022). In doing so, the government can leverage corporate resources and expertise to speed up AI deployment and achieve economies of scale. In addition, this approach offers Shanghai a competitive advantage vis-à-vis other cities in the attraction and nurturing of AI companies, because no other Chinese localities can arguably rival Shanghai in terms of quantity and variety of AI application scenarios.[144] This engagement-based approach is also appealing to AI companies, which compete to partner in government-led projects. First, as just mentioned, these projects create market opportunities for AI technologies and products (e.g., the City Brain developed by Alibaba in Hangzhou has been later implemented in more than 20 cities across Asia). This aspect is extremely valuable for AI firms, considering the existing difficulties in commercializing AI products.[145] Second, by cooperating in government-led projects, private firms can gain access to the rich data sources of Shanghai government agencies and databases, including in medical care, public security, education, smart transportation, and other areas that are often precluded to private companies (Chapter 2.2.3). By accessing these data sources, companies

人工智能应用场景拓展与产业创新发展是相辅相成的关系]". On the role of Chinese local governments in promoting this link, see also Deloitte China (2019, p. 14).

144 Yu, 2021 (cit.). The Shanghai Municipal Commission of Economy and Informatization, a key agency in Shanghai AI policy (Chapter 3.2), also emphasizes this point: "Currently, Shanghai is centering on the construction of an AI 'Shanghai Highland', giving full play to the advantages of Shanghai's super-large city application scenarios, and through the construction of AI application scenarios, making Shanghai into the 'best testing ground for intelligent technology' and 'super incubator for intelligent applications'" (SHEITC, 2020. The Third Batch of Requirements for AI Application Scenarios in Shanghai Is Officially Released, Waiting for You to Unveil the List! [上海市第三批人工智能应用场景需求正式发布, 等您来揭榜!], 13 July, http://www.sheitc.sh.gov.cn/gydt/20200713/6e86f1f9070440c482f360a4b1f20061.html).

145 Liu Shui, investment director at the incubator CAS Star, commented: "[I]t's very difficult to commercialize a [AI] product. First, finding funding is hard. And second, there isn't a lot of support to help transitioning from tech to a viable product". Source: Wang, L., 2019. The Cold Winter of AI Venture Capital, Why Only You Can't Find the Money [AI创投寒冬, 为什么只有你找不到钱]. *WeChat Post*, 12 August, https://mp.weixin.qq.com/s/S_vBIC3hi_AtO_eumjs_9w.

can optimize their technologies and products, since learning from real-world data may provide unique insights that cannot be acquired from synthetic data.[146] In addition to the AIOIPs discussed earlier, the System 206 again offers another illustrative example of this aspect. By cooperating with the Shanghai Supreme People's Court, iFlytek could train its AI system on approximately 45 million digital documents collected from Shanghai's tribunals, enforcement agencies, and other sources.[147] Similar considerations can be extended to the AI pilot application scenarios that involve public sector AI implementations (Chapter 5.3).

4.4.3 *Conclusions on the AI Company Indicator*

Shanghai has one of the highest concentrations of AI companies among Chinese cities, and it hosts a variety of AI firms that spans from "national champions" to unicorns and promising startups. In addition, Shanghai has been very active in supporting AI industrial development through direct financial handouts, manifold preferential policies, and by offering AI firms plentiful application scenarios to test their technologies and products. These indicators suggest that Shanghai's AI industry is one of the most advanced in China. While the statistics examined in this section are mostly drawn from the *AI@SH Report* and other sources close to the Shanghai government, which have logical interests in emphasizing the strengths of the local industry, various reports confirm the strong position of Shanghai in the company indicator.[148] Beyond the official

[146] A synthetic dataset is a repository of data that is generated programmatically; it is not collected by any real-life survey or experiment. Synthetic data are primarily used to train AI systems. A study in AI in healthcare showed that 92% of AI models trained on synthetic data have lower accuracy than those trained on real data (Rankin, D., Black, M., Bond, R., Wallace, J., Mulvenna, M. and Epelde, G., 2020. Reliability of Supervised Machine Learning Using Synthetic Data in Health Care: Model to Preserve Privacy for Data Sharing. *JMIR Medical Informatics*, 8(7), https://medinform.jmir.org/2020/7/e18910/).

[147] Cui, 2020 (cit.), p. 66.

[148] The *China New Generation AI Technology Industry Regional Competitiveness Evaluation Index (2019)* compiled by the China New Generation Artificial Intelligence Development Strategy Research Center ranked Shanghai third in China behind Beijing and Shenzhen. See: Nankai Economic Field Research, 2019. China New

narratives and statistics, there is a vibrant debate among Chinese experts on the actual competitiveness of China's AI industry in general. These discussions primarily focus on the innovation capacity of Chinese AI firms and the development prospects of the national AI industry[149] and do

Generation Artificial Intelligence Development Strategy Research Institute released two heavyweight reports [中国新一代人工智能发展战略研究院发布两份重量级报告]. *Nankai Economic Field Research* [南开经济调查], 18 May, http://www.nkear.com/news/201905/201905181542026.htm. Tsinghua University (2018, cit.) and Deloitte China (2019) also confirm this finding, among others. Recent data confirm that Shanghai has the second highest concentration of AI firms (296) after Beijing (537). See: People.cn, 2021. China Internet Development Report: The Scale of My China's AI Industry Was 303.1 Billion RMB in 2020 [中国互联网发展报告: 2020年我国人工智能产业规模为3031亿元]. *People.cn*, 14 July, http://finance.people.com.cn/n1/2021/0714/c1004-32157937.html.

[149] There are a number of Chinese-language commentaries on this topic published in various forms (paper, blogs, etc.). One of the most influential pieces is the essay by Prof. Cai Zixing (蔡自兴), an eminent AI expert who in 2016 observed that China's AI industrial policy has a short-term focus on economic gains (经济效益至上, 缺乏远大眼光). Many companies and local governments lack a long-term vision for AI development, neglecting that AI development is a process that requires time (AI发展应当遵循一定的规律, 需要一个过程, 需要一定的时间, 不能急于求成). Prof. Cai also warns to avoid "rushing headlong into mass action" because this would lead to disorderly competition (一哄而起可能导致无序竞争), as it happened in areas such as drones and robotics (Cai, 2016). Another commentary highly circulated online is a 2019 article published on the WeChat account *Huxiu.com* (虎嗅网), which argues that Baidu is the only Chinese company really researching, investing in, and developing AI among China's four major technology giants, i.e., Alibaba, Huawei and Tencent (Qian, D., 2019. A Map to Understand China's AI Close-Quarters Combat: Only Baidu and Huawei Are Really Doing AI [一图看懂中国AI肉搏战: 只有百度华为真在做AI]. *Huxiu.com*, 7 January, https://mp.weixin.qq.com/s/3BcoGMDzp-oOzvj9mijvrA?fbclid=IwAR1CckzxrXKmRPwYzT7Pg3CqmOFtSqFcC3oSSAX_wDmhxUE3Gc_pbs8dLfU. Other topics related to China's AI industry discussed by Chinese experts are well captured in articles such as: *Who killed that AI Unicorn?* which looks at China's four main computer vision companies (SenseTime, Megvii, Yitu and Cloudwalk) to examine the difficulties of Chinese AI firms to transition into a sustainable business model (Yu, D. and Zhang, X., 2020. Who Killed That AI Unicorn? [谁杀死了那只AI独角兽?], 13 July, https://mp.weixin.qq.com/s/hvg5Un3EjORhMg6kP_1rRA); *Who strangled the AI industry?*, which discusses various difficulties of China's industrial AI (i.e., non-commercial private-sector AI applications), and lists some of the barriers that industrial AI will need to overcome (Song, H., 2020. Who Strangled the AI Industry? [谁卡住了工业AI的脖子?]. *Synced* [机器之能], 29 November, https://mp.weixin.qq.com/s/3lNamVcFySeDEUfcNJ16Lg); or *The development of the AI industry still faces many challenges*, which discusses some foundational challenges to China's AI industry development (Xinhua Net, 2020. The development of artificial intelligence industry still faces many challenges [人工智能产业发展仍面临诸多挑战], World AI Conference WeChat Blogpost, https://mp.weixin.qq.com/s/y3iSgnkyUBlBBxgSGSqAFg.

not affect the general consensus that Shanghai has a solid AI industrial foundation.

A trait of Shanghai's approach to supporting AI companies that has important implications for public sector AI applications is the opportunity given to private firms to test their technologies in real-world scenarios, either in demonstration zones or in public sector AI projects. In particular, the direct engagement of AI companies in public sector AI projects replicates what is happening at the national level with the New Generation Artificial Intelligence Open Platforms (AIOIPs), whereby private sector enterprises are selectively granted access to public domains and associated data repositories, and are endorsed to apply AI solutions to optimize the operations of public institutions and the provision of public services. This relationship may have a net positive impact on public sector AI applications by allowing for better connections between the providers of AI technologies and the public sector areas where such technologies are needed, partly overcoming a barrier that traditionally limited the partnerships involving strategic assets and sensitive information to China's State-owned enterprises (Larsen, 2019). At the same time, the increasing interconnection between public and private sectors may generate challenges, including conflicts of interests[150] or contrasting visions about the use of AI in the public sector, among others. There are some specific downsides for industrial development too. For instance, the tendency to favor large firms that have a proven track record and substantial financial, human, and other resources, usually leaving relatively little room for small-medium enterprises. This possibly increases the influence of

[150] Conflict of interests were highlighted in studies on China's Internet Courts (互联网法院). For instance, one scholar emphasizes the dual positions of tech companies as sometime defendants as well as online judicial facilitators: "[Companies] may not simply influence how matters are resolved, but also how information about the parties to a case is held by them (as judicial facilitator) even when they may have an interest in a case (as a party)". See: Xu, A., 2017. Chinese Judicial Justice on the Cloud: A Future Call or a Pandora's Box? An Analysis of the 'Intelligent Court System' of China. *Information & Communications Technology Law*, 26(1), pp. 59–71, https://doi.org/10.1080/13600834.2017.1269873. Similar problems emerged with the Social Credit System. In early 2015, the PBoC selected eight companies to begin preparatory work for the establishment of a credit reporting system, and gave them six months to do so. After the trial period, these private credit initiatives were temporarily blocked because national authorities were concerned with private companies' practices of data collection and processing, as well as potential conflicts of interest (Creemers, 2018, p. 25; Kostka, 2019, pp. 1568–1569). See also Appendix I.

major players in the short term and stifles industrial development in the mid-term.[151] These considerations are further developed in Chapter 5.

The engagement of private AI companies is better understood in light of a broader phenomenon documented in earlier studies, which examine how Chinese local governments use their administrative capacity to attract and support selected firms by providing "special deals", such as preferential access to capital and land or market protection, among others.[152] In the case of AI, the novelty is that these "special deals" rely on central and local governments being the primary users of the technologies and solutions provided by the companies. This often makes AI firms highly dependent on central and local governments, which become their main customers[153] as well as key providers of essential resources like data (i.e., public data, 4.1), technological and physical infrastructure (4.2), financial support (e.g., government investment funds and subsidies,[154] 4.4), and a friendly regulatory environment.[155]

[151] Han, 2020; Deloitte China, 2019, p. 6; author interview with a consultant of the Shanghai municipal government on AI policy, open data consultant, and director of AI Space (details in Table 5.2).

[152] Bai, C., Hsieh, C. and Zheng, M., 2019. Special Deals with Chinese Characteristics. *NBER Working Paper Series*, National Bureau of Economic Research, May 2019, http://www.nber.org/papers/w25839.

[153] Ruehl, M., Riordan, P. and Olcott, E., 2021. Can SenseTime Become a Chinese AI Champion? *Financial Times*, 29 September, https://www.ft.com/content/c735e0f3-5704-47b5-a76f-7a02d53a1525. It shows that government agencies form a big chunk of the customer base of SenseTime.

[154] An article by economic news outlet Caijing states that several Chinese AI firms have not yet achieved a healthy growth in revenue and profits, relying on financing money to support their operations, including foreign acquisitions. See: Cajing Magazine, 2020. 2021 Will Be Even More Difficult for AI Companies [2021, AI公司将难上加难]. *Caijing Magazine* [财经杂志], *WeChat Post*, 29 November, https://mp.weixin.qq.com/s/vYWa6o8SwcPsHbCTnX-6TQ.

[155] "Autonomous driving is a case in point. The first company to go to market may not be the one that is the first to develop the technology but the one that operates in a country that is the first to develop a nation-wide regulatory framework that allows autonomous vehicles to legally drive on the road [...]" (Lewis, 2019, p. 16).

4.5 Social Acceptance

Social acceptance here indicates public confidence and trust in public sector AI implementations (Makasi et al., 2021). China's central and local governments can adopt with relative ease the laws and regulations that provide legal foundations for their AI initiatives. However, failing to address social considerations would make the implementation of AI more challenging, especially in activities where citizens can decide whether or not to engage with AI, in domains where AI-enabled public services would risk widening existing inequalities, or in case of incidents that would expose privacy, safety or other sensitive issues (Chui et al., 2018). Hence, social acceptance is examined as a resource needed to support the efficient rollout of AI initiatives in the public sector, following an approach adopted in previous studies (Castro et al., 2019). Indeed, "even if one takes the cynical view that everything the Chinese leadership does is aimed at consolidating Party rule, it must equally be recognised the leadership believes an efficient way of doing so is ensuring the population is, by and large, satisfied" (Creemers, 2020, p. 67).

To gauge the level of social acceptance of AI among the Chinese population and its possible impacts on the operational capacity of Shanghai to bring AI projects to fruition, this section analyzes four surveys and one study on the public perception of artificial intelligence in China. These sources are not targeted at the use of AI in the public sector, but they provide valuable information about what Chinese citizens think of several issues related to artificial intelligence, including attitudes toward AI development, views of the expected societal impacts of AI, and an attempt to gauge public acceptance of AI. These findings allow to extrapolate useful insights on the level of acceptance that AI-enabled public services may encounter among the Chinese population, including in Shanghai.

4.5.1 Surveys on Public Perception of AI in China

Tsinghua University's *China AI Development Report 2018* contains a section dedicated to the public perception of AI, which reports the main findings from a survey conducted by the popular AI-enabled news feed platform Jinri Toutiao (今日头条). Conducted in the period 9–13 May 2017, the survey collected 3,088 valid responses in total. According to the survey, the majority of respondents stated they had knowledge of

AI, which they primarily gathered from the news[156] (80.27%). In terms of social acceptance, 53.15% of respondents expressed support of the comprehensive development of AI. A more conservative support was expressed by 28.68% of the respondents, who believe that AI development should be confined to relatively low-risk projects. Other respondents did not oppose AI, but believed that the pace of development should slow down (15.77%). Only a minority of respondents (2.4%) opposed AI development (Tsinghua, 2018, p. 88). Tsinghua also observes that respondents were mostly interested in how AI development will affect them in terms of job displacement (46.14%), potential harms (43.61%), and AI legal and moral agency (40.36%). The report emphasizes that "all the three [topics] have negative implications, indicating that despite a supportive attitude toward AI development, people want to know more about the direct risks that AI might bring"[157] (Tsinghua, 2018, p. 87). In addition, the analysis of over 10,000 users' comments on popular AI-related articles on Jinri Toutiao in the period 2016–2017 shows a slight decrease in the positive attitude toward AI, from a score of 48.71 in 2016 to 46.37 in 2017, where a higher score indicates a more positive attitude. Tsinghua interprets this shift as "a gradually rational attitude towards AI" (Tsinghua, 2018, pp. 90–91).

Another survey on public perception of AI in China was conducted by Chinese AI and Internet giant Tencent and published in the book it edited with CAICT (Tencent and CAICT, 2017, pp. 4–20). The online survey was carried out between May and June 2017 on a sample of 2,968 individuals. The majority of the respondents (70%) agree that AI will have a positive impact on society, 27.2% believe that such positive influence is likely, and only 0.9% of the respondents does not agree that AI will have a positive societal impact. The survey contains a section dedicated to "public trust and acceptance" (人工智能的信任与接受程度), which

[156] Despite this high level of awareness, only 41.58% reported that they had used AI products, with 40.74% stating that they had never used any AI products, and 17.68% saying that they were not sure what makes a product an AI product. This latest phenomenon is known as the "AI effect" or "odd paradox": a pattern whereby AI technologies enter the common fold (e.g., speech recognition used in smartphones), people become accustomed to these technologies, and these technologies stop being considered AI (Stanford, 2016, p. 12; see also Haenlein and Kaplan, 2019).

[157] The most common AI-related concerns that emerged from the survey are "AI losing control and causing social crises" (54.9% of respondents), "AI making wrong decisions or judgments" (46.01%), and "AI losing control and causing personal injuries" (45.81%).

emphasizes that "users' trust in AI systems is the precondition for AI systems to generate social benefits".[158] Tencent surveyed public acceptance across nine AI applications that the company believes are already commonly used in society, namely: autonomous driving, virtual assistants, AI in education and research, financial services, medicine and medical diagnosis, art and design, legal practice, social relations, and industry and services. By looking at the percentage of interviewees stating preference for "human as principal, AI as support" (人类为主, 人工智能为辅助), Tencent infers that public acceptance is relatively low in education and research (57% of respondents replied that AI should only serve as human support), medicine and medical diagnosis (49%), social relations (43%), and legal practice (39%; Tencent and CAICT, 2017, p. 11–13). Finally, the survey examined respondents' attitude in terms of the responsibilities related to AI development and deployment. The majority of respondents (45% strongly agree, 30% agree) believe that "citizens should participate in the evaluation of AI social impacts" (对于社会影响力的人工智能做评估, 市民也应该参加). In terms of legal responsibility for damage or harm generated by AI systems in autonomous driving, medicine, and other areas, 20.7% of the respondents answered that the government should be legally responsible, a relatively low percentage compared to those who attribute legal responsibilities to companies (77.9%) or users themselves (43.1%; Tencent and CAICT, 2017, pp. 17–18).

In March 2018, State-run national broadcaster CCTV published the results of the annual China Economic Life Survey (中国经济生活大调查), which that year included a section on the Chinese public perception of AI edited in cooperation with Tencent Research. The survey interviewed 8,000 participants aged between 16 and 60 from China's first,

[158] In original: "用户对人工智能系统的信任，是人工智能系统产生社会效益的前提". Tencent and CAICT (2017, p. 10).

second and third tier cities.[159] Findings show a high level of AI awareness: 91.2% of the respondents think that AI will affect their life and work, of which 50.4% responded they already feel the impact of AI (已经产生了影响), and 40.8% said they believe it will affect them but were yet to feel it (目前还没有感受到). In terms of social acceptance, the findings show that 76.3% of respondents think that AI applications in certain areas are a threat to privacy. Despite this, 85.7% of respondents say that they would try a health-related applications of AI, and 90% would be willing to experience autonomous driving.

In June 2018, the Boston Consulting Group published the results of a global survey on AI that interviewed over 7,000 respondents in the period May–June 2018.[160] Respondents were almost equally distributed in seven countries, including China (1,011 respondents). Findings show that enthusiasm for AI is particularly high in China, where 94% of the respondents cite at least one positive feeling about AI. Findings also show that China is adopting AI at a faster rate than the other countries included in the survey, and the great majority of Chinese respondents believe that AI will have positive impacts on their results (92%), effectiveness (91%), and other work-related aspects. These findings are interesting considering that the survey also interviewed respondents from the public sector, although the specific breakdown of figures by country is not available. Still, in examining the main findings of the survey, some analysts argue that one possible explanation of Chinese respondents' enthusiasm for AI is related to public sector AI applications: "Indeed, in the public sector, Chinese mayors and other local officials began rushing to invest

[159] The results of the survey's findings related to AI are discussed in: Hersey, F., 2018. Almost 80% of Chinese Concerned About AI Threat to Privacy, 32% Already Feel a Threat to Their Work. *Technode*, 2 March, https://technode.com/2018/03/02/almost-80-chinese-concerned-ai-threat-privacy-32-already-feel-threat-work/; or Sohu. 2018. How Much Has AI Affected You? 30% of Respondents Feel Threatened to Their Jobs [AI对你影响有多大?3成受访者感受到对自己工作的威胁]. *Sohu* [搜狐], https://www.sohu.com/a/224746185_561670. Xinhua offers a more synthetic account focused on privacy, while also noticing that interviewees are willing to try the application of artificial intelligence technology (多数受访者愿意尝试人工智能技术的应用). Xinhua, 2018. AI Threats to Personal Privacy Becomes a Worry [人工智能威胁个人隐私成隐忧]. *Xinhua*, 3 March, http://xinhuanet.com/info/2018-03/03/c_137012166.htm.

[160] Boston Consulting Group, 2018. *Artificial Intelligence: Have No Fear*, BCG Gamma, https://www.bcg.com/fr-fr/press/20june2018-france-press-release (press release); https://de.slideshare.net/TheBostonConsultingGroup/artificial-intelligence-have-no-fear (slides with main findings).

in AI start-ups and adopt AI following the release of the State Council's *New Generation of Artificial Intelligence Development Plan* in 2017. By embracing AI, Chinese governments not only provide capital to AI firms, but also create use cases that demonstrate the benefits of AI" (Castro et al., 2019, p. 35).

Finally, in August 2021 the Massachusetts Institute of Technology (MIT) published a study on the dynamics that inform popular debates and public acceptance about the applications of facial recognition, which are widespread in China.[161] The study presents four cases from the previous three years in which facial recognition attracted great public attention in China. The study looks at intrusive applications in commercial settings (access to a wildlife park and to residential buildings, customers' profiling), but also in public sector applications in education (use of cameras in university classrooms) and public transport (facial recognition at metros' entrances). These cases sparked considerable domestic discussion on Chinese media, including State-run news outlets and popular social media such as WeChat and Weibo. Although it acknowledges the existence of some limitations,[162] the MIT study proposes that "while debates about facial recognition have indeed become more common, there is still broad-based public support for uses that promise increased security or convenience". The study suggests that public concern is primarily directed toward specific kinds of private uses, and that "the ultimate authority of the state to use facial recognition technology is broadly accepted". These conclusions confirm the findings of earlier studies that indicate Chinese citizens' support for technologies that are expected to improve the quality of life, even when there are trade-offs in terms of privacy (e.g., Kostka, 2019, which examines the findings of a survey on

[161] Brown, T., Statman, A. and Sui, C., 2021. Public Debate on Facial Recognition Technologies in China. *MIT Case Studies in Social and Ethical Responsibilities of Computing*, Summer 2021, https://doi.org/10.21428/2c646de5.37712c5c.

[162] According to its authors, the main limitations of the MIT report are: source bias (i.e., debates that are permitted to remain online are much more likely to capture challenges to commercial uses of the technology than those of the State); and statistical representativeness (i.e., four cases do not represent a full view of the Chinese public's opinions of facial recognition technologies). It must also be noted that facial recognition is the AI-based application with the highest level of awareness among Chinese citizens, as revealed by the Tencent-CCTV survey.

the AI-based Social Credit System). The MIT survey also further corroborates the considerations that were made on Chinese AI regulations and ethics principles (Chapter 2.2.3), as well as those on data privacy (4.1.3).

4.5.2 Conclusions on the Social Acceptance Indicator

Chinese and international surveys on public perception of AI in China conducted in the period 2017–2018 consistently show that Chinese citizens predominantly hold a positive or at least open attitude toward AI development and applications. These findings were confirmed in late 2021 by an IPSOS survey on global attitudes toward AI products and services. The IPSOS survey indicates that 78% of Chinese respondents feel that AI products and services have more benefits than drawbacks, compared to only 35% of American respondents (Stanford, 2023, pp. 323–324). An interesting feature that emerges from the sources examined in this section is that Chinese individuals can hold positive views of AI, while at the same time believing in several negative implications caused by the technology, as noted by previous research (Castro et al., 2019, p. 35). For instance, the Tsinghua report highlighted that despite a supportive attitude toward AI development, Chinese respondents are concerned about AI-induced job displacement and potential harms, among others. The Tencent-CCTV survey confirms the coexistence of positive and negative views among the Chinese public: nearly 80% of the survey respondents believe that AI has broad prospects for development and are willing to try AI applications, but are also concerned that AI applications in certain fields will threaten their privacy. The Boston Consulting Group produces similar findings. It shows that 53% of Chinese respondents believe that their job will no longer exist in the next ten years because of AI (compared to 26% of respondents in the United States and 27% in Germany), but it also shows that 51% of Chinese respondents believe AI will create job opportunities (compared to 19% in the United Kingdom and the United States, 26% in France, or 33% in Germany). And while Chinese respondents are concerned with AI-related workplace dangers like increased control and surveillance (84%) at higher rates than their Western counterparts, the survey shows that Chinese interviewees remain especially enthusiastic about AI.

While it is important to gauge citizens' acceptance for the reasons explained at the beginning of this section, there is scant evidence that negative public opinion of AI would have any tangible impact on the

AI policies and applications promoted by the Chinese government at the national or local levels. For instance, the implementation of facial recognition at the entrance of Beijing metro stations (examined by the MIT study) was not affected by ongoing public debates. In general, all AI applications somehow related to "public security"—an expanding concept that under the leadership of Xi Jinping includes public health, social stability, etc.—are clearly beyond the reach of any public debate, no matter how vibrant. This does not mean, however, that the Chinese government is disinterested in the social acceptance of AI. On the contrary, national and Shanghai AI plans emphasize the importance of societal support for AI development. The AIDP states that China will "fully use all kinds of traditional media and new media to quickly propagate new progress and new achievements in AI, to let the healthy development of AI become a consensus in all of society, and muster the vigour of all of society to participate in and support the development of AI".[163] The AIDP also calls for promoting various type of activities aimed at popularizing AI among Chinese citizens, and for comprehensively improving the level of cognition and application of AI in society (State Council, 2017, cit., section 5, par. 6). In Shanghai, the *Opinions* emphasize the importance of giving proper considerations to social issues as part of the "the sustainable and healthy development of artificial intelligence" (人工智能持续健康发展). In this regard, Shanghai is trying to popularize AI among local citizens. One initiative is particularly illustrative of these efforts. At the end of 2021, the Shanghai Municipal Commission of Economy and Informatization launched a media campaign on its official WeChat account, called "AI by your side" (AI在身边). This initiative aims to showcase the best practices of Shanghai in integrating AI in public health, transportation, urban governance, and other areas, in order to show the value that AI is creating for the local population of Shanghai.[164]

[163] In original: "充分利用各种传统媒体和新兴媒体，及时宣传人工智能新进展、新成效，让人工智能健康发展成为全社会共识，调动全社会参与支持人工智能发展的积极性" (State Council, 2017, cit., section 6, par. 4).

[164] For instance, one episode of the media campaign presents the AI-enabled system supporting pathological diagnosis developed by the Shanghai Hospital Development Center (上海申康医院发展中心, which manages the budget, staffing, and health-record sharing of all municipal-level hospitals), in cooperation with 8 local medical institutions and a number of well-known AI companies. The article reports that the AI-based diagnostic system reduces the diagnostic time from 30–40 minutes to 3 minutes per sample,

4.6 Main Findings

This chapter showed that Shanghai has a well-developed AI ecosystem. Shanghai occupies a leading position in China in access to data, technological and physical infrastructure, and AI companies. In terms of AI talents, Shanghai trails Beijing but remains among the top Chinese cities, especially if the talent repositories in private AI firms is considered. In terms of social acceptance, this research could not find surveys among the Shanghai citizens. However, national surveys suggest that the Chinese public holds an open attitude toward AI, and the Jinri Toutiao survey cited by Tsinghua University identified Shanghai respondents as the most AI-interested local users in China (Tsinghua, 2018, p. 88). Overall, the analysis of the Shanghai AI ecosystems showed that Shanghai has the operational skills and resources needed to implement public sector AI applications in practice.

The chapter also emphasized the ability of Shanghai to orchestrate the resources of the municipal AI ecosystem, arguing that this is a key component of its capacity to promote the implementation of AI in the public sector. Shanghai has deployed several policy initiatives to foster the sharing of public data, a critical asset for public sector AI implementations (4.1.2). The municipality is strengthening both its technological and physical infrastructure in a way that is conducive to the development of AI applications in the public sector (4.2.3). In human capital, Shanghai is expanding the municipal AI talent pool and involves its major knowledge sources in various government projects (4.3.3). In terms of AI companies, Shanghai has been actively engaging private firms in promoting the use of AI in the public sector by leveraging public infrastructure (the trial and demonstration zones), and directly involving private companies in public sector AI projects (4.4.2). Finally, Shanghai is showing attention to the popularization of AI as a way to bolster social acceptance among local citizens (4.5.2). These findings about the ability of Shanghai to orchestrate the resources needed for AI applications are consistent with earlier studies, which observe that the Chinese government is making better use of its resources than many other countries, and suggest that government

reaching a 90% accuracy rate. See: Shanghai Municipal Commission of Economy and Informatization, 2021. "AI by Your Side" AI in Hospitals, Smart-Aided Diagnosis ["AI在身边" AI在医院 智能助诊断]. *WeChat Post*, 10 December, https://mp.weixin.qq.com/s/UvV58bY40BiC6c-aUIiB1Q. Further examples are provided in Chapter 5.3.

prioritization of AI implementation may have a positive impact on actual AI applications (Oxford Insights and IDRC, 2020, pp. 5, 11).

Based on the extensive analysis of official reports, statistics, and other documentary sources on the Shanghai AI ecosystem, this chapter showed that Shanghai has developed a solid operational capacity to bring public sector AI applications to fruition. To account for the possible impacts of the sociotechnical complexities of AI on the capacity to implement AI in the public sector (Chapter 2.4), the findings on the AI ecosystem of Shanghai will be integrated with primary data gathered from in-depth key informant interviews (Chapter 5.1). The analysis of the Shanghai AI ecosystem already tried to account for these sociotechnical factors, examining not only technological resources, but also legal (data privacy) and social elements (social acceptance) that can affect operational capacity. Moreover, the possible impacts of ethical issues on public sector AI implementations in China have been discussed earlier (Chapter 2.2.3). The interviews will expand the findings of desk research, offering further insights into the availability of operational skills and resources in Shanghai, and how such skills and resources are mobilized and put to use to promote public sector AI implementations in the municipality. The refined results will serve as a starting point to examine the main policy initiatives that are fostering the use of AI in the public sector in Shanghai (Chapters 5.2 and 5.3).

References

CAICT (China Academy of Information and Communications Technology). 2021. *White Paper on China's Computing Power Development Index* [中国算力发展指数白皮书]. CAICT, No. 202110, September 2021, http://www.caict.ac.cn/kxyj/qwfb/bps/202109/t20210918_390058.htm. English translation excerpts by Jeffrey Ding: https://docs.google.com/document/d/1Mq5vpZQe7nrKgkYJA2-yZNV1Eo8swh_w36TUEzFWIWs/edit#heading=h.yx06um9bhugh.

CAICT, 2023. *White Paper on China's Computing Power Development Index* [中国算力发展指数白皮书]. CAICT, No. 202306, September 2023, http://www.caict.ac.cn/kxyj/qwfb/bps/202309/t20230914_461823.htm.

CAICT and AIIA (China Artificial Intelligence Industry Alliance), 2021. *White Paper on Artificial Intelligence Core Technologies Industry: The Era of AI Under the Drive or Deep Learning* [人工智能核心技术产业白皮书 – 深度学习技术驱动下的人工智能时代], CAICT, April 2021, http://www.caict.ac.cn/kxyj/qwfb/bps/202104/t20210419_374019.htm.

CAICT and BDA (Broadband Development Alliance), 2020. *Shanghai 5G and Broadband* [上海 "双千兆宽带城市" 发展白皮书]. CAICT, November 2020, http://www.caict.ac.cn/kxyj/qwfb/bps/202011/P020201111484158729811.pdf.

CAICT and CMG (China Media Group), 2020. *China Regional and Urban Digital Economy Development Report* (2020) [中国区域与城市数字经济发展报告 (2020年)]. CAICT, December 2020, http://www.caict.ac.cn/kxyj/qwfb/ztbg/202101/P020210104510830262645.pdf.

Castro, D. and McLaughlin, M., 2021. *Who Is Winning the AI Race: China, the EU or the United States?—2021 Update*. Center for Data Innovation, https://datainnovation.org/2021/01/who-is-winning-the-ai-race-china-the-eu-or-the-united-states-2021-update/.

Castro, D., McLaughlin, M. and Chivot, E., 2019. *Who Is Winning the AI Race: China, the EU or the United States?* Center for Data Innovation, https://www.datainnovation.org/2019/08/who-is-winning-the-ai-race-china-the-eu-or-the-united-states/.

CESI (China Electronics Standardization Institute), 2021. *Big Data Development Index Report of Key Cities (2021)* [重点城市大数据发展指数报告 (2021年)]. CESI [中国电子技术标准化研究院], http://www.cesi.cn/images/editor/20210719/20210719104506217.pdf.

Chui, M., Harryson, M., Manyika, J., Roberts, R., Chung, R., van Heteren, A. and Nel, P., 2018. *Notes from the AI Frontier: Applying AI for Social Good*. McKinsey Global Institute, https://www.mckinsey.com/featured-insights/artificialintelligence/applying-artificial-intelligence-for-social-good.

Creemers, R., 2018. China's Social Credit System: An Evolving Practice of Control, https://doi.org/10.2139/ssrn.3175792.

Creemers, R., 2020. The Ideology Behind China's AI Strategy. In: Elliott, H. ed., 2020. *The AI Powered State: China's Approach to Public Sector Innovation*. Nesta, May 2020, pp. 63–69, https://www.nesta.org.uk/feature/ai-powered-state/.

Deloitte China, 2019. *Scenarios and Potentials of AI's Commercial Applications in China*. Deloitte Digital Difference, https://www2.deloitte.com/cn/en/pages/innovation/articles/china-ai-industry-whitepaper-intelligence-driven-by-innovation.html.

Desouza, K., 2018. *Delivering Artificial Intelligence in Government: Challenges and Opportunities*. Washington DC, USA: IBM Center for the Business of Government, http://www.businessofgovernment.org/report/delivering-artificial-intelligence-government-challenges-and-opportunities.

Ding, J., 2018. *Deciphering China's AI Dream*. Oxford: University of Oxford, https://www.fhi.ox.ac.uk/deciphering-chinas-ai-dream.

Ding, J., 2019. *China's Current Capabilities, Policies, and Industrial Ecosystem in AI*. Testimony before the U.S.-China Economic and Security Review

Commission Hearing on Technology, Trade, and Military-Civil Fusion: China's Pursuit of Artificial Intelligence, New Materials, and New Energy, 7 June, https://www.uscc.gov/sites/default/files/June%207%20Hearing_Panel%201_Jeffrey%20Ding_China%27s%20Current%20Capabilities%2C%20Policies%2C%20and%20Indu.

Engin, Z. and Treleaven, P., 2019. Algorithmic Government: Automating Public Services and Supporting Civil Servants in Using Data Science Technologies. *The Computer Journal*, 62(3), pp. 448–460, https://doi.org/10.1093/comjnl/bxy082.

Ernst, D., 2020. *Competing in Artificial Intelligence Chips: China's Challenge amid Technology War*. Waterloo: Centre for International Governance Innovation, https://www.cigionline.org/publications/competing-artificial-intelligence-chips-chinas-challenge-amid-technology-war.

Gal, D., 2020. China's Approach to AI Ethics. In: Elliot, H. ed., 2020. *The AI Powered State: China's Approach to Public Sector Innovation*. Nesta, May 2020, pp. 53–61, https://www.nesta.org.uk/feature/ai-powered-state/.

Haenlein, M. and Kaplan, A., 2019. A Brief History of Artificial Intelligence: On the Past, Present, and Future of Artificial Intelligence. *California Management Review*, 61(4), pp. 5–14, https://journals.sagepub.com/doi/10.1177/0008125619864925.

Han, E., 2020. From Traffic Management to Smart Courts: China's Approach to Smart Cities. In: Elliott, H. ed., 2020. *The AI Powered State: China's Approach to Public Sector Innovation*. Nesta, May 2020, pp. 35–41, https://www.nesta.org.uk/feature/ai-powered-state/.

Kostka, G., 2019. China's Social Credit Systems and Public Opinion: Explaining High Levels of Approval. *New Media & Society*, 21(7), pp. 1565–1593, https://doi.org/10.1177/1461444819826402.

Larsen, C., 2019. China's National AI Team. The role of National AI Open Innovation Platform. In: Webster, G. ed., 2019. *AI Policy and China: Realities of State-Led Development*. Stanford-New America DigiChina Project, 29 October, pp. 16–20, https://www.newamerica.org/cybersecurity-initiative/digichina/blog/special-report-ai-policy-and-china-realities-of-state-led-development/.

Lee, C., 2022. *Artificial Intelligence in China: Players, Regulations, Prospects*. Webinar for the EU Delegation to China, 25 March 2022.

Lee, K. and Sheehan, M., 2018. *China's Rise in Artificial Intelligence: Ingredients and Economic Implications. China in an Emerging World*, Hoover Institution, Fall Series, Issue 218, https://www.hoover.org/research/chinas-rise-artificial-intelligence-ingredients-and-economic-implications.

Lewis, D., 2019. China's Techno-Utilitarian Experiments with Artificial Intelligence. *Digital Asia Hub*, 16 March, https://www.digitalasiahub.org/2019/03/16/chinas-techno-utilitarian-experiments-with-artificial-intelligence/.

Makasi, T., Tate, M., Desouza, K. and Nili, A., 2021. Value-Based Guiding Principles for Managing Cognitive Computing Systems in the Public Sector. *Public Performance & Management Review*, 44(4), pp. 929–959, https://doi.org/10.1080/15309576.2021.1879883.

Marcus, G. and Davis, E., 2019. *Rebooting AI: Building Artificial Intelligence We Can Trust*. New York: Pantheon Books.

Mikalef, P. and Gupta, M., 2021. Artificial Intelligence Capability: Conceptualization, Measurement Calibration, and Empirical Study on Its Impact on Organizational Creativity and Firm Performance. *Information & Management*, 58(3), pp. 1–20, https://doi.org/10.1016/j.im.2021.103434.

Misuraca, G. and van Noordt, C., 2020. *Overview of the Use and Impact of AI in Public Services in the EU*. Luxembourg: Publications Office of the European Union, https://doi.org/10.2760/039619.

Oxford Insights and IDRC (International Research Development Centre), 2020. *Government AI Readiness Index 2020*. Oxford Insights and IDRC, on file with the author.

Roberts, H., Cowls, J., Morley, J., Taddeo, M., Wang, V. and Floridi, L., 2020. The Chinese Approach to Artificial Intelligence: An Analysis of Policy, Ethics, and Regulation. *AI & Society*, 36, pp. 59–77, https://doi.org/10.1007/s00146-020-00992-2.

SHFDI (Shanghai Foreign Investment Development Board), 2020. *Shanghai Foreign Investment Guide 2020* [2020上海外商投资指南], https://www.investsh.org.cn/upload/index/2020%20Shanghai%20Foreign%20Investment%20Guide.pdf.

SHFDI, 2021. *Shanghai Foreign Investment Guide 2021* [2021上海外商投资指南], https://www.investsh.org.cn/upload/upload/channel/file/2021_2/4_30/04koko3pi67s.pdf.

SJTU, CAICT and SHEITC (Shanghai Jiatong University AI Institute, China Academy of Information and Communications Technology Easter China Institute and Shanghai Economic and Information Development Research Center), ed. 2019. *AI@SH Action Report. Exploration and Practice of Building an Artificial Intelligence Development Highland in Shanghai* [AI@SH 行动报告 - 上海打造人工智能发展高地的探索与实践]. SJTU, CAICT and SHEITC [上海交通大学人工智能研究院, 中国信息通信研究院华东分院, 上海市经济和信息化发展研究中心], on file with the author.

Stanford University, 2016. *Artificial Intelligence and Life in 2030: One Hundred Year Study on Artificial Intelligence*. Stanford: Stanford University, https://ai100.stanford.edu/2016-report.

Stanford University, 2019. *The AI Index 2019 Annual Report*. AI Index Steering Committee, Human-Centered AI Institute, Stanford: Stanford University, December 2019, https://hai.stanford.edu/sites/default/files/ai_index_2019_report.pdf.

Stanford University, 2021. *The AI Index 2021 Annual Report*. AI Index Steering Committee, Human-Centered AI Institute, Stanford: Stanford University, March 2021, https://aiindex.stanford.edu/report/.

Stanford University, 2023. *The AI Index 2023 Annual Report*. AI Index Steering Committee, Institute for Human-Centered AI, Stanford: Stanford University, April 2023, https://aiindex.stanford.edu/wp-content/uploads/2023/04/HAI_AI-Index-Report_2023.pdf.

State Council, 2017. *New Generation Artificial Intelligence Development Plan* [新一代人工智能发展规划]. Guo Fa (2017) 35, 8 July, http://www.gov.cn/zhengce/content/2017-07/20/content_5211996.htm.

Tencent and CAICT (Tencent Research Institute, Tencent AI Lab and China Academy of Information and Communications Technology), 2017. *Artificial Intelligence: A National Strategic Initiative for Artificial Intelligence* [人工智能: 国家人工智能战略行动抓手]. Beijing: China Renmin University Press.

Tsinghua University, 2018. *China AI Development Report 2018*. Beijing: China Institute for Science and Technology Policy at Tsinghua University, on file with the author.

United Nations, 2020. E-*Government Survey 2020. Digital Government in the Decade of Action for Sustainable Development*. New York: United Nations, https://publicadministration.un.org/en/Research/UN-e-Government-Surveys.

Woo, J., 2021. *Capacity-Building and Pandemics. Singapore's Response to Covid-19*. Singapore: Palgrave Macmillan.

Zeng, J., 2021. China's Artificial Intelligence Innovation: A Top-Down National Command Approach? *Global Policy*, 12(3), pp. 399–409, https://doi.org/10.1111/1758-5899.12914.

CHAPTER 5

Public Sector AI Applications in Shanghai

The analysis of the AI policy environment and the AI ecosystem provides solid and detailed documentary evidence about the policy capacity of Shanghai to implement AI in the public sector. The findings show that Shanghai has the analytical capacity to devise public sector AI applications that can contribute to achieving municipal goals in this area, the political capacity to create and sustain political support for these AI applications, and the operational capacity to orchestrate the resources of the AI ecosystem in order to implement public sector AI applications in practice. Policy capacity is vital to achieve the desired policy outputs and outcomes, and capacity deficits are considered a major cause of policy failure and sub-optimal outcomes. Thus, assessing Shanghai's policy capacity to implement AI in the public sector is the first, necessary step to examine whether Shanghai is improving public service provision by means of AI, because without adequate policy capacity Shanghai would not be able to develop, access, and mobilize the skills and resources necessary to foster the use of AI in the public sector efficiently and effectively.

At the same time, understanding whether Shanghai is fulfilling its goal to improve public service provision by means of AI also requires the examination of how this capacity translates into real-world policy initiatives that deploy AI in the public sector, and their implications for the delivery of public services. To examine these aspects, this chapter starts

D. Todaro, *The Use of Artificial Intelligence in the Public Sector in Shanghai*, https://doi.org/10.1007/978-981-97-0597-9_5

by refining and validating the findings on Shanghai's policy capacity that were derived from the analysis of the AI policy environment and AI ecosystem. Based on the information gathered from interviews with key stakeholders of Shanghai's AI policy, it provides evidence that Shanghai has ample resources and capabilities in all the three dimensions of policy capacity, and it offers a more precise understanding of how such capacities contribute to fostering public sector AI applications. The interviews provide a direct account of what Shanghai is doing to stimulate public sector AI applications in practice, bringing into focus the key features of Shanghai's strategy for AI in the public sector (Sect. 5.1). To understand how policy capacity enables the implementation of this strategy, the analysis of the case studies delves into the main policy initiatives that are actively using AI in the public sector in Shanghai: the Government Online-Offline Shanghai (Sect. 5.2.1), the Single Platform for Urban Management (Sect. 5.2.2), and the AI pilot application scenarios (Sect. 5.3). By combining primary and secondary data obtained from key informant interviews and extensive documentary research, the analysis of the case studies examines the analytical, operational, and political capabilities that determine the strengths and limitations of these policy initiatives in deploying AI in the public sector, and their implications for public service provision. Examining policy capacity and how it is put to use to promote public sector AI applications is consistent with theoretical stances that postulate the need to think about policy capacity in terms of resources as well as outputs and outcomes (Woo, 2021; Painter and Pierre, 2005). This analytical approach offers deeper insights into whether Shanghai is fulfilling its goal to improve public service provision by accelerating the integration of AI in public sector activities.

The chapter brings the analytical focus closer to the activities of the actors and organizations that are directly involved in the implementation of public sector AI applications in Shanghai, making theoretical and practical contributions to public sector AI research and public policy research. To researchers on AI in the public sector, this chapter provides empirical evidence to test the hypotheses on the correlation between the availability of enabling factors that make AI applications possible and actual AI implementations in the public sector (Oxford Insights and IDRC, 2020), and to assess the impacts that challenges in the implementation phase can bear on the success of public sector AI applications (Molinari et al., 2021). To scholars of public policy, the chapter sheds light on how policy capacities at the organizational level can add or detract from the capacities at the municipal level, and on the implications that policy capacity can have on real-world policy initiatives and their outcomes. In addition, this analysis provides unprecedented insights into how Shanghai is leveraging AI to improve the provision of public services. These insights are useful because the municipality has made rapid progress in public sector AI innovation, and there are practical lessons that can be drawn from the experience of Shanghai, as discussed in the conclusions of the book. In this perspective, the analysis of the case studies in Shanghai provides valuable inputs for researchers and practitioners beyond the scope of this work.

5.1 Capacity in Action: The Strategy of Shanghai for AI in the Public Sector

This section provides evidence that Shanghai has plenty of analytical, political, and operational skills and resources needed to use AI in the public sector. Based on in-depth interviews with key stakeholders of Shanghai's AI policy, it also zeroes in on how these skills and resources are mobilized to foster the use of AI in this area in practice. The focus on the actual impacts of policy capacity on public sector AI applications is motivated by two reasons. First, the need to *refine, validate, and expand the findings on Shanghai's policy capacity that were derived from documentary research*. The discussions in Chapter 2.4 highlighted that the sociotechnical complexities of AI in the public sector could affect the ability of public organizations to use AI in their work. Hence, it is instructive to integrate documentary research with direct accounts of how Shanghai's policy capacity is affecting the use of AI in the public sector in practice, in order to verify if the available policy skills and resources are actually contributing to promoting the use of AI in this area. This approach that focuses on outputs and outcomes will continue with the analysis of the case studies, as just explained.

Second, the focus on how policy skills and resources are mobilized to foster public sector AI applications in practice is also motivated by the need to *outline with greater precision the strategy of Shanghai for promoting the use of AI in the public sector*, as a basis for a comprehensive analysis of the case studies. By looking at how Shanghai is mobilizing its analytical, political, and operational capabilities to promote the deployment of AI in the public sector, the interviews lift important aspects about the coordinated, systemic, and proactive efforts undertaken by Shanghai to foster AI integration in public sector activities. Such efforts are consistent with the policy goals set by the municipal AI plans, which call for improving public service capacity and citizens' sense of gain by accelerating the use of AI in urban governance and public services. Understanding this strategy is a useful starting point to examine how public sector AI initiatives are unfolding in Shanghai, and it creates a sound basis to assess their similarities, differences, and complementarities.

Primary data on the policy capacity of Shanghai to implement AI in the public sector were mostly gathered from *semi-structured interviews*[1] Respondents were asked open-ended questions about the availability in Shanghai of the analytical, political, and operational resources and skills necessary to implement AI in the public sector. These questions were constructed upon the findings of previous research that identified a set of skills and capabilities considered important for using AI in public sector activities, and reflect the three dimensions of policy capacity. The majority of primary data on the policy capacities of Shanghai and their contribution to fostering public sector AI applications is obtained from these questions. At the same time, insights also emerged in the flow of the conversation or were derived from answers to other topics (the interviews also included a set of questions that explore strengths and limitations of the case studies in deploying AI in the public sector,[2] which are discussed in Sects. 5.2 and 5.3). The contents related to Shanghai's policy capacity and its impacts on public sector AI applications are presented in the following paragraphs, despite the questions that originated them (Table 5.1).

[1] Semi-structured interviews are based on a list of questions on specific topics, usually in the form of an interview guide (sample questions in Appendix V). At the same time, questions may be asked in a different order than the schedule of the interview guide. Moreover, the interviewer can add questions that were not originally included in the guide in response to what are considered significant replies by the interviewees. Despite this flexibility, all the questions in the interview guide were usually asked, using a similar wording across different interviewees so that their answers could be compared, and the contents coded into categories (Bryman, 2012, pp. 212, 471).

[2] The Government Online-Offline Shanghai and the Single Platform for Urban Management were selected as case studies when the interview program was already at an advanced stage, after their importance as conduits to the use of AI in the public sector had repeatedly emerged from the interviews. Hence, they were explicitly included only in the semi-structured interview with Shanghai INESA in May 2022. Primary data on the strengths and limitations of the Government Online-Offline Shanghai and the Single Platform for Urban Management in deploying AI in the public sector primarily come from unstructured interviews (see next paragraph).

Table 5.1 Interview questions on policy capacity

Capacity	*Skills and capabilities*	*Questions*
Analytical	Policymakers have a sound understanding of the technical underpinnings of AI and its expected impacts on social domains (Mishra et al., 2020; Scantamburlo et al., 2018; Mehr, 2017)	AI is a very complex field and decision-makers are not technical experts. What can be done to improve the communications between AI experts and government agencies[3]?
Political	There is sustained political support for AI in the public sector, resulting in an enabling environment for AI innovation (Desouza, 2021; Campion et al., 2020; Berryhill et al., 2019)	In recent years, Shanghai has issued various policies for AI development. How are these initiatives supporting the development of AI in Shanghai?[4]
Operational	Public organizations have the technical and non-technical resources to implement public sector AI applications in practice (Molinari et al., 2021; Misuraca et al., 2020)	What are the strengths and weaknesses of the Shanghai AI ecosystem? What should be done to realize the safe and beneficial deployment of AI[5]?

The semi-structured interviews were carried out with persons who are directly involved in, or have first-hand knowledge of, the municipal AI policy and public sector AI applications in Shanghai, including the case studies of this book. The semi-structured interviews took place between August 2020 and September 2021 in Shanghai,[6] they were mostly conducted in person, and primarily in Mandarin. The interviewees included: four public managers involved in the AI pilot application scenarios; a director of the Shanghai Data Exchange Center, the most important public–private data exchange platform in Shanghai

[3] In Chinese: "人工智能是一个技术含量很高的行业。同时，政府机构的领导不一定是内行。为了便于政府机构跟人工智能企业和其他AI专家有效、清晰地双方沟通，您认为要注意哪些方面?"

[4] In Chinese: "近几年，上海发布了促进AI发展的若干规划和行动计划。这些支持措施主要是在哪些方面有利于上海人工智能行业的发展?"

[5] In Chinese: "您认为上海AI生态圈有哪些强点?为了实现人工智能应用的安全、有益的部署，您认为要注意哪些方面?" The latter question was added to ensure that respondents also considered non-technical aspects.

[6] The only exception is the second interview with Shanghai INESA (Table 5.2, informant code 3INESA), which was carried out in May 2022.

(Chapter 4.1); the project coordinator of the Shanghai Artificial Intelligent Industry Association, a government-led platform that brings together the main industrial actors of Shanghai's AI policy and is actively involved in promoting public sector AI applications (Chapter 2.2.3); eight managers of AI companies that cooperate in the implementation of public sector AI projects in Shanghai, including the case studies of this book; the director of an AI accelerator partly owned by the Shanghai government (AI Space), and senior consultant of the municipal government on AI policy; a foreign professor member of the Shanghai Municipal Artificial Intelligence Strategy Advisory Expert Committee (上海市人工智能战略咨询专家委员会; Chapter 3.2), who also teaches artificial intelligence at Tongji University; a foreign professor based in Australia, who worked at the China Institute for Urban Governance at Shanghai Jiaotong University, and previously advised the Shanghai municipal government on technology policy; the head of the China research teams of McKinsey Global Institute in Shanghai; and a professor of Fudan University who is regarded as a principal expert on the philosophy of AI in China.

With 19 semi-structured interviews, this empirical investigation is on a par with other qualitative research that has dealt with the topic of adoption and use of AI in the public sector (Schaefer et al., 2021; Mikalef et al., 2019; Chen et al., 2019; Sun and Medaglia, 2019). It should also be noted that, following the semi-structured interviews, the author established an open and regular dialogue with some of the interviewees, namely: the Shanghai Data Exchange Center, AI Space, iFlytek, Shanghai INESA, and Shanghai Zhuofan. This dialogue was the basis for a set of *unstructured interviews*[7] that integrated the information on Shanghai's AI policy capacity derived from the semi-structured interviews, and their relevant contents are also presented in the following Sects. 5.1.1–5.1.3. On the other hand, the contents of unstructured interviews related to the strengths and limitations of the case studies in deploying AI in the public sector are discussed in Sects. 5.2 and 5.3. Table 5.2 provides an overview

[7] Unstructured interviews typically include only a brief list of topics or issues to be covered. The interviewee responds freely, while the interviewer follows up on contents of interests for the research. The interviewing is usually informal and often assumes a conversational style. The phrasing and sequencing of the interviewee questions varies from interview to interview, depending on the topic(s) to be covered (Bryman, 2012, pp. 213, 471).

of the interview data sources. In the remainder of the chapter, information gathered from unstructured interviews is marked by the letter "i" near the informant code (e.g., IFLYi).

5.1.1 *Analytical Capacity in Action*

Interviewees have different opinions on whether the AI policy agencies of Shanghai have adequate **knowledge resources** to devise AI applications that can improve public service provision. Some believe that these agencies are technically savvy. LING states that Shanghai decision-makers have a good understanding of autonomous vehicles and related issues, since some officials have a technical background and/or industrial experience. Similarly, ZJAI argues that many government agencies are staffed with technical experts, who are often drawn from State-owned enterprises. In addition, ZJAI observes that a number of government agencies have already introduced specialized departments dedicated to AI, mentioning SHEITC's AI Development Office (Chapter 3.2). Other interviewees disagree on the level of knowledge resources in Shanghai's AI policy agencies. Based on her experience in a big State-owned enterprise, CHUN bluntly states that "the government doesn't understand technology" (政府不懂技术). AISP confirms that the number of people in government agencies with the technical skills to understand AI is still limited. POAI notes that AI experts in government agencies often are not very useful, because they generally come from the academia and lack practical experience, or are retired officials who don't know state-of-the-art AI technologies. TUSI confirms that there is a disconnect between AI practitioners and the government in terms of understanding the features of contemporary AI technologies, noting that non-experts tend to attribute to AI far greater capabilities than those actually available. Similarly, talking about his company's experience in providing AI solutions for the judiciary (Chapters 4.4 and 5.3), IFLYi notes that government agencies often overestimate the capabilities of AI technologies. Finally, SDEC says that the leaders of municipal organizations that focus on sectors requiring specific technical knowledge are sometimes picked from the private sector (the interviewee himself has worked in a multinational IT company). But the staff of these organizations consists mostly of career civil servants, who do not have a technical background.

While Shanghai's AI policy agencies may lack in-house knowledge resources, they have established **channels of communications** with AI

Table 5.2 Overview of interview data sources (structured interviews: SI; unstructured interviews: UI)

Organization	*Position*	*Informant code*	*Date(s)*	*Length (min.)*	*No. of interviews*
Shanghai Jing'an Data Center	Vice Director	JADC	26 August 2020	50	1 SI
Shanghai Lingang Intelligent Connected Vehicles Comprehensive Demonstration Zone	Senior Supervisor of the Intelligent Connected Vehicle Innovation Center	LING	10 September 2020	45	1 SI
Shanghai Museum	Vice Director of the Information Center	SHMU	12 January 2021	60	1 SI
Zhangjiang AI Island	Project Manager	ZJAI	26 January 2021	50	1 SI
Shanghai Data Exchange Center	Director	SDEC	30 June 2020	65	1 SI
				–	Multiple UI
Shanghai Artificial Intelligent Industry Association	Head of Operations	SAIA	3 February 2021 21 April 2021	30 40	2 SI
iFlytek	Vice General Manager	IFLY	13 October 2020	40	1 SI
				–	Multiple UI
TuSimple	General Manager, CEO Executive Assistant	TUSI	4 February 2021	50	1 SI
Pony.AI	Public Relations Director	POAI	15 January 2021	35	1 SI
China Unicom	General Manager 5G+ AI center	CHUN	3 August 2021	60	1 SI
Shanghai Zhuofan	Head of R&D Center	SHZF	2 August 2021	40	1 SI
				–	Multiple UI
Shanghai INESA	Deputy General Manager CEO Assistant	1INESA 2INESA	1 September 2021	65	1 SI, multiple UI with 2INESA

(continued)

Table 5.2 (continued)

Organization	*Position*	*Informant code*	*Date(s)*	*Length (min.)*	*No. of interviews*
	Project Director	3INESA	28 May 2022	90	1 SI and multiple UI
AI Space	Director	AISP	16 November 2020	80	1 SI
				–	Multiple UI
Shanghai Municipal Artificial Intelligence Strategy Advisory Expert Committee	Member, AI expert	AIEXC	15 December 2020	50	1 SI
China Institute for Urban Governance at Shanghai Jiaotong University	Distinguished Research Fellow	SJTU	25 May 2021	35	1 SI
McKinsey Global Institute in Shanghai	Head of Research China	MGI	14 December 2020	30	1 SI
Fudan University, Faculty of Philosophy	Expert of philosophy of AI	FUDN	5 December 2020	50	1 SI

companies and AI experts through which Shanghai policymakers can gain access to specialized knowledge in AI. The interviewees say that AI policy agencies often reach out to companies to access their expertise. TUSI—whose company is the main technical partner of an AI pilot application scenario in autonomous driving—states that TuSimple is regularly communicating with various agencies of the Shanghai government, which consult them in relation to issues about AI-enabled transportation and the design of specific public sector AI projects. POAI also says that Chinese authorities are quite willing to listen to the opinions and suggestions of AI companies, and corporate expertise in the field is taken into account. 1INESA observes that the municipal government often communicates with companies to translate AI and technology policies into feasible and viable solutions. In addition to the bilateral communications with companies, AISP observes that government-endorsed associations like the Shanghai Artificial Intelligent Industry Association

(SAIA), and expert committees like the Shanghai Artificial Intelligence Strategic Advisory Expert Committee, work as a bridge between AI experts and the government. He also confirms that government officials often consider the advice of experts when drafting AI policy initiatives. This was corroborated by SAIA, who explained that the Strategic Advisory Expert Committee reports directly to the municipal leadership, and focuses on broad strategic issues related to AI development in Shanghai; while SAIA usually communicates with the Shanghai Municipal Commission of Economy and Informatization (SHEITC), and it is more focused on the operational aspects of AI development. Despite these channels of communications, AIEX—a member of the Strategic Advisory Expert Committee—doubts that the municipal leadership has a clear understanding of the public sector AI applications currently ongoing in Shanghai.

Importantly, despite their diverging opinions on the technological proficiency of Shanghai's AI policymakers, the interviewees emphasize that Shanghai has **the ability to devise public sector AI applications that can improve the provision of public services**. AISP observes that the Shanghai government is spearheading the use of AI in public services by becoming the main promoter of AI solutions. It does so in two ways, both of which leverage existing digital government platforms. First, Shanghai is actively integrating AI technologies in the provision of administrative services through the municipal platform Government Online-Offline Shanghai. Second, it is leveraging open government data, and the sharing of public and private data to develop novel AI applications in healthcare, medicine, and other applications like finance. As an example, he mentions the Shanghai Shenkang Hospital Development Center[8] and the Shanghai Data Exchange Center. Other interviewees confirm that digital platforms are a key component of Shanghai's strategy to accelerate the integration of AI in public services. 1INESA is Deputy General Manager of the government-owned municipal enterprise that acts as general contractor of the Government Online-Offline Shanghai

[8] The Shanghai Hospital Development Center (SHDC, 上海申康医院中心) was established in September 2005 and manages the budget, staffing, and health-record sharing of 37 of Shanghai's municipal hospitals. Website: https://www.shdc.org.cn/. Data sharing initiatives in the medical sector have also been promoted at the national level (e.g., in September 2020 China has started to compile its first national radiological image database, https://www.yicaiglobal.com/news/china-starts-national-medical-image-database-to-promote-smart-healthcare).

and the Single Platform for Urban Management. He says that Shanghai is following an approach known as “double middle platform” (双中台) popularized by Baidu and Alibaba, which uses a single digital platform to enable several AI applications. These observations are further corroborated by a director of the Shanghai Data Exchange Center (SDEC), who confirms that Shanghai is promoting the use of government data to develop AI applications in transport, urban governance, and other areas such as finance and commerce. CHUN also observes that in recent years the Shanghai government invested significant resources to build platforms and other infrastructure to support the widespread implementation of AI applications in the public sector, in order to improve its governance capabilities.

In addition to digital platforms, interviewees identify other methods used by the Shanghai government to leverage AI applications to improve the provision of public services. One method is the use of government-supervised industry associations to advance the use of AI in the priority areas identified by the municipality. In this regard, SAIA says that the association has been tasked by SHEITC to promote AI applications in urban governance, healthcare, transportation, and smart residential communities (智慧社区), all areas prioritized by the municipal AI plans. Another method is the upgrading of existing equipment. SHZF—a leading provider of AI solutions for public sector applications in Shanghai and nationally (including the case studies examined shortly)—says that Shanghai is actively promoting the integration of AI in administrative services to improve the quality, efficiency, and precision of public service provision. He argues that AI is attractive to the Shanghai government because it allows to improve public service provision, while also containing the number of government staff (控制公务人员编制). IFLY—which is a leading supplier of NLP and speech recognition solutions for education and other applications—says that many public schools in Shanghai have received active support from the municipal government to adopt AI, especially to improve teaching efficiency and reduce the workload of teachers. A third method is the use of State-owned enterprises as conduits to develop public sector AI applications. Apart from its role in developing the Government Online-Offline Shanghai platform and the Single Platform for Urban Management, 1INESA says that the municipal government assigned (定为) his company to develop Shanghai’s smart city, with a particular focus on public security and government services, and some projects in education and medicine. SDEC also observes that

Shanghai is leveraging government-owned companies, sometimes created ad-hoc (like the Shanghai Data Exchange Center), to promote the use of Big Data and artificial intelligence in the public sector.

Finally, the interviews provided additional insights on the priority areas for AI in the public sector in Shanghai. The municipal AI plans have a consistent focus on city operations (security, environment, basic infrastructures), public services (administrative services, judiciary, education, culture), transportation (urban traffic, maritime logistics), and public health (treatment assistance, elderly care, health prevention, and control). This focus was confirmed during the interviews and is corroborated by the analysis of the case studies. At the same time, 1INESA observes that while the Shanghai government is very active on the demand side (需求方), it is still **evaluating which AI applications could be more valuable** for the municipality. AISP also argues that "the Shanghai government really believes that AI technologies can make a contribution to improving the quality and efficiency of public services", but not all applications are deemed equally valuable. He states that AI in healthcare is the main priority pursued by the municipal government in the public sector, while AI in education is considered less important. AIEX makes a similar point, observing that the Shanghai government doesn't want to "put all the eggs in one basket", and is still exploring suitable AI applications in the public sector. This selective approach is also emphasized by MGI, who argues that the experimental approach of the AI pilot application scenarios is also due to the fact that there are not best practices in the implementation of AI in public services yet. Understanding this selective approach is important for two reasons. First, it provides further evidence of the analytical capacity of Shanghai, which is discerning—or at least trying to do so—which AI applications are most suitable to achieve the goals it set for AI in the public sector. Second, it explains that not all current implementations are necessarily the final word of public sector AI applications in Shanghai, as the municipality is pursuing experimental tactics as part of its diversified approach to the use of AI in the public sector (Sect. 5.3).

5.1.2 Political Capacity in Action

Shanghai has the political capacity to create and sustain support and legitimacy for public sector AI applications that can contribute to achieving municipal goals in this area. This ability is demonstrated by the concoction of an **enabling environment for public sector AI applications**

in the areas prioritized by the municipal government. This enabling environment encourages private actors and public institutions to experiment with AI within the boundaries set by the Shanghai government. Regarding private actors, TUSI states that Shanghai is providing significant policy support to the companies operating in autonomous driving, smart infrastructure, and other priority areas identified by the government. He mentions the availability of licenses to test driverless trucks on public roads and other forms of government support. Similarly, POAI argues that Shanghai has the most supportive policies for autonomous driving in China. This policy support is important, he argues, also because it signals the political determination of Shanghai to promote the development of smart transportation and related public infrastructure. Regarding public institutions, AISP observes that the Shanghai government provides policy support and political incentives to motivate district governments and public agencies to advance AI and other digital technologies in line with municipal priorities. 1INESA highlights the importance of the guiding role of the municipal government in smart city and urban digitalization. He says that Shanghai authorities provide a general framework that draws the boundaries within which public and private actors are actively encouraged to deploy AI and ICT technology. SHMU—the main history museum of Shanghai—argues that the efficient bureaucratic process to select the AI pilot application scenarios and fast-track other public sector AI applications is an important form of political support that facilitates the uptake of AI by public organizations. Easier paperwork is accompanied by financial and non-financial incentives for public organizations that make use of AI, thus encouraging the adoption of AI in the public sector. AISP says that another important manifestation of this enabling environment is a deregulated approach that leaves public organizations greater room to maneuver. He argues that this "experiment first and regulate later" approach is a crucial factor spurring AI adoption in Shanghai because it leaves space for growth, it allows public and private actors wider access to data, and thus creates opportunities for AI applications.

Another indicator of political capacity highlighted by the interviewees is the strong **political support for AI development coming from the top leadership of Shanghai**. SAIA argues that the vigorous support of the municipal leadership for the use of AI is the main competitive advantage of Shanghai in AI development. Starting from the top leaders—the interviewee mentions Party Secretary Li Qiang[9] and Mayor Gong Zheng—Shanghai is very open and supportive for AI development in the private and public sectors. AISP also states that support for AI development comes from the top leadership. He notes that Party Secretary Li Qiang was working in Hangzhou as Governor of the Zhejiang Province between 2012 and 2016, at a time when the cooperation between the city government and Alibaba resulted in the successful deployment of the City Brain (Chapter 2.2.2), one of the most famous early cases of public sector AI applications in China. Hence, AISP believes that a key factor affecting future developments of public sector AI applications in Shanghai is the political value that the Party will attach to the AI technology, saying that AI adoption will be fast if there are successful applications endorsed by the municipal leadership. SJTU observes that the Shanghai government is at the same time innovator, implementor, and evaluator of AI technologies, which obviously helps to create legitimacy and support for AI in the public sector. SHZF notes the practical implications of this political support. He underscores that government agencies at every level have been mobilized to share data on municipal platforms, and this is translating into a coordinated approach to the use of AI in government services. ZJAI argues that the support of the Shanghai leadership echoes the attention to AI development of the national government. He recalls a visit by Premier Li Keqiang to the Zhangjiang AI Island in summer 2019, during which Premier Li called for accelerating the expansion of the zone,[10] an advice that was promptly taken by the municipal government (see Appendix VI). AIEX argues that the support from the municipal leadership is particularly impactful considering that in Shanghai, like other municipalities and first-tier cities, mayors and Party leaders are very powerful. This allows them to quickly mobilize and distribute resources for AI development.

Although Shanghai has the political capacity to create support and legitimacy for public sector AI applications, this political endorsement is

[9] Li Qiang (李强) was the Party Secretary of Shanghai from 2017 to October 2022, when he was appointed to the Standing Committee of the CPC Politburo as its second highest-ranking member, and was nominated Premier in March 2023.

[10] Mu, X., 2019. Premier Li Stresses Greater Reform, Opening-Up. *Xinhua News Agency*, 24 July, http://www.xinhuanet.com/english/2019-07/24/c_138251823.htm.

not monolithic. LING observes that the Shanghai government encompasses various interest groups. Based on his experience at the Intelligent Connected Vehicle Innovation Center, he notes that some government agencies like SHEITC push for a faster deployment of AI in autonomous driving, while others like the Public Transportation Commission and the Public Security Bureau have a more cautious approach. AISPi also notes the existence of competing interest groups at the municipal level. He mentions that SHEITC—which traditionally promotes the integration of informatization and industrialization in Shanghai—is mostly interested in promoting AI applications, in the public and private sector alike. On the other hand, the Science and Technology Commission of Shanghai, another important actor of Shanghai's AI policy, is primarily focusing on scientific AI research, including the impact of AI technology on economy and society. He notes that at present the focus of the Shanghai leadership is clearly set on AI applications, and SHEITC has been tasked to actively promote AI implementations both in the public sector (i.e., the AI pilot application scenarios) and the industry.[11]

Finally, it was argued that assessments of the political capacity of Shanghai may be overinflated by incentives for local actors to show compliance to municipal AI plans (Chapter 2.4). This hypothesis is based on the analysis of the incentive structure institutionalized in China's bureaucratic system, and it was confirmed during the selection of the case studies drawn from the AI pilot application scenarios, which showed that some of the pilot projects (or applications within the projects) make

[11] A main initiative supervised by SHEITC to promote the local AI industry is the "AI major industrial projects" (人工智能重大产业项目). It consists of attracting investments by private companies across different districts of the municipality by offering them incentives to locate in Shanghai (subsidies, tax breaks, residence permit facilitations for the personnel, etc.). These projects are used to "guide" investments in sectors prioritized by the government, including in areas that could result in public sector applications (typically, smart transportation and healthcare). However, their primary objective is recruiting AI companies. In 2020, 36 projects were signed for a total value of 30 billion RMB. In 2021, 26 projects were signed for a total value of more than 10 billion RMB. See: Tencent Net, 2020. Total Investments for More Than 30 Billion RMB! 36 AI Major Industrial Projects Are Signed and Land in Shanghai [总投资超 300 亿元! 36 个人工智能重大项目签约落沪]. Tencent Net [腾讯网], 12 July, https://new.qq.com/omn/20200712/20200712A036G300.html; Wu, Q. and Sun, H., 2021. The 2021 World AI Conference Comes to an End: 26 AI Major Industrial Projects Are Signed, Total Investment Exceeds 10 Billion RMB [2021世界人工智能大会闭幕: 26个重大项目签约 总投资金额超百亿]. *Guangchazhe* [观察者], 11 July, https://www.guancha.cn/politics/2021_07_11_597931.shtml.

only superficial uses of AI (Sect. 5.3, list of exclusions). This topic could seldom be raised explicitly during the interviews due to the fact that most respondents are directly involved in the AI pilots and other public sector AI applications, and asking this question would have sounded confrontational; hence the findings are sparse. Nonetheless, there were some valuable insights from two interviewees who have direct access to Shanghai policymakers. AISP states that some AI pilot application scenarios were included in the list because "somebody thinks they are fancy". He specifically mentions education as a policy area where there won't be any real integration of AI in the foreseeable future, especially because there were lots of complaints about the use of some AI technologies in classes.[12] AIEX also says that some AI pilot application scenarios are "window dressing". But he also argues that this does not change the fact that the Shanghai government is genuinely interested in using AI to improve the life of citizens, for instance in areas like transportation and urban governance.

5.1.3 Operational Capacity in Action

To gain further insights into the operational capacity of Shanghai to implement public sector AI applications in practice and identify issues that could affect this capacity, the interviews inquired about the strengths and weaknesses of the Shanghai AI ecosystem. To ensure that non-technical aspects were considered, interviewees were also asked what should be done to realize the safe and beneficial deployment of artificial intelligence. The answers primarily highlight the strengths of the Shanghai AI ecosystem, confirming the findings of documentary research (Chapter 4). At the same time, they provide a more granular view of Shanghai's AI ecosystem, and identify some potential issues in using data and maintaining social acceptance.

Managerial Capabilities: interviewees say that managerial capabilities are a key strength of the Shanghai ecosystem. By making a comparison with Beijing and Shenzhen, two other major Chinese AI hubs, 1INESA says that the main comparative advantage of Shanghai is that the

[12] See, for instance, Xie, E., 2019. Artificial Intelligence Is Watching China's Students But How Well Can It Really See? *South China Morning Post*, 16 September, https://www.scmp.com/news/china/politics/article/3027349/artificial-intelligence-watching-chinas-students-how-well-can.

municipality is very "well managed". He says that efficient governance is facilitating the deployment of public sector AI applications because Shanghai is able to promote a coordinated approach to AI development. Similarly, POAI observes that Shanghai has "the mentality to provide services to companies", and this is smoothing the involvement of AI firms in the implementation of AI in the public sector.

Data: data is widely regarded as a major strength of Shanghai's AI ecosystem. JADC, the Vice Director of the government data center in Jing'an district, states her awareness that the data center has access to much more data than it would be possible in other countries. LING also confirms that his organization has access to great quantities of good-quality government and private data, which can be used to design and develop smart infrastructure in the municipality. AISP and IFYTi also agree that access to big volumes of data is a key strength of Shanghai's AI ecosystem. At the same time, SDECi and SHZF note that some public agencies are still not willing to share their data. 2INESAi argues that one reason is the lack of precise standards on data sharing.

Potential issues in the data dimension are related to **privacy and security**. JDAC highlights the complexity faced by the Jing'an Data Center in using data while at the same time ensuring privacy and security. She argues that it is challenging to find the right balance between the dual role of the government as regulator and user of data. SHMU, Vice Director of the Shanghai Museum Information Center, says that data privacy is a crucial issue, and his department is required to ensure the security of personal data collected from the visitors of the museum. AISP observes that Shanghai is trying to balance data privacy and use, observing that this problem is particularly sensitive in healthcare and finance, two priority areas where Shanghai is promoting AI applications. He argues that part of the solution depends on privacy policies and regulations, but technology should also play a part. Having extensive experience in government data sharing, SDECi argues that the attention of public organizations to data privacy and security improved a lot following the introduction of the *Personal Information Protection Law* in 2021 and the *Shanghai Data Regulations* in 2022 (Chapter 4.1). SHZF agrees that the Shanghai government is committed to do things according to the law (依法办事), and public organizations are very attentive to issues of data privacy and security when purchasing AI systems for administrative services. 1INESA also highlights the importance of ensuring data privacy in their work. AIEX confirms that in government circles there is great awareness of the data privacy and security issues related to AI, although these concerns do not influence AI applications in government agencies.

AI Companies: AI companies are a key resource of the Shanghai AI ecosystem. SAIA states that the Alliance has more than 300 members covering the whole value chain of AI, from semiconductors, hardware, cloud services, R&D, to technologies and applications in almost every area where is currently possible to deploy AI. ZJAI says that a key feature of the Zhangjiang AI Island is the high density and diversity of AI and hi-tech companies located in the park, which reflects the high density and diversity of AI companies in Shanghai. AISP notes that Shanghai has a rich commercial AI ecosystem, and the municipality is using financial and other incentives to attract the biggest domestic AI companies (e.g., SenseTime, Tencent), which in turn are expected to lure smaller but promising startups to move to Shanghai. As expected, nearly all technology companies (IFLY, SHZF, TUSI, POAI, INESA) highlight the strength of Shanghai's commercial ecosystem.

The interviews provide deeper insights into Shanghai's **ability to engage companies in public sector AI applications**. 2INESAi observes that Shanghai is successfully engaging AI companies, which actively compete to be selected for public projects. He argues that leveraging public sector AI projects is perceived by the government as a win–win solution to promote at the same time the development of the AI industry and public sector applications. SHZFi confirms that there is fierce competition between companies to be selected for public sector projects that make use of AI technologies, like the Government Online-Offline Shanghai. On a similar note, IFLYi argues that "Shanghai is developing the AI industry in a smart way". He says that municipality is actively leveraging public projects to attract AI leading companies from China and abroad, de facto requiring that companies participating in government-led projects are registered in Shanghai. AISP notes that Shanghai planned to develop 100 government-sponsored AI projects between 2019 and 2021. This would create market opportunities attractive to AI companies, while also steering them toward developing public sector AI applications. He notes that many applications include the use of AI in healthcare (he mentions the chatbots used by public hospitals, Sect. 5.3). MGI also says that initiatives like the AI pilot application scenarios can be an effective way to jumpstart AI applications in the public sector and promote industrial development: by becoming a customer of AI technologies, the government integrates AI in its activities and also contributes to create market for AI solutions. Interviewees argue that this dual strategy is helping the government to foster public sector AI applications and the AI industry, but has mixed impacts on companies. AISP states that Shanghai still doesn't offer a friendly environment for small-medium enterprises, because the monopolies held by government-owned enterprises in public services (e.g., transportation) represent a barrier to entry. 1INESA, whose company is a big State-owned enterprise (SOE), confirms that in public sector projects Shanghai prefers to cooperate with large firms because they are supposed to be more stable and trustworthy. 1INESA also notes that, other things being equal, the Shanghai government prefers to cooperate with SOEs because it has more control over them. IFLYi—whose company is a "national AI champion" (Chapter 2.2.3)—argues that their status as both a large and government-endorsed company allows them easier access to public projects at the national and local levels.

Human Capital: both public and private interviewees confirm that they can easily access qualified human resources with adequate AI skills (more details on this point are discussed in the case studies in Sect. 5.3). The interviewees observe that companies and research institutes cooperate in nurturing human capital under the guidance of the Shanghai government, consistently with the national indications to promote collaborations between government, enterprises, universities, research institutes, and end users in AI development. Like its national counterpart, SAIA states that the association is tasked to cooperate with local universities (e.g., Tongji University and Shanghai Jiaotong University) and research centers to facilitate internships, joint laboratories, and other forms of cooperation between academia and industry. This brings universities closer to the needs of the companies, while also transferring the expertise of companies to universities. ZJAI confirms that Zhangjiang Science City (owned and operated by the Shanghai government) is encouraging companies to closely cooperate with universities and research centers. He highlights the presence in the Zhangjiang AI Island of the Microsoft AI & IoT Insider Lab[13] and the Shanghai Research Institute for Intelligent Autonomous

[13] Established in partnership with the Zhangjiang Group, the AI & IoT Insider Lab in Shanghai is one of Microsoft's global R&D centers aiming to boost the innovation

Systems (上海自主智能无人系统科学中心) of Tongji University. AISP highlights that the Shanghai World AI Conference and the Pujiang Innovation Forum are two main channels through which Shanghai is promoting cooperation between private companies and research institutions to develop AI talents. This cooperation between government, companies, and research institutes is important for two reasons. First, it indicates that the ability of the Shanghai government to mobilize AI companies is not limited to projects where corporate participation is motivated by private interests, but extends to other government priority areas. Second, it suggests that Shanghai is actively connecting the public sector, leading tech companies, research institutes and networks of SMEs to drive technological advances and AI implementations. These "hybridized industrial ecosystems" (Ding, 2020) are important for public sector AI applications. As shown by the experience of other cities, like the Hangzhou AI Town (杭州人工智能小镇) and the China Speech Valley (中国声谷) in Hefei, these hybridized ecosystems often result in successful forms of public–private cooperation in AI.[14] Further indications that Shanghai is pursuing the creation of hybridized industrial ecosystems are offered by the "4+X" carrier spaces and the municipal AI pilot zones, which facilitate mutual exchanges among government, industry, and research institutions. By de facto institutionalizing the cooperation between public and private actors in AI, this approach could further strengthen the systematic involvement of private companies in public sector AI projects in Shanghai.

and industrialization of AI and IoT solutions and applications. It is the first of its kind in the Asia-Pacific region and the largest such lab/accelerator run by Microsoft Corporation in the world. Since the summer of 2018, Mr. Tan estimates that a total of nearly 300 enterprises have been approved as resident members of the Shanghai Microsoft AI & IoT Insider Lab, accelerating their AI products and solutions application thanks to the lab's full-range services from hardware and software support to cloud services and ecosystem support. The lab plans to drive the transformation and upgrading of traditional industries through its advanced AI technology and deep integration with the innovation and industry resources of Zhangjiang Science City.

[14] Alibaba City Brain in Hangzhou, or the first experiments of the later ubiquitous healthcare QR code that originated in that city, offer an example of a private company leveraging government data to develop AI applications. In describing the case of Hefei, where his company is the main pillar of the China Speech Valley together with the University of Science and Technology of China, IFLYi confirms that the local government is actively engaging private companies as part of the strategy to develop the local hybridized ecosystem.

Infrastructure: in terms of technological infrastructure, the importance of digital platforms in public sector AI applications was discussed in Sect. 5.1.1, and is thoroughly examined in the analysis of the case studies. In addition, LING and POAI note that the extensive 5G network of Shanghai is a main enabler for autonomous driving and smart connected vehicles. ZJAI also notes that 5G and Internet of Things are key resources for the various applications developed in the Zhangjiang AI Island park. As for physical infrastructure, its importance was emphasized by companies that develop autonomous vehicles. Both TUSI and POAI—whose companies are based in the two municipal experimental zones for autonomous driving in Jiading and Lingang (Chapter 4.2)—note that the possibility of testing autonomous vehicles on enclosed areas and public roads is a key strength of Shanghai's AI ecosystem. ZJAI also observes that the Zhangjiang AI Island creates a safe environment to test AI applications in various applications, from environmental management to public security and infrastructure maintenance (smart buildings, automatic street cleaning).

Social acceptance: AISP notes that generally speaking there is a high degree of acceptance of AI solutions by the Chinese society. Despite an increased debate on privacy issues related to the use of AI systems, citizens in Shanghai and other big cities have quickly adopted AI technologies such as facial recognition to make payment and access public service platforms, among others. FUDN also argues that there is lower resistance to AI adoption in China compared to other countries. SHMU says that the visitors of the Museum showed a high degree of acceptance to AI technologies, as they enrich their visiting experience. SHZF notes that AI applications in administrative services are improving the quality efficiency of public service delivery, so he does not foresee any issues related to social acceptance.

At the same time, SAIA notes that the current levels of social acceptance of AI solutions should not be taken for granted. The AI pilot application scenarios mostly involve small-scale applications actively endorsed by the government and public institutions. It remains to be seen what the real uptake of AI by society will be when these applications become more extensive. ZJAI makes a similar point. In discussing future AI applications, he observes that the real degree of social acceptance can be assessed only once AI technologies are widespread and more mature. Although he did not elaborate on the reasons, INESA argues that it will not be easy to promote the overall understanding and acceptance of AI among society, but this difficulty will ease over time. Referring to his experience in providing AI solutions for education, IFLYi argues that a key determinant of social acceptance is the perceived value generated by AI solutions, referring to both public institutions and end users. One specific aspect related to social acceptance is mentioned by SDECi, who notes that bridging the digital gap for elderly people in using AI technology was one of the priorities of Shanghai's digital transformation efforts in 2021. FUDN makes a similar point, and notes that speech recognition and Natural Language Processing do not support the Shanghai dialect, which is the main language for most elderly people.

In addition to potential issues related to specific components of the AI ecosystem, **safety** was identified as an overarching factor that could affect the operational capacity to bring AI applications to fruition in the public sector. Some interviewees argue that safety considerations are already influencing the deployment of AI solutions in Shanghai. LING states that safety is a major concern for the Shanghai government when it comes to the deployment of autonomous vehicles. He says that Shanghai is not planning to introduce autonomous vehicles in the short term because there are too many variables that AVs currently can still not handle, and it is also challenging to develop adequate infrastructure (V2X). ZJAI agrees that at present there are concerns about the safe deployment of AI systems. He also makes the example of autonomous vehicles, which are still not allowed to drive on public roads (besides designated areas) because of safety concerns. In discussing secure multiparty computation as a possible technical solution to data privacy, AISP observes that it is not widely used yet because public organizations are not willing to take the risk to test it and validate it. Similarly, CHUN highlights the importance of testing and validating (验收) AI technologies to ensure their safety before they are rolled out and implemented in society, and argues that the government will not adopt technologies that have not been fully vetted.

Among the main issues that the interviewees think could affect Shanghai's operational capacity to use AI in the public sector, only safety was identified as an actual obstacle. Data privacy and security, and possible shifts in social acceptance were rather indicated as issues that interviewees consider important in their work, or that should be paid attention to when deploying AI solutions in the public sector. Indeed, regarding data privacy and security, there is no evidence that the current regulatory framework is affecting the activities of public organizations (Chapter 4.1). When mentioning the growing attention of public organizations to issues of privacy and security, SDECi also notes that data regulations are not affecting the activities of the Data Exchange Center. Rather, the *Shanghai Data Regulations* are favoring data sharing. Despite this, the analysis of the case studies will highlight some possible limitations to the deployment of AI in the public sector related to data privacy and security. Regarding social acceptance, national surveys indicate that Chinese citizens are on average very open to the use of AI technologies, and to date there is no evidence of public sector AI applications that were dismissed due to public opposition (Chapter 4.5). Beyond their impacts in the short term, acknowledging the existence of potential obstacles to the use of AI in the public sector in Shanghai is important: by pursuing an approach that prioritizes fast-paced AI implementation over considerations about privacy, security, and ethical issues, the municipal government could exacerbate latent problems and compromise its ability to develop beneficial AI applications (Chapter 6).

5.1.4 Outlining Shanghai's Policy Strategy for AI in the Public Sector

By showing how analytical, political, and operational skills and resources are mobilized and deployed, the interviews provided deeper insights into the policy capacity of Shanghai to implement AI in the public sector. The interviews confirm the findings of documentary research, showing that Shanghai has ample skills and resources in all the three dimensions of policy capacity. Despite the sociotechnical complexities of AI, there is no evidence that these are significantly detracting from the ability of Shanghai to implement public sector AI applications. Instead, the interviews highlighted the depth and breadth of Shanghai's policy capacities, as explained shortly. Furthermore, the interviews also show that the municipal government is cleverly leveraging its skills and resources, thus effectively fostering the use of AI to enhance the provision of public services. The ability of Shanghai to mobilize policy resources and capabilities was already highlighted in the analysis of the AI policy environment and the AI ecosystem, based on documentary evidence. By providing a direct account of what the municipality is doing to promote the use of AI in the public sector in practice, the interviews outline with greater precision the policy strategy of Shanghai for improving public service delivery by means of AI.

This strategy has three main characteristics. First, it is **coordinated**. The interviews highlight that the political support for AI development and its public sector applications comes from the top leadership of Shanghai, including the Party and the municipal government. This high-profile endorsement ensures that public and private actors perceive the development of AI as politically important, and it contributes to mobilizing them toward the priorities set by the Shanghai government, including the use of AI in the public sector. In addition, the implementation of AI is currently centralized in the hands of two government agencies that translate this coordinated approach in practice: the Shanghai Government General Office, which oversees the design and deployment of the Government Online-Offline Shanghai and the Single Platform for Urban Management; and the Shanghai Municipal Commission of Economy and Informatization, which oversees the deployment of AI in public sector and industrial projects, including the AI pilot application scenarios. Coordination is helping Shanghai to make efficient use of the available resources, ensuring consistency of action over time and across policy areas, and possibly preventing the inefficient allocation of resources that characterized previous government-led efforts to develop emerging technologies in China (e.g., photovoltaics, industrial robots, new energy vehicles, semiconductors, etc.).

Second, the strategy of Shanghai for AI in the public sector is **systemic**. It is supported by resources and capabilities in the analytical, political, and operational spheres. Although they disagree on the level of knowledge resources among Shanghai's AI policymakers, the interviewees observe that the communication channels with experts are helping the Shanghai leadership to collect and interpret policy-relevant information that support decision-making in AI policy. This is corroborated by the fact that the interviewees confirm that the Shanghai government has the analytical capacity to devise public sector AI applications that can improve the provision of public services. Political capacity underpins the coordinated approach to AI in the public sector, as just explained. In addition, the interviews show that sustained political support has created an enabling environment for the use of AI in the public sector in the areas prioritized by the municipal government, which encourages public and private sectors to experiment with AI applications within the boundaries set by the Shanghai government. Finally, the interviews confirm that Shanghai has the operational skills and resources to implement AI in the public sector in practice, from rich data sources to advanced infrastructure, from human capital and companies to a high degree of social acceptance. Safety was identified as a potential obstacle, and the analysis of case studies will look for further evidence of its impacts on public sector AI applications. While the policy capacity framework postulates that capacities don't need to be present in equal measure or all at the same time, the alignment of analytical, political, and operational skills and capabilities is theorized to be more likely to lead to policy success (Wu et al., 2015, p. 168). Indeed, evidence gathered from the interviews suggests that this systemic strategy is enhancing the ability of Shanghai to implement AI in the public sector.

Third, the strategy of Shanghai for AI in the public sector is **proactive**. The interviews reveal that the Shanghai government is spearheading the use of AI in the public sector by becoming the first mover in promoting the uptake of AI solutions. It does so in several ways: by using digital government platforms that leverage AI to optimize existing government activities (e.g., administrative service provision) and develop novel AI-based applications in various policy realms; by promoting AI pilot applications in various policy areas; by mobilizing government-led industry associations to advance the use of AI in the priority areas identified by the municipality; by upgrading existing equipment in public agencies and public institutions; and by leveraging State-owned enterprises as conduits to develop AI applications. In addition, this proactive approach includes the engagement of private companies in public sector AI projects, as part of a strategy that pursues the promotion of industrial development as well as public sector applications. Interviewees also suggest that this ability to engage AI enterprises extends to other priority areas of Shanghai's AI policy like nurturing human capital, thus providing further evidence of the capacity of Shanghai to access the resources and expertise of companies in order to implement AI in the public sector. A proactive government approach is widely regarded as an essential resource to promote AI development in the public and private sectors[15] (Molinari

[15] "Broadly, there are three ways to develop thriving AI-based ICT. The first is by public institutions being the first and the largest clients for new technologies. In general, EU member states have not been systematic in this regard, and the EU has not necessarily stimulated such activity. [...] China is a contrasting case in point. The government is enabling the development of AI by making it a national priority and is pulling on all levers, including R&D and skills development. [...] Beyond funding, the Chinese government has become the main customer in AI ventures such as video

et al., 2021), and in this dimension Shanghai appears to be particularly strong.

This coordinated, systemic, and proactive strategy that leverages municipal-level policy capacities to foster AI integration in the public sector is consistent with the government goals to improve public service provision and citizens' sense of gain by means of AI (Chapter 3.2). To understand how policy capacity enables the implementation of this strategy, the analysis of the case studies delves into the main policy initiatives that are actively using AI in the public sector in Shanghai. These initiatives can be classified in two main approaches. One is a **platform-based approach** that uses two municipal digital platforms as conduits to integrate AI in the public sector. Namely: the Government Online-Offline Shanghai (一网通办) for the provision of administrative services to citizens and companies; and the Single Platform for Urban Management (一网统管) to support government operations and public service provision in transportation, infrastructure management, and other areas of urban governance (Sect. 5.2). The other is an **experiment-based approach** that consists of standalone AI pilot applications in various policy areas, under a coordinated program promoted by the municipal government. Namely: the AI pilot application scenarios (人工智能试点应用场景; Sect. 5.3). The analysis of the case studies examines how these three policy initiatives articulate in practice. It shows how municipal-level capacities interact with organizational-level capacities to determine the strengths and limitations of these policy initiatives in deploying AI in the public sector, and it gauges the implications of such initiatives for public service provision in Shanghai.

recognition". Bughin, J., Seong, J., Manyka, J., Hämäläinen, L., Windhagen, E. and Hazan, E., 2019. *Notes from the AI Frontier: Tackling Europe's Gap in Digital and Artificial Intelligence*. McKinsey Global Institute, February 2019, p. 43, https://www.mckinsey.com/~/media/mckinsey/featured%20insights/artificial%20intelligence/tackling%20europes%20gap%20in%20digital%20and%20ai/mgi-tackling-europes-gap-in-digital-and-ai-feb-2019-vf.ashx.

5.2 The Platform-Based Approach: "One City, Two Networks"

In the platform-based approach, the Shanghai government is using the Government Online-Offline Shanghai and the Single Platform for Urban Management as conduits to integrate AI into the activities of the public sector. Both digital platforms are complex, city-wide initiatives that primarily rely on municipal-level analytical, political, and operational resources for their successful implementation. Next sections present the main features of these policy initiatives, examine their strengths and limitations in deploying AI in the public sector, and discuss their implications for public service provision in Shanghai.

5.2.1 The Government Online-Offline Shanghai

Officially started in 2018, the Government Online-Offline Shanghai (abbreviated: GOS) is a major initiative for digital innovation in the public sector that has progressively integrated AI technologies in its operations. It consists of a **unified e-government platform for the provision of administrative services to citizens and enterprises**, from household registration to the renewal of ID cards or business licenses. Based upon a centralized system that integrates Big Data, AI, and other advanced technologies, the Government Online-Offline Shanghai has created a single platform for the acceptance, examination, approval, and issuance of administrative documents (一窗受理, 分类审批, 一口发证). Through this unified digital platform, government agencies at all administrative levels share and exchange data relevant to the provision of administrative services. At the time of this writing, approximately 3,670 administrative services are available on the Government Online-Offline Shanghai system, and their number continues to increase.[16] These AI-based administrative

[16] Sohu, 2023. Fifth Anniversary of the Government Online-Offline Shanghai | Five Years of Hard Work, Forging Ahead to Write a New Chapter ["一网通办" 五周年| 砥砺奋进已五载 锐意进取谱新篇]. *Sohu* [搜狐], 20 October, https://www.sohu.com/a/729761255_120720272. In December 2021, the number of administrative services available on the GOS platform was 3,458. See: China Central Government, 2022. Shanghai "Government Online-Offline Shanghai" Will Promote the "Enjoy Without Applying" Service [上海 "一网通办" 将推 "免申即享" 服务]. *China Central Government* [中华人民共和国中央人民政府], 5 January, http://www.gov.cn/xinwen/2022-01/05/content_5666509.htm.

services are accessible from several digital channels (e.g., PC, mobile) and hundreds of administrative service centers connected to the GOS platform, as explained shortly. The digital and physical channels of the Government Online-Offline Shanghai share and integrate information, so that: documents available in digital form do not need to be submitted in paper; documents containing information that can be verified through the GOS platform do not need to be submitted; and documents that have been collected during previous interactions do not need to be re-submitted (Suiyi, 2021). As a result, citizens and companies have a unified point of access to submit applications for administrative services and check their status online, obtain information on such services (including fees, required documents, processing time), or book appointments for visiting government service centers, among many others.

The Government Online-Offline Shanghai is **integrated into the activities of government departments and administrative service centers at all levels**: 55 government departments[17] at the municipal and district levels, 16 district-level administrative service centers (区行政服务中心), 7 administrative centers in the development zones (开发区中心), 220 subdistrict service acceptance centers[18] (街镇社区事务受理中心) and more than 1,200 service points (called 服务站, 延伸点 or 分中心) in the municipality are connected to this unified e-government platform. This integrated online-offline system has simplified administrative procedures, and increased the efficiency in the provision of administrative services to individuals and companies. Applications that previously required examinations and approvals (审批) from more than one government agency can now be completed entirely online through the GOS platform, or

[17] Hubei Government, 2020. [Walking through Shanghai, Zhejiang and Guangdong to study the business environment] The "Government Online-Offline Shanghai" Is Convenient as Online Shopping [[行走沪浙粤看营商环境] "一网通办" 办事像网购一样方便]. *Hubei Government Website*, 26 November, http://www.hubei.gov.cn/zwgk/hbyw/hbywqb/202011/t20201126_3053842.shtml.

[18] Shanghai Bendibao, 2019. Address List of Community Affairs Acceptance Service Centers in Every Shanghai District [上海各区社区事务受理服务中心地址一览]. *Bendibao* [本地宝], 8 January, http://m.sh.bendibao.com/cyfw/190662.html. The number of subdistrict service acceptance centers is higher than the number of 215 subdistricts (see Chapter 1) because in some districts there is more than one service acceptance center for each subdistrict (e.g., Fengxian district has 3 subdistricts and 8 towns, but 13 service acceptance centers; see https://finance.sina.com.cn/jjxw/2022-05-17/doc-imcwipik0409520.shtml?cre=tianyi&mod=pcpager_china&loc=37&r=0&rfunc=47&tj=cxvertical_pc_pager_spt&tr=174&wm=).

can be initiated online and often completed in one single visit at the administrative service centers. In addition, more than 260 services (mostly for individuals, 个人办事) can be completed at any administrative service center in the municipality, in spite of the applicant's residence.[19] In 2020, the Government Online-Offline Shanghai platform has been indicated as a best e-government practice by the United Nations (2020).

The analysis conducted in the following paragraphs is primarily based on: Chinese-language official documents, including the municipal plans and reports on the development of the Government Online-Offline Shanghai; academic articles in Chinese language; gray sources (news articles and specialized blogs[20]) in Chinese language; and interviews with people who have direct knowledge of the GOS project and its applications, namely: Shanghai Zhuofan (SHZF, a main supplier of AI technologies used in the GOS system); Shanghai INESA (3INESA, a State-owned enterprise specialized in smart city development, and general contractor of the GOS project); the Shanghai Data Exchange Center (SDEC, the main open government data platform in Shanghai); and a consultant of the municipal government on AI and open data policies (AISP).

Project Description

In 2018, the Shanghai government stated that it would create the Government Online-Offline Shanghai in order to "build a service-oriented government that the people are satisfied with, adhere to the

[19] For instance, a resident in Minhang District can now apply for her medical insurance card (医保卡) in any other of the 15 districts of the municipality. This was not possible before the introduction of the Government Online-Offline Shanghai, as citizens needed to apply for administrative services at relevant government service centers in the district where they reside.

[20] The main source for specialized blogs used in Sect. 5.2 is Zhihu, China's largest knowledge sharing community with 220 million registered users and more than 130 million user-generated answers in 2019. Apart from its Q&A section, similar to Quora, Zhihu also has a "Zhihu Column" (知乎专栏) for users who want to write articles about a specific topic (e.g., economics, technology, science). Publications must be approved, and applicants are required to state in their applications all their relevant experience about the topic they want to write about (educational background, working experience, certificates, etc.). Previous studies reveal that Zhihu's user base mostly consists of professionals in the tech industry, students of computer sciences, and other highly educated groups; hence, Zhihu is considered one of the best Chinese social media platforms to get professional expert insights on various topics (Mao and Shi-Kupfer, 2021, p. 3).

people-centered development concept, meet the requirements of the modernization of government management and service [...], further optimize the business environment, and enhance the sense of gain for citizens and enterprises".[21] The Government Online-Offline Shanghai was presented as "one net to handle all services" (进一网、能通办) for enterprises and citizens.[22] Since then, a unified e-government platform has been built upon an **integrated digital architecture** designed and controlled by the municipal government. This digital architecture is the backbone that supports all the online and offline operations of the Government Online-Offline Shanghai, and it consists of three layers. Namely: the government affairs extranet, the e-government cloud, and the Big Data exchange platform (Fig. 5.1).

Each layer includes one municipal-level infrastructure built and operated by the municipal government, and 16 district-level infrastructures built and operated by each district government according to the standards, specifications, and requirements set by the municipality. In each layer, district-level infrastructure is logically integrated into the city infrastructure and hierarchically subordinated to it. The result is a centralized architecture that is controlled by the municipal government, while district-level infrastructures (i.e., extranets, e-government clouds, and data centers) are modeled on the municipal-level infrastructure and support its operations. This centralized architecture was designed to prevent data dispersion, ensure that the Government Online-Offline Shanghai has consistent standards and functions, and—in the case of the cloud platforms—ensure sufficient computing power to support the applications of the GOS across the hundreds of government agencies participating in the Government Online-Offline Shanghai (SHZFi).

[21] General Office of the CPC Shanghai Municipal Committee, Shanghai Municipal Government, 2018. *Work Plan for Comprehensively Promoting the "Government Online-Offline Shanghai" to Accelerate the Construction of Smart Government* [全面推进 "一网通办" 加快建设智慧政府工作方案]. Huweibanfa (2018) 14, 30 March, https://www.shanghai.gov.cn/newshanghai/xxgkfj/yiwangtongban.pdf. Preamble, in original: "建设人民满意的服务型政府 [...], 坚持以人民为中心的发展思想, 适应政府管理和服务现代化发展需要 [...], 进一步优化营商环境, 提升群众和企业获得感".

[22] Shanghai Municipal Government, 2019. *Working Points for Promoting the "Government Online-Offline Shanghai" in Shanghai in 2019* [2019年上海市推进 "一网通办" 工作要点]. Hufubanfa (2019) 8, 26 March, https://www.shanghai.gov.cn/nw44388/20200824/0001-44388_58587.html. Preamble, in original: "实现面向企业和市民的所有政务服务 "进一网, 能通办" 目标".

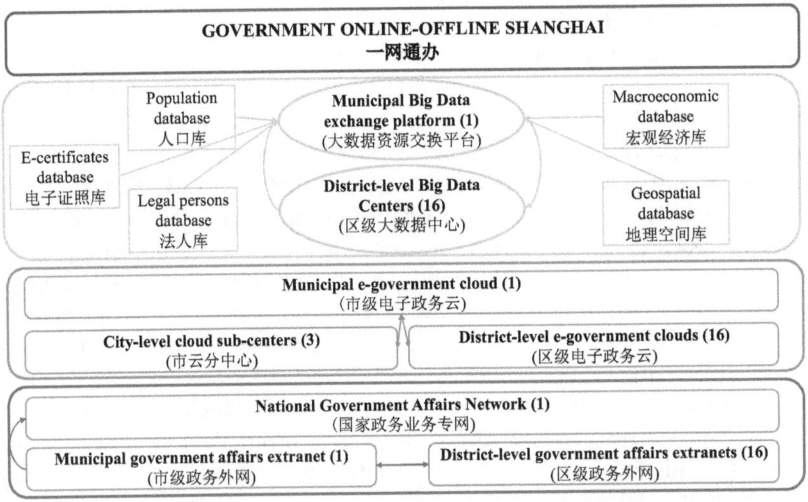

Fig. 5.1 Digital architecture of the Government Online-Offline Shanghai (author elaboration based on information from SHZF, SDEC, and Suiyi, 2021)

Starting from the foundations, the first layer of this integrated digital architecture consists of the **government affairs extranet** (政务外网). An extranet is a private network that only authorized users can access. These authorized users, both internal and external to the organization that owns the extranet (e.g., civil servants based in different departments), can exchange information or access services through the extranet without having to enter the host's (i.e., one specific government agency) main network. Shanghai's government extranet includes one municipal-level extranet (市级政务外网) and 16 district-level extranets (区级政务外网) connected to it. In turn, Shanghai municipal extranet is also linked to the National Government Affairs Network[23] (国家政务业务专网). The

[23] The National Government Affairs Network is part of the National E-Government Extranet (国家电子政务外网), which was built in the early 2000s in accordance with requirements set by the National Informatization Leading Group/国家信息化领导小组 (中办发 [2002] 17号文件, [2006] 18号文件). The National E-Government Extranet is the national extranet platform for Party committees, People's Congresses, government agencies, CPPCC, courts, procuratorates, and other government departments at all administrative levels. Within this framework, the National Government Affairs Network is mainly used for the transmission of non-confidential official documents and information between

government extranet in Shanghai carries services such as video conferencing, mobile offices, or government hotlines, among others. It typically requires Internet Protocol version 6 (IPv6) and high-performance broadband access (Chapter 4.2). It is the basic layer that supports the GOS architecture, connecting the components of the whole system.

The second layer consists of the **e-government cloud** (电子政务云). Cloud computing means the delivery of computing services—including servers, data storage, databases, networking, software, computing power, analytics, etc.—over the Internet, so that these can be used on demand.[24] Created in 2016, the e-government cloud of Shanghai includes one municipal-level e-government cloud (市级电子政务云), three city-level cloud sub-centers (市云分中心), and 16 district-level e-government clouds (区级电子政务云) connected to the municipal cloud. This system of cloud platforms provides the computing power, data storage, service support, and security guarantees needed to exchange data between government agencies in Shanghai.[25] The municipal cloud is the vertex of the system. It provides centralized and standardized cloud services to all government agencies in Shanghai via government purchase of services agreements (政府购买服务的方式; Suiyi, 2021). In turn, district-level cloud platforms provide services to government agencies within each district, and share the data that were collected in their jurisdictions on

government agencies in China. Source: https://zhuanlan.zhihu.com/p/283871806. See also: Du, P., Yu, S. and Yang, D. eds., 2019. *The Development of E-governance in China*. Singapore: Springer.

[24] Public clouds are owned and operated by third-party cloud service providers, which deliver their computing resources, like servers and storage, over the Internet. A private cloud refers to cloud computing resources used exclusively by a single business or organization. A private cloud can be physically located on the organization's on-site data center. Some organizations also pay third-party service providers to host their private cloud. Hybrid clouds combine public and private clouds, bound together by technology that allows data and applications to be shared between them. See: https://azure.microsoft.com/en-us/resources/cloud-computing-dictionary/what-is-cloud-computing/#uses (last accessed on 30 October 2023).

[25] Shanghai Municipal Government General Office, 2022. *Interim Measures for the Administration of Shanghai Municipal Government Affairs Cloud* [上海市政务云管理暂行办法], Hufubangui (2022) 6, 7 May, art. 2 and art. 5, http://www.echinagov.com/policy/322599.htm.

the municipal-level cloud platform. Government agencies are mandated by law to share all the non-confidential data generated by their activities via the e-government service cloud.[26]

The third layer consists of the **municipal Big Data exchange platform** (大数据资源交换平台) that supports all the operations of the Government Online-Offline Shanghai, whose core activities rely on data sharing across different government agencies. This centralized Big Data exchange platform is operated by the **Shanghai Municipal Big Data Center** (SBDC, 上海市大数据中心), a government entity created in April 2018 to foster the implementation of the GOS by promoting the collection, management, sharing, opening, application, and security of government data resources.[27] The municipal Big Data exchange platform is supported by 16 district-level Big Data Centers (区级大数据中心). The district-level Big Data Centers collect the data generated by the administrative activities of government agencies in their jurisdictions (e.g., data from relevant departments such as districts' social security bureaus), and share these data through the e-government cloud with the SBDC, which consolidates and synchronizes them on a daily basis (SDECi). The municipal Big Data exchange platform also includes five major databases on population, legal persons, geospatial information (地理空间), macroeconomic

26 Shanghai Municipal Government General Office, 2022, art. 7.

27 Huang, Y., 2018. Big Data Center Launched to Drive Smart Shanghai. *Shanghai Daily* [上海日报], 13 April, https://archive.shine.cn/business/it/Big-Data-center-launched-to-drive-smart-Shanghai/shdaily.shtml; Suiyi (2021).

information,[28] and electronic certificates.[29] These data are the "raw material" for the development of AI applications that support the provision of administrative services via the GOS platform. The exact size and contents of the municipal database are not public information, but it was reported that the database had approximately 14 billion data points in 2020 (United Nations, 2020, p. 157). To ensure the secure use of government data, the SBDC has established a unified security monitoring and supervision system, a risk assessment system, security review, data backup and daily monitoring mechanisms for data sharing (Suiyi, 2021; 3INESA).

The **Government Online-Offline Shanghai e-government Platform** is built on top of this three-layer digital architecture. Like its underlying structure, the GOS is centrally managed by the municipal government as a unified acceptance and processing platform (统一受理平台). The system is designed and supervised by two departments under the Shanghai Government General Office[30] (上海市人民政府办公厅): the Government Service Department (政务服务处) is in charge of the overall planning, promotion, and management of the services of the GOS; the Administrative Approval System Reform Office (行政审批制度改革处) is in charge of

[28] The population database contains information on natural persons, such as resident population, floating population (流动人口), permanent residents (户籍人口), employment, social security, real estate, personal accumulation fund (个人公积金, one component of China's social insurance), credit records; the legal person database contains information on legal persons, enterprises, social organizations, and other entities, including tax, corporate social security, corporate provident fund, electronic licenses, and other data; the geospatial information database contains information on Shanghai's administrative divisions, topography, land use, municipal facilities, rivers and lakes, and other related information; the macroeconomic information database contains information on economic and social development, such as fiscal revenues and expenditures, taxation, employment, industrial development, etc. (Suiyi, 2021, cit.).

[29] The electronic certificate database contains more than 380 kinds of common certificates such as ID cards, household registration book (户口本), real estate property certificate, enterprise business license, Sina, 2020. Reform of Shanghai's Government Online-Offline Shanghai: Data Integration and Sharing of More Than 380 Commonly Used Licenses [上海一网通办改革: 380多种常用证照数据整合共享]. *Sina Shanghai* [新浪上海] 21 May, http://sh.sina.cn/news/2020-05-21/detail-iirczymk2731129.d.html. See also: Shanghai Municipal Government, 2022. *Measures for the Administration of Electronic Licenses in Shanghai* [上海市电子证照管理办法], 25 June, https://www.pudong.gov.cn/14495.gkml_zcfgl/20220625/702865.html.

[30] Office of the Organization and Personnel Committee of the CPC Shanghai Municipal Committee (中共上海市委机构编制委员会办公室), Main Responsibilities and Internal Organizations of the General Office of the Shanghai Government General Office [上海市人民政府办公厅主要职责和内设机构], https://www.shbb.gov.cn/szfbgt/8994.jhtml.

deciding which services are provided through the GOS system (SHZFi). Operationally, the Government Online-Offline Shanghai is managed by the SBDC, which is also subordinated to the Shanghai Government General Office[31] The SBDC operates the municipal government cloud and coordinates the development of the whole cloud network.[32] In addition, the SBDC is in charge of the technological support, implementation, operation, and maintenance of the whole GOS system (SHZFi; SDECi; 3INESA). As the operator of the municipal Big Data exchange platform, the SBDC processes and analyzes the data contained in it, and uses these data to develop a set of standardized AI applications that support the provision of administrative services via the Government Online-Offline Shanghai. These AI applications are created in cooperation with AI companies, and they enable the automatic verification of the identity of applicants, or the automatic retrieval of data needed for the verification and approval of administrative documents, among others (see infra). The provision of AI-based administrative services is accessible from all the online and offline channels of the Government Online-Offline Shanghai: its website portal[33] (一网通办的门户网站), the mobile App "Suishenban" (随申办),[34] the "Suishenban" miniprograms on WeChat and Alipay, the citizen service hotline 12345, as well as the traditional service counters or the smart self-service kiosks (智慧自助服务设备/自动终端) in government administrative centers and service points in districts and subdistricts. All these digital and physical service channels are connected to the unified Government Online-Offline Shanghai platform operated by the SBDC,

[31] Zhu Zongyao (朱宗尧), Vice Director of the Shanghai Government General Office, is also Director of the SBDC.

[32] Shanghai Municipal Government General Office, 2022, art. 5: "The Municipal Big Data Center is the operation and management unit of the municipal government cloud, responsible for the specific construction, management, operation and maintenance, and security assurance of the municipal government cloud (excluding the government cloud special domains), and it provides guidance for the work the government cloud special domains as well as the district government clouds" [市大数据中心是市级政务云的运行管理单位, 负责市级政务云 (不含政务云专有域) 的具体建设, 管理, 运行维护和安全保障等工作, 对政务云专有域和区级政务云的有关工作开展业务指导].

[33] Government Online-Offline Shanghai Internet portal: https://zwdt.sh.gov.cn/govPortals/index.do.

[34] The name of the App is based on the assonance in Mandarin between the pronunciations of "follow Shanghai" ("sui shen"/随申) and "take along" ("sui shen"/随身).

thus ensuring the coordinated provision of AI-enabled administrative services throughout the GOS system (SHZFi, SDECi, Suiyi, 2021).

The Government Online-Offline Shanghai is a unified municipal platform supported by 16 district-level GOS subsystems developed and operated by the district-level Big Data Centers, according to the standards set by the municipal government. These subsystems are subordinated to the municipal platform and work as its interfaces (AISPi, SDECi). For instance, the district-level GOS subsystems are the gateways through which all the administrative service centers in one district are connected to the municipal e-government platform (SHZFi). Moreover, the district-level GOS subsystems are integrated into the municipal mobile App "Suishenban", which contains 16 district "flagship stores" (旗舰店). These local interfaces of the "Suishenban" App not only host the functions and applications developed by the SBDC (i.e., each district-level App displays information on all the services provided in the whole municipality, and share all the basic functions of the municipal-level GOS App); they can also offer applications designed for the specific needs of each district. Such applications—if considered successful—may be extended to the whole municipal platform, or are emulated by other districts. The Shanghai government chose this combination of municipal and district-level infrastructures and systems under an overarching, centralized city-level platform[35] because it is flexible, as it distributes operations across different nodes of the GOS; and because it allows for innovation and experimentation in districts and subdistricts, while at the same time maintaining centralized control and standardized services (SHZFi).

Finally, the centralized approach of the Government Online-Offline Shanghai is replicated in the services that support the functioning of the GOS system. This service structure, called "one beam and four pillars" (一梁四柱), includes: the citizen service hotline 12345; the unified log-in for the whole GOS system, which can be used for any online and

[35] Called in Chinese "统分方式", it is one of the three methods indicated by the State Council for the construction of e-government platforms at the provincial level. The other two methods are: the construction of separate provincial and city platforms that are linked only through their data exchange centers (called 分建方式); or the construction of a unified e-government platform with one single data exchange center for the whole province (called 统建方式). State Council, 2017. *Guidelines for the Construction of the Technical System of "Internet + Government Services"* ["互联网+政务服务" 技术体系建设指南], Guo Ban Han [2016] 108, 12 January, http://www.gov.cn/zhengce/content/2017-01/12/content_5159174.htm.

offline channel of the Government Online-Offline Shanghai; the unified online payment system that citizens and companies can use to pay for all the services provided by the platform, including traditional banking (China Union Pay) and third-party payment channels (e.g., WeChat, Alipay); and the unified logistic service provided by the government-owned Shanghai Postal Service, which delivers to the applicants those documents that cannot be provided in digital form or require a physical version (e.g., ID cards).

Strengths and Limitations in Deploying AI in the Public Sector

The Government Online-Offline Shanghai makes extensive use of AI technologies to support the provision of administrative services. It is a complex, city-wide initiative that primarily relies on municipal-level skills and resources for its successful deployment. Next paragraphs examine how Shanghai is leveraging its analytical, operational, and political capacities to integrate AI into the provision of administrative services via the GOS platform, and how municipal-level capacities interact with the organizational skills and resources of the government agencies participating in this digital platform. The analysis offers deeper insights into the capabilities that determine the strengths and limitations of this policy initiative in deploying AI in the public sector, and provides a solid basis to assess the resulting implications of the Government Online-Offline Shanghai for public service provision in the municipality.

Strengths

The municipality has set a clear goal for the Government Online-Offline Shanghai: "build a service-oriented government that the people are satisfied with" (Sect. 5.2.1.1). As a tool to achieve this goal, Shanghai aims to use AI technologies to improve the management and provision of administrative services. This is a daunting task that requires high levels of analytical capacity, as it involves hundreds of government agencies at different administrative levels, and thousands of services and related bureaucratic procedures. To promote the coordinated development of the GOS project, every year the Shanghai municipal government publishes work plans (工作方案, 工作要点) that set specific targets for the development of the Government Online-Offline Shanghai. For instance, completing the construction of the GOS portal, the unified data exchange platform, and the electronic certificates database by 2018; adding 100 individual services (个人事项) to the list of government services that can be applied for anywhere in the municipality in 2019 and 2020, etc. Taken together, these work plans form a well-articulated blueprint for the development of the Government Online-Offline Shanghai. Importantly, since the publication of the first work plan in 2018, Shanghai has been constantly reiterating the intention to integrate AI technologies in the GOS system in order to enhance the provision of administrative services, as shown in the table below.

In addition to formulating a well-articulated policy initiative that consistently plans the use of AI in administrative services, Shanghai has demonstrated **the analytical capacity to devise AI applications that can effectively improve the provision of administrative services** via the Government Online-Offline Shanghai. The AI-enabled chatbot of the GOS platform, called Xiao Shen (小申), offers an illustrative example of such capacity. The chatbot is accessible any time of the day through the GOS website, the mobile App "Suishenban", the "Suishenban" miniprograms on WeChat and Alipay, and on the websites of many government agencies. Xiao Shen uses Natural Language Processing (NLP) and a constantly growing knowledge base[36] to answer users' inquiries on various services and features of the GOS platform. In March 2021, the Shanghai government announced that it would "improve the service level of the online intelligent customer service Xiao Shen and promote the unified deployment of Xiao Shen on the websites of various agencies of the municipal government" (Table 5.3). Since then, the AI chatbot has been combined with the activities of human operators in a system known as "application assistance system" (帮办制度). This system integrates three modes of customer assistance: the hotline 12345, the AI chatbot Xiao Shen, and human operators specialized on some of the most common topics and services provided by the GOS. Such system is designed to help individuals and companies to address the difficulties they encounter when using the GOS and cannot be promptly addressed by extant customer service channels in isolation. Starting from the second half of 2021, the "application assistance system" was tested on the 35

[36] As explained in Chapter 1, "knowledge" base refers to the data, information, and past experiences about a certain domain, which are loaded into an AI system and allows it to answer questions related to that domain (e.g., the services and functions of the GOS platform). Knowledge-based systems can be subdivided into systems that base decision-making on prior case experience; and rule-based systems where the domain knowledge is coded in the form of event-condition-action, such as using IF-THEN or IF-THEN-ELSE rules (Engin and Treleaven, 2019, p. 450).

most common services inquired by individuals and companies[37] (e.g., residence registrations/住居登记, food business licenses/食品经营许可). The combination of AI chatbot and human operators aims to reduce the time of first response (首次响应) to less than one minute, further improving the efficiency of the GOS platform.[38] In January 2022, the new GOS work plan reiterated the intention to improve the "application assistance system", stating that the algorithms and knowledge base of Xiao Shen will be further improved so that the chatbot would be able to automatically answer 50% of the inquiries on the 100 most common services of the GOS system.

The "two exemptions from submission" (两个免于提交) provide another example of Shanghai's analytical capacity to devise AI applications that contribute to enhancing the provision of administrative services. This AI-based innovation is one of the hallmarks of the GOS, and it was announced in the 2020 work plan. In principle, all the materials (documents, certificates, licenses) issued by Shanghai government agencies are exempted from submission, and the materials for which there is a digital version are exempted from the submission of paper versions. Applicants can retrieve from the GOS website or the "Suishenban" App the digital documents (e.g., ID cards, marriage certificates, business licenses, construction permits, etc.) needed for the service of interest. When applying for such services, digital documents can be shown at the counters of the administrative service centers by using the "Present Certificate" (亮证) function of the "Suishenban" App. The staff at the service counters check the authenticity of the document by scanning its QR code, and verify on their computers the information contained in the GOS platform.[39] The "two exemptions from submission" is enabled by several AI applications: machine learning to retrieve and verify the data contained in

[37] The Paper, 2021. These 35 Items Will Be Covered Online by the End of This Year! One Picture to Understand the "Government Online-Offline Shanghai" Assistance System [今年底前将线上覆盖这35个事项!一图了解"一网通办"帮办制度]. *The Paper* [澎湃], 8 November, https://m.thepaper.cn/baijiahao_15285263.

[38] China Central Government, 2021. Shanghai Creates the "Government Online-Offline Shanghai" Application Assistance System [上海建立"一网通办"帮办制度]. *China Central Government* [中华人民共和国中央人民政府], 2 December, http://www.gov.cn/xinwen/2021-12/02/content_5655406.htm.

[39] The Paper, 2021. "Two Exemptions from Submission" Allow the Principle of Benefiting Enterprises and Citizens to Efficiently Penetrate Government Services! ["两个免于

Table 5.3 Work plans for the implementation of the Government Online-Offline Shanghai (2018–2022)

Document (year)	*AI in the Government Online-Offline Shanghai*
Work plan for comprehensively promoting the "Government Online-Offline Shanghai" and accelerating the construction of smart government[40] (2018)	"Use Big Data, artificial intelligence, Internet of Things and other technologies to improve the scientificity, precision and intelligentization of government service management[41]" "Actively use new technologies such as artificial intelligence and virtual reality to improve the personalization and intelligentization of online government services[42]" "Comprehensively promote the construction of intelligent public security, and apply advanced technologies and products such as Big Data, cloud computing, Internet of things and artificial intelligence to public security work through integrated innovation[43]"
Working points for promoting the "Government Online-Offline Shanghai" in Shanghai in 2019[44] (2019)	This document does not explicitly mention artificial intelligence, but several applications cited in the document imply the use of AI technologies[45]

40 General Office of the CPC Shanghai Municipal Committee, Shanghai Municipal Government, 2018 (cit.).

41 Ibid., section 1. In original: "应用大数据、人工智能、物联网等新技术, 提升政府管理科学化、精细化、智能化水平".

42 Ibid., section 3, par. 5.1. In original: "主动运用人工智能、虚拟现实等新技术, 提升网上政务服务个性化、智能化水平".

43 Ibid., section 5, par. 5.3. In original: "全面推进智慧公安建设, 将大数据、云计算、物联网、人工智能等先进技术和产品, 集成创新应用于公安工作".

44 Shanghai Municipal Government, 2019 (cit.).

45 For instance, section 1, par. 5.2 states that "materials that can be verified through data sharing or the network don't need to be submitted" (能够通过数据共享或网络核验的材料一律不需提交). These applications typically rely on machine learning and AI technologies for automatically reading and parsing documents (see, for instance, the 2022 work plan).

Document (year)	*AI in the Government Online-Offline Shanghai*
Working points for deepening the reform of the "Government Online-Offline Shanghai" in Shanghai in 2020[46] (2020)	"All districts and departments are encouraged to cooperate and use blockchain, Big Data, AI, 5G and other advanced technologies, and boldly explore and make trials in process optimization and reengineering, data integration and sharing, enterprise-friendly and people-friendly applications, 'AI + Government Online-Offline Shanghai' and other areas[47]"
Working points for comprehensively deepening the reform of the "Government Online-Offline Shanghai" in Shanghai in 2021[48] (2021)	"Give full play to AI empowerment, continuously improve the service level of the online intelligent customer service 'Xiao Shen' [*an AI chatbot*], and promote the unified deployment of 'Xiao Shen' on the websites of various departments of the municipal government[49]" "Improve the enabling level of 'AI + Government Online-Offline Shanghai'. Replicate and promote the pilot results of various districts and departments, focus on people's livelihood and business environment, deepen applications in 'AI + approval', 'AI + service' and 'AI + supervision', and realize the [AI-enabled] automatic approval of simple matters and [AI-assisted] auxiliary approval of complex matters[50]"

(continued)

46 Shanghai Municipal Government, 2020b. *Working Points for Deepening the Reform of the "Government Online-Offline Shanghai" in Shanghai in 2020* [2020年上海市深化"一网通办"改革工作要点], 24 February, https://www.shanghai.gov.cn/nw12344/20200813/0001-12344_64071.html.

47 Ibid., section 6, article 4 做好试点推广. In original: 鼓励各区, 各部门结合实际, 借助区块链, 大数据, 人工智能, 5G等前沿技术, 在业务流程优化再造, 数据资源整合共享, 便企利民应用, "AI + 一网通办" 等方面大胆探索、先行先试".

48 Shanghai Municipal Government, 2021. *Working Points for Comprehensively Deepening the Reform of the "Government Online-Offline Shanghai" in Shanghai in 2021* [2021年上海市全面深化"一网通办"改革工作要点], 12 March, https://www.shanghai.gov.cn/nw12344/20210312/4652749fb81d4e9c9ab4029322ff58c4.html.

49 Ibid., section 4 "Enhance the functions of the 'Government Online-Offline Shanghai' Platform" [提升"一网通办"平台能力], article 14. In original: "发挥AI赋能作用, 持续提高在线智能客服 '小申' 服务水平, 推动市政府各部门网站统一部署 '小申'".

50 Ibid., section 4, article 16. In original: "提升 'AI + 一网通办' 赋能水平。复制推广各区、各部门试点成果, 重点聚焦民生领域和营商环境领域, 深化 'AI + 审批' 'AI + 服务' 'AI + 监管', 推动实现简单事项自动审批、复杂事项辅助审批等目标".

Table 5.3 (continued)

Document (year)	*AI in the Government Online-Offline Shanghai*
Decision of the Standing Committee of the Shanghai Municipal People's Congress on further promoting and ensuring the reform of the Government Online-Offline Shanghai[51] (2021)	"Strengthen the standardization of administrative approval, and rely on Big Data, artificial intelligence and other technical means to meet the needs of the applicants[52]" "Promote the widespread [*lit., 'socialized'* 社会化] application of the individual healthcare QR code [随申码] and use this digital identification code to realize one code for individuals, enterprises and other market entities. Provide personalized, accurate, active and intelligent services based on the portals [of the Government Online-Offline Shanghai] dedicated to citizens and enterprises[53]"
Working points for comprehensively deepening the reform of the "Government Online-Offline Shanghai" in Shanghai in 2022[54] (2022)	"Use data sharing, Big Data analysis and artificial intelligence assistance to precisely identify and match companies and individuals that meet the conditions for automatically receiving administrative services[55]"

51 Shanghai Municipal People's Congress, 2021. *Decision of the Standing Committee of the Shanghai Municipal People's Congress on Further Promoting and Ensuring the Reform of the Government Online-Offline Shanghai* [上海市人民代表大会常务委员会关于进一步促进和保障"一网通办"改革的决定], 23 June, http://www.spcsc.sh.cn/n8347/n8467/u1ai236289.html#:~:text=%E3%80%8A%E4%B8%8A%E6%B5%B7%E5%B8%82%E4%BA%BA%E6%B0%91%E4%BB%A3%E8%A1%A8,7%E6%9C%881%E6%97%A5%E8%B5%B7%E6%96%BD%E8%A1%8C%E3%80%82.

52 Ibid., article 5. In original: "强化审批要素标准化建设, 依托大数据、人工智能等技术手段, 根据申请人的办事需求".

53 Ibid., article 10. In original: "本市推广 '随申码' 的社会化应用, 以 '随申码' 作为个人以及企业等市场主体的数字身份识别码, 实现一码通办。依托市民主页和企业专属网页, 提供个性、精准、主动、智能服务".

54 Shanghai Municipal Government, 2022. *Working Points for Comprehensively Deepening the Reform of the "Government Online-Offline Shanghai" in Shanghai in 2022* [2022年上海市全面深化 "一网通办" 改革工作要点], Hufubanfa (2022) 1, 5 January, https://www.shanghai.gov.cn/nw12344/20220114/9ac0208eb4024b61a20307c94831be40.html.

55 Ibid., section 2, par. 5.1. In original: "通过数据共享、大数据分析、人工智能辅助, 精准匹配符合条件的企业群众, 企业群众全程无需主动提出申请".

Document (year)	*AI in the Government Online-Offline Shanghai*
	"Improve the service level of the 'Xiao Shen + human' application assistance system […]. Optimize the services of the smart customer assistant 'Xiao Shen' by establishing a working mechanism for adding, linking, sharing and filling vacancies in its knowledge base. In principle, one working day before the implementation of new policies, the relevant questions and answers should be updated to the knowledge base [of 'Xiao Shen']. Improve the algorithms of 'Xiao Shen' and its ability to identify and analyze intentions, so that 'Xiao Shen' can achieve a 50% resolution rate[56]" [of inquiries related to the 100 most common services of the GOS system] "Consolidate the intelligent service base of the Government Online-Offline Shanghai by using algorithm models for speech recognition, image recognition (OCR), and semantic analysis (NLP) to enable fundamental applications […]. Strengthen algorithm modelling and machine deep learning in various fields, expand and enrich intelligent application scenarios[57]"

56 Ibid., section 4, par. 5.2. In original: "提升 "小申" + "人工帮办" 服务能级 […] 优化智能客服 "小申"服务, 建立知识库新增、关联、共享和查遗补缺工作机制, 原则上, 在新的政策文件实施前1个工作日, 应当将相关问答更新至知识库, 升级 "小申"算法能级, 提升意图识别分析能力, 实现 "小申"解决率达到50%".

57 Ibid., section 5, par. 5.4. In original: "夯实基于语音识别、图像识别 (OCR) 、语义分析 (NLP) 等算法模型的 "一网通办" 智能化服务底座, 赋能基层应用. […] 强化各领域算法模型建模和机器深度学习, 拓展和丰富智能场景应用".

the municipal database of electronic certificates and associate them to the applicants; the use of optical character recognition,[58] Natural Language Processing, robotic process automation, and algorithmic systems to automatically pre-check the information without human intervention[59]; as well as other AI applications embedded in the operations of the GOS platform, as described shortly.

AI applications for enhancing the provision of administrative services continue to expand. In October 2021, the GOS started to implement the "enjoy without applying" (免申即享), which was later included in the 2022 *Working Points* (Table 5.3). The "enjoy without applying" allows eligible parties to enjoy policy benefits and public services automatically or after confirming their willingness to apply, without any other initiatives being required. It is a type of predictive service delivery[60] that leverages Big Data analytics and artificial intelligence to identify enterprises and citizens entitled to certain policy benefits, such as students in difficulty, the disabled, the elderly, or retired soldiers. At present, the "enjoy without applying" focuses on 27 policy areas, and it is mostly directed to vulnerable groups. But this AI-based service will be progressively extended to

提交" 让利企便民原则高效渗透政务服务!]. *The Paper* [澎湃新闻], 6 November, https://www.thepaper.cn/newsDetail_forward_15259490.

[58] Optical character recognition is the use of technology to recognize printed or handwritten text characters inside digital images of physical documents, and translate the characters into code that can be used for data processing. It is typically used to convert physical documents into machine-readable text.

[59] Tencent Net, 2021. When "AI" Meets the "Government Online-Offline Shanghai", What Will Happen? Come and See Jing'an "Government Affairs Smart Application"! [当 "AI" 遇上 "一网通办", 会发生些什么?来看静安 "政务智能办" !]. *Tencent Net* [腾讯网], 1 December, https://new.qq.com/omn/20211201/20211201A053WH00.html.

[60] Predictive service delivery uses predictive analytics to improve outcomes and efficiently manage resources through automation, earlier intervention, and better prediction and targeting. Predictive analytics means the use of AI and related technologies to examine historical data in order to identify trends (patterns and relationships) that can be used to anticipate future needs. For an analysis of the expected benefits of predictive service delivery in the public sector, see: Trehan, V., 2021. Predictive Algorithms in the Public Sector. *Rutgers New Jersey State Policy Lab*, https://policylab.rutgers.edu/predictive-algorithms-in-the-public-sector/; Local Government Association, 2020. Using Predictive Analytics in Local Public Services. *Local Government Association*, https://www.local.gov.uk/publications/using-predictive-analytics-local-public-services#what-do-we-mean-by-predictive-analytics; Smith, R., 2018. The Future of Government: Moving from Reactive to Predictive Service Delivery. *Deloitte*, https://www2.deloitte.com/nz/en/pages/technology/articles/future-of-government.html.

other users. Zhu Zongyao, Director of the SBDC, explained: “Relying on data, our government departments should know when the masses may apply for what services”.[61]

In addition to the AI applications for administrative service provision designed and implemented by the municipal government, the GOS platform also promotes the use of AI applications that leverage the analytical capacity of districts. As noted earlier, district-level Big Data Centers not only host the functions and applications developed by the SBDC, but they can also offer applications designed for the specific needs of each district. Such applications—if considered successful—may be extended to the whole municipal platform or are emulated by other districts. This **policy design that combines guidance and flexibility is another important facet of analytical capacity**. On the one hand, it ensures the consistent development of the Government Online-Offline Shanghai across hundreds of government agencies, thousands of services, and related bureaucratic procedures. On the other, it also leaves room for districts to devise AI solutions for the provision of the administrative services that are most needed in their jurisdictions, based on their different socioeconomic characteristics.

These sound analytical capabilities are paired by Shanghai’s **operational capacity to efficiently develop and integrate AI applications for administrative services in the activities of government agencies, supporting their core operations**. The Government Online-Offline Shanghai is best understood as a “capability platform” designed and supervised by the Shanghai government (SDECi). By aggregating and coordinating the operational resources available in the municipality, Shanghai is making efficient use of its AI ecosystem to develop AI applications for administrative services. The Shanghai government leverages huge amounts of *data* (consolidated in the Big Data exchange platform), advanced *technological infrastructure* (the extranets, the e-government

61 China Central Government, 2021 (cit.); Tencent Net, 2022. Analysis of the Effects of the “Enjoy Without Applying” on Employment Applications [“免申即享” 政策对项目申报职业的影响分析]. *Tencent Net* [腾讯网], 22 June, https://new.qq.com/omn/20220622/20220622A0007U00.html; Shanghai Government General Office, 2022. *Work Plan for Accelerating the Promotion of the “Enjoying Without Applying” Preferential Policy and Service for Companies and Citizens Through the “Government Online-Offline Shanghai”* [依托“一网通办”加快推进惠企利民政策和服务“免申即享”工作方案], Hufubanzi (2022) 4, 8 March, https://www.shanghai.gov.cn/nw12344/20220322/79c9df1e95bd4287b03ad86b5dbea19f.html?siteId=1.

clouds, and the Big Data exchange platform), the know-how and ***human capital*** provided by ***AI companies*** and government technology agencies (the SBDC, the district Big Data Centers), and the municipal ability to promote the standardized development of the Government Online-Offline Shanghai. This coordinated deployment of municipal operational resources is producing several AI applications that are integrated into the activities of government agencies via the GOS platform to improve the provision of administrative services (e.g., the AI chatbot Xiao Shen, the "two exemptions from submission", the "enjoy without applying"). This process is further explained below.

In cooperation with AI companies, the Shanghai Municipal Big Data Center designs and implements a set of fundamental AI applications that are used to optimize the provision of administrative services, and it makes such applications available to all agencies connected to the e-government platform (3INESAi, AISPi, SDECi). The SBDC is mandated to "build the basic platform of 'AI + Government Online-Offline Shanghai', compile a general library of AI content learning, create a list of AI service directories, and provide a number of general algorithm models to solve common problems in government agencies and improve efficiency".[62] Doing so requires the coordination of several operational resources, including: an integrated technological infrastructure for the efficient collection and sharing of digital data and their timely transmission to the SBDC; the computing power, standardized databases, algorithms, and know-how to develop AI applications based on these data; and, again, the technological infrastructure through which these AI applications are made available to the organizations connected to the e-government platform. AI applications developed by the SBDC include computer vision-based OCR to extract contents from standardized document templates, convert the information into machine-readable data, and apply machine learning algorithms to analyze these data and verify the information needed to approve the emission of various administrative certificates (3INESAi). The SBDC also uses AI to verify the identity of individuals and companies, which are required to log on to the GOS platform using real-name registration

[62] Shanghai Development and Reform Commission, 2020. *Shanghai Action Plan for Promoting the Construction of New Infrastructure (2020–2022)* [上海市推进新型基础设施建设行动方案 (2020–2022 年)], Hufu (2020) 27, 12 May, section 3, par. 5.3. In original: "建设 "AI + 一网通办" 基础平台, 构建AI内容学习总库, 形成AI服务目录清单, 提供一批解决部门共性难题、提升效率的通用算法模型".

(e.g., mobile phone number for individuals, company business licenses, etc.). By leveraging AI to analyze the data it receives from the government agencies in the GOS system, the SBDC automatically verifies and compares information on users' identity, and it allows a one-time authentication for the whole platform: PC, mobile App, and smart terminals in the government service centers. Moreover, the SBDC can provide accurate digital profiles of the GOS users by mining data on their past interactions with the Government Online-Offline Shanghai (e.g., services required, offices visited, etc.). This profiling capability allows to predict users' service needs and provide personalized service recommendations at different stages of the administrative process (Suiyi, 2021), and it is one of the pillars of the "enjoy without applying" described earlier. The SBDC also uses AI to encrypt and decrypt data transferred among public organizations within the GOS system, ensuring the secure use and management of data (3INESA). Other AI applications available to all the organizations joining the GOS system include: an intelligent knowledge base of service guides, application manuals, and administrative documents that can be updated in real time by using machine learning, deep learning, NLP, and other technologies; or the use of NLP in the citizen service hotline 12345 to provide customer assistance, extract key contents, and monitor service quality (SHZFi; see also Sect. 5.2.2).

The AI chatbot Xiao Shen, the "two exemptions from submission", the "enjoy without applying", and the standardized AI applications developed by the Shanghai Municipal Big Data Center (e.g., OCR to extract contents from standardized document templates) all provide vivid examples of Shanghai's capacity to efficiently integrate AI technologies in the provision of administrative services by orchestrating municipal-level operational resources. At the same time, they also reveal the contribution given by skills and resources at the organizational level. For instance, the "two exemptions from submission" and the "enjoy without applying" require that district-level Big Data Centers cooperate with AI companies in developing the technical solutions needed to implement public sector AI innovation in their jurisdictions. District-level Big Data Centers are requested to identify, standardize, and digitalize the documents that will be included in the "two exemptions from submission" and the "enjoy without applying".[63] These activities are carried out under the supervision of the SBDC, which provides data and technical support, and determines the relevant technical and operational standards (SHZFi). But the technologies that enable the "two exemptions from submission" and the "enjoy without applying" must be developed by district-level Big Data Centers in cooperation with their technical partners. This ability to aggregate and coordinate the municipal and organizational resources of Shanghai's AI ecosystem is fostering the efficient implementation of AI applications for the provision of administrative services, and their integration into the activities of government agencies at each administrative level.

The **ability to engage AI firms** is another important operational resource to efficiently integrate AI in administrative services, since companies are essential partners to develop the AI applications used by the Government Online-Offline Shanghai, just like most other public sector AI applications (Chapters. 3.2.3 and 4.4). The Shanghai Municipal Big Data Center has established strategic partnerships with public and private companies that supply the technologies needed for the operations of the Big Data exchange platform and the development of AI applications for administrative services, including[64]: Shanghai INESA (上海仪电集团), a State-owned enterprise specialized in smart city development, which is also the general contractor of the main projects related to the GOS construction; Tencent (腾讯公司), an Internet giant and major AI company that provides data analytics technologies, among others; 360 Total Security (三六零安全科技股份有限公司), the leading Chinese company in Internet security; Shanghai Datatom (上海德拓信息技术股份有限公司), specialized in data storage, data mining, and data analysis; Primeton Sofware (普元信息技术股份有限公司), specialized in basic middleware, cloud applications and Big Data middle platforms; Tianran Intelligent Technology (上海天壤智能科技有限公司), specialized in artificial intelligence platforms for urban governance and traffic management;

[63] See for instance: Wenhui, 2021. The Capacity of the "Whole Process Online Management" Reaches 98.92%! The Third Anniversary of Xuhui's "Government Online-Offline Shanghai" Has Brought These "Benefits" ["全程网办" 能力达98.92%! 徐汇 "一网通办" 三周年, 这张网带来了这些 "福利" …]. *Wenhui* [文汇], 17 October, https://wenhui.whb.cn/third/baidu/202110/17/429149.html?sdkver=93de1a00.

[64] Shanghai Municipal Big Data Center, official website: https://www.shdata.com/PC/App/friends. Last accessed on 30 October 2023.

and iFlytek (科大讯飞), specialized in speech recognition and Natural Language Processing. Many of these companies are leaders in their respective fields. By establishing strategic partnerships with these key technology providers, the SBDC not only ensures a stable supply of AI technologies, and related know-how and human resources,[65] but it can also develop tailor-made solutions based on the operational requirements of the GOS system (3INESAi).

The cooperation with AI companies is also crucial for district-level Big Data Centers. As noted, district-level Big Data Centers operate the 16 subsystems that serve as interfaces of the unified Government Online-Offline Shanghai platform, build the technical solutions that support the implementation of AI-based administrative services promoted by the Shanghai government (e.g., the "two exemptions from submission"), and can design AI applications for the specific needs of each district (e.g., the AI applications discussed below in the "political capacity" section). In this perspective, the great number of technology suppliers available in Shanghai offers district governments a wide pool of potential partners[66] that can support the operations, maintenance, and development of the district Big Data Centers and the GOS subsystems (SHZFi, 3INESA). The interoperability of these solutions with the unified municipal e-government platform is ensured by a set of technical standards for the construction of the GOS system, as discussed in the next paragraph. At the same time, the fierce competition among suppliers encourages technology companies to provide solutions that usually exceed these standards, granting quantity as well as quality (SHZFi). Indeed, the participation in public sector AI projects is very attractive for AI firms: by cooperating with the public sector, companies have the opportunity to market their products, and they can also leverage the abundance of real-world government data to optimize their technologies (Chapter 4.4.2 and 5.1).

[65] IFLYi says that companies are usually required to assign a dedicated team to work with the SBDC.

[66] Shanghai Zhuofan estimates that there are approximately 300 suppliers of technologies used by the Government Online-Offline Shanghai. This estimate is confirmed by available online sources, for instance: Enet.com, 2020. 2020 Ranking of Suppliers of the "Government Online-Offline Shanghai" [2020 "一网通办" 解决方案提供商排行榜]. *Enet.com* [硅谷动力], 17 August, http://www.enet.com.cn/article/2020/0817/A202008171186600.html.

Another operational skill that is helping Shanghai to efficiently integrate AI in administrative services is the ability to **promote the standardized development of the Government Online-Offline Shanghai**. Standardization involves two interrelated aspects. One aspect is the *standardization of workflows and operating procedures*. Most of the AI applications used by this unified e-government platform—including the platform-wide applications as well as those developed by districts—are based on standardized procedures, document templates, and data classifications. If these standards change, such AI applications are no longer feasible (3INESAi). Hence, the ability to standardize the workflows and procedures of administrative services, promoting operational consistency across the agencies involved in the GOS platform, is essential for the efficient integration of AI in the Government Online-Offline Shanghai (SHZFi, 3INESAi, AISPi). Indeed, the municipal policy documents indicate that Shanghai pays great attention to the standardization of the procedures of administrative service provision. For instance, the 2020 GOS work plan states that Shanghai will promote the standardization of the application requirements and methods, acceptance modes, review procedures, issuance methods, and management structure of administrative services[67]; the standardization of the management practices of the administrative service centers[68]; and the standardization of government data that underpin the provision of administrative services.[69] A local expert emphasizes that this is an iterative (流程再造) process that aims to make workflows suitable for AI automation, and then standardizes them for fast implementation and easy replication (AISPi). These findings corroborate earlier studies observing that the innovation and optimization of workflows and operating procedure is a central feature of the GOS initiative.[70]

[67] Shanghai Municipal Government, 2020b (cit.), section 2, par. 1, point 1. In original: “明确申请条件、申报方式、受理模式、审核程序、发证方式、管理架构 ‘六个再造’ 实施标准”. See also section 2, par 1, point 6; and section 2, par. 5, point 5.

[68] Ibid., section 2, par. 5, point 1. In original: “出台我市政务服务中心标准化建设与管理的意见 […], 修订政务服务大厅地方标准。建立政务服务地图。细化量化线下窗口标准化管理”. See also next paragraph on the technical standardization of the government administrative centers.

[69] Ibid., section 2, par. 3, point 4. In original: “依托市公共数据标准化技术委员会, 强化全市公共数据标准统筹管理”.

[70] Chinese scholars carried out the content analysis of the three GOS work plans issued in the period 2018–2020 (Table 5.3), showing that concepts related to innovation in

The second aspect is *technical standardization*. District governments have to build and operate their Big Data Centers and GOS subsystems, devise the technical solutions that support the implementation of AI-based services promoted by the Shanghai government, and are also encouraged to experiment with AI applications for the provision of administrative services. In addition, each public agency and administrative service center is responsible for purchasing the equipment (e.g., smart cameras for facial recognition) needed to support the functions of the GOS platform. To ensure coordination and interoperability, Shanghai has set technical standards for the construction of the Government Online-Offline Shanghai. In 2018 and 2019, the municipal government issued a number of local standards that determine the technical specifications for the operations of the GOS platform.[71] In 2021, the municipal government also regulated the construction and operations of the brick-and-mortar administrative service centers[72] In addition, local

management (管理创新), service (服务创新), cooperation (合作创新), and governance (治理创新) occur 114, 61, 36 and 7 times, respectively, in these policy documents. They argue that these innovations are crucial to ensure that technology can be effectively integrated in the Government Online-Offline Shanghai. See: Chen, Z., Li, Z. and Wu, J., 2022. Digital Government Construction as Combinational Innovation: The Case of the "Government Online-Offline Shanghai" [作为组合式创新的数字政府建设 - 基于上海 "一网通办" 的案例分析]. *Comparative Economic and Social Systems* [经济社会体制比较], 2(220), p. 137. See also: Ding, Y. and Ye, Z., 2021. Research on Government Service Reform from the Perspective of "Seamless Government Theory": the Case of the "Government Online-Offline Shanghai" ["无缝隙政府理论" 视角下政府政务服务改革研究 - 以上海 "一网通办" 为例]. *Symposium* [经验交流], 9(371), pp. 61–62.

[71] The main standards include: *Service Specifications for the "Government Online-Offline Shanghai" Government Services* [政务服务 "一网通办" 业务规范], DB31/T1113-2018, which contains the requirements for project management, process optimization, data exchange and sharing, channels for the provision of administrative services, information disclosure, etc.; *Technical Specifications for the Whole Integrated Process of the Online Service Platform "Government Online-Offline Shanghai" for Government Services Part 1: Access to the Unified Acceptance Platform* [政务服务"一网通办" 全流程一体化在线服务平台技术规范 第1部分: 统一受理平台接入], DB31/T 1106.1-2018; *Technical Specifications for the Construction of the Electronic Certificate Databases of the "Government Online-Offline Shanghai"* [政务服务"一网通办"电子证照库建设技术规范], DB31/T1107-2018; and *Technical Specifications for Electronic Document Filing Management of "Government Online-Offline Shanghai" for Government Services* [政务服务"一网通办"电子文件归档管理技术规范], DB31/T 1152-2019.

[72] Shanghai Administration for Market Regulation, 2021. *Government Online-Offline Shanghai Specification for Construction and Operation of Administrative Service Centers* ["一网通办" 政务服务中心建设和运行规范], DB31/T 862-2021. This standard contains

standards require to comply with national standards on information security.[73] These standards do not explicitly refer to AI, but they regulate several aspects that are relevant for the implementation of AI technologies, from data and information security to the technical specifications for the provision of administrative services on the GOS platform. Compliance with the relevant standards is verified by experts during the project establishment, procurement, and acceptance phases (SHZFi). In addition, Shanghai INESA, the general contractor of the GOS project, has created a list of certified suppliers that comply with such standards (3INESA). This approach based on standards and certified suppliers is helping the efficient integration of AI in the GOS system because technology companies know from the start what are the technical requirements, and can adapt their solutions to the needs of the GOS platform. This makes the approval process faster, and ensures the replicability of the GOS system and related AI technologies at all administrative levels. This standardized approach also creates a pool of vendors that have experience in providing AI solutions for the GOS system (3INESA), and thus they can possibly compensate for some deficiencies in organizational-level capacities, as discussed shortly.

Finally, Shanghai's **political capacity to create and sustain support for the deployment of the Government Online-Offline Shanghai has led to the widespread use of AI in administrative services in the municipality via this digital platform**. Since its announcement in March 2018, the Government Online-Offline Shanghai has been elevated to a political priority of the Shanghai Party and municipal leadership.[74]

very detailed indications on informatization management (信息化管理), knowledge base management (知识库管理), and information security, among others.

[73] For instance: Information security technology—Information system security management requirements (GB/T 20269-2006, 信息安全技术-信息系统安全管理要求); Information security technology—Basic security technical requirements for networks (GB/T 20270-2006, 信息安全技术-网络基础安全技术要求); Information security technology—Common security techniques requirement for information system (GB/T 20271-2006, 信息安全技术-信息系统通用安全技术要求); and Information technology—Security techniques—Guidelines for the practice of information security control (GB/T 22081-2016, 信息技术 安全技术 信息安全控制实践指南). Source: Shanghai Administration for Market Regulation, 2021 (cit.), p. 7.

[74] CPC News, 2018. Li Qiang: The "Government Online-Offline Shanghai" Is the Key Link for a First-Class Business Environment [李强: "一网通办" 是一流营商环境关键环节]. *CPC News* [中国共产党新闻网], 6 July, http://cpc.people.com.cn/n1/2018/0706/c64094-30130775.html.

Subsequently, the Shanghai government has been regularly emphasizing the political importance of the project.[75] In addition, the work plans for the development of the Government Online-Offline Shanghai every year reiterate the attention of the municipal leadership to this initiative (Table 5.3), and they explicitly call for district and department leaders to implement the municipal plans for the development of the GOS.[76] The capacity of the Shanghai leadership to gain political support for the Government Online-Offline Shanghai also benefits from the focus on improving public service provision emphasized by the national authorities since the XVIII Party Congress (2012–2017), which called for "streamlining administration, delegating power, and optimizing government services[77]" ("简政放权、放管结合、优化服务").

This high-profile political support has resulted in high rates of adoption among government agencies in the municipality. When the Government Online-Offline Shanghai was launched on 1 July 2018, it already connected 46 government departments, 16 district-level and 220 subdistrict-level administrative service centers (Suiyi, 2021). The number of government departments joining the GOS platform has then increased

[75] Yicai, 2020. Ying Yong: This Year, We Will Continue to Promote the "Government Online-Offline Shanghai" to Make Service Applications as Convenient as "Online Shopping" [应勇: 今年继续推动 "一网通办", 让办事像 "网购" 一样方便]. *Yicai* [第一财经], 20 January, https://www.yicai.com/news/100474397.html; Sina Finance, 2022. Accelerate the Restoration of Market Expectations, Boost Development Confidence, and Strengthen New Momentum for Development! Li Qiang Thoroughly Visited and Investigated the Situation of Companies [加快修复市场预期、提振发展信心、壮大发展新动能!李强深入企业大走访大排查]. *Sina Finance* [新浪财经], https://finance.sina.com.cn/china/gncj/2022-06-22/doc-imizirau9996281.shtml.

[76] For instance, the 2018 work plan states that "[t]he main leaders of all districts and relevant departments, as the first responsible persons, should strengthen organizational leadership and deployment coordination" [各区, 各相关部门主要领导作为第一责任人, 要加强组织领导和部署协调]. The 2021 work plan states that "[a]ll departments [must] strongly support grassroots reform and innovation, respect grassroots initiatives, encourage grassroots pilots, and promote the transformation of relevant experience into city-wide standards. Financial departments at all levels shall ensure funds as needed, and support the construction of key projects of the 'Government Online-Offline Shanghai'" [各部门大力支持基层改革创新, 尊重基层首创, 鼓励基层试点, 推动相关经验转化为全市标准。各级财政部门按需做好资金保障, 支持 "一网通办" 重点项目建设].

[77] China Central Government, 2019. Promoting the Reform of "Streamlining Administration, Delegating Power and Optimizing Government Services": Connotation, Application, and Trend [推进 "放管服" 改革: 内涵、作用和走向]. *China Central Government* [中华人民共和国中央人民政府], 31 July, http://www.gov.cn/xinwen/2019-07/31/content_5417514.htm.

to 55. The ability of Shanghai to create political support for the use of the GOS can also be inferred by the fact that all district governments in the municipality are actively implementing this e-government platform in their jurisdictions (Table 5.4). Moreover, some districts are also particularly willing to experiment with new AI functions and applications for administrative services (SHZFi), as required by the municipal work plans.[78] For instance, the "Suishenban" App of Songjiang District introduced an AI application that leverages data mining to facilitate inpatient claims settlements for work-related injuries. This application has been considered successful, and the municipal government encouraged other districts to develop similar solutions.[79] Pudong New Area introduced an AI-based service called "smart handling" (智能办), which leverages AI technologies to assist companies in all stages of service provision, from the AI-enabled filling of forms to the automated verification of the submitted materials. The "smart handling" has also been indicated as a best practice that other districts should emulate.[80] Jing'an District has introduced AI solutions for the automatic generation of application materials based on user portraits (用户画像) and guided questions and answers, and a "smart pre-review" (智能预审) system that can automatically correct

[78] See the quotes from the *Working points for deepening the reform of the "Government Online-Offline Shanghai" in Shanghai in 2020* and the *Working points for comprehensively deepening the reform of the "Government Online-Offline Shanghai" in Shanghai in 2021* (Table 6.3).

[79] Songjiang District People's Government, 2021. Songjiang District Achieved Remarkable Results in Promoting the Reform of the "Government Online-Offline Shanghai"—Online Services Resemble Online Shopping, Offline Services Are Delivered at the Door [松江区推进 "一网通办"改革成效显著—线上办事如网购 线下服务到门口], 21 October, https://www.songjiang.gov.cn/xwzx/001001/20211021/aa3786a9-0bda-4916-805e-4a399733e3b2.html.

[80] Youshuzheng, 2022. One Picture to Understand: The "Smart Handling" Being Promoted in Various Places Turned Out to Be an Invention Patent of Pudong? [一图读懂 | 各地在推的 "智能办" 竟然是浦东的发明专利?]. *Youshuzheng* [有数政], 26 May, https://mp.weixin.qq.com/s/6Rg_1CumAWLNmEor6F0IAw; Sohu, 2021. Pudong's New Model of "Smart Handling of Government Affairs" Was Launched, and the Approval Rate Exceeded 98% [浦东 "政务智能办" 新模式上线 审批一次通过率超过百分之九十八]. *Sohu* [搜狐], 21 March, https://www.sohu.com/a/456566941_162758; Shanghai Government, 2021. Pudong Will Create a New Model of the "Government Online-Offline Shanghai" [浦东将打造 "一网通办" 新模式], 21 October, https://www.shanghai.gov.cn/nw4411/20211021/f34cd0398b6e4a11b582cf78b45561ee.html.

wrong information and fill in the application forms for selected administrative services, among others.[81] Other districts also report cases of local experiments with the Government Online-Offline Shanghai (see, for instance, the articles on Changning, Fengxian, and Putuo in Table 5.4).

The capacity of Shanghai to obtain political support for the Government Online-Offline Shanghai is important because there are two main factors that could create opposition to the adoption of this e-government platform. First, joining the GOS can be onerous and complex for public agencies, and this generates various forms of resistance that can be overcome only if there is clear political endorsement for the project[82] (SHZFi). As noted, district governments are required to operate and maintain the district-level extranets, e-government clouds, Big Data Centers, and GOS subsystems that support the operations of the Government Online-Offline Shanghai. District governments are also responsible for coordinating the deployment of the GOS under their jurisdictions (e.g., collect data from district and subdistrict agencies, ensure the diffusion of the GOS system, promote local applications, etc.). Moreover, government organizations and administrative service centers at each level are also required to create protocols and systems for data sharing, to upgrade their facilities to integrate online and offline activities and make efficient use of the functions of the Government Online-Offline Shanghai, or to meet the standards for the construction and operations of the offline administrative centers mentioned earlier. In short, while the GOS system is helping to reduce the workload of government agencies and increase their efficiency in the provision of administrative services, it is a complex project that requires that public agencies invest significant financial, human, and time resources.

Second, the resistance to the adoption of the Government Online-Offline Shanghai could also stem from the fact that the GOS platform makes supervision and inspection very intrusive, allowing a high level of scrutiny that is frequently opposed by government agencies (SHZF;

[81] Tencent Net, 2021 (cit.). See also: Shanghai Government, 2021. "Government Online-Offline Shanghai" in Jing'an: Online Speed, Offline Warmth, Smart Services Do Not Close ["一网通办" 在静安: 线上有速度、线下有温度, 智能服务不打烊], 9 December, https://www.shanghai.gov.cn/nw4411/20211209/55cd403f9f2f4983a8889821f649b231.html.

[82] In the words of Shanghai Zhuofan: "体系过于复杂. [...] 很多工作推动阻力很大, 也需要有明确的依据来做支撑".

Table 5.4 Implementation of the Government Online-Offline Shanghai in the 16 districts of Shanghai

Baoshan District: The "Government Online-Offline Shanghai" turns three! Let's take a look at some of the results in Baoshan ["一网通办" 三岁啦!一起来看宝山的这些成果], https://www.shbsq.gov.cn/shbs/bsdt/20211018/322813.html	**Jinshan District**: The "Government Online-Offline Shanghai" in Jinshan: these "intelligent" systems make government services more convenient, accurate, and efficient ["一网通办"在金山: 这些"智能"系统让政务服务更便捷精准高效], https://jinshan.gov.cn/ywdt-zhxx/20211122/824058.html
Changning District: Shanghai Changning: the "Government Online-Offline Shanghai" has brought these benefits to the lives of citizens [上海长宁: "一网通办" 为居民的生活带来了这些便利], http://sh.wenming.cn/cnwmw/cn_yw/202110/t20211018_6206086.htm	**Minhang District**: "Government Online-Offline Shanghai, in Minhang it's easy"! From today, all services have one single entry point, convenient! ["一网通办, 闵行好办" !今后办事都进一扇门, 方便!] https://sghexport.shobserver.com/html/baijiahao/2021/05/26/443924.html?sdkver=93de1a00
Chongming District: The "Government Online-Offline Shanghai" makes services for companies even more convenient ["一网通办" 让企业办事更便捷], https://www.shcm.gov.cn/xwzx/002003/20211025/ecdef4f5-1134-4934-a490-c0c97224558f.html	**Pudong New Area**: Shanghai Pudong continues to optimize the "Government Online-Offline Shanghai" to improve the level of government services [上海浦东新区持续优化 "一网通办" 提升政务服务能级], https://www.saac.gov.cn/daj/c100198/202201/7b30b552f6b64e52b127e77c3f407521.shtml
Fengxian District: The "Government Online-Offline Shanghai" in Fengxian district is further upgraded, the model of "integrating the two clients" makes applying for services even more convenient [奉贤区 "一网通办" 再升级 "两端融合" 模式让办事更便捷], https://www.fengxian.gov.cn/shfx/dxal/20211227/4318.html	**Putuo District**: Easily reach the full virtual space! "Putuo Digital Government Hall" goes online! [轻松触达虚拟化全景空间! "普陀数字政务大厅" 上线啦!], https://sghexport.shobserver.com/html/baijiahao/2022/07/23/806061.html?sdkver=93de1a00

(continued)

Table 5.4 (continued)

Hongkou District: Deepening the "Government Online-Offline Shanghai", new software helps to make government services in Hongkou district "easy and fast" [深化"一网通办", 新点软件助力虹口区政务服务"好办、快办"], http://science.china.com.cn/2021-09/27/content_41686069.htm	**Qingpu District**: Continue to promote the integration of the "Government Online-Offline Shanghai" into industrial parks and residential communities, and give full play to the brand effect of "it's easy in Qingpu" [持续推进"一网通办"进园区、进社区, 切实发挥"青浦好办"品牌效应], https://www.shanghai.gov.cn/qpq/20210916/8e7982e352794f76b2ed39c85c0bd675.html
Huangpu District: Deeply promote the "Government Online-Offline Shanghai" for administrative services, build a new service model with "6+10" at the core [深入推进政务服务"一网通办"构建以"6+10"为核心的服务新模式], https://fgw.sh.gov.cn/hp/20200303/0025-40641.html	**Songjiang District**: Optimize the "Government Online-Offline Shanghai" to support the development of the district, the CPPCC in Songjiang district organizes consultation activities on key proposals [优化"一网通办"助力区域发展 松江区政协组织开展重点提案办理协商活动], https://www.shszx.gov.cn/shzx/dqzx/content/24c19d4c-5e39-4d3a-af33-3f2bf3947c80.html
Jiading District: From "two-way rush" to "one click" approval, the "Government Online-Offline Shanghai" in Jiading again realizes the "zero visit" [从"双向奔赴"到"一键式"审批, 嘉定"一网通办"再现"零跑动"], https://www.cnr.cn/shanghai/qqlb/20211119/t20211119_525665232.shtml	**Xuhui District**: Comprehensively promote the "zero difference acceptance" of online and offline applications under the "Government Online-Offline Shanghai" [全面推进"一网通办"线上线下"零差别受理"], https://fgw.sh.gov.cn/xh/20200303/0025-40709.html
Jing'an District: Shanghai deepens the reform of the "Government Online-Offline Shanghai", the satisfaction rate at government affairs service counters reaches 99.78% [上海静安深化"一网通办"改革, 政务窗口好评率99.78%], https://www.jiemian.com/article/4269994.html	**Yangpu District**: Services updated in the "Government Online-Offline Shanghai" of Yangpu, citizens can apply for services even more conveniently [杨浦"一网通办"服务上新 市民办事更加便捷], https://www.shanghai.gov.cn/nw15343/20211021/e6dd2a3a3aa84feab0afa3db38403771.html

SDECi). The Government Online-Offline Shanghai embeds a supervision system that monitors government activities during and after the provision of administrative services. This supervision system was created in compliance with the "double randomness, one disclosure" (双随机, 一

公开) inspection policy launched by the State Council in 2015.[83] All matters that are subject to supervision are linked to the "comprehensive supervision platform" (综合监管平台) built within the GOS system. By aggregating all relevant data, this "comprehensive supervision platform" strengthens the inspections across departments and districts. In addition, almost all activities leave digital footprints on the backend of the GOS platform, including information on handling progress, service evaluation, or the division of responsibilities for processing administrative services between different agencies. As data are shared between government agencies and the activities of public organizations become more easily traceable, the GOS reduces information asymmetry between upper and lower levels of government, facilitating inspections and supervision (Suiyi, 2021).

Limitations

Local experts have identified some possible limitations to the deployment of AI in the public sector via the Government Online-Offline Shanghai. Although Shanghai's operational and political capacities have resulted in the efficient integration and widespread use of AI applications for administrative services, interviewees observe that there are still **varying degrees of AI assimilation in the activities of the government agencies** that join the Government Online-Offline Shanghai. These differences are mostly related to two ancillary aspects of the GOS platform. The first difference is the development of the district-level applications for administrative services mentioned earlier. While all districts are actively implementing the GOS in their jurisdictions (Table 5.4), some districts are proving more capable than others to develop their own AI solutions for administrative services (3INESA, SHZFi). These localized solutions expand the set of standardized AI applications offered by the Government Online-Offline Shanghai. If these experiments are deemed successful by the municipal government, they may be later extended to the whole

[83] CPC Shanghai Committee and Shanghai Municipal Government, 2018 (cit.), section 5, par. 2; Shanghai Municipal Government, 2019 (cit.), art. 37, in original: "全面推行 '双随机、一公开'监管". The "double randomness, one disclosure" consists of randomly selecting inspection targets during the supervision process, randomly selecting the law enforcement inspectors, and disclosing the results of these inspections and investigations to the public in a timely manner. See: Baidu Baike [百度百科], https://www.baike.com/wikiid/6165050202305102534?prd=mobile&view_id=w0ioatpd4ls00.

GOS platform. However, the absence or paucity of district-specific applications does not reduce the number of services that citizens or companies can apply to via the GOS platform, nor it affects the fundamental operations of the Government Online-Offline Shanghai. Interviewees argue that the differences in district-level applications are mostly due to analytical capacity. They note that district-level Big Data Centers, which are mainly responsible for developing these technical solutions, have similar operational resources (e.g., data, digital infrastructure, access to companies). However, some district governments have clear objectives about how they want to use AI in administrative services, while others do not, and not all district governments are able to identify how AI technologies can help them to improve the provision of administrative services (3INESAi, SHZFi).

The second difference in the degree of AI assimilation in administrative services is related to the availability of intelligent equipment in the brick-and-mortar services centers at each administrative level. Such equipment includes service desks (政务服务工作台) that use AI models to extract structured information from application materials and other AI technologies that support civil servants in data collection and processing document submissions. It also includes the smart self-service kiosks (自助服务终端) that allow applicants to access their digital records, automatically fill in application forms and prepare other materials before going to the service counters, or complete service applications autonomously.[84] The lack of this smart equipment does not hinder the operations of the GOS platform. As noted, by connecting to the Government Online-Offline Shanghai to perform their activities, each administrative service center is supported by the same set of fundamental AI applications that make their work more efficient. To connect and use the GOS platform, government agencies only need a standard computer connected to the

[84] For instance, the smart service desks use machine learning to automatically sort digital documents by type, and leverage a combination of Big Data and AI to extract structured information from application materials, automatically comparing and verifying their contents against preset rules. The smart self-service kiosks use facial recognition technology to confirm the identity of the user by comparing her face with the picture of the ID card stored in the municipal database. These kiosks also deploy smart voice and video assistance to guide users through the application process, or use OCR technology and machine learning to automatically pre-check (预审) the validity of the documents submitted by the applicants, among others. Source: Shanghai Zhuofan product brochures, on file with the author.

Internet, a printer, a high-quality OCR-based scanner, a QR code scanner, a webcam, and an ID card/social insurance card reader. The absence of smart desks and self-service kiosks does not reduce the quantity of administrative services provided or the capacity of government service centers to use the functions of the unified e-government platform; it only reduces the efficiency of service provision as it may take longer to complete service applications[85] (SHZFi, 3INESA). Differences in the dotation of smart equipment are mostly due to operational capacity. In general, subdistricts, towns, and townships have less financial, human, and technological resources than organizations at higher level of governments, affecting their ability to purchase and deploy smart equipment for the provision of administrative services[86] (SHZFi, 3INESA, AISPi).

At the time of this writing, the varying degrees of AI assimilation in the activities of the government agencies are not resulting in the uneven provision of administrative services, because such differences are mostly related to ancillary aspects of the Government Online-Offline Shanghai. Nonetheless, acknowledging the varying degrees of AI integration is important because they reveal analytical and operational capacity deficiencies at the organizational level (e.g., district Big Data Centers, administrative service centers in subdistricts), which must be taken into account if the benefits of AI-based administrative services are to be universalized through the public sector (Chapter 6). On the other hand, these limitations in analytical and operational capacities are mitigated by an approach that promotes the technical standardization of the GOS platform. As noted, the standardization of technical requirements and workflows of the Government Online-Offline Shanghai requires that AI solutions can be replicated across different public agencies at different administrative levels. This creates a pool of technology suppliers that have experience in providing standardized, replicable AI tools for administrative services, and can help public organizations in districts and

[85] WeChat conversation with Shanghai Zhuofan (SHZF), 4 June 2022. In original: "服务窗口主要是用普通电脑, 加通用设备: 打印机、高拍仪、扫码枪摄像头等等, 和部分专用设备: 身份证/社保卡读卡器, 接入到横向的政务服务外网 [...]. 理论上自助服务只是一网通版的其中一个渠道, 一种客户端的形式, 没有的话不影响网点的业务办理。只是服务持续时间和效率会下降而已".

[86] A search on the public procurement website of Shanghai (上海公共资源交易平台, https://www.shggzy.com/) using the keywords "AI" (人工智能) and "Government Online-Offline Shanghai" (一网通办) confirms that most purchases of equipment for the GOS platform are at the municipal or district levels (last accessed on 28 June 2022).

subdistricts to devise and implement AI solutions that are aligned with the requirements of the unified e-government platform, compensating for their analytical and operational shortcomings (AISPi). This interpretation is corroborated by Shanghai INESA, who explains that his company provides a complete service to government service centers, from design to implementation and training (3INESA). Similarly, Shanghai Zhuofan says that his company helps government agencies to design technical solutions suitable to their conditions and resources, providing training to civil servants and after-sales assistance (SHZF).

A second limitation to the deployment of AI in the public sector via the Government Online-Offline Shanghai is the persistence of **data barriers between government agencies**. These barriers are generated by the operational and political capacity deficits of some organizations participating in the GOS platform. Operational factors are related to the existence of "systems within the system" that can hinder data sharing across government agencies. As explained by Shanghai Zhuofan: "Over the years, some government agencies in charge of administrative processes (审批单位) – like the Shanghai Administration for Market Regulation, the Public Security Bureau, Tax Bureau or the Human Resources and Social Security Bureau – have created their own service systems (业务系统). We call these systems 'vertical systems' (垂直) because they are not cross-department systems. [...] We are still in the phase where both [standalone and cross-department] systems exist side by side, or where some departments use their standalone special networks [...] to provide services" (SHZFi). Political capacity deficits are related to the low level of support for data sharing in some public organizations, which are still reluctant to share their data, resulting in the persistence of "information islands" (Suiyi, 2021; SHZFi, SDECi).

At the time of this writing, there is no evidence suggesting that data barriers are hampering the deployment of the Government Online-Offline Shanghai or its AI applications: the number of AI-based services on the e-government platform continues to expand, and the efficiency in public service delivery is constantly improving (Sect. 5.2.1.3). Moreover, Shanghai is actively addressing the problem of data barriers. The municipal government is progressively connecting all government departments to the unified government cloud and government extranet, eliminating duplicates and solving problems of data sharing (SHZFi). Government agencies are also mandated by law to share their data on the government cloud, and the municipality is actively promoting a policy of open government data (Chapter 4.1). Nonetheless, the problem of data barriers should not be overlooked as it indicates that obstacles in the data sharing among public organizations still exist in Shanghai.

Finally, a third limitation to the deployment of AI in the public sector via the Government Online-Offline Shanghai is related to **data privacy and security risks**. In an analysis of the GOS platform, the director of the SBDC Zhu Zongyao observed: "With the wide application of emerging technologies such as Big Data, the large concentration of data has brought new breakthroughs to the government's informatization construction; at the same time, there are also some hidden problems, and the most prominent is how to ensure the safety of data. […] The government faces a trade-off between the benefits of data concentration and the costs caused by the decline in data security".[87] Data privacy and security risks are arguably engrained in any system that makes extensive use of data and technological infrastructure like the Government Online-Offline Shanghai. At the same time, the municipality has shown the analytical capacity to identify such risks, as demonstrated by the work plans for the implementation of the GOS.[88] These documents state that the municipality will strengthen information security management and improve the overall security of the e-government platform, and will establish a "security test, warning, and emergency response system" (安全检测预警和应急响应机制) to guard against attacks, intrusions, and sabotage of the Government Online-Offline Shanghai, as well as to prevent

[87] Zhu, Z., 2021. Government Affairs Graph: Framework Logic and Its Theoretical Interpretation—Based on the Practice of the "Government Online-Offline Shanghai" in Shanghai [政务图谱: 框架逻辑及其理论阐释 — 基于上海 "一网通办" 的实践]. *E-goverment* [电子政务], 4(220), p. 49. In original: "随着大数据等新兴技术的广泛应用, 数据的大集中为政府的信息化建设带来了新的突破口, 但同时也潜藏着一些问题, 最为突出的便是如何确保数据的安全. […] 政府面临着数据集中的收益与数据安全下降导致的成本之间的权衡".

[88] See for instance: Shanghai Municipal Government, 2019. *Working Points for Promoting the "Government Online-Offline Shanghai" in Shanghai in 2019* (cit.), articles 43 and 45; Shanghai Municipal Government, 2020b. *Working Points for Deepening the Reform of the "Government Online-Offline Shanghai" in Shanghai in 2020* (cit.), section 2, par. 3, point 6; *Working points for comprehensively deepening the reform of the "Government Online-Offline Shanghai" in Shanghai in 2021* (cit.), art. 28; Shanghai Municipal Government, 2022. *Working Points for Comprehensively Deepening the Reform of the "Government Online-Offline Shanghai" in Shanghai in 2022* (cit.), section 5, par. 1, 2, and 6.

accidents that could affect its normal operations.[89] Shanghai will also reinforce the protection of personal privacy, refine public data management and the information security protection system.[90] In addition, Shanghai has shown the operational capacity to address these risks. The Shanghai Municipal Big Data Center implements various advanced measures to ensure the secure use of government data, and it sets similar requirements for the district-level Big Data Centers (Sect. 5.2.1.1). Technical solutions to ensure data privacy and security include physical isolation, virus protection, encryption and desensitization, data backup, identity authentication, access rights, blockchain, and other technical means.[91] But threats to data privacy and security are always latent, as demonstrated by the data leak of the Shanghai police department that was revealed in July 2022.[92]

Implications of the Government Online-Offline Shanghai for Public Service Provision

By leveraging municipal-level policy capacities, Shanghai is promoting the effective, integrated, and widespread use of AI in the public sector via the Government Online-Offline Shanghai, fostering the assimilation of AI technologies into the provision of administrative services. The strengths of this policy initiative in deploying AI in the public sector are summarized as follows:

[89] Shanghai Municipal Government, 2019. *Working Points for Promoting the "Government Online-Offline Shanghai" in Shanghai in 2019* (cit.), articles 43 (加强信息安全管理, 全面提升平台安全防护能力) and 45 (对攻击、侵入和破坏政府网站的行为以及影响政府网站正常运行的意外事故进行防范). A similar focus on data security is reiterated by the other policy documents that regulate the implementation of the GOS platform: Shanghai Municipal Government, 2020b. *Working Points for Deepening the Reform of the "Government Online-Offline Shanghai" in Shanghai in 2020* (cit.), section 2, par. 3, point 6.

[90] Shanghai Municipal Government, 2021. *Working Points for Comprehensively Deepening the Reform of the "Government Online-Offline Shanghai" in Shanghai in 2021* (cit.), art. 28. Data privacy is also mentioned in: Shanghai Municipal Government, 2022. *Working Points for Comprehensively Deepening the Reform of the "Government Online-Offline Shanghai" in Shanghai in 2022* (cit.), section 5, par. 1 and 2.

[91] Zhu, 2021 (cit.), p. 49.

[92] Xiong, Y., Ritchie, H. and Gan, N., 2022. Nearly One Billion People in China Had Their Personal Data Leaked, and It's Been Online for More Than a Year. *CNN*, 6 July, https://edition.cnn.com/2022/07/05/china/china-billion-people-data-leak-intl-hnk/index.html.

- Shanghai has demonstrated the analytical capacity to ensure that AI effectively contributes to improving the provision of administrative services via the Government Online-Offline Shanghai. The municipality has designed and introduced AI applications that enhance the efficiency and convenience of public service delivery to citizens and enterprises, such as: the AI chatbot Xiao Shen; the AI applications enabling the "two exemptions from submission", the "enjoy without applying", and the "one industry, one license[93]"; or the AI applications for epidemic control mentioned at the end of this section. In addition to the AI applications designed by the municipal government, the GOS platform also leverages the analytical capacity of districts. Successful AI applications for administrative services developed and tested at the district level may be included in the municipal e-government platform.
- The Government Online-Offline Shanghai shows that Shanghai has the operational capacity to bring public sector AI applications to fruition. This is manifested in the creation of a city-wide "capability platform" that aggregates and coordinates the resources and skills needed to implement AI-based administrative services in practice. Shanghai is leveraging the resources of the municipal AI ecosystem to efficiently develop and implement AI applications for the provision of administrative services, and via the Government Online-Offline Shanghai it has integrated such applications into the activities of government agencies in order to support their core operations.
- Shanghai has the political capacity to create and sustain support for the deployment of the Government Online-Offline Shanghai. This is instrumental in achieving high rates of adoption among government

[93] The "one industry, one license" system integrates multiple licenses and certificates involved in a given industry (e.g., business licenses, hygiene certificates, etc.) into a "comprehensive license" (综合许可证), significantly simplifying the approval procedures. It uses AI technologies like OCR, NLP, and machine learning for the automatic classification and examination of a large number of licenses and materials, and RPA systems to facilitate data sharing between government departments, among others. See: Sina, 2021. Shanghai: Digital Empowerment of the Reform of the "One Industry, One License", the "Government Online-Offline Shanghai Launches a Dedicated Service Column [上海: 数字赋能 "一业一证" 改革 "一网通办" 开通服务专栏]. *Sina Kandian* [新浪看点], 28 April, http://k.sina.com.cn/article_6145283913_m16e49974902001cu45.html.

agencies, leading to the diffusion of AI in public sector activities. The GOS platform connects 55 government departments, 16 district-level administrative service centers, 7 administrative centers in the development zones, 220 subdistrict-level service acceptance centers, and more than 1,200 service points. Through this network, Shanghai is fostering the widespread use of AI in the provision of administrative services in the municipality, reaching the majority of the population.

The deployment of AI in administrative services via the Government Online-Offline Shanghai is also facing some limitations. These include varying degrees of AI assimilation in government organizations, the persistence of data barriers, and concerns about data privacy and security. However, the Shanghai government has already taken the initiative to address many of these problems, and there are no indications that they are hampering the development of the Government Online-Offline Shanghai or the deployment of AI in administrative services. On the contrary, evidence indicates that the GOS: (i) is improving the *efficiency* of administrative service provision; (ii) has become a catalyst for the *continuous integration* of AI in administrative services in Shanghai; and (iii) is *extending the reach* of AI-enabled administrative services to the majority of citizens. These three major implications for public service provision are examined below.

First, the Government Online-Offline Shanghai is **improving the efficiency of administrative service provision**. In 2021, the rate of administrative services that were processed entirely online reached 69.3%.[94] In addition, more than 320 administrative services could be completed in only one visit to the administrative service centers, without submitting any paper document (SHFDI, 2021). By combining online and offline activities, the GOS platform on average reduced the time needed to process administrative services by 59.8%, and lowered the number of documents required for administrative procedures by 52.9% (SHFDI, 2021). In addition, since 2021 a group of 27 administrative services that are considered particularly important to citizens and companies—such as medical expenses, childbirth documents, tax compliance, and low-rent housing

[94] China Central Government, 2022 (cit.).

applications (廉租房申)—can now be applied for in one unified administrative process, known as "single thing" ("一件事"). On average, this unified process reduced the number of procedures (平均实现减环节) by 70%, reduced the processing time by 58%, lowered the number of documents required by 77%, and reduced the number of visits to government administrative centers needed to complete each application by 72%.[95] The efficiency gains brought by the GOS platform continue to expand. At the end of October 2023, the number of administrative services under the "single thing" unified process reached 55 items across the "individual" (服务个人), "corporate" (服务企业) and "miscellaneous" (综合服务) categories. Moreover, 13 new services in the "individual" category are being trialed by the districts of Pudong, Changning, Hongkou, Baoshan, Jiading, and Yangpu, among others.[96]

This enhanced efficiency is also documented by national statistics. According to the *Investigation and evaluation report on the integrated government service capacity of provincial governments and key cities (2021)*, Shanghai ranked first in China with a score of 95.38.[97] This is the best result achieved by the municipality since the introduction of this evaluation. In 2018, Shanghai ranked 15th, and it then rose rapidly to the fifth place in 2019 and second place in 2020, finally reaching the top spot in 2021. Local commentators highlight that this upward trajectory completely coincides with the development of the Government Online-Offline Shanghai, arguing that the platform is achieving concrete efficiency gains.[98] Improved efficiency has also resulted in the

[95] Ibid.

[96] Government Online-Offline Shanghai website, https://zwdt.sh.gov.cn/govPortals/column/ot/detail.html?tabIndex=0, last accessed on 30 October 2023. The services currently trialed by district governments further corroborate the considerations made earlier about the role of district-level GOS subsystems in testing applications that may later be extended to the municipal platform.

[97] Central Party School (National School of Administration) E-Government Research Center, 2021. Investigation and Evaluation Report on the Integrated Government Service Capacity of Provincial Governments and Key Cities (2021) Is Released ["省级政府和重点城市一体化政务服务能力调查评估报告 (2021)" 发布], *Central Party School (National School of Administration) E-Government Research Center* [中央党校 (国家行政学院)电子政务研究中心], 26 May, http://zwpg.egovernment.gov.cn/art/2021/5/26/art_1329_6339.html.

[98] NetEase, 2021. Behind the "Government Online-Offline Shanghai" | Shanghai Municipal Big Data Center: There Is Nothing "Difficult to Do" in Shanghai [走进 "一网

high rates of satisfaction of individuals and enterprises. In 2021, the platform achieved an approval rate of 99.7% (SHFDI, 2021). In October 2023, the service ratings published on the GOS website reported 92.85 million feedbacks indicating a high level of user satisfaction (非常满意), with positive ratings of the platform equal to 99.97% of the comments registered since 29 October 2019.[99]

Second, through the Government Online-Offline Shanghai, **AI applications for administrative services continue to expand and have become increasingly integrated in the provision of citizen services**. In December 2021, the number of services provided via the GOS platform was 3,458 items,[100] covering the most relevant needs in the lives of individuals and companies. In October 2023, this figure increased to 3,668 items.[101] In addition, at the height of the Covid-19 pandemic in China in February 2020, the "Suishenban" App introduced the "health QR code" (健康码), called "Suishenma" (随申码) in Shanghai. This is a contact tracing tool that gauges the probability of an individual having contracted the virus.[102] The "Suishenma" QR code has progressively become an

通办" 的背后|上海大数据中心: 在魔都没有 "难办" 的事]. *NetEase* [网易号], 18 August, https://www.163.com/dy/article/GHML2CFG0550DDYR.html.

99 Government Online-Offline Shanghai official website, https://zwdt.sh.gov.cn/govPortals/appr/apprIndex, last accessed on 30 October 2023.

100 China Central Government, 2022 (cit.).

101 Sohu, 2023 (cit.).

102 Initially developed by Internet giants Alibaba and Tencent, the "health code" is known by different names in different cities. In Shanghai, it is called "Suishenma" (随申码), and it can be accessed in real time on the "Suishenban" App as well as the App Alipay or WeChat. The health code uses self-reported travel histories and medical information, and automatically collected travel and medical data that are stored on the municipal data exchange platform managed by the SBDC. These data are provided by both government agencies and public and private companies. They include information relating to personal identity (public security offices), state of health (health system), domicile, geolocation, and digital tracking (district committees, airlines and railways, mobile phone data, digital payments, etc.). Data are then processed and merged into a dynamic QR code that can be green, yellow, or red. It indicates whether citizens have been at risk of contagion and must be quarantined (red), confined for further observation (yellow), or if they have unhindered access to public spaces (green). The result is transmitted to health authorities, allowing them to monitor compliance with the quarantine measures and implement them coercively if necessary. During the pandemic, public spaces like office buildings, public transport, or shopping malls could only be accessed with a green QR code, and the use of the health code became de facto mandatory in Shanghai. See: Kostka, G. and Habich-Sobiegalla, S., 2021. Covid-19 Contact Tracing Apps: Why They Are So Popular

integrated tool that Shanghai citizens can swipe to take public transport such as buses, subways, and ferries. The "Suishenma" is also used to obtain personal information on the citizens, who can scan their QR code when they apply for public services in the administrative services centers. The Shanghai government has stated its intentions to continue with this approach that integrates several functions into one code (多卡汇一码) and extends the applications of the "Suishenma".[103] Indeed, following the Covid-19 outbreak of Shanghai in spring 2022, the mobile App "Suishenban" introduced two new AI applications linked to the "Suishenma". One is the "nucleic acid code" (核酸码), which was used for on-site nucleic acid sampling registration and whose results were displayed as part of the "health QR code" function. The other is the "venue code" (场所码), which had to be scanned with the Suishenban, Alipay, or WeChat mobile Apps before entering nearly every public and private venues in Shanghai in order to check the identity, health information, and latest nucleic acid test result of the visitors, and digitally trace their presence. While its public health-related functions have progressively disappeared with the retreat of the pandemic, the "Suishenma" QR code continues to be widely used for identifying citizens that apply for administrative services. In addition, in July 2023 the Shanghai government confirmed that the functions of the "Suishenma" will continue to expand both for citizens and enterprises, and the "Suishenma" QR code will become a "city code" (城市码) that further integrates AI applications in administrative services and other areas like medical services and urban transport.[104]

Third, the Government Online-Offline Shanghai is **extending the reach of AI-enabled administrative services to the majority of citizens**. As noted, 55 government departments, 16 district-level, and 220

in China. *MERICS*, 5 March, https://merics.org/en/short-analysis/covid-19-contact-tracing-apps-why-they-are-so-popular-china; Todaro, D., 2020. Tecnologia e azione pubblica in Cina: il codice sanitario individuale e le principali tendenze delle politiche digitali cinesi contemporanee [Technology and public action in China: The individual health code and the main trends in contemporary Chinese digital policies]. *IAI Papers*, 20(46), https://www.iai.it/en/pubblicazioni/tecnologia-e-azione-pubblica-cina.

103 China Central Government, 2022 (cit.). See also Table 5.3, Shanghai Municipal People's Congress, 2021 (cit.), art. 10.

104 People.cn, 2023. Shanghai Will Promote the Progressive Upgrade of the "Suishenma" to the "City Code" [上海: 将推动 "随申码" 迭代升级为 "城市码"]. *People.cn* [人民网], 10 July, http://sh.people.com.cn/n2/2023/0710/c134768-40487963.html.

subdistrict-level administrative service centers are connected to the GOS platform, in the effort to promote the seamless combination of online and offline services. Consistently, the number of users that registered to the GOS system has been growing steadily. At the end of 2018, the number of real-name registered users was around 10 million. In November 2020, the English version of the platform was launched, and more than 400,000 foreigners reportedly registered to use the platform. In October 2021, the number of real-name registered users had risen to 57 million individuals and 2.3 million companies.[105] In October 2023, this figure reached 81.46 million.[106] In addition, the number of administrative services performed via the Government Online-Offline Shanghai platform also indicates its high rates of penetration among citizens and enterprises. By the end of 2021, the number of services processed via the GOS platform reached 173,000 items daily (SHFDI, 2021). "Over 60% of government issues, for both companies and individuals, have been processed through the platform as of May [2021]", Zhu said.[107] This is double the 30% rate of 2018. By the end of 2021, the rate of government services processed by the GOS reached 77%, according to official statistics.[108] The reach of the Government Online-Offline Shanghai continues to expand. In October 2023, the number of services processed via the GOS platform amounted to 370,000 items daily, rising the rate of government services processed by the GOS further to 81.6%, according to official statistics.[109]

The potential of AI technologies to improve the efficiency of administrative service provision, the growing number and progressive integration of AI applications in the Government Online-Offline Shanghai, and the

[105] China Central Government, 2021. Shanghai: The Convenience of the "Government Online-Offline Shanghai" Penetrates the Daily Life of Citizens [上海: "一网通办"便利渗入市民日常生活]. *China Central Government* [中华人民共和国中央人民政府], 17 October, http://www.gov.cn/xinwen/2021-10/17/content_5643113.htm.

[106] Shanghai Municipal Office for Port Services, 2023. Fifth Anniversary of the Government Online-Offline Shanghai Went Online, the Real-Name Registered Users Reach 81.46 Million, the Compounded Number of Processed Services Overcomes 400 Million [上海"一网通办" 上线5周年, 实名用户已有81.46万, 累计办件超过4亿件]. *Shanghai Municipal Office for Port Services* [上海市口岸服务办公室], 27 October, https://kab.sww.sh.gov.cn/xwzx/001001/20231027/8770f881-b4ab-4605-a507-cf9e2c88c30e.html.

[107] Yang, J., 2021. Shanghai's e-Governance Platform Highlighted at WAIC. *SHINE*, 9 July, https://www.shine.cn/news/metro/2107091804/.

[108] China Central Government, 2022 (cit.).

[109] Shanghai Municipal Office for Port Services, 2023 (cit.).

extending reach of AI-based administrative services documented by the increasing number of users and their growing engagement with the GOS platform all indicate that Shanghai will continue to use artificial intelligence to enhance the provision of administrative services. This approach also enjoys the political support of the national leadership. In March 2022, the State Council restated that China would use new technologies such as Big Data, AI, and the Internet of Things to improve the level of intelligent, precise, and personalized services for enterprises and individuals. It said that China would expand applications such as QR codes and the intelligent approval of administrative processes, as well as AI-based services like the "enjoy without applying" (免申即享) or the "one code service" (一码办事), among others.[110] As AI technologies are becoming inextricably embedded in the lives and activities of Shanghai citizens and enterprises via the Government Online-Offline Shanghai, the use of AI in administrative services offers useful insights into the possible development trajectories of public sector AI applications in the municipality, as discussed in the conclusions of this book.

5.2.2 *The Single Platform for Urban Management*

The Single Platform for Urban Management (一网统管; abbr.: SPM) is another major project for digital innovation in the public sector that integrates AI technologies in its operations. Officially initiated in 2020, it consists of a **unified digital platform for urban governance** that enables the detection and coordinated management of a wide range of situations: from city-scale events, such as flood and typhoon prevention or traffic control[111]; to more localized issues, such as bikes being left in front of gates, boxes blocking fire rescue routes, and other small-scale safety risks.[112] By leveraging Big Data, Internet of Things and

[110] State Council, 2022. *Guiding Opinions of the State Council on Accelerating the Promotion of Standardization, Regularization and Facilitation of Government Services* [国务院关于加快推进政务服务标准化规范化便利化的指导意见], Guofa (2022) 5, 1 March, section 4, point 6, http://www.gov.cn/zhengce/zhengceku/2022-03/01/content_5676259.htm.

[111] Shanghai Investment Promotion Bureau, 2021 (cit.).

[112] Zhou, W., 2021. Shanghai Builds on Its Smart Approach. *China Daily*, 31 March, https://www.chinadailyhk.com/article/161931#Shanghai-builds-on-its-smart-approach; Li, J., 2020. Shanghai Xuhui Urban Operation Center Started, version 3.0 of the "Single Platform for Urban Management" Efficiently Handles Issues [上海徐汇城运

AI technologies, the Single Platform for Urban Management performs real-time monitoring of the municipality, and provides warnings against possible emergencies so that precautions can be timely taken.[113] For instance, it can provide precise weather forecasts for areas as small as one square kilometer for the coming hour, or it can regulate traffic lights based on the volume of vehicles on the roads to ensure smooth flows during peak hours.[114] The Single Platform for Urban Management is currently deployed to promote smart urban governance in **public security**, **market supervision**, **environmental protection**, **emergency response**, and **daily urban management**, the five areas prioritized by the municipal government in the policy documents examined shortly.

The Single Platform for Urban Management collects real-time data at the municipal, district, and subdistrict levels, and uses these data to support the urban governance operations of public agencies and enforcement units at all administrative levels in Shanghai. In 2021, over 1,700 types of data relevant for urban governance (e.g., weather and traffic conditions, water and electricity consumption), for a total of 39 billion data entries, were integrated into the SPM system to improve the efficiency of urban management in the municipality (Han, 2021, p. 12).[115] In June 2022, the SPM every day collected, shared, and exchanged over 1 billion data.[116] These data are gathered from surveillance cameras, traffic monitoring systems, and a network of approximately 5.1 million Internet of Things (IoT) sensors that in 2021 generated more than 34

中心启用, 3.0版 "一网统管" 高效处置一件事]. *The Paper News* [澎湃新闻], 4 November, https://www.thepaper.cn/newsDetail_forward_9847638.

113 Shi, J., 2020. Shanghai's Government Services Get Smart Upgrade. *China Daily*, 13 April, http://global.chinadaily.com.cn/a/202004/13/WS5e940de8a3105d50a3d15d53.html.

114 Zhou, 2021 (cit.).

115 See also: Shi, 2020 (cit.); Chen, R. and Wang, Y., 2021. Shanghai Digitizes Urban Management to Keep Mega City Ticking. *Yicai* [第一财经], 1 July, https://www.yicaiglobal.com/news/shanghai-digitizes-urban-management-to-keep-mega-city-ticking; SHFDI, 2021; People.cn, 2020. Shanghai Builds the "Single Platform for Urban Management" Platform to Make the City Smarter [上海建设 "一网统管" 平台, 让城市更智慧]. *People.cn* [人民网], 29 April, http://scitech.people.com.cn/n1/2020/0429/c1007-31692649.html.

116 Guomai Digital Government Network, 2022. Data Empowerment, Driving the Modernization of Governance in Megacities [数据赋能, 牵引带动超大城市治理现代化]. *Echinagov.com*, 16 June, http://www.echinagov.com/news/324985.htm.

million data items daily (Chen, 2021; Sun and Zhao, 2021). Data are also generated by the activities of the organizations connected to this unified digital platform of urban governance. These include: more than 70 government departments at the municipal and district levels (e.g., Public Security Bureau, Shanghai Meteorological Service, the Shanghai Water Authority, the Shanghai Municipal Health Commission); and 16 district-level and 215 subdistrict-level **Urban Operation Management Centers** (城市运行管理中心; abbr.: Urban Operation Centers). The Urban Operation Centers are joint command-and-control units responsible for urban governance at every administrative level in Shanghai. They are in charge of coordinating the activities of the departments, agencies, and entities involved in urban governance in their jurisdictions, such as public security bureaus, health commissions, Urban Management and Law Enforcement teams/城管人员队伍, among others.[117] By leveraging online technology to support offline activities, Shanghai seeks to "modernize the governance capabilities and governance system of a super-large city".[118] For instance, by 2025 Shanghai aims to use the Single Platform for Urban Management to improve its ability to deal with serious epidemics and public health emergencies, making the municipality one of the safest cities in terms of public health across the globe (SHFDI, 2021, p. 62).

The analysis conducted in the following paragraphs is primarily based on: Chinese-language official documents, including the municipal plans on the development of the Single Platform for Urban Management; academic articles in Chinese language; gray sources (news articles and specialized blogs); and interviews with people who have direct knowledge of the Single Platform for Urban Management and its applications, namely Shanghai Zhuofan (SHZF, a main supplier of AI technologies used in the SPM system), Shanghai INESA (3INESA, State-owned enterprise specialized in smart city development, and general contractor of the SPM project), the Shanghai Data Exchange Center (SDEC, the main open government data platform in Shanghai), and a consultant of the municipal government on AI and open data policies (AISP).

[117] CPC Shanghai Committee, Shanghai Government General Office, 2020. *Three-Year Action Plan for the Construction of the "Single Platform for Urban Management" for Urban Operation in Shanghai (2020–2022)* [上海市城市运行 "一网统管" 建设三年行动计划 (2020–2022)]. Huwei Banfa (2020) 19, 8 May, section 2, par. 2, https://www.digitalelite.cn/h-pd-1136.html.

[118] Ibid., section 1.

Project Description

The origins of the Single Platform for Urban Management in Shanghai can be traced back to 2017, when the Pudong New Area started the construction of the first smart system for urban governance in the municipality (Modaxia, 2021). This was soon followed by the construction of similar systems in Xuhui, Jing'an, Putuo, and other districts of Shanghai.[119] In early 2019, Shanghai Party Secretary Li Qiang announced that the municipality would create "one screen to view the whole area, one network to manage the whole city" (一屏观全域、一网管全城), thus making Shanghai the first locality in China to propose the creation of a comprehensive digital platform for urban management.[120] In February 2020, the construction of the Single Platform for Urban Management officially started. The goal of the SPM is to "make the city more intelligent and wiser, [and] let the masses have a deeper sense of gain, happiness and security".[121] To do so, Shanghai intends to use Internet, Big Data, artificial intelligence, and other information technologies to foster the modernization of urban governance[122] Through the Single Platform for Urban Management, Shanghai is actively integrating online and offline resources to solve urban governance problems down to the lowest administrative level, at the earliest time, with relatively minimum costs and maximum effectiveness.[123]

[119] China News Network, 2021. Shanghai "Single Platform for Urban Management" Debuts at the Digital China Construction Summit [上海"一网统管"亮相数字中国建设峰会]. *China News Network* [中信网], 26 April, https://www.chinanews.com.cn/gn/2021/04-26/9464725.shtml.

[120] Min, J., 2022. Create a New Miracle, Show a New Atmosphere, Welcome the 12th Party Congress of the Municipality [创造新奇迹 展现新气象 迎接市第十二次党大会]. *Xinmin Evening Post* [新民晚报], 16 June 2022, https://img1.xinmin.cn/xmwb/2022-06-16/50616.pdf.

[121] CPC Shanghai Committee, Shanghai Government General Office, 2020 (cit.), section 1. In original: "让城市更聪明、更智慧, 让群众更有获得感、幸福感、安全感".

[122] Shanghai Municipal Government, 2020. *Several Opinions on Further Accelerating the Construction of Smart Cities* [关于进一步加快智慧城市建设的若干意见], 10 February, section 1, par. 2, https://www.shanghai.gov.cn/nw44142/20200824/0001-44142_63566.html.

[123] CPC Shanghai Committee, Shanghai Government General Office, 2020 (cit.), section 1. See also: Guomai Digital Think Tank, 2021. Theory. Analyze the Policies and Trends of the "Single Platform for Urban Management" in Urban Governance [理论丨浅析城市治理"一网统管"的政策及趋势]. *Tencent Open Content Platform*, 21 September, https://page.om.qq.com/page/OC2_OgA-Gq1dMUBQ8o8MnfeQ0; Sohu,

The Single Platform for Urban Management is deeply interlinked with the Government Online-Offline Shanghai. In May 2022, the Shanghai Municipal People's Congress reiterated that "the municipality promotes the integrated development of the Government Online-Offline Shanghai and the Single Platform for Urban Management. Relying on Big Data resource platforms, and including data, applications and systems, it promotes the two-way integration and mutual coordination of the 'two networks' (两张网)".[124] Indeed, these "two networks" present three fundamental similarities. First, like the Government Online-Offline Shanghai, the Single Platform for Urban Management is **built upon an integrated digital architecture** designed and controlled by the municipal government. This digital architecture consists of the three layers examined earlier (Sect. 5.2.1): the government affairs extranets, the e-government clouds, and the network of Big Data Centers connected to the Big Data exchange platform. Each layer includes one municipal-level infrastructure built and operated by the municipal government, and 16 district-level infrastructures built and operated by each district government according to the standards, specifications, and requirements set by the municipality. In addition, the Shanghai government explicitly requires that the Single Platform for Urban Management forms a "six ones technical support system" (六个一技术支撑体系). This consists of: one map of urban governance items, one network for interconnection, one data lake for data collection, one cloud for the city brain (see infra), one platform for system development, and one platform for mobile applications.[125] By leveraging this unified "technical support system" and digital

2020. Xu Huili: This Is How We Understand the Relationship Between Shanghai's "Single Platform for Urban Management" and Data Elements [徐惠丽. 我们这样理解上海"一网统管"和数据要素的关系]. *Sohu* [搜狐], 20 October, https://www.sohu.com/a/427486082_657456 (at the time of the article, Ms. Xu Huili was the deputy director of the Shanghai Urban Operation Management Center examined shortly, and in March 2021 she became its director).

[124] Shanghai Municipal People's Congress, 2022. *Decision of the Standing Committee of the Shanghai Municipal People's Congress on Further Promoting and Guaranteeing the Construction of the "Single Platform for Urban Management" for Urban Operations* [上海市人民代表大会常务委员会关于进一步促进和保障城市运行"一网统管"建设的决定], (XV) 109, 24 May, art. 11, http://www.spcsc.sh.cn/n8347/n8467/u1ai246617.html. In original: "本市推进'一网通办''一网统管'融合发展, 依托大数据资源平台, 围绕数据、场景、系统, 推动'两张网'双向融合、相互协同".

[125] CPC Shanghai Committee, Shanghai Government General Office, 2020 (cit.), section 1. In original: "打造 "三级平台、五级应用" 逻辑架构, 形成

architecture, Shanghai aims to create an urban governance platform based on integrated infrastructure, standardized data, standardized operating platforms, and coordinated deployment.[126]

The second similarity with the GOS is that the operations and development of the Single Platform for Urban Management are also **coordinated and supervised by the Shanghai Government General Office** (上海市人民政府办公厅). The Shanghai General Office orchestrates the activities of the Single Platform for Urban Management in two main ways. First, it controls the **Shanghai Municipal Big Data Center** (SBDC; Sect. 5.2.1). Like in the GOS, the Shanghai Municipal Big Data Center is the operational core for data management of the whole Single Platform for Urban Management, and it can be understood as the "IT department" of the SPM system (SHZFi, AISPi). The SBDC is in charge of the collection, management, sharing, application, and security of the data resources used by the Single Platform for Urban Management. The SBDC operates the municipal Big Data exchange platform that consolidates the data on urban governance it receives from government departments and district-level Big Data Centers. The latter collect data within their jurisdictions (district government agencies, subdistricts, residential communities, etc.), and share them on the Big Data exchange platform. This coordinating role of the Shanghai Municipal Big Data Center is officially stated in the main blueprint issued by the Shanghai government for the development of the SPM platform.[127] Second, the Shanghai Government General Office also

"六个一" (治理要素一张图、互联互通一张网、数据汇集一个湖、城市大脑一朵云、系统开发一平台、移动用户一门户) 技术支撑体系". See also: Han (2021) (cit.), pp. 12–13.

[126] Shanghai Municipal Government, 2020 (cit.), section 4, point 9. See also: Zhianjun (2022a) and CESI (2022, p. 8).

[127] The *Three-year action plan for the construction of the "Single Platform for Urban Management" for urban operations in Shanghai (2020–2022)* indicates that the SBDC shall guide the construction of district-level e-government clouds according to the requirements of the Single Platform for Urban Management, creating a unified government cloud network for urban governance, and strengthening the real-time collection of urban governance data to create a solid basis for the development of urban governance systems and applications at each administrative level (attachment, section 1, points 1 and 4). The SBDC and the Shanghai Urban Operation Management Center are also required to develop an urban operation middle platform (城运中台) that integrates data, applications, and artificial intelligence, guiding the construction of urban operation platforms in districts, neighborhoods, and townships (attachment, section 2, point 10). See: CPC Shanghai Committee, Shanghai Government General Office, 2020 (cit.).

oversees the operations of the **Shanghai Urban Operation Management Center** (上海市城市运行管理中心, SUOC), which was established in March 2020 to coordinate the monitoring, analysis, and early warning of urban governance issues in the whole municipality as part of the Single Platform for Urban Management. The SUOC reports to the Administrative Approval System Reform Office(行政审批制度改革处) and the Transfer Office (职转处) of the Shanghai Government General Office (SHZFi).[128]

The third fundamental similarity with the GOS is that **the Single Platform for Urban Management also integrates online and offline activities**. The Shanghai Urban Operation Management Center coordinates a network of 16 district-level Urban Operation Centers (区级城运中心) and 215 subdistrict-level Urban Operation Centers (街镇级城运中心). These are subordinated to the SUOC, in a top-down organizational structure where higher-level Urban Operation Centers guide, supervise, and inspect the operations of lower-level Urban Operation Centers,[129] at the same time providing various forms of support to promote smart urban governance at lower levels (Zhianjun, 2022b; Sun and Zhao, 2021; see detailed analysis in Sect. 5.2.2.2). Like the administrative service centers in the GOS, the Urban Operation Centers are all connected to the SPM platform and are its physical "carriers" (载体). This organizational structure is called "three-level platforms, five-level applications[130]" (三级平台, 五级应用; Fig. 5.2). Its key features are explained below.

Subdistrict Urban Operation Centers are the "front line" of the Single Platform for Urban Management. They deal with specific urban governance problems at the grassroots level, promote the enforcement

[128] Ms. Xu Xuili (徐惠丽), director of the Shanghai Urban Operation Management Center, has been vice director of the Shanghai Government General Office from March 2020 to August 2021, when she was promoted to Deputy Secretary General of the Municipal Government [上海市人民政府副秘书长]. She continues to follow the development of smart urban governance. See for instance: https://english.shyp.gov.cn/ywb/yangpunews/20220215/403124.html.

[129] The *Three-year action plan (2020–2022)* states that the SUOC and other municipal government departments shall "establish a unified system and norms at the municipal level, and guide the working rules for Urban Operation Centers of districts and townships". CPC Shanghai Committee, Shanghai Government General Office, 2020 (cit.), attachment, art. 60. See also: Shanghai Municipal People's Congress, 2022 (cit.), art. 3, par. 1.

[130] CPC Shanghai Committee, Shanghai Government General Office, 2020 (cit.), section 1.

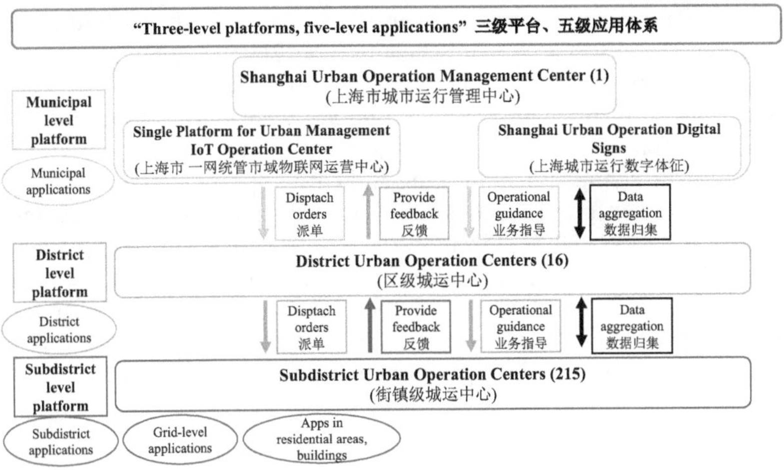

Fig. 5.2 Organizational structure of the Single Platform for Urban Management (author elaboration based on policy documents in Table 5.5 and sources provided by Shanghai Zhuofan)

of laws and regulations, and coordinate operations in subdistricts, towns, and townships.[131] Subdistrict Urban Operation Centers are responsible for management, enforcement, and inspection. They handle urban governance issues directly or report them to the district-level Urban Operation Centers. They are also the first point of collection of data that are then fed into the SPM platform. Subdistrict Urban Operation Centers distribute the orders coming from higher authorities to the relevant departments in townships and subdistricts, grid stations[132] (网格站), residential areas

[131] Shanghai People's Congress, 2022 (cit.), art. 3, point 4. In original: "乡镇、街道城市运行管理机构应当加强一线协调处置能力，依托基层综合执法、联勤联动机制，协调处置基层治理中的具体问题".

[132] The Single Platform for Urban Management has its organizational foundations in the "urban gridization management system" (城市网格化管理体系) introduced in Shanghai in 2004, one of the first cities in China to adopt this system. Urban gridization aims to improve urban management efficiency by dividing the municipality into a network of "grids", whose dimensions vary, but are on average as small as one road intersection. Grid supervisors (网格监督员) appointed by the relevant district authorities coordinate the patrolling and inspections within each grid to identify a variety of urban governance problems, from environmental issues to road maintenance or potential safety and security risks. Grid management in each district is coordinated by "urban

(社区), or property service companies (物业服务公司), according to their respective responsibilities (Zhianjun, 2022b). They are required to build a joint response and emergency team available at any time, which includes government agencies like the Public Security Bureau, the Urban Management and Law Enforcement Bureau,[133] the Market Supervision Bureau, or the Shanghai Landscaping and City Appearance Administrative Bureau.[134] Urban governance issues at the grassroots level are managed based on the "1+3+N" "gridization system", whereby: "1" indicates the municipal grid of Shanghai; "3" indicates the urban governance issues that are assigned to subdistricts authorities, which include (i) general governance (综合治理), (ii) market inspection and supervision, and non-policing issues reported through the police emergency number 110; and

grid management command and disposal centers" (城市网格化管理指挥处置中心), which dispatch relevant entities to address the reported problems and supervise their solutions. In 2015, Shanghai published the *Shanghai urban grid integrated management standard (for trial implementation)* [上海市城市网格化综合管理标准(试行)]. This document sets the technical specifications of an integrated information system for urban grid management at the municipal, district, and subdistrict levels, which has been incorporated in the "three-level platforms, five-level applications" of the SPM. For an overview of the urban gridization management system, see: Qian, G., 2018. China Under the Grid. *China Media Project*, 7 December, https://chinamediaproject.org/2018/12/07/china-under-the-grid/. For the link between the Single Platform for Urban Management and the urban gridization system, see: Liu (2021, p. 127); China Construction Journal, 2022. How to Integrate Gridization into the Modernization of Urban Governance—Taking the Exploration Path of Urban Governance in Shanghai as an Example [网格化如何融入城市治理现代化 - 以上海市城市治理探索路径为例]. *Zhihu* [知乎], 10 February, https://zhuanlan.zhihu.com/p/465630369; NetEase, 2021. Make Every Effort to Create the Single Platform for Urban Management 3.0 for Urban Operations, and Promote the Digital Transformation of Urban Governance! This Is What Jing'an Does [全力打造城市运行一网统管3.0, 推动城区治理数字化转型!静安这么干]. *NetEase* [网易号], 6 May, https://www.163.com/dy/article/G9AVB9SE0514CCT2.html.

[133] The Urban Management and Law Enforcement Bureau (城市管理综合行政执法局) is a government agency created in 2017 under the Ministry of Housing and Urban-Rural Development (住房和城乡建设部). Similarly, the Shanghai Urban Management and Law Enforcement Bureau (上海市城市管理行政执法局) is under the jurisdiction of Shanghai Housing and Urban-Rural Development and Management Commission, and it has branches in every district of the municipality (see Chapter 1).

[134] CPC Shanghai Committee, Shanghai Government General Office, 2020 (cit.), section 3, par 4.

"N" indicates the several governance issues that may arise at the grassroots level.[135]

District Urban Operation Centers perform connecting and coordinating functions.[136] They link the Urban Operation Centers at the subdistrict level with the Shanghai Urban Operation Management Center at the municipal level. They share data and relevant information between upper and lower levels of government, and convey the instructions from the municipality to urban governance agencies at the grassroots level. They are also responsible for coordinating the emergency response and daily management of urban operations in their district, and for increasing the efficiency of handling urban governance issues[137] in the five policy areas prioritized by the municipal government (i.e., emergency response, urban daily management, public security, market supervision, and environmental protection). District Urban Operation Centers collect, process, and analyze data on urban governance issues in their district, and reroute information or dispatch orders on such issues to the relevant departments based on the type of intervention required and the territorial jurisdiction (Zhianjun, 2022b). These governance issues are communicated or discovered through the various channels that feed information into the Single Platform for Urban Management, such as: the citizen service hotline 12345,[138] the urban construction service hotline 12319, each district's WeChat public account, the network of IoT sensors and surveillance cameras, grassroots inspections, and governance issues reported by the subdistrict Urban Operation Centers (Zhianjun, 2022b).

At the vertex of this organizational structure, the **Shanghai Urban Operation Management Center** formulates the management strategy

[135] CPC Shanghai Committee, Shanghai Government General Office, 2020 (cit.), section 2, par 3; attachment, point 13.

[136] Shanghai People's Congress, 2022 (cit.), art. 3, point 3. In original: "区城市运行管理机构应当加强上下联通和资源整合"; Modaxia (2021).

[137] Shanghai People's Congress, 2022 (cit.), art. 3, point 3: "提升区域城市运行日常管理和应急联动协调能力，提高城市运行综合管理事项的处置效率".

[138] The 12345 is the unified citizen service hotline, which is also used by the Government Online-Offline Shanghai. Since June 2020, the hotline has been equipped with a "smart dispatch and data analysis perception system" (智能派单和数据分析感知系统). This system serves to route the phone inquiries to the competent departments at the municipal, district and subdistrict levels, and use data analysis to understand and forecast public sentiment (CPC Shanghai Committee, Shanghai Government General Office, 2020, attachment 1, point 20).

and development plan for smart urban operations of the whole municipality in public security, market supervision, environmental protection, emergency response and management, and urban daily management. It is mandated to set standards and norms for intelligent urban governance, strengthen the monitoring, analysis, and early warning of urban operations, establish a command-and-control system based on different administrative levels and types of issues, and coordinate the joint emergency response to major emergencies.[139] The SUOC determines the logical framework (逻辑框架) of the entire Single Platform for Urban Management, formulates operational procedures, and develops AI applications for the municipal-level urban governance platform (Zhianjun, 2022a). Based on data it receives from over 70 government departments at the municipal and district level as well as from the Urban Operation Centers in districts and subdistricts, the SUOC performs real-time monitoring of the city at the macro level. It provides early warnings and forecasts about possible emergencies so that precautions can be taken, and it coordinates the management of emergency incidents.[140] It is a command-and-control center that empowers existing urban governance agencies to carry out their everyday operations according to their responsibilities, it does not replace them.

The functions and capabilities of the SUOC are continuously expanding. In October 2020, Shanghai unveiled the **Shanghai "Single Platform for Urban Management" Internet of Things Operation Center** (上海市"一网统管"市域物联网运营中心), the first city-level IoT operation center officially created in China. Under the supervision of the SUOC, the IoT Operation Center collects the data generated by IoT sensing devices at all administrative levels in Shanghai, coordinates the orderly construction of Shanghai's IoT infrastructure, and allows to monitor in real time issues ranging from smoke and gas leaks

[139] Shanghai People's Congress, 2022 (cit.), art. 3, point 2. In original: "市城市运行管理机构负责拟订全市城市运行智能化管理战略和发展规划，研究制定标准规范，加强城市运行状态监测、分析和预警，健全分层分类指挥处置体系，统筹协调重大突发事件应急联动处置".

[140] Shi, 2020 (cit.); Peng, Y., 2020. Shanghai Urban Operation and Management Center Officially Established and Operational, the Shanghai Platform for Urban Management Quickly Advances [上海市城运中心正式建设运作"一网统管"将加快推进]. *Yicai* [第一财经], 13 April, https://www.yicai.com/news/100590789.html.

to water quality, extending its reach to the level of residential communities.[141] In June 2021, the capabilities of the SUOC were further strengthened with the introduction of the **Shanghai Urban Operation Digital Signs** (上海城市运行数字体征), the first system of its kind in China. By using algorithms and AI models to analyze data collected from government departments at various levels and Urban Operation Centers in districts and subdistricts, this system offers a comprehensive, real-time view of urban operations based on over 1,000 indicators grouped into 55 categories (e.g., meteorological information, garbage disposal, traffic conditions, people flow[142]). The system examines trends in urban operations, detects potential risks in advance, and accurately gives early warning to relevant agencies, from fire departments to the neighborhood committees in residential areas.[143]

By using Urban Operation Centers as pivots to connect urban governance agencies at each administrative level, the organizational structure of the Single Platform for Urban Management efficiently distributes urban governance tasks across the municipality. "Shanghai leverages the Single Platform for Urban Management to create a five-level application system that includes the municipality, districts, subdistricts, gridded areas, and residential communities and buildings, it strengthens command coordination and on-site deployment, and through online-offline coordination realizes the efficient disposal of single issues".[144] In this "five-level application system", "[w]hen urban governance issues are discovered

[141] Chen (2021) (cit.), pp. 10–11; China News Network, 2021 (cit.); CNR, 2021. Helping Urban Governance, Shanghai Urban Operations Hall Let Numbers "Speak" [助力城市治理 上海市城运大厅让数字 "说话"]. CNR [央广网], 13 October http://www.cnr.cn/shanghai/tt/20201021/t20201021_525305143.shtml.

[142] Modaxia (2021) lists among the main indicators: actual population present in the municipality; air quality index; traffic passenger flow in the city; water supply load; and water quality. These indicators are updated in real time.

[143] NetEase, 2021. The First in the Country! Shanghai Urban Operation Digital Signs version 1.0 is online, see what it can do [国内首个!上海城市运行数字体征1.0版上线, 看看它都能干什么]. *NetEase* [网易号], 10 June, https://www.163.com/dy/article/GC4SRNLQ05506BEH.html; Xinhua, 2021. Shanghai Urban Operation Digital Signs Is Online [上海城市运行数字体征上线]. *Xinhua News*, 11 June, http://m.xinhuanet.com/sh/2021-06/11/c_1310001820.htm.

[144] Shanghai People's Congress, 2022 (cit.), art. 5. In original: "本市依托 "一网统管" 平台, 建立市、区、乡镇和街道、网格化区域、社区和楼宇五级应用体系, 加强指挥协调和现场处置, 实现线上线下协同高效处置一件事".

by the Single Platform for Urban Management platform, urban operation management agencies according to their authority shall dispatch and coordinate relevant departments and units to intervene in a timely manner".[145] In this system, Urban Operation Centers are the hubs that oversee cross-departmental coordination in urban governance in their jurisdictions. They leverage data and technology to analyze, predict, and process urban management issues, promoting the "intelligentization" of urban governance at all administrative levels,[146] under the supervision of the Shanghai municipal government. Understanding this organizational structure is important because it has direct implications for the use of AI in the Single Platform for Urban Management. First, it preserves the coordinating role of the municipal government, while also empowering lower levels of governments. As such, Shanghai can guide the development of the Single Platform for Urban Management by indicating the priority areas for the use of AI in urban governance, at the same time allowing districts and subdistricts to devise the AI solutions that best fit their conditions and capabilities. Second, by making the Urban Operation Centers the hubs for coordinating urban governance operations at each administrative level, the "three-level platforms, five-level applications" structure creates single "entry points" for the use of AI in urban management. Through the Urban Operation Centers, AI technologies are applied to various areas of urban governance, helping to integrate AI in urban operations and bringing AI applications to the grassroots level. These and other aspects are examined in the next subsection.

Strengths and Limitations in Deploying AI in the Public Sector

The Single Platform for Urban Management makes extensive use of AI technologies to optimize urban governance and urban management services in various policy areas. It is a complex, city-wide initiative that primarily relies on municipal-level policy capacities for its successful implementation. Next paragraphs examine how Shanghai is leveraging its analytical, operational, and political capacities to integrate AI in urban governance via the Single Platform for Urban Management, and how

[145] Shanghai People's Congress, 2022 (cit.), art. 5, par. 2. In original: "对依托 "一网统管" 平台发现的城市运行中的问题, 城市运行管理机构按照管理权限, 派单调度相关部门和单位及时进行处置".

[146] CPC Shanghai Committee, Shanghai Government General Office, 2020 (cit.), section 2, par. 2. See also: Xinji (2021).

municipal-level capacity interacts with the organizational capabilities of the government agencies participating in such platform. The analysis offers deeper insights into the skills and resources that determine the strengths and limitations of this policy initiative in deploying AI in the public sector, and it provides a solid basis to assess the implications of the Single Platform for Urban Management for public service provision in the municipality.

Strengths

The Single Platform for Urban Management uses AI, Big Data, IoT, and other technologies to "make the city more intelligent and wiser, [and] let the masses have a deeper sense of gain, happiness and security".[147] Leveraging AI technologies to improve urban governance in a city of nearly 25 million people extending over 6,300 Km^2 requires high levels of analytical capacity. As noted for the GOS, building an integrated, city-wide digital platform requires that the Shanghai government has the ability to align hundreds of government agencies at different administrative levels toward the achievement of the goals set by the municipality. Over the years, the Shanghai municipal government has published a number of policy documents that outline a consistent plan for the coordinated construction of the Single Platform for Urban Management. These documents set specific timelines and targets for the implementation of the SPM (e.g., strengthening the construction of IoT and smart sensors for buildings, roads, water supply, and other applications by October 2020[148]). These policy documents form a well-articulated blueprint for the development of the Single Platform for Urban Management. Importantly, since the publication of the first policy document mentioning the SPM in February 2020, Shanghai has been constantly reiterating the intention to use AI technologies in urban governance, as shown in Table 5.5.

In addition to formulating a well-articulated policy initiative that systematically plans the use of AI in urban governance, Shanghai has demonstrated **the analytical capacity to devise AI applications that can**

[147] CPC Shanghai Committee, Shanghai Government General Office, 2020 (cit.), section 1. In original: "让城市更聪明、更智慧, 让群众更有获得感、幸福感、安全感".

[148] Ibid., attachment, points 9 and 16.

Table 5.5 Policy documents for the implementation of the Single Platform for Urban Management (2020–2022)

Document (year)	*AI in the Single Platform for Urban Management*
Several opinions on further accelerating the construction of smart cities[149] (February 2020)	"Continue the construction of the city as 'one integrated chessboard', make more use of the Internet, Big Data, artificial intelligence and other information technologies, promote the innovation of urban governance systems, models, and means, and improve the level of scientificity, refinement, and intelligentization of urban management[150]" "Take data as the core resource of the 'city brain', rely on the Shanghai Municipal Big Data Center to optimize the quality of public data collection, realizing the centralized aggregation of public data [...]. Explore the construction of a digital twin city,[151] digitally simulate all the resources of the urban ecosystem, and build a digital base for the intelligent operations of the city[152]" "Build a new model of urban Internet of Things (IoT) network that integrates IoT, digital connectivity and intelligent connectivity, deploy urban neuron nodes and perception platforms, and build an 'urban neuron system' to help expand the functions and services of the 'city brain'[153]"

(continued)

149 Shanghai Municipal Government, 2020 (cit.).

150 Ibid., section 1, par. 2 "Construction Goals". In original: "坚持全市 "一盘棋、一体化" 建设, 更多运用互联网、大数据、人工智能等信息技术手段, 推进城市治理制度创新、模式创新、手段创新, 提高城市科学化、精细化、智能化管理水平".

151 The digital twin is the virtual representation of a physical object or system across its life cycle. It uses real-time data and other sources to enable learning, reasoning, and dynamically recalibrating for improved decision-making. This means creating a highly complex virtual model that is the exact counterpart (or twin) of a physical thing. See: Armstrong, M., 2020. Cheat Sheet: What Is Digital Twin? *IBM*, 4 December, https://www.ibm.com/blogs/internet-of-things/iot-cheat-sheet-digital-twin/.

152 Shanghai Municipal Government, 2020, section 2 "Coordinate and improve the 'city brain' structure", par. 3. In original: "将数据作为 '城市大脑' 的核心资源, 依托市大数据中心, 优化公共数据采集质量, 实现公共数据集中汇聚 [...]. 探索建设数字孪生城市, 数字化模拟城市全要素生态资源, 构建城市智能运行的数字底座".

153 Ibid., section 6, art. 22. In original: "打造物联、数联、智联三位一体的新型城域物联专网, 部署城市神经元节点及感知平台, 构筑 "城市神经元系统", 助力 "城市大脑" 功能拓展、服务延伸".

Table 5.5 (continued)

Document (year)	*AI in the Single Platform for Urban Management*
Guiding opinions on strengthening data governance and promoting the Single Platform for Urban Management for urban operations[154] (April 2020)	This document set the unified requirements for data governance of the Single Platform for Urban Management (Chen, 2021, cit., p. 7)
Three-year action plan for the construction of the "Single Platform for Urban Management" for urban operations in Shanghai (2020–2022)[155] (May 2020)	"Build an ecosystem of intelligent applications that can 'see everything, manage accurately, and prevent effectively', […] move from digitalization and intelligentization towards wisdom, making the city more intelligent and wiser, [and] let the masses have a deeper sense of gain, happiness and security[156]" "Through the use of modern information technologies such as Big Data, cloud computing, blockchain, artificial intelligence, and the Internet of Things, create a digital twin of the city's vital signs [生命体征], achieve comprehensive situational awareness, intelligent trend prediction, coordinated resource scheduling, and human-machine cooperation[157]" "Speed up the construction of the urban operation platforms at the municipal, district and subdistrict levels, focus on building the three major functions of applications, data, and artificial intelligence, and promote the urban operation platforms to become application hubs, command platforms and enabling carriers of the urban operation system[158]"

(continued)

154 Original title: 关于加强数据治理促进城市运行 "一网统管" 的指导意见. This policy document is mentioned by various sources. However, the author could not retrieve a copy of the document.

155 CPC Shanghai Municipal Committee, Shanghai Government General Office, 2020 (cit.).

156 Ibid., section 1. In original: "营造 '观全面、管到位、防见效' 的智能应用生态 […] 让城市更聪明、更智慧, 让群众更有获得感、幸福感、安全感".

157 Ibid., section 2 "Work structure", par. 1. In original: "通过运用大数据、云计算、区块链、人工智能、物联等现代信息技术, 对城市生命体[体征]进行数字孪生, 实现态势全面感知、趋势智能预判、资源统筹调度、行动人机协同".

158 Ibid., Section 3 "Main Tasks", par. 1. In original: "市、区、街镇要加快城运中台建设, 着重打造业务、数据和人工智能三大功能, 推动城运中台成为城运系统的应用枢纽、指挥平台和赋能载体".

Table 5.5 (continued)

Document (year)	*AI in the Single Platform for Urban Management*
	"In the development of intelligent application scenarios, encourage and support each department and institution to focus on actual problems, and to develop intelligent application scenarios[159]" "Create an expert advisory committee including specialists in Big Data, cloud computing, blockchain, artificial intelligence, Internet of Things and other IT technologies, as well as experts in urban management and social governance, that will provide high-level decision-making consultancy[160]" "Develop the first phase of the middle platform for urban operations (城运中台) that includes data, applications, and artificial intelligence[161]" "Use artificial intelligence and Big Data analysis for the smart cognition, early warning and risk assessment of major issues related to public opinion in Shanghai, preventing harmful information on the Internet[162]"
Decision of the Standing Committee of the Shanghai Municipal People's Congress on Further Promoting and Guaranteeing the Construction of the "Single Platform for Urban Management" for Urban Operations[163] (May 2022)	"The municipality will use modern information technologies such as Big Data, cloud computing, Internet of Things, blockchain, and artificial intelligence to build the 'Single Platform for Urban Management'[164]"

(continued)

[159] Ibid., Section 3, par. 6. In original: "在智能应用场景开发方面, 鼓励和支持各部门、各单位结合实际、聚焦问题, 开发智能应用场景".

[160] Ibid., Section 4, par. 1. In original: "建立由大数据、云计算、区块链、人工智能、物联网等方面互联网技术 (IT) 精英, 以及城市管理和社会治理领域专家学者等组成的专家咨询委员会, 提供高端决策咨询".

[161] Ibid., attachment, point 10. In original: "首期开发集成数据、应用、人工智能的城运中台". The notion of "middle platform" was expounded in Sect. 5.1.

[162] Ibid., attachment, point 14. In original: "通过人工智能、大数据分析技术, 实现涉沪重大舆情智能感知、预警分析与风险评估, 做好互联网有害信息防阻工作".

[163] Shanghai Municipal People's Congress, 2022 (cit.).

[164] Ibid., art. 4. In original: "本市运用大数据、云计算、物联网、区块链、人工智能等现代信息技术, 建设"一网统管"平台".

Table 5.5 (continued)

Document (year)	*AI in the Single Platform for Urban Management*
	"The municipality promotes the construction of a digital sign system [数字体征系统] for urban operations, it scientifically creates an urban operation signs index system [城市运行体征指标体系], and it relies on the Single Platform for Urban Management and an intelligent perception system to strengthen the real-time, dynamic, intelligent and accurate monitoring of the status of urban operations[165]"

effectively improve urban governance operations and urban management services. The *Several opinions on further accelerating the construction of smart cities* and the *Three-year action plan for the construction of the "Single Platform for Urban Management" for urban operations in Shanghai* not only consistently indicate five policy areas where Shanghai wants to use AI and advanced technologies to optimize urban governance[166]; they also outline some types of AI applications that can be used to promote smart urban management in each of these policy areas. In details:

- *Emergency response*: (1) "Improve the rapidity of response and the efficiency of joint disposal capabilities. [...] Carry out data analysis of urban operations, strengthen comprehensive analysis and evaluation, and enhance the monitoring, early warning, emergency response, and cross-sectoral coordination capabilities for comprehensive urban management, in order to promote efficient and unified handling [of

[165] Ibid., art. 9. In original: "本市推动建设城市运行数字体征系统, 科学设定城市运行体征指标体系, 依托"一网统管"平台和智能感知系统, 加强对城市运行状态的实时动态、智能精准监测".

[166] These areas are also reiterated in other policy documents related to the SPM. For instance, the Shanghai Development and Reform Commission calls for the SPM to "fully integrate data resources such as rail transit, road situation, public health, food safety, water and electricity, finance, market supervision, and economic and social risks". See: Shanghai Development and Reform Commission, 2020 (quoted in Chapter 3.4), section 3, paragraph 4. In original: "全面融合轨道交通、道路实况、公共卫生、食品安全、水电气、金融、市场监管、经济社会风险等数据资源".

urban governance issues][167]"; (2) "In emergency management, [...] build an intelligent early warning system for urban safety covering safe manufacturing, construction, hazardous chemical products, fire prevention, civil defense (民防), typhoon and flood prevention, public health and other areas, [...] implement a comprehensive safety supervision and intelligent comprehensive command; [...] speed up the intelligent management of emergency measures, and develop an intelligent system for the dissemination of emergency information".[168]

- *Public security*: (1) "Effectively improve the ability to utilize data, promote in-depth applications of new information technology for the monitoring and early warning of large crowds, urban security and crime repression, thus creating a national benchmark for smart policing[169]"; (2) "In social management and control, extend the achievements of smart public security construction [...]; realize smart cognition, early warning and risk assessment of major issues related to public sentiment in Shanghai; [...] effectively enhance intelligent perception functions".[170]
- *Market supervision*: "In economy and market supervision, use data resources such as market entities, social credit and financial credit for the smart forecast of market risks [...]; carry out intelligent and dynamic risk identification".[171]
- *Environment*: (1) "Strengthen the real-time acquisition, analysis, and assessment of the city's ecological and environmental protection

[167] Shanghai Municipal Government, 2020 (cit.), section 4, art. 10. In original: "提升快速响应和高效联动处置能力水平。[...] 开展城市运行数据分析, 加强综合研判, 增强城市综合管理的监控预警、应急响应和跨领域协同能力, 实现高效处置 '一件事'".

[168] CPC Shanghai Municipal Committee, Shanghai Government General Office, 2020 (cit.), section 3, par. 1. In original: "在应急管理方面, 紧盯安全生产、工程建设、危险化学品、消防、民防、防台防汛、公共卫生等, 构建智能化城市安全预警体系, [...] 实施全周期安全监管和智能化综合指挥; [...] 加快预案智能化管理, 开发智能应急信息发布系统".

[169] Shanghai Municipal Government, 2020 (cit.), section 4, art. 11. In original: "切实提高数据利用能力, 推动信息新技术在大人流监测预警、城市安防、打击犯罪等领域深度应用, 打造国内智慧警务标杆".

[170] Ibid., section 3, par. 3.2. In original: "在社会面管控方面, 放大智慧公安建设成果 [...]; 实现涉沪重大舆情智能感知、预警分析与风险评估; [...] 确实增强智能感知功能".

[171] Ibid., section 3, par. 3.3. In original: "在经济运行和市场监管方面, 应用市场主体经营、社会信用、金融信贷等数据资源, [...] 开展智能动态识险".

data, such as water, air, woodland, soil, noise and radiations, and improve the digital management and control capabilities of ecological resources[172]"; (2) "In environment, deepen the integrated use of multiple data sources [including those on] water, air, noise and soil, and improve the level of informatization of environmental governance and ecological restoration".[173]

- *Urban daily management*: (1) "Promote the application of IoT sensing and intelligent prediction in the fields of water supply and drainage, gas, and urban construction, and comprehensively improve the security capability of urban operations. Continue to improve the flexibility and compatibility of smart electricity grids [...], build a food and drug information traceability system and a public health early warning system. Promote the application of real-time data analysis, computer vision, and other technologies in the field of intelligent transportation to improve service efficiency[174]"; (2) "In urban daily management, comprehensively collect public data (公共数据) on 3D maps, rail transit, road situation, large passenger flows, food safety, water, electricity, gas and others, [in order to] strengthen intelligent applications for comprehensive urban management, explore innovation [...] in smart application scenarios and digital solutions for various hot problems [e.g., maintenance of historical building, overhead electricity cables, etc.]".[175]

By indicating priority areas and reference applications for AI in urban governance, the municipal government provides **policy guidance** for the coordinated construction of the Single Platform for Urban Management.

[172] Shanghai Municipal Government, 2020 (cit.), section 4, art. 13. In original: "加强对水、气、林、土、噪声和辐射等城市生态环境保护数据的实时获取、分析和研判, 提升生态资源数字化管控能力".

[173] Ibid., section 3, par. 3.4. In original: "在生态环境方面, 深化多数据综合应用 [...] 落实水、空气、噪音、土壤等方面多维度采集, 提高环境治理、生态修复的信息化水平".

[174] Shanghai Municipal Government, 2020 (cit.), section 4, art. 12. In original: "推动物联传感、智能预测在给排水、燃气、城市建设领域的应用, 全面提升城市运行安全保障能力. 持续提升智能电网灵活性和兼容性, [...] 建设食品药品信息追溯体系和公共卫生预警体系。推动实时数据分析、计算机视觉等在智能交通领域的应用, 提升服务效率。推动实时数据分析、计算机视觉等在智能交通领域的应用, 提升服务效率".

[175] Ibid., section 3, par. 3.5. In original: "在城市日常管理方面, 全面汇集三维地图、轨道交通、路道实况、大客流、食品安全、水电气等公共数据, [...] 强化城市综合管理智能化应用, 探索创新 [...] 热点难点问题的智能应用场景和数字化解决方案".

This guidance is important considering the myriad possible applications of AI in this field: "[t]he Single Platform for Urban Management can use AI recognition algorithms to 'analyze' from which floor and household in the community the cigarette butts are thrown, and notify the staff of the neighbourhood committees [...]; at any time it can check whether there is stagnant water in the city, whether the workers in construction sites are wearing safety helmets, whether there are anomalies in the manhole covers on the roads, etc."[176] At the same time, the Shanghai government allows the **flexibility to devise AI solutions** that best fit the conditions and requirements of districts and subdistricts, based on their demographics, urban structure, and socioeconomic characteristics, among others (AISPi). Such flexibility is consistent with the goal of "solving the most prominent urban governance problems with the maximum effectiveness, at the lowest administrative level, at the earliest time, and with relatively minimum costs".[177] While the municipal policy documents indicate five priority areas for AI in urban governance and suggest possible activities (e.g., analysis, monitoring, early warning), these documents only indicate general applications (e.g., "deepen the integrated use of multiple data sources"). As such, districts and subdistricts have ample room for adaptation, as long as localized solutions fall within the five priority areas for AI in urban governance and are consistent with the types of AI applications indicated by the municipality. This has translated into a practice whereby—within the general framework set by the Shanghai government—districts and subdistricts devise the AI applications they want to use in urban governance in a bottom-up fashion (SHZFi). This **policy design that combines guidance and flexibility is another important facet of analytical capacity**. On the one hand, it ensures the consistent development of the Single Platform for Urban Management, preventing disparate applications that would be difficult to reconcile under a unified digital platform that coordinates urban governance operations from the municipal level to single residential communities. On the other hand, this

[176] Wang, X., 2022. The "Single Platform for Urban Management" Empowers the Digital Transformation of Urban Governance ["一网统管" 赋能城市治理数字化转型]. *Shanghai Municipal People's Congress*, 6, p. 9. 10.16702/j.cnki.cn31-1590/d.2022.06.047.

[177] CPC Shanghai Committee, Shanghai Government General Office, 2020 (cit.), section 1. In original: "在最低层级、最早时间、以相对最小成本, 决绝最突出的问题, 取得最佳综合效应".

policy design facilitates the creation of AI applications that can effectively improve urban governance, since districts and subdistricts are allowed to devise AI solutions that can be fine-tuned to the needs that arise at different administrative levels and under different conditions (3INESAi, SHZFi).

Based upon this policy design, Shanghai is leveraging its **operational capacity to efficiently develop and integrate AI applications for urban governance in the activities of government agencies, supporting their core operations**. Like the GOS, the Single Platform for Urban Management is best understood as a "capability platform" designed and supervised by the Shanghai government (SDECi). By aggregating and coordinating the operational resources available in the municipality, Shanghai is making efficient use of its AI ecosystem to develop AI applications for the Single Platform for Urban Management. Most of the operational resources and capabilities involved are very similar to those of the Government Online-Offline Shanghai (Sect. 5.2.1.2). Hence, they are just briefly recalled here. The Single Platform for Urban Management relies on an advanced *technological infrastructure* (the extranets, the e-government clouds, the Big Data exchange platform, IoT sensors, surveillance cameras) to collect, share, and process troves of *data* that are used to create AI applications for urban governance. These AI applications leverage the know-how and *human capital* provided by *AI companies* and government technology agencies (i.e., the Urban Operation Centers, Big Data Centers). As noted earlier, the SBDC has established strategic partnerships with leading AI firms that ensure a stable supply of AI and other advanced technologies, as well as qualified human capital. Similarly, the Shanghai Urban Operation Management Center cooperates with several AI companies such as: Tencent Cloud WeDa (Chen, 2021, p. 10), a low-code development platform[178]; Guanyuan Technology, which supplies encryption technologies for e-government clouds; or DAS-Security, which

[178] Low-code development platforms help organizations to quickly create and deliver digital applications without having to rely on a large amount of manual programming or user training. It is a method of software and application development that allows individuals with very little or no coding experience or knowledge to create digital apps for their organizations, using various functionalities that simplify the app-building process. See: Microsoft, n.d. Why Low-Code Development Matters. *Microsoft*, https://powerapps.microsoft.com/en-us/what-is-low-code/. Last accessed on 25 November 2022.

provides cybersecurity solutions for urban governance.[179] By cooperating with these and other technology suppliers, the SUOC is able to develop tailor-made solutions for urban governance based on the operational requirements of the Single Platform for Urban Management. The great number of technology suppliers[180] in the Shanghai AI ecosystem also provides public organizations with a wide choice of potential partners that can develop technical solutions for urban governance at each administrative level (SHZFi, 3INESA). At the district-level, Shanghai INESA is involved in the construction of most Urban Operation Centers and their "city brains" (see below) as a major contractor of the SPM project, and it often works as an aggregator of technology suppliers for urban governance applications (3INESA, AISPi). At the subdistrict-level, cooperation with AI companies is crucial for the construction of the "city brains" of the Urban Operation Centers in subdistricts and townships, and for developing mobile applications and devices that enable smart governance at the grassroots level, as illustrated shortly with some examples.

The efficient integration of AI in urban governance is also supported by the ability of Shanghai to **promote the rationalized development of the Single Platform for Urban Management**. Like the GOS, the Single

[179] Guanyuan Technology, 2021. Work Together to Build a Unified Data Security Platform, Guanyuan Technology Helps Build a Smart City [携手共建一网统管数据安全保障平台, 观源科技助力智慧城市建设]. *Guanyuan Technology*, 3 December, https://baijiahao.baidu.com/s?id=1718117755903208659&wfr=spider&for=pc.

[180] Shanghai Zhuofan and Shanghai INESA did not quantify the number of technology suppliers of the Single Platform for Urban Management. However, it is reasonable to assume that this figure is in the same region of the 300 suppliers mentioned by Shanghai Zhuofan for the Government Online-Offline Shanghai. In fact, many of the main suppliers of the GOS are also suppliers of the Single Platform for Urban Management. For instance, in addition to Shanghai Zhuofan and Shanghai INESA, other suppliers of both platforms include: Huawei (华为), Dahua Technology (大华科技), Hikvision (海康威视), SenseTime (商汤科技), Wanda Information (万达信息), Xindian Software (国泰新点软件), Tencent, Baidu, and iFlytek, among others (SHZFi). This inference is corroborated by available online sources, which not only show that there are hundreds of suppliers of technical solutions for the SPM, but also that many of these suppliers coincide with the providers of technical solutions for the GOS platform (Sect. 5.2.1). See: Smart City Team, 2021. The Top 100 e-Government and Smart City Solution Providers in 2020 [2020电子政务与智慧城市解决方案提供商TOP 100]. *Smart City Team* [智慧城市行业分析], 3 February, https://www.smartcity.team/investment/companies/2020%E7%94%B5%E5%AD%90%E6%94%BF%E5%8A%A1%E4%B8%8E%E6%99%BA%E6%85%A7%E5%9F%8E%E5%B8%82%E8%A7%A3%E5%86%B3%E6%96%B9%E6%A1%88%E6%8F%90%E4%BE%9B%E5%95%86top100/.

Platform for Urban Management is an initiative where the use of AI and advanced technologies is developing alongside the governmental attempts to optimize the workflow and procedures of urban governance, making them more logical and efficient (SHZFi, AISPi). Rationalization involves two aspects. First, Shanghai is actively promoting the ***standardization of workflows and operational procedures*** of the agencies involved in the Single Platform for Urban Management (SHZFi, 3INESAi, AISPi). As discussed in the analysis of the Government Online-Offline Shanghai, the efficient integration of AI applications into digital platforms that connect different government organizations requires standardized operating procedures and data classification, among others. Indeed, the municipal policy documents indicate that Shanghai pays great attention to the standardization of the Single Platform for Urban Management. For instance, Shanghai intends to "standardize the working process and internal working system of the three-level urban operation platforms, and clarify the construction standards and application standards. Further unify data standards and usage specifications, [...] provide standards and basis for effective system interconnection and operational collaboration".[181] In addition, the SBDC and the SUOC are also mandated to set the standards and the operational logic of the whole Single Platform for Urban Management, as noted earlier.[182] Like for the GOS, a local expert emphasizes that such rationalization is an iterative process that aims to make workflows suitable for AI automation, and then standardizes them for fast implementation and easy replication (AISPi). These findings corroborate earlier studies observing that the optimization of government operations is a key component of the SPM initiative.[183] Moreover, although at present

[181] CPC Shanghai Committee, Shanghai Government General Office, 2020 (cit.), section 4, par. 3. In original: "规范三级城运平台的业务流程和内部工作制度，明确建设标准和应用标准。进一步统一数据标准和使用规范, [...] 为系统有效互联、业务协同联动提供标准和依据".

[182] See for instance footnotes 32 (SBDC), and 129 and 139 (SUOC). See also: CPC Shanghai Committee, Shanghai Government General Office, 2020 (cit.), attachment, art. 59 ("progressively create and improve local standards [for the SPM], and create technical standards for the Urban Operation Centers", 逐步建立健全相关地方标准, 建立城运中心相关技术标准).

[183] Chinese experts observe that the core of this initiative "is not only the innovation of technical means, but also the innovation of management mode, the reshaping of administrative mode, and the reform of system and mechanism" aimed at improving urban governance (Modaxia, 2021). Other analysts agree that the Single Platform for

there are no technical standards for the construction of the Shanghai Platform for Urban Management,[184] the standardization of workflows and operational procedures has benefits similar to the technical standardization of the GOS platform: technology suppliers know from the start what are the operational requirements of Big Data Centers and Urban Operation Centers; hence, they can adapt their solutions to the needs of urban governance agencies at each administrative level. In addition, this approach creates a pool of vendors that have experience in providing AI solutions for the SPM platform, and thus they can possibly compensate for some deficiencies in organizational-level capacities (3INESA, AISPi), as discussed later.

Rationalization is also manifested in the *coordinated distribution of urban governance tasks* between the government agencies involved in the Single Platform for Urban Management. In the "three-level platforms, five-level applications" structure, Urban Operation Centers are the focal points that oversee cross-departmental coordination of urban governance operations in their jurisdictions. Due to this function, Urban Operation Centers are the main "entry point" for AI applications in public security, market supervision, environmental protection, emergency response, and urban daily management. Through the Urban Operation Centers, such AI applications are efficiently integrated both horizontally and vertically.[185] Horizontal integration means that the Urban Operation Centers

Urban Management "is not simply the application of digital technology [...]. [The Single Platform for Urban Management] not only detects problems that need to be dealt with in a timely manner, but it also breaks through departmental barriers with data sharing, forming a joint force of 'whole-of-government' deployment, so that the city's governance resources can be more effectively used". See: Wenhui Daily, 2022. Data Empowerment Drives the Modernization of Governance in Megacities [数据赋能, 牵引带动超大城市治理现代化]. *Wenhui Daily* [文汇报], 16 June, retrieved from: http://www.echinagov.com/news/324985.htm. See also: Liu (2021, cit. in 5.2.2).

[184] In December 2021, the Ministry of Housing and Rural-Urban Development published the *Technical standard of urban operation management service platform* [城市运行管理服务平台技术标准], https://www.mohurd.gov.cn/gongkai/fdzdgknr/zfhcxjsbwj/202112/20211216_763467.html. However, Shanghai Zhoufan argues that this standard is narrow (狭隘) as it covers only certain aspects of the Single Platform for Urban Management (SHZFi).

[185] "Based on the logical structure of the 'three-level platforms, five-level applications', open up the disconnected tree-like structure of the segmented operating systems to form a connected structure that extends horizontally to edge, vertically to the bottom, and is interconnected" [基于"三级平台、五级应用"的逻辑架构, 打通条块业务系统互不相连的

use AI to support all government agencies participating in urban governance in their jurisdictions. Vertical integration means that AI applications are deployed from the municipal to the grassroots levels, extending the reach of AI applications for urban governance to residential communities, industrial parks, and single buildings.[186] This distribution of urban governance tasks is paralleled by a technological arrangement in which AI applications for urban management are mainly developed at each administrative level (AISPi, SHZFi). Urban Operation Centers at the municipal, district, and subdistrict levels cooperate with AI companies to develop AI applications for urban governance, leveraging the data provided by the Big Data Centers at their administrative level,[187] as well as data collected and shared via the network of Urban Operation Centers[188] (SHZFi, SDECi). These AI applications are implemented through the so-called city brains, which are the "smart hubs" (智能中枢) that enable the AI-based operations of the Urban Operation Centers. City brains are intelligent systems that combine Big Data, cloud computing, Internet of Things, artificial intelligence, blockchain, and digital twins to perform

树状结构, 形成横向到边、纵向到底、互联互通的矩阵结构], CPC Shanghai Committee, Shanghai Government General Office, 2020 (cit.), section 2, par. 3. This combination of horizontal and vertical integration is sometimes described using the Chinese character for "king" (王), see: Xinji (2021) (cit.), p. 25.

186 Shanghai People's Congress, 2022 (cit.), art. 5. In original: "本市依托 "一网统管" 平台, 建立市、区、乡镇和街道、网格化区域、社区和楼宇五级应用体系, 加强指挥协调和现场处置, 实现线上线下协同高效处置一件事". CPC Shanghai Committee, Shanghai Government General Office, 2020 (cit.), section 2, par 3. In original: "依托移动应用, 支持基层自治组织和单位、园区、楼宇等参与社会治理".

187 The data used for AI applications developed by the subdistrict Urban Operation Centers are provided by the district-level Big Data Centers, since there are no Big Data Centers in subdistricts. With some possible exceptions in very specific usages, there are no standard applications developed by the SUOC and made available on the whole SPM platform (SHZFi). Shanghai INESA also did not mention unified applications developed by the SUOC (3INESAi).

188 In the SPM, data are also collected and shared via the network of Urban Operation Centers, depending on the source of data. For instance, IoT-generated data are often transmitted to the relevant Urban Operation Centers at the municipal, district, or subdistrict level, and can be directly shared between them, as Urban Operation Centers are also connected via the e-government clouds (SHZFi). There are many possible configurations, and the situation is constantly evolving as the SPM progressively expands its data sources. The existence of multiple channels for data sharing does not diminish the importance of the Big Data Centers in storing and transferring data for urban governance.

smart analysis, prediction, planning, and other functions in urban governance (CESI, 2022, p. 22).[189] AI applications implemented by the Urban Operation Centers typically focus on command and coordination activities, while AI applications in residential communities and other grassroots scenarios mainly use mobile devices for on-site deployment (Zhianjun, 2022a).

This ability of Shanghai to aggregate and coordinate the resources of its AI ecosystem has resulted in the efficient use of AI to empower the core operations of urban governance agencies at all administrative levels. Some examples illustrate this point. At the municipal level, the Shanghai Municipal Urban Operation Center uses AI to control the accumulation of stagnant water on the roads. Data collected in real time from 157 water level monitoring stations, 550 rainfall monitoring stations, 26 meteorological monitoring stations, and video surveillance information are combined with data gathered from 1,418 drainage pumping stations, nearly 28,000 kilometers of underground drainage pipe network, 64 flood-prone points, 14,000 residential communities, more than 100 flood control teams and vehicles, and other data sources. Based upon this information, the SUOC coordinates relevant agencies so that pump trucks are promptly dispatched to flooded areas, according to early warnings and following optimal routes calculated by AI algorithms. Moreover, data on water accumulation are shared with public security and traffic administration bureaus in real time, so that they can close the roads that are flooded. In public health, the SUOC leveraged the data provided by the Shanghai Municipal Health Commission to coordinate the operations of health commissions, public security bureaus and other departments involved in the joint prevention and control activities during the Covid-19 pandemic. AI models supported more than 263,000 health officials, and tracked 295 people that were later transferred to medical institutions.[190] Another example is the use of AI for the maintenance of urban infrastructure. More than 30,000 digital sensors monitor the municipal water supply network in districts and subdistricts to locate potential problems,

[189] See also: The Paper, 2020. Create a "City Brain", Explore "Digital Twins", Keep Well the "Urban Arteries" [打造 "城市大脑" 探索 "数字孪生" 守好 "城市动脉"]. *The Paper News* [澎湃新闻], 9 December, https://m.thepaper.cn/baijiahao_10330184.

[190] Both applications are discussed in People.cn, 2020 (cit.).

so that warnings about water pipe failures can sometimes be sent to the relevant agencies even before residents ask for help.[191]

At the district level, the Xuhui District Urban Operation Center merged 38.5 million pieces of data gathered from public security, civil affairs, medical insurance, and public health departments of the district. It used these data to profile elderly residents and their families, providing them with tailor-made services and supervising their situation.[192] In the Pudong New Area, the local branches of the Construction and Traffic Commission and the Environmental and Landscaping Bureau are using AI to reduce the problems caused by construction debris. They upload data about construction sites and lorries destinations on the district Big Data Center, so that the Pudong Urban Operation Center can share such information with the Pudong traffic police and urban management officials. Cameras installed on roadsides and intersections are programmed to distinguish lorries carrying construction debris from other vehicles. If rules are not respected, like failing to properly cover debris and trash loaded on the lorries, police and relevant authorities are notified in real time.[193] In Jing'an District, the local Urban Operation Center receives data from the smart water meters installed in the houses of many elderly people living alone. These smart water meters update data every half an hour during the whole day, sending a warning if water usage time and consumption change abnormally, so that staff in the residential communities can promptly contact the elderly to check their health status.[194] Some historical buildings in Huangpu District are equipped with sensors connected to the district Urban Operation Center, which can detect safety risks related to visitor flow, fire threats, or the malfunctions of elevators and escalators, sending an immediate alert to the smart portable devices of the security staff of the buildings.[195] Some districts like Xuhui and Pudong are also developing mini-Apps that allow citizens to use images,

[191] Zhou, 2021 (cit.).

[192] Li, J., 2020 (cit.).

[193] Li, Q., 2022. Pudong's Futuristic 'City Brain' Can Foresee the Future. *SHINE*, 21 June, https://www.shine.cn/news/in-focus/2206217030/.

[194] China Central Government, 2020. Shanghai Explores the "Single Platform for Urban Management" to Solve the Problems of Urban Operations 上海探索 "一网统管" 解城市运行难题]. *China Central Government* [中华人民共和国中央人民政府], 18 January, http://www.gov.cn/xinwen/2020-01/18/content_5470432.htm.

[195] Zhou, 2021 (cit.).

videos, and text messages to report to relevant authorities several issues like littering, improper parking, and road surface anomalies, among others (Chen, 2021, p. 8; Liu, 2021, p. 129).

In subdistricts, Urban Operation Centers enable granular applications that integrate artificial intelligence in urban governance activities in areas as small as residential communities, single buildings, and street blocks. For instance, the Urban Operation Center of the Jiangsu Road Subdistrict (Changning District) uses computer vision to analyze the images and videos collected by traffic and surveillance cameras to identify littering, bicycles parked in forbidden areas, and other issues. Once anomalies are detected, the system promptly notifies human operators (street cleaners, urban management and law enforcement agents) by sending an alert to applications installed on their mobile devices, so that they can go to solve the problem.[196] The Urban Operation Center of Kangqiao Town (Pudong New Area) started to use AI in public health when the Covid-19 pandemic first broke out in early 2020. Smart cameras and sensors were used at the entrances of offices, factories, residential compounds, and public spaces to locate people that should stay at home under quarantine, and promptly notify the neighborhood committee via similar mobile applications.[197] Likewise, the residential area of Kangningqiang in Xuhui District used AI for pandemic control. It provided mini-Apps to community workers that surveyed residents' travel history and potential contacts with confirmed or suspected Covid-19 cases. This mini-App progressively integrated more and more functions (e.g., resumption of work record), effectively supporting grassroots urban governance.[198] Another example of grassroots applications can be found in elderly care. Dongping Township in Chongming District has launched an application for the elderly living alone and affected by dementia or disability. By installing "smart door magnets" (智能门磁) at the house doors, the subdistrict Urban Operation Center receives data when doors open and close. If the system

[196] Xinhua, 2020. Fine City Governance, Shanghai's "Single Platform for Urban Management: Enhances the City's "Intelligent Governance" [精细治城, 上海 "一网统管" 提升城市 "智治力"]. *Xinhua News*, 8 June, http://www.xinhuanet.com/2020-06/08/c_1126088136.htm.

[197] Li, 2022 (cit.).

[198] Xinhua, 2020 (cit.).

detects abnormal patterns, the platform sends a warning to the family of the elderly and the neighborhood committee via SMS and phone.[199]

These examples are not exhaustive. AI applications for urban governance continue to evolve, and there are also many AI applications that are not publicly disclosed as they involve sensitive topics (SHZFi). At the same time, these examples provide a useful indication of the breadth and depth of AI applications supported by the Single Platform for Urban Management, showing that Shanghai has the operational capacity to efficiently develop AI applications for urban governance and integrate them in the core activities of public organizations at every administrative level. The number of such applications is expected to grow, since they rely on a set of AI technologies that are mature and commercially available. For instance, the Single Platform for Urban Management makes wide use of technologies such as: computer vision to recognize and track individuals and vehicles; NLP to monitor public sentiment and other applications; digital twins to monitor, simulate and predict various situations of urban governance; image recognition and speech recognition (SHZFi); IoT sensors in various applications, including smoke detection (SHZFi, 3INESAi); and video structuring[200] for the analysis of illicit behaviors such as throwing objects from high-rise buildings (3INESAi). The technologies mentioned by the interviewees correspond to those reported by other expert sources (CESI, 2022, pp. 27, 38, 40–45; Modaxia, 2021). In addition to the increasing availability of mature technologies, another incentive to pursue AI solutions for urban governance comes from the strong political push of the Shanghai municipal government, which has clearly set the development of the Single Platform for Urban Management as a political priority.

199 Chongming District Government, 2021. The "Single Platform for Urban Management" Enables Grassroots Governance ["一网统管" 为基层治理赋能]. *Chongming District Government*, 13 October, https://www.shcm.gov.cn/xwzx/002003/20211013/426da6e6-1104-414d-99fa-a22bd3304703.html.

200 Video structuring (or video structuring, video structure analysis, or video segmentation) is the process of hierarchically decomposing videos into units (e.g., scenes, shots) and building their relationships, so that video data can be more easily accessed and analyzed. Video structuring can be regarded as a part of activity recognition in videos (see Chapter 1.1.2). On video structuring, see: Wang, M. and Zhang, H., 2009. Video Content Structuring. *Scholarpedia*, 4(8), p. 9431, http://www.scholarpedia.org/article/Video_Content_Structuring.

In fact, Shanghai's **political capacity to create and sustain support for the deployment of the Single Platform for Urban Management has led to the widespread use of AI in urban governance in the municipality via this digital platform**. Since its announcement in 2019, the construction of the SPM has been elevated to a political priority of the Shanghai government.[201] The Shanghai Party leadership regularly emphasizes the political importance of this project, periodically visiting the Shanghai Municipal Urban Operation Center, and reiterating that the construction of the Single Platform for Urban Management is a crucial work ("牛鼻子" 工作) for the modernization of urban governance.[202] To make this political endorsement even more tangible, the municipal policy documents explicitly state that progress in the construction of the Single Platform for Urban Management must be included among the indicators of the annual performance appraisal of Shanghai officials,[203] making

[201] The Observer, 2019. "Government Online-Offline Shanghai" for Administrative Services, the "Single Platform for Urban Management" for Urban Governance! Today Li Qiang Inspected the Construction of Platform and System for Urban Operations [政务服务 "一网通办" 、城市运行 "一网统管" !李强今天调研城运系统平台建设]. *The Observer* [观察者], 17 September, https://www.guancha.cn/politics/2019_09_17_518254.shtml; Yicai, 2020. Ying Yong: Shanghai Urban Governance, "One Screen to View the Whole Area, One Network to Manage the Whole City" [应勇: 上海城市治理 "一屏观天下, 一网管全城"]. *Yicai* [第一财经], 20 January, https://www.yicai.com/brief/100474433.html.

[202] China Construction News, 2020. Municipal Party Secretary Li Qiang Yesterday Inspected the Construction of the "Single Platform for Urban Management" [上海市委书记李强调研城市运行 "一网统管" 建设]. *China Construction News* [中华建设网], 23 April, https://www.zhjsw.cn/news/show-22302.html; Eastday.com, 2020. Municipal Party Secretary Li Qiang Yesterday Inspected the Construction of the "Single Platform for Urban Management" for City Operations [市委书记李强昨调研城市运行 "一网统管" 建设]. *Eastday.com* [东方网], 14 October, https://j.eastday.com/p/1602644326022214; The Paper, 2021. Municipal Party Secretary Li Qiang Inspected the "Single Platform for Urban Management" and the Urban Operation Digital Signs System [上海市委书记李强调研 "一网统管" 和城市运行数字体征系统]. *The Paper News* [澎湃新闻], 17 August, https://www.thepaper.cn/newsDetail_forward_14087047.

[203] CPC Shanghai Committee, Shanghai Government General Office, 2020 (cit.), section 4, par. 1: "The progress of construction of the Single Platform for Urban Management shall be included in the scope of the annual performance appraisal" [将 "一网统管" 建设推进情况纳入年度绩效考核范畴]; attachment 1, art. 60 (same wording); Shanghai People's Congress, 2022 (cit.), art. 18: "The municipal and district people's governments shall strengthen the assessment of the effectiveness of the Single Platform for Urban Management construction work of the people's governments and relevant departments at lower levels, and use the assessment results as an important basis for the annual performance appraisal and comprehensive assessment and evaluation of leading cadres".

the development of the SPM a metric to determine career advancements under the evaluation system for promotion (Chapter 2.3.3). This political capacity has resulted in high rates of adoption of the Single Platform for Urban Management among government agencies at every administrative level, leading to the extensive use of AI in urban governance across Shanghai. As of December 2020, the Shanghai Municipal Urban Operation Center, the 16 district-level, and 215 subdistrict-level Urban Operations Centers were completed. In addition, the number of government departments joining the SPM platform has been constantly growing: from 30 departments in September 2019, to 50 departments in August 2021, to more than 70 departments in June 2022, according to local media.[204] In addition, Shanghai's political capacity to gain support for the Single Platform for Urban Management can also be inferred from the fact that all 16 districts of Shanghai are fostering the construction and implementation of this digital platform in their jurisdictions (Table 5.6).

The capacity of Shanghai to obtain political support for the Single Platform for Urban Management is important because there are two main factors that could generate resistance to its adoption by government agencies. These factors mirror those highlighted in the analysis of the Government Online-Offline Shanghai, consistently with the similarities between the two platforms stressed earlier. First, joining the Single Platform for Urban Management is onerous for government agencies, and this is likely to generate various forms of resistance that can be overcome only if there is clear political support for the SPM project[205]

[市、区人民政府应当加强对下级人民政府和有关部门“一网统管”建设工作成效的考核，并将考核结果作为年度绩效考核和领导干部综合考核评价的重要依据].

[204] The Observer, 2019 (cit.) mentions "more than 30 departments" in September 2019. By August 2021, the number had risen to "more than 50 departments", see: The Paper, 2021. Municipal Party Secretary Li Qiang Inspected the "Single Platform for Urban Management" and the Urban Operation Digital Signs System [上海市委书记李强调研“一网统管”和城市运行数字体征系统]. *The Paper News* [澎湃新闻], 17 August, https://www.thepaper.cn/newsDetail_forward_14087047. In June 2022, more than 70 government departments at the municipal and district levels were connected to the SPM, see: Guomai Digital Government Network, 2022 (cit.).

[205] Shanghai Zhuofan observes that one important determinant in the use of the SPM at each administrative level is the political "determination" (决心) of the leadership. Similarly, AISPi notes that political support from district authorities is a key factor affecting the adoption of smart urban governance in their jurisdictions.

Table 5.6 Implementation of the Single Platform for Urban Management in the 16 districts of Shanghai

Baoshan District: The "Single Platform for Urban Management" helps to make Baoshan urban management more refined! ["一网统管", 助力宝山城市管理更精细!], https://new.qq.com/omn/20211116/20211116A0C3PY00.html	**Jinshan District**: Task list of Jinshan District for the "Single Platform for Urban Management" in 2021 [2021 年金山区 "一网统管" 任务清单], https://www.jinshan.gov.cn/qfb-ybwj/20210508/813197.html
Changning District: The three-year action plan for digital transformation of (2022–2024) by the Construction Management Committee of Changning District is officially implemented, digital intelligence enables urban construction management [长宁区建管委数字化转型三年行动计划 (2022-2024年) 正式实施, 数字智慧赋能城建管理], https://www.shcn.gov.cn/col5683/20220301/1211836.html	**Minhang District**: Three-year action plan for the construction of "Single Platform for Urban Management" for urban operations in Minhang District (2020–2022) [闵行区城市运行 "一网统管" 建设三年行动计划(2020-2022年)] http://xxgk.shmh.gov.cn/mhxxgkweb/html/mh_xxgk/xxgk_gmjd_ghjh_zx/2021-09-01/Detail_117857.htm
Chongming District: Three-year action plan for the construction of "Single Platform for Urban Management" for urban operations in Chongming District (2020–2022) [崇明区城市运行 "一网统管" 建设三年行动计划(2020-2022年)], http://cmb.shcm.gov.cn/html/2020-11/28/content_20978_12688265.htm	**Pudong New Area**: Pudong New Area comprehensively promotes the XIV Five-Year Plan of urban digital transformation [浦东新区全面推进城市数字化转型 "十四五" 规划], https://phone.pudong.gov.cn/shpd/infoopen/InfoDetail.aspx?CategoryNum=006021011&InfoId=4650d9ac-8dce-4068-af42-29716b99af3b
Fengxian District: New application scenarios for the "Single Platform for Urban Management". Fengxian urban management uses data to "speak" ["一网统管" 应用场景上新啦 奉贤城市管理用数据 "说话"], https://j.eastday.com/p/1637653850048540	**Putuo District**: Three-year action plan for the construction of "Single Platform for Urban Management" in Putuo District [普陀区 "一网统管"《三年行动计划》] https://www.shpt.gov.cn/shpt/ztlh-zixun/20210121/545100.html
Hongkou District: Hongkou District Urban Operation Center held a public open-day event to reveal the secrets of the brain of the "Single Platform for Urban Management" [虹口区城运中心举行公众开放日活动 揭秘一网统管大脑] https://www.shanghai.gov.cn/hkq/20210916/446404c5a75b4df5a3fa3a2613dc8d5e.html	**Qingpu District**: Looking back at the XIII Five-Year Plan: the Single Platform for Urban Management, "intelligent" urban governance in one screen [十三五回眸: 一网统管, 一块屏幕里的城市 "智" 理], https://www.shqp.gov.cn/shqp/qpyw/20210218/819704.html

(continued)

Table 5.6 (continued)

Huangpu District: Working points of Huangpu District for the promotion of the district digital transformation in 2021 [2021年黄浦区推进城区数字化转型工作要点], https://www.shhuangpu.gov.cn/yqyw/010001/010001004/010001004005/20211111/30070fcc-11a2-4b7a-9183-54be8d2b96ff.html	**Songjiang District**: Songjiang District "Implementation Opinions on Strengthening the Construction of Urban Operation Management Centers in Subdistricts (Economic Development Zones)" [松江区 "关于加强街镇 (经开区) 城市运行管理中心建设的实施意见"], https://www.songjiang.gov.cn/govxxgk/SHSJ31/2021-09-23/8557632a-3a22-49f6-93af-f909259b017a.html
Jiading District: A "smart brain" helps flood control and epidemic prevention. Scenario upgrade and function optimization of the "Single Platform for Urban Management" in Jiading ["智慧大脑" 助力防汛防疫 嘉定 "一网统管" 场景升级、功能优化], *Eastday.com* [东方网], 24 June, https://j.eastday.com/p/1656055969045005	**Xuhui District**: Work plan of Xuhui District for accelerating the construction of the advanced areas of the "Single Platform for Urban Management" for urban operations [徐汇区关于加快推进城市运行 "一网统管" 先行区建设工作方案], http://www.xuhui.gov.cn/xwzx_zwxx/20200603/267827.html
Jing'an District: Make every effort to create the Single Platform for Urban Management 3.0 for urban operations, promote the digital transformation of urban governance! This is what Jing'an does [全力打造城市运行一网统管3.0, 推动城区治理数字化转型!静安这么干], https://www.163.com/dy/article/G9AVB9SE0514CCT2.html	**Yangpu District**: Action plan for building Shanghai digital transformation demonstration zone and comprehensively promote urban digital transformation in Yangpu District (2021–2023) [打造上海市数字化转型示范区全面推进杨浦区城市数字化转型行动方案(2021-2023年)], http://ssme.sh.gov.cn/policy/knowledge!knowledgeDetail.do?id=2c91c28d797f6b5a017983140c69026a

(SHZFi, AISPi). Even without considering the district-level extranets, e-government clouds, and Big Data Centers that are already in place as part of the technological infrastructure of the GOS, district governments have to build the Urban Operation Centers and related city brains. They are also responsible for installing smart cameras, IoT sensors, and other devices that collect data from the environment and are crucial to support urban governance activities (AISPi). Likewise, subdistricts have to build their own Urban Operation Centers and the related city brains. Furthermore, district- and subdistrict-level Urban Operation Centers have to ensure the successful deployment of the SPM in their jurisdictions. This means they have to connect and coordinate the operating systems and activities of bureaus and public organizations, promoting local applications, etc. In short, while the Single Platform for Urban Management helps to enhance efficiency in urban governance, it is a complex project that requires that public agencies invest significant financial, human, and time resources.

Second, resistance to the adoption of the Single Platform for Urban Management could also stem from the fact it makes inspections very intrusive. Under the "three-level platforms, five-level applications" structure, higher-level Urban Operation Centers are requested not only to guide, but also to supervise and inspect the operations of lower-level Urban Operation Centers.[206] Furthermore, information related to urban governance activities are shared on the SPM platform. As explained by a Chinese analyst: "By digitalizing governance, the Single Platform for Urban Management leaves traces of government administrative activities throughout the process, making it easy to trace back such activities. [T]he whole-process supervision function (全程监督功能) of the Single Platform for Urban Management […] allows to share information between superior and subordinate departments, or departments at the same level within a public organization, as well as across different organizations, and it can offer a warning and supervision function for dereliction of duty, inaction, and disorderly conduct. […] It is thus evident that the Single Platform for Urban Management governance platform provides a more direct, fast, and comprehensive digital supervision channel".[207] Like for the GOS, interviews confirmed that the use of technologies that enable timely and thorough supervision are often opposed by the leaders of government agencies, whose administrative discretion is now constrained by the fact that higher-level authorities can have a complete and detailed view of urban governance issues at lower levels of government (SDECi).

[206] Shanghai Municipal People's Congress, 2022 (cit.), art. 3, par. 1. In original: "上级城市运行管理机构应当加强对下级城市运行管理机构的业务指导和督促检查".

[207] Chen (2021) (cit.), p. 9. In original: "'一网统管' 通过引入数字化治理, 使政府行政行为全程留痕, 便于追溯。'一网统管' 治理平台的全程监督功能 […] 可以让上下级部门、同级部门和跨部门之间共享信息, 能够对工作失职、不作为和乱作为等行为形成警示作用与监督功能 […]. 可见, "一网统管"治理平台提供了更为直接、快捷和全面的数字监督渠道".

Limitations

Local experts have identified a number of possible limitations to the deployment of AI in the public sector via the Single Platform for Urban Management. Some of these limitations are similar to those examined in relation to the Government Online-Offline Shanghai. Such similarities can be logically expected, considering that both the GOS and the Single Platform for Urban Management are based on the intensive use of data and technological infrastructure, and are trying to extend the use of AI to all levels of government.

First, albeit Shanghai's operational and political capacities have resulted in the efficient integration and widespread use of AI for urban governance via the Single Platform for Urban Management, there are still **varying degrees of AI assimilation in the activities of urban governance agencies**. Differences in AI assimilation can be gauged by looking at the features and activities of the Urban Operation Centers, which host the main technological infrastructure for implementing AI in urban governance at each administrative level. Leaving aside the Shanghai Urban Operation Management Center, which has no counterparts, the main differences at the district and subdistrict levels are highlighted below:

- Districts display varying degrees of AI assimilation in urban governance. Evidence suggests that Jing'an, Xuhui, Pudong, Huangpu, Jiading, Qingpu, and Songjiang are making a more extensive use of

AI applications in urban governance than other districts.[208] Interviewees argue that the differences in AI integration between districts are primarily due to analytical capacity. Districts have similar operational resources in terms of data, digital infrastructure, access to companies and financial resources when it comes to developing the Single Platform for Urban Management. In addition, there are no significant differences in the technological development of the district-level Urban Operation Centers (AISPi, SHZFi). All districts are also actively promoting the SPM in their jurisdictions, suggesting similar levels of political capacity (Table 5.6). In terms of analytical capacity, however, Shanghai INESA and Shanghai Zhuofan both argue that not all district governments are able to identify how AI technologies can help them to improve urban governance operations. As such, some district Urban Operation Centers make more intensive use of AI applications for urban governance than others.

- District-level Urban Operation Centers are usually technologically more advanced than subdistrict Urban Operation Centers. These differences are mostly due to operational skills and resources: district Urban Operation Centers have more financial, human, and other operational resources, and greater ability to coordinate them (SHFZi). While some subdistricts have high levels of ability in

[208] At the Global Cities Forum in November 2020, Jing'an, Xuhui, Pudong, Huangpu, Jiading, Qingpu and Songjiang received several awards for applications related to smart urban governance. See: Wenming Shanghai, 2021. "Best Practices of Urban Governance in Shanghai" Are Selected ["上海城市治理最佳实践案例" 评选出炉]. *Wenming Shanghai* [文明上海], 11 March, http://sh.wenming.cn/YW/202011/t20201102_5835415.html. Jing'an and Xuhui are widely acknowledged as two of the most innovative districts in smart urban governance in Shanghai, as corroborated by latest evidence. For Xuhui: Law & Security Net, 2022. 126 million RMB, Tencent Cloud adjudicates the Shanghai Xuhui District "Single Platform for Urban Management" Project [1.26 亿, 腾讯云中标上海市徐汇区 "一网统管" 项目]. *Law & Security Net* [法安网], 10 November, https://m.faanw.com/biaoxunjijin/12233.html. For Jing'an: Shanghai Jing'an, 2023. The New Command-and-Control Hall of the Jing'an District Urban Operation Center Starts Operations, the "Single Platform for Urban Management" 4.0 Is Officially Online [静安区城运中心新建指挥大厅启用, "一网统管" 4.0平台正式上线]. *Jing'an District WeChat Account*, 22 December, https://mp.weixin.qq.com/s/7e15DJKPkQenaH0Vfpmr5w. Pudong and Huangpu, together with Changning and Hongkou, were mentioned again as best practices of implementing the Single Platform for Urban Management two years after the Global Cities Forum of 2020. See: Xinhua Daily Telegraph, 2022. People's City, from Shanghai to the World [人民城市, 从上海走向全球]. *Xinhua Daily Telegraph* [新华每日电讯], 3 November, http://www.news.cn/mrdx/2022-11/03/c_1310672875.htm.

identify AI solutions for urban governance (analytical capacity), this cannot compensate for the differential in operational resources (3INESAi). Hence, districts on average make more intensive use of AI in urban governance than subdistricts. These differences are consistent with the roles and tasks assigned to districts and subdistricts in urban governance under the “three-level platform, five-level applications” structure. In other words, such differentials are contemplated by an arrangement whereby district Urban Operation Centers provide subdistricts with technical support to develop AI applications at the grassroots level, as explained shortly.

– Varying degrees of AI assimilation are most evident at the subdistrict level. Subdistrict belonging to districts that are making more intensive use of AI in urban governance have on average a higher level of AI integration in urban management than those in other districts.[209] This is because in the interlocked organizational structure of the SPM, district Urban Operation Centers empower those at lower levels. At the same time, AI assimilation at the subdistrict level also depends on localized capabilities. Operational resources for the construction, maintenance, and operation of subdistrict Urban Operation Centers come primarily from the budget of the subdistricts.[210] In addition, the analytical capacity of subdistricts is also important to determine the successful use of AI in urban governance[211] (3INESAi, SHZFi). This is because the policy design of the SPM requires that districts and subdistricts devise AI applications that best fit their requirements, as noted. As a result, the degree of

[209] See, for instance, examples drawn from subdistrict Urban Operation Centers in Jing’an District: The Paper News, 2020. Ye Qiang Visits the Daning Road and Jing’an Temple Subdistricts to Carry Out Supervision by the Democratic Parties of the “Single Platform for Urban Management” [叶强赴大宁路街道, 静安寺街道开展“一网统管”专项民主监督]. *The Paper News* [澎拜新闻], 10 June, https://m.thepaper.cn/baijiahao_7776109.

[210] Shanghai People’s Congress, 2022 (cit.), art. 15. In original: “各级人民政府应当将‘一网统管’建设经费纳入本级财政预算, 实施项目库管理, 建立与“一网统管”建设相适应的科学高效的项目审批机制, 落实项目资金保障”. See also: Songjiang government (cit., Table 5.6.), section 6, point 4. In original: “加强经费保障。各街镇 (经开区) 要结合实际, 保障城运中心软硬件设施建设、维护、配套设施设备配置、安全保障及日常运行经费”.

[211] The Gumei Road Subdistrict in Minhang District offers an example of a well-articulated plan for the use of AI in urban governance at the subdistrict level. See: http://xxgk.shmh.gov.cn/mhxxgkweb/html/mh_xxgk/xxgk_gmjd_ghjh_zx/2021-09-01/Detail_117857.htm.

> AI assimilation at the subdistrict level is very variegate. For instance, while some subdistrict Urban Operation Centers are technologically sophisticated, others simply consist of "a nice dashboard with key input data feeds from sensors and recommendations by AI to support decision making" (AISPi). Varying degrees of AI assimilation are also displayed at the level of residential communities: some communities are experimenting advanced solutions, like the use of smart devices to monitor the health status of elderly people living alone, while others stick to extremely basic applications like smoke detectors, sensors for car parking, or AI-enabled video surveillance, or are yet to implement any AI application at all (3INESAi).

At the time of this writing, there are not indications that varying degrees of AI assimilation in urban governance are resulting in the uneven provision of public services in Shanghai. The impact of *differences between districts* is hard to quantify. Like the district-level applications experimented in the Government Online-Offline Shanghai, it seems that varying degrees of AI assimilation in the Single Platform for Urban Management are mostly related to applications that make incremental improvements in smart urban governance, rather than fundamental differences that create significant disparities among districts. First, districts enjoy similar access to data, AI companies, and financial resources, and have almost identical technological infrastructure (e.g., e-government cloud, Big Data Centers), suggesting a similar level of technological development. Second, as just noted, the core AI applications of the SPM platform are enabled by mature, commercially available technologies like computer vision and NLP, among others. Third, when the Urban Operation Centers contract out the construction of their "city brains" or other technology services, they usually require that the technology suppliers also develop AI applications for urban governance, suggesting that a certain level of AI integration is equally diffused among districts (AISPi). Finally, all districts in Shanghai are actively pursuing the development of the SPM. Considering that the Single Platform for Urban Management is a complex, long-term project of public sector AI innovation,[212] it is possible that the aforementioned differences in analytical capacities

[212] In September 2021, Modaxia (2021) argued that "at present, we are still in the initial stage of the 'Single Platform for Urban Management'" (当前还只是"一网统管"的起步阶段). In July 2022, Shanghai Zhuofan said that local governments are still exploring

will reduce over time, leveling the degree of AI assimilation in urban governance across districts.

The different degrees of AI assimilation between ***districts and subdistricts*** are part of the "three-level platforms, five-level applications" structure of the Single Platform for Urban Management. Under this organizational structure, districts and subdistricts have the flexibility necessary to devise AI solutions that best fit their conditions and requirements. However, as lower levels of government have less operational resources, lesser AI assimilation in subdistricts is to be expected. At the same time, in the organizational structure of the Single Platform for Urban Management, district Urban Operation Centers offer technical support to subdistricts, empowering urban governance at the grassroots level. For instance, the Xuhui District Urban Operation Center shares and exchanges data in real time with all the subdistrict Urban Operation Centers in its jurisdiction (Chen, 2021, p. 9). The Songjiang District Urban Operation Center coordinates the design of algorithms for AI applications in the whole district, it empowers Urban Operation Centers in subdistricts and townships, and it also supports the mobile applications used at the grassroots level.[213] Moreover, subdistricts can request district Urban Operation Centers to provide data and other forms of technical support based on specific requirements (3INESA, AISPi). These forms of "intra-district" support are important to raise the average level of AI integration within one district. But the ***degree of AI assimilation in urban governance in subdistricts*** is also dependent on localized operational and analytical capabilities. Considering that subdistrict authorities have to "implement the construction requirements of the 'Single Platform for Urban Management' in grassroots governance, promote practical applications, and improve grassroots governance efficiency",[214] some Chinese analysts emphasize that enhancing the capabilities of subdistricts will be

the construction of the Single Platform for Urban Management ("一网统管全国各地正在探索阶段"; SHZFi).

213 Songjiang Government (cit., Table 5.6), section 5 (深耕技术创新, 做强 "一网统管" 平台), point 3. In original: "为避免重复建设和提高效率, 区城运中心统筹全区应用场景AI算法并赋能街镇, 街镇城运中心按需配置相应算力"; section 5, point 5, in original: "街镇应用小程序由区城运中心统一进行整合归并, 实现对区、街镇移动端应用的有机衔接".

214 Shanghai People's Congress, 2022 (cit.), art. 2, par 4. In original: "乡镇人民政府、街道办事处应当在基层治理中, 落实 "一网统管" 建设要求, 推进实战应用, 提升基层治理效能".

crucial to ensure the long-term sustainable development of the SPM and the uniform provision of smart urban governance services at the grassroots level (Chen, 2021, p. 11).

Indeed, the Shanghai government is **aware of the importance of nurturing the capabilities of districts and subdistricts in smart urban governance**. To accelerate the construction of the Single Platform for Urban Management, the Shanghai leadership requires that municipal and district authorities support the development of digital capabilities of subdistricts, townships, residential areas, and villages.[215] In this regard, the Shanghai government has pledged to provide *financial support* by creating a database of SPM-related projects ("一网统管" 项目库) to ensure funding for the development and application of the Single Platform for Urban Management.[216] A case study on the SPM in Minhang district confirms that this system has been put in place, and it has partly relieved financial difficulties for the construction of the SPM at the district and subdistrict levels.[217] Shanghai also emphasizes the importance of nurturing adequate *human resources* to support the development of the SPM. The municipality calls for government authorities at all levels to improve the technical competencies of their staff by recruiting professional and technical personnel, and by including contents related to the Single Platform for Urban Management and digital governance in the training of grassroots staff, civil servants, and leading cadres.[218] The recruiting criteria of civil servants are not public information. However, an

[215] Shanghai Municipal Government, 2020 (cit.), art. 14. In original: "提升基层社区治理水平。加强党建引领, 建设 "社区云", 推进街镇、居村各类信息系统归集, 有效支撑居村委会减负增能。支持基层综合管理应用, 完善基层事件发现机制, 丰富市、区协同处置主体。创新社区治理O2O模式, 建设数字化社区便民服务中心, 推进社区治理共建共治共享".

[216] CPC Shanghai Municipal Committee, Shanghai Government General Office, 2020 (cit.), attachment 1, point 57. In original: "探索建立 '一网统管' 项目库, 实施入库项目滚动管理, 在此基础上, 建立科学、高效的项目审批机制, 并落实项目资金保障。按照轻重缓急, 优先安排财政资金用于开发 '一网统管' 应用". An almost identical wording is used in the same policy document, section 4.4.

[217] Li, H. and Meng, Z., 2022. The Creation of Urban Digital Governance and the Prevention and Control of Its Risks: A Case Study of the "Single Platform for Urban Management" in the M District of Shanghai [城市数字治理的生成及其风险防控: 以上海市M 区 "一网统管" 为例]. *Contemporary Economic Management* [当代经济管理], 44, p. 5, https://kns.cnki.net/kcms/detail/13.1356.F.20220628.1613.003.html.

[218] Shanghai People's Government, 2022 (cit.), art. 16. In original: "各级人民政府应当根据 '一网统管' 建设需要, 创新人才保障机制, 通过聘任制公务员、引进专业技术人才等方式, 加强人员配备, 提升能力素质, 并将 '一网统管' 和数字治理等专业知识纳入基层工作人员、公务员和领导干部培训内容".

interviewee confirmed that the Shanghai Urban Operation Management Center regularly organizes seminars and training courses for the personnel of district and subdistrict Urban Operation Centers on various issues, including the use of databases for developing urban governance applications (AISPi). Finally, the municipal government also provides *technical support* to facilitate urban governance operations at the grassroots level. For instance, Shanghai requires that municipal and district government departments (e.g., Public Security, Human Resources, Social Security Bureaus) provide basic data on population, legal persons, or housing to subdistrict offices (街道办事处), town governments (镇人民政府), and township governments (乡人民政府) in order to empower grassroots governance.[219] Moreover, the Shanghai Urban Operation Management Center has selected leading AI enterprises, and commissioned them to design mini-Apps to support urban governance activities typically carried out in neighborhoods, townships, and residential communities. These mini-Apps are made available to grassroots operators who are now using them in public health, environmental protection, public security, and market supervision, among others.[220] In addition to these forms of government support, the limited capacities at the grassroots level are also partly mitigated by the rationalization of the working procedures of the SPM. The standardization and coordination of workflows in the Single Platform for Urban Management require that AI solutions can be replicated across different public agencies at different administrative levels. This creates a pool of technology suppliers that have experience in providing standardized, replicable AI tools for urban governance. These

[219] Shanghai People's Congress, 2022, cit., art. 13. In original: "市、区有关部门应当依托"一网统管"平台, 整合、归并业务系统, 加强数据共享, 减少重复派单和报送信息, 支持乡镇人民政府和街道办事处依法履行服务与管理职能, 为基层减负增能。公安、市场监管、住房城乡建设管理、规划资源、民政、经济信息化、卫生健康、人力资源社会保障等部门应当依法向乡镇人民政府和街道办事处提供人口、法人、房屋等基础数据, 赋能基层治理".

[220] Zhou, 2021 (cit.); Wenhui Net, 2021. Changning "Single Platform for Urban Management" Version 2.0 Is Online, the Intelligent Screening of High-Rise Residential Buildings and Real-Time Supervision of Construction Sites Are All "Arranged" [长宁"一网统管"2.0版上线, 高层住宅智慧体检、在建工地实时监管统统"安排"]. *Wenhui Net* [文汇网], 22 June, https://www.whb.cn/zhuzhan/cs/20210622/410595.html. These applications are developed by the "Single Platform for Urban Management" Light Applications R&D and Empowerment Center (上海"一网统管"轻应用研发及赋能中心), an agency of the Shanghai Urban Operation Management Center created in March 2021. More details in Sect. 5.2.2.3.

companies can help public organizations in districts and subdistricts to devise and implement AI solutions that are aligned with the requirements of the SPM platform, compensating for their analytical and operational shortcomings (3INESA, AISPi, SHZFi).

A second limitation to the deployment of AI in the public sector via the SPM platform is the persistence of **data barriers** between government agencies. Data barriers in the Single Platform for Urban Management are generated by the operational and political capacity deficits of some organizations participating in the initiative. In terms of operational capacity, despite the constant efforts made by Shanghai to standardize formats and protocols to facilitate data sharing, incompatibilities among government agencies still remain. These incompatibilities are mainly due to the fact that some urban governance agencies are connected to the SPM via their preexisting information systems (SHZFi). As a result, "different data management modes and different data quality in various sectors such as government affairs, housing development, human resources and social security, transportation, public security, medical care, and education make it difficult to aggregate, correlate and match data. [T]here are still problems such as unclear data governance responsibilities, irregular governance processes, unclear quality standards, unclear ownership of property rights, and difficulty in data sharing and exchange" (CESI, 2022, p. 17). Political capacity deficits are related to the low level of support for data sharing in some public organizations, which are still reluctant to exchange their data on the Single Platform for Urban Management (SHZFi, SDECi). Local experts observe that "some government departments regard their data and information as their property and are unwilling to share them with each other, thus forming information barriers between government departments and between different levels of government" (Chen, 2021, p. 11). However, there is no evidence that data barriers are hampering the deployment of the Single Platform for Urban Management and its AI applications: urban governance agencies at each administrative level are continuously integrating AI in their activities, and AI is improving the efficiency of urban governance operations, as demonstrated shortly (Sect. 5.2.2.3). Moreover, Shanghai is actively addressing the problem of data barriers. The municipal government is progressively connecting all government departments to the unified government cloud and government extranet, eliminating duplicates, and solving problems of data sharing (SHZFi); government agencies are mandated by law to share their data on the government cloud; and the municipality is actively promoting a policy of open government data (SDECi, Chapter 4.1). Nonetheless, the problem should not be overlooked as it indicates that obstacles in the data sharing among public organizations still exist in Shanghai.

A third limitation to the deployment of AI in the public sector via the Single Platform for Urban Management is related to **data privacy and security risks**. In the SPM framework, information that was originally stored and used only within one government department is shared among different agencies at different administrative levels. As a result, there are bigger risks of personal and other information being leaked, and public organizations must pay great attention to issues of data privacy and security (Chen, 2021, p. 11; Han, 2021, p. 14). Moreover, the intensive use of technological infrastructure like smart sensors and IoT devices, the aggregation and processing of Big Data, and the integrated analysis of multiple data sources have increased risks related to equipment security, information loss, and identity thefts (CESI, 2022, p. 17). Data privacy and security risks are arguably embedded in any system that makes extensive use of data and technological infrastructure. The Shanghai government has shown the analytical capacity to identify such risks. In fact, municipal policy documents require that departments and agencies joining the SPM platform establish and improve mechanisms for risk assessment, security review, daily monitoring, emergency response, and strengthen the protection of data and personal information in accordance with the law.[221] Shanghai has also shown the operational capacity to address such threats. As examined earlier, the Shanghai Municipal Big Data Center implements various measures to ensure the secure use of government data, and it sets similar requirements for the district-level Big Data Centers (Sect. 5.2.1.1). Nonetheless, data privacy and security risks cannot be eliminated. Moreover, these risks are further increased by

[221] Shanghai People's Congress, 2022 (cit.), art. 17. See also: CPC Shanghai Committee, Shanghai Government General Office, 2020 (cit.), section 4, par. 2 ("Information security guarantees"/信息安全保障); and Shanghai Municipal Government, 2020 (cit.), art. 23 ("Strengthen the security of critical information"/增强关键信息安全韧度), 24 ("Improve the speed of response to information security incidents/提升信息安全事件响应速度) and 25 ("Improve the protection of public data and personal information"/完善公共数据和个人信息保护). These articles are contained in a section of the document that is not specifically referred to the SPM; hence, they also refer to the GOS and the construction of Shanghai's digital economy, the two other main topics of this policy document.

analytical and operational capacity deficits in some districts and subdistricts, where evidence suggests that urban governance staff often has scarce awareness of, familiarity with, and operational resources to address issues related to personal privacy and information security.[222]

In addition to the aforementioned limitations that overlap with those faced by the GOS, local experts have also identified two criticalities specific of the Single Platform for Urban Management. These limitations are related to analytical and operational capacity deficits that can emerge both at the municipal and organizational levels. In terms of analytical capacity, Big Data analysis, AI, and other advanced technologies provide powerful tools to support public decision-making in urban governance. However, overreliance on technology may lead to erroneous and unfair judgments, or to neglect other methods such as on-site inspections and in-depth investigations that can better reveal the complexity of urban governance problems (Chen, 2021, p. 13).[223] In terms of operational capacity, despite Shanghai's ability to foster the rationalization of the working procedures of the Single Platform for Urban Management, there are still some issues that requires further refinement. These include: the coordination between departments, districts, and policy areas; the creation of mechanisms to clearly define which urban governance issues should be included in the joint management system of the Single Platform for Urban Management; or the establishment of methods for determining accountability, assign responsibility, and solve conflicts that may arise in joint operations of urban governance (Chen, 2021, p. 12; Han, 2021, pp. 13–14).

Implications of the Single Platform for Urban Management for Public Service Provision

By leveraging municipal-level policy capacities, Shanghai has promoted the effective, integrated, and widespread use of AI in the public sector via the Single Platform for Urban Management, fostering the assimilation of AI technologies in urban governance. The strengths of this policy initiative in deploying AI in the public sector are summarized as follows:

[222] Li and Meng, 2022 (cit.), pp. 8, 10.

[223] See also: China Construction Journal, 2022 (cit.).

- Shanghai has demonstrated the analytical capacity to ensure that AI can effectively contribute to improving urban governance operations and urban management services via the Single Platform for Urban Management. The AI applications of the SPM platform are enhancing urban governance capabilities in public security, environmental protection, emergency response, and the other priority areas indicated by the municipality. Moreover, the Shanghai government is skillfully coordinating the development of this urban governance platform at each administrative level: the municipality has drafted a comprehensive and consistent blueprint for the SPM, while at the same time it leverages the analytical capacity of districts and subdistricts to devise AI solutions that can effectively address the governance requirements that arise at different administrative levels
- Operational capacity is manifested in the creation of a city-wide "capability platform" that aggregates and coordinates the resources and skills needed to implement AI-based urban governance operations and urban management services in practice. Shanghai is leveraging the resources of the municipal AI ecosystem to efficiently develop and implement AI applications for urban governance at each administrative level, and via the Single Platform for Urban Management it has integrated such applications into the activities of government agencies in order to support their core operations.
- The political capacity of Shanghai to create and sustain support for the Single Platform for Urban Management is instrumental in achieving high rates of adoption among government agencies in the municipality, leading to the diffusion of AI in public sector activities. The Single Platform for Urban Management connects 70 government departments, 16 district-level Urban Operation Centers, and 215 subdistrict-level Urban Operation Centers, and through the latter thousands of residential communities, townships, and buildings. Shanghai is leveraging this extensive network to foster the widespread use of AI in urban governance in the municipality, reaching the majority of the population.

The deployment of AI in urban governance via the Single Platform for Urban Management is also facing some limitations. These include varying degrees of AI assimilation in urban governance organizations, the persistence of data barriers, concerns about data privacy and security, issues related to the possible overreliance on technology, and the need to further improve the coordinating mechanisms of the SPM. However, the Shanghai government has already taken the initiative to address most of these problems, and there are no indications that these limitations are hampering the development of the Single Platform for Urban Management or the deployment of AI in urban governance. On the contrary, evidence indicates that the SPM: (i) is improving the *efficiency* of urban management services and urban governance operations; (ii) has become a catalyst for the *continuous integration* of AI in urban governance in Shanghai; and (iii) is *extending the reach* of AI-enabled urban management services to the majority of citizens. These three major implications for public service provision are examined below.

First, while there are less quantifiable indicators compared to the Government Online-Offline Shanghai (Sect. 5.2.1.3), several documented cases indicate that the Single Platform for Urban Management is **improving the efficiency of urban management services and urban governance operations at each administrative level**. For instance, the Single Platform for Urban Management is helping Shanghai to improve the maintenance of public infrastructure in the municipality. During the rigid winter of 2021, more than 30,000 digital sensors in the municipal water supply network monitored water volumes in neighborhoods and spotted potential problems, sending warnings about water pipe failures before residents made phone calls asking for help. When Shanghai experienced a similar cold spell in 2016, the water supply authority received 230,000 calls about pipe failures. In 2021, only 20,000 such calls were received, and repairs were completed more quickly.[224] In traffic management, traffic lights in the municipality are equipped with sensors and cameras to collect data that are used by the Single Platform for Urban Management to elaborate optimal routing solutions. Since the early stages of the introduction of this intelligent traffic management system, the vehicle congestion index in Shanghai fell by 15% and the average speed increased by 10%.[225] Similarly, Pudong New Area is using digital twin functions to monitor and control traffic in one of Shanghai's busiest intersections, resulting in improved traffic flows and in a

[224] Zhou, 2021 (cit.).

[225] Xinhua, 2020 (cit.).

30% reduction of car accidents.[226] Pudong is also using AI to improve the efficiency in monitoring safe production. For example, the district Urban Operation Center uses AI technology for the automatic discovery of problems such as workers not wearing safety helmets or electric sparks in construction sites, greatly reducing the workload of on-site supervisors (Liu, 2021, p. 128). The use of AI in the Single Platform for Urban Management allows the efficient handling of urban governance issues at a very granular level. In 2022, a subdistrict in Hongkou District reported that mobile AI applications greatly improved the efficiency of inspections in market supervision and workplace safety: inspections that previously required more than 60 inspectors now employ less than 20 people, and are completed within 3 days.[227] Similarly, the Hongqiao Subdistrict in Changing District reported that the use of algorithms and other smart technologies embedded in the SPM platform led to significant efficiency gains in garbage sorting and collection, saving a considerable amount of time: issues that first required at least two hours can now be solved in 15 minutes the fastest.[228] The use cases described in Sect. 5.2.2.2 provide further examples of how the Single Platform for Urban Management is improving the efficiency of urban management services and operations at each administrative level in Shanghai.

One common trait shared by the aforementioned examples and those provided in Sect. 5.2.2 is the willingness of Shanghai authorities at each administrative level to use the Single Platform for Urban Management and its AI applications to solve practical problems of urban governance. While several Chinese cities have introduced smart systems for urban

[226] CCTV, 2020. [Thirty and a New Journey] Practicing the Concept of a City for the People and Create a High-Quality Life [[三十而立启新程]践行人民城市理念 打造高品质生活]. *CCTV News*, 11 November, https://news.cctv.com/2020/11/11/ARTIVnkuWt1nXVIQ7ftbftUL201111.shtml.

[227] Hongkou District Government, 2022. The Single Platform for Urban Management of Quyang Road Neighborhood in Hongkou District Shows Quyang's "Wisdom" [虹口区曲阳路街道一网统管尽显曲阳 "智慧"]. *Hongkou District Government Website*, 18 February, http://www.shhk.gov.cn/xwzx/002005/20220218/69ee1193-2a7e-4709-97f2-02fb7d801edf.html.

[228] Shanghai Landscaping and City Appearance Bureau, 2023. Digital Response and Refined Management, the Single Platform for Urban Management Supports New Trends [数字化响应精细化管理 "一网统管" 助力新时尚]. *Shanghai Landscaping and City Appearance Bureau* [上海市绿化和市容管理局], 22 March, https://lhsr.sh.gov.cn/ywdt/20230322/83766da8-68ae-4274-8612-74d368f75f44.html.

management, what sets Shanghai apart is its determination to use AI, Big Data, IoT, and other digital technologies to actually improve the efficiency of urban management services and urban governance operations, not just to monitor them (SDECi). This determination is bringing fruits, and local experts argue that the Single Platform for Urban Management is helping Shanghai to improve urban governance capabilities in several aspects (Chen, 2021; Modaxia, 2021).[229] First, the SPM *increases the accuracy of urban governance*. By using data mining and AI technologies to identify people and situations that require intervention, government agencies can provide timely services and even identify problems before they are reported. Second, it *facilitates monitoring and provides early warnings*. The SPM uses IoT, smart sensors, and smart cameras for the real-time collection of data, which are quickly processed by the Urban Operation Centers using AI technologies. This increases monitoring efficiency of various indicators like air quality, smoke, water supply, and water quality, among others. Third, the Single Platform for Urban Management *supports decision-making*. It uses data analysis to support the assessment of various urban governance situations, providing reliable data to decision-makers at each administrative level. Fourth, it *helps the coordination between urban governance agencies* in different districts, different policy areas, and at different administrative levels. By combining data collected from various sources and agencies, the Single Platform for Urban Management facilitates joint operations and management of governance issues, ensuring the quick and coordinated dispatch of personnel to resolve problems as soon as they arise. Fifth, the Single Platform for Urban Management provides a *comprehensive view of urban governance issues* in the municipality. As noted earlier regarding the supervisory functions of the SPM, information related to urban governance activities are shared in real time on the unified digital platform. As such, higher-level authorities have a complete and detailed view of urban governance issues within their jurisdictions as well as at lower levels of government. This enables administrators to monitor the operations of the municipality from both macro and micro perspectives, and it helps to effectively coordinate the mobilization of resources in Shanghai.

[229] See also: Tencent Net, 2022. Research on the Construction System of the Urban Operation Platform "Single Platform for Urban Management" for Digital Government [数字政府 "一网统管" 城运平台建设体系研究]. *Tencent Net* [腾讯网], 22 January, https://new.qq.com/omn/20220121/20220121A03XQ300.html.

The second major implication for public service provision is that **AI applications for urban governance continue to expand and have become increasingly integrated in the provision of public services** via the Single Platform for Urban Management. In March 2021, the Single Platform for Urban Management Light Applications R&D and Empowerment Center (上海 "一网统管" 轻应用研发及赋能中心) was established under the Shanghai Urban Operation Management Center. It serves as an aggregator of developers of AI and digital solutions for urban governance. Since its creation, the Empowerment Center has published online more than 200 digital solutions for urban governance, spanning from epidemic control to market supervision. Its first project was the creation of an open platform that provides a unified service interface for urban government agencies at each administrative level. This open platform has a particular focus on AI applications for subdistricts and townships, where the lack of technical expertise and other operational resources often hampers the use of AI technologies. Urban governance agencies at grassroots level can log on to the platform to search and download the desired applications, some of which are made available free of charge. In addition, the Empowerment Center also develops customized applications for urban governance. Subdistricts can send their requests to the Empowerment Center, which aggregates companies that can develop applications for environmental protection, fire prevention, and data analysis, among others. At the same time, the Empowerment Center also reviews and supervises the applications offered through its platform in order to ensure the quality of the digital solutions provided to government agencies (Chen, 2021, p. 9).[230] Another example of the growing use of AI in urban management services is the adoption of digital twin technologies. In February 2022, the Shanghai Urban Operation and Management Center announced that Shanghai has started to adopt digital twin technologies at scale. Urban Operation Centers in Jiading, Hongkou, Pudong New Area, and other districts have developed digital twins of selected pilot areas in their jurisdictions. These digital representations of the real world can reach a level of detail that

[230] See also: Zhou, 2021 (cit.); Tencent Net, 2021. "Single Platform for Urban Management" Light Applications R&D and Empowerment Center Established to Effectively Reduce the Burden on the Grassroots [上海 "一网统管" 轻应用开发及赋能中心成立切实为基层减负]. *Tencent Net* [腾讯网], 25 March, https://new.qq.com/omn/20210325/20210325A0B01600.html.

includes not only public and private buildings, streetlamps, road signs, dustbins, greenery, or other infrastructure and urban objects, but also the layout and floor plans of each building. Digital twins are used by the Urban Operation Centers to support various urban governance operations and services, from providing health authorities with accurate information about the residents for epidemiological investigation, to optimizing the collection and disposal of urban waste or the allocation of charging stations for electric scooters.[231] The use of AI in urban governance in Shanghai continues to expand. In 2023, for instance, Jiading district introduced six new AI applications, including the use of AI for preventing the floods of underpasses, controlling river pollution, and supporting fire hazard inspections at small venues. These applications are based upon the collection of 280,000 pieces of information from underground pipelines, construction sites, and residential communities, among others.[232]

The third implication for public service provision is that the Single Platform for Urban Management is **extending the reach of AI-enabled urban management services to the majority of citizens**. As noted, more than 70 government departments, 16 district-level Urban Operation Centers, and 215 subdistrict-level Urban Operation Centers are connected to the SPM platform. The examples presented in the previous paragraphs and in Sect. 5.2.2.2 clearly show that AI applications for urban governance in Shanghai are reaching the grassroots level. Through the "three-level platforms, five-applications" structure and the integrated network of Urban Operation Centers, the Single Platform for Urban Management is bringing AI applications to subdistricts, townships, residential communities, and single buildings. While varying degrees of AI integration exist at the grassroots level, the Shanghai government is aware of the importance of nurturing the capabilities of subdistricts, and it is providing financial, human capital, and technical support to develop AI-based smart urban governance at the lower levels of government. As such, the penetration of smart urban management services is expected to continue, reaching a growing number of Shanghai citizens in the near term. The aforementioned Single Platform for Urban Management Light

[231] Zhu, Y., 2022. Shanghai Harnessing 'Digital Twin' Technology to Improve City Management. *SHINE*, 15 February, https://www.shine.cn/news/metro/2202151932/.

[232] SASAC, 2023. CETC Empowers Urban Management Through Digital Network. *State-owned Assets Supervision and Administration Commission of the State Council*, 30 October, http://en.sasac.gov.cn/2023/10/30/c_16124.htm.

Applications R&D and Empowerment Center—which helps to bring AI applications down to the grassroots level—further corroborates this point.

The potential of AI technologies to improve the efficiency of urban governance, the growing number and progressive integration of AI applications in the Single Platform for Urban Management, and the extending reach of AI-based urban management services to the majority of citizens indicate that Shanghai will continue to use artificial intelligence to enhance its governance capabilities and the provision of services in public security, market supervision, environmental protection, emergency response, and daily urban management. The appeal of technological tools that can improve urban governance capabilities is hardly surprising to a "super-large city" of nearly 25 million residents and 14,000 residential communities, which every day has a volume of over 2 million vehicles on its roads in the city center, dispatches more than 7,000 Urban Management and Law Enforcement teams[233] (城管人员队伍) and 22,000 cleaning workers, has 600 buildings taller than 100 meters and managed a total of 174 warnings for severe weather in 2020 (Xinji, 2021).[234] Furthermore, the use of AI and digital technologies to improve urban governance enjoys the strong political support of the national leadership. During his visit to Shanghai in November 2018, President Xi Jinping emphasized that urban governance is an important part of the modernization of the national governance system and capacity, and encouraged Shanghai to continuously improve the level of scientific, refined, and intelligent urban management.[235] Between March 2019 and July 2021, the national government published several documents related to the use of Big Data, AI, and other advanced technologies in urban governance (CESI, 2022, pp. 3–5). This political support is expected to continue in the long term. This can be inferred by the fact that the *14th Five-Year Plan for National Economic and Social Development* (2021–2025) and the related "Vision 2035" call for using technology to innovate urban governance, improve the level of urban intelligence and comprehensively enhance operational efficiency and liveability, implementing the unified digital management of urban infrastructure, and promoting the

[233] China Central Government, 2020 (cit.).

[234] See also: Chen and Wang, 2021 (cit.).

[235] Xinhua, 2018. Xi Jinping Inspects Shanghai [习近平在上海考察], *Xinhua News* [新华网], 7 November, http://www.xinhuanet.com/politics/leaders/2018-11/07/c_1123679389.htm.

Single Platform for Urban Management.[236] As Shanghai is poised to increasingly integrate artificial intelligence and other advanced technologies in urban governance via the Single Platform for Urban Management, the use of AI in this area offers useful insights into the possible development trajectories of public sector AI applications in the municipality, as discussed in the conclusions of this book.

5.2.3 *Conclusions on the Platform-Based Approach*

The Government Online-Offline Shanghai and the Single Platform for Urban Management are two complex, city-wide initiatives that primarily rely on municipal-level analytical, political, and operational resources for their effective deployment. Section 5.2 presented the main features of these policy initiatives, examined their strengths and limitations in deploying AI in the public sector, and discussed the resulting implications for public service provision. By leveraging municipal-level policy capacities, Shanghai has promoted the effective, integrated, and widespread use of AI in the public sector via the Government Online-Offline Shanghai and the Single Platform for Urban Management, fostering the integration of AI technologies in the provision of administrative services and urban management services. The two projects also share some common limitations, such as varying degrees of AI assimilation among government organizations, the persistence of data barriers, and concerns about data privacy and security. These limitations must be acknowledged in order to gain a comprehensive, nuanced view of these policy initiatives. However, they are not hampering the development of the two platforms. On the contrary, evidence indicates that the Government Online-Offline Shanghai and the Single Platform for Urban Management: (i) are improving the efficiency of public service provision; (ii) have become a catalyst for the continuous integration of AI in public

[236] State Council, 2021. *The 14th Five-Year Plan for National Economic and Social Development of the People's Republic of China and Outline of the Vision 2035* [中华人民共和国国民经济和社会发展第十四个五年规划和2035年远景目标纲要], 12 March, http://www.gov.cn/xinwen/2021-03/13/content_5592681.htm. See for instance: chapter 16, section 2 (以数字化助推城乡发展和治理模式创新，全面提高运行效率和宜居度。分级分类推进新型智慧城市建设，将物联网感知设施、通信系统等纳入公共基础设施统一规划建设，推进市政公用设施、建筑等物联网应用和智能化改造) and chapter 29, section 2 (升城市智慧化水平，推行城市楼宇、公共空间、地下管网等 "一张图" 数字化管理和城市运行一网统管).

services; and (iii) are extending the reach of AI-enabled public services to the majority of the Shanghai citizens. The main findings of the analysis carried out in Sect. 5.2 are summarized in Table 5.7.

The similarities between these two policy initiatives in their strengths in deploying AI in the public sector, and the resulting implications for public service provision, should not be surprising. The Government Online-Offline Shanghai and the Single Platform for Urban Management share the three fundamental features that characterize Shanghai's strategy for AI in the public sector (Sect. 5.1). First, **the platform-based approach is coordinated**. The Government Online-Offline Shanghai and the Single Platform for Urban Management are politically endorsed by the top leadership of Shanghai (i.e., the municipal CPC Party Secretary and the Mayor), which directly oversees and coordinates the implementation of both initiatives by means of policy documents and work plans regularly published by the municipal government (see next paragraph). In addition, the deployment of the Government Online-Offline Shanghai and the Single Platform for Urban Management is centrally orchestrated by the municipal government: both platforms are built upon an integrated digital architecture designed and controlled by the municipality; and their daily operations are coordinated and supervised by dedicated municipal agencies (i.e., the Shanghai Municipal Big Data Center and the Shanghai Urban Operation Management Center) that respond to the Shanghai Government General Office.

Second, **the platform-based approach is systemic**, as it deploys a combination of municipal-level analytical, political, and operational capacities to foster the use of AI in the public sector. The Shanghai municipal government has the *analytical capacity* to devise AI applications that can effectively leverage AI to improve administrative services and urban governance via the Government Online-Offline Shanghai and the Single Platform for Urban Management, and it has published consistent, well-articulated blueprints for the development of both policy initiatives (Table 5.3 and 5.5). The Shanghai Municipal Big Data Center and the Shanghai Urban Operation Management Center have the *operational resources* (data, infrastructure, supply of AI technologies) to efficiently translate these policy initiatives into practice. They also have the skills and resources to centrally direct and supervise the implementation of the GOS and the SPM by means of an integrated digital architecture that they control, and by setting standards and operational procedures for these

Table 5.7 Platform-based approach: strengths, limitations, and implications for public service provision

Government Online-Offline Shanghai

Strengths	Limitations	Implications for public service provision
The use of AI is effectively designed to improve the provision of administrative services in Shanghai. The municipality has developed and introduced AI applications that can enhance the efficiency of public service provision to citizens and enterprises, and it also leverages the skills of district governments to devise AI applications for administrative services AI applications for the provision of administrative services are efficiently developed and implemented, and via the Government Online-Offline Shanghai they are integrated into the activities of government agencies in order to improve their core operations High rates of adoption among government agencies are fostering the widespread use of AI in administrative service provision across the municipality, leading to the diffusion of AI in public sector activities in Shanghai	Varying degrees of AI assimilation among government organizations, administrative service centers Persistence of data barriers Concerns about data privacy and security	(1) AI is improving the efficiency in the provision of administrative services: – In 2021, the rate of administrative services that were processed entirely online reached 69.3% – More than 320 administrative services can be completed in one visit to the relevant government agency, without submitting any paper document issued by government departments – The time needed to process administrative services has reduced by 59.8% on average – The number of documents required for completing administrative procedures has reduced by 52.9% on average (2) The number of AI applications for administrative services of the Government Online-Offline Shanghai is continuously expanding, and such applications are becoming increasingly integrated in the provision of administrative services: – the number of services provided via the GOS platform reached 3,668 items, covering the most relevant needs in the lives of individuals and companies

Government Online-Offline Shanghai

Strengths	Limitations	Implications for public service provision
		– the functions of the "Suishenma" will continue to expand both for citizens and enterprises, and the "Suishenma" will become a "city code" (城市码) that further integrates AI applications in administrative services and other areas (3) Through the Government Online-Offline Shanghai, AI is used in the provision of administrative services at each administrative level and in a great number of government agencies, extending the reach of AI-enabled administrative service provision to the majority of citizens: – 55 government departments, 16 district-level, and 220 subdistrict-level administrative service centers are connected to the GOS platform – the GOS platform reached 81.46 million real-name registered users – the rate of government services processed by the GOS reached 81.6%

(continued)

Table 5.7 (continued)

Government Online-Offline Shanghai		
Strengths	Limitations	Implications for public service provision
Single Platform for Urban Management		
Strengths	*Limitations*	*Implications for public service provision*
The use of AI is effectively designed to improve urban governance operations and urban management services, leveraging municipal guidance as well as the skills of districts and subdistricts to devise AI applications targeted to the urban governance needs at their administrative levels AI applications for urban governance are efficiently developed and implemented, and via the Single Platform for Urban Management they are integrated into the activities of government agencies in order to improve their core operations High rates of adoption among government agencies are fostering the widespread use of AI in urban governance across the municipality, leading to the diffusion of AI in public sector activities	Varying degrees of AI assimilation among urban governance organizations, Urban Operation Centers Persistence of data barriers Concerns about data privacy and security Possible overreliance on technology Need to further improve the coordinating mechanisms of the SPM	(1) AI is improving the efficiency of urban governance and urban management services: – There are several documented cases of efficiency gains in urban governance following the introduction of AI applications – Scholars and analysts agree that the SPM is helping Shanghai to: (i) increase the accuracy of urban governance; (ii) facilitate monitoring and provide early warning; (iii) support decision-making in urban governance; (iv) facilitate the coordination between urban governance agencies; and (v) provide a holistic view of urban governance issues in the municipality (2) The number of AI applications for urban governance of the Single Platform for Urban Management is continuously expanding, and such applications are becoming increasingly integrated in urban operations and urban management services: – digital twin technologies have been introduced to support urban governance operations and services

Government Online-Offline Shanghai		
Strengths	Limitations	Implications for public service provision
		– a growing number of mobile Apps for urban governance is made available on a dedicated municipal platform (3) Through the Single Platform for Urban Management, AI is used in urban governance at each administrative level and in a great number of government agencies, extending the reach of smart urban governance to the majority of citizens: – more than 70 government departments, 16 district-level, and 215 subdistrict-level Urban Operation Centers are connected to the SPM platform – the integrated network of Urban Operation Centers is bringing AI applications to subdistricts, townships, residential communities, and single buildings

unified e-government platforms. Finally, the Shanghai municipal government and the Shanghai CPC Committee have the *political capacity* to obtain and sustain support for the GOS and the SPM from municipal departments and government authorities in districts and subdistricts, as shown by the high rates of adoption of the two digital platforms among government agencies at each administrative level of the municipality.

Municipal-level capacities refer not only to the resources and skills of municipal organizations, but also to the ability of the Shanghai government to orchestrate the policy resources and capabilities available in the whole city (Chapter 2.3). The analysis showed that the Shanghai government has established channels of communications with AI experts and companies through which municipal policymakers can gain access to specialized knowledge in AI. The municipality is also leveraging the analytical skills of districts and subdistricts to devise applications for citizen services and urban governance based on the specific needs of each district and neighborhoods. In terms of political capacity, the Shanghai government incentivizes district governments to foster AI in administrative services and urban governance, ensuring that they are actively promoting the use of both platforms within their jurisdictions (Tables 5.4 and 5.6). Finally, the Shanghai government aptly leverages the operational resources of the municipal AI ecosystem in order to implement AI applications for administrative services and urban governance. These operational resources include: the data generated in the provision of administrative services and urban governance operations in districts and subdistricts; the existence of a ramified technological infrastructure that spreads throughout the municipality reaching the neighborhoods (i.e., district-level extranets, e-government clouds and databases, and the "city brains" in Urban Operation Centers at each administrative level); and the availability of AI companies and government technology agencies in the municipality (i.e., the district-level Big Data Centers, and the Urban Operation Centers in districts and subdistricts).

Third, **the platform-based approach is proactive**. The Shanghai government is spearheading the use of AI in the public sector by using the Government Online-Offline Shanghai and the Single Platform for Urban Management as conduits to assimilate AI technologies in the activities of public organizations and the provision of public services. The Shanghai municipal government is directly and actively involved in building the required technological infrastructure, gathering the necessary data resources, standardizing government workflows and procedures, and developing novel AI applications for administrative services and urban governance. In doing so, Shanghai is also actively engaging State-owned enterprises and private companies in public sector AI projects, consistently with an approach that aims to promote the development of the local AI industry as well as AI applications in the public sector (Chapter 4.4 and 5.1).

As noted, the Government Online-Offline Shanghai and the Single Platform for Urban Management are deeply interlinked. In May 2022, the Shanghai Municipal People's Congress reiterated that the municipality promotes the joint development of these two digital platforms, and will continue to foster the integration and mutual coordination of the "two networks[237]" (两张网). The Government Online-Offline Shanghai and the Single Platform for Urban Management have become the pillars of the "urban digital transformation[238]" (城市数字化转型) of Shanghai. Hence, these two platforms offer a vantage point to gauge the possible development trajectories of public sector AI applications in the municipality (Chapter 6).

Next section integrates the analysis of the main policy initiatives that promote public sector AI applications in Shanghai. It examines the experiment-based approach to the use of AI in public service provision, the strengths and limitations of this approach in deploying AI in the public sector, its implications for public service provision, and its similarities and differences with the platform-based approach.

[237] Shanghai Municipal People's Congress, 2022 (cit.), art. 11. See also Wang, 2022 (cit.), p. 8.

[238] This remark was made by the Vice Director of the Shanghai Municipal Big Data Center Liu Yingfeng (刘迎风) at the 2021 World Artificial Intelligence Conference in Shanghai. In original: "在城市数字化转型方面, 上海两个核心应用是政务服务 '一网通办' 和城市运行 '一网统管'". Quoted in: NetEase, 2021. Behind the "Government Online-Offline Shanghai" | Shanghai Municipal Big Data Center: There Is Nothing "Difficult to Do" in Shanghai [走进 "一网通办" 的背后|上海大数据中心: 在魔都没有 "难办" 的事]. *NetEase* [网易号], 18 August, https://www.163.com/dy/article/GHML2CFG0550DDYR.html.

5.3 Experiment-Based Approach: The AI Pilot Application Scenarios

The experiment-based approach to the use of AI in public service provision aims to accelerate the implementation of AI technologies in various policy areas by means of standalone trial projects. These trial projects are part of a program coordinated by the Shanghai government, called "AI pilot application scenarios" (人工智能试点应用场景). Next subsections present the main features of the AI pilot application scenarios, examine their strengths and limitations in deploying AI in the public sector, and discuss the resulting implications for public service provision.

5.3.1 Project Description

In December 2018, the Shanghai Municipal Commission of Economy and Informatization (SHEITC)—which oversees the deployment of AI in public sector and industrial projects (Chapters 3.2 and 5.1)—published the *Notice on the launch of the first collection of solutions for artificial intelligence applications in Shanghai.*[239] This is the first of three municipal calls[240] for the creation of AI pilot application scenarios that aim to "accelerate the first use in Shanghai of new AI technologies, products and models, create a benchmark for innovative AI applications at the municipal level, and significantly improve the degree of intelligence of [Shanghai as] a smart city and the citizens' perception of it".[241] In two years, this policy initiative led to the approval of 40 government-endorsed AI trial

[239] SHEITC Notice, 2018. *Notice on the Collection of Solutions for the First Batch of AI Application Scenarios in Shanghai* [关于开展本市首批人工智能应用场景解决方案征集工作的通知]. Hujingxintui (2018), no. 963, 14 December, http://www.shpt.gov.cn/kw/tongzhi/20181214/365807.html.

[240] The other two calls for the collection of AI pilots are: SHEITC Notice, 2019b. *Notice on the Collection of the Second Batch of Solutions for AI Application Scenarios in Shanghai* [关于征集本市第二批人工智能应用场景解决方案的通知]. Hujingxintui (2019), no. 402, 12 June, http://sheitc.sh.gov.cn/xxfw/20190612/0020-682748.html; and SHEITC Notice, 2020a. *Notice on the Collection of the Third Batch of Solutions for AI Application Scenarios in Shanghai* [关于征集本市第三批人工智能应用场景解决方案的通知]. Hujingxintui (2020), no. 506, 16 July, http://www.sheitc.sh.gov.cn/xxfw/20200717/aeec0bd27b7742518c4be5e4a55df642.html.

[241] SHEITC Notice, 2018, preamble. In original: "快推进人工智能新技术新产品新模式在上海率先运用，打造人工智能城市级创新应用标杆，显著提升智慧城市智敏化水平和市民感知度".

projects. When the first batch of projects was officially announced in April 2019, municipal authorities stated that the goal of the AI pilot application scenarios is to "improve citizens sense of gain and satisfaction, [and] effectively use artificial intelligence to solve practical bottlenecks and pain points".[242] Through the AI pilot application scenarios, Shanghai wants to leverage AI trial projects to identify solutions that can be disseminated at city-scale in various policy areas. The pilots must "strive to form replicable and referential experience models that can be applied to the whole city",[243] and "the work units (单位) where each application is located shall [...] actively demonstrate the progressive construction results of the application scenarios".[244]

In essence, the AI pilot application scenarios are a policy initiative that matches the demand of public organizations that want to use AI technologies in their activities with the supply of such technologies. For explanatory purposes, this process can be divided into four steps, all of which happen under the coordination and supervision of the SHEITC. First, the "scenario organizations" (场景单位) that want to host the trial projects—e.g., public entities like schools, hospitals, museums, neighborhood committees, utility providers, State-owned companies, or industrial parks—publish their "requirements for AI application scenarios" (人工智能应用场景需求) through the official notices issued by the SHEITC. These project requirements are quite brief, typically consisting of descriptions of 300–400 characters, and include the details of the contact persons of each scenario organization.[245] Second, technology

[242] SHEITC Notice, 2019a. *Notice of the Shanghai Municipal Commission of Economy and Informatization on the Announcement of the First Batch of AI Pilot Application Scenarios in Shanghai* [上海市经济信息化委关于公布本市首批人工智能试点应用场景的通知]. Hujingxintui (2019), no. 238, 19 April, http://app.sheitc.sh.gov.cn/xxfw/682323.htm, art. 2. In original: "提升市民的获得感和满意度 [...] 切实运用人工智能解决实际的瓶颈、痛点问题". The same wording is repeated in the announcement of the second batch of AI pilots in August 2019.

[243] Ibid., art. 5. In original: "力争形成可复制、可借鉴的经验模式, 在全市进行推广应用".

[244] Ibid., art. 4. In original: "各场景所在单位应严格按照实施进度 [...] 积极展示应用场景阶段性的建设成效".

[245] SHEITC Notice 2018, 2019b and 2020a, attachment 1, "Application form for requirements for the Shanghai AI pilot application scenarios" [人工智能试点应用场景需求列表]. The details of the contact persons of scenario organizations are indicated in the second and third batches of project requirements.

suppliers submit their candidatures to the SHEITC to provide AI solutions for the application scenarios. Aspirant technology partners have to indicate the specific pilot project they apply to, and explain how they can contribute to meeting the project requirements. In addition to the presentation of their company or institution, technology suppliers have to indicate: the number of personnel they intend to assign to the pilot project (拟投入人员数量); outline, in a summary and dedicated attachment, proposed "scenario construction solutions" to address the specific application requirements (结合具体的应用场景需求, 提出场景建设解决方案); and explain their competitive advantages compared to other potential technical partners,[246] among others. The aspirant technology partners primarily consist of private AI companies, although universities and State-owned enterprises can also be suppliers of AI technologies (Sect. 5.3.2.3). After the "scenario organizations" have identified their preferred technical partners, the third step is the selection of the projects that become "AI pilot application scenarios". The selection process is carried out by the SHEITC and its affiliated expert committees, like the Shanghai Municipal Artificial Intelligence Strategy Advisory Expert Committee (AISPi). The selection criteria are not public, and the official documents only state that pilots are chosen "through the match of supply and demand, field assessment, expert review, and other work".[247] The selection process usually

[246] SHEITC Notice 2018, 2019b and 2020a, attachment 2, "Application form for solutions for the Shanghai AI pilot application scenarios" [上海市人工智能应用场景解决方案申报表].

[247] SHEITC Notice 2019a; SHEITC Notice, 2019c. *Notice of the Shanghai Municipal Commission of Economy and Informatization on the Announcement of the Second Batch of AI Pilot Application Scenarios in Shanghai* [上海市经济信息化委关于公布本市第二批人工智能试点应用场景的通知]. Hujingxintui (2019), no. 663, 26 August, http://www.sheitc.sh.gov.cn/xxfw/20190902/0020-683526.html; and SHEITC Notice, 2020b. *Notice of the Shanghai Municipal Commission of Economy and Informatization on the Announcement of the Third Batch of Application Scenarios for Artificial Intelligence Pilots Shanghai* [上海市经济信息化委关于公布本市第三批人工智能试点应用场景的通知]. Hujingxinwei (2020) 1084, 16 December, http://www.sheitc.sh.gov.cn/xxfw/20201216/5f61e1fa133a42408d51a98cda582fa3.html. In original: "经过供需对接、实地评估、专家评审等工作, 确定上海市市西中学等12家单位列入本市首批人工智能试点应用场景" (2019a, preamble); "经过供需对接、实地评估、专家评审等工作, 确定上海电气集团股份有限公司等19家单位列入本市第二批人工智能试点应用场景" (2019c, preamble); "经过实地评估、供需对接、专家评审等工作, 确定上海集成电路研发中心有限公司、上海机场 (集团) 有限公司、吴淞口投资 (集团) 有限公司等9家单位列入本市第三批人工智能试点应用场景" (2020b, preamble).

does not modify the main requirements set by the "scenario organizations", since SHEITC only sets some broad targets that the projects must fulfill.[248] Fourth, the selected "AI pilot application scenarios" are finally announced by official notices published by SHEITC.

The official duration of the trial period (执行期, 试点期) is one year starting from the inclusion of the project in the list of AI application scenarios. After that, the AI pilots are reviewed and evaluated by the Shanghai municipal authorities, and the most valuable projects are awarded the title of "municipal-level AI demonstration application scenarios[249]" (市级人工智能示范应用场景). After the conclusion of the trial period, projects usually continue their due course, as it happened for all the case studies examined in this section. In December 2020, Shanghai announced the "municipal-level AI demonstration application scenarios" selected from the first batch of AI pilots approved in April 2019 (the delay was arguably due to the outbreak of the Covid-19 pandemic in the first months of 2020). All the four projects that the Shanghai government chose as best practices consist of public sector AI implementations. More specifically, these are projects in education (Shanghai World Foreign Language Education Group), healthcare (Shanghai No. 10 People's Hospital), residential community management (Beixinjing Subdistrict in Changning District), and industrial park management (Zhangjiang AI

[248] SHEITC requires that "the units where each application scenario is located should [...] carry out the construction of the application scenarios based on the fundamental starting points of high-quality development of AI-enabled economy, high-quality life of citizens, and safe and efficient urban operations" (SHEITC Notice, 2019a, art. 2). In original: "各场景所在单位应 [...] 以人工智能赋能经济高质量发展、市民高品质生活、城市安全高效运行为根本出发点, 开展场景建设工作". The same wording is repeated in the other two announcements of AI application scenarios in August 2019 and December 2020.

[249] SHEITC Notice, 2019a, art. 4.

Island).[250] At the time of this writing, no other "municipal-level AI demonstration application scenarios" have been announced.

In December 2020, nearly two thirds of the AI pilot application scenarios (25 projects out of 40) were nominally using AI for the provision of public services in various policy areas (Table 5.8). In details: education (6 projects); hospitals and public health (5 projects); transportation (5 projects); culture and tourism (3 projects); government affairs (2 projects); residential community (2 projects); urban management (1 project); and the judiciary (1 project).

Next paragraphs provide an overview of the 40 AI pilot application scenarios, briefly outlining the main contents of the AI pilots that were not selected as case studies for analysis (see infra for exclusions). The AI pilots selected as case studies are described in detail in Appendix VI, and their main features are examined in Sect. 5.3.2.

An Overview of the AI Pilot Application Scenarios

The intention of Shanghai to create AI pilot application scenarios was articulated in the two main policy documents for the promotion of AI development in the municipality (Chapter 3.2). In October 2017, the *Implementation Opinions on Promoting the Development of a New Generation Artificial Intelligence in Shanghai* stated that the municipality would create 60 "AI in-depth application scenarios" (人工智能深度应用场景), and more than 100 "AI application demonstration projects" (人工智能应用示范项目). In September 2019, the *Action Plan on Building Shanghai into an AI Highland and Creating First-Class Innovation Ecosystem (2019–2021)* reiterated this commitment by stating that Shanghai will build 100 "AI in-depth application scenarios" (人工智能深度应用场景) in 10 categories (not specified in the document).

In between these two policy documents, the collection of AI pilot application scenarios already started. In December 2018, the SHEITC

[250] SHEITC Notice, 2020c. *Notice of the Shanghai Municipal Commission of Economy and Informatization on the Announcement of the City's First Batch of AI Model Application Scenarios* [上海市经济信息化委关于公布本市首批人工智能示范应用场景的通知]. Hujingxintui (2020), no. 1085, 14 December, http://www.sheitc.sh.gov.cn/xxfw/20201216/259fd0aedd5049c29c73631164654014.html. It should be noted that the project in education is operated by a private company. On the other hand, the project labeled "AI + industrial park" (AI+ 园区) mainly consists of applications in environmental protection and public security (see the selection criteria of the case studies in Sect. 5.3.2, and detailed project descriptions in the Appendix at the end of this chapter).

Table 5.8 Artificial intelligence pilot application scenarios in Shanghai (December 2020)

Collection date	*Approval date*	*Application area*	*Projects*
14 December 2018	19 April 2019	AI+ school (AI+ 学校)	3
		AI+ hospital (AI+ 医院)	2
		AI+ residential community (AI+ 社区)	2
		AI+ industrial park (AI+ 园区)	2
		AI+ transport (AI+ 交通)	1
		AI+ government affairs (AI+ 政务)	1
		AI+ finance (AI+ 金融)	1
12 June 2019	26 August 2019	AI+ education (AI+ 教育)	3
		AI+ medicine (AI+ 医疗)	3
		AI+ culture and tourism (AI+ 文化旅游)	2
		AI+ transport (AI+ 交通)	2
		AI+ manufacturing (AI+ 制造业)	2
		AI+ industrial park (AI+ 园区)	2
		AI+ assorted applications (AI+ 综合)	1
		AI+ finance (AI+ 金融)	1
		AI+ urban management (AI+ 城市管理)	1
		AI+ judiciary (AI+ 司法)	1
		AI+ agriculture (AI+ 农业; initially termed AI+ 村庄)	1
16 July 2020	16 December 2020	AI+ manufacturing (AI+ 制造)	1
		AI+ transport hubs (交通枢纽)	2
		AI+ business circles (AI+ 商圈)	2
		AI+ culture and tourism (AI+ 文化旅游)	1
		AI+ government affairs (AI+ 政务)	1
		AI+ industrial park management (AI+ 园区)	1
		AI+ finance (AI+ 金融)	1
		Total AI pilot applications	**40**

published the first call for trial projects. The document includes 19 projects in 10 areas, with a marked prevalence (14 projects) of public sector applications: four projects in education; three projects in medicine; two projects in government affairs, residential communities, and transportation, respectively; and 1 project in public security. From these 19 projects, in April 2019 the Shanghai government selected the **first batch of 12 AI pilot application scenarios,**[251] which have a clear focus on public sector AI applications. The selected pilots include:

- three projects in *schools* (AI+ 学校): the (i) Minhang Qiangwei Primary School, (ii) Shanghai Shixi High School, and (iii) Shanghai WFL Education Group (see Sect. 5.3.2 and Appendix VI);
- two projects in *hospitals* (AI+ 医院): the (i) Shanghai No. 10 People's Hospital, and (ii) the Fudan University Cancer Hospital (see Sect. 5.3.2 and Appendix VI);
- two projects in *residential communities* (AI+ 社区): the (i) Beixinjing Subdistrict in Changning District, and (ii) the Xietu Road Subdistrict in Xuhui District (see Sect. 5.3.2 and Appendix VI);
- two projects in *industrial parks* (AI+ 园区): the (i) Zhangjiang AI Island (see Sect. 5.3.2 and Appendix VI), and (ii) the Changyang Innovation Valley project, which consists of demonstrative applications in intelligent logistics, unmanned sales and intelligent office, and virtual reality technology to popularize science education among the users and visitors of the park;
- one project in *transport* (AI+ 交通): the Lingang Autonomous Vehicles Testing Base (see Sect. 5.3.2 and Appendix VI);
- one project in *government affairs* (AI+ 政务): the Jing'an Government Data Management Center (see Sect. 5.3.2 and Appendix VI);
- one project in *finance* (AI+ 金融): the China Construction Bank Shanghai central branch project, which uses AI for the predictive maintenance of ATM machines and other IT equipment, and carries out AI-based forecast of the total amount of cash required by each ATM machine.

[251] SHEITC Notice, 2019a.

In June 2019, Shanghai published a second notice on the collection of AI solutions for 28 pilot application scenarios.[252] The list of candidate projects again displays a prevalence of public sector applications: five projects in medicine; five projects in education; four projects in culture and tourism; three projects in transportation; one project in the judiciary, and one project in urban management. From these 28 projects, in August 2019 the Shanghai government approved the **second batch of 19 AI pilot application scenarios**,[253] which include:

- three projects in *medicine* (AI+ 医疗): (i) the Shanghai Children's Hospital Eastern Medical Complex (Pudong and Fengxian Districts), (ii) the Shanghai Ruijin Hospital (for both projects see Sect. 5.3.2 and Appendix VI), and (iii) the joint project by Xuhui District Health Management Development Center, Zhongshan Hospital and the Xuhui District Central Hospital, which uses AI for the early detection of key cardiovascular diseases and the identification of high-risk groups, and AI-powered IoT equipment for health monitoring and assessment in the rehabilitation period following cardiovascular disease treatment;
- three projects in *education* (AI+ 教育): (i) the Luwan No. 1 Central Primary School (see Sect. 5.3.2 and Appendix VI); (ii) the Shanghai Institute of Physical Education (上海体育学院), a project that leverages computer vision to create a "smart table tennis teacher" that uses data collected from professional athletes for teaching and demonstration, and also introduced a table tennis robot arm that is capable of confronting human players; and (iii) the Shanghai University project for the creation of a smart campus that uses smart surveillance service robots, as well as computer vision and other AI technologies for visitor management and intelligent detection of security and safety risks in the campus;
- two projects in *culture and tourism* (AI+ 文化旅游): (i) the Shanghai Museum (see Sect. 5.3.2 and Appendix VI), and (ii) the project of the Shanghai Media Group (a State-owned broadcaster) that uses AI to edit video and audio contents, improve image clarity to meet

[252] SHEITC Notice, 2019b.

[253] SHEITC Notice, 2019c.

ultra-high-definition requirements, automatically generate news and information contents, and create a virtual news anchorman;

- one project in ***urban management*** (AI+ 城市管理): the State-owned Shanghai Chengtou Environment Group (上海城投环境 (集团) 有限公司) uses computer vision and other AI technologies installed on garbage trucks to automatically sort and classify the wet garbage that is loaded on the vehicles, and send warnings in case of impurities in the garbage or when non-wet garbage is erroneously collected. This project also uses AI systems and smart robots in the garbage collection points to identify recyclable garbage and harmful garbage, and place them in different recycling and treatment containers;
- two projects in ***transport*** (AI+ 交通): (i) the Shanghai Subway (see Sect. 5.3.2 and Appendix VI), and (ii) the Donghai Bridge project for smart road management and maintenance, which uses AI to extract, classify and analyze information on vehicles such as license plates and vehicle models, automatically detect car accidents or vehicles illegally parked on the bridge, and identify safety risks like road surface defects (pits, cracks, etc.);
- one project in the ***judiciary*** (AI+ 司法): the Shanghai Financial Court (see Sect. 5.3.2 and Appendix VI);
- one project in ***miscellaneous applications*** (AI+ 综合): the Shanghai Expo Park project, which consists of demonstrative applications in "smart business", including smart restaurants (e.g., augmented reality menus and immersive dining experience), smart clothing stores (e.g., collect data on customers to recommend clothes and virtually try them on), and other demonstrative applications (e.g., music concerts performed by AI systems and robots);
- two projects in ***manufacturing*** (AI+ 制造): the State-owned companies (i) Shanghai Electric (上海电气集团) and (ii) State Grid of China Shanghai branch (国网上海市电力公司) developed projects focused on predictive equipment maintenance, intelligent diagnosis of equipment faults, and safe production and operations;
- two projects in ***industrial parks*** (AI+ 园区): (i) the State-owned real-estate developer West Bund Group (上海西岸集团) uses AI to provide smart services and support management activities in the West Bund Media Port Smart Industrial Park (西岸传媒港智慧园区), such as assistance in finding available parking lots, registration and monitoring of visitors, and the monitoring of fire risks; and (ii) Wangpu Logistics Equipment Co., Ltd. (网普物流装备) uses AI

for warehouse automation (e.g., service robots for stacking, sorting, handling, packaging, unpacking, loading, and unloading in the warehouse), stock management and logistics operations (e.g., use AI to optimize the loading rate of vehicles, to support inventory and the location of goods, or to arrange the dispatch of goods);

- one project in *agriculture* (AI+ 农业): the Zhouzha Village of Tingling Town in Jinshan District (金山区亭林镇周栅村) uses computer vision for soil monitoring, and agricultural robots to perform labor-intensive agricultural work (e.g., watering, sowing, weeding and fertilizing) and carry out automatic operations such as pruning, combing and automatic picking of fruit from trees;
- one project in *finance* (AI+ 金融): the China Foreign Exchange Center (中国外汇交易中心) project uses AI and data mining to detect abnormal transactions and provide early warnings, suggest users options for financial trading that reduce the risks of losses, carry out predictive maintenance of its IT equipment, and create AI-enabled e-brokers that can improve the quality and efficiency of customer service.

Finally, following a similar pattern, in July 2020 Shanghai published a third notice on the collection of AI solutions for 11 pilot application scenarios,[254] including three projects in transportation, one project in in culture and tourism, and one project in government affairs. From these 11 projects, in December 2020 the Shanghai government approved the **third batch of 9 AI pilot application scenarios.**[255] These include:

- one project in *manufacturing* (AI+ 制造): the Shanghai Integrated Circuit R&D Center (上海集成电路研发中心有限公司) uses AI to improve production efficiency (e.g., automatic classification and analysis of product defects), optimize the R&D of integrated circuits (e.g., AI models analyze and simulate the performance of key materials used for integrated circuit production, shortening the R&D cycle), and carry out predictive maintenance and smart diagnosis of integrated circuit equipment;

[254] SHEITC Notice, 2020a.

[255] SHEITC Notice, 2020b.

- two projects in *transport* (交通枢纽): (i) the Shanghai Pudong International Airport combines data on air and land traffic, and leverages AI models to predict the demand for taxis of arriving passengers and help identify available parking lots in the parking areas of the airport. It also uses AI models to monitor and optimize traffic management in the airport area, combining data from air and land traffic, weather conditions, etc. The project at (ii) the Wusong International Cruise Terminal uses AI to simplify customs clearance procedures for tourists, optimize the traffic connections between the port and the city reducing the congestion points, and provide intelligent solutions for safe and efficient operations of the terminal;
- two projects in *business circles* (AI+ 商圈): the project on (i) the East Nanjing Road pedestrian street, one of the main commercial venues of Shanghai, uses augmented reality (AR) to create a virtual guide integrating commercial information and recommendations for touristic routes. It also uses AI and IoT technologies for the real-time monitoring and prediction of people flows in key areas and identify potential safety risks. The (ii) State-owned retailer Bailian Group (上海百联) uses AI models for the analysis of customer data in order to improve the service in some of its shopping malls, for instance providing smart shopping guides that integrate information from various merchants and ongoing activities in the mall;
- one project in *culture and tourism* (AI+ 文化旅游): the Bingjiang Forest Park (滨江森林公园) uses AI and Big Data to provide visitors with personalized recommendations for touring the park, virtual reality presentations, driverless shuttle bus, and other services. AI, data mining, and smart robots provide unmanned cleaning services and other park maintenance operations (e.g., smart sprinkler irrigation, pesticide application, weeding, grass cutting, and other maintenance services). Finally, AI is also used to improve park security (e.g., monitoring the risks of fire, preventing theft and other illegal activities, etc.);
- one project in *government affairs* (AI+ 政务): the Shanghai Customs Technology Innovation Center (上海科创中心海关) uses AI to support the supervision and inspection of imported large-scale equipment, instruments, and R&D materials (e.g., raw materials, reagents). It also uses AI to facilitate customs clearance for selected groups of people (e.g., top talents in the field of science and technology);

- one project in ***industrial parks*** (AI+ 园区): the National Intelligent Connected Vehicle (Shanghai) Pilot Demonstration Zone (国家智能网联汽车 (上海) 试点示范区) in Jiading district[256] (Chapter 4.2) replicates some applications similar to those of the aforementioned Lingang Autonomous Vehicles Testing Base. In some circumscribed areas, it also tests unmanned express delivery (small packages, correspondence) and unmanned meal delivery;
- one project in *finance* (AI+ 金融): the Industrial and Commercial Bank of China (中国工商银行) Shanghai branch uses AI for the personalized recommendation of products and services to its customers, carry out risk assessments for the provision of credit, and improve service efficiency by integrating online and offline operations.

5.3.2 Strengths and Limitations of the AI Pilots in Deploying AI in the Public Sector

The AI pilot application scenarios are a program designed and coordinated by the Shanghai municipal government via the SHEITC. The development and execution of the trial projects are supported in various forms by municipal-level policy skills and resources, as discussed shortly. At the same time, each AI pilot application scenario is a standalone project, in which the use of AI to improve the provision of public services is primarily dependent on the skills and resources of the public organization implementing the pilot project. Therefore, to understand how this experiment-based approach fosters the use of AI in public sector activities, next paragraphs examine the strengths and limitations in deploying AI in the public sector determined by this combination of organizational and municipal-level capabilities, and assess the resulting implications for public service delivery in Shanghai.

The problem of pursuing this analytical stance is that the variety of AI pilot applications scenarios complicates the identification of strengths and limitations that can be generalized to the entire experiment-based approach. Even after the selection of the case studies reduces the scope of

256 This project was already proposed in the first call for AI solutions published in December 2018 (SHEITC, 2018). At that time, it was labeled as "AI + transport" (AI+ 交通) and was not selected as a pilot application scenario.

the investigation (see infra), the AI pilots still display a great diversity of trial applications distributed across several policy areas.[257] Namely: *education* (AI+ school/education, case studies #1–4); *health* (AI+ hospital/ medicine, case studies #5–8); *housing and community amenities* (AI+ residential community, case studies #9–10); *environmental protection, public order and safety* (AI+ industrial park, case study #11); *economic affairs* (AI+ transport,[258] case studies #12–13); *general public services* (AI+ government affairs, case study #14); *recreation, culture, and religion* (AI+ culture and tourism, case study #15); and *public order and safety* (AI+ judiciary,[259] case study #16). In addition, within each policy area and case study, AI technologies are used to enable several public sector activities (Chapter 2.2.2). For instance: *public service delivery and engagement* (all case studies but Lingang, case study #12); *enforcement* (e.g., smart campus security in case study #1, street security in residential communities in case studies #9–10, smart security of industry park in case study #11 and subway stations in case study #13, and the use of AI in smart trials in case study #16); *internal operations* (e.g., smart teacher training system in case study #1, AI-assisted outpatient appointments in case study #6, personnel management in case study #13, restoration of cultural relics in case study #15); *public infrastructure management* (e.g., in neighborhoods in case studies #9–10, in industrial parks in case study #11, in transport in case studies #12–13, in museum buildings in case study #15); or *public policy research, analysis and monitoring* (in urban planning and market supervision, case study #14).

To ensure that the analysis lifts important aspects to understand the impacts of the experiment-based approach on public service provision in Shanghai, next paragraphs identify *cross-cutting features* that characterize all the case studies of AI pilot application scenarios, and examine the strengths and limitations in deploying AI in the public sector related

[257] Case studies are grouped here by policy area based on the OECD's first-level Classification of the Functions of Government (COFOG), which classifies government expenditure data from the System of National Accounts by the purpose for which the funds are used (Chapter 2.2). The categorization is based on the main content of each AI pilot, whose classification according to SHEITC documents (Table 5.8) is reported in brackets.

[258] "Transport" is a second-level classification of "economic affairs" in the COFOG classification.

[259] "Law courts" is a second-level classification of "public order and safety" in the COFOG classification.

to these features. This approach offers two key advantages. First, it ensures that *the analysis is representative*, as it examines strengths and limitations that are relevant to all the AI pilots, and thus are most suited to characterize the experiment-based approach as a whole. Second, it ensures that *the analysis is significant*. By examining the strengths and limitations that best represent the experiment-based approach, it highlights the organizational policy capacities that are most important to gauge the impacts of the AI pilot application scenarios on the use of AI in public sector activities, and their interactions with municipal-level capacities. By offering deeper insights into the strengths and limitations of the experiment-based approach in deploying AI in the public sector, next subsections provide a solid basis to assess the implications of the AI pilot application scenarios for the provision of public services in Shanghai.

The analysis of the strengths and limitations of the experiment-based approach and the resulting implications for public service provision is based on the in-depth review of 16 case studies (Table 5.9), which are drawn from the list of the total 40 AI pilot application scenarios approved by the SHEITC. The case studies include: 15 of the 25 AI pilots that are nominally using AI in the public sector (i.e., they were classified as projects related to public service delivery, e.g., "AI + education"); and one pilot application scenario labeled "AI + industrial park" that is actually testing AI applications in environmental protection and public order and safety. The selection criteria are explained below:

- **Public-service Relevance**: the analysis considers AI pilot projects related to the delivery of public services, intended as services of general interest provided by public organizations to benefit all the people in a particular society or community (Chapter 2.2.2). Public organizations indicate entities owned or controlled by the national or local governments, subject to administrative law, and financed by public money. The only case study that does not involve a public organization is case study #3. This is implemented by a private education group, but was included in the analysis because in December 2020 it was chosen as one of the "municipal-level demonstration projects" that are officially recommended to be replicated by other public organizations in Shanghai. On the other hand, the project of State-owned broadcaster Shanghai Media Group labeled as "culture and tourism" (August 2019) was not considered because it solely focuses on the use of AI for editing video and audio content,

Table 5.9 The AI pilot application scenarios selected as case studies (approval date), and their main AI usages. Details of each case study are provided in Appendix VI

(1) Minhang Qiangwei Primary School (April 2019)

1. *Smart campus security*: it uses AI to fully cover campus security. For instance, it leverages computer vision to count the number of students arriving at the school, monitor and track the outside people, and identify dangerous individuals. This application also registers student behavioral patterns, and monitors students' activities in real time between classes to discover potential health and safety problems (e.g., children's chasing or quarreling)
2. *Smart teacher training system*: it uses AI technologies to evaluate teaching performance based on criteria such as their voice and speech rate. It also uses data mining technology to automatically segment and match videos that can support teaching activities based on the contents of each class, and automatically extracts relevant teaching video clips that teachers can use for their lessons. This application has then evolved into a "smart classroom evaluation system" (智能课堂评价系统) that uses facial expression recognition and speech recognition to automatically detect and record student behaviors (e.g., raising hands, yawning) to make correlations between learning status, classroom effectiveness, and learning interest
3. *Smart promotion of traditional Chinese culture*: based upon a list of traditional physical exercises (e.g., the Yi Jin Jing), it uses an AI system that displays the standard movements of the exercises, and uses AI models to correct the movements and postures of the students by means of interesting games

(2) Shanghai Shixi High School (April 2019)

1. *AI education laboratory*: it provides AI software that students can use to acquire and analyze images and videos generated within the school; a demonstration area of AI technologies, including facial check-in, facial recognition technologies; and a demonstration area of AI equipment, among others
2. *Intelligent teaching and learning platform*: it uses AI to examine data generated by the students' online learning activities in the "online classrooms" (网学课堂) and other digital learning platforms created by the school. Based on information on study time and content, test results, and other data, the AI system makes teaching suggestions targeted at the characteristics of each student
3. *Smart classrooms*: it uses AI technologies such as computer vision and Natural Language Processing to support the teaching of subjects like English language (e.g., speech-to-text conversion to boost listening and speaking training). It also uses AI for the recognition of letters, numbers, Chinese characters, and mathematical expressions, supporting students in doing their homework assigned on the school's digital learning platforms

(3) Shanghai World Foreign Language Education Group (April 2019)

1. *Adaptive learning system*: it uses Big Data analysis and machine learning to help teachers timely recommend exercises and learning resources suitable to the level of each student, promoting personalized teaching in three disciplines: mathematical calculus, macroeconomics, and statistics. The system includes functions such as student grading, daily practice suggestion, and automatic collection of wrong answers

(continued)

Table 5.9 (continued)

2. *Classroom real-time analysis system*: it uses AI technologies such as computer vision for behavioral analysis through real-time video recording in the classrooms. This application uses AI models to infer students' learning habits, points of interest, and classroom attention, in order to improve teaching efficiency in classrooms
3. *Pronunciation correction system*: designed for English language teaching, it includes multidimensional AI evaluation, correction suggestions, independent practice scoring, and a self-study system for English reading practice

(4) Luwan No. 1 Central Primary School (August 2019)

1. *Smart teaching support*: it uses AI technologies to promote tailor-made teaching solutions for students. It generates digital portraits (数字画像) of students, allowing teachers to infer the learning process and habits of each student in order to provide personalized tutoring and teaching recommendations
2. *Smart assistance for emotional education*: it uses AI to assist the school in "emotional education" (情感教育) activities. The aforementioned "digital portraits" also support teachers to recognize the emotional state of the students and promote personalized emotional education (个性化情感教育). This system is a variation of classroom real-time analysis systems used in other case studies (#1 and 3), and it measures five key indicators of students' behavior: "standing up", "reading", "writing", "listening and reading", and "lying down on the desk". The system also uses data collected from "cloud watches" (云手表) that record the physical state of students, measuring their average fatigue and exercise frequency

(5) Shanghai No. 10 People's Hospital (April 2019)

1. *Smart emergency auxiliary diagnosis and treatment system*: it consists of three main components:
   (i) Intelligent consultation. Accessible via smartphone or on-site, it supports voice, handwriting, and Natural Language Processing to assist doctors in the pre-diagnosis of outpatient cases. It uses machine learning to predict and grade the criticality of patients, and gives advice on the medical treatment, automatically recommending the most suitable physical examinations and health checks. It also automatically generates medical records and stores them on the database. (ii) Service robot. The system uses an AI service robot that collects data such as blood pressure, pulse, body temperature of patients. (iii) Smart diagnostic system. It includes a multi-specialty smart diagnostic system that leverages an AI knowledge base on diseases of the cardiovascular, digestive, respiratory, and nervous systems, and other specialized diseases
2. *Intelligent CT auxiliary imaging diagnosis*: it leverages AI to shorten the examination time and improve the accuracy rate of CT imaging diagnosis and screening

(continued)

Table 5.9 (continued)

3. *Eyeground disease multimodal intelligent screening*: it uses AI to examine optical coherence tomography images and color fundus images.[260] It offers ophthalmic auxiliary diagnostic tools (e.g., the automatic calculation model of arterial-vein ratio/cup-to-disc ratio), and conducts Big Data analysis of the ophthalmic screening results

(6) Fudan University Cancer Hospital (April 2019)

1. *Outpatient appointment accuracy*: it uses Natural Language Processing and speech recognition to collect medical history data, description of medical symptoms, and other information when registering a patient. The AI system makes an assessment of the patient's condition, and evaluates whether the patient needs to see a specialist outpatient clinic. When collecting the patient's information, the system can also automatically determine whether the patient's conditions require to perform clinical trials in the hospital
2. *Management of medications*: the medication guidance function (用药指导功能) provides patients with a personalized medication guidance plan, based upon a prescription formulated by a doctor and revised and approved by a pharmacist. When the patient starts the chemotherapy treatment, AI can intelligently generate a personalized medication plan, and can also activate reminders to ensure that patients take medications on time. The system also creates a reporting channel for adverse drug reactions experienced by patients
3. *Communications between hospital and patients*: it uses AI to allow patients to communicate with the hospital via a smart chatbot (智能对话机器人) embedded in the hospital's official WeChat account. This AI system supports voice, text, and pictures, so that patients can receive timely information about the whole process of medical treatment before, during and after the diagnosis
4. *Early tumor screening*: it leverages AI to generate a preliminary risk assessment based on the information provided by the users. Based on the resulting tumor risk assessment, the system provides different professional suggestions, depending on the users' risk profile
5. *Statistics management*: it consists of a visualization system of survival rate of tumor patients (肿瘤患者生存率可视化系统), which makes it simpler to interpret the statistics of patient survival rates, so that the hospital's relevant departments can quickly obtain and visualize the data
6. *Outpatient medical history and examination report management*: the AI-enabled voice recording function uses speech recognition to support the accurate and efficient transcription of medical records, helping doctors to quickly generate medical records and reports, reducing the time spent on this task

(continued)

[260] Optical coherence tomography (OCT) is a non-invasive imaging method that uses reflected light to create pictures of the back of the eye to diagnose and manage diseases like diabetes-related retinopathy and glaucoma. Fundus imaging is the process whereby reflected light is used to obtain a two-dimensional representation of the 3D, semi-transparent, retinal tissues projected on to the imaging plane. See: https://my.clevelandclinic.org/health/diagnostics/17293-optical-coherence-tomography and https://www.sciencedirect.com/topics/medicine-and-dentistry/fundus-imaging.

Table 5.9 (continued)

7. *Mammography Intelligent Auxiliary Diagnosis System*: it uses deep learning algorithms to improve diagnostic accuracy in mammography, reducing the incidence of missed diagnosis and misdiagnosis of lesions
8. *Cervical cancer screening*: it uses deep learning techniques, image recognition, and other AI technologies to extract key features of cervical cells, and automatically identify cancerous areas and types of cells

(7) Shanghai Children's Hospital, Eastern Medical Complex (August 2019)

1. *Smart consultation*: parents can briefly describe the symptoms of their children using the smart consultation system available on the hospital's WeChat account. The system then analyzes the information through semantic recognition, and it automatically recommends the relevant hospital department according to the reported symptoms
2. *Pre-diagnosis inspection*: it uses an AI pre-diagnosis inspection system that provides recommendations about medical checks that can be done before face-to-face consultations with doctors. The system relies on a knowledge base of clinical practice guidelines and expert experience
3. *Smart auxiliary diagnosis*: it uses AI to support the collection of medical information, reducing the time spent by doctors in writing medical records. After the doctor completes the medical record, the system can automatically extract information from it, and uses algorithms to screen and locate the main symptoms, suggest possible diagnoses, and recommend possible treatments
4. *Remote consultation*: the hospital uses smart robots to conduct ward rounds, allowing direct but contactless communication between doctors and patients. It also introduced smart auscultation equipment (breath sounds, heart sounds, etc.) that automatically updates medical data on the hospital's cloud system, providing the basis for real-time data analytics

(8) Shanghai Ruijin Hospital (August 2019)

1. *Smart authentication*: it uses facial recognition technologies to verify the identity of patients during medical treatment, admission and discharge, nursing, surgery, and other steps
2. *Smart pre-check and pre-diagnosis*: it uses AI to facilitate communications with patients before the medical check through voice, text, and images, assisting and guiding patients to choose a department or specialist. It uses AI to generate a pre-diagnostic report for doctors' reference, based on the information provided by the patients
3. *Smart medical records*: by combining the medical history information provided by the patients in the smart pre-diagnosis system (see above), this AI application assists doctors in selected departments by using speech recognition to enable the voice input of medical records
4. *Smart image recognition*: it leverages AI to identify lesions in the images of thyroid, breast, cerebral hemorrhage, lumbar spine and other diseases, assisting doctors to carry out the medical diagnosis
5. *Chronic disease management and follow-up*: it uses smart wearable or portable devices to collect follow-up data, smart phone follow-up, supporting the management of chronic disease patients

(continued)

Table 5.9 (continued)

6. *Smart remote ward rounds*: it uses AI-enabled robots and other technologies so that doctors can conduct remote ward rounds. Technologies like computer vision and 5G also allow the hospital to perform remote medical checks with partner institutions

(9) Beixinjing Subdistrict, Changning District (April 2019)

1. *Smart community services*: it includes several functions. The "smart government affairs" function (智慧政务) leverages speech recognition technology, computer vision and Natural Language Processing to provide services to businesses and community residents. The "smart business" function (智慧商业) consists of 24-hour unattended convenience stores and other services. Other, more demonstrative applications use AI to support cultural and sports activities, such as "smart walking trails" (智能步道), etc.
2. *Smart elderly care services*: this application collects data from various sources such as the elderly care center, community health station, etc., and leverages AI to provide smart and personalized health management services for the elderly people. For instance, it introduced a "wireless network biological detection system" (无线网络生物探测系统) designed for the elderly who are living alone
3. *Smart life*: it uses AI to support management and services in the neighborhood, such as smart garbage classification, smart parking, smart cleaning
4. *Smart security*: this application leverages AI and IoT technologies for the real-time monitoring of public security in the neighborhood, including fire prevention, smoke detection, water accumulation detection, monitoring the elevators, etc.
5. *Smart community*: the "community brain" (社区大脑), fully connected to the Single Platform for Urban Management (Sect. 5.2.2), uses AI technologies such as computer vision, speech recognition and Natural Language Processing. It performs "smart video patrol" (智能巡屏) that can automatically discover problems in the residential community almost in real time: from removing shared bikes or garbage to clear passageways, to more complex problems that require the intervention of higher-level authorities

(10) Xietu Road Subdistrict, Xuhui District (April 2019)

1. *Smart brain*: it consists of an AI-enabled digital platform that was later connected to the municipal Single Platform for Urban Management (Sect. 5.2.2). It gathers data from different urban governance agencies to improve community management through traffic monitoring (流量监测), notification and early warning, smart evacuation, and other services
2. *Smart security*: it uses facial recognition, smart smoke detectors, and other smart sensors to improve the security of public spaces in the neighborhood. The security equipment also leverages AI to collect data that are fed into the "smart brain" platform to improve the quality of public service provision in the neighborhood
3. *AI+ medicine and healthcare*: it consists of self-service clinics (社区自助诊所) where residents can use smart voice technology to ask doctors for remote diagnoses for minor ailments, or order medicines from nearby pharmacies. This system is designed to support the services provided by community hospitals (社区医院)

(continued)

Table 5.9 (continued)

4. *AI+ administrative services*: it consists of an "unmanned reception stations" (无人值守受理站) equipped with AI-enabled systems (e.g., smart ID card readers, service robots, smart kiosks, and file cabinets), which allow citizens to handle selected administrative services by themselves (see the smart equipment discussed in Sect. 5.2.1)
5. *AI+ relatives and neighbor interactions* (AI+ 亲邻互动): it uses AI to profile the residents in the neighborhood, and it serves as a match-making platform that pairs the most common needs of the local residents (e.g., disabled and elderly care, childcare, culture and sports, etc.) with relevant resources (e.g., volunteers, community activities)

(11) Zhangjiang AI Island (April 2019; on-site visit: January 2021)

1. *Park management*: it uses AI and IoT technologies in various activities within the park: (i) "smart security" consists of using AI and IoT technologies, cloud computing, mobile Internet, smart surveillance cameras, security robots and a smart visitor management system to improve security management and control; (ii) "smart lampposts" use an IoT network to improve the utilization rate of resources through the intelligent management of street lights, smart e-charging stations and other methods; (iii) "smart parking" uses AI-based automatic license plate recognition and IoT technologies to optimize car parking in the AI Island; (iv) "fire prevention" uses intelligent smoke detectors, smart sensing equipment for temperature and humidity detection, or systems for the security scanning of vehicles, in order to avoid potential fire and safety hazards; (v) "smart energy management" leverages AI for the remote, real-time monitoring of electrical equipment and other energy systems, providing accurate information for energy management and conservation; (vi) "environmental monitoring" uses AI to control water and air quality, to check the maintenance of garbage bins and manhole covers, and to manage an automatic irrigation system; and (vii) " machine intelligence" (机器智能) consists of promoting real-world applications of drones, cleaning robots, security robots, and unmanned vehicles in the park
2. *Park services*: it integrates augmented reality (AR) and virtual reality (VR) technologies in the activities of the AI Island security staff, who can rely on these technologies during their tours and patrols of the park. It also combines AR and VR technologies with the activities and data collected by the security service robots (see above)
3. *Smart buildings*: this application implements smart systems for office management (e.g., intelligent control of office environment such as temperature, humidity, and air quality), and it uses AI to support the activities of the command center (智能指挥中心) of the AI Island. For instance, it uses AI-based audio and video technologies to monitor park activities, provide early warnings, or support decision-making
4. *Park Smart Brain*: the data collected and generated by the AI applications within the park (i.e., park management, park services, and smart buildings) feed the "Park Smart Brain" (园区智脑). This is an AI system that leverages speech recognition, Natural Language Processing and other AI technologies for data collection and analysis, supporting applications like identity authentication and other park operations

(continued)

Table 5.9 (continued)

(12) Lingang autonomous vehicles testing base (April 2019; on-site visit: September 2020)

1. *Demonstration area for unmanned intelligent connected vehicles*: this area focuses on AI technologies for public transport (unmanned taxis, unmanned buses) and infrastructure management and maintenance (smart traffic infrastructure, unmanned street-sweeping cars). It also helps companies to develop commercial applications that can be later deployed by the public sector (unmanned delivery vehicles, unmanned truck logistics). AI supports the smart traffic infrastructure of the demonstration zone, to which the autonomous vehicles are connected through a V2X (vehicle-to-everything) coordination system. In addition, computer vision and IoT allow the control center of the zone to monitor and collect in real-time the information on the operations of vehicles, drivers, and other activities, gathering images from more than 70 smart cameras installed in the demonstration area
2. *Low-altitude demonstration area for drones*: the area has built an overall supervision system for low-altitude drones, and is testing demonstrative applications of drones in urban security and logistics
3. *Unmanned boat demonstration area*: applications of unmanned boats, underwater robots, underwater acoustic instruments are being tested in some parts of the Dishui Lake, which is located in the area

(13) Shanghai Subway (August 2019; on-site visit: January 2021)

1. *Passenger flow detection and early warning*: it uses computer vision to monitor real-time passenger flows in the subway stations, including the actual number of people in each station, the speed of passenger flows, and the total passenger volumes of the day, among others. This application also uses an AI-based geospatial model[261] (地理空间模型) that performs real-time quantitative monitoring of key areas, and it triggers congestion alerts based on a set of parameters (number of people, congestion index, density, and flow speed, etc.). This model also monitors the passenger flows in the whole subway network, including real-time analysis and forecast of passenger flows at designated stations and on the entire railway network
2. *Personnel management and behavior identification*: it uses facial recognition technology to verify the identity of subway staff for entrance to restricted areas, to conduct automatic inspections (自动巡检), and to carry out other staff management operations. In addition, the "behaviour identification" application (行为识别) monitors signs of fatigue on train drivers or irregular operations of the subway staff; it also monitors a variety of situations inside the subway stations, including irregular or dangerous behaviors on the escalators, other irregular or dangerous activities (e.g., begging, not paying the ticket, quarreling, etc.), and the clearing of passengers when the stations close at night

(continued)

[261] Geospatial artificial intelligence (GeoAI) is the combination of AI (especially machine learning and deep learning techniques) with spatial computing to develop a better understanding, using geospatial data, of geographical phenomena and dynamics at the levels of individuals, communities, cities, nations, and the planet. See: Song, G., 2021. Geospatial Artificial Intelligence (GeoAI). *Oxford Bibliographies*, 24 March, https://www.oxfordbibliographies.com/view/document/obo-9780199874002/obo-9780199874002-0228.xml.

Table 5.9 (continued)

3. *Smart maintenance*: it uses machine learning, computer vision, and other AI technologies for the online monitoring and fault diagnosis of key subway equipment and infrastructure, such as subway trains and traffic signals
4. *Autonomous driving lines*: it uses AI, IoT, and other technologies to fully automate the subway transport. In some subway lines, the whole process of entry and exit of trains from the warehouses, train driving, stopping, and turn-backs are entirely automatic, with no human intervention

(14) Jing'an Government Data Management Center (April 2019; on-site visit: August 2020)

1. *Smart population forecasts*: these forecasts use AI models to analyze data on the resident population, and make long-term demographic projections. A combination of AI models and computer vision is also used for making real-time people flow projections. Long-term population forecasts are used for urban planning (see next point). Real-time people flow forecasts are used to monitor population agglomeration in key areas of Jing'an district (such as touristic spots, office areas, commercial areas), in order to assist decision-makers in various government departments
2. *Smart planning*: it uses AI to design policies based on the aforementioned long-term population forecasts, and other demographic and spatial data. It projects the future needs of the district's residents, in order to plan the creation of educational, medical, cultural, sports, commercial, and other facilities. It also uses machine learning to simulate the evolution of urban planning policies, and predict the impacts of urban planning on the target area and its surroundings
3. *Smart business*: it applies AI-enabled data analytics to support the activities of the economic and industrial departments of the district, like the Investment Promotion Bureau. It also examines various corporate data (e.g., data on the sales revenues of companies in the main shopping centers in the district) to create clusters of companies, for instance by trying to concentrate luxury brands of similar level in the same area of Jing'an district
4. *Smart supervision*: it uses AI to carry out credit assessment and risk warning for companies and other business entities within the district jurisdiction. It also tracks illegal enterprises and forecasts related risks, thus improving the efficiency of supervision and law enforcement
5. *Smart district sentiment*: this application (智能区情) uses Natural Language Processing, computer vision, and other AI technologies to "capture, classify, analyze and assess public sentiment in a comprehensive way" (进行全方位的舆情抓取, 归类, 分析和研判), thus supporting urban governance activities

(15) Shanghai Museum (August 2019; on-site visit: January 2021)

1. *Smart guided tours*: this application uses AI to analyze data on visitors and recommend personalized tours of the museum, including visiting routes and other activities. Such data (e.g., demographics, reason of the visit, duration of the visit, sections visited, etc.) are collected during the online registration phase (visitors are required to fill in an online form to book a visit to the Shanghai Museum), as well as by monitoring the visiting routes of the guests. This application also uses AI to provide the visitors with a more immersive experience by allowing virtual reality tours, or smart interactions with the museum exhibits through augmented reality and mixed reality

(continued)

Table 5.9 (continued)

2. *Smart management and control*: it uses AI technologies and IoT sensors to monitor the electricity and water consumption of the Shanghai Museum, and other building functions (e.g., monitoring visitor entries and routes)
3. *Smart restoration of cultural relics*: it deploys augmented reality and AI techniques (e.g., machine learning) to support the restoration of cultural relics and assist specialists in their work. It provides restoration experts with full images of incomplete cultural relics as a basis for restoration plans, in order to improve restoration accuracy, reliability, and efficiency
4. *Smart research on ancient books and documents*: it leverages Big Data and machine learning techniques to create a smart search tool that examines the characteristics of ancient written documents such as punctuation, text alignment, etc., to facilitate the retrieval of the full book and the analysis of the documents
(16) Shanghai Financial Court (August 2019)
1. *Smart litigation*: it uses AI for the smart classification and filing of financial cases. It consists of a "smart case filing system" (智助立案系统) that uses OCR and Natural Language Processing to check legal documents submitted by lawyers. Based on the complexity of each case, it asks lawyers whether they are willing to accept mediation. In case the lawyers opt for mediation, they can immediately contact professional mediators online through the working station of the court, which has an area dedicated to "smart dispute resolution" (智源解纷区). The "smart litigation" application can also provide guidance and assistance directly to the litigants, who can choose the preferred litigation method (mediation or filing) based on the suggestions of the court's "smart case filing system"
2. *Smart trials*: smart trials use AI technologies to assist the courts in solving procedural problems that may arise during the trials of financial cases, such as incomplete evidence review. By using AI to create model cases based on the sentences of senior judges, this application also provides the courts with reference verdicts to adjudicate financial cases, in order to improve the efficiency of the trials and the consistency of court rulings
3. *Smart profiling*: it uses Big Data, OCR, machine learning, Natural Language Processing, and other AI technologies to mine and analyze information about the assets and whereabouts of the person required to fulfill the obligations set forth in the court judgment (被执行人智能画像). It also automatically identifies, parses, and analyzes lawsuits, enforcement cases, and other information related to person who must fulfill the court obligations

and the creation of a virtual news anchorman. This selection criterion set the initial scope at 25 case studies.

- **Duration**: the analysis is restricted to the first and second batch AI pilot application scenarios, that is the projects that were approved in April and August 2019. This choice was made to ensure that the case studies had completed the one-year trial period required by SHEITC when the fieldwork started in August 2020, so that: (i) sufficient information could be gathered both from on-site visits and documentary research; and (ii) the impacts of these projects were more apparent, assuming that the AI trial projects need some time to mature and deliver the intended results, as suggested by literature on AI in the public sector (Desouza, 2021; Molinari et al., 2021; Misuraca and van Noordt, 2020). This led to the exclusion of the four public sector-related AI applications scenarios approved in December 2020, namely: two projects in transportation, one in culture and tourism, and one in government affairs. This selection criterion reduced the scope to 21 case studies.

- **Activity Relevance**: the analysis focuses on application scenarios that deploy AI technologies in the core activities of public organizations. This led to the exclusion of two pilot projects: the "smart table tennis trainer" of the Shanghai Institute of Physical Education (August 2019), which has a highly demonstrative nature and focuses on a limited part of the educational activities of the Institute; and the AI pilot for smart road maintenance on the Donghai Bridge (August 2019), which adds only marginal applications to the Lingang autonomous vehicles project that was approved in April 2019 (case study #12). This selection criterion reduced the scope to 19 case studies.
- **Information Availability**: the analysis examines the AI pilot application scenarios for which information is publicly available. This led to the exclusion of three public sector-related projects, for which to the best of the author's knowledge there are no sufficient public sources of information. Namely: the AI+ medicine project for cardiovascular disease, jointly developed by the Xuhui District Health Management Development Center, Zhongshan Hospital and the Xuhui District Central Hospital (August 2019); the AI+ education project of the Shanghai University for the creation of a smart campus (August 2019); and the AI+ urban management project for garbage sorting and collection implemented by Shanghai Chengtou Environment Group (August 2019). This selection criterion led to the final list of 16 case studies, which are summarized in Table 5.9.

Next sections identify *three cross-cutting features that characterize all the case studies of AI pilot application scenarios*. Namely: organizational experiments under municipal lead (Sect. 5.3.2.1); deregulated approach to AI innovation (Sect. 5.3.2.2); and engagement of private companies (Sect. 5.3.2.3). For each of these cross-cutting features, the strengths and limitations in deploying AI in the public sector are examined. The analysis is primarily based on: Chinese-language official documents, including the official notices on the AI pilot application scenarios released by SHEITC, one official report on the first batch of AI trials published in 2019 (SJTU, CAICT, and SHEIC, 2019), and other accounts on the AI pilots published on the SHEITC and other government websites; gray sources (news articles and specialized blogs) in Chinese language; interviews with people who participate in or have direct knowledge of this experiment-based approach; and field visits to five of the 16 case studies (Table 5.9).

Organizational Experiments Under Municipal Lead

The AI pilot application scenarios are a program designed and coordinated by the Shanghai municipal government. This program aims to spur the use of AI technologies in Shanghai starting from the promotion of trial projects in the public sector and other areas. Consistently with the design of this policy initiative, a cross-cutting feature of the experiment-based approach is the use of municipal-level analytical, political, and operational resources to create the basic conditions for public organizations to experiment with AI in their activities. This use of municipal-level policy capacities to support organizational experiments is a **strength** in deploying AI in the public sector because it helps to **jumpstart public sector AI pilot applications that, if successful, can be applied at city-scale.**

Municipal-level analytical capacity is a necessary precondition to devise a sound policy initiative for promoting, testing, and assessing public sector AI solutions that can be disseminated in Shanghai. As noted earlier (Sect. 5.1.1), interviewees emphasize that the trial approach of the AI pilot application scenarios is a valuable way to scope suitable public sector AI applications: it would not be sensible to "put all the eggs in one basket" (AIEX), especially because there are not best practices in the implementation of AI in public services yet (MGI). In addition, through the collection and selection of the AI pilot application scenarios, the municipality is steering the creation of AI applications that are more likely to be disseminated because they coincide with the areas prioritized by the Shanghai government for the use of AI in the public sector. The municipal AI plans require that government agencies and public organizations in Shanghai use AI to optimize *city operations* (i.e., public security, environmental monitoring, infrastructures operation and maintenance); improve the quality and efficiency of *public services* (i.e., administrative services, judiciary, education, culture); improve efficiency of *transport and shipping* (i.e., urban traffic, maritime logistics); and promote the accuracy and inclusiveness of *medicine and healthcare*[262] (i.e., medical care, elderly care, public health prevention, and control). The AI pilot application scenarios cover all these priority areas. In *city operations*: 1 project in environmental monitoring (case study #11), and 2 projects in infrastructure operation and maintenance (case studies #9–10). As for public security, a number of pilots contain public security components (see Table 5.9, case studies #1, 9–11, 13). In *public services*: 1 project in administrative services (case study #14), 1 project in the judiciary (case study #16), 4 projects in education (case studies #1–4), and 1 project in culture (case study #15). In *transport and shipping*: 2 projects in urban traffic (case studies #12–13). In *medicine and healthcare*: 4 projects in medical care (case studies #5–8). This overlap between the AI pilot application scenarios and the areas prioritized by the Shanghai government for the use of AI in the public sector is confirmed by looking at the public sector AI pilots that were not included in the case studies examined in this section.[263]

[262] Shanghai Municipal People's Government, 2017 (cit.), section 2, par. 2.3, "Strengthen intelligent perception and optimize comprehensive city operations" (强化智能感知优化城市综合运行); section 2 , par. 2.4 "Strengthen decision-making assistance to improve the quality and efficiency of public services" (强化决策辅助促进公共服务提质增效); section 2, par. 2.5 "Focus on intelligent recognition to improve transportation and shipping efficiency" (聚焦智能识别提升交通航运效率); and section 2, par. 2.6 "Focus on cognitive computing to promote the accuracy and inclusiveness of medicine and healthcare" (聚焦认知计算推进医疗健康精准普惠). The 2019 *AI Highland Plan* (SHEITC, 2019d, cit.) reiterates that education, administrative services, smart courts, urban management, public security and garbage classification, transportation, and medicine are the main areas where Shanghai wants to leverage AI to improve public sector operations and enhance public service provision. See Chapter 3.2 for details.

[263] In city operations: 1 project in environmental monitoring (Shanghai Chengtou Environment Group for garbage collection and disposal); 1 project in infrastructure operation and maintenance project (Donghai Bridge). In public services: 2 projects in education (Shanghai Institute of Physical Education, Shanghai University); 1 project in government affairs (the Shanghai Customs Technology Innovation Center); and 1 more project in culture (Bingjiang Forest Park, culture and tourism). In transport and shipping: 2 projects in urban traffic (Shanghai Pudong airport transport hub and the intelligent connected vehicle pilot demonstration zone in Jiading district), 1 project in maritime logistics (Wusong cruise terminal management). In public health: 1 project in medical care

Municipal-level political capacity is helping the deployment of AI in the public sector by creating support for the AI pilot application scenarios. This ensures high rates of participation in this policy initiative, and the widespread uptake of AI trial applications in several policy areas. Between December 2018 and August 2020, SHEITC collected proposals for AI trial projects from 56 public organizations, government agencies, and State-owned entities (and two private companies). This created a representative basis of AI applications from which best practices can potentially be identified and replicated. Political capacity also serves to enlist the cooperation of policy actors that can support the startup and execution of the AI pilot application scenarios. When announcing the AI pilots approved by the municipal government, SHEITC requests relevant authorities in districts, industrial parks, and other sites hosting the application scenarios to "give priority to support [the pilot projects] in terms of special funds and resource matching, in combination with their own relevant policies".[264] The Beixinjing Subdistrict AI pilot (case study #9) offers an illustrative example of the importance of such political sponsorships. In executing the project, the subdistrict committee can count on the support of the Changning District Science and Technology Commission and several State-owned enterprises controlled by Changning Changing District (区属国企).[265] Similarly, the pilot on autonomous driving and smart traffic infrastructure (case study #12), managed by the Lingang Sci-Tech City (上海临港科技创新城经济发展有限公司), is actively supported by two specialized government entities that contribute to the activities of the pilot: the Shanghai Motor Vehicle Inspection Certification & Technology Innovation Center (上海机动车检测认证技术研究中心有限公司), and the China Academy of Information and Communications (CAICT) Easter China Institute (中国信息通信研究院华东分

(the joint project by Xuhui District Health Management Development Center, Zhongshan Hospital, and the Xuhui District Central Hospital).

264 SHEITC, 2019a, art. 4. In original: "鼓励各区、园区管委会等结合自身相关政策, 在专项资金、资源配套等方面优先予以支持". The same announcement is repeated in the announcements of August 2019 (SHEITC, 2019c, art. 4.) and December 2020 (SHEITC, 2020b, art. 4).

265 Sohu, 2020. Beixinjing Subdistrict Is the Only "AI + Residential Community" in the City to Be Selected into the First Batch of Artificial Intelligence Demonstration Application Scenarios in Shanghai [北新泾街道作为全市唯一 "AI + 社区", 入选上海首批人工智能示范应用场景]. *Sohu* [搜狐], 9 December, https://www.sohu.com/a/437304389_99893471?sec=wd.

院). Similarly, the Qiangwei Primary School (case study #1) is actively supported by the government authorities in Minhang District,[266] and the AI pilot in Xietu Road (case study #10) is officially endorsed by the Communist Party Committee of Xuhui District.[267] Indeed, all the public sector AI pilots of the first batch formally have a "sponsor organization" (推荐单位), which is almost always a government agency: the Municipal Education Commission for the trials in education (case studies #1–3); the Shanghai Hospital Development Center (上海申康医院发展中心) for the pilot in health (case study #5); the district governments of Changning and Xuhui for the pilots in residential communities (case studies #9–10); the Pudong New Area district government for the project in industrial park (case study #11); the Lingang Special Area Management Committee (临港新片区管理委员会) for the project in transport (case study #12); and the Jing'an District government for the project in government affairs (case study #14). Finally, municipal-level political support for AI development has created an enabling environment that encourages a fast-paced approach to experimentation with AI in the public sector, as discussed earlier (Sect. 5.1) and further elaborated in the next Sect. 5.3.2.2.

Finally, municipal-level operational capacity is helping the deployment of AI in the public sector by aggregating and coordinating the resources needed to implement the AI pilot application scenarios in practice. First, through the calls for AI pilots published by the SHEITC, the Shanghai government acts as a "matchmaker" between public organizations and AI companies that provide the technical solutions for the trial projects. This has mobilized AI companies, and created a venue to pair public agencies with technology suppliers and other sources of specialized knowledge of the Shanghai AI ecosystem (more details in Sect. 5.3.2.3). In addition, the availability in Shanghai of rich data sources and advanced infrastructure is also important to kick-start the AI pilot application scenarios. For instance, the Ruijin Hospital (case study #8) has

266 Minhang District Government, 2020. Minhang District CPPCC Education and Sports Committee Visited Qiangwei Primary School to Carry Out Pre-consultation Investigation on "Smart Education Construction" [闵行区政协教体委莅临蔷薇小学开展 "智慧教育建设" 协商前调研]. *Minhang District Government* [上海市闵行区人民政府], 10 June, http://www.shmh.gov.cn/shmh/zwdt-jyj/20200616/483583.html.

267 CPC Xuhui District Committee, 2019. The Party Committee of the District's Science and Technology Commission Promotes the In-depth Application of AI and Solves Bottleneck Problems in Many Industries [区科委党委推进人工智能深度应用, 破解多个行业瓶颈问题]. *CPC Xuhui District Committee*, 2 July, http://dj.xh.sh.cn/HTML/xhdj/kw_bmdt/2019-07-02/Detail_180806.htm.

implemented an AI-based system that generates pre-diagnostic medical reports. This system combines the information provided by the patients during the online registration with the data collected from all medical institutions in Shanghai via digital platforms like the Government Online-Offline Government Shanghai, the Municipal Health Cloud (健康云), and the Shanghai Medical Federation (上海医联).[268] The AI pilots in Zhangjiang AI Island (case study #11) and Lingang (autonomous vehicles testing base, case study #12) leverage the well-developed digital infrastructure of the municipality, including an extensive network of 5G and Internet of Things, as well as dedicated physical spaces to test AI applications. In terms of digital infrastructure, the AI pilots in the Beixinjing and Xietu Road subdistricts (case studies #9–10) and the Jing'an Government Data Management Center (case study #14) are connected to the government extranet, e-government cloud, and municipal Big Data exchange platform examined in Sect. 5.2.1. Finally, another municipal operational resource that is helping the deployment of the AI pilot application scenarios is the provision of financial support for the trial projects. In many cases, public organizations alone would hardly be able to bear the costs of implementing the AI solutions adopted in the pilot, if they had not access to financial support from the government (IFLYi). For instance, the AI-related equipment purchased by the Shixi High School (case study #2) in April 2020 costed nearly 1.5 million RMB,[269] a sum that a public school could hardly afford for teaching equipment. The Shanghai municipal government has pledged various forms of financial support for AI projects, including the AI pilot application scenarios.[270]

[268] Xinmin Evening Post, 2021. The "Hospital of the Future" Is Here! Medical Visits Are More Intelligent, the Ruijin Hospital Has the Solution for Handling Documents ["未来医院" 来了!看病更智慧, 瑞金医院交卷解题思路]. *Xinmin Evening Post* [新民晚报], 7 May, https://baijiahao.baidu.com/s?id=1699076962184314485&wfr=spider&for=pc.

[269] China Government Procurement Net, 2020. Bid Winning Announcement of Shanghai Shixi Junior High School Artificial Intelligence Laboratory Procurement Project [上海市市西初级中学人工智能实验室采购项目中标公告]. *China Government Procurement Net* [中国政府采购网], 10 April, http://www.ccgp.gov.cn/cggg/dfgg/zbgg/202004/t20200410_14133520.htm.

[270] For instance, the 2018 *Implementation measures for accelerating the high-quality development of artificial intelligence in Shanghai* (Chapter 3.2) pledge various forms of financial support for AI applications, including "AI application demonstration projects", "towns with AI characteristics", and "demonstration parks with AI characteristics" that apply the technologies and products of AI companies based in Shanghai.

This support is often matched by district governments. Minhang District offers an example. The district has pledged to match the amount of financial support given by the municipal government to the projects identified by relevant municipal departments as AI pilot application scenarios, AI demonstration application scenarios, or "AI application demonstration areas" (人工智能应用示范区), for a maximum of 3 million yuan.[271]

Municipal-level policy capacities facilitate the deployment of AI in the public sector by creating the basic conditions for public organizations to experiment with AI technologies in their activities, in line with the program requirements of the AI pilot application scenarios. However, the creation of "replicable and referential experience models that can be applied to the whole city" needs **organizational-level capacities to transition from pilots to established applications** that are integrated in the activities of public agencies. Previous studies on AI in the public sector identified the existence of a gap between the phase where AI is tested and evaluated for potential use in public service, and the phase where the AI technology is stably embedded in the functions of the public sector organizations (Desouza, 2021; Molinari et al., 2021; Misuraca and Van Noordt, 2020). These studies indicate that, in order to create replicable experiences, trial projects like the Shanghai AI pilots should evolve into established applications that can show how "developed AI solutions work in practice and whether they are obtaining intended results successfully, which is crucial for establishing a common knowledge base to share best practices among public administrations [...]" (Molinari et al., 2021, p. 9). To make the most of the opportunities for innovation in the public sector and use AI to advance organizational goals, every public agency must develop its own unique ability to select, orchestrate, and leverage its AI-specific organizational resources (Mikalef and Gupta, 2021, p. 8; Engstrom et al., 2020, p. 92). However, developing these organizational-level capacities is a complex process that entails a combination of several types of skills and resources, all of which are necessary to make the transition from pilots to established applications[272] (Desouza,

[271] Xinmin Net, 2019. Minhang Primary School Will Appear at the World Artificial Intelligence Conference. The first "AI + School" Is as Cool as Iron Man! [闵行这所小学将亮相世界人工智能大会, 首家 "AI + 学校" 像钢铁侠一样酷!]. *Xinmin Net* [新民网], 26 July, http://shanghai.xinmin.cn/xmsq/2019/07/26/31562300.html.

[272] In one of the most systematic and updated organizational studies found during the literature review, Desouza (2021) proposes a maturity model consisting of five levels

2021; Mikalef and Gupta, 2021; Molinari et al., 2021). The AI pilot application scenarios provide empirical evidence of the importance of developing the organizational-level capacities needed to make this transition. In the AI pilots, the "scenario organization" must decide—when drafting the project requirements published by the SHEITC—how to use AI technologies in its activities (analytical capacity); it must accrue and put to use the resources (data, infrastructure, human capital, etc.) needed to translate the AI pilots in practice, in cooperation with its technical partners (operational capacity); and it must obtain and sustain support for the use of AI technologies within the organization (policy capacity).

Developing **organizational-level capacities to transition from pilots to established applications** is challenging for public organizations, and it **could become a limitation to the deployment of AI in the public sector via the AI pilot application scenarios**. This aspect was highlighted by the interviewees. Regarding *analytical capacity*, the Shanghai Artificial Intelligence Industry Alliance observes that public organizations that want to implement AI in their activities often lack the ability to "translate" (翻译) their organizational needs in terms that can be addressed by the use of AI technologies (SAIA). Shanghai INESA agrees that it is crucial that public organizations learn how to identify which aspects of their activities they want to improve and optimize by deploying AI technologies. While observing progress in recent years, he stresses the importance of nurturing the ability of public organizations to identify AI applications that can contribute to achieving organizational objectives (INESA). The Shanghai Museum (case study #15) also emphasizes that organizational-level analytical capacity is a key factor for the successful implementation of AI in public organizations. He highlights two components: on the one hand, the Museum leadership must set

of AI integration in public organizations. Namely: ad hoc, experimentation, planning and deployment, scaling and learning, and enterprise-wide transformation. The passage from one maturity level to the next entails the development and management of technical elements (Big Data, AI systems, and analytical capacity) and organizational elements (innovation climate, governance and ethical frameworks, and strategic visioning). The notion of "AI capability" for organizations developed by Mikalef and Gupta (2021) also highlights that there are several types of skills and resources involved in integrating AI in the activities of public agencies. Namely: tangible resources (data, technology, time, and financial resources), human resources (technical skills and business skills), and intangible resources (inter-departmental coordination, organizational change capacity, and risk proclivity).

an overall vision for the implementation of AI in the Museum's activities; on the other, "specialized" departments like the Information Center (headed by the interviewee) have to translate this vision into real-world applications that support the activities of the Museum. AISPi argues that organizational-level analytical capacity would benefit from regular exchanges with government-endorsed entities like the Shanghai Artificial Intelligence Strategic Advisory Expert Committee, which is involved in the selection of the AI pilots and would be a valuable source of specialized AI knowledge for public organizations. However, "most people working on the ground don't have really access to these experts' expertise and [don't] work closely with them" (AISPi), as the Expert Committee mostly limits its interactions to the municipal leadership and government agencies (SAIA).

In terms of *operational capacity*, Shanghai INESA observes that many public organizations still do not have sufficient data quality, the financial resources, or the sufficient level of informatization (信息化水平) to efficiently implement AI in their activities (2INESAi). Public organizations in Shanghai can potentially access qualified human resources in terms of AI knowledge (Sect. 5.1). But technical prowess alone is not enough. The Shanghai Museum (case study #15) highlights the difficulties in recruiting people who have both a solid technical knowledge of AI and a deep understanding of the activities and goals of the Museum, arguing that this combination is crucial to successfully implement AI in the activities of public organizations (SHMU). Other interviewees agree that it is important to train the civil servants to ensure the effective integration of AI solutions in public organizations (INESA, SHZF). However, the case studies suggest that the creation of people that combine technical and organizational knowledge is difficult to achieve. The Jing'an Data Management Center (case study #14) says that they do not know how the algorithms that support their activities are developed and implemented (JDAC). Moreover, due to budgetary constraints, the staff of government agencies is often quite limited, reducing the chances to have staff that could combine technical knowledge with the understanding of the activities of the public organization (SDECi). The lack of in-house staff was confirmed by the author's visit to the AI pilot in Lingang (case study #12), where the Shanghai Lingang Intelligent Connected Vehicle Innovation Center—the organization that operates the pilot—employs a dozen employees, many of whom do not have a technical background.

In addition, two visits to the SAIA Secretariat confirmed that the Association—which, among its tasks, has to contribute to the use of AI in the public sector—only employs around five people, a limited number considering its broad operational mandate and high political importance (Chapter 2.2.3).

In terms of *political capacity*, the interview with the Shanghai Museum (case study #15) indicates that there is often organizational inertia, and even some form of resistance to the introduction of AI technologies. Some departments are quite conservative (保守), while others do not see actual benefits of using AI in their activities and consider this technology as an additional burden, or something that overlaps with their usual work. Hence, the political skills of the organizational leadership are crucial to instill a sense of priority in implementing AI (SHMU). Shanghai INESA—whose company is a general contractor for a number of undisclosed AI pilots—also observes some resistance to the introduction of AI technologies in certain public organizations, which he attributes to the fact that many people still consider AI very complex and almost intimidating (INESA). Shanghai Zhuofan—whose company is the main technical partner of the Xuhui District Government Affairs Center, which applied for the first batch of AI pilots—notes that government officials in Shanghai are very pragmatic. They focus on the benefits that technology can bring to their work in terms of increased efficiency, and on the safe and legal use of the technologies. At the same time, public managers often resist the use of AI applications that allow to scrutinize the activities of their organizations, such as systems that use emotion recognition technology to assess the satisfaction rate of citizens when using public services (SHZF).

Deregulated Approach to AI Innovation

Earlier discussions on the AI policy capacity of Shanghai (Chapters 3.2 and 5.1 and 5.2) underscored that the ability of the municipal government to gain and sustain support for AI development has created an enabling environment for implementing policy initiatives that foster the use of AI in the public sector and other areas prioritized by the Shanghai government. In this environment, private actors and public organizations are encouraged to develop and test AI applications in government-designated areas. The platform-based approach offers an example of highly coordinated AI applications for the public sector, whereby districts and subdistricts are allowed some degree of freedom to develop AI solutions that are consistent with the design and functions of the Government Online-Offline Shanghai and the Single Platform for Urban Management. In addition to such highly coordinated public sector AI applications, AISP observes that another important manifestation of this enabling environment is a more deregulated approach that leaves public organizations greater room to maneuver when experimenting with AI in their activities (Sect. 5.1). He argues that this deregulated approach is crucial to spur AI adoption in Shanghai because it leaves space for growth, it allows public and private actors wider access to data, and thus creates opportunities for AI applications. MGI and AIEX also observe that the primary concern of Shanghai authorities in the pilot application scenarios is promoting the use of the AI technology, while regulatory issues will be addressed at a later stage.

This deregulated approach to public sector AI innovation is a cross-cutting feature of the AI pilot application scenarios. It is embedded in the nature of the AI pilots, which are designed to "accelerate the first use in Shanghai of new AI technologies, products and models, [and] create a benchmark for innovative AI applications at the city level". This extremely agile approach is a **strength** that facilitates the deployment of AI in the public sector in three main ways. First, it is a **trial-and-error tactic that spurs AI innovation in the public sector by encouraging public organizations to use AI in their activities**. Experimentation is critical for AI innovation, but public agencies often eschew it due to a risk-averse mentality that overemphasizes the risks of failure and wastage of public resources (Desouza, 2021, p. 16; Mikalef and Gupta, 2021, p. 6). By formally encouraging public organizations to experiment with AI technologies in their activities, the AI pilot application scenarios remove a fundamental obstacle to public sector AI innovation, and support the political capacity of public agencies to create consensus for the adoption of AI in their operations. This paved the way to a variety of public sector AI applications across all the policy areas of the AI pilot application scenarios:

- in *education* (AI+ school/education), the Qiangwei Primary School (case study #1) has developed a "smart teacher training system" that uses AI and data mining technology to automatically segment teaching videos and match them to the contents of different classes and subjects, extracting videoclips that teachers can use for their lessons. The Shanghai Shixi High School (case study #2) uses AI to provide personalized education (个别化教育) targeted to the characteristics of each student. The AI system examines data generated by the online learning activities of the students, collecting and summarizing information related to study time and content, test results and other information. Based on these data, the AI system evaluates the learning level and abilities of the students, and identifies the shortcomings in their learning process in order to provide personalized recommendations. Similar applications for personalized education and tutoring have been promoted by the Shanghai World Foreign Language Education Group (case study #3) and the Luwan No. 1 Central Primary School (case study #4);

- in *health* (AI+ hospital/medicine), the Shanghai No. 10 People's Hospital (case study #5) is using AI technologies like OCR, Natural Language Processing, and speech recognition to support doctors in pre-diagnosis of outpatient cases, and introduced an AI system that automatically suggests further examinations and checks. The hospital also uses machine learning to assess the criticality of patients and give advice on the next medical treatment (e.g., see an outpatient clinic or get emergency treatment), including which department to visit, and what preparations should be made before the visit. The Fudan University Shanghai Cancer Hospital (case study #6) has developed an AI-based "medication guidance function" (用药指导功能) for chemotherapy that provides patients with a personalized medication plan, based upon the prescription of human doctors and revision by pharmacists. The system also collects information on adverse drug reactions, so that doctors can quickly obtain feedback from patients and adjust the therapy if needed. The Shanghai Children's Hospital (case study #7) has implemented an AI-enabled "pre-diagnosis inspection" (诊前检验) system that—using a knowledge base of clinical practice guidelines and expert experience—provides recommendations about medical checks that can be done before medical consultation, thus shortening the treatment process. The Ruijin Hospital (case study #8) has also developed an AI-based pre-diagnosis system that combines the information on medical history provided by the patients with data collected from all medical institutions in Shanghai via the Government Online-Offline Shanghai, the Health Cloud, and the Shanghai Medical Federation. The system generates a pre-diagnostic report that doctors can consult for their reference, thus reducing the waiting time for patients and the workload of doctors, while increasing the interaction time between doctors and patients during the visit;

- in *housing and community amenities* (AI+ residential community), the Beixinjing Subdistrict (case study #9) is implementing AI applications similar to those examined in the Single Platform for Urban Management. For instance, the local "community brain" (社区大脑, now part of the subdistrict Urban Operation Center) uses computer vision, speech recognition, and Natural Language Processing to automatically perform "smart video patrols" (智能巡屏) that can discover problems in selected residential communities almost in real time, from cracked road surface to garbage littering. Similarly, in the Xietu Road Subdistrict (case study #10), the "smart brain" (智慧大脑, now also part of that subdistrict Urban Operation Center) leverages AI technologies such as facial recognition, compounded by smart smoke detectors and other smart sensors, to improve the security of public spaces in the subdistrict. In addition, both pilot projects are testing other AI applications to improve public service provision. For instance, the Beixinjing Subdistrict has equipped the community health service stations with smart medical devices that assist doctors in making health checkups. The data collected during the visits are uploaded on the municipal Health Cloud, so that residents can check their health records and make appointments for expert visits at Shanghai's municipal hospitals. The Xietu Road Community Health Service Center introduced an AI-enabled "smart pharmacy" (智慧药房) that automatically picks and dispenses the medicines while the pharmacist double-checks the information with the recipient, stores the medicines and updates the inventory, and automatically flags abnormal situations in medical prescriptions such as excessive dosages;
- in *environmental protection, public order, and safety* (AI+ industrial park), Zhangjiang AI Island (case study #11) uses a combination of Internet of Things, cloud computing, mobile Internet, and AI technologies like computer vision (smart surveillance cameras), security robots and an AI-based visitor management system to improve security in the park, including the monitoring and prevention of fire risks. It also uses AI for environmental applications, like monitoring water quality, air quality, the maintenance of road surface and manhole cover, and to control an automatic irrigation system and smart lampposts. Various forms of machine intelligence (机器智能) also enable

the deployment of drones, cleaning robots, security robots, and unmanned vehicles in the park. Moreover, Zhangjiang AI Island has introduced a "smart energy management" (智能能源管理) application that leverages AI for the remote, real-time monitoring and management of electrical equipment and energy systems;

- in *economic affairs* (AI+ transport), the Lingang Intelligent Connected Vehicles Comprehensive Demonstration Zone (case study #12) is testing autonomous driving technologies and applications in public transportation, street cleaning, and logistics. This project has developed smart traffic infrastructure to which the autonomous vehicles are connected through a V2X (vehicle-to-everything) coordination system (V2X 车路协同系统) based on AI and 5G technologies. This pilot also uses computer vision, smart sensors, and other technologies to monitor in real-time the information on the operations of vehicles, drivers, and the smart infrastructure. The Shanghai Subway (case study #13) has introduced the "smart metro station" (智慧车站) application, which uses computer vision to monitor real-time passenger flows in the subway stations (e.g., the number of people in each station, the speed of passenger flows, total passenger volumes of the day, real-time analysis, and forecast of passenger flow on the entire road network). It also uses a geospatial model that triggers congestion alerts based on a set of parameters (number of people, congestion index, density and flow speed, etc.). The Shanghai Subway also uses AI in the "behaviour identification" (行为识别) application that ensures safe and secure operations of the subway ecosystem: it can identify signs of fatigue in train drivers or irregular driving operations; it also monitors irregular or dangerous activities in the subway stations, like passengers falling on the escalators, not paying the ticket, quarreling, etc.;
- in *general public services* (AI+ government affairs), the Jing'an Government Data Management Center (case study #14) uses AI models for long-term demographic projections of the resident population in the district to support urban planning decision (e.g., construction of educational, medical, and other public facilities). This project also uses machine learning to simulate the evolution of urban planning policies, and predict the impacts of urban planning

on the target area and its surroundings. Specifically, it uses generative adversarial networks[273] to train its AI models on data derived from international cities like New York, London, and Tokyo. In addition, this project leverages AI for applications related to urban governance like those discussed in the analysis of the Single Platform for Urban Management. For instance, AI models for real-time people flow predictions (实时人流预测) are used to ensure security in this bustling downtown district;

- in *recreation, culture, and religion* (AI+ culture and tourism), the Shanghai Museum (case study #15) uses AI technologies to support the restoration of cultural relics and assist archaeologists and other specialists of the museum in their work (e.g., providing restoration experts with full images of incomplete cultural relics as a basis for restoration). The museum also deploys Big Data and machine learning techniques for the study of ancient books and other written documents;
- in *public order and safety* (AI+ judiciary), the Shanghai Financial Court (case study #16) uses AI in the "smart trial of financial cases" (金融案件智慧审判), an application assisting the courts in solving problems that may arise during the trial, such as "inconsistent case handling[274]" (办案思路不统一) or incomplete evidence review. By using AI to create reference cases based on the sentences of senior

[273] These are deep learning-based generative models that can train a system to produce new data similar to an existing dataset. These new data can be used to provide more material for training AI models in complex domains or domains with a limited amount of data (Amazon Web Services, n.d. What Is a GAN? *Amazon Web Services*, https://aws.amazon.com/what-is/gan/?nc1=h_ls, last accessed on 10 October 2022).

[274] The so-called inconsistent case handling is related to the "judicial accountability system" (司法责任制) introduced in 2015 by the Supreme People's Court. It requires that courts carry out a search on the sentences handed down in similar cases before issuing a verdict, in order to ensure the consistency of judgment criteria. This practice is known as the "mandatory search and reporting mechanism for similar cases" (类案强制检索与报告机制). See: *Several Opinions of the Supreme People's Court on Improving the Judicial Accountability System* (最高人民法院关于完善人民法院司法责任制的若干意见) issued in 2015; and *Opinions of the Supreme People's Court on Implementing the Judicial Accountability System and Improving the Trial Supervision and Management Mechanism (for Trial Implementation)* (最高人民法院关于落实司法责任制完善审判监督管理机制的意见 (试行)) and the *Opinions of the Supreme People's Court on the Implementation of the Judicial Accountability System (for Trial Implementation)* (最高人民法院司法责任制实施意见 (试行)) issued in 2017. The link between the judicial accountability system and the use of AI in Chinese courts is examined in: Yu, M. and Du, G., 2019. Why Are

judges, the system helps to improve the efficiency of the trials and consistency of verdicts. This pilot also uses Big Data, OCR, machine learning, NLP, and other AI technologies to mine information about the assets and whereabouts of the persons required to fulfill the obligations set forth in the court judgment (被执行人). In addition to support the internal operations of the courts, this pilot also uses AI technology to assist users. For instance, it introduced a system that uses NLP and other technologies to automatically check the documents submitted by lawyers, and based on the complexity of each case it asks the applicants whether they are willing to accept mediation.

The second **strength** of this deregulated approach in deploying AI in the public sector is that it facilitates the creation of **success stories that can build momentum for scaling up AI applications within the pilot organizations**. As AI applications are rolled out in great numbers, promising results start to emerge in various policy areas, showcasing the successful integration of AI in the activities of public agencies (see above). These success stories reinforce the political capacity of public agencies to create support for continuing and expanding the use of AI in their activities. In fact, literature on AI in public organizations agrees that developing a clear narrative explaining how AI can assist public sector employees to better deliver services is a crucial resource to promote the use of AI in public agencies (Berryhill et al., 2019, p. 92). The availability of case studies showcasing the successful integration of AI in the activities of public agencies can help organizational leadership to make a case for continuing and expanding the use of AI, breaking the organizational status quo, and creating environments that are supportive of the development of AI in the public agency (Desouza, 2021, p. 23; Mikalef and Gupta, 2021, p. 6; Desouza, 2018, p. 34). Indeed, evidence suggests that all the case studies of pilot application scenarios in Shanghai have integrated AI in their activities, making the transition from AI pilots to established applications, and in most cases expanding the use of AI in their operations (see analysis in Sect. 5.3.3).

Chinese Courts Turning to AI? *The Diplomat*, January 2019, https://thediplomat.com/2019/01/why-are-chinese-courts-turning-to-ai/.

Finally, the third **strength** in deploying AI in the public sector related to this deregulated approach is that it **combines fast-paced implementation with attention to safety**. A key requirement of the AI pilot application scenarios is to "accelerate the first use in Shanghai of new AI technologies"; hence, these projects have a clear focus on the quick uptake of AI. At the same time, the AI pilots serve as sandboxes and innovation testbeds for creating safe and secure public sector AI applications that can eventually be extended at city-scale. When announcing the projects selected as AI pilot application scenarios, the SHEITC recommends that the organizations hosting the projects have to "benchmark against the highest international standards and best levels", and ensure information security and protect data privacy, among others.[275] In this regard, a key function of the AI pilots is to conduct experimentation in set-aside, controlled environments. While the scope of the AI pilots varies (e.g., from single classrooms in schools to the whole subway network), the AI trial applications are all tested for a limited time frame (they are evaluated after 12 months), and on a predefined number of participants (the students and teachers of a school; the visitors of one hospital or one museum; the residents of one neighborhood; the vehicles of the Lingang Intelligent Connected Vehicles Comprehensive Demonstration Zone; the users of the Shanghai subway; the judges, lawyers, and litigants of one court; etc.). This approach fosters innovation in a controlled way. It gives public organizations the opportunity to test AI applications in real-life scenarios and learn about the potential of AI in their activities, while it also allows the municipal government to evaluate the impacts of public sector AI applications starting from supervised, circumscribed scenarios. The use of sandboxes and testbeds confirms Shanghai's intentions to develop the safe and secure use of AI in the public sector, as noted earlier (Sects. 5.1 and 5.2). It also shows the analytical capacity of the Shanghai government to devise policy solutions conducive to safe and secure AI innovation, as the use of sandboxes and testbeds is recognized as a best practice in this area by the literature on AI in the public sector. Berryhill et al. (2019, pp. 94–95) observe that a number of governments (e.g., Estonia, Lithuania, Finland) are using sandboxes to develop public sector AI solutions and accelerate their uptake. Engstrom et al. (2020, p. 73) call for

[275] See for instance: SHEITC Notice, 2019a, 2019c, and 2020a, art. 2 (各场景所在单位应对标国际最高标准、最好水平) and art. 3 (做好信息安全、 [...] 个人隐私等保护工作).

public agencies in the United States to develop sandboxes that allow for iterative evaluation of AI applications and for sharing lessons across the organization. Similarly, the OECD (2019, p. 105) suggests that public organizations should provide controlled environments for testing of AI systems, including regulatory sandboxes, as a way to foster public sector AI innovation. The literature also highlights that the use of sandboxes has some shortcomings, as the actual impacts of technology cannot be easily predicted until it is extensively developed and widely used (Misuraca and van Noordt, 2020, p. 51). Despite these shortcomings, the use of sandboxes and innovation testbeds, corroborated by Shanghai's attention to AI safety, offer a good compromise between fast-paced implementation and secure applications.

Sandboxes and innovation testbeds, however, cannot prevent the emergence of problematic AI applications. Indeed, a **potential limitation** in deploying AI in the public sector related to these highly experimental tactics is that some AI pilot application scenarios introduced **intrusive AI applications that enable pervasive control**. A risk inherent to an approach that gives public agencies ample room to trial AI in their activities is that insufficient organizational-level analytical capacity may lead to controversial AI solutions. For instance, the Qiangwei Primary School (case study #1) is deploying a "campus smart security system" (校园智能安保) that also monitors whether students smile, greet teachers, pick up garbage, line up neatly, and display other desirable behaviors, or instead run fast, quarrel or perform other dangerous actions. The school also uses a "smart classroom behaviour analysis system" (智能课堂行为分析系统) that leverages AI to monitor the conduct of students in classrooms, like sitting, raising hands, standing, or yawning. The system then uses these data to make assessments on the learning status and interest level of students, or classroom effectiveness.[276] The Shanghai World Foreign Language Group (case study #3) introduced a similar "classroom real-time analysis system" (课堂实时分析系统) that leverages computer vision (facial expression recognition) and other technologies to monitor the attitude of students in the classroom. Through the analysis of data collected from real-time videos in the classrooms, this AI application

[276] Tencent Open Content Platform, 2019. AI+ Primary School: Capture Children's Posture Through AI to Assess Learning Interest and Effect [AI+ 小学: 通过AI捕捉孩子姿态 评估学习兴趣与效果]. *Tencent Open Content Platform* [腾讯内容开放平台], 24 August, https://page.om.qq.com/page/O5W-pZrn5_f08eqr7l4GExMQ0.

infers students' learning habits, points of interest, and classroom attention, in order to improve classroom teaching efficiency (SJTU, CAICT, and SHEIC, 2019, p. 107). The Luwan No. 1 Central Primary School (case study #4) also introduced a "smart behaviour evaluation" (智能行为评测) application that uses AI to monitor the conduct of students and their physiological data (through "cloud watches" / 云手表 that monitor students' physical functions[277]). It also deployed a system for "smart assistance for emotional education" (智能情感教育辅助) that uses "tri-dimensional digital portraits" (一幅立体的 "数字画像") of the students to help teachers recognize the emotional state of their pupils, and promote personalized emotional education (个性化情感教育). The Jing'an Big Data Management Center (case study #14) has deployed a "smart district sentiment" (智能区情) application that leverages computer vision and other AI technologies to "capture, classify, analyze and assess public sentiment in a comprehensive way" (进行全方位的舆情抓取、归类、分析和研判), allowing relevant departments to grasp the trends in public opinion in the district in real time, and adopt a proactive approach in propaganda (宣传), service provision, and governance (SJTU, CAICT, and SHEIC, 2019, p. 132). Experts agree that ethical issues in AI in the public sector have different importance in different societies, and there is no evidence that privacy or ethical concerns are creating barriers to the use of AI in the public sector in Shanghai or other Chinese cities (Chapters 2.3.3, 4.1 and 6.1.3). At the same time, several surveys indicate that the Chinese public is attentive to issues like the potential harms and privacy violations generated by AI (Chapter 4.5.1). Hence, it can be reasonably argued that the aforementioned AI applications are invasive also by Chinese standards, and they could turn out to be a limitation in deploying AI in the public sector if they started to be opposed by the target population. These intrusive AI applications demonstrate analytical deficiencies not only because public organizations roll out AI solutions that could be opposed by the target population, but also because such applications are not aligned with the goal of the AI pilot application scenarios to improve citizens' perception of Shanghai as a smart city via these trial projects. Moreover, intrusive

[277] SHEITC Notice, 2019b; The Paper, 2019. How to Teach Students in Accordance with Their Aptitude on a Large Scale? Every Child in This Primary School in Shanghai has a "Digital Portrait" [如何大规模因材施教?上海这所小学每个孩子都有 "数字画像"]. *The Paper* [澎湃新闻], 21 August, http://m.thepaper.cn/yidian_promDetail.jsp?contid=4217660&from=yidian.

AI applications are not aligned with the broader objective to promote social acceptance for AI in the public sector in Shanghai (Chapter 4.5.2), which local experts agree is important to apply AI solutions at scale in the municipality (Sect. 5.1.3). Evidence from the AI application scenarios indicates that these controversial applications are circumscribed to a handful of cases. However, the insufficient organizational-level analytical capacity to identify these problematic applications—combined with a lapse in municipal-level analytical capacity, since the Shanghai government de facto endorsed such applications by including them in the AI pilot application scenarios—demonstrate the difficulties in reconciling fast-paced implementation with safety guarantees and attention to ethical concerns, a topic further examined in Chapter 6.

A second **limitation** in deploying AI in the public sector under this deregulated approach to AI innovation is that **the lack of standards and regulations can become an obstacle to scaling up AI applications beyond the pilots**. Obstacles to scaling up AI applications due to the lack of rules and standards are evident in autonomous driving. On the one hand, Shanghai is providing policy and infrastructural support for trialing autonomous vehicles on selected public roads (Chapter 4.2 and 5.1). On the other, the Shanghai Lingang Intelligent Connected Vehicle Innovation Center (case study #12) observes that real-life applications of autonomous vehicles also need a regulatory framework that clarifies issues like the liability in case of accidents, among others (LING). Pony AI—a company testing its autonomous driving taxis in the streets of Jiading district, as part of the AI pilot project approved in August 2019 mentioned earlier—also notes that there is a policy vacuum in autonomous driving, and the applications of autonomous vehicles will be limited until there are clear regulations for driverless cars on public roads (POAI). The limits of a deregulated approach are manifested also in the lack of standards. Shanghai INESA argues that it is hard to deploy AI applications at scale if companies and public organizations do not have enforceable standards they can refer to (2INESAi). China Unicom—which developed several 5G-based applications in the Zhangjiang AI Island (case study #11)—also states that standardization is important, not only to ensure a safe and secure use of AI technologies, but also to support government procurement and deployment of these technologies. For instance, she asks how the government can assess the characteristics of the AI systems it purchases and implements, if there are not standards it can refer to (CHUN). Finally, the lack of regulations can become an obstacle to scaling up AI applications also in terms of the transition costs that are expected to accompany the passage from a permissive to a more tightly regulated environment. If AI technologies mature and must be applied at scale, at some point they will have to be regulated to ensure they are beneficial to society (ZJAI, case study #11). And once regulations are in place, the financial and policy costs of implementing AI solutions will increase, as it already happened with the Internet sector (AISP), and other cases of technological integration in the social domain, from online sales to car-hailing services.[278] The limitations related to scaling up AI applications under a deregulated approach can be associated to municipal-level analytical capacity, since this "experiment first and regulate later" feature is embedded in the policy design of the AI pilot application scenarios. At the same time, the analysis of the Government Online-Offline Shanghai and the Single Platform for Urban Management demonstrated that Shanghai is also pursuing a more standardized approach to foster the use of AI in the public sector. Hence, the limitations in scaling up AI applications under a deregulated approach should not necessarily be interpreted as a lack of municipal-level analytical capacity, but rather as part of a broader policy strategy that attempts to leverage both the structured methods of the platform-based approach, and the experimental tactics of the pilot application scenarios, in order to foster AI integration in the public sector (Sect. 5.4).

Engagement of Private AI Companies

The third cross-cutting feature of the experiment-based approach is the engagement of private companies in the implementation of the AI pilot application scenarios, a process supported by the capacity of the Shanghai government to mobilize AI enterprises (Chapters 4.4 and

[278] See for instance: the hefty fines faced by online retailer Alibaba, which in April 2021 was sanctioned to pay 18.3 billion RMB for anti-competitive behavior (Murdoch, S. and Stanway, D., 2021. China Fines Alibaba Record $2.75 Bln for Anti-monopoly Violations. *Reuters*, https://www.reuters.com/business/retail-consumer/china-regulators-fine-alibaba-275-bln-anti-monopoly-violations-2021-04-10/); or the investigations on the ride-hailing company Didi Chuxing by the Cybersecurity Review Office of the Cyberspace Administration of China in July 2021, which one year later resulted in an 8-billion RMB fine (Ma, S. and Cao, Y., 2022. Ride-Hailing Giant Didi Fined over 8 Billion Yuan. *China Daily*, 21 July, https://www.chinadaily.com.cn/a/202207/21/WS62d95801a310fd2b29e6db39.html).

5.3.2.1). A great number of technology suppliers—mostly private companies—submitted proposals to provide AI technologies to the trial projects, promptly responding to the SHEITC "collections of solutions for AI application scenarios" (人工智能应用场景解决方案征集工作). As noted in the analysis of the platform-based approach, the engagement of AI companies is a **strength** in deploying AI in the public sector because it supports the capacity of public organizations in several ways. In the AI pilot application scenarios, the cooperation with AI firms helps to **promote the adoption, integration, and refinement of AI technologies in public sector activities**, supporting the analytical and operational capacities of public organizations.

First, the engagement of AI companies **grants public organizations access to the technologies needed to implement AI in their activities**. Private firms—not State-owned enterprises or other government-affiliated institutions—are the key suppliers of AI technologies and products. Hence, private companies are essential partners that need to be engaged to spur AI adoption in public organizations via the AI pilot application scenarios. While not all projects disclose their technical partners, evidence shows that the major Chinese AI companies and a number of emerging local firms are involved in the AI pilots, along with some State-owned enterprises. For instance, the AI laboratory of Shanghai Shixi High School (case study #2) is developed in cooperation with SenseTime (商汤). The AI applications in the schools of the Shanghai World Foreign Language Group (case study #3) are developed in cooperation between the technology company of the group (Shiwai Intelligence Education Technology) and other undisclosed technical partners. The Shanghai No. 10 People's Hospital (case study #5) developed some of its AI applications in cooperation with Ping'an Technology (平安科技) and Synyi AI (森亿智能). Fudan University Cancer Hospital (case study #6) uses a visualization system of survival rate of tumor patients developed by Tencent, a mammography intelligent diagnostic system that applies deep learning algorithms developed by AI company YITU (依图), and a cervical cancer screening system developed in cooperation with Shanghai Shenxin (上海深芯) and Ping'an Technology. The Shanghai Children's Medical Center (case study #7) uses AI systems provided by Synyi AI (森亿智能). The Ruijin Hospital (case study #8) also uses AI systems provided by Synyi AI, 4Paradigm (第四范式) and Fosun AITrox (复星杏脉), while the smart robot Ruijin Xiaobai (瑞金小白) used for ward rounds was jointly developed with the Shanghai Jiaotong University School of Medicine, to which the hospital is affiliated. The Beixinjing Subdistrict pilot (case study #9) introduced "smart health cabins" (智慧健康小屋) equipped with AI-based medical devices provided by iFlytek (科大讯飞), DeepBlue (深兰科技), and other AI companies. The Xietu Road Subdistrict project (case study #10) assessed ten AI companies as technology suppliers, including Unisound (云知声), China Telecom (中国电信), Pactera (中电文思海辉) and Sangtian Smart Technology (桑田智能技术), among others. The Zhangjiang AI Island pilot (case study #11) mostly uses technologies developed by Chinese and international companies and research institutes located in the park, including IBM, CloudWalk (云从科技), Tongji University's Research Institute for Intelligent Autonomous Systems, and Microsoft AI & IoT Insider Lab. The Lingang Intelligent Connected Vehicles pilot (case study #12) was developed in cooperation with autonomous vehicle company TuSimple (图森未来), and it uses smart transportation infrastructure supplied by Human Horizons (华人运通). The Shanghai Subway uses autonomous driving and smart signal technologies produced by Casco (卡斯柯信号). The Jing'an Government Data Management Center (case study #14) was developed in cooperation with Tencent. The Shanghai Museum (case study #15) uses smart speech technologies provided by iFlytek and AI-assisted restoration technologies developed by the Tongji University Design AI Lab (设计人工智能实验室). The Shanghai High People's Court (case study #16) also uses speech recognition and OCR technologies provided by iFlytek. Without associating them to specific projects, public sources indicate that 85 private AI companies were involved in the first batch of AI pilot application scenarios.[279] In addition to the aforementioned enterprises, these include Baidu, Alibaba, Huawei, Yanchuang Technology (亚创科技), Megvii (旷视科技), Liulishuo (流利说), and Xiao-i robots (小i机器人), among others.

Second, the engagement of AI companies **facilitates the integration of AI in public organizations by leveraging corporate expertise**. The technical expertise of AI companies helps public organizations to identify suitable technological solutions that meet their requirements (supporting organizational-level analytical capacity), and it also provides the operational resources and skills to deploy these solutions in practice

[279] AI Beetle, 2019. The First Batch of 12 AI Pilot Application Scenarios Will Be Built in Shanghai! [全国首批12个人工智能试点应用场景, 将在上海开建!]. *Zhihu* [知乎], 26 April, https://zhuanlan.zhihu.com/p/63904329.

(supporting organizational-level operational capacities). This integration process fostered by corporate resources and know-how can happen in two ways.[280] One is the provision of *standardized products and services*. As observed by the interviewee of the Zhangjiang AI Island (case study #11), the AI trial projects often use mature AI technologies that companies have been testing in commercial applications for at least 3–4 years (ZJAI). Similar considerations apply to the AI technologies deployed in other pilots. For instance: the use of computer vision for smart public security in schools (case study #1) and subdistricts (case studies #9–10), or for monitoring the large flow people in subway stations (case study #13) and districts (case study #14); the use of facial recognition for the identification of hospital patients (case study #8) and subway personnel (case study #13); the use of computer vision and NLP for detecting emotions and behaviors in smart classroom applications (case studies #1, 3–4), for monitoring the operations and signs of fatigue of subway drivers (case study #13), or for monitoring public opinion (#14); the use of NLP and speech recognition to collect and record medical information from patients registering for a visit (case studies #5–8); or the use of OCR, NLP, and speech recognition to grade student compositions (case studies #2–3), help doctor generate medical reports (case study #6–8) and extract information from such reports (case study #7) or from legal documents (case study #16). In many cases, these technologies still need some fine-tuning to the specific context of each organization (Molinari et al., 2021; Chui et al., 2018). But the use of mature technologies makes public sector AI adoption faster, as it starts from standard solutions that can be quickly integrated in the activities of public organizations by leveraging the know-how and experience of companies in providing commercial applications (SHZF, IFLYi, INESA). In addition, the use of market-tested products also facilitates after-sales assistance and continued access to some level of AI-related skills needed to maintain the systems. In this regard, the AI pilot applications scenarios confirm the findings of earlier studies, which observe that one of the main lessons that can be derived from China is

[280] In addition to the integration of AI solutions in standalone trial projects described here, corporate expertise can also support AI integration in public organizations in the context of city-wide, unified projects like the Government Online-Offline Shanghai and the Single Platform for Urban Management. In this case, corporate expertise mainly helps public organizations to devise and implement AI solutions that comply with the technical and operational requirements set by the municipal government, as examined earlier.

that public sector AI innovation does not require cutting-edge technical solutions, but is often down to rapid deployment and scaling of existing AI technologies (Elliott, 2020).

Another way in which the engagement of AI companies facilitates AI integration in public organizations is the ***development of tailor-made AI solutions***. In addition to mature, market-tested technologies, some AI pilot applications scenarios also use highly specialized AI systems that are built in close collaboration between public organizations and technical teams of the technology supplier, based on the specific requirements of the public agency. For instance, the AI system used to promote traditional physical education in the Qiangwei Primary School (case study #1) was jointly developed by the school's physical education teachers, experts from the University of Chinese Medicine (to which the school is affiliated), and the (undisclosed) technical partner. The eyeground disease multi-modal intelligent screening (眼底疾病多模态智能筛查) implemented by the Shanghai No. 10 People's Hospital (case study #5) was jointly developed and validated by three medical teams of Tongji University, Fudan University, and Shanghai Jiaotong University in cooperation with AI partner Ping'an Technology. The X-ray mammography intelligent diagnosis system (乳腺X 线智能诊断系统) of the Fudan University Cancer Hospital (case study #6) applies YITU's deep learning algorithms to medical data under the strict review and control of hospital doctors in order to improve the accuracy of medical diagnoses. The application "smart trial of financial cases" (金融案件智慧审判) of the Shanghai High People's Court (case study #16), which creates standard cases that judges can refer to when adjudicating similar controversies, was jointly developed by legal experts of the Shanghai High People's Court and technical experts of iFlytek. The importance of leveraging corporate expertise to integrate complex public sector AI solutions is confirmed by projects that precede the AI pilot application scenarios[281] It is also corroborated by extant literature on AI in the public sector, which emphasizes that public–private agreements for AI need to be more collaborative than traditional ITC sourcing projects, because it is unlikely that public agencies are able to specify AI requirements in as much detail as traditional systems (Desouza, 2018, p. 30).

281 See the discussions in Chapter 4.4 about the case-handling system for criminal trials, called System 206 (206系统), started in February 2017 by the Shanghai High People's Court (same sponsoring organization and technology partner of case study #16).

Third, the engagement of AI companies in public sector projects creates mutually beneficial arrangements that incentivize continuous public–private cooperation. This stable cooperation allows to **refine the capabilities of AI systems and adjust them to the needs of public organizations**. As examined earlier (Chapters 4.4 and 5.1.3), the Shanghai government values public–private cooperation in AI development because it helps to promote both the development of the AI industry and public sector applications, two goals of the municipal AI plans. For public organizations, cooperating with private AI firms is valuable not only because it boosts their analytical and operational capacities (as discussed in the previous paragraph), but also because it can bring economic benefits[282] and prestige[283] to the public agency. For AI companies, public sector AI projects create market opportunities for their technologies and products. These projects also give private firms access to the rich data sources of Shanghai government agencies and databases, which private companies can use to optimize their technologies and products. The benefits for AI companies are also emphasized by the official report on the first batch of AI pilot application scenarios.[284] As public organizations and AI

[282] For instance, the Shanghai No. 10 People's Hospital (case study #5) expects that its AI-based CT auxiliary imaging diagnostic system generates income for the hospital, as it can be the foundation of a specialist outpatient clinic. For the Zhangjiang AI Island (case study #11), the main source of income is the taxes paid by the companies that locate in the park (ZJAI). Economic benefits are also related to the reduction of costs deriving from efficiency gains, like some of those examined in Sect. 5.3.3.

[283] The Fudan University Cancer Hospital (case study #6) expects that its AI-based Mammography Intelligent Auxiliary Diagnosis System provides technical support for the construction of an oncology specialist medical alliance in Shanghai, with the hospital as a pivot. The Shanghai Children Medical Center (case study #7) in October 2020 was awarded as one of the "Top Ten Innovative Measures for Shanghai Medical Reform" for its use of AI. The Luwan No. 1 Central Primary School was selected as one of the "Shanghai educational informatization applications benchmark schools" for its successful use of AI technologies (references in Appendix VI). The smart elderly care application of Beixinjing Subdistrict (case study #9) was selected as a national smart elderly care applications demonstration site (智慧健康养老应用示范点; see Appendix VI). The smart elderly care applications of Xietu Road Subdistrict (case study #10) received the same award (see: Shanghai Xuhui, 2020. Good News! Xietu Subdistrict Awarded "National Smart Elderly Care Applications Trial Demonstration Subdistrict" [喜报!斜土街道荣获 "国家智慧健康养老应用试点示范街道"]. *The Paper News* [澎拜新闻], 4 January, https://m.thepaper.cn/newsDetail_forward_5438563).

[284] For instance, the review of the Fudan University Cancer Hospital pilot (case study #6) highlights that "[t]his project will bring great economic benefits to industrial cultivation. The market for hospital and medical AI systems is huge. If the products cultivated

companies have incentives to cooperate, their continuous collaborations can lead to the development of increasingly sophisticated AI tools that are progressively fine-tuned to meet the requirements of public agencies, thus reinforcing their operational capacity to implement AI in their activities. As noted, AI systems based on machine learning algorithms—the majority of AI systems in use today—learn while being deployed, from the infusion of more data and interactions with humans and their environment (Chapter 2.1). Hence, it is important that technical experts can closely work with public organizations to improve the accuracy of AI systems, enhance their performance threshold, extract meaningful output from AI technologies, and ensure that AI tools are both usable and compliant to the obligations of public organizations (Engstrom et al., 2020; Berryhill et al., 2019; Chui et al., 2018; Desouza, 2018).

Despite the importance of engaging private companies to promote the use of AI in public organizations and the mutual benefits that can derive from public–private partnerships, cooperation with AI firms also entails some difficulties that could **limit** the deployment of AI in the public sector via the AI pilot application scenarios. A common issue identified by the interviewees is the existence of **difficulties in reconciling the requirements of the pilot organizations with those of private AI companies**. In terms of analytical requirements, the person in charge of the Shanghai Museum pilot project emphasizes that it is necessary that AI technologies contribute to the realization of the core mission of public institutions (SHMU). However, AISPi observes that most AI technologies implemented in the pilot application scenarios are developed by private companies driven by a profit-making logic. This profit-making logic does not match the fundamental objective of public service provision, which must ensure that everyone has the right to access essential

by this project can occupy a large share of this market in the future, the participating enterprises will develop into a multi-billion industrial cluster". Similarly, the review of the Beixinjing Subdistrict pilot (case study #9) also emphasizes the benefits that this public sector application can bring to AI companies: "Connecting AI capabilities with the needs of the residential community [...] is conducive to further promoting the agglomeration of the AI industry, [...] accelerating application of AI enterprises and business model innovation, and improving economic benefits. [...] AI+ residential community construction provides application scenarios for new AI technologies, products and business models. See SJTU, CAICT and SHEIC (2019). In original: "将AI 所能与社区所需相衔接 [...] 有利于进一步助推人工智能产业集聚, [...] 加速AI 企业应用落地及商业模式创新, 提高经济效益" (p. 115). "AI + 社区建设为人工智能提供了新技术、新产品和新商业模式的应用场景" (p. 117).

goods and services. SJTU, who advised the Shanghai municipal government on technology policy, argues that reliance on private outsourcing can be highly problematic for public organizations due to conflict of interests and different values. CHUN, manager of a State-owned enterprise, observes that the use of AI in the public sector should increase convenience for the citizens. However, she argues that private companies are profit-driven and their priorities clearly diverge from those of the government. In terms of operational requirements, earlier chapters observed that public organizations are subject to more complex and often more stringent ethical, legal, and socioeconomic obligations than the private sector when using AI technologies, such as ensuring the safe, secure, benign, and inclusive use of AI, or fulfill a high level of transparency, fairness, and accountability, among others (Chapter 2.2.2). Indeed, AISPi notes that private companies don't pay particular attention to issues related to the governance of AI, such as ethical issues or the implications of transferring decision-making authority to machines, which instead are crucial in public sector AI applications. SJTU agrees that different requirements in terms of data privacy can be a major operational obstacle in public–private partnerships for AI. Similarly, CHUN notes that cooperating with private companies entails the risk that private actors leverage public resources (e.g., government data) for their own interests. She argues that the Shanghai government is aware of the problem and is trying to keep control on public service delivery.[285] FUDN agrees that the Shanghai government is aware of the challenges of cooperating with private companies, but it cannot develop AI technologies by itself; hence, it is "kidnapped by the companies" that are assuming a dominant role in the provision of technologies for public sector applications. The difficulties in reconciling the analytical and operational requirements of public organizations with those of private AI companies are confirmed by Shanghai INESA, who observes that the government prefers to cooperate with SOEs like his company because it has more control over them and can align them with government priorities.

[285] The interviewee makes the example of taxi service. She mentions the State-owned taxi-hailing platform Shencheng Transport (申城出行), created in September 2020 by the Shanghai government with State-owned automotive giant SAIC Group (https://www.guancha.cn/economy/2022_05_18_640275.shtml). She argues that the platform was introduced as an alternative to the privately-owned Didi Chuxing.

5.3.3 *Implications of the AI Pilots for Public Service Provision*

In the experiment-based approach, the interactions of municipal-level and organizational-level policy capacities generate a number of strengths and limitations in deploying AI in the public sector, which are summarized in Table 5.10. The resulting implications for public service provision in Shanghai are discussed in the next paragraphs in relation to the two main objectives set by the municipal government for the AI pilot application scenarios. Namely:

(i) improving the operations of public organizations and the provision of public services ("improving citizens sense of gain and satisfaction, [and] effectively using artificial intelligence to solve practical bottlenecks and pain points[286]"); and
(ii) leveraging AI trial projects to develop AI applications that can be replicated in the whole city ("striving to form replicable and referential experience models that can be applied to the whole city[287]").

Available evidence indicates that **the AI pilot application scenarios are improving the efficiency of public sector operations and public service provision**, the first objective of the experiment-based approach. While there are intrusive applications in a small number of trial projects, the majority of AI pilots are fostering positive innovation in the public sector (Sect. 5.3.2.2). AI adoption has led to several efficiency gains, which have been quantified by the organizations involved. For instance, the "emergency auxiliary diagnosis and treatment system" (急诊辅助诊疗系统) of the Shanghai No. 10 People's Hospital (case study #5) increased the triage accuracy rate from 69 to 95% in the diagnosis of 450,000 emergency patients.[288] Moreover, the AI-based smart CT auxiliary imaging diagnostic system of the hospital improved the diagnosis efficiency of

[286] SHEITC Notice, 2019a, art. 2.

[287] Ibid., art. 5.

[288] China Youth Journal, 2020. Why Are These Four Projects in the First Batch of Shanghai AI Demonstration Application Scenarios? New Trends in Future Scenario Construction [首批上海人工智能示范应用场景为何是这四家?未来场景建设有何新趋向]. *China Youth Journal* [中国青年报], 11 December, retrieved from https://baijiahao.baidu.com/s?id=1685771160240538427; Chen, J. and Sheng, X., 2020. "AI + medicine" Helps Accurate Diagnosis "Hospital of the Future" in Shanghai "Comes True"

Table 5.10 Experiment-based approach: strengths and limitations in deploying AI in the public sector

Organizational experiments under municipal lead	
Strengths	*Limitations*
Municipal-level policy capacities are helping to *jumpstart public sector AI applications* by creating the basic conditions for organizational experiments with AI technologies that, if successful, can be applied in the whole city: – The Shanghai municipal government has designed a sound policy initiative for developing, testing, and assessing public sector AI solutions that can be replicated in the city. Through this policy initiative, it steers the creation of AI pilots that are more likely to be disseminated because they coincide with the municipal priority areas for the use of AI in the public sector – Shanghai has created political support for the AI pilot application scenarios. This ensures the widespread uptake of AI trial projects in several policy areas, serves to enlist the cooperation of policy actors that can politically support the startup and execution of the AI pilot application scenarios, and creates an enabling environment that encourages a fast-paced approach to experimentation with AI in the public sector – The Shanghai AI ecosystem has plenty of operational skills and resources that help the deployment of AI in the public sector via the AI pilot application scenarios. These include the availability of AI companies and the ability to engage them, rich data sources, advanced infrastructure, and financial support	It is difficult to develop the organizational-level policy capacities needed to *make the transition from pilots to established applications* integrated in the activities of public organizations, a necessary condition to creating viable models that can be replicated by other public organizations in Shanghai: – Public organizations often have difficulties in identifying AI applications that are conducive to organizational goals. They also lack the ability to "translate" the needs of the public organization in terms that can be addressed by AI, and to align the use of AI technologies with organizational objectives. Public agencies have difficulties in gaining regular access to government-led AI expert committees – Public organizations sometimes display inertia when it comes to adopting AI, and there are also various forms of resistance to the introduction of AI technologies in public organizations – Public organizations can have limited data quality, scanty financial resources, or insufficient level of informatization to efficiently implement AI in their activities. Public organizations also face difficulties in recruiting people who have both technical AI knowledge and an understanding of public sector activities

(continued)

Table 5.10 (continued)

Deregulated approach to public sector AI innovation	
Strengths	*Limitations*
Municipal-level political capacity has created an enabling environment that helps to promote AI innovation in the public sector by *encouraging public organizations to use AI in their activities*. This supports the political capacity of public agencies to create consensus for the adoption of AI in their operations, and it paved the way to a variety of public sector AI applications across all the policy areas of the AI pilot application scenarios Fast-paced experimentation has created *success stories of AI integration in the public sector that can build momentum for scaling up AI applications* in the pilot organizations, reinforcing the political capacity of public agencies to create support for continuing and expanding the use of AI in their activities The policy design of the AI pilot application scenarios allows the Shanghai government to pursue a *combination of fast-paced implementation with attention to safety*. The AI pilots serve as sandboxes and innovation testbeds that try and evaluate public sector AI applications in controlled environments	Insufficient organizational-level analytical capacity and ineffective oversight by municipal authorities resulted in some *experiments with intrusive AI applications*. There is no evidence that privacy or ethical concerns are hindering the AI pilots. But these applications are invasive also by Chinese standards, and they could turn out to be a limitation in deploying AI in the public sector if they started to be opposed by the target population and negatively affected social acceptance for the use of AI The *lack of regulations and standards can become an obstacle to scaling up AI applications* in the mid-term, hindering large-scale applications that extend beyond the AI pilots. In addition, experience from other cases of deep integration of technology in the social domain suggests that financial and policy costs are expected to accompany the transition from a permissive to a more tightly regulated environment
Engagement of private companies	
Strengths	*Limitations*
The municipal-level operational capacity to mobilize AI companies *grants public organizations access to the technologies needed to implement AI in their operations*. Private companies are key suppliers of AI technologies, and must be engaged if the pilot application scenarios have to spur AI adoption in public organizations Engaging private companies can *facilitate the integration of AI in public organizations by leveraging corporate expertise*, fostering the analytical and operational capacities of public agencies to use AI in their activities. Corporate expertise can help both in the provision of mature AI technologies as well as ad-hoc, highly specialized AI solutions jointly developed with public organizations	Public organizations have *difficulties in reconciling their analytical and operational requirements with those of private AI companies*. Most AI technologies implemented in the AI application scenarios are developed for commercial purposes; hence, they do not necessarily match the priorities of public organizations, and there can be conflicting interests and values. In addition, public organizations are subject to more complex and often more stringent ethical, legal, and socioeconomic obligations than the private sector when deploying AI technologies in their activities

(continued)

Table 5.10 (continued)

Engaging private companies generates beneficial arrangements that create the premises for lasting collaborations, which are crucial to *adjust AI systems to the needs of public organizations and refine the capabilities of such systems*. This reinforces the operational capacity of public organizations to implement AI in their work by providing increasingly sophisticated AI systems that can be better integrated in their activities

doctors by 30–50%, while maintaining high-level accuracy. In an assessment made during the first months of the pilot, the hospital reported various benefits from the use of AI: it allows doctors to have more time to serve patients; it reduces the workload of doctors, while providing accurate diagnostic suggestions, suggesting tailor-made medical plans, and helping the management of patients; AI also contributes to improving satisfaction of the patients and enhancing quality of hospital management, among others. At the Fudan University Shanghai Cancer Hospital (case study #6), the AI-based outpatient appointment system has reduced the average waiting time for specialist visits by 7.4 days, and the appointment rate increased by about 20%. The "medication guidance function" maps the adverse reactions of 47 common chemotherapy drugs used by the hospital, helping 350 patients per day on average, greatly reducing the work pressure of outpatient medical staff, and improving consultation efficiency. In the diagnosis and treatment of cervical carcinoma, another area where the hospital is using AI, the 5-year survival rate of patients reached 98.6%.[289] At the Ruijin Hospital (case study #8), the smart pre-check and pre-diagnosis system reduced the waiting time for patients and the

to Benefit Patients ["AI + 医疗" 助力精准诊断 "未来医院" 上海 "成真" 造福患者]. *CN-Healthcare* [健康界], 10 December, https://www.cn-healthcare.com/article/20201210/content-547446.html.

[289] Fudan University, 2021. The 90th Anniversary of the Fudan University Cancer Hospital: Becoming a World-Class Hospital, the 5-Year Overall Survival Rate of Tumor Patients Has Reached 71.3% [复旦大学附属肿瘤医院建院90周年: 跻身国际一流, 肿瘤患者5年总生存率达到71.3%]. *Fudan University*, 15 November, https://news.fudan.edu.cn/2021/1115/c4a110579/page.htm.

workload of doctors, thus increasing the interaction time between doctors and patients during the visit. In addition, the use of speech recognition to input medical records reduces the time of drafting patients' medical history from 5 to 1.5 minutes on average. The Beixinjing Subdistrict (case study #9) introduced an AI system that performs "smart video patrols" (智能巡屏) and discovers problems in the residential community mostly (95%) within one hour. In the Lingang demonstration area (case study #12), autonomous driving trucks reduce fuel consumption by 7–15%, contributing to the reduction of polluting emissions. In road safety, intelligent networked vehicles can avoid 90–95% of traffic accidents caused by human errors (SJTU, CAICT, and SHEIC, 2019, pp. 128–129). In the Shanghai Subway (case study #13), the use of computer vision and machine learning for monitoring and maintenance of key subway equipment (e.g., trains and traffic signals) reduced the inspection time by 25%, while increasing inspection reliability by 10%. The probability of equipment failure decreased by 20%, and the reliability of equipment increased by 61%. AI technologies have also reduced the time required to open and close the subway stations (e.g., activate equipment in the morning, evacuate passengers at night) from more than 1 hour to only 10 minutes. Thise not only reduces the workload of the staff, but also saves two hours of time for the maintenance of the subway.[290] In the Shanghai Financial Court (case study #16), AI helps to analyze the contents of legal documents submitted to the tribunal, improving efficiency in documents submission. As a result, service counters have been reduced from ten to two (execution and filing), allowing to better allocate the staff of the court.[291] Further examples are provided in Appendix VI.

The second objective of the experiment-based approach is to develop AI applications that can be replicated in the whole municipality. To assess whether the AI pilot application scenarios have achieved this goal, it is useful to proceed in two steps. The first step is to observe if the AI pilots have transitioned from trial projects to established applications

[290] SAIA, 2021. Shanghai Subway Intelligent Transportation System [上海地铁智慧交通系统]. *Shanghai AI Industry Association* [上海人工智能行业协会], 30 June, http://www.sh-aia.com/dynamics/detail364.htm.

[291] Shanghai Law Journal, 2020. Face Recognition! Smart Case Filling! The Shanghai Financial Court Litigation Service Center Gathers "Wisdom" and Makes an Upgraded Appearance! [人脸识别!智助立案!上海金融法院诉讼服务中心 "智慧" 云集, 升级亮相!]. *Shanghai Law Journal* [上海法治报], 11 June, retrieved from: https://baijiahao.baidu.com/s?id=1669134008192482050&wfr=spider&for=pc.

that are integrated in the activities of public organizations. As noted, this is a necessary condition to create "model experiences" that can be replicated by other public organizations in Shanghai. The interviews highlighted the difficulties in developing the organizational-level capabilities needed to make this evolution. At the same time, **a key strength of the experiment-based approach is that it leverages municipal-level skills and resources to enhance the ability of public agencies to use AI in their activities**, mitigating the reported deficiencies in organizational policy capacities. Specifically: (i) the promotion of AI experiments under municipal lead creates the basic conditions for jumpstarting AI trial projects, supporting the analytical, operational, and political capacities of public organizations; (ii) a deregulated approach to public sector AI innovation helps create consensus for AI adoption and scaling up AI applications in public organizations, supporting their political capacity; and (iii) the engagement of private companies grants public organizations steady access to AI technologies, leverages corporate expertise to promote AI integration, and creates lasting collaborations that allow to adjust the AI systems to the needs of public organizations and refine their capabilities, thus boosting the analytical and operational capacities of public agencies.

Indeed, evidence indicates that **all the AI pilots have integrated AI technologies in the provision of public services, making the transition from trial projects to established applications**. In addition to the AI applications examined in Sect. 5.3.2.2 and the examples of efficiency gains presented in the previous paragraph, there are several other indicators of successful AI integration in public service delivery via the AI pilots. For instance, the Qiangwei Primary School (case study #1) has broadened the scope of application of its "smart campus security", which is also used to discover potential health and safety problems (e.g., children's chasing or quarreling in between classes). In fall 2019, the Luwan No. 1 Central Primary School (case study #4) was awarded by the Shanghai Education Commission for its successful integration of AI and digital technologies in classroom teaching. In October 2020, the Shanghai Children's Medical Center (case study #7) was awarded as one of the "Top Ten Innovative Initiatives of Shanghai Medical Reform" (上海医改十大创新举措) for its successful establishment of a mobile AI platform for outpatient service.[292] In 2021, evidence showed that the AI applications in the Beixinjing Subdistrict (case study #9) had received a continuous upgrade over the years.[293] Similarly, the government report on AI applications in the Xietu Road Subdistrict (case study #10) also listed several achievements in 2021.[294] The Zhangjiang AI Island not only has successfully developed the AI technologies indicated in the project requirements of the pilot application scenario, but it also added new AI applications (e.g., unmanned aerial vehicles for safety inspection, and unmanned ships for water quality monitoring, etc.). The Shanghai Museum (case study #15) is determined to replicate and expand its AI applications in the East Branch of the Shanghai Museum (上海博物馆东馆) once it opens. The Museum aims to further integrate AI in smart museum management, from BIM[295] to the supervision of the exhibition areas (SHMU). Publicly

[292] Shanghai Children's Medical Center, 2020. Shanghai Children's Medical Center Has Built a Mobile Platform for AI Outpatient Service, and Won the Third "Top Ten Innovative Measures for Shanghai Medical Reform" [上海儿童医学中心打造人工智能门诊患者服务移动平台，荣膺第三届 "上海医改十大创新举措"]. *Shanghai Children's Medical Center WeChat Official Account*, 10 October, https://mp.weixin.qq.com/s?__biz=MzA3OTY2NDEyNA==&mid=2650928449&idx=1&sn=9b4a8188f10d8630e2d6236d41fc95da&chksm=844553d2b332dac49930aca5667461dbfd795b4a73ffcb448a7f69cc1a9adaeb54ac09dbc7f5#rd.

[293] Shanghai Party Construction Service Center, 2021. Changning District Beixinjing Subdistrict: Party Building Leads the "Single Platform for Urban Management", Refines Community Governance [长宁区北新泾街道：党建引领 "一网统管" 社区治理更精细]. *Shanghai Party Construction Service Center* [上海市党建服务中心], 8 February, https://www.shjcdj.cn/djWeb/djweb/web/djweb/newestindex/newestindex!info.action?articleid=ff8080817745095401777c8cc0f4036a; Sohu, 2021. The "Grounded Gas" Practice of a Digital Benchmarking Community in Shanghai [一个申城数字化标杆社区的 "接地气" 实践]. *Sohu* [搜狐], 19 December, http://news.sohu.com/a/509743789_120244154; Zhang, Y. and Lu, J., 2021. Beixinjing Subdistrict|Technology Empowers "Old and Small", the Xinjing No. 6 Community Is Transformed into an "AI + community" [北新泾街道|科技赋能 "老旧小"，新泾六村变身 "AI + 社区"]. *Morning News* [新闻晨报], 24 January, retrieved via: https://baijiahao.baidu.com/s?id=1689695521711702661&wfr=spider&for=pc.

[294] Xuhui District People's Government, 2022. Dare to Take on the Mission, Dare to Be the Pioneer, Compose a New Miracle, and Comprehensively Promote the New Development of Xietu—Report at the First Meeting of the Sixth Assembly of the Xietu Community [勇担使命 敢为先锋 谱写新奇迹 全面推动斜土新发展—在斜土社区第六届代表会议第一次会议上的报告], 18 February, http://www.xuhui.gov.cn/H/xhxxgkN/xhxxgk_xt_ghlxx_ghjh/Info/Detail_65312.htm.

[295] Building Information Modelling (BIM) is a 3D model-based process used in architecture and engineering to efficiently plan, design, construct, and manage buildings and infrastructure. Advanced BIM models incorporate AI techniques, e.g., the optimization

available information, field visits, and conversations with key informant interviewees confirm that all the case studies have integrated AI in their activities. Moreover, in many cases, the AI pilots have also progressively introduced further AI applications (see Appendix VI for details of each case study).

The second step to assess if the experiment-based approach produced AI applications that can be disseminated to the whole city is to look for evidence that the "model experiences" of the AI pilots have been replicated in other projects in Shanghai. A preliminary consideration to be made is that the "scenario organizations" of the AI pilots display a unique set of organizational skills and resources. Hence, the existence of model experiences is a necessary but not sufficient condition to spur AI applications via the trial projects, since other public agencies in Shanghai do not necessarily have the same level of skills and resources of the AI pilot organizations they want to emulate.[296] These skills and resources include:

- *the proven ability to promote digital innovation in the public sector*. The Qiangwei Primary School (case study #1) started to build an "AI smart campus system" (AI 智慧校园系统) as early as 2018, leveraging surveillance cameras and three sets of "AI + school" systems to solve issues encountered in traditional teaching.[297] The Shixi High School (case study #2) created its Internet learning platform (网络学习平台) in 2014, and in 2016 upgraded it to a "smart learning platform[298]" (智能学习平台). Since 2017, the school also introduced AI courses and an AI

of energy performance using convolutional neural networks. See for instance: Xu, F., and Liu, Q., 2023. Building Energy Consumption Optimization Method Based on Convolutional Neural Network and BIM. *Alexandria Engineering Journal*, 77, pp. 407–417, https://doi.org/10.1016/j.aej.2023.06.084.

[296] The only case study not included in the following list is the Shanghai WFL Education pilot (case study #3), which as noted is managed by a private group.

[297] Xinmin Net, 2019. Minhang Primary School Will Appear at the World Artificial Intelligence Conference. The first "AI + School" Is as Cool as Iron Man! [闵行这所小学将亮相世界人工智能大会，首家 "AI + 学校" 像钢铁侠一样酷!]. *Xinmin Net* [新民网], 26 July, http://shanghai.xinmin.cn/xmsq/2019/07/26/31562300.html.

[298] Eastday.com, 2018. Shanghai Shixi High School: Building the School of the Future and Ushering in the Era of Artificial Intelligence [上海市西中学: 建构未来学校 迎来人工智能时代]. *Eastday.com* [东方网], 20 September, http://edu.021east.com/node2/jypd/n5/n708/u1ai15713_K20.html.

laboratory.[299] The Luwan No. 1 Central Primary School (case study #4) introduced several digital applications since the mid-2010s, including: a "cloud platform" (云平台)[300]; "cloud class-rooms" (云课堂) that integrate digital technologies (i.e., tablets) in classroom activities,[301] and a smart library that records data on the books read by the students and feed them to teachers, who can then provide personalized reading recommendations.[302] The AI pilot in Zhangjiang AI Island (case study #11) is operated by the Zhangjiang Group (张江集团), a State-owned company that has 30 years of experience in promoting technological innovation in the Zhangjiang Hi-tech Industry Park (张江高新技术产业开发区), a main hub of technological development in Shanghai.[303] The Shanghai Subway (case study #13) introduced autonomous driving technologies since 2010s. And the Shanghai Museum (case study #15) in May 2018 had already established the first museum digital platform in China (博物馆数字化管理平台), which uses digital technology to monitor

299 Whale Media, 2019. At the Shanghai Shixi High School AI Approves Writing Compositions, Should AI Redefine Teachers? [上海市市西中学AI批作文, AI要重新定义教师?]. *Whale Media* [鲸媒体], 29 August, retrieved via: https://baijiahao.baidu.com/s?id=1643167213919372703&wfr=spider&for=pc. See also: SJTU, CAICT and SHEIC (2019, p. 103).

300 Luo, Y., 2014. Luwan No. 1 Central Primary School in Huangpu District, Shanghai: Creating a Personalized Learning Space Anytime, Anywhere [上海市黄浦区卢湾第一中心小学: 随时随地随需创建个性化学习空间]. *Shanghai Education* [上海教育], 2014 (07A).

301 Wu, R. and Ji, Y., 2016. Effective Integration of Digital Media to Form a New Integrated Teaching Method—The Innovative Practice of "Cloud Classrooms" in Luwan No. 1 Central Primary School in Huangpu District, Shanghai [有效整合数字媒体 形成融合式新教学方式—上海市黄浦区卢湾一中心小学"云课堂"的创新实践]. *Modern Teaching* [现代教学], 2016(9), pp. 72–73.

302 Chen, Z., 2018. Luwan No. 1 Central Primary School: Caiyun Library Uses Intelligence to Serve Wisdom [卢湾一中心小学: 用智能服务智慧的彩云图书馆]. *Shanghai Education* [上海教育], April 2018 (B).

303 The Zhangjiang Hi-tech Industry Park was established in 1992. In 2011, the park obtained the status of National Innovation Demonstration Zone (国家自主创新示范区), technology hub sponsored by the national government to promote the indigenous development of advanced technologies.

the real-time flow of people in each exhibition hall, and automatically sends warning if the crowd density overcomes the preset threshold[304];

- *the affiliation to leading technology institutions that provide public agencies with in-house resources to integrate AI in their activities*. The hospitals hosting the AI pilot application scenarios are all affiliated to elite Shanghai universities that offer AI undergraduate majors and carry out important AI research projects (Chapter 4.3.1): the Shanghai No. 10 People's Hospital (case study #5) is affiliated to Tongji University; the Fudan University Cancer Hospital (case study #6) is affiliated to Fudan University, and already started AI applications for outpatient appointment accuracy in 2018[305]; the Shanghai Children Medical Center (case study #7); and the Shanghai Ruijin Hospital (case study #8) are affiliated to the Shanghai Jiaotong University. The Lingang pilot project in transport (case study #12) is managed by Lingang Sci-Tech City (上海临港科技创新城经济发展有限公司), an organization created in 2015 with proven experience to promote technological innovation in the Lingang New Area in Pudong. In addition, this project is also associated with two leading technology institutions, the Shanghai Motor Vehicle Inspection Certification & Technology Innovation Center and the China Academy of Information and Communications (CAICT) Easter China Institute;
- *the participation in other public sector digital innovation programs that give public agencies access to a supplementary set of municipal-level resources*, in addition to those deriving from being part of the AI pilot program of SHEITC (Sect. 5.3.2.1). The Beixinjing and Xietu Road subdistricts (case studies #9–10) since 2019 have been absorbed into the Single Platform for Urban Management and benefit from its operational "capability platform", which boosts their ability to integrate AI in their activities (Sect. 5.2.2). Similarly, the Jing'an Government Data Management Center (case study #14) benefits from its inclusion in both the Single Platform for Urban

[304] Sina News, 2018. The Shanghai Museum Has Built the First Museum Digital Management Platform in China [上海博物馆今建成国内首家博物馆数字化管理平台]. *Sina News* [新浪新闻中心], 3 May, https://k.sina.com.cn/article_6145283913_16e499749020007aqd.html.

[305] Fudan University Shanghai Cancer Hospital, 2019. [Jiefang Daily] in Addition to Identifying "Scalpers", It Can Also Accurately Triage [[解放日报] 除了识别 "黄牛" 还能精确分诊]. *Fudan University Cancer Hospital*, 26 November, https://www.shca.org.cn/Home/news/content/id/308/pid/6037.html.

Management and the Government Online-Offline Shanghai, being part of the network of Big Data centers that characterize these platforms. In addition, Jing'an district was among the first in the municipality to establish a district-level data management center in January 2018, showing its ability to promote digital innovation in the public sector. Finally, the use of AI in the Shanghai Financial Court (case study #16) is part of a national initiative for the creation of "smart courts" (智慧法院), and thus it enjoys high-profile political endorsement and operational support to test AI in the judiciary.

As for solid evidence that the "model experiences" of the AI pilot application scenarios have been replicated in other projects in Shanghai, it is difficult to establish a causal relationship between the introduction of the AI pilots and the increased public sector AI activity in the municipality. In fact, there are several concurring programs and policy initiatives that are spurring the "digitalization" (数字化) and "informatization" (信息化) of the public sector in the same areas of the AI pilot application scenarios. For instance, in October 2018 the Shanghai municipal government published the *Shanghai Education Informatization 2.0 Action Plan (2018–2022)* (上海市教育信息化2.0行动计划 [2018–2022]). Among other things, this action plan promotes the creation of "Shanghai educational informatization applications benchmark schools" (上海市教育信息化应用标杆学校) that integrate AI and other digital technologies in teaching and school management at all levels (kindergartens, primary schools, middle schools, high schools, vocational schools, and universities[306]). In November 2021, Shanghai published the *Implementation plan for the digital transformation of education in Shanghai (2021–2023)* (上海市教育数字化转型实施方案 [2021–2023]), spurring a wave of digitalization in local schools.[307] This was followed

306 Tencent, 2019. Shanghai Has Established 54 Benchmark Schools for the Application of Educational Informatization to Create the Most Suitable Education for Each Student [上海创建54所教育信息化应用标杆学校, 为每位学生创造最适合的教育]. *Tencent Open Content Platform* [腾讯内容开放平台], 10 October, https://page.om.qq.com/page/OThWXFSV657X6aRn8cwRnpaw0.

307 Shanghai Observer, 2021. Changning, Baoshan, and Xuhui Release Plans for Education Digital Transformation Experimental Zones [长宁、宝山、徐汇发布教育数字化转型实验区方案]. *Shanghai Observer* [上观], 17 November, https://sghexport.shobserver.com/html/baijiahao/2021/11/17/588683.html.

by the *14th Five-Year Plan for the Digital Transformation of Education in Shanghai* (上海市教育数字化转型 "十四五" 规划), which further expands the efforts to promote the digitalization of education in the municipality.[308] In public health, since 2014 Shanghai has been promoting the integration of Internet and digital technologies in healthcare management, elderly care, vaccination records, and other areas.[309] The municipality has introduced several digital initiatives in various areas of public health, making Shanghai a pioneering city in this field in China. These initiatives mention the use of AI in "Internet hospitals[310]" (互联网医院), and state that AI, 5G, and Big Data are the three pillars of the comprehensive digital transformation of Shanghai's medical and health service system.[311] In line with these initiatives, in October 2017 the municipality introduced the initiative called "Top Ten Innovative Measures for Shanghai Medical Reform" (上海医改十大创新举措). Since the first edition in 2018, this initiative rewards medical institutions that leverage Big Data and digital technologies in their activities.[312] In urban management, Shanghai has been promoting various smart city initiatives since as early as 2010.[313] The smart city plan published in 2020

[308] Ministry of Education, 2022. Shanghai Actively Promotes Education Digital Transformation and Development [上海市积极推进教育数字化转型发展]. *Ministry of Education*, 28 June, http://www.moe.gov.cn/jyb_xwfb/s6192/s222/moe_1740/202206/t20220628_641459.html.

[309] SHEITC, Municipal Health Commission, Municipal Human Resources Bureau, Municipal Civil Affairs Bureau and Municipal Food and Drugs Administration, 2014. *Shanghai Working Solution for the Promotion of Internet Healthcare* [上海市健康物联网推进工作方案], https://www.zhihuichengshi.cn/XinWenZiXun/ChengShiZhuanLan/21432.html.

[310] Shanghai Municipal Health Commission, 2019. *Shanghai Internet Hospitals Management Guidelines* [上海市互联网医院管理办法], Huweigui [2019] 004, 16 July, http://wsjkw.sh.gov.cn/yzgl3/20190812/0012-64913.html.

[311] Shanghai Municipal Health Commission, Shanghai Development and Reform Commission, SHEITC, Shanghai Shenkang Hospital Development Center, Shanghai Data Exchange Center, Shanghai Finance Bureau, 2021. *Shanghai "Convenient Medical Service" Digital Transformation Work Plan* [上海市 "便捷就医服务" 数字化转型工作方案], Huwei Xinxi [2021] 5, 4 June, http://wsjkw.sh.gov.cn/zhgl2/20210607/6cab5f1b39f44211a60c1fcb2a5f1d06.html.

[312] China Central Government, 2018. Top 10 Innovative Measures of Shanghai Medical Reform [上海医改十大创新举措评出]. *China Central Government* [中华人民共和国中央人民政府], 5 January, http://www.gov.cn/xinwen/2018-01/15/content_5256648.htm.

[313] The 2016 municipal government plan on smart cities write: "Since 2010, Shanghai has been comprehensively promoting the construction of the future smart city, and

stated that by 2022 Shanghai would be a global leading smart city, which makes extensive use of the Internet, Big Data, AI, and other information technologies to promote urban governance and "improve the level of scientification, precision and intelligentization of city management".[314] In addition, in early 2019 Shanghai announced the creation of the Single Platform for Urban Management, a major initiative that makes extensive use of AI, Big Data, IoT, and other technologies in urban governance, and it encompasses some of the case studies examined earlier (the pilots of Beixinjing and Xietu Road subdistricts, and some applications of the Jing'an Government Data Management Center). In transport, in January 2019 Shanghai launched the "AI + transportation scenario program" (AI+ 交通场景计划; SJTU, CAICT, and SHEIC, 2019, p. 28), which contributed to make the municipality the national leader in applications for of AI-enabled autonomous vehicles (Chapter 4.4). In administrative services, the integration of AI in the activities of public organizations is actively spurred by the Government Online-Offline Shanghai, which also encompasses some of the case studies examined earlier (the Jing'an Government Data Management Center, and some applications of the Beixinjing and Xietu Road pilots). In the judiciary, Shanghai has been a pioneer city in China in the construction of "smart courts" that integrate AI technologies in the activities of the tribunals since as early as February 2017 (Chapter 4.4 and Appendix VI), and it has continued to promote the digitalization of the local courts[315] in line with national plans

the level of urban digitalization, network connection and intelligence have been clearly enhanced" [2010年以来, 本市全面推进面向未来的智慧城市建设, 城市数字化、网络化、智能化水平显著提升]. Shanghai Municipal Government, 2016. *Thirteen Five-Year Plan for Promoting the Construction of a Smart City in Shanghai* [上海市推进智慧城市建设"十三五" 规划], Hufufa (2016) 80, 19 September, https://www.shanghai.gov.cn/nw12344/20200814/0001-12344_50147.html.

[314] Shanghai Municipal Government, 2020. *Several Opinions on Further Accelerating the Construction of a Smart City* [关于进一步加快智慧城市建设的若干意见], 10 February, https://www.shanghai.gov.cn/nw44142/20200824/0001-44142_63566.html. Section 4, in original: "到2022年, 将上海建设成为全球新型智慧城市的排头兵, [...] 更多运用互联网、大数据、人工智能等信息技术手段, 推进城市治理制度创新、模式创新、手段创新, 提高城市科学化、精细化、智能化管理水平".

[315] Supreme People's Court of China, 2021. Deepen the Construction of Smart Courts and Better Serve the Masses. Shanghai Court Launches Full-Process Online Case Handling System Version 2.0 [深化智慧法院建设 更好为群众办实事 上海法院推出全流程网上办案体系2.0版]. *Supreme People's Court of China* [中华人民共和国最高人民法院], 19 April, https://www.court.gov.cn/zixun-xiangqing-296901.html.

in this area.[316] Finally, establishing causal relationship between the introduction of the AI pilots and the increased public sector AI activity in the municipality is further complicated by the fact that even when the same public organizations that hosted the AI pilot application scenarios continue the integration of AI in their activities, they usually do not mention the "AI pilot application scenario" program,[317] since the official trial period officially lasts for 12 months.

To sum up, the analysis on the dissemination of AI applications following the introduction of the AI pilots shows that: (i) the organizations in the AI pilots display a unique set of organizational resources and capabilities; and (ii) it is difficult to establish a causal relationship between the introduction of the AI pilots and the increased public sector AI activity in Shanghai. In addition, it was already observed that the lack of regulations and standards that characterize the experiment-based approach can become an obstacle to scaling up and duplicating the applications of the AI pilots (Sect. 5.3.2.2). As a result, it is not possible to make a conclusive assessment on the extent to which the "model experiences" of the AI pilot application scenarios can, have been, or will be actually replicated in other projects in Shanghai. Nonetheless, indications derived from public sector AI literature as well as the practices of Shanghai to support AI development suggest that the AI pilot applications scenarios can give an **important contribution to spurring the diffusion of AI-based public services** in the municipality in three main ways.

First, given the paucity of empirical evidence on public sector AI applications (Chapter 2.1), the existence of well-known, government-endorsed

[316] See for instance: Supreme People's Court, 2017. *Opinions of the Supreme People's Court on Accelerating the Construction of Smart Courts* [最高人民法院关于加快快建设智慧法院的意见], Fafa (2017) 12, 12 April 2017, http://gongbao.court.gov.cn/Details/5dec527431cdc22b72163b49fc0284.html.

[317] For instance, when purchasing AI systems in August 2022, the Luwan No. 1 Central Primary School (case study #4) did not mention the AI pilot application scenarios, but the initiative on "Shanghai educational informatization applications benchmark schools". See: Shanghai Bid Center, 2022. Huangpu District Shanghai Huangpu District Luwan No.1 Central Primary School Government Procurement Intention from August to September 2022—Smart Campus Service Based on AI Face Recognition Technology [黄浦区上海市黄浦区卢湾一中心小学2022年8月至9月政府采购意向-基于AI人脸识别技术的智慧校园服务]. *Shanghai Bid Center* [上海招标网], 12 August, https://sh.bidcenter.com.cn/diqucontent-190099424-2.html. Similar considerations apply to the 2020 public procurement bid of the Shanghai Shixi High School mentioned earlier.

case studies that successfully integrated AI technologies in the provision of public services provides **valuable learning experiences for other public agencies in Shanghai**, which can draw useful insights from the AI pilot application scenarios when gauging possible AI implementations in their organizations. Scholars of AI in the public sector observe that the existence of shareable experiences of public sector AI applications can foster the process of AI adoption across different public agencies, because best practices help to address the scarce knowledge about the organizational challenges faced at different stages of AI development in the public sector, providing evidence of successful management strategies that public agencies can employ when adopting AI (Molinari et al., 2021; Campion et al., 2020, pp. 10, 20; Berryhill et al., 2019, p. 27). By providing real-world examples of AI solutions that improve public service provision and are integrated into the activities of public organizations in several policy areas, the AI pilot application scenarios offer useful lessons to other public organizations that are considering to adopt AI technologies.

Second, the AI pilot application scenarios display **success stories that can help to foster social acceptance for public sector AI applications** among the Shanghai citizens. Social acceptance is a resource that the Shanghai government considers important to promote the sustainable development of AI in the public sector and other areas in the long term, when AI applications are expected to become more widespread and integrated in the lives and activities of Shanghai citizens and companies (Sects. 5.1.3 and 5.3.2.3). As noted, Shanghai is trying to popularize AI among local citizens, and in 2021 SHEITC launched a media campaign aiming to showcase the best practices of Shanghai in integrating AI in public health, transportation, urban governance, and other areas, in order to show the value that AI is creating for the local population (Chapter 4.5). In this context, the AI pilots are often presented as success stories of AI applications. The AI pilots of the Shanghai World Foreign Language Group in education (case study #3) and the Beixinjing subdistrict in urban governance (case study #9) were included among the best practices publicized in the media campaign,[318] together with the AI pilots for smart transport

[318] Shanghai Observer, 2021. [AI by Your Side] Smart Home Beixinjing, Creating a Community Model for Digital Transformation [[AI在身边] 慧居家园北新泾，打造数字化转型社区样板]. *Shanghai Observer* [上观], 1 December, https://sghexport.shobserver.com/html/baijiahao/2021/12/01/599420.html; SHEITC, 2022. [AI by your side] Intelligent teaching, AI tries your hand [[AI在身边] 智慧教学 AI一试身手]. *SHEITC*

in Jiading district.[319] In addition, the pilots for “AI + business circles” in the East Nanjing Road pedestrian street and the shopping mall operated by State-owned Bailian Group[320] were also included in the media campaign.

Third, the AI pilot application scenarios **contribute to Shanghai’s efforts to build an enabling environment for public sector AI innovation**, because they provide further evidence that the municipal government is committed to accelerating the use of AI in public sector operations and public service provision. The AI pilots not only are enshrined in the municipal plans for AI development, but they are also explicitly used to pursue the integration of AI in all the policy areas prioritized by the Shanghai government: city operations, public services, transport and shipping, and medicine and healthcare. By spearheading the use of AI in the public sector under a municipal program, the AI pilot application scenarios confirm Shanghai’s high-profile political endorsement and consistent policy vision for the use of AI in this area. In the upward accountability system of the Chinese bureaucracy, where public officials at every level are evaluated based on performance criteria set by higher authorities, the AI pilots provide a clear signal that encourages public organizations in Shanghai to implement AI-based public services in the policy areas prioritized by the municipal government, as local officials know that they will be rewarded if they succeed in doing so.

The SHEITC did not officially explain why it didn’t publish any other notices for the collection of AI pilot application scenarios after the last batch in December 2020. A local expert, who has frequent interactions with the Commission, argues that—based on the experience of the first

Website, 13 January, http://sheitc.sh.gov.cn/gydt/20220113/27dba4f07fcf4b9085d4bd46277656c9.html.

[319] SHEITC, 2022. [AI by Your Side] Smart Cars and Smart Roads [[AI在身边] 聪明的车与智慧的路]. *SHEITC WeChat Account*, 13 January, https://mp.weixin.qq.com/s/bBbo8i3-JEZIi-jiow6jmg.

[320] SHEITC, 2021. [AI by Your Side] Smart Nanjing Road, There Are Really “Numbers” to Play [[AI在身边] 智慧南京路 玩转真有 “数”]. *SHEITC Website*, 18 November, https://app.sheitc.sh.gov.cn/gydt/691168.htm; SHEITC, 2021. [AI by Your Side] Smart River Mall, New Experience of Future Shopping Street [智慧世博源, 未来商街新体验], *SAIA WeChat Account*, 29 November, https://mp.weixin.qq.com/s?__biz=Mzg3NjUxNjg4NQ==&mid=2247504123&idx=4&sn=4d210d9388b9b9ca099edb57ce5eae97&chksm=cf339381f8441a97d8abdd96eb33820c8abc6bd5a7e6cdba3774ff98e269604fa97d1cb5fdc4&scene=178&cur_album_id=2175035792270655488#rd.

three batches—SHEITC is trying to coordinate the development of more complex AI applications. These would include multiple, interconnected scenarios within the same policy area (he mentions public health), or across different sectors (e.g., the combination of smart transport and smart services). These more complex scenarios would provide more solid evidence to showcase the successes of Shanghai in AI development to the political leadership of the municipality[321] (AISPi). These considerations are corroborated by some policy documents on urban digital transformation issued in 2021 and 2022, which clearly state that Shanghai will continue to use pilot applications and model scenarios to promote large-scale integrated AI implementations in the public sector and other areas (see Chapter 6).

Despite possible future implementations of more complex trial projects, the analysis of the case studies shows that **the AI pilot application scenarios have significantly contributed to improving public service provision and fostering AI integration in the public sector in Shanghai**. First, the AI pilot application scenarios have produced several AI solutions that enhanced public sector operations and public service provision in the policy areas prioritized by the municipal government. Second, the AI pilots have successfully transitioned from trial projects to established AI applications, thus contributing to deepening the integration of AI in public service delivery in Shanghai. Third, the AI pilots have created "replicable and referential experience models" that can spur the diffusion of AI-based public services in Shanghai by providing valuable learning experiences for other public agencies, displaying success stories that can foster social acceptance for public sector AI applications, and by concurring to the municipal efforts to build an enabling environment for public sector AI innovation.

[321] The interviewee said: "What they [SHEITC] desire to do is, if one day the mayor wants to know how well AI is developed in Shanghai, he can be taken to one hospital, where he can go through multiple AI applications helping patients or doctors. For instance, a robot may welcome you at the door, then patients can be quickly diagnosed and sent to test, doctors can read the test results delivered by [AI] machines and give advice based upon AI recommendations". WeChat conversation with AISP, 25 August 2022.

5.4 Main Findings from Public Sector AI Applications in Shanghai

Sections 5.2 and 5.3 examined the main policy initiatives that are actively implementing AI in public service provision in Shanghai. They assessed the analytical, operational, and political capabilities that determine their strengths and limitations in deploying AI in the public sector, and discussed their implications for public service provision in the municipality. These policy initiatives can be categorized in two main approaches. One is a platform-based approach that consists of using two municipal digital platforms—the Government Online-Offline Shanghai and the Single Platform for Urban Management—as conduits to integrate AI in the provision of administrative services and urban management services. The other is an experiment-based approach that aims to foster the use of AI in the public sector by promoting AI trial projects in various policy areas under a program coordinated by the Shanghai government, the "AI pilot application scenarios". Next paragraphs compare the approaches and the impacts of these policy initiatives.

5.4.1 *Shanghai's Strategy for AI in the Public Sector: Comparing the Approaches*

The empirical investigation focused on the Government Online-Offline Shanghai, the Single Platform for Urban Management, and the AI pilot application scenarios for two main reasons. First, these policy initiatives are *significant*. They are major projects through which Shanghai is actively fostering the use of AI in the public sector. In addition to their political importance and the scale of their applications, the Government Online-Offline Shanghai and the Single Platform for Urban Management have officially become the pillars of Shanghai's "urban digital transformation", as noted earlier (Sect. 5.2.3). The AI pilot application scenarios are the only municipal policy initiative with the explicit mandate to promote the integration of AI in all the policy areas prioritized by the Shanghai government. Hence, these policy initiatives offer a vantage point to observe what Shanghai is actually doing to improve public service provision by means of AI, and gauge possible development trajectories for the use of AI in the public sector in the municipality. Second, these policy initiatives are *illustrative*. The Government Online-Offline Shanghai, the Single Platform for Urban Management, and the AI pilot application scenarios vividly demonstrate that Shanghai is promoting a coordinated, systemic, and proactive strategy that integrates and disseminates AI in the public sector in order to enhance public service provision. By comparing the platform-based approach and the experiment-based approach across the three dimensions of Shanghai's AI policy strategy—coordination, systematization, and proactivity—it is possible to highlight their similarities and differences, thus gaining a holistic view of the methods adopted by Shanghai to promote AI in the public sector. This improved understanding will support the discussions made in the conclusions of this book.

Coordination

The platform-based approach and the experiment-based approach are both masterminded and coordinated by the Shanghai municipal government. This top-down policy design, however, has different nuances:

- The platform-based approach is *tightly coordinated*. The Government Online-Offline Shanghai and the Single Platform for Urban Management are endorsed by the top political and government leadership of Shanghai, which directly oversees and coordinates the implementation of both initiatives by means of policy documents and work plans regularly published by the main AI policy agencies in Shanghai. In addition, the GOS and the SPM are unified municipal e-government platforms, and their deployment is closely orchestrated by the municipal government: both platforms are built upon an integrated digital architecture designed and controlled by the municipality, and their daily operations are coordinated and supervised by dedicated municipal agencies (i.e., the Shanghai Municipal Big Data Center and the Shanghai Urban Operation Management Center) that respond to the Shanghai Government General Office, which in turn directly reports to the municipal leadership on various policy matters.[322]

[322] Among other things, the Shanghai Government General Office is responsible for supervising and inspecting the implementation of the decisions and instructions of the municipal government leaders in all departments and district governments of Shanghai, and report to the leaders of the municipal government. See: Office of the Organization and Personnel Committee of the CPC Shanghai Municipal Committee (中共上海市委机构编制委员会办公室), Main Responsibilities and Internal Organizations of the General

– The experiment-based approach is *loosely coordinated*. The AI pilot application scenarios are politically endorsed by the municipal government via the Shanghai Commission of Economy and Informatization (SHEITC). The Commission plays an important supervisory role in coordinating the collection, selection, and evaluation of the AI pilot application scenarios. However, these are standalone trial projects, and SHEITC did not create ad-hoc municipal entities like the Shanghai Municipal Big Data Center and the Shanghai Urban Operation Management Center through which it closely orchestrates the day-to-day operations of the AI pilots. In other words, SHEITC coordinates and facilitates the AI trial projects, consistently with its institutional mandate to promote the integration of informatization and industrialization in Shanghai; but it does not intervene in their daily activities.

Systematization

The platform-based approach and the experiment-based approach combine and leverage analytical, operational, and political capacities at the municipal and organizational levels. However, the mixture and interactions of municipal-level and organizational-level policy capacities differ between the two approaches:

– The platform-based approach mainly relies on *municipal-level policy capacities*. By leveraging analytical, political, and operational capacities at the municipal level, the Shanghai government has promoted the effective, integrated, and widespread use of AI in the public sector via the Government Online-Offline Shanghai and the Single Platform for Urban Management. Besides the skills and resources of municipal organizations (e.g., the Shanghai Municipal Big Data Center, the Shanghai Urban Operation Management Center, the Shanghai Government General Office), the Shanghai government is skillfully aggregating and steering the policy skills and resources of the whole municipality in order to integrate AI in the activities of government agencies at every level through the GOS and SPM platforms, as discussed in Sect. 5.2.3.

Office of the Shanghai Government General Office [上海市人民政府办公厅主要职责和内设机构], https://www.shbb.gov.cn/szfbgt/8994.jhtml, point 4.

– The experiment-based approach mainly relies on *organizational-level policy capacities*. The successful integration of AI in each pilot application scenario mostly depends on the policy capacities of the public organization responsible for the trial project. The "scenario organization" must decide—when drafting the project requirements—how to use AI in its activities (analytical capacity); it must accrue and put to use the resources (data, infrastructure, human capital, etc.) needed to translate the AI pilots in practice, in cooperation with its technical partners (operational capacity); and it must obtain and sustain support for the use of AI technologies within the organization (policy capacity). These organizational-level policy capacities are crucial to make the transition from pilots to established applications that integrate AI in the activities of public agencies.

Despite having a different combination of municipal-level and organizational-level policy capacities, both approaches highlight the difficulties in developing organizational-level capacities for AI in the public sector. In the platform-based approach, deficits in organizational-level capabilities can lead to varying degrees of AI assimilation in the activities of the public agencies, create data barriers, and aggravate issues related to data privacy and security risks. In the experiment-based approach, interviewees pointed to the difficulties in developing the analytical, operational, and political capacities that public organizations need to make the transition from AI pilots to applications that are integrated in their activities. The experiment-based approach also showed that deficits in organizational-level capabilities can result in controversial applications, and that it can be difficult for public organizations to ensure that private companies are aligned with the analytical and operational requirements of public agencies. At the same time, the analysis of the case studies in Shanghai also showed that municipal-level capacities can support policy capacities at the organizational level:

– In the platform-based approach, the integrated digital architecture underpinning the Government Online-Offline Shanghai and the Single Platform for Urban Management supports the operational capacity of public agencies at each administrative level by giving them access to resources (data, AI applications, etc.) beyond those available within the single organization. Moreover, the ability of the Shanghai government to standardize the technical requirements and workflows of the Government Online-Offline Shanghai and the Single Platform for Urban Management creates AI solutions that can be replicated across different public agencies at different administrative levels. This nurtures a pool of technology suppliers that have experience in providing standardized, replicable AI tools for administrative services and urban governance, and thus can help public organizations in districts and subdistricts to devise AI solutions that are aligned with the requirements of the unified e-government platforms (analytical capacity), and translate them into practice (operational capacity). In addition, in the SPM platform, the government has adopted various initiatives to nurture the policy capabilities of public agencies in smart urban governance. Finally, the political capacity of Shanghai to create support for the GOS and the SPM helps the diffusion of AI across public organizations, which are incentivized to join the municipal initiatives for promoting AI in administrative services and urban governance, are mandated to share their data, and are encouraged to experiment with AI in their activities under tight coordination of the municipal government.

- In the experiment-based approach, Shanghai leverages municipal-level skills and resources to enhance the ability of public agencies to use AI in their activities. The Shanghai government is promoting organizational experiments under municipal lead. In this arrangement, municipal-level analytical, operational, and political capacities support the policy capabilities of public organizations by creating the basic conditions for jumpstarting AI trial projects. In addition, municipal-level political capacity has created an enabling environment manifested in a deregulated approach to public sector AI innovation, which supports the political capabilities of public organizations to create consensus for the adoption of AI in their operations as well as for scaling up AI applications. Finally, municipal-level operational capacity has created an institutional mechanism (i.e., the call for solutions for the AI pilot application scenarios) that efficiently engages private companies in public sector AI applications. The cooperation with AI firms is boosting the analytical and operational capacities of public organizations: private companies are key suppliers of AI technologies needed to implement AI in the public sector, they can help public agencies to identify suitable technological solutions based on the requirements of public agencies, and they also provide the resources and skills to deploy and refine these solutions in practice.

Proactivity

In both the platform-based approach and experiment-based approach, the Shanghai government is spearheading the use of AI in the public sector by becoming the first mover in promoting the uptake of AI solutions. This proactivity also entails the engagement of private companies in public sector AI projects, not only because AI firms are key suppliers of technology and know-how, but also because the municipal government aims to promote industrial development as well as applications in the public sector. However, consistently with the aforementioned differences in coordination and systematization, the Shanghai government has different levels of operational involvement in these two approaches:

- In the platform-based approach, the municipality has a *direct operational involvement* in promoting the uptake of AI solutions in the public sector. The Shanghai government uses two municipal platforms—the Government Online-Offline Shanghai and the Single Platform for Urban Management—as conduits to directly integrate AI in the public sector, and it plays a prominent role in the construction and operation of the digital architecture that underpin these unified e-government platforms. The municipal government is also the focal point for gathering the necessary data resources that enable the operations of the Government Online-Offline Shanghai and the Single Platform for Urban Management (i.e., the Shanghai Municipal Big Data Center), and for standardizing workflows and procedures that serve to integrate AI in public sector activities via the two platforms (i.e., the Shanghai Municipal Big Data Center and the Shanghai Urban Operation Management Center).
- In the experiment-based approach, the municipality has an *indirect operational involvement* in promoting the uptake of AI solutions in the public sector. The Shanghai government is spearheading the use of AI in public organizations by launching a municipal program that elicits and supports the collection of AI pilot applications for the public sector and other areas. It also acts as a facilitator that creates the conditions for the successful rollout of such program, and it encourages organizational experiments with AI technologies.

But the focal points for the implementation of the AI pilot application scenarios remain the public agencies responsible for each pilot project, which must primarily rely on their own operational resources and skills to integrate AI in their activities.

5.4.2 *Shanghai's Strategy for AI in the Public Sector: Comparing the Impacts*

The platform-based approach is a very structured method that mainly leverages municipal-level capacities to foster the integration of AI in the provision of administrative services and urban management services in the whole municipality, under the tight control and direct operational involvement of the municipal government. The experiment-based approach is a more explorative method that mainly leverages organizational-level capacities to test standalone AI applications that can result in replicable experiences in several policy areas prioritized by the municipality, under the loose coordination and indirect operational involvement of the municipal government. Sections 5.2 and 5.3 presented a detailed analysis of these approaches. They examined the strengths and limitations in deploying AI in the public sector of the Government Online-Offline Shanghai, the Single Platform for Urban Management, and the AI pilot application scenarios, and assessed their implications for public service provision in the municipality. The main research findings are summarized in Table 5.11 at the end of this section.

The analysis demonstrated that both the platform-based approach and the experiment-based approach have contributed to achieving the goal of the Shanghai government to improve public service provision by accelerating AI integration in public sector activities in various policy areas:

1. Both the platform-based and experiment-based approaches have contributed to **improving the efficiency of public service provision**. The Government Online-Offline Shanghai and the Single Platform for Urban Management are improving the efficiency of public service delivery and public sector operations in the areas of

administrative services and urban governance. The AI pilot application scenarios have produced several AI solutions that enhance the efficiency of public sector operations and the provision of public services in various policy areas prioritized by the municipal government, from education to public health and transport.

2. Both the platform-based and experiment-based approaches have contributed to **accelerating the integration of AI in public services**. The Government Online-Offline Shanghai and the Single Platform for Urban Management have become catalysts for the continuous, progressive assimilation of AI in administrative services and urban management services. In the AI pilot application scenarios, the organizations hosting the trial projects have successfully integrated AI in the provision of public services, making the transition from pilots to established applications. Many pilot organizations have also gradually adopted further AI solutions for the provision of public services.
3. In addition, both the platform-based and experiment-based approaches have contributed to fostering the **diffusion of AI-based public services across the municipality**. By disseminating public sector AI applications at each administrative level and in a great number of government agencies, the Government Online-Offline Shanghai and the Single Platform for Urban Management are extending the reach of smart administrative services and smart urban governance to the majority of citizens in Shanghai. In creating "replicable and referential experience models", the AI pilot application scenarios can spur the diffusion of AI-based public services by providing valuable learning experiences for other public agencies in Shanghai, displaying success stories that can foster social acceptance for AI in the public sector, and concurring to the municipal efforts to build an enabling environment for public sector AI innovation.

This chapter brought the analytical focus closer to the activities of the actors and organizations that are directly involved in public sector AI applications in Shanghai. By providing an improved understanding of the main municipal initiatives that foster AI integration in public services, the findings from expert interviews and the analysis of the case studies make theoretical and practical contributions to research in public policy and the use of AI in the public sector.

To researchers on AI in the public sector, the analysis of the case studies provides empirical evidence to test the hypotheses on the correlation between the availability of enabling factors that make AI applications possible, and actual AI implementations in the public sector. The analysis shows that Shanghai has aptly leveraged its available skills and resources to promote the use of AI in the public sector. In doing so, this research corroborates the findings of previous studies arguing that, in terms of implementation, China is making better use of its AI capabilities than many other countries (Oxford Insights and IDRC, 2020, p. 11). The analysis of the case studies also lifts important aspects about the impacts that limitations in the implementation phase can bear on the success of public sector AI applications. It shows that obstacles in AI deployment do not necessarily affect the improvements in public service provision that can be achieved by means of AI, as demonstrated by the overall positive impacts of the Government Online-Offline Shanghai, the Single Platform for Urban Management, and the AI pilot application scenarios, despite their respective limitations. In doing so, this work expands the findings of previous research on the sustainable implementation of AI in public services (Molinari et al., 2021).

To scholars of public policy, the analysis of the case studies confirms that the combination of adequate analytical, political, and operational capacities leads to improved policy outputs and outcomes, as postulated by the policy capacity framework (Wu et al., 2015). In the platform-based approach, this combination has resulted in the effective, integrated, and widespread deployment of AI in the public sector. In the experiment-based approach, this combination has helped to make the transition from pilots to established applications that integrate AI in the activities of public agencies. In both cases, the resulting policy outcomes are enhanced public service provision and public sector operations. The analysis also sheds light on the interactions of policy capacities at different levels. It shows the possible coexistence, within the same city, of policy initiatives that propose different combinations of municipal-level and organizational-level capacities, whereby municipal-level capabilities can be the main drivers (i.e., platform-based approach) or the enablers (i.e., experiment-based approach) of public sector AI applications, depending on the design and objectives of such policy initiatives. Finally, the analysis indicates that municipal-level capacities can support policy capacities at the organizational level, mitigating the difficulties in developing organizational-level capacities for AI in the public sector that were identified by the literature and confirmed by the fieldwork in Shanghai.

In addition, this empirical analysis provides practitioners in the fields of public policy and public sector AI research with unprecedented insights into the methods adopted by Shanghai to promote public sector AI innovation. These insights are useful because the municipality has made rapid progress in leveraging AI to enhance public service provision through the Government Online-Offline Shanghai—an internationally recognized best practice in e-government (United Nations, 2020), the Single Platform for Urban Management, and the AI pilot application scenarios. Hence, the experience of Shanghai can contribute new knowledge about improving public sector operations and public services by means of AI. In the closing chapter, the findings on the capacity of Shanghai to implement AI in the public sector, the characteristics of the main policy initiatives that foster AI integration in this area, and their implications for public service provision are examined in relation to key research topics identified by previous studies on AI in the public sector. By using Shanghai's experience to gain deeper and practical insights on issues that are relevant to the whole field of public sector AI research, the conclusions lift important aspects to consider when examining the use of AI in the public sector, and provide useful indications to gauge the possible development trajectories of public sector AI applications in Shanghai. In doing so, the significance and contribution of this work are extended beyond its findings on public sector AI applications currently ongoing in China's "AI highland".

Table 5.11 Summary of the strengths, limitations, and implications for public service provision of Shanghai's main policy initiatives that promote AI in the public sector (see Tables 5.7 and 5.10 for details)

Government Online-Offline Shanghai		
Strengths	*Limitations*	*Implications for public service provision*
The use of AI is effectively designed to improve the provision of administrative services in Shanghai. The municipality has developed and introduced AI applications that can enhance the efficiency of public service provision to citizens and enterprises, and it also leverages the skills of district governments to devise AI applications for administrative services AI applications for the provision of administrative services are efficiently developed and implemented, and via the Government Online-Offline Shanghai they are integrated into the activities of government agencies in order to improve their core operations High rates of adoption among government agencies are fostering the widespread use of AI in administrative service provision across the municipality, leading to the diffusion of AI in public sector activities in Shanghai	Varying degrees of AI assimilation among government organizations, administrative service centers Persistence of data barriers Concerns about data privacy and security	(1) The use AI of in the Government Online-Offline Shanghai is improving the efficiency in the provision of administrative services (e.g., the time needed to process administrative services has reduced by 59.8% on average) (2) Through the Government Online-Offline Shanghai, the number of AI applications for administrative services is expanding, and such applications are becoming increasingly integrated in the provision of administrative services (e.g., over 3,660 services provided via the GOS platform cover the most relevant needs of individuals and companies; the functions of the "Suishenma" continue to expand both for citizens and enterprises) (3) Through the Government Online-Offline Shanghai, AI is used in the provision of administrative services at each administrative level and in a great number of government agencies, extending the reach of AI-enabled administrative services to the majority of citizens (e.g., the GOS platform reached 81.46 million real-name registered users)

Single Platform for Urban Management		
Strengths	*Limitations*	*Implications for public service provision*
The use of AI is effectively designed to improve urban governance operations and urban management services, leveraging municipal guidance as well as the skills of districts and subdistricts to devise AI applications targeted to the needs at their administrative levels AI applications for urban governance are efficiently developed and implemented, and via the Single Platform for Urban Management they are integrated into the activities of government agencies in order to improve their core operations High rates of adoption among government agencies are fostering the widespread use of AI in urban governance across the municipality, leading to the diffusion of AI in public sector activities	Varying degrees of AI integration among urban governance organizations, Urban Operation Centers Persistence of data barriers Concerns about data privacy and security Possible overreliance on technology Need to further improve the coordinating mechanisms of the SPM	(1) AI is improving the efficiency of urban governance and urban management services (e.g., evidence indicates it increases governance accuracy, facilitates monitoring and provides early warning, supports decision-making, eases the coordination between urban governance agencies, etc.) (2) Through the Single Platform for Urban Management, the number of AI applications for urban governance is expanding, and such applications are becoming increasingly integrated in urban operations and urban management services (e.g., digital twin technologies, mobile Apps for urban governance) (3) Through the Single Platform for Urban Management, AI is used in urban governance at each administrative level and in a great number of government agencies, extending the reach of smart urban governance to the majority of citizens (e.g., the integrated network of Urban Operation Centers is bringing AI applications to the grassroots level)

(continued)

Table 5.11 (continued)

AI pilot application scenarios		
Strengths	*Limitations*	*Implications for public service provision*
The promotion of organizational experiments under municipal lead jumpstarts public sector AI applications by creating the basic conditions for organizational experiments with AI technologies that, if successful, can be applied in the whole city	The promotion of organizational experiments under municipal lead entails difficulties in developing the organizational-level policy capacities needed to make the transition from pilots to established applications integrated in the activities of public agencies	(1) The AI pilot application scenarios have produced AI solutions that are improving the efficiency of public sector operations and public service provision in the organizations hosting the pilot projects across all the policy areas prioritized by the municipal government
The deregulated approach to public sector AI innovation: (i) encourages public organizations to use AI in their activities, paving the way to a variety of public sector AI applications across several policy areas; (ii) creates success stories of AI integration in the public sector that can build momentum for scaling up AI innovation in the pilot organizations; and (iii) combines fast-paced implementation with attention to safety, creating sandboxes and innovation testbeds that try and evaluate public sector AI applications in controlled environments	In the "experiment first and regulate later" approach, some AI pilots introduced intrusive AI applications that could start to generate opposition from the target population. In addition, the lack of regulations and standards can become an obstacle to scaling up AI applications in the mid-term, and financial and policy costs are expected to accompany the transition from a permissive to a more tightly regulated environment	(2) The AI pilot application scenarios have successfully integrated AI in the provision of public services in the public organizations hosting the trial projects, making the transition from pilot projects to established applications
	The cooperation with private companies can generate conflicts of interests and values, as well as difficulties in reconciling the ethical, legal, and socioeconomic obligations of public organizations with the commercial practices of private firms	(3) The AI pilot application scenarios have created "replicable and referential experience models" that can spur the diffusion of AI in public services by: (i) providing valuable learning experiences for other public agencies in Shanghai; (ii) displaying success stories that can foster social acceptance for public sector AI applications; and (iii) contributing to the municipal efforts to build an enabling environment for public sector AI innovation

The engagement of private companies (i) grants public organizations access to the technologies needed to implement AI in their activities; (ii) facilitates the integration of AI in public organizations by leveraging corporate expertise; and (iii) generates lasting collaborations that are needed to develop increasingly sophisticated AI systems that can be better integrated in the public sector

Appendix V: Interview Sample Questions

The semi-structured interviews were designed to: (i) refine the validity of the findings on Shanghai's policy capacity to implement AI in the public sector, which were derived from documentary research; and (ii) gain deeper knowledge of the policy initiatives that are fostering the use of AI in the public sector in Shanghai, including their strengths and limitations in deploying AI in this area. Interviewees were asked open-ended questions about two main topics: the resources and skills that enable public sector AI applications in the municipality; and the advantages and difficulties in using AI in the public sector in Shanghai, based on their involvement in, or first-hand knowledge of, the AI pilot application scenarios[323] Sample questions are provided below.

- AI is a very complex field and decision-makers are not technical experts. What can be done to improve the communications between AI experts and government agencies?
  [人工智能是一个技术含量很高的行业。同时，政府机构的领导不一定是内行。为了便于政府机构跟人工智能企业和其他AI专家有效、清晰地双方沟通，您认为要注意哪些方面?]
- What skills do decision-makers and civil servants need to develop in order to better manage and utilize AI applications in (*policy area*)?
  [为了更好地管理和利用人工智能技术在（...）领域的应用，领导和公务人员需要具备哪些技能?]
- In recent years, Shanghai has issued various policies and action plans for AI development. How are these initiatives supporting the development of AI in Shanghai?
  [近几年，上海发布了促进AI发展的若干规划和行动计划。根据您的经验，这些支持措施主要是在哪些方面有利于上海人工智能行业的发展?]
- What are the strengths and weaknesses of the Shanghai AI ecosystem?
  [您认为上海AI生态圈有哪些强点?]
- What should be done to realize the safe and beneficial deployment of AI?

[323] As explained earlier, the Government Online-Offline Shanghai and the Single Platform for Urban Management were selected as case studies only when the interview program was already at an advanced stage; hence, they were only explicitly included in the semi-structured interview with Shanghai INESA in May 2022, after the importance of these policy initiatives as conduits to the use of AI in the public sector in Shanghai had repeatedly emerged from previous semi-structured interviews.

[为了实现人工智能应用的安全、有益的部署, 您认为要注意哪些方面?]

- Can you present the main AI applications used in the (*project name*)? In these applications, what is the added value of AI technologies?
  [请问, 可以介绍 (…) 的主要AI应用吗? 在这些应用场景, 人工智能技术实现了哪些增值功能?]
- How did (*managers, staff, users*) react to the application of AI technologies in (*their work/the provision of a given set of public services*)?
  [(管理者, 工作人员, 用户) 对于AI技术在 (…) 的应用有什么反应?]
- What are the advantages that (*Shanghai/the pilot organization*) can leverage in implementing AI technologies in (*the public sector* via *the AI pilot application scenarios/main applications of the AI pilot*)?
  [在实施人工智能在 (…) 的应用, (…) 可以利用哪些优势?]
- What difficulties do you think (*Shanghai/the pilot organization*) is facing in implementing AI in (*the public sector via the AI pilot application scenarios/main applications of the AI pilot*)?
  [您认为 (…) 在实施人工智能在 (…) 的应用会遇到什么困难?]
- What skills are needed to overcome these difficulties and make better use of existing advantages?
  [为了更好地利用现有的优势而穿越面临的困难, 您认为需要具备哪些技能?]
- Based on your experience, what do you think will be the future developments of AI in (*public sector applications/policy area*)?
  [根据您的经验, 您可以分享一下AI在 (…) 领域的未来发展趋势吗?].

Appendix VI: AI Pilot Application Scenarios—Case Studies

Case Study 1: Minhang Qiangwei Primary School (闵行蔷薇小学)

The Minhang Qiangwei Primary School is a public school affiliated to the Shanghai University of Traditional Chinese Medicine (上海中医药大学) and located in Minhang District (periphery of Shanghai). Selected as an AI pilot application scenario in April 2019, the project uses AI technologies in the following applications[324]:

- *Smart campus security*: based on the use of AI, IoT technologies, and Big Data analysis, the school has introduced a new model of intelligent "prevention, management and control" for campus security. This smart monitoring system uses computer vision to count the number of students arriving at the school. It monitors and tracks the outsiders, identifies dangerous individuals, and checks potentially dangerous situations within the campus providing early warnings. The system aims to comprehensively improve the level of prevention and management of campus security.
- *Smart teacher training system*: it uses computer vision, speech recognition, and other AI technologies to evaluate teaching effectiveness based on criteria such as voice, speech rate, movements, and facial orientation of teachers when giving classes. In addition, it uses data mining technology to automatically segment and select videos that can support teaching activities based on the course contents, and automatically extracts "exemplar teaching clips" (优秀教学片段) that teachers can use for their classes. The system can also recommend relevant teaching clips to teachers. AI technologies are also used to enhance the utilization rate and output efficiency of the existing teaching equipment, but no further details are provided.
- *Smart promotion of traditional Chinese culture*: experts from the University of Chinese Medicine and the school's physical education teachers have contributed to developing an AI system that supports the learning of traditional physical exercises (e.g., the Yi Jin Jing). The system displays the standard movements of the exercises, and

[324] SJTU, CAICT and SHEIC (2019, p. 105); Minhang District Government, 2020. Minhang District CPPCC Education and Sports Committee Visited Qiangwei Primary School to Carry Out Pre-consultation Investigation on "Smart Education Construction" [闵行区政协教体委莅临蔷薇小学开展 "智慧教育建设" 协商前调研]. *Minhang District Government* [上海市闵行区人民政府], 10 June, http://www.shmh.gov.cn/shmh/zwdt-jyj/20200616/483583.html; Sohu, 2019. AI+ Primary School, Artificial Intelligence Should Start from "Grasping" Kids? [AI+ 小学, 人工智能要从娃娃 "抓" 起?]. *Sohu* [搜狐], 27 August. https://www.sohu.com/a/336705445_642762; Xinmin Net, 2019. Minhang Primary School Will Appear at the World Artificial Intelligence Conference. The First "AI + School" Is as Cool as Iron Man! [闵行这所小学将亮相世界人工智能大会, 首家 "AI + 学校" 像钢铁侠一样酷!]. *Xinmin Net* [新民网], 26 July, http://shanghai.xinmin.cn/xmsq/2019/07/26/31562300.html.

uses algorithms to correct the students' movements and postures by means of interesting games, thus promoting children's physical and mental development with the support of AI.

The use of AI in the Minhang Qiangwei Primary School has expanded.[325] The "smart campus security" application has broadened its scope, extending its functions to the registration of student behavioral patterns and the analysis of students' activities in real time between classes to discover potential safety problems (e.g., children's chasing or quarreling). The "smart teacher training system" has soon been expanded to a "smart classroom evaluation system" (智能课堂评价系统). This upgraded system not only evaluates teaching effectiveness, but also uses AI technologies like computer vision and speech recognition to automatically detect and record students' behaviors such as raising hands, standing, yawning, or sitting improperly, making correlations between learning status, classroom effectiveness, and learning interest. In doing so, the system offers an overall evaluation of the classroom effectiveness and "continuously corrects bad habits in children's learning" (不断纠正孩子学习中的不良习惯).[326] Additional AI applications have been implemented. In November 2021, the school reported the successful introduction of augmented reality (AR) technologies in teaching Chinese language to third-year students, a system called "easy learning" (易学), as well as the implementation of data-based education (基于数据的教学) that aims to promote "precise teaching" (精准教学). The school stated its intentions to continue to timely collect data generated by the students during classroom activities in order to implement individualized teaching.[327]

325 Shanghai Education, 2020. Qiangwei Primary School: AI-Enabled Smart e-Campus [蔷薇小学: AI赋能下的智慧 "E" 校园]. *Shanghai Education* [上海教育], 2020 (28), October, p. 48.

326 Qilu Evening News, 2020. [5G+ AI绘就未来 "新基建" 蓝图]. *Qilu Evening News* [齐鲁晚报], 14 July, retrieved from: https://baijiahao.baidu.com/s?id=1672172898201285285&wfr=spider&for=pc.

327 Minhang Qiangwei Primary School, 2021. Technology Lights Up the Classroom, Learning Partners Help Grow—A Large-Scale, Data-Based Teaching Innovation Experiment Supports the Display of a Service Project [技术点亮课堂 学伴助力成长—数据支持下大规模因材施教的教学创新实验支持服务项目展示]. *Minhang Qiangwei Primary School*, 29 November, https://qwxx.mhedu.sh.cn/schoolweb/web/qiangwei/home!info.action?articleid=ff8080817bc490fb017d75bda0a363ce&catalogid=4028824652b4f64e0152b4fba9090005.

Case Study 2: Shanghai Shixi High School (上海市市西中学)

The Shanghai Shixi High School is a public high school located in Jing'an District, downtown Shanghai. Selected as an AI pilot application scenario in April 2019, the project uses AI technologies in the following applications[328]:

- *AI laboratory*: the school designed and built a curriculum-based AI laboratory, which includes five components: (1) a "supercomputing center" for data sharing within the school's campus network, which is connected to a data center operated by AI company SenseTime. The "supercomputing center" allows students to use AI software packages, with which they can acquire and analyze images and videos generated within the school; (2) demonstration area of AI technologies, including facial check-in, facial recognition technologies, classroom emotion recognition demonstration (课堂情绪识别演示), air quality screening, etc.; (3) an IT lab where students can learn Python language, coding and debugging, and study various applied topics related to AI; (4) a "chip workshop" where the AI programs written by the students can be burnt into chips, so that they can be integrated into real hardware and make the students experience the process of transforming AI technology into products; and (5) a demonstration area of AI equipment, which includes models of unmanned vehicles and aircrafts, and motion-controlled robots in order to show possible implementations of the knowledge learned by the students.
- *Intelligent teaching and learning platform*: the "intelligent teaching and learning platform" (教与学平台) leverages AI to provide individualized education (个别化教育) targeted to the characteristics of each student. The platform examines data generated by the students' online learning activities in the "online classes" (网学课堂) and other

[328] SJTU, CAICT and SHEIC (2019, pp. 103–104); Whale Media, 2019. At the Shanghai Shixi High School AI Approves Writing Compositions, Should AI Redefine Teachers? [上海市市西中学AI批作文，AI要重新定义教师?]. *Whale Media* [鲸媒体], 29 August, retrieved via: https://baijiahao.baidu.com/s?id=1643167213919372703&wfr=spider&for=pc; Shanghai Shixi High School, 2019. Our School Participated in the Exhibition Activities of the 2019 World Artificial Intelligence Conference [我校参加2019世界人工智能大会展示活动]. *Shanghai Shixi High School*, 9 September, http://www.shixi.edu.sh.cn/sx/jwxw/87895.htm.

digital learning platforms created by the school in previous years (e.g., cloud-based systems called 云平台 and 睿易云). The "intelligent teaching and learning platform" collects data related to study time and contents, test results, and other information. Based on these data, the platform then uses AI models to evaluate the learning level and ability of students, and it identifies the shortcomings and deficiencies in their learning process in order to provide personalized recommendations. The platform can also recommend suitable classes and make suggestions to improve the learning process, supporting the teachers based on the analysis of the learning characteristics of different student groups.

- *Smart classrooms*: this application uses AI technologies such as computer vision and natural language processing to support teaching of subjects like English language (e.g., speech-to-text conversion to boost listening and speaking training). It also uses AI for the recognition and identification of letters, numbers, Chinese characters, and mathematical expressions to support students in performing their assignments on the school digital platforms.

The Shanghai Shixi High School pilot is expanding the use of AI applications. In summer 2019, the school stated that by 2020 it would introduce AI technologies to help teachers assess and grade the compositions and translations in Chinese and English. It also said that AI applications would be extended to teaching physics, chemistry, and biology (e.g., using audio and image recognition technologies to support classroom experiments in these subjects).[329] Indeed, in March 2021 the "teacher AI mini program" (teacher AI 小程序) was already applied in assessing English homework, and the school reiterated its commitment to use technology to provide "customized learning" (学习的 "个性定制") to its students.[330]

[329] Xu, L., 2019. AI+ High School: Shanghai Shixi High School Students Learn "Reptiles", and AI Helps Teachers to Approve Writing Compositions [AI+ 高中: 上海市西中学学生学 "爬虫", AI帮老师批作文]. *The Paper* [澎湃新闻], 27 August, retrieved via: https://news.cctv.com/2019/08/27/ARTIyU4uFJxlRMJUB14Cfj3q190827.shtml.

[330] Tencent Net, 2021. Improve the Management and Evaluation Mechanism to Achieve "Customized" Learning. Shixi High School Helps Students Develop in a Comprehensive Way [完善管理评价机制 实现学习 "个性定制" 市西中学助力学生全面发展]. *Tencent Net* [腾讯网], 24 March, https://new.qq.com/rain/a/20210324A0F8X100.

Case Study 3: Shanghai World Foreign Language Education Group (WFL, 上海世外教育集团)

The Shanghai World Foreign Language (WFL) Education Group is a private education group (民办教育集团) that belongs to the conglomerate Juneyao Group.[331] Its schools are renowned in Shanghai, and there is intense competition to enroll. Selected as an AI pilot application scenario in April 2019, the project uses AI technologies in the following applications[332]:

- *Adaptive learning system*: designed for high-school students, the adaptive learning system (自适应学习系统) uses Big Data analysis and machine learning to help teachers recommend exercises and learning resources suitable to the level of each student. The system promotes personalized teaching in mathematical calculus, macroeconomics, and statistics. The system includes functions such as student grading, daily practice suggestion, and the automatic collection of wrong answers provided by the students. The system helps teachers to grade students, and supports AI-enabled adaptive learning and practice. Shiwai Smart Education Technology Co., Ltd. (世外智慧教育科技有限公司), a technology branch of the WFL group, in cooperation with other technology companies also developed a mathematics adaptive learning application software (the Jinshan Shiwai AP Math Adaptive Question Pushing System/金山世外AP 数学自适应推题系统), which was released in the summer 2019. After a pilot use in 3 schools at the end of 2019, in 2020 the system was extended to 16 schools affiliated to the World Foreign Language Education Group (seven of which are located in Shanghai).
- *Classroom real-time analysis system*: the classroom real-time analysis system (课堂实时分析系统) is also designed and developed by Shiwai Smart Education Technology. It helps to improve teaching efficiency through data analysis and expert advice. The system

[331] At the time of this writing, the WLF Group operates nearly 70 schools from kindergarten to high-school levels in Shanghai, Zhejiang, Anhui, and other provinces. See WLF Group website: https://www.shwfl.edu.cn/main.htm (last accessed on 9 November 2023).

[332] SJTU, CAICT and SHEIC (2019, pp. 106–108); SAIA, 2021. Innovative Combination of Education and Artificial Intelligence [教育与人工智能的创新结合]. *Shanghai AI Industry Association*, 24 June, http://www.sh-aia.com/policy/detail292.htm.

leverages computer vision (facial expression recognition) and other technologies to monitor the behavior of students. Through the analysis of data collected from real-time video recording in the classrooms, this application infers students' study habits, points of interest, and classroom attention in order to improve classroom teaching efficiency. The system was first tested at the Qingpu World Foreign Language School, which was equipped with classroom recording and broadcasting equipment. It was then extended to the Baoshan World Foreign Language School. Since then, it has become a highly publicized product offered by Shiwai Smart Education Technology[333]

- *Pronunciation correction system*: this system (口语语音矫正) leverages speech recognition to support teachers in correcting pronunciations in spoken English. The system, developed by Shiwai Smart Education Technology, offers an accurate speech evaluation model for students and correction suggestions. In the summer 2019, the system was put into use in 12 schools of the WFL Group. At that time, the optimization of various dimensions of the voice evaluation was being tested.

In December 2020, the Shanghai World Foreign Language Education Group AI application scenario was nominated "AI demonstration application scenario" (人工智能示范应用场景). In January 2022, the three aforementioned AI applications were implemented in 30 schools of the WFL Group in Shanghai and the Yangtze River Delta, and they were included in the media campaign "AI by your side" (AI在身边) promoted by SHEITC to popularize AI applications among Shanghai citizens[334] (Chapter 4.5).

Case Study 4: Luwan No. 1 Central Primary School (卢湾一中心小学)

Luwan No. 1 Central Primary School is a public school located in Huangpu District, downtown Shanghai. Before being selected as an AI pilot application scenario in August 2019, the school had already

333 SAIA, 2021 (cit.).

334 SAIA, 2021; SHEITC, 2022. [AI by Your Side] Intelligent Teaching, AI Tries Your Hand [[AI在身边] 智慧教学 AI一试身手]. *SHEITC*, 13 January, http://sheitc.sh.gov.cn/gydt/20220113/27dba4f07fcf4b9085d4bd46277656c9.html.

introduced several digital applications. These include: a "cloud platform" (云平台), consisting of a Basic Data Management Subsystem (基础数据管理子系统) and other eight digital subsystems launched in 2014 to support personalized teaching in mathematics, Chinese language, natural sciences and other subjects[335]; "cloud classrooms" (云课堂) that integrate digital technologies (i.e., tablets) in classroom activities[336]; and a smart library system that records data on the books read by the students, and feed such records to teachers who can then provide personalized reading recommendations.[337]

The Luwan No. 1 Central Primary School pilot application scenario uses AI in the following applications[338]:

- *Smart teaching support*: it uses digital writing boards equipped with a "cloud pen" (云笔) to record the learning habits of every student (e.g., the number and speed of strokes when they answer a question in writing). These data are analyzed by AI models that allow teachers to infer the learning process and habits of each student, and provide personalized recommendations. Based on the information collected through writing boards, each of the over 1,300 students at the school receives an AI-generated, tri-dimensional "digital

[335] Luo, Y., 2014. Luwan No. 1 Central Primary School in Huangpu District, Shanghai: Creating a Personalized Learning Space Anytime, Anywhere [上海市黄浦区卢湾第一中心小学: 随时随地随需创建个性化学习空间]. *Shanghai Education* [上海教育], 2014 (07A).

[336] Wu, R. and Ji, Y., 2016. Effective Integration of Digital Media to Form a New Integrated Teaching Method—The Innovative Practice of "Cloud Classrooms" in Luwan No. 1 Central Primary School in Huangpu District, Shanghai [有效整合数字媒体 形成融合式新教学方式—上海市黄浦区卢湾一中心小学 "云课堂" 的创新实践]. *Modern Teaching* [现代教学], 2016(09), pp. 72–73.

[337] Chen, Z., 2018. Luwan No. 1 Central Primary School: Caiyun Library Uses Intelligence to Serve Wisdom [卢湾一中心小学: 用智能服务智慧的彩云图书馆]. *Shanghai Education* [上海教育], April 2018 (B).

[338] SHEITC Notice, 2019b; The Paper, 2019. How to Teach Students in Accordance with Their Aptitude on a Large Scale? Every Child in This Primary School in Shanghai Has a "Digital Portrait" [如何大规模因材施教?上海这所小学每个孩子都有 "数字画像"]. *The Paper* [澎湃新闻], 21 August, http://m.thepaper.cn/yidian_promDetail.jsp?contid=4217660&from=yidian; Luwan No. 1 Central Primary School, 2020. Special Feature [特色展示]. *Luwan No. 1 Central Primary School*, 19 March, https://lwyzx.hpe.cn/P/C/533363.htm; Huangpu District Government, 2021. Different experience, smart management, precise teaching, the campuses in Shanghai are full of wisdom [别样体验 聪明管理 精准教学 申城校园充满智慧]. *Huangpu District Government*, 16 April, https://www.shhuangpu.gov.cn/xw/001009/20210416/c46488aa-f0be-4e76-8746-6a06bb78f01a.html.

portrait" (一幅立体的 "数字画像") that is meant to support teaching activities by providing individualized tutoring (个性化的指导) and stimulate students' interest to learn.

- *Smart assistance for emotional education*: this system is a rebranding of classroom real-time analysis systems used in other case studies (#1 and 3). It uses AI technologies to support "emotional education" (情感教育). The aforementioned "digital portraits" also serve to recognize the emotional state of the students, thus helping teachers to promote personalized emotional education (个性化情感教育). The system measures five key indicators of student behavior: "standing up", "reading", "writing", "listening and reading", and "lying down on the table". The system also uses data collected from "cloud watches" (云手表) that record the physical state of students, measuring their average fatigue and exercise volume.[339]

The school has successfully integrated AI in its activities. In fall 2019, it was selected as one of the "Shanghai educational informatization applications benchmark schools" (上海市教育信息化应用标杆学校) by the Shanghai Education Commission (上 海 市 教 育 委 员 会) for its use of AI to promote personalized education, and for deepening information technology in classroom teaching.[340] The success of the school in promoting digital innovation in education is also highly publicized on local media, with dedicated reports aired on Shanghai television channels.[341] In addition, the Luwan No. 1 Central Primary School continues to play a pivotal role in the Shanghai government plans to promoted AI

[339] Tencent, 2021. Children Learn to Write Characters "on the Cloud", This "Smart Campus" in Shanghai Is so Amazing! [孩子学习画像搬上 "云端", 上海这座 "智慧校园" 也太赞了!]. *Tencent Net* [腾讯网], 1 August, https://new.qq.com/rain/a/20210801A03UGF00.

[340] Tencent, 2019. Shanghai Has Established 54 Benchmark Schools for the Application of Educational Informatization to Create the Most Suitable Education for Each Student [上海创建54所教育信息化应用标杆学校, 为每位学生创造最适合的教育]. *Tencent Open Content Platform* [腾讯内容开放平台], 10 October, https://page.om.qq.com/page/OThWXFSV657X6aRn8cwRnpaw0.

[341] Sina, 2020. Huangpu District Luwan No. 1 Central Primary School, Information Technology Creates a "Cloud" Campus [黄浦区卢湾一中心小学 信息技术打造 "云" 校园]. *Sina Kandian* [新浪看点], 19 September, https://k.sina.com.cn/article_6145283913_m16e4997490200163ef.html.

education in primary and secondary schools[342] (Chapter 4.3). The integration of AI at the Luwan No. 1 Central Primary School progresses steadily. In the summer 2021, the school initiated the construction of a "smart campus" (智慧校园) that uses AI to identify suspicious persons staying in front of the school, check whether the manhole covers of the campus are loose, and detect any other safety hazards. In August 2022, the construction of the "smart campus" was expanding.[343]

Case Study 5: Shanghai No. 10 People's Hospital (上海市第十人民医院)

The Shanghai No. 10 People's Hospital is a Grade III A[344] (三甲) public hospital affiliated to Tongji University. Selected as an AI pilot application scenario in April 2019, the hospital created an AI-enabled "emergency auxiliary diagnosis and treatment system" (急诊辅助诊疗系统), which consists of three subsystems: smart emergency auxiliary diagnosis (智能急诊辅助诊断), smart CT auxiliary imaging diagnosis (智能CT 辅助影像

[342] Sina Finance, 2021. The Shanghai Youth Activity Center Signed an Agreement with 7 Primary and Secondary Schools to Carry Out Artificial Intelligence Education for Teenagers [上海市青少年活动中心与7所中小学签约开展青少年人工智能教育]. *Sina Finance* [新浪财经], 28 August, https://finance.sina.com.cn/jjxw/2021-08-28/doc-iktzqtyt2671126.shtml.

[343] Tencent, 2021; Shanghai Bid Net, 2022. Huangpu District Shanghai Huangpu District Luwan No. 1 Central Primary School Government Procurement Intention from August to September 2022—Smart Campus Service Based on AI Face Recognition Technology [黄浦区上海市黄浦区卢湾一中心小学2022年8月至9月政府采购意向-基于AI人脸识别技术的智慧校园服务]. *Shanghai Bid Net* [上海招标网], 12 August, https://sh.bidcenter.com.cn/diqucontent-190099424-2.html.

[344] The Chinese classification system categorizes hospitals into Grades I, II, and III (一级, 二级, 三级) according to their specialization and activities. Grade I hospitals include community health centers and township health centers that focus on prevention, basic medical care, and rehabilitation services. Grade II hospitals provide comprehensive medical services to a region (city, province, etc.), and undertake some teaching and scientific research. Grade III hospitals provide high-level, specialized medical services, and undertake advanced teaching and scientific research. These grades are further subdivided into three levels, A (甲), B (乙), and C (丙), based on the hospital's scale, service provision, medical equipment, medical research, and other criteria. In addition, there is a special level, called 3AAA (三级特等), which is reserved to the most specialized hospitals. See for instance: Li, L., Du, T. and Hu, Y., 2020. The Effect of Different Classification of Hospitals on Medical Expenditure from Perspective of Classification of Hospitals Framework: Evidence from China. *Cost Effectiveness and Resource Allocation*: C/E, 18, 35. https://doi.org/10.1186/s12962-020-00229-5.

诊断), and the eyeground disease multimodal intelligent screening (眼底疾病多模态智能筛查). In details[345]:

- *Smart emergency auxiliary diagnosis*: this subsystem consists of three main components:
- Smart consultation is accessible via smartphone or at dedicated smart stations in the hospital hall. This application uses speech recognition, optical character recognition, and Natural Language Processing to collect patient information that support doctors in the pre-diagnosis of outpatient cases. It then uses machine learning to predict and grade the criticality of patients, give advice on the most suitable medical treatment (e.g., visit an outpatient clinic or an emergency room, which department to visit), and it suggests preparations to be made before the visit. The smart diagnosis application can automatically recommend patients the most suitable physical examinations, using an algorithmic model that analyzes risk factors such as medical history, allergies, age, etc. It also gives advice on drug prescription, and it automatically generates medical records and saves them on the dedicated database.
- Intelligent inspection and classification. It uses an AI service robot to collect data such as blood pressure, pulse, body temperature, blood pressure saturation, respiratory rate, etc. It then uses the Emergency Severity Index (ESI), the Glasgow Coma Scale (GCS), the Modified Early Warning Score (MEWS), and other medical classification methods to accurately categorize injuries and medical conditions.
- Intelligent multi-specialty diagnosis. Provide doctors with multi-specialty diagnosis and differential diagnosis advice, and make accurate diagnosis. It leverages an AI knowledge map on diseases of the

345 SJTU, CAICT and SHEIC (2019, pp. 109–111). SAIA, 2021. Shanghai No. 10 People's Hospital Smart Medicine Comprehensive Application Scenario [第十人民医院智慧医疗综合应用场景]. *Shanghai AI Industry Association*, 30 June, http://www.sh-aia.com/dynamics/detail363.htm; Sohu, 2020. Three Major AI Application Scenarios at the Shanghai No. 10 People's Hospital Have Been in Use for More Than a Year and Have Attracted Countless Fans [上海市第十人民医院三大人工智能应用场景投用一年多来圈粉无数]. *Sohu* [搜狐], 10 December, https://www.sohu.com/a/437477793_362042?sec=wd; China News, 2020. AI+ Medicine Helps Accurate Diagnosis, the "Hospital of the Future" in Shanghai "Becomes a Reality" to Benefit Patients ["AI + 医疗" 助力精准诊断 "未来医院" 上海 "成真" 造福患者]. *China News* [中国新闻网], 10 December, retrieved from: https://baijiahao.baidu.com/s?id=1685683604742085522&wfr=spider&for=pc.

cardiovascular, digestive, respiratory, and nervous systems, among others.

- *Smart CT auxiliary imaging diagnosis*: this subsystem uses AI to support CT image diagnosis of common emergency conditions such as cerebral hemorrhage, establishing a unified reading standard that shortens the time and improves the accuracy rate of medical diagnoses. This subsystem ensures that doctors can efficiently and accurately detect and diagnose lesions. Clinical practice indicates that this smart diagnostic system can improve the efficiency rate of doctors by 30–50%, while maintaining high-level accuracy. The subsystem is expected to generate income for the hospital, as it can be the foundation of a specialist outpatient clinic, and ensure that the radiology department can improve the detection rate of lesions. Finally, this subsystem system can greatly improve the ability to effectively cure patients, reduce the medical burden and insurance expenses, and improve the reputation and academic status of the hospital.
- *Eyeground disease multimodal intelligent screening*: this subsystem uses AI to examine OCT images and color fundus images. It supports ophthalmic auxiliary diagnostic tools (e.g., the automatic calculation model of arterial-vein ratio/cup-to-disc ratio) and screening models, and it conducts big data analysis of the ophthalmic screening results. In May 2019, the system was validated on 784 samples by three clinical teams from Tongji University (Prof. Wang Fang, who practices at the No. 10 People's Hospital), Fudan University (Prof. Sun Xinghuai), and Shanghai Jiaotong University (Prof. Xu Xun), with technical support by Ping'an Smart Medical Technology Company. The accuracy rates of the OCT screening system were 99.2% for image quality evaluation, 98.6% for lesion detection, and 96.7% for urgency assessment.

Because of the successful integration of AI in the aforementioned applications, in December 2020 the Shanghai No. 10 People's Hospital was nominated "AI demonstration application scenario" (人工智能示范应用场景). The integration of AI in the activities of the hospital is expanding. In 2020, the hospital introduced an AI system for the intelligent prediction, auxiliary diagnosis, and treatment system of deep vein thromboembolism[346] (VTE). In addition, since 2020 every time patients visit the hospital, their information feed the hospital database in real time. Such data are then used to train an AI model based on deep learning techniques, which supports several AI applications in the hospital.[347]

Case Study 6: Fudan University Shanghai Cancer Hospital (复旦大学附属肿瘤医院)

The Fudan University Cancer Hospital is a Grade III A public hospital affiliated to the Medical School of Fudan University. Selected as an AI pilot application scenario in April 2019, the project uses AI technologies in the following applications[348]:

- *Outpatient appointment*: this application uses Natural Language Processing and speech recognition to collect information on medical history, medical symptoms, and other information when registering patients. The AI system assesses the conditions of the patients, and it evaluates whether they need to see a specialist outpatient clinic, in which case the patients are automatically registered for a visit. Otherwise, the patients receive recommendations on the most suitable medical treatments. Since its introduction in 2018, this application can support 15 common tumor diseases. The hospitalization rate of those using the system surpassed 40%, the average waiting time for specialist visits was reduced by 7.4 days, and the appointment rate increased by about 20%.
- *Management of clinical trials*: when collecting information about the patients, the aforementioned AI system can also automatically determine whether the patient conditions require to perform clinical trials in the hospital (临床试验). In doing so, the AI system helps

[346] CN-Healthcare, 2020. Shanghai Accelerated the Promotion of the Deep Application of AI+ Medical Care, the first VTE Intelligent Diagnosis and Treatment in China [上海加快推动AI+ 医疗深度应用 全国首个VTE智能化诊疗落地]. *CN-Healthcare* [健康界], 9 July, https://www.cn-healthcare.com/article/20200709/content-539195.html.

[347] Sohu, 2020 (cit.).

[348] SJTU, CAICT and SHEIC (2019, pp. 112–114). Fudan University Shanghai Cancer Hospital, 2019. [Jiefang Daily] in Addition to Identifying “Scalpers”, It Can Also Accurately Triage [[解放日报] 除了识别 “黄牛” 还能精确分诊]. *Fudan University Shanghai Cancer Hospital*, 26 November, https://www.shca.org.cn/Home/news/content/id/308/pid/6037.html.

to improve the accuracy and efficiency of clinical trials and patient admissions. The system was initially tested on a small set (five types) of advanced esophageal and liver cancer, and it helped doctors to speed up patient admissions by four times.

- *Management of medications*: the "medication guidance function" (用药指导功能) provides patients with a personalized pharmacological plan based on prescriptions formulated by doctors, and revised and approved by pharmacists. When a patient starts chemotherapy treatment, this AI system generates a personalized medication plan, and can also activate a notification service to remind patients via WeChat, SMS, and other channels to take medicines on time. The AI system also creates a reporting channel for adverse drug reactions, so that pharmacists can quickly obtain direct feedback from patients and collect data on adverse drug reactions. During the silent online testing phase (静默上线测试阶段), this function mapped the adverse reactions of 47 common chemotherapy drugs used by the hospital, helping 350 patients per day on average, greatly reducing the work pressure of outpatient medical staff and improving consultation efficiency.
- *Hospital-patient communications*: the smart Q&A function (智能问答功能) allows patients to communicate with the hospital via a smart chatbots (智能对话机器人) embedded in the official WeChat account of the hospital. The AI-enabled chatbots support voice, text and images, and they can answer questions about the whole process of medical treatment before, during, and after the diagnosis. The system is operational 24/7.
- *Follow-up patient assistance*: before being discharged from the hospital, patients affected by thyroid tumors can opt to participate in a personalized follow-up plan. Patients joining such plan receive a reminder from the hospital to schedule a follow-up medical check, when time arrives. In addition, after re-examination, patients can also send the medical report back to the hospital for an additional revision made by an AI system, which can provide further guidance and feedback.
- *Early tumor screening*: the "tumor early-risk smart assessment" (肿瘤早筛智能风险评估) uses AI to make a preliminary risk assessment based on the information provided by the users. Based on the results, the system provides medical suggestions targeted at the users' risk profile. If the system identifies the need for further examinations,

it advises the user to go to hospital for further examinations, and it recommends relevant hospitals and departments for early tumor screening.

- *Statistics management*: the visualization system of survival rate of tumor patients (肿瘤患者生存率可视化系统) uses a visual database (可视化数据库) developed by Tencent, which makes it simpler to interpret the statistics of survival rates of tumor patients, so that the hospital's relevant departments can quickly obtain and interpret data.
- *Outpatient medical history and examination report*: this AI-enabled voice recording function leverages speech recognition to support the efficient transcription of medical records. With an accuracy rate that can reach more than 97%, it helps doctors to quickly generate medical records and reports, reducing the time spent on this task. This voice recording function greatly reduces the workload of medical staff, and it also digitally records the whole diagnostic and treatment process. Data collected via this voice recording functions are also used to support applications in precision medicine.
- *Mammography Intelligent Auxiliary Diagnosis System*: the system, called "care.aiTM X ray mammography intelligent diagnosis system" (care.aiTM 乳腺X 线智能诊断系统), applies deep learning algorithms developed by AI company YITU (依图) to a large number of medical data, under the strict review and control of the doctors of the hospital. The system has reached a level of accuracy similar to senior physicians. At the same time, the system maintains high consistency and stability, and reduces the incidence of missed diagnoses and misdiagnoses of lesions. The system is expected to provide technical support for the construction of an oncology medical alliance in Shanghai.
- *Cervical cancer screening*: the hospital is cooperating with Shanghai Shenxin (上海深芯) and Ping'an Technology (平安科技) to leverage deep learning, image recognition, and other AI technologies to extract key features of cervical cells, and automatically identify cancerous areas and types of cells. This will ultimately shorten the screening time, reduce the rate of missed diagnosis and misdiagnosis, and support smart cervical cytology. The AI model can detect mutant cells, and it covers the seven major cervical cancer risks (ASC-H, HSIL, SCC, ASC-US, LSIL, AGC, AC).

In 2021 and 2022, the Fudan University Cancer Hospital reported that the use of AI technologies consistently contributed to improving the activities of the hospital. AI technologies helped to shorten the time required for medical visits, while at the same time enhanced the quality and precision of medical diagnoses, among others.[349]

Case Study 7: Shanghai Children's Medical Center, Eastern Medical Complex (Pudong and Fengxian Districts) (上海儿童医学中心东部儿科医疗联合体 (浦东新区、奉贤区))

Affiliated to the Shanghai Jiaotong University, the Shanghai Children's Medical Center is considered the first smart children hospital in China. It was selected as an AI pilot application scenario in August 2019, and it uses AI technology in the following applications[350]:

- *Smart consultation* (智能导诊): this application recommends which hospital department to visit according to the reported symptoms. Parents briefly describe the symptoms of the child on the smart consultation system accessible through the WeChat account of the

[349] Fudan University, 2022. "Fudan Tumor" Triple Negative Breast Cancer Diagnosis Now Has a "Smart Solution" ["复旦肿瘤" 三阴性乳腺癌诊断今起有了 "智能方案"]. *Fudan University*, 20 July, https://news.fudan.edu.cn/2022/0720/c40a131986/page.psp; Fudan University, 2021. The 90th Anniversary of the Fudan University Cancer Hospital: Becoming a World-Class Hospital, the 5-Year Overall Survival Rate of Tumor Patients Has Reached 71.3% [复旦大学附属肿瘤医院建院 90 周年: 跻身国际一流, 肿瘤患者5年总生存率达到 71.3%]. *Fudan University*, 15 November, https://news.fudan.edu.cn/2021/1115/c4a110579/page.htm.

[350] Si, Z., 2020. Is Artificial Intelligence Reliable for Children's Medical Visits? Shanghai Children's Medical Center Is Already Using It [孩子看病, 人工智能靠谱吗?上海儿童医学中心已经用上啦]. *The Shanghai Observer* [上观], 8 July, https://www.shobserver.com/news/detail?id=267159; Shanghai Children's Medical Center, 2020. Shanghai Children's Medical Center Has Built a Mobile Platform for AI Outpatient Service, and Won the Third "Top Ten Innovative Measures for Shanghai Medical Reform" [上海儿童医学中心打造人工智能门诊患者服务移动平台, 荣膺第三届 "上海医改十大创新举措"]. *Shanghai Children's Medical Center*, 10 October, https://mp.weixin.qq.com/s?__biz=MzA3OTY2NDEyNA==&mid=2650928449&idx=1&sn=9b4a8188f10d8630e2d6236d41fc95da&chksm=844553d2b332dac49930aca5667461dbfd795b4a73ffcb448a7f69cc1a9adaeb54ac09dbc7f5#rd; Guangming Net, 2020. From Guide to Auxiliary Diagnosis, AI Is Involved in the Whole Process of Clinical Diagnosis and Treatment [从导诊到辅助诊断, AI投身临床诊疗全流程]. *Guangming Net Technology* [光明科技], 5 August, https://tech.gmw.cn/2020-08/05/content_34059003.htm.

Shanghai Children Medical Center. The system analyzes the information through semantic recognition, automatically recommends the department for treatment, and provides the corresponding information for appointment registration.

- *Pre-diagnosis inspection* (诊前检验): this application uses AI to improve the efficiency of the existing pediatric diagnosis and treatment process (registration, consultation, visit, supplementary examination, visit, diagnosis). It relies on a knowledge base of clinical practice guidelines and expert knowledge to recommend medical checks that can be done before face-to-face consultation with doctors. As such, it shortens the treatment process and reduces queuing time in outpatient clinics.
- *Smart auxiliary diagnosis* (智能辅诊): this application uses AI to support the collection of medical information before diagnosis, reducing the time spent by doctors in writing medical records and improving the quality of medical reporting. When doctors finish to write the medical records, the AI system can automatically extract information from them. It uses an algorithm to screen and locate the main symptoms, recommend possible diagnoses, and provide suggestions for treatment. This system is based on a "clinical evidence-based brain" (临床循证大脑) that use AI to parse a medical database of common pediatric diseases, improving diagnostic accuracy.
- *Remote consultation* (远程问诊): it deploys AI-enabled auscultation equipment (breath sounds, heart sounds, etc.) that automatically updates medical data on the cloud system of the hospital, providing real-time data analysis. It also introduced the service robot Xiaobai (小白) to conduct ward rounds, allowing direct but contactless communication between doctors and patients. This solution was launched during the Covid-19 pandemic to reduce the risks of cross-infection, improve the efficiency of expert consultation in the hospital, and save medical protection resources.

The integration of AI in the activities of the Shanghai Children Medical Center has steadily continued. In October 2020, the hospital was awarded in the third edition of the "Top Ten Innovative Measures for Shanghai Medical Reform" (上海医改十大创新举措) by the Shanghai Medical

Reform Office, the Municipal Health Commission, and the Municipal Medical Insurance Bureau for its successful establishment of an "AI-enabled mobile platform for outpatient service".[351]

Case Study 8: Shanghai Ruijin Hospital (上海交通大学医学院附属瑞金医院)

Affiliated to the Medical School of the Shanghai Jiaotong University, the Shanghai Ruijin Hospital was selected as an AI pilot application scenario in August 2019. The project uses AI technologies in the following applications[352]:

- *Smart authentication*: it uses facial recognition technology to verify the patient's identity during medical treatment, admission, discharge, nursing, surgery, and other interactions between the patient and the hospital.
- *Smart pre-check and pre-diagnosis*: it uses AI to facilitate communications with patients before the medical visit through voice, text, and images, assisting and guiding patients to choose a department or specialist. The system combines the information provided by the patient during the online registration with data collected from all medical institutions in the municipality via the Government Online-Offline Shanghai, the Health Cloud (健康云), and the Shanghai Medical Federation (上海医联) platform. On this basis, the system generates a pre-diagnostic report for doctors' reference and it recommends appointment with the appropriate department, reducing the waiting time for patients. Smart pre-consultation also reduces the workload of doctors, and it increases the interaction time between doctors and patients during the visit.

[351] Shanghai Children's Medical Center, 2020 (cit.).

[352] Zuo, Y., 2021. "The Hospital of the Future" Is Here. How to Become More Intelligent in Seeing a Doctor? Let's Take a Look at This Hospital's Problem-Solving Ideas ["未来医院" 来了, 看病如何变得更加智慧?来看这家医院的解题思路]. *Xinmin Evening Post* [新民晚报], 6 May, http://shanghai.xinmin.cn/xmsq/2021/05/06/31951291.html; Sun, Z., 2020. The AI Medical Robot "Ruijin Xiaobai" Is Used in the Front Line of Wuhan's Covid-19 Epidemic Prevention and Control [人工智能医护机器人 "瑞金小白" 投入武汉新冠肺炎疫情防控一线使用]. *Xinmin Evening Post* [新民晚报], 24 February, http://newsxmwb.xinmin.cn/xinminyx/2020/02/24/31669127.html.

- *Smart medical records*: by combining data on medical history provided by patients in the aforementioned smart pre-diagnosis system, this application uses speech recognition for the automatic transcription of medical records, assisting doctors in selected departments. The system relies on 255 knowledge databases covering 80% of the hospital's departments. According to Ruijin Hospital's statistics, this application reduces the time of drafting patients' medical history from 5 to 1.5 minutes on average. In addition, the Shanghai Medical Federation (上海医联) platform allows the Ruijin Hospital to check medical records collected at other hospitals in the municipality. All medical institutions at any level in Shanghai are interconnected, and the municipality established a "single network" ("一张网") of medical examination records that covers 44 items.
- *Smart image recognition*: it leverages AI to identify lesions in the diagnostic imaging of thyroid, breast, brain, lumbar spine, and other body parts, assisting doctors to carry out the diagnosis. In combination with 5G and other technologies, the Ruijin Hospital also uses its smart diagnostic imaging system to perform remote medical checks (e.g., ultrasounds) for patients in other hospitals of Shanghai.
- *Chronic disease management and follow-up*: it uses wearable and portable sampling devices to collect follow-up data from patients and send them notifications via phone, in order to better assist patients affected by chronic diseases.
- *Smart remote ward rounds*: by using AI service robots and other technologies, doctors can conduct remote ward rounds. The robot Ruijin Xiaobai (瑞金小白), jointly developed by Shanghai Jiaotong University School of Medicine and its affiliated Ruijin Hospital, is equipped with lidar, infrared radar, 5G communication 3D visual recognition sensors, and AI chips. Technologies like computer vision and 5G also allow the hospital to perform remote medical checks, rehabilitation, and medical training with partner institutions.

The digital transformation of the Ruijin Hospital is progressing. The hospital is testing the integration of Internet of Thing technologies in the "smart wards" (智慧病房), which are equipped with: a smart floor with embedded sensors that can detect patients falling and send immediate warnings; smart hospital beds that detect the bed status and the weight of patients in bed in real time; and other non-invasive technologies that can detect patients' medical parameters like heartbeat and breathing.

Clinical services and nursing assistance provided by smart robots are also expected to reduce the workload of the medical staff. In 2020 and 2021, the hospital signed agreements with AI companies 4Paradigm (第四范式) and Fosun AITrox (复星杏脉) to further integrate AI in its activities.[353] In August 2022, the hospital published a tender for the procurement of an AI online adaptive radiotherapy system[354] (人工智能在线自适应放射治疗系统).

Case Study 9: Changning District Beixinjing Subdistrict (长宁区北新泾街道)

Located in Changning District in downtown Shanghai, the Beixinjing Subdistrict has over 49,000 residents. This project was selected as an AI pilot application scenario in April 2019. According to the *General Construction Framework of Beixinjing Subdistrict Smart Community* (北新泾街道智慧社区总体建设框架), this project is focusing on the integration of AI in community services, governance and the intelligentization of life. It is organized into "one platform, two communities, and three roads": "one platform" indicates the "community comprehensive management service platform" (社区综合管理服务平台) of the subdistrict; "two communities" are the Xinjing Liucun and Yuanfeng Tianshan Garden residential communities; "three roads" are Jinzhong Road, Tianshan West Road, and Pingtang Road. The pilot uses AI technologies in the following applications[355]:

353 Fosun, 2020. Fosun AITrox signed 5G+ AI strategic cooperation with Shanghai Ruijin Hospital [复星杏脉与上海瑞金医院签署 5G+ 人工智能战略合作]. *Fosun*, 25 December, https://www.fosun.com/content/details74_5222.html; Diankeji, 2021. 4Paradigm reaches a strategic cooperation with Ruijin Hospital, and jointly explore new heights of AI medical care [第四范式与瑞金医院达成战略合作 强强联手共探AI医疗新高度]. *Diankeji* [电科技], 20 December, http://www.diankeji.com/news/42771.html.

354 China Government Procurement Net, 2022. Ruijin Hospital affiliated to the Medical College of Shanghai Jiaotong University International Public Bidding for Artificial Intelligence Online Adaptive Radiotherapy System [上海交通大学医学院附属瑞金医院人工智能在线自适应放射治疗系统国际公开招标采购招标公告]. *China Government Procurement Net* [中国政府采购网], 9 August, http://www.ccgp.gov.cn/cggg/dfgg/gkzb/202208/t20220809_18423845.htm.

355 SJTU, CAICT and SHEIC (2019, pp. 115–117). Sohu, 2020. Beixinjing Neighborhood, Is the Only "AI + Residential Community" in the City to Be Selected into the First Batch of Artificial Intelligence Demonstration Application Scenarios in Shanghai [北

- *Smart community services*: these include a set of AI applications for "smart government affairs" (智慧政务), which use speech recognition, computer vision, and NLP to provide services to businesses and community residents like those of the Government Online-Offline Shanghai. AI applications also support "smart business" (智慧商业) services such as 24-hour unattended convenience stores, or other highly demonstrative applications like smart service robots, "smart vegetable markets". Finally, AI also empowers "smart culture" (智慧文化) and "smart sports" (智慧运动) services, such as a "smart studio" (智慧书房), "smart walking trails" (智能步道), etc. (details below).
- *Smart elderly care services*: at the end of 2018, nearly 40% of the Beixinjing residents was over 60 years old. To optimize the use of available medical resources, Beixinjing collects data from the local elderly care center, community health service stations (社区卫生服务站), and other sources, and it leverages AI to provide personalized health management services to the elderly. For instance, it introduced a "wireless biological detection system" (无线网络生物探测系统) designed for the elderly living alone. Developed by AI company Baizhilong (百芝龙), this AI system uses tailor-made wireless devices installed in the houses of elderly people to infer physiological characteristics such as breathing and heartbeat, and to detect unexpected events such as falls, automatically sending alerts when necessary.[356] Beixinjing also introduced a 24-hour smart consultation and health service system, which in cooperation with local health institutions provides medical support at any time.
- *Smart life*: it leverages AI technologies to facilitate community management and services in the neighborhood, such as smart garbage classification, smart parking, or smart street cleaning, supporting the activities of the local property management companies (i.e., companies that are primarily responsible for routine maintenance in neighborhoods and residential communities).

新泾街道作为全市唯一 "AI + 社区", 入选上海首批人工智能示范应用场景]. *Sohu* [搜狐], 9 December, https://www.sohu.com/a/437304389_99893471?sec=wd.

[356] Sohu, 2019. Just Now! Baizhilong Uses Wireless Biological Detection Technology to Save the Elderly Around the World! [刚刚!百芝龙用无线生物探测技术拯救全球老人!]. *Sohu* [搜狐], 29 August, https://www.sohu.com/a/337286669_100037449.

- *Smart security*: it leverages AI and IoT technologies for real-time monitoring in public security, including areas like fire prevention, smoke detection, water accumulation detection, monitoring of elevators, and other activities like those of the Single Platform for Urban Management. To support these applications, the subdistrict has been improving the local 5G coverage.
- *Smart residential community*: it uses AI to create a "community comprehensive management service platform" that combines public services, public management, and public safety. This AI-based "community brain" (社区大脑), now integrated in the Single Platform for Urban Management, collects and analyzes data that support the aforementioned smart applications in the subdistrict.

In December 2020, the Beixinjing Subdistrict was nominated "AI demonstration application scenario" (人工智能示范应用场景). The expert committee stated that the project is characterized by "a high grade of involvement, strong innovation, and remarkable application results".[357] Indeed, based on available evidence, most of the applications of this pilot scenario have been implemented as planned and further expanded[358]:

- *Smart elderly care services*: the community health service stations have been upgraded to "smart health cabins" (智慧健康小屋).

[357] Sohu, 2020 (cit.).

[358] Sohu, 2020 (cit.); Shanghai Observer, 2022. Unimaginable! The Future "Digital Home" of Changning People Is Like This... [难以想象!长宁人未来的"数字家园"是这样的...]. *Shanghai Observer* [上观], 21 January, https://sghexport.shobserver.com/html/baijiahao/2022/01/21/640421.html; Shanghai Party Building Service Center, 2021. Changning District Beixinjing Subdistrict: Party Building Leads the "Single Platform for Urban Management", Refines Community Governance [长宁区北新泾街道: 党建引领"一网统管"社区治理更精细]. *Shanghai Party Construction Service Center* [上海市党建服务中心], 8 February, https://www.shjcdj.cn/djWeb/djweb/web/djweb/newestindex/newestindex!info.action?articleid=ff8080817745095401777c8cc0f4036a; Sohu, 2021. The "Grounded Gas" Practice of a Digital Benchmarking Community in Shanghai [一个申城数字化标杆社区的"接地气"实践]. *Sohu* [搜狐], 19 December, http://news.sohu.com/a/509743789_120244154. Zhang, Y. and Lu, J., 2021. Beixinjing Neighborhood|Technology Empowers "Old and Small", the Xinjing No. 6 Community Is Transformed into an "AI + Community" [北新泾街道|科技赋能"老旧小", 新泾六村变身"AI + 社区"]. *Morning News* [新闻晨报], 24 January, retrieved via: https://baijiahao.baidu.com/s?id=1689695521711702661&wfr=spider&for=pc.

These allow elderly and other community residents to remotely see a doctor, collect medicines, and receive drips without leaving the neighborhood. These smart health cabins are equipped with smart medical devices provided by iFlytek, DeepBlue, and other AI companies. This AI-based equipment can assist doctors in doing health checkups, monitoring chronic diseases, and conducting early screening for eye diseases. Data collected from these smart cabins are uploaded on the municipal "health cloud" (健康云), allowing residents to check their health records (medical history, examination reports, medication records), and also to make appointments for expert visits at second- and third-level hospitals in Shanghai. This application has been particularly successful, and it became a "national demonstration site for smart elderly care applications" (全国的智慧健康养老应用示范点). In addition, the subdistrict has implemented a "cloud guardianship" (云守护) system for the elderly over 80-year old who live alone. This system combines the "community brain" platform with smart door sensors introduced during the peak of the Covid-19 pandemic to monitor people in quarantine. If an elderly person does not open the door for more than 48 hours, the "community brain" platform issues an early warning. The volunteers in charge of elderly care will also simultaneously receive a notification on their mobile phones, and will contact the elderly by phone or by visiting in person. Finally, Beixinjing has also introduced an AI chatbot that calls local residents affected by high blood pressure, diabetes, and other chronic diseases to check their conditions and record medical data such as blood sugar levels or blood pressure.

- *Smart community services*: the subdistrict introduced smart facilities like "smart studios" (智慧书房), service points where books can be borrowed and returned without interactions with human operators; "smart sports" (智慧运动), a gym where residents receive personalized suggestions for exercise from an "AI personal trainer", based on their individual health records; "smart walking trails (智能步道) equipped with digital screens (which, however, do not appear to be AI-enabled); and "smart government affairs" (智慧政务) applications in the administrative centers in the pilot, which installed smart equipment that—through the municipal online platform Government Online-Offline Shanghai—allows residents to apply and perform more than 70 government services online.

- *Smart community*: the "community brain" (社区大脑) has been fully connected to the municipal online platform Single Platform for Urban Management. By leveraging AI technologies such as computer vision, speech recognition, and Natural Language Processing, the "community brain" automatically performs "smart video patrol" (智能巡屏) that can discover problems in the residential community almost in real time—mostly (95%) within one hour—and dispatch relevant personnel for a follow-up, such as removing shared bikes (which cannot be parked into residential communities) or garbage to clear passageways, to more complex problems that require the intervention of higher-level authorities).

Case Study 10: Xuhui District Xietu Road Subdistrict (徐汇区斜土路街道)

Located in Xuhui District in downtown Shanghai, the Xietu Road Subdistrict has approximately 60,000 residents. Selected as an AI pilot application scenario in April 2019, the project uses AI technologies in the following applications[359]:

- *Smart brain*: this application consists of an AI-enabled digital platform that gathers information by interconnecting data from different government departments and agencies through a fast interoperability mechanism (互通机制). This "smart brain" (智慧大脑) platform offers "online customization, offline service" (线上定制, 线下服务) to the residents of the Xietu Road Subdistrict. The platform improves management precision (提升精细化管理水平) through traffic monitoring (流量监测), notification and early warning, "atmosphere creation" (氛围营造), smart evacuation and other services. The smart brain is now integrated in the Single Platform for Urban Management.

[359] SJTU, CAICT and SHEIC (2019, pp. 118–119); CPC Xuhui District Committee, 2019. The Party Committee of the District's Science and Technology Commission Promotes the In-depth Application of AI and Solves Bottleneck Problems in Many Industries [区科委党委推进人工智能深度应用, 破解多个行业瓶颈问题]. *CPC Xuhui District Committee* [中共徐汇区委员会], 2 July, http://dj.xh.sh.cn/HTML/xhdj/kw_bmdt/2019-07-02/Detail_180806.htm.

- *Smart security*: it leverages AI technologies such as face recognition, smart smoke detection, "smart protection" (智慧看护), and smart lampposts to improve the security of public spaces in the neighborhood. The security equipment also uses AI to collect and analyze data that are fed into the aforementioned "smart brain" platform to improve public service provision in the subdistrict.
- *AI+ medicine and healthcare*: similar to the Beixinjing pilot, the Xietu Road Subdistrict introduced self-service clinics (社区自助诊所) where residents can use smart voice technology to remotely consult doctors about minor ailments and order medicines from nearby pharmacies. These smart self-service clinics support the services provided by the community hospitals (社区医院).
- *AI+ administrative services*: it consists of an "unmanned reception station" (无人值守受理站) that relies on AI-enabled equipment (e.g., smart ID card readers, fingerprint readers, service robots, intelligent file cabinets). Such equipment allows users to handle selected administrative services by themselves (see the smart equipment discussed in the Government Online-Offline Shanghai, Sect. 5.2.1). The self-service station is always operational, and residents can use it at any time.
- *AI+ relatives and neighbor interactions* (AI+ 亲邻互动): it uses AI models to analyze data of the residents in the neighborhood. It serves as a match-making platform that pairs the most common needs of the local residents (e.g., disabled and elderly care, childcare, culture and sports, etc.) with relevant resources (e.g., volunteers, community activities). In doing so, it aims to "promote the interaction and harmonious relationship between relatives and neighbors" (促进亲邻互动和谐关系).
- *AI+ popularization of science education* (AI+ 科普教育): it consists of immersive AI education projects for children that entail robots, programming, and other demonstrative applications. The goal is to attract young "future scientists" to observe and experiment AI innovation, thus cultivating the scientific spirit and digital literacy of youngsters. This application also provides opportunities for citizens to experience the innovations produced by AI enterprises in the neighborhood.
- *AI+ Communist Party building services* (AI+ 党建服务): it leverages AI technologies such as Natural Language Processing and speech recognition to support grassroots Party building by providing more

precise and personalized services and contents for the training of local Party members.

The Xietu Road pilot has integrated AI in public sector operations. The official work report of the neighborhood committee of a residential community in the pilot listed several AI-related achievements in 2021.[360] In elderly care, the community's Nursing Home No. 2 introduced experimental "smart rooms" for the elderly, which leverage Natural Language Processing and other technologies (e.g., infrared monitoring, etc.) to support functions such as emergency call, automatic lighting, and warnings in case the elderly fall in the bathroom or leave their beds. The system transmits such alerts to the nursing home's management platform or the family. In public security, several smart fire-prevention facilities (e.g., control and monitoring systems, smoke detectors) were installed in the neighborhood. In medical care, the Xietu Community Health Service Center introduced an AI-enabled "smart pharmacy" (智慧药房) that automatically picks and dispenses the medicines, while the pharmacist double-checks the information with the recipient, stores the medicines, and updates the inventory. The "smart pharmacy" automatically flags abnormal situations in medical prescriptions, such as excessive dosages. If the doctor still confirms the prescribed dosages, the pharmacist is notified through the system, and the medicine is issued to the patient after a further review by the pharmacist.[361]

The integration of AI in public sector activities was planned to continue in 2022.[362] The "AI + relatives and neighbour interactions" (AI+ 亲邻互动), later rebranded "neighbour reunions" (邻里汇), was due to further expansion and integration in the West Bund AI cluster (Chapter 4.2). The

[360] Xuhui District People's Government, 2022. Dare to Take on the Mission, Dare to be the Pioneer, Compose a New Miracle, and Comprehensively Promote the New Development of Xietu—Report at the First Meeting of the Sixth Assembly of the Xietu residential Community [勇担使命 敢为先锋 谱写新奇迹 全面推动斜土新发展—在斜土社区第六届代表会议第一次会议上的报告]. *Xuhui District People's Government*, 18 February, http://www.xuhui.gov.cn/H/xhxxgkN/xhxxgk_xt_ghlxx_ghjh/Info/Detail_65312.htm.

[361] Morning News, 2022. AI Review + Pharmacist Approval, This Smart Pharmacy in Xuhui Is Full of Future [AI审方 + 药师审核, 徐汇这家智慧药房未来感十足]. *Morning News* [新闻晨报], 17 March, retrieved via: https://xw.qq.com/cmsid/20220317A0AZ7Q00.

[362] Xuhui District People's Government, 2022 (cit.).

digitalization of governance (治理数字化) and related data integration were accelerated by the further assimilation of the Xietu Subdistrict urban governance system into the municipal Single Platform for Urban Management, and the creation of micro digital platforms in selected residential areas of the neighborhood that to improve community management. Finally, the "smart elderly care model" (智慧养老模式) started to be strengthened by integrating AI, IoT, and other technologies to provide better services for the elderly and people with cognitive impairment.

Case Study 11: Zhangjiang Artificial Intelligence Island (张江人工智能岛)

Established in 2018, the Zhangjiang Artificial Intelligence Island (ZJAIsland) is the first demonstration park in Shanghai dedicated to real-life applications of AI, IoT, and 5G technologies. It is also part of the four municipal AI clusters (Sect. 5.2). Selected as an AI pilot application scenario in April 2019, it was visited by the author in January 2021. At the time, the ZJAIsland covered an area of 100,000 m^2 and had more than 20 buildings. It already hosted Chinese and international AI and tech companies (IBM, CloudWalk, Alibaba's semiconductor division Pingtouge), research institutes (the Tongji University's Research Institute for Intelligent Autonomous Systems/上海自主智能无人系统科学中心, Microsoft AI & IoT Insider Lab), and financial investors (Sequoia Capital). By 2025 ZJAIsland is planned to expand "from an island to a district" (由 "岛" 变 "区"), covering 3.5 million square meters. By then, it will be named "Zhangjiang AI Gathering Area" (张江人工智能集聚区). The ZJAIsland pilot uses AI technologies in the following applications[363]:

- *Experience center* (体验中心): it is an exhibition hall that showcases AI applications in smart living (智能生活), including AI+ home (AI+ 家居), AI+ school campus (AI+ 校园), and AI+ medicine (AI+ 医疗), as well as some applications of smart manufacturing (AI+ 智能制造). These demonstrative applications complement the AI+ security (AI+ 安防), AI+ traffic (AI+ 交通), and AI+ park management (园

[363] SJTU, CAICT and SHEIC (2019, pp. 120–123). Field visit, January 2021. Shanghai Observer, 2021. See the Future on the Zhangjiang Artificial Intelligence Island [在张江人工智能岛上看见未来]. *Shanghai Observer* [上观], 6 May, https://sghexport.shobserver.com/html/baijiahao/2021/05/06/426349.html.

区) applications that are deployed in real-life inside the ZJAIsland park (see below).

- *Park management* (园区管理): it entails the use of AI and IoT technologies in various activities within the park. *Smart security* applies AI and IoT, cloud computing, computer vision (smart surveillance cameras), service robots, and intelligent visitor management systems to enhance security management and control. The goal is to leverage digital technologies to implement a smart security system based on forecasting (事先预测) rather than ex-post investigation (事后调查), thus improving the efficiency of public security. *Smart lampposts* leverage the IoT network of the park to improve the utilization rate of basic resources. This application includes the smart management of streetlights, but also smart e-charging stations (智能充电桩) and other methods. *Smart parking* (智慧停车) consists of the adoption of automatic license plate recognition (a commonly used AI application), IoT, and other technologies to optimize car parking in the ZJAIsland. *Fire prevention* (消防管理) consists of using smart smoke detectors and other smart sensors for temperature and humidity, and systems for the security scan of motor vehicles, in order to prevent potential fire and safety hazards. *Smart energy management* (智能能源管理) uses AI for the remote real-time monitoring and recording of the status of electrical equipment and energy systems, providing accurate information for energy management and conservation. *Environmental monitoring* (环境监测) uses AI to monitor water and air quality, the maintenance of garbage bins and manhole covers, and to manage an automatic irrigation system. Finally, *machine intelligence* (机器智能) consists of promoting real-world applications of drones, cleaning robots, security robots, and unmanned vehicles in the park.
- *Park services* (园区服务): it embeds augmented reality (AR) and virtual reality (VR) technologies in the patrolling activities of the security staff of the ZJAIsland, who can also access the data collected by the security service robot. Other ancillary services include: a "smart restaurant" that uses AI to optimize the management of the canteen that serves the park, mostly through online orders and self-service applications; and "smart retail", which includes both smart vending machines that support face recognition technologies, and autonomous vehicles that drive inside the park selling food and beverage.

- *Smart buildings* (智能楼宇): this application implements smart systems for office management, such as the smart control of office environment (e.g., temperature, humidity, and air quality). It also uses AI to support the activities of the command-and-control center (智能指挥中心) of the ZJAIsland, for instance using AI-based voice and video technologies to monitor park activities, provide early warnings, and support decision-making.
- *Park Smart Brain*: the aforementioned AI applications in the park (i.e., park management, park services, and smart buildings) generate data that feed the "Park Smart Brain" (园区智脑, later renamed 张江人工智能岛数字化管理中心). This is an AI system that leverages speech recognition, natural language processing, and other AI technologies for data collection and analysis, supporting applications like identity authentication and other park operations.

The Zhangjiang AI Island was nominated "AI demonstration application scenario" (人工智能示范应用场景) in December 2020, and all the aforementioned AI applications were fully operational when visited by the author in January 2021. In addition, conversations with a manager of the project in March 2022 and available evidence confirm not only that the Zhangjiang AI Island has integrated AI in its activities, but also that it added new AI applications, such as unmanned aerial vehicles

Fig. 5.3 The "experience center" and two autonomous vehicles in Zhangjiang AI Island (*Source* Author)

for safety inspection, and unmanned ships for water quality monitoring (Fig. 5.3).[364]

Case Study 12: Shanghai Lingang Intelligent Connected Vehicles Comprehensive Demonstration Zone (上海临港智能网联汽车综合测试示范区)

Selected as an AI pilot application scenario in April 2019, the Lingang Intelligent Connected Vehicles Comprehensive Demonstration Zone focuses on autonomous driving in public transportation, street cleaning, and logistics, all of which are priority applications set forth in the Shanghai municipal AI plans. The demonstration zone covers a bounded area of 3.2 km^2 physically separated from the surrounding public streets, which includes 4.7 km of roads for testing autonomous vehicles (AVs). The demonstration zone is located at the extreme Southeastern margins of Shanghai, near the Donghai Bridge (东海大桥) that leads to the Yangshan Deepwater Port (洋山港), Shanghai's main container port. The construction of the demonstration zone started in August 2019. The "scenario organization" of the AI pilot is the Lingang Sci-Tech City (上海临港科技创新城经济发展有限公司), which is supported by two other main government entities: the Shanghai Motor Vehicle Inspection Certification & Technology Innovation Center (上海机动车检测认证技术研究中心有限公司), and the China Academy of Information and Communications (CAICT) Easter China Institute (中国信息通信研究院华东分院). The private autonomous trucks company TuSimple is one of the main technical partners of the AI pilot. The demonstration zone is also part of the four municipal AI clusters (Chapter 4.2).

[364] Tencent Net, 2022. In Zhangjiang AI Island, You Can See How the Future Looks Like [在张江人工智能岛，看见未来的模样]. *Tencent Net* [腾讯网], 25 June, https://new.qq.com/rain/a/20220625A00R1W00; Shanghai Office for Promoting the Construction of Science and Technology Innovation Center, 2021. Shanghai Technological Innovation. "From an Island to a District"! In 2025, There Will Be More Than 2,500 Enterprises in the Zhangjiang Artificial Intelligence Cluster [科创上海 | "由岛变区" !2025年张江人工智能集聚区企业将超2500家]. *Shanghai Office for Promoting the Construction of Science and Technology Innovation Center* [上海推进科技创新中心建设办公室], 13 July, https://www.zjsfq.gov.cn/html/1/168/151/152/1706.html; Fangsheng Research, 2021. Zhangjiang AI Island—A Leading Artificial Intelligence Gathering Area [张江人工智能岛—龙头林立的人工智能集聚区]. *Zhihu* [知乎], 11 October, https://zhuanlan.zhihu.com/p/420118502.

The Lingang Demonstration Zone aims to develop technologies for public transport (unmanned taxis, unmanned buses) and infrastructure management (smart traffic infrastructure, unmanned street-sweeping cars). It also provides a venue for private companies to test commercial applications that can be later deployed by the public sector (unmanned delivery vehicles, unmanned truck logistics). After approval from the SMVIC, AVs tested in the demonstration zone are allowed to conduct trials on a number of authorized public roads surrounding the demonstration zone, with a total length of over 26 Km. When visited by the author in September 2020, the Lingang Demonstration Zone was using several AI technologies in the area of unmanned and intelligent connected vehicles, as reported by local sources.[365] Specifically:

- *Smart traffic infrastructure*: the autonomous vehicles tested in the demonstration zone use a V2X (vehicle-to-everything) coordination system (V2X 车路协同系统) that connects them in real time to a state-of-the-art smart traffic infrastructure, which combines computer vision, IoT, 5G, and other digital technologies
- *Data collection and analysis*: the Operation Center of the Shanghai Lingang Intelligent Connected Vehicle Innovation Center uses computer vision (i.e., more than 70 smart cameras) and IoT technologies to monitor and collect in real time the data generated by the operations of vehicles, drivers, and other activities in the zone.

At the time of the field visit, the Lingang pilot application scenario was already fully operational. The demonstration zone was entirely covered by 5G signal to support V2X applications, autonomous trucks were being tested in a mix environment with normal vehicles on the Donghai Bridge,

[365] SJTU, CAICT and SHEIC (2019, pp. 127–129); field visit, September 2020; The Paper, 2020. Shanghai AI Industrial Park Exploration Camp: Can Self-Driving Cars Hit the Road? [上海AI产业园区探营: 自动驾驶汽车可以上路了吗]. *The Paper* [澎湃], 3 July, https://m.thepaper.cn/newsDetail_forward_8086763?from=message; Jiefang Daily, 2020. The Automatic Driving Line Is Fixed, and There Is No Commercial Use at Present [自动驾驶线路固定, 目前没有商用]. *Jiefang Daily* [解放日报], 2 July, https://www.jfdaily.com/journal/2020-07-02/getArticle.htm?id=295746; Shanghai Observer, 2020. The Wind Is Coming from Lingang | Tesla Is Happy! Wanlihai Road Becomes a Ten-Minute Drive, and the Logistics Cost Is Almost Zero [风从临港来| 特斯拉乐了!万里海路变成十分钟车程, 物流成本几乎为零]. *Shanghai Observer* [上观], 16 August, https://web.shobserver.com/wxShare/html/279671.htm?from=timeline.

and the demonstration zone was using traffic lights and other equipment to simulate real-life driving conditions, including urban scenarios (e.g., parked vehicles, dummies of pedestrians and cyclists), a tunnel (the longest for testing AVs in China), and water pipes that simulate raining conditions. When visiting the SICVIC Operation Center, the control panel showed that on 10 September 2020 there were 11 vehicles being tested inside the zone, and two on authorized public roads. Detailed information on each vehicle, driver, and activity were displayed on the screen. Autonomous driving applications are progressing fast. In February 2021, the interview with TuSimple confirmed that AV technologies developed in the zone allow five trucks to drive autonomously while maintaining a stable distance at a speed of 70–80 km/h, so that only the first truck needs a safety operator in it, while the other vehicles automatically keep distance and drive accordingly to the behavior of the leading truck (Fig. 5.4).

Available evidence confirms that the Lingang Demonstration Zone has integrated AI in its activities.[366] The demonstration zone also started to implement AI applications that were included in the project requirements,

Fig. 5.4 Testing square for autonomous vehicles (left) and SICVIC Operation Center (right) in the Shanghai Lingang Intelligent Connected Vehicles Comprehensive Demonstration Zone (*Source* Author)

366 Xinmin Evening Post, 2022. Hit the Leading Area | Lingang: AI Driven Smart City [直击引领区丨临港: AI驱动的智慧之城]. *Xinmin Evening Post* [新民晚报], 5 January, retrieved via: https://baijiahao.baidu.com/s?id=1721098191406934196&wfr=spider&for=pc;%20%20https://www.pcauto.com.cn/jxwd/2834/28340189.html.

but were not seen during the field visit. Namely: a low-altitude demonstration area for drones in applications such as urban security and logistics; and trial applications of unmanned boats, underwater robots, underwater acoustic instruments in some parts of the Dishui Lake, which is adjacent to the demonstration zone.[367]

Case Study 13: Shanghai Subway (上海地铁集团)

In 2022, the Shanghai subway network consisted of 18 metro lines, more than 500 subway stations, and the longest operating mileage in the world with more than 800 km of railroads.[368] It is operated by the government-owned Shanghai Shentong Subway Group (上海申通地铁集团有限公司). Selected as an AI pilot application scenario in August 2019, this project uses AI technologies in the following applications[369]:

- *Passenger flow detection and early warning*: also called "smart metro station" (智慧车站), this application uses computer vision to monitor real-time passenger flows in the subway stations, including the actual number of people in each station, the speed of passenger flows, and total passenger volumes of the day, among others. Part of this information is made available to subway users on the Metro App

[367] Tencent Net, 2021. The Demonstration Service Platform of UAV Digital Application Is Launched in the Lingang New Area, Which Will Explore Low Altitude Digital Application Scenarios [临港新片区启用无人机数字化应用示范服务平台，将探索低空数字化应用场景]. *Tencent Net* [腾讯网], 16 March, https://new.qq.com/rain/a/20210316A0D3KE00; Sina, 2021. The Construction of Dishui Lake Unmanned Boats Pilot Zone Has Further Promoted the Development of "Blue Economy" [滴水湖无人船试验区建设更进一步 临港海洋创新园推动"蓝色经济"加速发展]. *Sina Finance* [新浪财经], 26 October, https://finance.sina.com.cn/jjxw/2021-10-26/doc-iktzqtyu3695456.shtml.

[368] Shanghai Fabu, 2022. These Rail Transit Lines in Shanghai Run in the "Air"! Is There Anyone That You Often Take? [上海这些轨道交通线路行驶在"空中"!有你常乘坐的吗?]. *Shanghai Fabu* [上海发布], 15 August, https://mp.weixin.qq.com/s/EqKM4uE7n3NJcr2R4aTQAw.

[369] SHEITC, 2019b. Sohu, 2020. How to Use AI in Rail Transit Operation and Maintenance? At the 2020 World Artificial Intelligence Conference Opening Ceremony Shanghai Metro Appears Worldwide [轨交运维如何运用人工智能?2020世界人工智能大会开幕式 上海地铁亮相全球]. *Sohu* [搜狐], 10 July, https://www.sohu.com/a/406871702_249521; Jiang Z., Zhang, L. and Deng, R., 2021. Shanghai Rail Transit Smart Station Technology Research and Demonstrative Applications [上海轨道交通智慧车站技术研究与示范应用]. *China Metros* [城市轨道交通], 2021 (9), pp. 36–38.

(Metro大都会), which also allows to check the congestion levels and temperature of different subway cars. In addition, the passenger flow application uses a geospatial model (地理空间模型) for the real-time quantitative monitoring of key areas. The model triggers congestion alerts based on a set of parameters such as number of people, congestion index, density and flow speed, etc. This model also monitors the passenger flows in the whole subway network, including real-time analysis and forecast of passenger flows at designated stations and on the entire railway network (e.g., real-time data on entries and exits at each station, analysis of passenger flow that change lines, etc.).

- *Personnel management and behavior detection*: the "personnel management" application uses facial recognition to verify the identity of the subway staff and allow their entrance to restricted areas, conduct automatic inspections (自动巡检), and carry out other operations related to staff management. The "behavior detection" (行为识别) function is not only targeted at the subway staff (e.g., monitors signs of fatigue on train drivers or irregular operations); it also monitors a variety of situations inside the subway stations, including irregular or dangerous behaviors on the escalators (e.g., passenger falling, people running or going in the forbidden direction, etc.), irregular or dangerous behaviors by metro users (e.g., begging, falling, not paying the ticket, quarreling, etc.), and the clearing of passengers when the subway stations close at night (e.g., monitoring that all passengers left the stations and that there are not irregular situations, such as people who didn't clear the station or got wedged between the roller shutters, etc.).
- *Smart maintenance*: it uses machine learning techniques, computer vision, and other technologies for the online monitoring and fault diagnosis of key subway equipment and infrastructure, such as vehicles and traffic signals. With the support of AI technology, the Shanghai subway is able to ensure the safe and reliable operation of more than 6,000 trains every day.[370]
- *Autonomous driving lines*: Shanghai subway line 10 was the first autonomous driving subway line introduced in China in April 2010. Since then, it reached the highest standard level for the automatic

[370] Sohu, 2020 (cit.).

> operation for passenger trains (UTO GOA4[371]). Its operations are fully automatic: the whole process of trains' power on, check, entry and exit from the warehouses, driving, stopping at stations, and turn-backs are completed automatically, with no human intervention. In December 2021, Shanghai had five fully automated subway lines (lines 10, 14, 15, 18, and the Pujiang Line), for a total of 167 km, the longest in the world.[372]

These AI applications are monitored by the Shanghai Rail Transit Network Operation Coordination and Emergency Command-and-Control Hall (上海轨道交通网络运营协调与应急指挥调度大厅). In January 2021, the author visited the Shanghai Railway Transportation Engineering Research Center for Driverless Train Control (上海轨道交通无人驾驶列控系统工程技术研究中心) operated by Casco (卡斯柯信号有限公司), one of the main technical partners of Shanghai Shentong Subway Group. This research center includes the Urban Railway Transport Command Lab (城轨运输指挥实验室), which closely reproduces the functions of the Command-and-Control Hall of the Shanghai Subway. During the visit, all the aforementioned applications were presented, showing the integration of AI in the operations of the Shanghai subway network. Available sources confirm that the Shanghai Subway has embedded AI in its activities, and it also added further applications, like service robots that carry out automatic patrol inspections and provide

[371] Unattended Train Operation, Grade of Automation Level 4 (unattended train operations), where the train is automatically controlled without any staff on board (Office of Rail and Road, 2022. *Goal-Setting Principles for Railway Health and Safety*, January 2022, https://www.orr.gov.uk/sites/default/files/2022-01/railway-safety-principles-factors-for-safe-operation-of-goa4-uto-trains-consultation.pdf). The Shanghai Metro line 10 initially operated in GoA2 (Semi-automated train operation) and GoA3 (driverless train operation), and transitioned to GoA4 in 2020.

[372] Sh.people, 2021. For the First Time, the Scale of Shanghai Metro's Fully Autonomous Driving Lines Has Jumped to the World's First for the First Time [上海地铁全自动驾驶线路规模首度跃升世界第一]. *Sh.people* [人民网上海], 29 December, http://sh.people.com.cn/n2/2021/1229/c138654-35072981.html. The Pujiang Line since March 2018, Line 18 since December 2020, line 15 since January 2021, and line 14 since December 2021.

Fig. 5.5 Shanghai Railway Transportation Engineering Research Center for Driverless Train Control (*Source* Author)

passengers with information about train schedules and station facilities, among others (Fig. 5.5).[373]

Case Study 14: Jing'an Government Data Management Center (静安政务数据管理中心)

Jing'an District in downtown Shanghai has a resident population of more than one million citizens. Due to its focus on retail, leisure, services, and recreational activities, every day there are on average more than two million people in the district. The creation of the Jing'an Government Data Management Center was announced in January 2018, among the first in the municipality.[374] This projects, also called Jing'an District Government Affairs Brain (静安区政务大脑), was originally established to support the operations of the Government Online-Offline Shanghai as one of its district-level Big Data Centers, and it is located inside the

[373] SAIA, 2021. Shanghai Subway Intelligent Transportation System [上海地铁智慧交通系统]. *Shanghai AI Industry Association* [上海人工智能行业协会], 30 June, http://www.sh-aia.com/dynamics/detail364.htm.

[374] China Central Government, 2018. Shanghai Jing'an Will Be the First to Establish a Government Data Management Center [上海静安将率先成立政务数据管理中心]. *China Central Government* [中华人民共和国中央人民政府], 12 January, http://www.gov.cn/xinwen/2018-01/12/content_5255843.htm.

Jing'an District Government Service Center (上海市静安区行政服务中心). Selected as an AI pilot in April 2019, the Jing'an Government Data Management Center uses data mining and AI-based data analytics to help Jing'an policymakers to "solve the pain points they encounter in planning and decision-making" (解决当前区内公共政策制定机构在规划决策工作中遇到的痛点问题). The ultimate goal is to build an efficient and intelligent "middle platform" (中台, see Sect. 5.1), and become a "benchmark demonstration project" (标杆性示范项目) for AI applications in Shanghai. The applications included in this AI pilot focus on urban governance, and coincide with those of the Single Platform for Urban Management. Developed in cooperation with Tencent, the Jing'an Government Data Management Center uses AI in the following applications[375]:

- *Smart population forecasting* (智能人口预测): it uses AI models to analyze data on the resident population and produce long-term demographic projections (人口长期预测) of the district's residents. During the visit, the author was shown data on the gender and age composition of the population residing in various areas of Jing'an District, and related demographic projections until 2035. These long-term population projections are used for urban planning (see next point). A combination of AI models and computer vision is also used for real-time people flow predictions (实时人流预测). These real-time predictions are used to monitor population agglomeration in key functional areas of the district (such as scenic spots, office areas), in order to assist the decision-makers in various government departments.
- *Smart planning* (智能规划): it includes two main functions. The "facilities smart location" function (设施智能选址) uses AI to analyze population forecasts and other population and spatial data. Based on the projected future needs of the district's residents and

[375] SJTU, CAICT and SHEIC (2019, pp. 130–132); field visit, August 2020; Tencent Net, 2019. The First Batch of Artificial Intelligence Pilot Application Scenarios in China Unveiled, Tencent Helps Shanghai to Build an AI Highland [全国首批人工智能试点应用场景揭榜 腾讯助力上海打造AI高地]. *Tencent Net* [腾讯网], 25 April, https://new.qq.com/cmsn/20190425/20190425009384.html?pc; NetEase, 2019. The "Jing'an Government Affairs Brain" Uses Cutting-Edge Technology to Build a Platform-Based AI Center ["静安政务大脑" 运用前沿技术构建平台型人工智能中枢]. *NetEase* [网易号], 30 August, https://www.163.com/dy/article/ENQQCS2G053469KO.html.

long-term demographic predictions, this AI application helps Jing'an decision-makers to plan the construction of educational, medical, cultural, sports, commercial, and other facilities. The "planning solutions analysis and modelling" (规划方案分析模拟) consists of a machine learning-based AI model that simulates the evolution of urban planning policies, predicting their impacts on the target area and its surroundings. Specifically, this application uses generative adversarial networks (GAN) to train the AI model on data derived from New York, London, Tokyo (all of which make their urban management data publicly available), and other international cities that Jing'an district considers best practices of urban planning.

- *Smart business* (智能营商): this application also includes two main functions. The "industry mapping" (产业地图) function surveys companies operating in Jing'an district, and it uses data analytics to support the activities of economic and industrial district departments, like the Jing'an Investment Promotion Bureau. The "industry analysis" (产业分析) function examines various corporate data (e.g., data on the sales revenues of companies in the district's main shopping malls) in order to create clusters of companies. For instance, it supports Jing'an decision-makers' efforts to concentrate luxury brands of similar level in the same area of the district, as it was explained during the field visit.
- *Smart supervision* (智能监管): this application monitors the business activities and the credit ratings (信用评估打分) of companies located in the district. During the visit, the author was shown business licenses and other financial data of companies operating in Jing'an district. Based on these and other data, Jing'an authorities use AI to carry out credit assessment and risk warning for companies and other business entities within their jurisdiction, track illegal enterprises, and forecast related risks, thus improving the efficiency of market supervision and law enforcement.
- *Smart district sentiment* (智能区情): this application uses Natural Language Processing, computer vision, and other technologies to "capture, classify, analyze and public sentiment in a comprehensive way" (进行全方位的舆情抓取, 归类, 分析和研判). According to the official project presentation, this application allows relevant departments to grasp the dynamics of the district in real time and adopt a proactive approach in propaganda (宣传), service and governance.

This application was not illustrated to the author during the field visit.

The Jing'an Government Data Management Center was visited by the author in August 2020. Fifteen months after the announcement of the AI pilot application scenario, all the aforementioned AI applications were implemented, as illustrated by the Vice Director of the Data Center with the support of big screens that showed the relevant data in real time. As noted, the only application that was not presented during the visit is the "smart district sentiment". However, evidence from similar projects in the Single Platform for Urban Management suggests that this application is also in use. Publicly available information further confirms that the Data Center has integrated AI in its activities.[376]

Case Study 15: The Shanghai Museum (上海博物馆)

Selected as an AI pilot application scenario in August 2019, the Shanghai Museum uses AI in the following applications[377]:

- *Smart guided tours of the museum*: this application has two main functions. First, it uses AI to analyze data on the visitors (e.g., demographics, reason and duration of the visit, sections visited, etc.), and recommend personalized tours of the museum, including visiting routes and other activities. Such data are collected during the online

[376] SHEITC, 2021. "AI + Supervision" Helps Jing'an to Ensure the Accuracy of Protection ["AI + 监管" 助力静安护险精准保障]. *SHEITC*, 26 November, http://dt.sheitc.sh.gov.cn/gqdt/1398.jhtml. In July 2022, the Jing'an Government Data Management Center purchased a remote transaction processing system valued 870,000 RMB. See: http://www.ccgp.gov.cn/cggg/dfgg/cjgg/202207/t20220712_18249012.htm.

[377] SHEITC Notice, 2019b; field visit January 2021; Science and Education Writer, 2020. iFlytek Signs Contract with Shanghai Museum to Create a Benchmark for "Smart Museum" [科大讯飞签约上海博物馆，打造 "智慧化博物馆" 标杆]. *Science and Education Writer* [科教撰稿人], 7 January, retrieved via: https://baijiahao.baidu.com/s?id=1655066491286477614&wfr=spider&for=pc; The Paper, 2020. The Shanghai Museum Will Build a "Smart Venue": AI Exhibition Hall Guidance and AI Cultural Relics Research Take the Lead [上博将打造 "智慧场馆": AI展厅导览和AI文物科研先行]. *The Paper News* [澎湃新闻], 6 January, retrieved via https://baijiahao.baidu.com/s?id=1654975756590652994&wfr=spider&for=pc; Xinhua, 2020. AI Company Helps Shanghai Museum "Go Smart". *Xinhua News*, 7 January, http://www.xinhuanet.com/english/2020-01/07/c_138685760.htm.

registration phase (visitors are required to fill in an online form to book a visit to the Shanghai Museum), and by monitoring the visiting routes of the guests (e.g., checking which audio guides the visitors connect to during their visit, as they use their smartphones to scan the QR code associated to various smart stations/智能展柜). Second, AI is used to provide the visitors with a more immersive experience. The museum allows virtual reality tours, smart interactions with the exhibits on display through augmented reality and mixed reality,[378] and it has multilingual service robots that can answer visitors' standard queries. By January 2021, the Shanghai Museum had tried such applications in different sections of the exhibition area, and it was evaluating where these technologies offer better outcomes.

- *Smart museum management and control*: initially, the Shanghai Museum planned to use AI to manage and control a broad range of activities, such as applying intelligent capture[379] (智能抓取) to the information collected via the online visit reservations system (see above), or using facial recognition for the supervision of the exhibition areas. After encountering unspecified difficulties, the museum decided to focus on smart building management. It applies AI to monitor the electricity and water consumptions of the museum, and other building functions (e.g., monitoring visitors' entries). Despite narrowing the initial scope of smart management, the Vice Director of the Museum Information Center said that the experience accumulated would support deeper AI integration in this area in the new East Branch of the Shanghai Museum (上海博物馆东馆). Once it opens, the East Branch would deploy several AI applications in smart museum management, from BIM[380] to smart supervision of the exhibition areas, according to the Vice Director.

[378] Mixed reality is an extension of augmented reality that allows real and virtual elements to interact in an environment.

[379] Intelligent capture is the process of identifying and extracting critical information from paper and electronic documents without extensive guidance from a user, converting them in digital content. Intelligent capture is based on AI technologies such as Natural Language Processing (NLP) and other AI technologies to trawl through reams of documents to detect, analyze, and classify tables.

[380] Building Information Modeling (BIM) is an intelligent 3D model-based process used in architecture, engineering, and construction to more efficiently plan, design, construct, and manage buildings and infrastructure. Recently some BIM models have

- *AI-assisted restoration of cultural relics*: it uses augmented reality and AI techniques (e.g., machine learning algorithmic analysis) to support the restoration of cultural relics. It provides restoration experts with reconstructed images of incomplete cultural relics that they can use as a basis for restoration, thus improving restoration accuracy, reliability, and efficiency. For instance, restorers and art conservators can virtually project the missing parts of cultural relics, elaborate 3D renderings of the inner parts of vases and other objects, etc. This application also includes a smart platform that facilitates the communications between researchers affiliated to the Shanghai Museum, who are working on the same topic but often are not physically based in the same place.
- *Intelligent research on ancient books and documents*: it leverages Big Data and machine learning to create a smart search tool that examines characteristics of ancient written documents, such as punctuation, text alignment, in order to facilitate the retrieval of the full book. In January 2021, this application was still in the trial phase with the Tongji University.

The Shanghai Museum was visited by the author in January 2021. One and half year after the official start of the project, all the aforementioned AI applications were implemented, as illustrated by the Vice Director of the Museum Information Center. Publicly available information further confirms that the Shanghai Museum has integrated AI in its activities.[381]

Case Study 16: Shanghai Financial Court (上海金融法院)

Selected as an AI pilot application scenario in August 2019, this project focuses on the smart litigation of financial cases (金融案件智慧诉讼). It is promoted by the Shanghai Financial Court, the first specialized financial

started to incorporate AI techniques, for instance in the optimization of BIM model energy performance using Deep Neural Networks.

[381] Tuya, 2021. AI Application Scenario in Smart Museum Solutions [智慧博物馆解决方案之人工智能的场景应用]. *Tuya* [涂鸦], 26 July, https://www.tuya.com/cn/industry-details/Kas9mb535rwvd.

court in China,[382] under the auspices of Shanghai High People's Court. This pilot uses AI in the following applications[383]:

- *Smart litigation* (智慧诉讼): it uses AI for the smart classification and filing of financial cases. It consists of a "smart case filing system" (智助立案系统) that uses OCR and NLP to check legal documents submitted by lawyers. Based on the complexity of each case, the system asks lawyers whether they are willing to accept mediation. In case the lawyers opt for mediation, they can immediately contact professional mediators online through the working station of the court, which has an area dedicated to "smart dispute resolution" (智源解纷区). The "smart litigation" application is also designed to provide guidance and assistance directly to the litigants, who can choose the preferred litigation method (mediation or filing) based on the suggestions of the court's "smart case filing system". In addition, the court created a "smart service area" (智慧服务区) that visually displays the real-time data of the court's litigations, and provides a "one-stop litigation service" by integrating the functions of case inquiry, case filing, application review, payment of litigation fees, communication with judges, and other services.
- *Smart trial of financial cases* (金融案件智慧审判): this application uses AI technologies to assist the courts in solving procedural problems that may arise during the trial. These include "inconsistent case handling[384]" (办案思路不统一), incomplete evidence reviews,

[382] The Shanghai Financial Court was established in April 2018. Shanghai Financial Court website: http://www.shjrfy.gov.cn/jrfy/English/about.jsp. Last accessed on 18 August 2022.

[383] SHEITC Notice, 2020a; Shanghai Law Journal, 2020. Face Recognition! Smart Case Filling! The Shanghai Financial Court Litigation Service Center Gathers "Wisdom" and Makes an Upgraded Appearance! [人脸识别!智助立案!上海金融法院诉讼服务中心 "智慧" 云集, 升级亮相!]. *Shanghai Law Journal* [上海法治报], 11 June, retrieved from: https://baijiahao.baidu.com/s?id=1669134008192482050&wfr=spider&for=pc; Eastday.com, 2020. The Shanghai Financial Court Litigation Service Center Has Been Upgraded! A New "One-Stop" Smart Litigation Service Model Has Been Created [上海金融法院诉讼服务中心升级亮相!打造 "一站式" 智慧诉讼服务新模式]. *Eastday.com* [东方网], 15 June, http://shzw.eastday.com/shzw/n1102226/n1201286/u1ai20580251.html.

[384] The "inconsistent case handling" refers to the "judicial accountability system" (司法责任制) introduced in 2015 by the Supreme People's Court. To prevent excessive inconsistency in sentences, the Supreme People's Court requires that courts carry

or irregular exercise of the right of discretion (自由裁量权行使不规范). By using AI to create model cases based on the sentences of senior judges, this application provides the courts with reference verdicts to adjudicate financial cases, in order to improve the efficiency of the trials and the consistency of court rulings.

- *Smart profiling of the person subject to execution* (被执行人智能画像): this application uses Big Data analysis, OCR, machine learning, NLP, and other AI technologies to mine and analyze information about the assets and whereabouts of the person required to fulfill the obligations set forth by a court ruling. It also serves to automatically identify, parse, and analyze the lawsuits, enforcement cases, and other information related to the person who must fulfill the court obligations.

This AI pilot application scenario of the Shanghai Financial Court builds upon the successful experience of an AI system for supporting judges and prosecutors in criminal trials,[385] which kicked off in February 2017 and started the implementation phase in August 2018. This project, known as System 206 (206工程), was assigned to the Shanghai High People's Court by the national Supreme People's Court nearly two years before the first batch of AI pilot application scenarios. Both the System 206 of the Shanghai High People's Court and the smart litigation of financial cases of the Shanghai Financial Court have been developed in cooperation with iFlytek, a leading AI company specialized in language processing

out a search on the sentences handed down in similar cases before issuing a verdict, in order to ensure that the consistency of judgment criteria. This practice is known as the "mandatory search and reporting mechanism for similar cases" (类案强制检索与报告机制). See: *Several Opinions of the Supreme People's Court on Improving the Judicial Accountability System* (最高人民法院关于完善人民法院司法责任制的若干意见), issued in 2015; and *Opinions of the Supreme People's Court on Implementing the Judicial Accountability System and Improving the Trial Supervision and Management Mechanism (For Trial Implementation)* (最高人民法院关于落实司法责任制完善审判监督管理机制的意见 (试行)), and the *Opinions of the Supreme People's Court on the Implementation of the Judicial Accountability System (For Trial Implementation)* (最高人民法院司法责任制实施意见 (试行)), both issued in 2017. The link between the judicial accountability system and the use of AI in Chinese courts is examined in Yu, M. and Du, G., 2019. Why Are Chinese Courts Turning to AI? *The Diplomat*, January 2019, https://thediplomat.com/2019/01/why-are-chinese-courts-turning-to-ai/.

[385] Cui, Y., 2020. *Artificial Intelligence and Judicial Modernization*. Shanghai: Springer.

technologies. In June 2021, the author had a conversation about the AI pilot for the smart litigation of financial cases with a manager of iFlytek, who confirmed that the Shanghai Financial Court is actively using AI in its operations. Publicly available information further corroborates that the Court has integrated AI in its activities.[386]

References

Berryhill, J., Kok Heang, K., Clogher, R. and McBride, K., 2019. Hello, World: Artificial Intelligence and Its Use in the Public Sector. *OECD Working Papers on Public Governance*, No. 36, https://doi.org/10.1787/726fd39d-en.

Bryman, A., 2012. *Social Research Methods*. 4th ed. New York: Oxford University Press.

Campion, A., Gasco-Hernandez, M., Mikhaylov, S. and Esteve, M., 2020. Managing Artificial Intelligence Deployment in the Public Sector. *Computer*, 53, pp. 28–37, https://www.computer.org/csdl/magazine/co/2020/10/09206418/1npxF00DQru.

Chen, S., 2021. Operational Logic of Governance Platforms in the Digital Ear: The Case of the "Single Platform for Urban Management" in Shanghai [数字时代平台治理的运作逻辑: 以上海 "一网统管" 为例]. *E-government* [电子政务], 8(224), p. 8. https://doi.org/10.16582/j.cnki.dzzw.2021.08.001.

Chen, T., Ran, L. and Gao, X., 2019. AI innovation for advancing public service: The case of China's first Administrative Approval Bureau. *Proceedings of dg.o 2019: 20th Annual International Conference on Digital Government Research*, June 18–20, Dubai, United Arab Emirates. ACM, New York: USA, https://doi.org/10.1145/3325112.3325243.

China Electronics Standardization Institute (CESI), 2022. *White Paper on City Brain Development (2022 edition)* [城市大脑发展白皮书 (2022 版)]. *China Electronics Standardization Institute* [中国电子技术标准化研究院], 5 January, https://www.cesi.cn/202201/8200.html.

Chui, M., Harryson, M., Manyika, J., Roberts, R., Chung, R., van Heteren, A. and Nel, P., 2018. *Notes from the AI frontier: Applying AI for Social Good*. McKinsey Global Institute, https://www.mckinsey.com/featured-insights/artificialintelligence/applying-artificial-intelligence-for-social-good.

Desouza, K., 2018. Delivering Artificial Intelligence in Government: Challenges and Opportunities. *IBM Center for the Business of Government*,

[386] Sohu, 2021. Shanghai Financial Court Explores Parallel Cases and Innovative Practices to Build Intelligent, Intensive, and Professional "Three-in-One" Courts [上海金融法院探索平行案件创新实践建设智能、集约、专业 "三化合一" 法院]. *Sohu* [搜狐], 16 July, https://www.sohu.com/a/477771477_121123741.

Washington, DC: USA, http://www.businessofgovernment.org/report/delivering-artificial-intelligence-government-challenges-and-opportunities.

Desouza, K., 2021. Artificial Intelligence in the Public Sector: A Maturity Model. *IBM Center for the Business of Government*, Washington D.C.: USA, https://www.businessofgovernment.org/report/artificial-intelligence-public-sector-maturity-model.

Ding, J., 2020. Promoting Nationally, Acting Locally: China's next generation AI approach. In: Elliott, H. ed., 2020. *The AI Powered State: China's approach to public sector innovation*. Nesta, May 2020, pp. 11–16, https://www.nesta.org.uk/feature/ai-powered-state/.

Elliott, H. ed., 2020. *The AI Powered State: China's Approach to Public Sector Innovation*. Nesta, May 2020, https://www.nesta.org.uk/feature/ai-powered-state/.

Engin, Z. and Treleaven, P., 2019. Algorithmic Government: Automating Public Services and Supporting Civil Servants in using Data Science Technologies. *The Computer Journal*, 62(3), pp. 448–460, https://doi.org/10.1093/comjnl/bxy082.

Engstrom, F., Ho, D., Sharkey, C., and Cuéllar, M., 2020. *Government by Algorithm: Artificial Intelligence in Federal Administrative Agencies*. Report Submitted to the Administrative Conference of the United States, https://ssrn.com/abstract=3551505.

Han, Z., 2021. Research and Reflection on the Construction of Shanghai "Single Platform for Urban Management" [上海"一网统管"建设探研与思考]. *Shanghai Informatization* [上海信息化], http://www.qikanzj.com/lwfw/dzfw/34226.html.

Liu, W., 2021. Technology Operations and the Construction of a New Organizational Model of "Single Platform for Urban Management" Network [技术运行与"一网统管"新型组织模式的建构]. *Administrative Tribune* [行政论坛], 3(165).

Mao, Y. and Shi-Kupfer, K., 2021. Online public discourse on artificial intelligence and ethics in China: context, content, and implications. *AI & Society*, 16 November, https://doi.org/10.1007/s00146-021-01309-7.

Mehr, H., 2017. Artificial Intelligence for Citizen Services and Government. *Harvard Kennedy School Ash Center for Democratic Governance and Innovation*, August 2017, https://ash.harvard.edu/files/ash/files/artificial_intelligence_for_citizen_services.pdf.

Mikalef, P., Fjørtoft, S. and Torvatn, H., 2019. Artificial Intelligence in the Public Sector: A Study of Challenges and Opportunities for Norwegian Municipalities. *Proceedings of the 18th IFIP WG 6.11 Conference on e-Business, e-Services and e-Society*, 18–20 September, 2019, Trondheim: Norway, pp. 267–277, https://doi.org/10.1007/978-3-030-29374-1.

Mikalef, P. and Gupta, M., 2021. Artificial Intelligence Capability: Conceptualization, Measurement Calibration, and Empirical Study on Its Impact on Organizational Creativity and Firm Performance. *Information & Management*, 58(3), pp. 1–20, https://doi.org/10.1016/j.im.2021.103434.

Mishra, S., Clark, J. and Perrault, C., 2020. *Measurement in AI policy: opportunities and challenges*, 22 September, https://arxiv.org/abs/2009.09071.

Misuraca, G. and van Noordt, C., 2020. *Overview of the Use and Impact of AI in Public Services in the EU*. Luxembourg: Publications Office of the European Union, https://doi.org/10.2760/039619.

Misuraca, G., van Noordt, C. and Boukli, A., 2020. The use of AI in public services: results from a preliminary mapping across the EU. *Proceedings of the 13th International Conference on Theory and Practice of Electronic Governance (ICEGOV 2020)*, 23–25 September 2020, Athens: Greece, pp. 90–99, https://doi.org/10.1145/3428502.3428513.

Modaxia, 2021. How to Manage the "Single Platform for Urban Management" ["一网统管" 怎么管]. *Zhihu* [知乎专栏], 21 September, https://zhuanlan.zhihu.com/p/412455354.

Molinari, F., van Noordt, C., Vaccari, L., Pignatelli, F. and Tangi, L., 2021. *AI Watch. Beyond Pilots: Sustainable Implementation of AI in Public Services*. Luxembourg: Publications Office of the European Union, https://publications.jrc.ec.europa.eu/repository/handle/JRC126665.

OECD (Organisation for Economic Co-operation and Development), 2019. *Artificial Intelligence in Society*. Revised version, August 2019. Paris: OECD Publishing, https://doi.org/10.1787/eedfee77-en.

Oxford Insights and IDRC (International Research Development Centre), 2020. *Government AI Readiness Index 2020*. Oxford Insights and IDRC, on file with the author.

Painter, M. and Pierre, J., 2005. Unpacking Policy Capacity: Issues and Themes. In: Painter M. and Pierre, J. eds., 2005. *Challenges to State Policy Capacity: Global Trends and Comparative Perspectives*. Basingstoke: Palgrave Macmillan, pp. 1–18.

Scantamburlo, T., Charlesworth, A. and Cristianini, N., 2018. Machine decisions and human consequences. On file with the author.

Schaefer, C., Lemmer, K., Kret, K., Ylinen, M., Mikalef, P. and Niehaves, B., 2021. Truth or Dare? – How can we Influence the Adoption of Artificial Intelligence in Municipalities? *Proceedings of the 54th Hawaii International Conference on System Sciences*, pp. 2347–2356, http://hdl.handle.net/10125/70899.

SHFDI (Shanghai Foreign Investment Development Board), 2021. *Shanghai Foreign Investment Guide 2021* [2021上海外商投资指南], https://www.investsh.org.cn/upload/upload/channel/file/2021_2/4_30/04koko3pi67s.pdf.

SJTU, CAICT and SHEIC (Shanghai Jiatong University AI Institute, China Academy of Information and Communications Technology Easter China Institute and Shanghai Economic and Information Development Research Center), ed. 2019. *AI@SH Action Report. Exploration and Practice of Building an Artificial Intelligence Development Highland in Shanghai* [AI@SH 行动报告 - 上海打造人工智能发展高地的探索与实践]. SJTU, CAICT and SHEITC [上海交通大学人工智能研究院, 中国信息通信研究院华东分院, 上海市经济和信息化发展研究中心], on file with the author.

Suiyi, 2021. The Current Situation and Future of "Government Online-Offline Shanghai", I Think It's Better to Make Some Analysis (Forwarded Article) ["一网通办" 现状与未来, 我觉得分析最好的 (转文)]. *Zhihu* [知乎专栏], 1 July, https://zhuanlan.zhihu.com/p/385640455#:~:text=%E4%B8%8A%E6%B5%B7%E2%80%9C%E4%B8%80%E7%BD%91%E9%80%9A%E5%8A%9E%E2%80%9D,%E4%B8%80%E4%BD%93%E5%8C%96%E6%94%BF%E5%8A%A1%E6%9C%8D%E5%8A%A1%E3%80%82.

Sun, T. and Medaglia, R., 2019. Mapping the challenges of artificial intelligence in the public sector: Evidence from public healthcare. Government Information Quarterly, 36 (2), pp. 368–383, https://www.sciencedirect.com/science/article/abs/pii/S0740624X17304781.

Sun, L. and Zhao, N., 2021. Research on the Construction System of the "Single Platform for Urban Management" Urban Operation Platform for Digital Government [数字政府 "一网统管" 城运平台建设体系研究], *Electronics Quality* [电子质量], 12(417).

United Nations, 2020. E-Government Survey 2020. *Digital Government in the Decade of Action for Sustainable Development*. New York: United Nations, https://publicadministration.un.org/en/Research/UN-e-Government-Surveys.

Woo, J., 2021. *Capacity-building and Pandemics. Singapore's Response to Covid-19*. Singapore: Palgrave Macmillan.

Wu, X., Ramesh, M. and Howlett, M., 2015. Policy capacity: A conceptual framework for understanding policy competences and capabilities. Policy and Society, 34, pp. 165-171, https://www.tandfonline.com/doi/full/10.1016/j.polsoc.2015.09.001.

Xinji, 2021. Wisdom First, and Security at Its Escort: Exploration and Practice of Shanghai "Single Platform for Urban Management" [智慧先行 安全护航 - 上海 "一网统管" 的探索与实践], *Informatization Construction* [信息化建设], 2021 (5).

Zhianjun, 2022a. "Shanghai Platform for Urban Management" Name Definition and Operational Structure ["一网统管" 名词定义与运行主体构架], 29 March, https://zhuanlan.zhihu.com/p/489378822.

Zhianjun, 2022b. The Division of Work and Responsibilities Between the Three Levels of Urban Operation Centers [三级城运中心职责分工]. *Zhihu* [知乎专栏], 31 March, https://zhuanlan.zhihu.com/p/490678850.

CHAPTER 6

Ambition, Capacity, Reality, Insights, and Prospects

Since 2017, the Shanghai government has set ambitious targets for AI development, stating that the municipality would become a "national AI development highland" (国家人工智能发展高地). This means that Shanghai aspires to be "China's leading source of AI innovation, demonstration site for applications, industry cluster and talent highland, reaching the world's most advanced levels in some fields".[1] In this context, Shanghai elevated the use of AI in the public sector to a priority of its AI development plans, saying that it would improve public service capabilities and citizens' sense of gain by accelerating the in-depth application of AI in urban governance and public services. In particular, the Shanghai government indicated its intentions to foster the use AI to optimize city operations (i.e., public security, environmental monitoring, infrastructures operation, and maintenance), enhance the quality and efficiency of public services (i.e., administrative services, judiciary, education, culture), improve efficiency of transport and shipping (i.e., urban traffic, maritime logistics), and increase the accuracy and inclusiveness of medicine and healthcare (i.e., medical care, elderly care, public health prevention and control). As the municipality embarked on a journey to promote AI in the public sector, this book examined whether Shanghai is fulfilling its

[1] Shanghai Municipal Government, 2017. *Opinions* (cit.), section 2, preamble. In original: "成为全国领先的人工智能创新策源地、应用示范地、产业集聚地和人才高地，局部领域达到全球先进水平".

D. Todaro, *The Use of Artificial Intelligence in the Public Sector in Shanghai*, https://doi.org/10.1007/978-981-97-0597-9_6

goal to improve public service provision by accelerating AI integration in public sector activities in various policy areas. To do so, this work asked the following research questions: (1) does Shanghai have the capacity to use AI in the public sector? (2) How does this capacity translate into real-world policy initiatives, and what are their strengths and limitations in deploying AI in the public sector? (3) What are the implications of these policy initiatives for public service provision in the municipality?

Answering these questions must confront the fact that scholarship on AI in the public sector provides growing but still limited empirical evidence on the use of AI in public organizations. Accordingly, scholars agree that establishing a common conceptual understanding of AI in this area is a prerequisite for examining opportunities and challenges of AI in the public sector, and it has significant downstream effects on the assessment of the factors that influence the use of AI in the activities of public organizations. Hence, clarifying the meaning of AI in the public sector is a necessary precondition for the in-depth analysis of public sector AI applications in Shanghai, and it has been the starting point of the book. To tackle the problem of conceptualizing AI in the public sector, this work adopted a sociotechnical framework that examines the technical and social factors affecting the use of AI in public sector activities. Guided by this framework, it systematized the prevalent research approaches in public sector AI scholarship in order to derive a set of criteria for the comprehensive study of the technical and social factors that shape the use of AI in the public sector.

Based on these criteria, the book offered a clear conceptualization of "AI in the public sector in China". It presented a workable and technically precise explanation of some key features of contemporary AI systems, at a level suitable for public sector AI research. It identified the main activities where public organizations are currently applying AI and examined the sociotechnical factors that are driving and hindering the use of AI in public organizations. Finally, it examined the country-specific dynamics affecting the use of AI in the public sector in China. By examining these technical, social, and country-specific factors, it defined AI in the public sector as the use of AI systems to support public organizations in performing a range of activities that currently include communicating with the public about its rights and obligations, managing internal resources and public infrastructure, enforcing regulatory mandates, adjudicating government benefits and rights, and monitoring and analyzing public policies. The use of AI in the public sector is driven by the need to improve the operations of public organizations in terms of increased efficiency and effectiveness, improved resource allocation, and enhanced decision-making capabilities; at the same time, the use of AI is hindered by a complex aggregation of technical, legal, ethical, and socioeconomic challenges that reflect the multiple obligations of public sector activities. In addition, in-depth research on the use of AI in the public sector in China must consider the existence of governance mechanisms in central-local relations and the national innovation system that foster the implementation of AI in public sector activities in the country, as well as the implications of the emerging Chinese responses to the regulatory and ethical challenges of AI in the public sector.

This definition of "AI in the public sector in China" outlined with greater precision the domain of investigation of the book. It also provided a solid basis to approach the study of public sector AI applications in Shanghai, because it brought into focus a set of important elements to assess Shanghai's capacity to implement AI in the public sector and its impacts on public service provision. In terms of cross-cutting factors, the analysis argued that the findings on policy capacity derived from documentary research should be refined and validated by fieldwork investigation, in order to account for the sociotechnical complexities of AI in the public sector that could detract from the ability of Shanghai to use AI in this area in practice. The analysis also explained the need to examine the strengths and limitations in AI deployment of real-world policy initiatives that foster public sector AI applications in Shanghai. This serves to identify possible issues that affect the implementation phase, and gain deeper insights into how these policy initiatives impact on public service provision. The examination of country-specific factors showed that the well-known importance of Chinese local administrations in policy implementation is increased by the general-purpose nature of the AI technology. AI projects require the proactive contribution of local governments. Hence, municipal-level policy capacities are crucial for the success of public sector AI applications in Shanghai, and they constitute the primary focus of the analysis. Moreover, country-specific factors showed that the Chinese State maintains its traditional guiding role also in AI policy, confirming that municipal-level policy capacities must be examined in relation to national-level capabilities. This is consistent with the nested model of policy capacity of this book, which examines how the interactions between municipal-level and organizational-level capabilities affect the deployment of AI projects in Shanghai. Finally, country-specific factors highlighted that private companies are key partners for implementing AI in the public sector in China. As such, examining the engagement of private companies in public projects is important not only to assess the policy capacity of Shanghai to bring AI projects to fruition, but also to scope how the dynamics between public agencies and private firms affect public service provision in the municipality.

Building upon these considerations, the book examined whether Shanghai is fulfilling its goal to improve public service provision by accelerating the integration of AI in public sector activities. The analysis was structured in two parts that address the research questions guiding this work. First, it used the policy capacity framework to assess the ability of Shanghai to develop, access, and mobilize the skills and resources necessary to use AI in the public sector. The analysis of the municipal AI policy environment and AI ecosystem provided solid and detailed documentary evidence that Shanghai has the analytical capacity to devise public sector AI applications that can contribute to achieving municipal goals in this area, the political capacity to create and sustain political support for these public sector AI applications, and the operational capacity to orchestrate the resources of the AI ecosystem in order to implement public sector AI applications in practice. Policy capacity is vital to achieve the desired policy outputs and outcomes, and capacity deficits are considered a major cause of policy failure and sub-optimal outcomes. Thus, assessing Shanghai's policy capacity to implement AI in the public sector has been the first, necessary step to examine whether Shanghai is improving public service provision by accelerating the use of AI in public sector activities, because without adequate policy capacity Shanghai would not be able to develop, access, and mobilize the skills and resources necessary to foster the use of AI in the public sector efficiently and effectively.

After demonstrating that Shanghai has a sound policy capacity to use AI in the public sector, the book examined how this capacity translates into real-world policy initiatives that promote the use of AI in this area and gauged their implications for the delivery of public services in the municipality. The analysis started by providing additional evidence on the availability in Shanghai of the skills and resources necessary to use AI in the public sector, showing how these skills and resources are mobilized and put to use to foster public sector AI applications in practice. This focus on the actual impacts of policy capacity on public sector AI applications was motivated by the need to refine and validate the findings of documentary research on Shanghai's AI policy capacity, considering that the sociotechnical complexities of AI in the public sector could detract from the ability of Shanghai to implement AI in this area in practice. This empirical focus was also motivated by the need to outline with greater precision the strategy of Shanghai for AI in the public sector, as a basis for a comprehensive analysis of the case studies. The insights gathered from interviews with key stakeholders of Shanghai's AI policy confirmed and expanded the findings of documentary research, showing that Shanghai has ample policy skills and resources, and it is aptly leveraging them to promote the use of AI in the public sector. By providing a direct account of what Shanghai is doing to stimulate public sector AI applications in practice, the interviews revealed that Shanghai has a coordinated, systemic, and proactive strategy to foster the integration and diffusion of AI in the public sector. This strategy is consistent with the goals of the municipal AI plans to improve public service capacity and citizens' sense of gain by accelerating the in-depth application of AI in urban governance and public services.

To understand how Shanghai's policy capacity enables the implementation of this strategy, the analysis examined the strengths and limitations in deploying AI in the public sector of the main policy initiatives that are fostering public sector AI applications in Shanghai, and it assessed the implications of these initiatives for public service provision. These initiatives can be categorized in two main approaches. One is a platform-based approach that consists of using two municipal digital platforms—the Government Online-Offline Shanghai and the Single Platform for Urban Management—as conduits to integrate AI in the provision of administrative services and urban management services, respectively. The other is an experiment-based approach that aims to foster the use of AI in the public sector by promoting AI trial projects in various policy areas under a program coordinated by the Shanghai government, the "AI pilot application scenarios". The platform-based approach is a very structured method that mainly leverages municipal-level capacities to foster the deep integration of AI in the provision of administrative services and urban management services in the whole municipality, under the tight control and direct operational involvement of the municipal government. The experiment-based approach is a more explorative method that mainly leverages organizational-level capacities to test standalone AI applications that can result in replicable experiences in several policy areas prioritized by the municipality, under the loose coordination and indirect operational involvement of the municipal government.

Both the platform-based and the experiment-based approaches have contributed to improving public service provision by accelerating AI integration in public sector activities in various policy areas: (i) the Government Online-Offline Shanghai and the Single Platform for Urban Management are improving the efficiency in the provision of administrative services and urban management services, while the AI pilot application scenarios have produced several AI solutions that are improving the efficiency of public service delivery in the policy areas prioritized by the municipal government; (ii) the Government Online-Offline Shanghai and the Single Platform for Urban Management have become catalysts for the continuous, progressive integration of AI in administrative services and urban management services, while the AI pilot application scenarios have successfully integrated AI in the provision of public services in the public organizations hosting the trial projects, making the transition from pilots to established applications, and often resulting in the pilot organizations adopting further AI solutions for public service provision; and (iii) the Government Online-Offline Shanghai and the Single Platform for Urban Management are extending the reach of smart administrative service provision and smart urban governance to the majority of citizens in Shanghai by disseminating the use of AI in the public sector at each administrative level and in a great number of government agencies, while the AI pilot application scenarios have created "models" that can spur the diffusion of AI in the public sector by providing valuable learning experiences for other public agencies, displaying success stories that can foster social acceptance for AI in the public sector, and concurring to the municipal efforts to build an enabling environment for public sector AI innovation.

By combining the examination of primary and secondary data, this book showed that Shanghai has solid analytical, political, and operational capacities to implement its ambitious plans for AI in the public sector. These capacities are mobilized in a coordinated, systemic, and proactive strategy, which is manifested in the Government Online-Offline Shanghai, the Single Platform for Urban Management, and the AI pilot application scenarios. The analysis of these case studies highlighted the policy capacities that determine their strengths and limitations in deploying AI in the public sector. It showed that these policy initiatives have improved the provision of public services by successfully integrating AI in public sector activities and have contributed to spurring the diffusion of public sector AI applications in Shanghai. By providing evidence-based insights into the actual ability of Shanghai to implement AI in the public sector and its implications for service delivery, the book demonstrated that the municipality is fulfilling its goal to improve public service provision by accelerating the use of AI in public sector activities in various policy areas.

6.1 Insights and Prospects from China's "AI Highland"

This book offers unprecedented insights into the ambition, capacity, and reality of using AI in the public sector in Shanghai. The significance of these findings goes beyond the study of Shanghai, and the results of this analysis can be used to obtain an improved understanding of key research topics identified by the literature on AI in the public sector. By using Shanghai's experience to gain deeper and practical insights into topics that are relevant to the larger context of research in this area, next paragraphs contribute new knowledge about the use of artificial intelligence to improve public sector operations and the provision of public services. In addition, by assessing the advantages and shortcomings of Shanghai's AI strategy in light of the broader findings of public sector AI scholarship, it is possible to identify the lessons that can be learnt and the unanswered questions that emerge from the experience of the municipality. Bringing into focus these advantages and shortcomings also provides useful elements to gauge the possible development trajectories of public sector AI applications in Shanghai. In these ways, the conclusions of this book provide valuable inputs to researchers and practitioners who are working in the field of AI in the public sector in China and other countries, extending the contribution of this work beyond the findings on current public sector applications in China's "AI highland".

Next paragraphs focus on three research topics. Namely: setting policy goals for AI in the public sector; cooperating with private companies in public sector AI projects; and managing the ethical barriers of AI in the public sector. These topics were chosen for three reasons. First, they cover all stages of the policy cycle[2]; hence, they allow to leverage

[2] Scholars of public policy often conceive the interrelated processes that form policymaking as a policy cycle. Despite being a simplification of the policymaking process, the policy cycle offers a useful heuristic to illustrate how public policies are designed, implemented, and evaluated. It consists of five stages summarized as follows. *Agenda setting* refers to the identification of a problem that requires government intervention. The main

Shanghai's experience to gain an improved understanding of research issues that are important to all the main phases of the use of AI in the public sector. Setting policy goals entails discussions about the problems AI should address (agenda setting), the definition of policy options to tackle the problems that entered the government agenda (policy formulation), and the choice of the particular course of action that relevant policy actors will undertake to address these problems and achieve the desired policy objectives (decision-making). The cooperation with private companies highlights the role of AI companies in translating policy initiatives into practice, and how the dynamics between public agencies and private firms can affect public service provision (policy implementation). The management of AI ethical barriers brings into focus a set of ethical issues that can emerge during the deployment of public sector AI applications and deserve proper consideration—even when, like in Shanghai, ethical concerns do not hinder the adoption of AI (policy implementation and evaluation). The second reason for choosing these research topics is that they are considered important by both the Chinese and English language literature on AI in the public sector. Hence, these topics are useful to draw insights that can contribute new knowledge about the use of AI in this area in both the Chinese and the international contexts, providing valuable inputs to researchers and practitioners

actors involved in agenda setting are public officials, the bureaucracy, the mass media, and interest groups. Their relative influence depends on the characteristics of each socioeconomic and institutional context. The problems that policymakers decide to address enter the policy agenda. *Policy formulation* implies the definition of policy objectives, and the selection of the most appropriate policy instruments and courses of action to achieve these objectives by tackling the problems on the policy agenda. *Decision-making* refers to the formal uptake of a particular policy alternative by government institutions. It is determined by a variety of factors that range from political bargaining to considerations about public opinion or the type of State organization (e.g., federal, unitary). *Implementation* refers to putting the chosen policy alternative into effect. This requires an entity that has sufficient resources and capacity to translate the policy objectives into an operational framework and that is accountable for its actions. Typically, bureaucracies are the principal actors in the implementation stage, although there are several factors that influence how they implement government decisions. *Evaluation* consists of assessing the chosen policy alternative in terms of efficiency (using the least resources to the maximum effect) and effectiveness (achievement of the intended policy goals), among other possible evaluation criteria. Policy evaluation provides a feedback loop, which enables policymakers to draw lessons from each particular policy, identify new policy problems, and set in motion the policymaking process once again. For a more detailed account of these policy processes, see: Knill and Tosun (2008, pp. 9–22), Howlett and Ramesh (2003).

who are interested to examine public sector AI applications in China or in other countries and cities. Third, these are research topics where the experience of Shanghai is particularly illustrative. The case studies not only offer empirical evidence to corroborate the findings of extant public sector AI scholarship, but they also add new elements on how issues related to setting AI policy goals, engaging private companies, and managing AI ethics play out in real-world scenarios. These practical insights are especially important considering that academic research on AI in the public sector still provides limited empirical evidence on the use of AI in this context (Chapter 2.2), thus making the experience of Shanghai extremely valuable to expand knowledge in these areas.

6.1.1 Setting Policy Goals for AI in the Public Sector

Literature on AI in the public sector indicates that the use of AI in this area benefits from having clear policy goals, and from the ability to determine whether and how artificial intelligence is a valuable tool to achieve such goals. Scholars argue that the question should not be how to use AI to solve a given policy problem, but what policy problem must be solved, and how AI can help to solve it (Mehr, 2017, p. 11). When evaluating the use of AI in social domains, public sector decision-makers should focus on determining if and how to apply AI systems and recognize the possibility that the best solution to a problem may not involve technology in the first place (Stanford, 2021b, p. 64; Selbst et al., 2019, pp. 63, 66). Scholars recommend to balance a "tech-first approach" (i.e., assessing which types of social problems can be effectively addressed by current AI technical capabilities) with a "social-first approach" that identifies key public sector problems and determine if and how AI could contribute to resolving them (Chui et al., 2018, pp. 4–5). Similarly, other scholars observe that just because some tasks can be automated or supported by AI technologies, this doesn't mean they should, since not all technically-viable solutions are necessarily adding value to public sector activities (Eggers et al., 2017, p. 18). Indeed, policymakers—like other potential AI users—should first try to clarify and specify the technology support they want to achieve in performing their activities; and in a second, independent step evaluate whether AI can fulfill their requirements.[3] Chinese scholarship also highlights the importance of setting clear goals for AI in the public sector. Policymakers should ensure that AI enhances the quality and value of public service provision in order to improve people's life (Tao, 2020), guaranteeing the "proper use" (恰当运用) of AI in the public sector (Zhang, 2019). In fact, the impacts of AI in this area depend on political choices that strike a balance between the "meaningful prospects" (有意义的前景) and the "crises and challenges" (危机和挑战) that AI can bring to public governance (Mei, 2018). Adopting a top-level design (顶层设计) that defines the priorities for AI development according to China's current socioeconomic conditions is considered necessary to effectively guide AI applications in the public sector (Wu, 2021). Similarly, other scholars observe that the guiding role of policies has been crucial for the sound development of a smart society (智慧社会) in China (Zhang et al., 2019). The need to combine a "tech-first approach" with a "social-first approach" advocated by some international literature is echoed by Chinese scholars, who also argue that public managers "need to find a balance between public value and technical value" (在公共价值和技术价值之间寻找平衡; Yu, 2020).

Literature on AI in the public sector also notes that there are various mechanisms to define the policy goals that AI should achieve in the public sector and the policy options to achieve them. In their comprehensive study, Berryhill et al. (2019) indicate two main approaches that public organizations can use to identify specific problems which AI has the potential to resolve and decide the courses of action to address such problems. In "decentralized, demand-driven approaches", public managers or civil servants in operational roles identify problems that AI can help address and bring in the relevant expertise to realize public service transformation. This decentralized approach facilitates problem-driven iterative adaptation, but it would not necessarily lead to effective prioritization or consistent approaches across government. In "centrally-driven, transformational leadership", potential AI applications are mapped

[3] Email interview with Prof. Wolfgang Bibel, 3 September 2020. Prof. Bibel is a German computer scientist, mathematician and Professor emeritus at the Department of Computer Science of the Technische Universität Darmstadt. He was one of the founders of the research area of artificial intelligence in Germany and Europe and was named as one of the ten most important researchers in the German artificial intelligence history by the Gesellschaft für Informatik.

across government, and expertise and attention are oriented toward areas and problems deemed most likely to benefit from AI. This centralized approach enables consistency, effective prioritization, and systemic approaches, but could lead to missing opportunities better perceived at the ground level. Intermediate solutions that address some weaknesses of these two approaches include: (i) centrally-determined missions or challenges, to which experts both inside and outside government can pitch solutions; (ii) promoting and allocating resources to communities of interest or networks of practitioners, enabling them to collaborate and share expertise across organizational boundaries; and (iii) building up central funds or teams of AI experts, and then encouraging public managers to identify fruitful areas for AI exploration and bid for their time or resources (Berryhill et al., 2019, pp. 98–99).

In addition to these different modulations of government-driven efforts, scholars observe that the use of AI in social domains requires broader discussions that extend beyond government and public agencies. By taking education as an example, Cristianini and Scantamburlo (2019, p. 14) state that the deployment of AI in schools is not only a technical matter, but a decision premised on various assumptions that requires discussions at different levels, from families to the board of teachers (e.g., do all families have access to digital devices? Do all stakeholders agree on the educational values of certain AI uses?). Hager et al. (2017, p. 14) also note that the use of AI in the public sector is ultimately about information and decisions that directly affect the lives of individuals. As such, it is necessary to understand and frame the policy problems that AI should address with respect to the social context, the dynamics, and preferences of the population in question. To support their argument in favor of a broader stakeholder involvement, Selbst et al. (2019, p. 64) emphasize that each relevant social group has a specific idea of what problems the technology needs to solve, and these differences should be accounted for in the design of AI systems in social domains. Chinese scholars also highlight the importance of broader societal engagement in setting the goals for AI in the public sector. Wang and Wang (2019) argue that it is important to promote government-led cooperation between State, companies, and society to ensure that the use of AI in public governance reflect societal needs. Similarly, Zhang (2019) notes the importance to establish a more active interaction between the public and the government when it comes to the use of AI in the provision of public services, and Meng and

Jun (2021) call for strengthening public participation to compensate the shortcomings of a centralized approach to AI in the public sector.

The findings on the use of AI in the public sector in Shanghai offer deeper and practical insights into these research topics. The analysis of the case studies confirms that having clear policy goals for AI in the public sector and well-articulated plans to achieve them is important to develop policy initiatives that efficiently and effectively use AI to improve public service provision. In Shanghai, the processes that define these goals, the possible policy alternatives, and the action plans to pursue such goals are centrally determined by the municipal government. This top-down policy design for AI in the public sector is consistent with Shanghai's coordinated strategy for AI in this area, and it materialized in the programmatic municipal plans that establish the guidelines for the use of AI in the public sector in Shanghai (Chapter 3.2). This top-down policy design is also replicated in the main policy initiatives through which Shanghai is actively integrating AI in the public sector, whereby the municipal government uses official policy documents to set the goals for AI in various policy areas and outline how it will pursue such goals. In the Government Online-Offline Shanghai, the municipality publishes yearly work plans (Table 5.3) that indicate how AI will help to "build a service-oriented government that the people are satisfied with, adhere to the people-centered development concept, meet the requirements of the modernization of government management and service […], further optimize the business environment, and enhance the sense of gain for citizens and enterprises".[4] In the Single Platform for Urban Management, the CPC Shanghai Municipal Committee, the Shanghai Municipal Government, and the Shanghai Government General Office published four policy documents that outline how Shanghai would use AI, Big Data, IoT, and other technologies to "make the city more intelligent and wiser, [and] let the masses have a deeper sense of gain, happiness and security" (Table 5.5).[5] In the AI pilot application scenarios, the Shanghai Municipal

[4] General Office of the CPC Shanghai Municipal Committee, Shanghai Municipal Government, 2018. *Work Plan for Comprehensively Promoting the "Government Online-Offline Shanghai" to Accelerate the Construction of Smart Government* (cit.), preamble, in original: "建设人民满意的服务型政府 […], 坚持以人民为中心的发展思想, 适应政府管理和服务现代化发展需要 […], 进一步优化营商环境, 提升群众和企业获得感".

[5] CPC Shanghai Committee, Shanghai Government General Office, 2020 (cit.), section 1. In original: "让城市更聪明、更智慧, 让群众更有获得感、幸福感、安全感".

Commission for Economy and Informatization selected 40 pilot projects that aim to "improve citizens sense of gain and satisfaction, effectively use artificial intelligence to solve practical bottlenecks and pain points",[6] and it stated that Shanghai would strive to "form replicable and referential experience models that can be applied to the whole city[7]" in the priority areas indicated by the municipal AI plans.

Within the boundaries defined by the Shanghai government, this top-down policy design allows for some decentralization in deciding the means to achieve the goals for AI in the public sector set by the municipal leadership. This approach—which public sector AI scholarship suggests could facilitate problem-driven iterative adaptation (see the "decentralized, demand-driven approaches" above)—is consistent with China's established policymaking practice of "experimentation under hierarchy" (Heilmann, 2008) that focuses on finding innovative policy instruments to achieve policy objectives defined by higher authorities (Chapter 2.3.1). In Shanghai's AI policy, such decentralization has varying degrees, depending on the level of coordination that characterize the policy initiatives through which the municipality is integrating AI in the public sector (Chapter 5.4). In the platform-based approach, the Shanghai Government General Office and its dedicated agencies (i.e., the Shanghai Municipal Big Data Center and the Shanghai Urban Operation Management Center) maintain tight control. In the Government Online-Offline Shanghai, districts can introduce new AI applications for the provision of administrative services, as long as these applications contribute to achieving the goals of the unified e-government platform set by the municipal government. If considered successful, these locally-devised applications may be extended to the whole municipality or emulated by other districts. In the Single Platform for Urban Management, districts and subdistricts have room to devise the AI solutions for urban governance that best meet their requirements, as long as they fall within the five policy areas prioritized by the municipal government and

6 SHEITC Notice, 2019a. *Notice of the Shanghai Municipal Commission of Economy and Informatization on the announcement of the first batch of AI pilot application scenarios in Shanghai* (cit.), art. 2. In original: "提升市民的获得感和满意度 [...] 切实运用人工智能解决实际的瓶颈、痛点问题". The same wording is repeated in the announcement of the second batch of AI pilots in August 2019.

7 Ibid., art. 5. In original: "力争形成可复制、可借鉴的经验模式，在全市进行推广应用".

are consistent with the types of AI-based applications for urban governance indicated by the municipality. In the experiment-based approach, municipal control is looser, and public organizations are encouraged to test AI technologies in their activities based on their organizational needs. At the same time, the AI pilot application scenarios take place under a government program coordinated by the Shanghai Municipal Commission for Economy and Informatization; hence, these organizational experiments must align with and contribute to the goals set by the municipality, which evaluates the results of the projects at the end of the trial period. As such, the pilots promote the use of AI in activities prioritized by the municipal plans for AI development (e.g., use AI to optimize public security and infrastructure maintenance, improve the quality and efficiency of medical and educational services, improve urban traffic management, etc.).

The findings of this book demonstrate that **Shanghai's top-down policy design for AI in the public sector, which allows varying degrees of decentralization in deciding the means to achieve the municipal AI policy goals, facilitates the efficient and effective deployment of AI in public sector activities**. In this perspective, the case studies in Shanghai corroborate the scholarship on AI in the public sector, which argues that intermediate solutions are needed to alleviate the weakness displayed by entirely "centrally-driven" or "demand-driven" methods. At the same time, the experience of Shanghai expands the findings of the literature by offering interesting insights into how "demand-driven" methods can be part of a policy design masterminded by higher level authorities. In Shanghai, public managers and civil servants are given room to decide the most suitable means to achieve the goals set by the municipality under a top-down policy design coordinated by the Shanghai government, which always maintains a clear guiding role in AI policy and steers bottom-up initiatives. The improvements in public service provision achieved by the Government Online-Offline Shanghai, the Single Platform for Urban Management, and the AI pilot application scenarios indicate that Shanghai's capacity to nest some degree of decentralization under an overarching top-down policy design for AI in the public sector can enable consistency, effective prioritization, and systemic approaches, while also intercepting some opportunities that are better perceived at the ground level. The experience of Shanghai shows that this policy design can be a valid intermediate solution between a rigid top-down approach and entirely bottom-up agenda methods, adding a new policy option in the spectrum between these two extremes.

On the other hand, there are no indications that Shanghai will pursue the broader societal engagement in AI policy advocated by the literature. In fact, this seems unlikely in light of China's non-democratic political system and the emphasis of the current national leadership on "top-level design" (顶层设计), which greatly strengthens the roles of central leading groups in the reform and policymaking process in every sector.[8] While there are regular communications between the Shanghai municipality and private companies and expert committees, they mostly serve to provide technical advice to assist the municipality in identifying suitable solutions to achieve government-defined policy goals (Chapter 5.1 and next section). Indeed, evidence indicates that Shanghai intends to maintain a top-down approach to promoting the use of AI in the public sector. On the one hand, the municipal government continues the copious production of policy documents that indicate how AI technologies shall be used in the public sector and it sets the pace for their adoption, as discussed from different angles in the next sections (6.1.2 and 6.1.3). On the other hand, AI development in the public sector has been further consolidated as political priority of the municipal government. AI technologies have officially been encapsulated in a broader masterplan for the digitalization of Shanghai. This masterplan sets goals for using AI and other advanced technologies in economic development, public services, and urban governance, and it outlines how the municipality will pursue these goals. Through this highly-touted masterplan that extends to 2025, the Shanghai leaderships continues to mastermind and coordinate the use of AI in the public sector and the economy, as discussed in the concluding paragraphs.

Despite the good results obtained by Shanghai's top-down policy design for AI in the public sector that incorporates some degree of decentralization, the lack of societal engagement could hinder the effectiveness of the municipal AI strategy. This lack of societal participation does not mean that Shanghai is uncaring of the public service needs of its citizens; it means that, to identify and anticipate such needs, the municipality is primarily relying on technological tools. Shanghai is using data mining,

[8] He, A., 2020. Top-level Design for Supremacy: Economic Policy Making in China under President Xi. *CIGI Papers No. 242*—May 2020, Centre for International Governance Innovation.

advanced profiling, and predictive service delivery to match demand and offer of public services (i.e., the "enjoy without applying"/免申即享 in the Government Online-Offline Shanghai). Shanghai is also leveraging AI-enabled monitoring (e.g., computer vision, smart sensors) to detect and address various urban governance problems as soon as they emerge (i.e., the Single Platform for Urban Management). These technological tools offer promising opportunities to identify and address citizens' needs. However, many of the problems that Shanghai aims to tackle by means of artificial intelligence are "unsolvable", in that they do not have a clear end point where they cease to be a problem. Education, healthcare, public safety, and other areas prioritized by the municipal AI plans are complex societal issues, which public policy scholars sometimes call "wicked" problems because they are long-term, chronic, and/or ill-defined problems that are rooted in many thorny and interdependent causes (Howlett and Ramesh, 2003, p. 192). **If AI has to make an impact on these complex societal issues, policymakers must establish deep and sustained interactions with the target communities**. This is important not only to give "voice" to people in areas where AI directly affects their lives in a critical and personal way (Stanford, 2021b), but also because the effects of AI-enabled policy interventions in these areas are not easily measurable only by algorithms or AI models,[9] and may only become apparent over a period of years or decades (Mishra et al., 2020; Hager et al., 2017). Therefore, "those living with the impact of AI systems will be the most expert on the context and outcome of AI systems", and the regular feedback from the population in question is crucial to better understand the effects of AI on the lives of individuals, and adjust policies when needed (Crawford and Whittaker, 2016). In light of these considerations, can Shanghai effectively use AI to improve the provision of services in education, healthcare, and other complex areas that directly affect the quality of life of its population, if the feedback from those who are meant to benefit from AI is mostly excluded from public sector AI policy? How can Shanghai combine the potential of technological tools with some forms

[9] For instance, controlled trial may be difficult or impossible to construct, and often involve non-discrete (difficult to measure), hidden variables such as engagement/happiness of students in school, satisfaction of patients in hospitals, sense of security of people in a community, etc. (Hager et al., 2017). Other studies also observe the current lack of agreed-upon methods for measuring and assessing the social and economic impacts of AI systems (Mishra et al., 2021; Crawford and Whittaker, 2016).

of societal engagement that allow the municipality to be more responsive to the public service demands of citizens, especially in relation to complex social problems?

6.1.2 *Cooperating with Private Companies in Public Sector AI Projects*

Literature on AI in the public sector underscores the importance and benefits of harnessing private sector expertise and resources to implement public sector AI applications. This focus is not surprising, considering that internationally, like in China, private companies are the main developers and suppliers of AI technologies.[10] Berryhill et al. (2019, p. 89) observe that public organizations need to find efficient ways to access talent, products, and services of the private sector in order to develop their AI capabilities. Wirtz et al. (2019, p. 597) also note that public–private partnerships are crucial to foster public sector AI applications. Based on an extensive literature review, Reis et al. (2019, p. 249) argue that partnering

[10] Molinari et al. (2021, p. 21) report that approximately 70% of global AI investment came from private companies in the period 2012–2018. Other studies confirm this point, while also observing that comparisons between public and private investment volumes are challenging for a number of reasons: nations have different classifications of what constitutes AI R&D; some countries do not report AI R&D figures nor distinguish between private and public money in their announcements; there are no accounting standards for public investment or expenditure in AI; and there is also no standard consensus on labeling AI investment in the private sector (Castro and McLaughlin, 2021, p. 9; Stanford, 2019, p. 98). Nonetheless, available indicators confirm that private investments in AI outpace public ones. Castro and McLaughlin (2021, p. 5) report that in 2019 private investments for AI firms (venture capital and private equity funding) in the United States (estimated USD 14.3 billion), China (estimated USD 5.6 billion) and the European Union (estimated USD 3.2 billion) totalled approximately USD 23.1 billion. By considering statistics that include private investment, public offerings, M&A, and minority stakes, Stanford (2021a, p. 93) sets total corporate investments in AI at a much higher figure of USD 48.8 billion in 2019. These data can be compared with available statistics on government expenditures in the same regions: the United States spent nearly USD 970 million on non-defense AI R&D and roughly USD 3 billion on defense AI R&D in 2019 (Stanford, 2019, pp. 95–97); China estimated expenditure on AI R&D vary widely between USD 2 billion and 8 billion in 2018 (Castro and McLaughlin, 2021; Acharya and Arnold, 2019); and the European Commission announced it planned to invest USD 1.7 billion in AI under its research and innovation program Horizon 2020 (Castro and McLaughlin, 2021, p. 9). Even considering the highest estimate of China's public spending on AI (8 billion USD), government AI spending totaled approximately 13.6 billion USD globally, that is less than 2/3 of the most conservative estimates of private investment (23.1 billion USD) in the same period.

with private companies can improve the ways in which public services are delivered to citizens. Similar considerations on the benefits of harnessing private sector AI expertise can be found in several other English language studies (Stanford, 2021a; Desouza et al., 2020; Engstrom et al., 2020; Oxford Insights and IDRC, 2020; Chui et al., 2018; Hager et al., 2017). In this context, scholars also observe that public procurement—the main channel to engage private sector expertise in public sector AI projects[11]—is an important policy instrument to promote the use of AI in the public sector. Molinari et al. (2021, pp. 12, 50) state that by leveraging its large purchasing power, the government can be the prime mover and a leader in promoting the introduction of AI within the public sector. Misuraca and Van Noordt (2020, p. 85) also recommend the use of "innovative public procurement" to stimulate and speed up AI adoption in the public sector, and they provide several examples of European countries trying to improve their procurement processes to better engage private companies. Scholarship in Chinese language also highlights the importance and benefits of engaging private companies in public sector AI projects. As noted in Appendix I, Chinese scholars argue that the government should establish effective cooperation mechanisms with AI companies to ensure that technological developments in the private sector are applied to public governance (Wu, 2021). The government should also cooperate with AI companies to promote the organic implementation of AI in the public sector, strengthen the planning of smart platforms, and promote the coordinated construction of relevant infrastructure, among others (Kang and Tang, 2021). "Technology is the most direct force for the development

[11] Non-commercial solutions to involve private companies in public sector AI projects are possible, but their importance remain limited compared to the engagement via public procurement. Desouza (2018, p. 33) mentions cases of government agencies using competitions like hackathons to engage external parties, including private companies, in developing solutions for the public sector. Chui et al. (2018) identified about 160 use cases of AI applications of "noncommercial benefit of society" worldwide, which consist of private sector initiatives, or partnerships among the private sector, public sector and/or civil society. Mikhaylov et al. (2018, p. 18) note that cross-sectoral collaborations between government, businesses and universities for public service delivery are emerging in the United Kingdom and internationally, but in several cases, they do not achieve the desired results. Similarly, Engstrom et al. (2020, p. 90) observe that non-commercial initiatives involving private companies in public sector AI projects may be insufficiently attuned to the complexities of tasks of public organizations, they often have problems scalability remain, and in the United States there is mostly no evidence of government adoption or intended adoption of AI solutions created in these initiatives.

of a smart society" (Zhang et al., 2019), and the government should strike a balance between regulating AI companies and reserving space for the development of this new technology, in the public sector like in other areas (Li, 2019). The importance of engaging private companies in public sector AI innovation highlighted by the English and Chinese literature is confirmed by a study of 33 national AI plans, which shows that in most cases national governments acknowledge the critical role the IT sector will play in terms of developing their capacity for AI (Fatima et al., 2020, p. 185).

In spite of being crucial for implementing AI in the public sector, the cooperation with private companies also entails some complexities that have been captured by both the English and Chinese literature. In examining public–private cooperation in AI projects in the United States, Engstrom et al. (2020, pp. 88–90) observe that contracting out AI solutions to private companies has benefits (e.g., it may yield more technically sophisticated AI tools than technologies built in-house, which also are often cheaper than internally-sourced ones). But cooperation with private companies can also make it more difficult for public organizations to obtain well-tailored, policy compliant, and accountable tools; it can impose heavy monitoring and transaction costs; and it raises concerns related to possible conflicts of interests. In a similar study in China focused on public–private partnerships in e-government, scholars also observe that technical and efficiency gains are often paired by challenges like risks in information security and privacy protection, and diverging missions and visions, among others.[12] Berryhill et al. (2019, p. 122) confirm the existence of monitoring and transaction costs in the cooperation with the private sector, as it is the responsibility of the government to ensure the appropriate design and use of the AI solutions provided by private firms, and the compliance of these AI tools with policies and laws. In terms of conflicts of interests and diverging principles, Desouza et al. (2020, p. 211) observe that public organizations must consider the value of AI more holistically than the efficiency gains typically pursued by private firms. In the literature in Chinese language, scholars point to the risks

[12] Liu, T., Yang, X. and Zheng, Y., 2020. Understanding the Evolution of Public–Private Partnerships in Chinese e-Government: Four Stages of Development. *Asia Pacific Journal of Public Administration*, 42(4), pp. 222–247, https://doi.org/10.1080/23276665.2020.1821726.

of government dependence on large enterprises that master the advantages of big data and AI technology (Chen, 2019). They stress that the government should strengthen the regulations of the "data monopoly enterprises" (数据垄断企业) that are deeply involved in public administration and government services (Tao, 2020). The government should also consider the existing forms of "algorithmic coercion" (算法强制) and inducement based on specific commercial interests, as well as the problem of "platform monopoly" (平台垄断), which means that only software in line with the corporate strategy of the platform developer will be accepted by the platform (Li, 2019). Government reliance on technologies developed by the private sector creates risks such as information disclosure and blurs the boundary between the public and private spheres to the point that all kinds of intelligent platforms collect personal information, creating a contradiction between the benefits of information disclosure and the need to protect personal privacy (Wu, 2021). Overall, these research findings on the difficulties in cooperating with the private sector are consistent with a larger corpus of literature emphasizing that public organizations using AI are confronted with a set of ethical, legal, and socioeconomic requirements that can be mostly skirted by private companies.

The findings on the use of AI in the public sector in Shanghai offer an improved knowledge of these research topics, providing further insights into the benefits and complexities of cooperating with private companies. Regarding the benefits of such collaborations, evidence from the interviews and the case studies indicates that the ability to engage private companies is crucial to efficiently develop and implement public sector AI applications. This is because AI companies can support the analytical and operational capacities to implement AI in the public sector both at the municipal and the organizational levels:

- at the municipal level, the Shanghai government has established channels of communications with AI companies through which municipal policymakers can gain access to specialized knowledge in AI. The interviewees revealed that the Shanghai government often communicates with companies to identify feasible and viable technical solutions that can achieve the AI policy goals set by the municipality, and these exchanges are considered important to support the analytical capacities of the Shanghai government to implement AI in the public sector (Chapter 5.1). Cooperation with private companies also supports municipal-level operational capacities. This clearly emerged in the analysis of the platform-based approach, which mainly leverages municipal-level capacities for its successful deployment. The Shanghai Municipal Big Data Center—which is the operational core for data management in both the Government Online-Offline Shanghai and the Single Platform for Urban Management—has established strategic partnerships with private enterprises to support its operations. By cooperating with key technology providers, the Shanghai Municipal Big Data Center not only ensures a stable supply of AI, related technologies, and human resources, but it can also develop tailor-made solutions based on the operational needs of the GOS and SPM systems. Similarly, in the Single Platform for Urban Management, private AI companies are fundamental technical partners of the Shanghai Urban Operation Management Center. They provide the key operational resources needed for the construction of the Shanghai Urban Operation Management Center as well as the functioning of its "city brain", which uses technologies such as Big Data, cloud computing, Internet of Things, artificial intelligence, blockchain and digital twins to perform smart analysis, prediction and planning in urban governance in the whole municipality;

- at the organizational level, in the platform-based approach the standardization of technical requirements and workflows favors the creation of AI solutions that can be replicated across different public agencies joining the Government Online-Offline Shanghai and the Single Platform for Urban Management at different administrative levels. While the ability to standardize is an indicator of municipal-level operational capacity, it nurtures a pool of technology suppliers that have experience in providing replicable AI tools for administrative services and urban governance and thus can support the analytical capacities of public organizations in districts and subdistricts to devise AI solutions aligned with the requirements of the unified e-government platforms. Private companies are also key partners to translate such solutions into practice, thus supporting organizational operational capacities. For instance, in the GOS private firms help district-level Big Data Centers to implement the AI-based services and supply the technologies used by brick-and-mortar administrative service centers; in the SPM, enterprises provide the AI technologies, smart sensors and other digital tools used by the "city brains" of the Urban Operation Centers in districts and subdistricts. In the experiment-based approach, corporate skills and resources support the analytical capacity of public organizations to devise suitable AI solutions for the specific requirements of each AI pilot application scenario. Private sector expertise is a valuable resource for identifying mature AI technologies that have been market-tested for years and can be swiftly integrated in public sector activities, as well as for designing tailor-made, highly-specialized AI solutions jointly developed with the public organizations in charge of the AI pilot application scenarios. In terms of operational capacity, AI companies provide public organizations with the technologies needed to implement AI solutions in each trial project, and the know-how to integrate AI in public organizations and fine-tune such technologies to the needs of public agencies;

The case studies in Shanghai also confirm the complexities of cooperating with private companies in public sector AI projects, which were identified by the literature. The analysis of the AI pilot application scenarios highlighted the difficulties in reconciling the analytical and operational requirements of public organizations with those of private AI companies. In terms of analytical requirements, most AI technologies implemented in the AI application scenarios are developed by private companies, which are driven by a profit-making logic that does not match the policy priorities of public organizations and the provision of public goods and services. This is expected to result in conflicting interests and values between the public and private actors cooperating in public sector AI applications, something that was already documented in earlier national policy initiatives that integrate digital technologies in the public sector in China, like the Social Credit System or the creation of smart courts (see discussions in Chapter 4.4). In terms of operational requirements, the interviewees emphasized that private companies often do not give adequate attention to ethical, legal, and other obligations that instead characterize the activities of public organizations. On the other hand, the analysis of the platform-based approach did not highlight particular complexities in cooperating with private AI companies, neither in academic articles, grey sources nor expert interviews. While there are alternative explanations for not mentioning these complexities,[13] a reasonable interpretation

[13] A possible explanation is self-censorship in both documentary sources and interviews. As noted, public–private cooperation in AI development is endorsed by both the national

is that the difficulties in public–private cooperation in AI projects are not perceived as critical in the Government Online-Offline Shanghai and the Single Platform for Urban Management. In fact, the platform-based approach keeps public agencies in a controlling position that helps to ensure government policy priorities and operational requirements are met when using AI in the public sector, as elaborated below.

This ability to harness AI companies relies on two features that characterize the platform-based approach. First, the development and deployment of the Government Online-Offline Shanghai and the Single Platform for Urban Management are *tightly coordinated* by the municipal government. Both policy initiatives are directly overseen by the top leadership of Shanghai (i.e., the municipal CPC Party Secretary and the Mayor), which guides their implementation by means of policy documents and work plans regularly published by the municipal government and the Shanghai Government General Office—consistently with the top-down policy design for AI in the public sector just examined (6.1.1). In addition, the operations of the Government Online-Offline Shanghai and the Single Platform for Urban Management are centrally orchestrated by the municipal government: both platforms are built upon an integrated digital architecture designed and controlled by the municipality; and their daily activities are coordinated by dedicated municipal agencies like the Shanghai Municipal Big Data Center and the Shanghai Urban Operation Management Center, which supervise the whole network of administrative service provision and urban governance operations down to the

and municipal leaderships: the national government supports it via initiatives like the AI Open Innovation Platforms (AIOIPs) and the Artificial Intelligence Industry Alliance (Chapter 2.2.3.2), while the municipal AI plans also identify public–private cooperation as a key to promote both the AI industry and the use of AI in the public sector (Chapters 4.5 and 5.1, and further elaborated in next paragraphs). Hence, it can hardly be expected that Chinese experts would be keen to criticize such strategic posture in the context of two high-profile policy initiatives like the Government Online-Offline Shanghai and the Single Platform for Urban Management. Regarding the interviews, it must also be noted that among the four respondents that provided the bulk of information on the strengths and limitations of the GOS and the SPM in deploying AI in the public sector: one works for a private company deeply involved in both projects (Shanghai Zhuofan); one works for the State-owned general contractors that coordinates hundreds of private suppliers of the GOS and the SPM (3INESA); and one works for a government entity tasked to promote data exchange between public and private sectors (SDEC). Hence, it is also unlikely that these interviewees would highlight the complexities in public–private AI cooperation. Indeed, even in the AI pilot application scenarios, the challenges in public–private AI cooperation were only mentioned by AI experts or State-owned enterprises.

subdistrict level. Second, the platform-based approach is ***highly standardized***. The construction and operations of the Government Online-Offline Shanghai, both online and offline, are regulated by several local and national standards, which span from the layout and functions of the brick-and-mortar administrative service centers connected to the e-government platform, to information security and other relevant aspects for the use of AI technologies. Companies that want to be suppliers of the GOS have to conform to these standards, and compliance is verified by experts during the project procurement and acceptance phases. In the Single Platform for Urban Management, Shanghai is also striving to unify standards for data collection and usage and to improve the interoperability between the IT systems of the public organizations working together on the e-platform for urban governance. While many of these standards are still developing, there are already indications on how the municipality is using standardization to harness companies' participation in AI projects. For instance, the Light Applications R&D and Empowerment Center of the Shanghai Urban Operation Management Center aggregates, reviews, and supervises the AI tools for urban governance provided to government agencies by private developers, in order to ensure that these technological solutions meet the operational requirements set by the Shanghai government (Chapter 5.2.2). The tightly coordinated and highly standardized methods of the platform-based approach require that AI companies that want to cooperate in the Government Online-Offline Shanghai and the Single Platform for Urban Management conform to the goals and standards set by the Shanghai government, leaving enterprises little room to deviate from the policy priorities and operational requirements of the municipality.

Consistently with the experience accumulated in reaping the benefits and mitigating the complexities of cooperating with AI companies, **Shanghai continues to proactively pursue the engagement of private firms in public sector AI projects, under a framework that prioritizes high levels of coordination and standardization**. In August 2022, the Standing Committee of the Shanghai Municipal People's Congress published the *Regulations of the Shanghai Municipality on Promoting* *the Development of the Artificial Intelligence Industry (draft)*,[14] a well-articulated document that clearly shows the intention of the municipal authorities to coordinate the development of the AI industry, steering it toward applications that local leaders deem beneficial. The *Regulations* call for AI companies to ensure the provision of the AI technologies and products for public sector applications that the Shanghai government wants to see implemented in various policy areas. In smart education (智能教育, art. 53), private companies are encouraged to provide AI technologies that can be integrated "into the whole process of teaching, management, resource construction and other applications", and to "provide more flexible, intelligent, accurate and personalized learning services in a variety of learning scenarios". In smart medical care (智能医疗, art. 54), Shanghai will support private companies that develop intelligent medical systems based on human–machine collaboration as well as flexible, wearable, and biocompatible systems for smart physiological monitoring.[15] It also calls for companies to develop AI technologies for intelligent auxiliary diagnosis, surgical, and other applications and to cooperate with medical institutions to jointly explore use of AI-based medical devices in clinical applications. In smart elderly care (art. 55), enterprises are encouraged to use public data to develop innovative, intelligent and suitable-to-the-elderly healthcare and elderly care products and services,[16] and public institutions are called upon to adopt them in their activities. In urban governance (section 4, 城市治理应用), the municipal government reiterates that it will continue to promote smart government services (art. 56, 智能政务). Shanghai will deepen the integration of the Government Online-Offline Shanghai and the Single Platform for Urban Management, further increasing the use of AI technologies and related

[14] Standing Committee of the Shanghai Municipal People's Congress, 2022. *Regulations of the Shanghai Municipality on Promoting the Development of the Artificial Intelligence Industry (Draft)* [上海市促进人工智能产业发展条例 (草案)], *SHEITC WeChat account*, 30 August, https://mp.weixin.qq.com/s/VUU5zzxIzO6b4tgoAvxhZA. The *Regulations* became effective on 1 October 2022. The number and order of articles in the final version slightly changed, but the contents relevant for this analysis remained unchanged.

[15] Ibid., art 54. In original: 支持医疗机构、企业等应用开发人机协同的智能医疗系统和柔性可穿戴、生物兼容的智能生理监控系统.

[16] Ibid., art 55. In original: 鼓励企业应用公共数据, 为市民开发更多创新、智能化、适老化的健康养老产品和服务.

investments to build an AI platform for government services, decision-making, and urban operations. In doing so, the government will build smart urban infrastructure (art. 57) and a "smart hub for urban operations", and it encourages enterprises to "develop AI general technology components for various application scenarios in digital cities" in the areas prioritized by the Single Platform for Urban Management[17] (art. 58–59). Art. 60 confirms that the use AI for the analysis of judicial cases and legal documents, evidence collection, and other applications of "smart justice" (智慧司法) remains a priority of the Shanghai government. Finally, the *Regulations* emphasize the importance of industry governance (section 5, 产业治理). They reiterate that the Shanghai government guides the development and safety of the AI industry, and relevant municipal departments will carry out safety inspections and supervision on AI applications (art. 61). AI applications will be evaluated by relevant government departments based on their risk level, application area and expected "impact scope" (影响范围, art. 63). The *Regulations* indicate the AI technologies that Shanghai wants to see implemented in public sector applications and reiterate the guiding political role of the municipality in the development of the AI industry. In doing so, the *Regulations* confirm that the municipal leadership will maintain a controlling position when engaging private companies in public sector AI projects, steering them toward the policy priorities set by the Shanghai government.

The August 2022 *Regulations* also confirm that the engagement of AI companies in public sector applications will take place in an increasingly standardized environment. The *Regulations* state that Shanghai will set standards for data labeling (数据标注, art. 16), the hardware and software of smart robots (art. 40), and it will spearhead the mutual recognition of technical AI standards in the Yangtze River Delta (art. 10). The document also contains an article dedicated to the "Shanghai standards" (art. 35, 上海标准). It states that the Market Supervision Bureau and the SHEITC will promote the formulation of local standards for artificial intelligence and will also guide enterprises and industry associations to propose the formulation of industrial AI standards in areas

[17] Ibid., art 58. In original: 鼓励企业开发面向数字城市不同应用场景的人工智能通用技术组件. Art. 59 reiterates that the priority areas for urban governance applications include "government services, community governance, public safety, traffic management, emergency management, planning and construction, market supervision, ecological environment".

such as algorithm performance, data security, privacy protection, product compatibility, and performance testing. In addition, after voluntary application and evaluation by a third-party institution, companies that meet leading domestic and international requirements will be granted the logo "AI Shanghai standard" (人工智能上海标准). The importance of AI standardization was already highlighted in the guidelines and regulations on using and sharing public data in the municipality (Chapter 4.1.2), and it is reiterated by the *14th Five-Year Plan for the Development of Shanghai Artificial Intelligence Industry*.[18] This consistent attention to standardization confirms that the Shanghai government will continue to use standards as a tool to ensure that companies meet the operational requirements set by the municipality. Indeed, while companies are actively involved in the formulation of AI standards, government-driven technical organizations ensure that municipal priorities prevail over the interests of enterprises in standard setting. A case in point, the Shanghai Municipal Technical Committee for AI Standardization (上海市人工智能标准化技术委员会), created in July 2021, has been very active in promoting local AI standards in cooperation with the government-led Shanghai AI Industry Association.[19] It should also be emphasized that the standardization of processes and technical requirements offers several advantages to the use of AI in the public sector that go beyond meeting the operational requirements set by the government. As noted, a standardized approach facilitates the integration of AI by favoring the creation of AI solutions that can be replicated across public organizations (5.2 and earlier in this section); it can contribute to addressing the challenges of scaling up AI applications, as discussed in the analysis of the AI pilot application scenarios (5.3); and it can help to tackle emerging challenges related to

[18] SHEITC, 2021. *14th Five-Year Plan for the Development of Shanghai Artificial Intelligence Industry* [上海市人工智能产业发展 "十四五" 规划], Hujingxinzhi (2021) 1195, 27 December, http://sheitc.sh.gov.cn/cyfz/20211228/29259791c2fd46a2aff8b0dc09d4f8e6.html. Specifically: section 3, "Development goals" (发展目标); section 4, "Main tasks" (主要任务), par. 2, point 3 "improve data basic support system" (完善数据基础支撑体系); section 4, par. 6 "Optimize the overall environment and create a vibrant industrial ecology" (优化综合环境, 打造活力迸发的产业生态).

[19] The Paper, 2021. Shanghai AI Standardization Technical Committee was established, and recently completed the preparation of the standard system [上海市人工智能标准化技术委员会成立, 近期完成标准体系编制]. *The Paper* [澎湃新闻], 10 July, https://www.thepaper.cn/newsDetail_forward_13518010. The AI standardization committees works under the guidance of the Shanghai Municipal Market Supervision Commission.

data privacy and security (5.2, 6.1.3). In public sector like in other applications, setting standards for AI is also a way to promote the political and economic interests of the Chinese government, both nationally and internationally.[20] Among these different motivations of AI standardization, Shanghai shows that setting standards is a useful policy instrument to ensure that enterprises follow the operational requirements set by the government in public sector AI projects, establishing some benchmarks that companies have to meet in practice even if they are not formally compulsory.

The experience of Shanghai expands the findings of the literature by providing practical insights on the importance and benefits of engaging private companies. The analysis of the case studies indicates that companies can provide a package of technical and managerial solutions to

[20] Experts of China's AI policy identify a number of drivers for the Chinese government standardization efforts. These include: domestic policy-oriented standards act like a form of regulation, spelling out requirements that companies can be audited against, even if they are not formally binding; standardization can generate more value out of AI technologies by facilitating data pooling and improving the interoperability of systems (as noted in this work in Chapter 5.2); standardization can strengthen the commercial competitiveness of Chinese companies globally, as standards include patents for which companies receive royalties when other firms build equipment using their patents; standardization can improve the quality of AI products and services, thus reducing the risks of societal backlash to technology, consistently with China's efforts to ensure that AI does not disrupt social stability (see discussions about social acceptance in Chapter 4.5); and standardization can help China to take a leading role in international governance on the safety (and ethics) of AI, reflecting long-standing concerns that Chinese representatives were not at the table to help set the rules of the game for the global Internet. See: Ding, J., Triolo, P. and Sacks, S., 2018. Chinese Interests Take a Big Seat at the AI Governance Table: Government and Industry Team to Shape Emerging AI Standards-Setting Process. *New America*, blog post, 20 June, https://www.newamerica.org/cybersecurity-initiative/digichina/blog/chinese-interests-take-big-seat-ai-governance-table/. Similar considerations on the use of standards to increase China's international influence can be found in commentaries related to *China Standardization 2035*, a 15-year blueprint that lays out Chinese plans to set the global standards for the next-generation technologies, including AI. See for instance: Smart Manufacturing, 2020. "China Standards 2035" ready to come out, this is the real key to Sino-U.S. tech competition [《中国标准2035》呼之欲出，这才是中美科技竞争的关键]. *Smart Manufacturing* [智能制造], 26 September, https://mp.weixin.qq.com/s/U07bu0YL7J0NQSGf732xgg?fbclid=IwAR239LpawuFVM0mJAgf74ducrk3SaNiLvQHhvU9WxcIaIWLfF8kNcBZbkBE; Wilson, N., 2020. China Standards 2035 and the Plan for World Domination—Don't Believe China's Hype. *Council on Foreign Relations*, blog post, 3 June, https://www.cfr.org/blog/china-standards-2035-and-plan-world-domination-dont-believe-chinas-hype.

support the analytical and operational capacities of public organizations to implement AI in the public sector, at the municipal level as well as the organizational level. In doing so, the analysis identifies with greater precision the contribution that can be made by the private sector to improve public service provision and public sector operations. Case studies in Shanghai also highlight the complexities of cooperating with private companies in public sector AI projects. The analysis confirms the findings of the literature in relation to the experiment-based approach, while also providing novel insights on how the tightly coordinated and highly standardized methods of the platform-based approach can address such complexities, keeping the public sector in a controlling position and thus helping to ensure that government policy priorities and operational requirements are met when using market-sourced AI in public sector activities. Pilot applications continue to exist, as they are instrumental in accelerating the integration of AI in the public sector, which remains a central feature of Shanghai's AI strategy (see infra, 6.1.3 and 6.2). At the same time, the development plans of the local AI industry and the ongoing efforts to promote AI standardization in the municipality indicate that Shanghai will prioritize high levels of coordination and standardization in order to better harness private sector expertise and resources in public sector AI projects. This evidence is further corroborated by interviews with local AI experts, who state that the SHEITC was displeased by the fact that some AI pilot application scenarios were primarily driven by corporate interests rather than the requirements of public organizations, and the Commission will likely seek greater control over private firms in public sector AI projects (AISPi). Seeking increased control over AI companies is also in line with existing national trends. In September 2022, the Central Commission for Comprehensively Deepening Reform presided by Xi Jinping called for stricter Party leadership and more centralized decision-making "to achieve breakthroughs in core technologies in key fields", optimizing the allocation of "innovation resources" based on China's strategic needs.[21]

[21] National Committee of the Chinese People's Political Consultative Conference, 2022. Xi stresses improving system for achieving breakthroughs in core technologies in key fields. *National Committee of the Chinese People's Political Consultative Conference*, 7 September, http://en.cppcc.gov.cn/2022-09/07/c_808759.htm.

Literature agrees that harnessing private sector expertise and resources in AI is crucial to improve the ways in which public services are delivered to citizens. The case studies show that Shanghai has been very successful in involving private AI companies in public sector projects: it ensured that public organizations at each administrative level can have access to the technologies needed to foster AI adoption in their activities; it leverages the skills and resources of private firms to support the analytical and operational capacities of public organizations to implement AI in the public sector; and it has the ability to engage AI firms in a way that ensures that government policy priorities are met in public sector AI projects. However, earlier research also suggests that harnessing private sector expertise and resources is per se not sufficient to ensure that the benefits of AI-based public services are evenly accessible to the majority of the population. First, if the benefits of AI are to be universalized through existing public sector systems, it is important to create sufficient capabilities across the public organizations that have to deliver AI-based public services to society (Engstrom et al., 2020; Liu, 2020; Sun and Medaglia, 2019). Shanghai has shown great attention to this aspect, and it is leveraging municipal-level capacities—and the skills and resources of private firms—to support and nurture policy capacities of public organizations across the city (5.4). Evidence suggests that Shanghai has been quite successful in this respect: the varying degrees of AI assimilation in public organizations currently are not resulting in the uneven provision public services (5.2.1.2, 5.2.2.2), and the AI pilot application scenarios have integrated AI in public organizations in various policy areas (5.3.3). In addition, both the platform-based and experiment-based approach have contributed to fostering the diffusion of public sector AI applications across public agencies in the municipality (5.4). Second, previous studies also indicate that **ensuring that the benefits of AI in the public sector reach the majority of citizens requires inclusive innovation policies.** Such policies address not only the capabilities of public organizations, but also the variety of factors that can create a digital gap among citizens, from different levels of digital literacy to socioeconomic disparities and other elements affecting equal access to AI-based services[22] (Stanford, 2021b; Liu, 2020; Crawford and Whittaker, 2016). In this context, the experience of Shanghai elicits a fundamental question about ensuring that the benefits of public sector AI innovation are equally shared by a broad section of society. By successfully engaging private AI companies in public sector projects, Shanghai has gained access to the technologies and expertise needed to increase the effectiveness and efficiency of the public services being provided to its citizens. Can Shanghai also ensure equity of access to such services, so that the benefits of AI technologies are universalized through the public sector? In addition to supporting the capabilities of public organizations, which additional policy actions are needed to ensure that the use of AI in the public sector enhances the quality of life of the majority of the population, avoiding the risk that public sector AI innovation widens inequalities and exacerbates the marginalization of certain social groups?

6.1.3 *Managing the Ethical Challenges of AI in the Public Sector*

Literature on AI in the public sector notes that there are several ethical challenges related to the use of AI in this area. These challenges were presented in Chapter 2.2.2 and are briefly recalled here. Scholarship in English and Chinese language emphasizes that public organizations must consider issues of explainability and transparency, including the consequences deriving from possible misjudgements in AI-based decision-making, or the fact that the process that led to AI-based decisions may not be interpreted by humans (Engstrom et al., 2020; Henman, 2020; Kankanhalli et al., 2019; Sun and Medaglia, 2019; Chui et al., 2018). Scholars also observe the challenge of creating ethical consistency among AI systems and humans (Dwivedi et al., 2021; Wirtz et al., 2019). Moral dilemmas can be a barrier to AI applications in the public sector (Xu and Xu, 2020; Kankanhalli et al., 2019; Wirtz et al., 2019), just like the challenges related to AI discrimination arising from the profiling capabilities of AI systems, the absorption of human prejudices through the design of AI algorithms, or the use of datasets that include biases (Kang and Tang,

[22] See for instance: Stanley, I., Glennie, A. and Gabriel, M., 2018. *How Inclusive is Innovation Policy? Insights from an International Comparison*. Nesta, https://media.nesta.org.uk/documents/How_inclusive_is_innovation_policy__Insights_from_an_international_comparison_v3.pdf.

2021; Li and Li, 2021; Henman, 2020; Chen et al., 2019; Dwivedi et al., 2021; Tinholt et al., 2019; Chui et al., 2018). Public sector AI scholarship also identifies issues related to administrative ethics (i.e., can machines have the same legitimacy of civil servant? Chen et al., 2019), the unethical use of data sharing and potential cases of privacy abuses (Wu, 2021; Sun and Medaglia, 2019), or the challenge of evaluating the ethical costs and benefits of using AI in public organizations (Desouza, 2021; Hager et al., 2017).

Literature on AI in the public sector also states that the responses to these ethical challenges are highly context-specific. This means that the impacts of such challenges on the adoption and implementation of AI in the public sector vary across different socioeconomic milieus. Experts about AI in social domains observe that the ethical concerns in the use of technology may have different importance in different societies (Wirtz et al., 2019). Scantamburlo et al. (2018) agree that the nature and degree of observance of the normative principles that should regulate AI systems change according to cultural and disciplinary expectations. Based upon these insights, Chapter 2.2.3 reviewed six AI ethics initiatives issued by Chinese government institutions between 2017 and 2022, independently or in collaborative efforts with private companies and/or public research institutes. It concluded that there is no evidence that these initiatives are creating any barriers of AI adoption and implementation in the public sector in China. The review highlighted that: (i) Chinese AI ethics initiatives are scarcely actionable and not embedded in the processes and institutions that shape decision-making within government (like most other AI ethics initiatives worldwide; Stanford, 2021a; Berryhill et al., 2019; Calo, 2017); (ii) the State remains the final judge of the ethical values that should regulate the AI technology, meaning that the Party-State is the arbitrator of how and to whom these values should apply (Lee, 2022); (iii) despite these AI ethics initiatives, there is evidence that the State is making an extensive use of technology for social control, and China has established "a culture of pervasive monitoring of citizens" (Creemers, 2020; Gal, 2020); and (iv) despite some signs of change, Chinese AI ethics guidelines have an "opaque nature" and a low level of engagement with international initiatives (Arcesati, 2021; Ding, 2018). While Chinese initiatives in AI ethics dispel misconceptions that the country lacks debate around the ethical use of AI, they do not hinder the deployment of AI technologies in the public sector.

Against this background, Shanghai displays a counterintuitive combination of two apparently irreconcilable elements. On the one hand, *there are high levels of attention to AI ethics*, codified in the main municipal plans for AI development and in the major public sector AI initiatives (see next paragraph). Such attention has translated into practices that aim to mitigate the ethical risks of AI (e.g., standards on data privacy and security, Chapter 5.2; sandboxes, Chapter 5.3). It also resulted in a growing awareness of issues related to AI ethics in Shanghai public organizations (e.g., privacy and safety, see Chapter 5.1). On the other hand, the case studies confirm that *ethical issues are not creating perceptible barriers to AI implementation in the public sector*, as demonstrated by the existence of a number of AI pilot application scenarios that introduced intrusive applications that infringe on personal privacy and raise ethical concerns[23] (Chapter 5.3). By examining these two conflicting elements in light of Shanghai's AI policy environment, it is possible to derive useful insights into the context-specific factors that shape the responses to the ethical challenges of AI in the public sector in the municipality, and argue that such insights can be generalized to other socioeconomic contexts.

The municipal policy documents for AI development emphasize the importance of ensuring ethical AI applications in economic development, urban governance, and public services. In October 2017, the *Opinions* stated that Shanghai would "strengthen research on AI ethics, legal protection, and social issues, and establish institutional norms and ethical frameworks to ensure the healthy development of AI".[24] In September 2019, the *AI Highland Plan* reiterated that Shanghai "encourages relevant parties to carry out research on information security, privacy protection, ethics, laws and regulations in the field of AI". It also called for the creation of an expert working group to carry out research on

[23] These intrusive applications were examined as a potential limitation of the AI pilots in deploying AI in the public sector because they could start to generate opposition from the target population. However, it was also observed that these intrusive applications have not been halted due to ethical concerns (Appendix VI).

[24] Shanghai Municipal People's Government, 2017. *Implementation Opinions on Promoting the Development of a New Generation Artificial Intelligence in Shanghai*, cit., section 5, par. 6 (加强人工智能伦理道德、法制保障和社会问题研究，建立保障人工智能健康发展的制度规范和伦理道德框架).

AI governance in areas such as information security and privacy protection.[25] The main public sector AI initiatives in Shanghai reiterate and operationalize this attention to AI ethics. In the platform-based approach, the municipality emphasizes the importance to address data privacy and security risks, two ethical concerns in the use of AI in the public sector commonly indicated by Chinese AI ethics initiatives (Appendix II). In the Government Online-Offline Shanghai, the municipality states that it will "strengthen the creation of institutionalized rules (制度规则) for data flow, technical security, privacy protection, ethics and other aspects". In the Single Platform for Urban Management, the Shanghai government requires that departments and agencies establish and improve mechanisms for risk assessment, security review, daily monitoring, emergency response, and strengthen the protection of data and personal information in accordance with the law. In the experiment-based approach, the SHEITC recommends public organizations in the AI pilot application scenarios to ensure information security and protect data privacy. In addition, the AI pilot application scenarios serve as sandboxes and testbeds for evaluating public sector AI applications in controlled environments—which the literature considers a best practice to combine public sector AI innovation with attention to safety. The attention of Shanghai to the ethical concerns raised by AI in the public sector was also emphasized during the interviews, which showed that public organizations in the municipality have a growing awareness of issues such as data privacy and security, possible shifts in social acceptance, and AI safety.

Despite this policy attention to AI ethics, the analysis of the case studies shows that in Shanghai there are some public sector AI applications that raise ethical concerns. The analysis of the AI pilot application scenarios highlighted a number of intrusive applications that infringe on personal privacy. For instance, the "campus smart security systems" (校园智能安保) and "smart classrooms" (智能课堂) use AI to monitor and analyze the behavior of students (e.g., whether pupils say hello to teachers, line up orderly, etc.), including in classroom activities (e.g., monitoring actions like sitting, raising hands or yawning, and examine

[25] SHEITC, 2019d. *Action Plan on Building Shanghai into an AI Highland and Creating First-Class Innovation Ecosystem (2019–2021)*, cit., art. 18 (鼓励有关方面开展人工智能领域信息安全、隐私保护、道德伦理、法规制度等研究) and Special Action 7: Take the lead in building an institutional system for AI governance (组件人工智能信息安全、隐私保护、知识产权、大数据等专家工作组, 围绕人工智能治理开展相应研究).

these data to make assessment on learning status, classroom effectiveness, and learning interest). Some AI pilot applications also potentially violate civil liberties. The "smart district sentiment" (智能区情) application leverages NLP, computer vision, and other technologies to capture and monitor public opinion. In addition, the Government Online-Offline Shanghai and the Single Platform for Urban Management also include AI applications that could raise potential ethical concerns. For instance, the Government Online-Offline Shanghai leverages the ability of AI systems to profile individuals and groups based on environmental characteristics (e.g., user information) and previous interactions in order to provide personalized service recommendations and predict users' needs. While these profiling capabilities are currently being used to optimize citizen services, they are potentially problematic because they could lead to new forms of discrimination.[26] On a similar note, the Single Platform for Urban Management makes extensive use of computer vision to analyze the images and videos collected by traffic and surveillance cameras to identify various urban governance issues. While this improves the efficiency of urban management services at each administrative level, it also extends the penetration of AI-enabled control to residential communities and each single street in the municipality. In addition, both the Government Online-Offline Shanghai and the Single Platform for Urban Management collect and combine huge quantities of personal information to support their activities, creating risks related to data privacy[27] and

[26] AI systems profiling capabilities can create groups of people based on more varied characteristics (e.g., habits, online and offline activities, network of personal relationships, etc.) than other demographic criteria (age, race, gender, marital status, etc.). This more detailed profiling can have positive effects, such as enabling tailor-made or predictive public services, but it can also potentially lead to broader discrimination by creating new collectives (Makasi et al., 2021, p. 12).

[27] Some information that is not sensitive when used alone could significantly undermine privacy, if used in combination with other data contained in municipal databases or other sources. Previous studies demonstrated that the vast majority of American citizens can be identified using only three pieces of "anonymized data": ZIP code, birthdate, and gender. See: Sweeney, L., 2000. *Simple demographics often identify people uniquely*. Carnegie Mellon University, Data Privacy Working Paper 3. See also, Malin, B., Sweeney, L. and Newton, E., 2003. *Trail re-identification: learning who you are from where you have been*. LIDAP-WP12, Carnegie Mellon University. Making an example from the private sector, other scholars observe that data on movie recommendations and viewing habits combined with movie database could potentially identify sexual and political information, which in some countries can put individuals in physical or psychological danger (Chui et al., 2018, p. 39).

security (as exposed by the data leak of the Shanghai police department revealed in July 2022, mentioned earlier).

By examining this counterintuitive combination of ethical awareness and problematic applications in light of the AI policy environment of Shanghai, it is possible to derive useful insights into the context-specific factors that shape the responses to the ethical challenges of AI in the public sector. In particular, **the experience of Shanghai shows the influence that public sector AI strategies exert on the management of ethical issues in a certain socioeconomic context**. As noted, Shanghai is pursuing a strategy that actively accelerates AI integration in the public sector, consistently with the goals of the municipal AI plans to improve public service capacity and citizens' sense of gain by fast-tracking the use of AI in urban governance and public services. This strategy has translated in policy initiatives that clearly prioritizes the rapid implementation and diffusion of AI in the public sector (Chapter 5). In this context, addressing the ethical concerns arising from public sector AI applications is of secondary importance. Indeed, as just recalled, there is no evidence that ethical concerns are hindering the fast deployment of AI in public organizations in Shanghai. This corroborates the findings of earlier studies arguing that public sector AI applications in Chinese cities are currently driven by a "development imperative" that prioritizes speeding up technological advances, data collection and implementing pilots over issues like risk management and data privacy (Han, 2020; Oxford Insights and IDRC, 2020). At the same time, the experience of Shanghai expands previous research by showing that this "development imperative" can be explicitly codified into an AI policy strategy, and by providing empirical insights into how such strategy shapes the management of AI ethics in the public sector in practice. Clearly, there are other context-specific factors that concur to determine the responses to AI ethical issues arising in the provision of public services. In China, these factors include: unique ethical, cultural and philosophical foundations, and debates around how to apply concepts derived from these foundations (e.g., the notion of "harmony") to AI ethics (Gal, 2020); an entrenched techno-utilitarian approach that considers technology a tool to strengthen State authority and achieve national strategic goals, and a broad connotation of social governance that traditionally pursues engineering-type solutions to gain a holistic control of society (Chapter 1); the ideological view that AI is a useful tool to improve the provision of public services as well as a channel for more effective social and political control (Chapter 3.1); or Chinese citizens' high level of social acceptance for AI (Chapters 4.5 and 5.1), and their general willingness to share personal data in exchange for convenient public services (Chun, 2020); among others. However, the existence of disparate context-specific elements does not diminish the influence that public sector AI strategies exert on the management of ethical issues arising in public sector activities. In fact, the government is the main regulator of and gatekeeper to AI applications in public organizations in virtually every socioeconomic context (Dwivedi et al., 2021; Misuraca and van Noordt, 2020; Berryhill et al., 2019; Mikhaylov et al., 2018). Therefore, the AI policy strategies pursued by governments are expected to have direct and tangible impacts on the management of ethical issues in public organizations. As such, they offer a useful framing device to interpret the decisions made about transparency, accountability, privacy, security, and other ethical issues in public sector AI applications in a given socioeconomic context, while also providing a valuable heuristic to gauge how public organizations in different localities will address the ethical issues of using AI. This inference drawn from the experience of Shanghai is corroborated at the macro level. The importance of AI strategies in guiding AI development is widely acknowledged by several studies, and an emerging body of research is trying to assess how the relative importance attributed to AI ethics in national AI plans impacts on AI applications (Fatima et al., 2021; Stanford, 2021a; Oxford Insights and IDRC, 2020). In addition, previous researchers also highlighted how different strategic approaches to AI development between China and other countries influence the management of ethical issues in AI applications in the public sector and other areas (Lee, 2022; Elliot, 2020; Roberts et al., 2020).

The experience of Shanghai demonstrates that actively fostering the integration and diffusion of AI in public sector activities can help the government to improve the efficiency and convenience of administrative service provision (the Government Online-Offline Shanghai), enhance public security, urban management, emergency response and other urban management services (the Single Platform for Urban Management), and improve public service provision in areas spanning from education to health and public transport (the AI pilot application scenarios). The capacity to rapidly assimilate AI in public sector activities can also help the government to be more reactive in addressing policy problems as they emerge. Shanghai's response to the Covid-19 pandemic is a case in point, despite some ethical concerns mentioned shortly. In light of these benefits, it is perhaps not surprising that **Shanghai continues to**

focus on accelerating the implementation of AI in the public sector, as indicated by the major plans for the AI industry issued in 2021 and 2022. While confirming the attention to AI ethics,[28] these plans strongly emphasize the municipal intentions to foster the practical applications of AI in the public sector, bringing AI technologies to fruition in this area. The *14th Five-Year Plan for the AI industry* confirms that Shanghai will deepen the use of AI and promote larger-scale integrated applications[29] (更大规模的融合应用) in economic development, citizen services (medical care, education, security in residential communities, transport, public services), and urban governance (government services, urban management, community governance, traffic management, emergency management, planning and construction, market supervision, environment).[30] To accelerate these applications, Shanghai will continue to explore the use of pilots and sandboxes.[31] The *Regulations* convey the same message. Shanghai will continue to foster the implementation of AI

[28] The *14th Five-Year Plan for the AI Industry* states that Shanghai will deepen research on the ethics of AI technology, formulate ethical standards for AI systems, establish and improve industry supervision mechanisms, formulate codes of conduct for practitioners, and strengthen ethics education and training. See: Section 4 "Main tasks", par. 6 "Optimize the overall environment and create a vibrant industrial ecology" (优化综合环境, 打造活力迸发的产业生态), subparagraph "Forming an institutional supply system for agile governance" (形成敏捷治理的制度供给体系). The *Regulations* states that Shanghai will create an expert committee on AI ethics to promote ethical self-discipline in the field of AI and evaluate the potential risks of AI applications in key areas such as life, health and public safety. See: art. 64 (本市设立人工智能伦理专家委员会, 推动建立人工智能领域伦理道德自律规范, 对涉及生命健康、公共安全等重点领域人工智能应用的潜在风险开展评估). The *Regulations* also require that "relevant entities shall not conduct unreasonable differential treatment when using technologies such as big data and algorithms in the process of providing AI products and services", and it states that municipal authorities will strengthen the control on the use of biometric information, supervising and guiding the activities of biometric service providers". See: art. 66, in original: "相关主体在提供人工智能产品和服务过程中, 使用大数据与算法等技术时, 不得进行不合理的差别待遇。[…] 市网信部门应当对生物识别信息加强监管, 监督指导生物识别服务提供者提供相关服务".

[29] SHEITC, 2021. *14th Five-Year Plan for the Development of Shanghai Artificial Intelligence Industry*., section 3, par. 2 "Basic principles" (基本原则). In original: "深度应用。持续打造更加泛在的超级场景, 充分利用上海超大型城市的超级场景, 推动更大规模的融合应用, 推动人工智能赋能千行百业, 深入千家万户, 创造智能时代的经济新模式、生活新体验、治理新方式".

[30] Ibid., section 4, par. 4, subparagraphs "Serve citizens' high quality of life" (服务市民高品质生活) and "promote efficient urban governance" (推动城市高效能治理).

[31] Ibid., section 4, par. 6.

in the economy (经济应用), in citizens' services (生活应用, i.e., education, medical care, elderly care), and in urban governance (城市治理应用, i.e., administrative services, community governance, traffic management, emergency management, planning and construction, market supervision and environment). To accelerate these applications, Shanghai will carry out AI experiments, explore sandbox regulations[32] and create AI application scenarios.[33]

Despite its benefits, **a policy strategy that prioritizes the rapid integration and diffusion of AI in the public sector is bound to leave many unresolved ethical concerns**—even when it gives attention to AI ethics, adopts best practices like regulatory sandboxes and pilot applications, and promotes standards regulating issues such as data privacy and security. Evidence shows that the intrusive AI applications that emerged in the AI pilots in schools have been evolving and expanding (see case studies #1, 3 and 4 in Appendix VI). Similarly, the use of AI to monitor public sentiment has been included among the types of AI applications prioritized by the Single Platform for Urban Management,[34] through which it continues to be implemented at scale. Moreover, the Government Online-Offline Shanghai showed that some public sector AI applications (e.g., the health QR code in combination with the "venue code", etc.) can at the same time improve the efficiency of public service provision and also enable invasive forms of surveillance[35] (i.e., it allowed digital tracking at the micro-level, recording each single location accessed by an individual via the "venue code"). In this regard, Shanghai's AI

[32] Standing Committee of the Shanghai Municipal People's Congress, 2022. *Regulations of the Shanghai Municipality on Promoting the Development of the Artificial Intelligence Industry (Draft)*, cit., art. 63. In original: "市相关部门 […] 在特定区域和范围开展应用测试, 探索沙盒监管".

[33] Ibid., art. 45, in original: "本市建立人工智能应用场景开放制度。市经济信息化部门应当建立完善相关激励机制, 定期征集和发布应用场景需求和示范解决方案清单, 搭建真实场景测试环境, 促进场景培育、发现、实施和示范性场景推广".

[34] Shanghai Municipal Government, 2020 (cit. in 6.2.2), Section 3, par. 3.2. "In social management and control, […] realize smart cognition, early warning and risk assessment of major issues related to public sentiment in Shanghai" (在社会面管控方面, […] 实现涉沪重大舆情智能感知、预警分析与风险评估; […] 确实增强智能感知功能).

[35] For earlier considerations on this facet of the health QR codes, see: Li, H., 2020. Have you made preparations to use "health codes" all the time? [你做好一直使用 "健康码" 的准备了吗?]. *Vistopia* [看理想], 7 April, https://mp.weixin.qq.com/s/xDKKicV22IBRGnNnNStOVg?utm_source=substack&utm_medium=email. A translation of this article is available through Jeffrey Ding's ChinAI newsletter #203 (14 November 2022).

strategy reflects some fundamental ethical tensions that animate the use of AI in the public sector. As it continues to pursue the rapid uptake of AI in the public sector, will Shanghai use data accumulation, increasing computational capacity, new algorithmic learning procedures and increasingly advanced AI systems to refine public service provision and make life more convenient for its citizens? Or will Shanghai go toward building "a new society engineered around the power of digital surveillance[36]"? How will Shanghai navigate through the various possible permutations that exist between a beneficial digital utopia and dystopian AI-powered applications? The analysis of the case studies in Shanghai confirms that both extremes are technically possible, and that both extremes can coexist in the same socioeconomic context: from AI-based administrative services that help vulnerable groups, to intrusive applications that monitor children in schools, public opinion in society and extend video surveillance to every corner of the city. The ethical tensions generated by the use of AI in public sector activities are not relevant only to China or Shanghai, as demonstrated by the growing body of literature on the ethical challenges of AI in the public sector. Nor are these tensions new to China or Shanghai, as documented by earlier methods that deeply integrate digital technologies in State activities in public security and other areas (Chapter 1). These tensions between beneficial and problematic applications of AI are also entrenched in the aforementioned ideological view that AI is a useful tool both to improve the provision of public services and achieve more effective social and political control, as it has been crystallized in China's national AI strategy. While they are not unique to the municipality, addressing the ethical concerns of AI in the public sector is expected to become especially urgent in Shanghai: by successfully pursuing a policy strategy that prioritizes the rapid integration and diffusion of AI in public sector activities, Shanghai is deemed to face the ethical tensions of AI in public services earlier and at a larger scale than other localities, as artificial intelligence is becoming increasingly entrenched in the lives of Shanghai citizens in many policy areas.

[36] Chin, J. and Lin, L., 2022. *Surveillance State: Inside China's Quest to Launch a New Era of Social Control*. New York: St. Martin's Press.

6.2 What's Next? AI in the Urban Digital Transformation of Shanghai

Since the end of 2020, AI policy has progressively been encapsulated in a broader masterplan that promotes the digitalization of Shanghai in three key areas: economy (i.e., industrial and economic activities); life (i.e., public services in healthcare, education and other areas); and governance (i.e., administrative service provision and urban management, corresponding to the areas covered by the Government Online-Offline Shanghai and the Single Platform for Urban Management). This masterplan consists of two main programmatic documents centered upon the topic of "urban digital transformation" (城市数字化转型). Namely: the *Opinions on Comprehensively Promoting the Urban Digital Transformation of Shanghai*,[37] released at the end of 2020 (abbr.: *Digital Opinions*); and the *Shanghai Municipal "14th Five-Year" Plan for comprehensively promoting urban digital transformation*,[38] published in October 2021 (abbr.: *Digital 5YP*). These documents regulate several advanced technologies that the Shanghai government considers important to enhance the "core competitiveness" of the municipality[39], such as artificial intelligence, Big Data, blockchain, 5G, IoT, AIoT, and digital twins, among others.

Urban digital transformation is a top priority of the Shanghai leadership: the *Digital Opinions* and the *Digital 5YP* were issued by high-profile government bodies (i.e., Shanghai CPC Municipal Committee, Shanghai Municipal Government, Shanghai Government General Office), and they were soon prepped up by a set of actionable plans to support their implementation. These documents have a time horizon that extends

[37] Shanghai CPC Municipal Committee, Shanghai Municipal Government, 2021. *Opinions on Comprehensively Promoting the Digital Transformation of Shanghai City* [关于全面推进上海城市数字化转型意见], Shanghai Digital Transformation [上海城市数字化转型], 8 January, http://dt.sheitc.sh.gov.cn/szzc/573.jhtml. Shanghai Digital Transformation is an official government website operated by SHEITC, and dedicated to all the initiatives related to the digital transformation of Shanghai.

[38] Shanghai Government General Office, 2021. *Shanghai Municipal "14th Five-Year" Plan for comprehensively promoting urban digital transformation* [上海市全面推进城市数字化转型 "十四五" 规划], Hufubanfa (2021) 29, 24 October, https://www.shanghai.gov.cn/nw12344/20211027/6517c7fd7b804553a37c1165f0ff6ee4.html.

[39] Shanghai Government General Office, 2021 (cit.), preamble (全面推进城市数字化转型, 是 [...] 巩固提升城市核心竞争力和软实力的关键之举).

to 2025, so looking at them offers valuable insights into the possible evolutions of the digital innovation of the public sector in Shanghai in the mid-term. They confirm that the municipality will continue to promote the digitalization of public sector activities along the three main trajectories highlighted in the previous sections. Namely: (i) a top-down policy design for the digitalization of the public sector that preserves the dominant role of the municipal government in technology policy, while allowing for some decentralization in deciding the means to achieve the goals set by the municipality; (ii) the proactive engagement of AI and technology companies in public sector activities under a framework that prioritizes high levels of coordination and standardization, enlisting private actors in a way that meets policy goals and operational requirements of the Shanghai government; and (iii) a strategic focus on the fast-paced implementation and diffusion of AI and other advanced technologies in the public sector, which prioritizes accelerating and expanding digitalization in various policy areas over the management of ethical issues.

First, through the masterplan for the digitalization of Shanghai, **the municipal leadership continues to adopt a top-down policy design to set the goals and plans for the use of AI and advanced technologies in economy, life, and governance.**[40] These are three areas that Shanghai has been consistently prioritizing since its first programmatic document for AI development was published in October 2017. The masterplan for urban digital transformation states that Shanghai will create a "data-driven digital city" (数据驱动的数字城市), which uses advanced technologies to "realize scientific government decision-making, efficient public service, and precise social governance".[41] Shanghai will continue to foster the use of digital technologies in administrative services and urban operations, in order to further improve the quality and efficiency

[40] Shanghai CPC Municipal Committee, Shanghai Municipal Government, 2021 (cit.). Section 3, par. 1 (Promote the digital transformation of the economy, improve the quality of economic development/推动经济数字化转型, 提高经济发展质量); par. 2 (Promote the digital transformation of life, improve the quality of urban life/推动生活数字化转型, 提高城市生活品质); and par. 3 (Promote the digital transformation of governance, improve the efficiency of modern governance/推动治理数字化转型, 提高现代化治理效能).

[41] Shanghai CPC Municipal Committee, Shanghai Municipal Government, 2021 (cit.). Section 4 (坚持全方位赋能, 构建), point 4 ("实现政府决策科学化、公共服务高效化、社会治理精准化").

of public services and comprehensively enhance its governance capabilities by 2025.[42] Shanghai will also use digitalization to promote more balanced, accurate, and adequate conditions in public health, healthcare, education, elderly care, employment, and social security.[43] To chart the course to achieve these goals, Shanghai issued three dedicated policy documents[44] that operationalize the indications of the *Digital Opinions* and the *Digital 5YP*. These three policy documents are meant to mobilize the municipal bureaucracy to concretely follow up to the indications provided by *Digital Opinions* and the *Digital 5YP*. Similar to the action plans examined earlier (Chapter 5.2), these documents list a set of tasks and the government agencies responsible to perform them[45] (the 责任部门) or provide a set of core indicators to be achieved within

[42] Shanghai CPC Municipal Committee, Shanghai Municipal Government, 2021 (cit.). Section 1 ("上海重点推进政务服务"一网通办"、城市运行"一网统管", 加快建设新型智慧城市"). Section 2 ("到2025年, [...] 公共服务质量和效率进一步提升, 构建充满活力的数字生活服务生态, 构建充满活力的数字生活服务生态, 形成人人享有更具品质、更加美好的数字生活新范式。治理能力全面跃升, 数字规则更加完备, 数据要素高效流动, 形成引领全国的超大城市数字治理新模式"). On urban operations, see also Section 5, par. 9. On promoting the Government Online-Offline Shanghai and the Single Platform for Urban Management as part of the urban digital transformation, see also: Shanghai Government General Office, 2021 (cit.), Section 3.

[43] Shanghai CPC Municipal Committee, Shanghai Municipal Government, 2021 (cit.). Section 3, par. 2 ("以数字化推动公共卫生、健康、教育、养老、就业、社保等基本民生保障更均衡、更精准、更充分 [...]).

[44] The three operational policy documents that focus on the digitalization of the public sector are: (i) the *Action plan for promoting the digital transformation of life in Shanghai and build a high-quality digital life (2021–2023)* [推进上海生活数字化转型构建高品质数字生活行动方案 (2021—2023年)], published in July 2021 by the Shanghai Municipal Government (abbr. *Action Plan for Digital Life*), http://dt.sheitc.sh.gov.cn/szzc/575.jhtml; (ii) the *Several policy measures of Shanghai to promote urban digital transformation* [上海市促进城市数字化转型的若干政策措施], published in July 2021 by the Shanghai Development and Reform Commission (abbr. *Measures for Urban Digital Transformation*), http://dt.sheitc.sh.gov.cn/szzc/1200.jhtml; and (iii) the *Action plan for promoting the digital transformation of governance and realizing high-efficiency governance (2021–2023)* [推进治理数字化转型 实现高效能治理行动方案 (2021–2023)], published in December 2021 by the Shanghai Municipal Government (abbr. *Action Plan for Digital Governance*), http://dt.sheitc.sh.gov.cn/szzc/1761.jhtml. In July 2021, the municipality also published an action plan on the digital transformation of the economy, the third core topic of the digital transformation masterplan: *Action plan for promoting the digital transformation of Shanghai's economy and empowering high-quality development (2021–2023)* [推进上海经济数字化转型 赋能高质量发展行动方案 (2021–2023)].

[45] The *Action Plan for Digital Life* and the *Measures for Urban Digital Transformation*.

a certain time frame.[46] Taken together, these three operational plans outline a consistent blueprint for using digital technologies in the areas prioritized by the Shanghai government: medicine, healthcare, education, employment services, residential services, transportation, and culture.[47] These plans also confirm the focus on the digitization of administrative services and urban operations, two areas where Shanghai reiterates the key role of the Government Online-Offline Shanghai and the Single Platform for Urban Management in spurring public sector innovation.[48] Within this framework set by the Shanghai government, there is room for some decentralization in deciding the means to achieve the municipal goals for urban digitalization, and districts are encouraged to "adjust measures to local conditions and highlight local characteristics".[49] At the same time, the urban digitalization policy remains controlled by the Shanghai Urban Digital Transformation Leading Group (上海市城市数字化转型工作领导小组), which coordinates analogous leading groups at the district level. In addition, societal engagement in digital policy will continue to be limited, and it can exist only under government guidance.[50] "Digitally-empowered diversified social governance" (数字赋能多元化社会治理), even at the grassroots level, is possible only under the

[46] The *Action Plan for Digital Governance*.

[47] *Action Plan for Digital Life*, Section 3 (推进智惠基本民生), par. 1 (健康慧服务, 提升获得感), par. 2 (成长全赋能, 提升成就感), par. 3 (居住数空间, 提升归属感); Section 4 (推进智享质量民生), par. 1 (出行畅体验, 提升便捷感), par. 2 (文旅智享受, 提升时尚感). *Measures for Urban Digital Transformation*, Section 3 (建立全面提升生活数字化服务能力的新制度).

[48] *Action Plan for Digital Governance*, Section 2, par. 2 (提升社会治理数字化水平, 共建美好和谐社会), par. 3 (提升城市治理数字化水平, 建设标杆智慧城市); and Section 3 (深化 "两张网" 改革举措). *Measures for Urban Digital Transformation*, Section 4 (建立全面提升生活数字化服务能力的新制度).

[49] Shanghai CPC Municipal Committee, Shanghai Municipal Government, 2021 (cit.). Section 6, par. 14 (支持各区因地制宜、凸显特色). Similarly, the *Action Plan for Digital Life* calls for "giving full play to the role of the main battlefield of digital transformation in each district" (Section 2, par. 1, point 3), and for districts to promote digitalization efforts based on their characteristics (section 6, par. 1). The *Action Plan for Digital Governance* also "encourage all districts and units to carry out innovative practices based on their own characteristics" (section 5, par. 2).

[50] Shanghai CPC Municipal Committee, Shanghai Municipal Government, 2021 (cit). Section 5, par. 11 (Improve the organization and implementation mechanism/健全组织实施机制); Shanghai Government General Office, 2021 (cit.), Section 6, point 1 (Strengthen the overall coordination and promotion mechanism/强化统筹协调推进机制).

command (统领) of the Party, and citizens will be guided (引导) so that they can develop a better awareness of issues like data management, credit maintenance, privacy protection, and collaborative governance.[51]

Second, the masterplan for urban digitalization confirms that **Shanghai will continue to actively engage private companies in the digital innovation of the public sector, under a framework that prioritizes high levels of government-led coordination and standardization**. This will help Shanghai harnessing private sector technologies and expertise in a way that meets policy priorities and operational requirements set by the municipality. Under the guidance of the government, Shanghai will mobilize market players and encourage them to participate in and support digital transformation, innovation, and application,[52] exploring the formation of a "joint innovation model of government-enterprise collaboration" whereby the public and private sectors promote their reciprocal strengths.[53] Shanghai will "vigorously guide and support the construction of various digital public platforms" in urban governance, public services, and other areas, attracting "various innovation elements and innovative resources" in order to promote collaborative innovation in the public sector and the economy.[54] The municipality will "explore a new

[51] Shanghai CPC Municipal Committee, Shanghai Municipal Government, 2021 (cit). Section 5, par. 7 ("引导市民重塑数字时代的认知能力与思维模式, 更加注重自身数据管理、信用维护、隐私保护、协同共治, 使人人都成为数据的生产者、治理者、使用者、获益者, 以数字化激发城市生命体每一个细胞的活力"). Shanghai Government General Office, 2021 (cit.), Section 4, par. 3, point 4 (Improve new achievements in social governance/提升社会治理新成效).

[52] Shanghai CPC Municipal Committee, Shanghai Municipal Government, 2021 (cit). Section 5, par. 10 ("导市场主体参与数字化转型场景运营, 全面激发社会创造力和市场活力"). Shanghai Government General Office, 2021 (cit.), Section 2, par. 2 ("在政府引导下, 调动市场主体的积极性, 鼓励市场力量参与和支持数字化转型创新应用 [...]"), and Section 6, par. 3 ("引导市场主体参与数字化转型项目建设和场景运营").

[53] Shanghai Government General Office, 2021 (cit.), Section 5, par. 2 ("探索形成政企协同、各扬所长的联合创新模式"). This concept is reiterated by the *Action Plan for Digital Life*, which states that by 2023 Shanghai will cultivate more than ten leading companies in areas such as Big Data, 5G and AI, and incubate more than 50 innovative companies in key fields such as healthcare, medical care, education, culture, and transport (section 1, par. 3, main goals/主要目标).

[54] Shanghai CPC Municipal Committee, Shanghai Municipal Government, 2021 (cit). Section 5, par. 10 (大力引导、支持建设各类数字化公共平台, 吸引各类创新要素、创新资源集聚, 打造成为链接协同创新的开放平台, 链接产业发展的赋能平台, 链接城市治理的智慧平台, 链接美好生活的服务平台, 形成共建共治共享的数字城市创新生态圈").

model for market entities to participate in social governance services[55]" and will strengthen the matching of supply and demand of technology under a framework "guided by the government, led by the market, and participated by the whole society[56]". Market players are encouraged to participate in the development and construction of digital application scenarios, following a mid- and long-term roadmap (路线图) based on the goals and vision of Shanghai's urban development strategy.[57] In this context, the creation of application scenarios, the sharing of government data,[58] and the "reveal the rankings" (揭榜挂帅) scheme[59] will continue to be key tools to engage private companies and integrate public and private resources in fostering the digital innovation of the public sector. In addition to coordination, Shanghai will maintain a standardized approach to promote the use of advanced technologies in the public sector. Shanghai will build a unified standard system for the construction and operation of the "urban digital base" (城市数字底座) that enables digital applications in the whole municipality, creating a "Shanghai standard" in the field of digital transformation.[60] Focusing on the "public service requirements of urban digital transformation" (城市数字化转型的公共服务需求), Shanghai will promote a standardized approach based on various types of "public application tools" (公共应用工具) and "public technology tools" (公共技术工具), and will strengthen the establishment

[55] Shanghai Government General Office, 2021 (cit.), Section 2, par. 2 ("探索市场主体参与社会治理服务新模式, 构建多方协同治理格局").

[56] Shanghai CPC Municipal Committee, Shanghai Municipal Government, 2021 (cit). Section 6 ("强化动态调整和供需匹配, [...] 形成政府引导、市场主导、全社会共同参与的城市数字化转型工作格局").

[57] Shanghai Government General Office, 2021 (cit.), Section 5, par. 5 (Application scenarios joint construction project/应用场景共建工程).

[58] Shanghai CPC Municipal Committee, Shanghai Municipal Government, 2021 (cit.), Section 6, par. 13 ("发市场主体活力。充分发挥市场主导作用, 将场景和数据开放作为育商招商的重要力量").

[59] See: *Action Plan for Digital Life*, section 2, par. 3, point 6. The *Measures for Urban Digital Transformation* explicitly require to use the "reveal the rankings" scheme to involve companies in the development and implementation of the Government Online-Offline Shanghai and the Single Platform for Urban Development (Section 5, point 18). The "reveal the rankings" scheme relies on competitive methods to select the most capable companies to work on important government projects (Chapter 4.4.2).

[60] Shanghai Government General Office, 2021 (cit.), Section 5, par. 3 ("打造城市数字底座标准体系, 坚持标准引领战略, 建立统一、开放、可操作的数字底座建设标准体系和评价指标体系, 创建数字化转型领域'上海标准'").

of a common technical basis. The Shanghai government will also speed up the improvement of regulations and standards for the digitalization of public governance, industrial development, and social operations, it will introduce a number of local digital standards and norms that are "usable, useful, and easy to use", and at the same time it will encourage enterprises to create industry-specific guidelines.[61]

Finally, the masterplan for urban digitalization confirms that **Shanghai will continue to foster the rapid application of AI and advanced technologies in the public sector, keeping the strategic focus on accelerating and expanding digitalization in various policy areas**. Attention to safety, security and ethical issues remains coded in policy.[62] But the prevalent focus on fast-paced implementation is clearly emphasized in the policy documents on urban digital transformation. The Shanghai government will spearhead the use of digital technologies to "comprehensively enhance the modernization of urban governance capabilities and governance levels, and create a beautiful digital life for the citizens".[63] The municipality will "[m]ake urban digital transformation an innovation pilot field, encourage innovative practices of cutting-edge technologies and applications, accelerate the elimination of institutional barriers to digital transformation, improve an inclusive and open development environment, and establish technical, normative and policy systems that adapt to digital transformation".[64] In this context, Shanghai will strengthen the digital infrastructure that supports smart public services (e.g., AIoT, smart sensors, 5G, fast broadband connection, computing power, data exchange

[61] Shanghai Government General Office, 2021 (cit.), Section 5, par. 4 (Leading digital rules project/数字规则引领工程).

[62] Shanghai CPC Municipal Committee, Shanghai Municipal Government, 2021 (cit.), Section 5, par. 8 ("重构数字时代的社会管理规则"). Shanghai Government General Office, 2021 (cit.), Section 4, par. 3, point 5 (深化智慧政法新应用), and Section 6, par. 5 (完善数字安全发展环境). The *Action Plan on Digital Life* and the *Action Plan on Digital Governance* have sections dedicated to data security and other "security guarantees" (安全保障). The *Measures for Urban Digital Transformation* have a paragraph dedicated to network security (加强网络安全制度供给).

[63] Shanghai CPC Municipal Committee, Shanghai Municipal Government, 2021 (cit.), Section 2.

[64] Shanghai Government General Office, 2021 (cit.), Section 2, par. 2 (以城市数字化转型为创新试验田, 鼓励前沿技术和应用的创新实践, 加快消除数字化转型的制度门槛, 完善包容开放的发展环境, 建立适应数字化转型的技术体系、规范体系和政策体系).

centers[65]), will further improve the openness and effectiveness of public data sharing,[66] and will accelerate the use of AI in public service delivery in the following areas:

- in *medical care and public health*, Shanghai will create "key application scenarios" for precise medical appointments, intelligent pre-consultation, electronic medical records, nucleic acid tests and vaccinations, intelligent first aid, medical information interconnection and mutual recognition, "future hospitals", and a new digital medical process covering the whole diagnostic process[67];
- in *education*, the municipality will continue to build digital campuses and use digital technologies to improve and innovate teaching modes, learning methods, and evaluation methods in order to achieve higher levels in education[68];
- in *public transport*, Shanghai will promote the digitalization of basic transportation facilities and smart highways, smart stations, smart

[65] Shanghai Government General Office, 2021 (cit.), Section 3, par. 1 (Improve urban AIoT infrastructure/完善城市AIoT基础设施), par. 2 (Build urban data hub system/构建城市数据中枢体系), and par. 3 (Build a technology enabling platform for the whole city/打造城市共性技术赋能平台); Section 5, par. 3 (Digital base empowerment project/数字底座赋能工程). On the same topics: Shanghai CPC Municipal Committee, Shanghai Municipal Government, 2021 (cit.), Section 4, par. 5 ("加快建设数字基础设施, 推动千兆宽带、5G、卫星互联网等高速网络覆盖, 建设高性能公共算力中心, 打造人工智能、区块链、工业互联网等数字平台, 坚实支撑经济发展、市民生活和城市治理等各领域的数字化应用"); and par. 6 ("打造 "物联、数联、智联" 的城市数字底座。构建城市运行生命体征指标体系, 纳入地理空间、生态环境、建筑结构、物品标识、人员活动、车辆状态、安全监测、能源状态、设施设备运行等数据。系统规划 "城市神经元系统", 科学部署视频图像、监测传感、控制执行等感知终端, 实现城市要素全面AIoT化").

[66] Shanghai Government General Office, 2021 (cit.), Section 5, par. 1 (Data value enhancement project/数据价值提升工程).

[67] Shanghai Government General Office, 2021 (cit.), Section 4, par. 2, point 1 ("聚焦就医、公共卫生、体育运动等健康服务, 以数字化助力打造更有温度的健康上海。以患者为中心, 打造精准预约、智能预问诊、电子病历卡 (医保电子记录册) 、核酸检测和疫苗接种、智慧急救、医疗信息互联互通互认等重点应用场景, 构建涵盖诊前、诊中、诊后全流程数字化医疗新流程。建立全域协同的智慧医疗应急体系, 试点打造数字健康城区和未来医院").

[68] Shanghai Government General Office, 2021 (cit.), Section 4, par. 2, point 2 ("建设数字校园为重点, 变革教学模式、改进学习方式、创新评价方法、强化学生关爱, 实现教育更高层次发展").

airports, smart parking lots, and will accelerate the construction of a digitally-enabled traffic management system[69];

- in *administrative services*, Shanghai will continue to promote the implementation of the Government Online-Offline Shanghai to make the provision of administrative services more efficient and convenient. The municipality will fully implement the "two exemptions from submission" (Chapter 5.2.1), achieving full coverage of services for citizens and enterprises. Shanghai will create a digital system that covers the entire lifespan of citizens from birth to old age, in areas such as education, healthcare, transportation, housing, and support for the weak and elderly care.[70] Shanghai will also continue to expand and deepen the applications of the mobile App "Suishenban" and its individual digital QR code (随申码) in medical care, healthcare, public transportation, and other areas[71];
- in *urban governance*, Shanghai will continue to promote the implementation of the Single Platform for Urban Management. Through it, the municipality will further integrate and apply technologies such as digital twin cities, Big Data and AI to support "a new model of scientific, precise and smart" digital governance in public security, emergency management, planning and construction, urban grid management, traffic management, market supervision, environmental protection, and other key areas.[72] The municipality will foster the integration of digital technologies in urban infrastructure and public facilities to monitor urban operations in real time, use

[69] Shanghai Government General Office, 2021 (cit.), Section 4, par. 2, point 4 ("加快数字化赋能静态交通能力建设和设施管理，深入拓展全流程数字化停车服务 [...] 。推进基础交通设施数字化，打造智慧高速公路、智慧车站、智慧机场、智慧停车场等新亮点").

[70] Shanghai Government General Office, 2021 (cit.), Section 4, par. 3, point 1 (构建政务服务新体系).

[71] Shanghai Government General Office, 2021 (cit.), Section 3, par. 3 (打造城市共性技术赋能平台), point 1 (完善随申码功能和标准，推动"多卡并一码"，在医疗健康、交通出行、特殊药品监管等场景，持续拓展深化随申码应用).

[72] Shanghai CPC Municipal Committee, Shanghai Municipal Government, 2021 (cit), Section 3, par. 3 ("打造科学化、精细化、智能化的超大城市"数治"新范式. [...] 深化"一网统管"建设，聚焦公共安全、应急管理、规划建设、城市网格化管理、交通管理、市场监管、生态环境等重点领域). The same topics are reiterated in more details in: Shanghai Government General Office, 2021 (cit.), Section 4, par. 3, point 2 (Strengthen the new resilience of urban operations/强化城市运行新韧性).

data to support urban management and planning,[73] and continue to promote smart security, smart elderly care and smart government services in residential communities, fostering the integration of online and offline activities.[74]

- Shanghai also confirms that it will continue to deepen digital applications in *public security* and the *judiciary*.[75]

To accelerate the creation of a "digital public service system" (数字化公共服务体系), Shanghai will establish "digital demonstrative applications" (数字化示范场景) that include smart hospitals, digital school campuses, and digital residential communities.[76] In doing so, Shanghai will create a batch of comprehensive application scenarios that have "vast driving influence" (带动面广) and offer replicable models for the digital transformation of the municipality and the whole country.[77] As noted, the Shanghai government also outlines quantitative targets for various "core indicators" (主要指标, 核心指标) of public service digitalization in healthcare, medicine, education,[78] administrative services, and urban

[73] Shanghai CPC Municipal Committee, Shanghai Municipal Government, 2021 (cit), Section 5, par. 9: (塑造数字时代的城市全新功能。融合应用数字孪生城市、大数据与人工智能等技术, 推动城市"规建管用"一体化闭环运转, 实现城市决策"一张图"、城市治理"一盘棋", 为城市精细管理和科学决策提供"说明书"。推进城市建筑、市政设施和地下管线的数字化管理系统建设和信息备案, 实时监测感知建筑设施运行态势, 利用城市运行数据, 前瞻规划和动态推演, 科学设计、合理布局城市公共基础设施).

[74] Shanghai Government General Office, 2021 (cit.), Section 4, par. 2, point 3 ("推进社区智能安防、智慧康养等终端设施合理布设。依托"社区云"等数字化平台和线下社区服务机构, 强化居民线上获得社会化服务和政务服务的能力").

[75] Shanghai Government General Office, 2021 (cit.), Section 4, par. 3, point 5 (Deepen new application of smart judiciary and public security/深化智慧政法新应用).

[76] Shanghai CPC Municipal Committee, Shanghai Municipal Government, 2021 (cit.), section 3, par. 2 ("打造智慧医院、数字校园、社区生活服务等一批数字化示范场景").

[77] Shanghai CPC Municipal Committee, Shanghai Municipal Government, 2021 (cit.), section 6, par. 14 ("打造一批综合性强、带动面广的应用场景, 形成一批可复制可推广的示范案例, 为全市乃至全国数字化转型创造经验、提供样板"); Shanghai Government General Office, 2021 (cit.), Section 5, par. 6 (Transformation Benchmarking Demonstration Project/转型标杆示范工程).

[78] The *Action Plan on Digital Life* states that by 2023 Shanghai will build 30 model "digital transformation hospitals", digital campus coverage will exceed 90%, and digital push-to-talk service (一键通服务) for the elderly will achieve full coverage of the elderly in difficulties (section 1, par. 3, Main goals/主要目标). A few months later, the *Digital 5YP* reiterates these benchmarks, stating that by 2025 Shanghai will build 50 model "digital transformation hospitals" and 200 "informatization model schools".

management.[79] These targets set the pace for the digitization of the public sector, focusing on major issues that affect the lives of citizens and on solving difficult problems in the governance of megacities.[80] In addition to pilot applications and quantitative targets, Shanghai will also adopt an "innovative regulatory system" that facilitates digital innovation in the public sector. Such system will include regulatory sandboxes and other mechanisms to eliminate the policy barriers to the development of new technologies, new business patterns, and new models that enable digital transformation.[81]

6.3 A Window on the Future

The development trajectories outlined by the urban digital transformation masterplan indicate that Shanghai will continue to pursue a coordinated, systemic, and proactive strategy to foster the integration of AI and other advanced technologies in the public sector. This strategy clearly preserves the dominant role of the Shanghai government in technology policy, while allowing for some degree of decentralization in deciding the most suitable means to achieve the goals set by the municipal leadership (coordination). It leverages the analytical and political capacities of the Shanghai government to devise and support policy initiatives that promote digital innovation in the public sector, combining government operational capacities with the analytical and operational abilities

[79] The *Digital 5YP* states that by 2025 the rate of administrative services that will be processed entirely online via the Government Online-Offline Shanghai will reach 80%, and that and the "benchmark scenarios" (标杆场景) of smart urban governance of the Single Platform for Urban Management will reach 50 in 2025. The *Action Plan on Digital Governance* reiterates and expands these benchmarks. It states that the basic coverage of key application scenarios (重点应用场景基层覆盖率) in urban governance and administrative services shall reach 90% in 2022 and 100% in 2023; the rate of administrative services that will be processed entirely online via the Government Online-Offline Shanghai will reach 80% by 2023; the number of active monthly users of the mobile App "Suishenban" for administrative services will reach 15 million in 2023; and the "benchmark scenarios" (标杆场景) of smart urban governance of the Single Platform for Urban Management will reach 35 in 2023, among others.

[80] Shanghai Government General Office, 2021 (cit.), Section 5, par. 5 (Application scenarios joint construction project/应用场景共建工程).

[81] Shanghai CPC Municipal Committee, Shanghai Municipal Government, 2021 (cit.), Section 5, par. 8 (支持创新的监管制度, 试点"监管沙箱"等创新支持机制, 着力消除数字化转型过程中新技术、新业态、新模式发展的政策性门槛).

of technology companies to translate these policy initiatives into practice (systematization). Finally, besides actively engaging AI companies, the Shanghai government is also spearheading the fast-paced implementation of AI and digital technologies in various policy areas as the first user of technology, the promoter of pilots and demonstrative applications, and the creator of a regulatory system that facilitates the use of advanced technologies in the public sector and the economy (proactivity).

This book demonstrated that a coordinated, systemic, and proactive strategy, underpinned by high levels of policy capacity, has improved public service provision in Shanghai by accelerating the use of AI in public sector activities. The key advantages of this strategy were examined in light of the findings of the literature on AI in the public sector, and they are expected to benefit the urban digital transformation of Shanghai. First, nesting some degree of decentralization under an overarching top-down policy design for the digitalization of the public sector enables consistency, effective prioritization, and systemic approaches to public sector innovation, while also intercepting some opportunities that are better perceived at the ground level. Second, harnessing technologies companies using highly coordinated and standardized methods keeps the government in a controlling position, helping to ensure that municipal policy priorities and operational requirements are met when cooperating with private actors and using market-sourced technologies in public sector activities. Third, pursuing a fast-paced approach that quickly brings public sector AI applications to fruition helps the government to find new and effective solutions to tackle entrenched policy problems and allows to be more responsive in addressing policy issues when they emerge. As it keeps on developing along these lines, Shanghai is expected to continue to improve public service provision by efficiently and effectively integrating AI and other advanced technologies in the public sector.

At the same time, building upon extant debates in public sector AI scholarship, it was possible to identify some shortcomings and related unanswered questions that arise from Shanghai's AI strategy. From different angles, these shortcomings and unanswered questions revolve around the ability of Shanghai to use AI and advanced technologies not only to improve the efficiency of public service provision, but also to enhance "citizens' sense of gain". Since the publication of the *Opinions* in October 2017, the Shanghai government has stated its intentions to enhance public services and citizens' lives by means of technological innovation, and these goals have been reiterated by the masterplan for the urban digital transformation of the municipality.[82] This book demonstrated that Shanghai has been very successful in using AI and advanced technologies to improve its governance capabilities and the efficiency of public service provision in various policy areas. However, if the Shanghai government is committed to improve citizens' lives by means of AI, it will need to conduct deeper reflections about the outcomes of this technology in public service delivery and their impacts on the local population, going beyond the current focus on efficiency gains, improving governance capabilities, and strengthening existing institutions.

Answering the open questions raised in Sect. 6.1 can be a good starting point to delve into the outcomes of AI in public service delivery and their impacts on citizens. These questions lift some fundamental aspects about the possible contribution of AI and advanced technologies to improving peoples' lives. These include: the need to better understand the actual effects of AI-based interventions on the lives of the population, so that AI policies can be adjusted also based on the feedback provided by the citizens; the necessity to ensure equity of access to AI and digital services, so that the benefits and convenience of public sector digital innovation can reach the majority of citizens, including disadvantaged social groups; and the need to respond to the ethical tensions of AI and digital technologies in public services, ensuring that advanced technologies increasingly entrenched in many policy areas are beneficial to the lives of citizens. Shanghai has initiated to reflect on some of these issues and coded them in policy. In addition to ethical considerations (6.1.3), the municipal

82 About using technology to improve public service provision and governance capabilities, *Digital Opinions*, Section 3, par. 3, "打造科学化、精细化、智能化的超大城市 '数治' 新范式"; Section 4, par. 4, "逐步建立完善城市数据资源体系, 实现政府决策科学化、公共服务高效化、社会治理精准化"; Section 5, par. 9 "融合应用数字孪生城市、大数据与人工智能等技术, [...] 为城市精细管理和科学决策提供 '说明书'". *Action Plan for Digital Life*, Section 3, "通过数字化推动各类基本民生服务提质增效, 实现更精细、更准确、更及时的基本民生服务体验". *Action Plan for Digital Governance*, Section 1, "全力打造科学化、精细化、智慧化的超大城市 '数治' 新范式"; Section 2, par. 3, "提高治理精细化水平, 让城市更有序、更安全、更干净". About using technology to improve citizens' life, *Digital Opinions*, Section 1, "必须充分运用数字化方式探索超大城市社会治理新路子, 回应人民对美好生活的新期待"; Section 6, art. 15, "不断提升广大主体的获得感、幸福感、安全感". *Action Plan for Digital Governance*, Section 1, par. 1 Guiding Principles (指导思想), "不断提升人民群众的获得感、幸福感、安全感". *Action Plan for Digital Life*, Section 1, par. 1 Guiding Principles (指导思想), "让人民生活更有品质、更有尊严、更加幸福". The policy focus on public service provision and governance capabilities is preponderant, as discussed shortly.

government has been paying attention to the needs of social groups that typically have limited access to technology, like the elderly, the disabled, and the minors, among others.[83] On the other hand, discussions on broader stakeholder engagement in AI policy are virtually non-existent[84] at present. These reflections are ongoing, and Shanghai is likely to keep on considering how advanced technologies can improve the lives of its citizens. As noted by previous studies, "even if one takes the cynical view that everything the Chinese leadership does is aimed at consolidating Party rule, it must equally be recognised the leadership believes an efficient way of doing so is ensuring the population is, by and large, satisfied. This is often couched in economic terms and GDP growth rates but perhaps equally important is the provision of social services to an

[83] The masterplan for urban digital transformation shows consistent attention to the elderly, the disabled, the minors and other technologically disadvantaged groups. See: the *Digital Opinions* (Section 3, par. 2 "着力解决'数字鸿沟'问题，倡导各类公共服务'数字无障碍'，面向老年人和残障人士推进相关服务的适应性改造，创造无处不在、优质普惠的数字生活新图景"); the *Digital 5YP* (Section 4, par. 2, point 8, "优化数字无障碍环境, 面对代际差别、收入差别、教育差别、地域差别等造成的数字化应用能力不平衡，鼓励电信服务向残疾人、农村居民、老年人等特殊群体倾斜，鼓励企业研发适应重点受益群体个性服务需求的数字产品和服务, 提升各类公共服务的'数字无障碍'水平"); the *Action Plan for Digital Life* (Section 5, "关注老年人、残障人、低收入等弱势群体的诉求, 通过数字化进一步摸清底数, 优化服务配置, 让全体市民享受均衡、普惠的数字化生活服务"; Section 5, par 2, point 23 "优化银发关爱服务" and point 24 "推动数字鸿沟弥合"); and the *Action Plan for Digital Governance* (Section 3, par. 1, " 提高普惠化服务水平, 开展'长者智能技术运用能力提升行动'和适老化、无障碍改造, 推进传统服务与智能创新相结合, 提升各类人群办事便利度"). The *Regulations* on the AI industry (August 2022) also recommend to give full consideration to the needs of the elderly and the disabled when providing intelligent public services, and avoid creating obstacles to their daily lives (Standing Committee of the Shanghai Municipal People's Congress, 2022, cit., art. 68). In addition, the *Shanghai 14th Five-year Plan for the Development of Services for the Elderly* (上海市老龄事业发展"十四五"规划) published in June 2021 also sets among its main tasks (重点任务) the use of AI technologies, smart services and products to support the elderly (section 4, par. 6).

[84] The masterplan for urban digital transformation confirms the focus outlined in 6.1.1, whereby the government maintains a top-down approach that uses technology to identify the needs of its citizens. The *Digital 5YP*, Section 4, par. 2, point 7, states: "Focus on urban and rural subsistence allowances, people with special difficulties, low-income families and other assistance objects, build individual digital portraits (个人数字画像) in the field of public assistance, and further understand the basics through digitalization, and realize the transformation from 'people looking for policies to policies looking for people'". Similar concepts on using technologies to identify the needs of the citizens are reiterated in the *Digital Opinions* (Section 5, par. 7) and the *Action Plan for Digital Life* (Section 5, par. 1, point 21).

ever more demanding populace" (Creemers, 2020, p. 67). In this regard, future research may want to explore if and how these reflections about the use of advanced technologies to improve citizens' lives will evolve over time, and whether Shanghai will follow up to them in practice[85] in order to adapt itself to the growing demands for better services and quality of life coming from its population.

As it steadily proceeds on a journey to become a leading international "AI highland", Shanghai will continue to try to stay ahead of most other cities in the world in terms of its rate of experimentation and adoption of AI and digital technologies in the public sector, and its breadth and depth of AI applications for public service provision. In this perspective, Shanghai will continue to provide valuable insights for researchers and practitioners who are working in the field of AI in the public sector in China and other countries. The experience of Shanghai offers a nuanced understanding of the use AI and advanced technologies in public sector activities, showing the opportunities and challenges that applying AI to the provision of public services carries with it. The advantages of the municipal strategy for AI in the public sector highlight practical lessons that can be learnt from Shanghai's ability to improve public service delivery by means of AI, eliciting new ideas on promising approaches and solutions. Not everything is applicable to other socioeconomic contexts, and the analysis also underscored some shortcomings and unanswered questions that arise from use of AI and digital technologies in public governance in Shanghai.

[85] Due to the demographic composition of its population – in 2020, 23.4% of the local residents or approximately 5.8 million people was aged 60 or above (Chapter 1) – Shanghai has shown particular attention to elderly people, and it started some initiatives targeted at this group. For instance, in 2021 Shanghai launched the "Digital partner program" (数字伙伴计划) to enhance the digital skills of elderly people, in cooperation with public and private entities like the Shanghai Elderly People University (上海老年大学), Alipay of Alibaba Group, and the local branches of telecom providers China Telecom, China Mobile, and China Unicom. In addition, in 2016 Shanghai introduced a municipal digital platform for services dedicated to the elderly (上海养老服务平台, https://shyl.mzj.sh.gov.cn/homePage). Since 2019, this platform has been using AI, Big Data and other technologies to provide "intelligent services" like AI-assisted inquiries and other functions. See: China Central Government, 2019. The "Shanghai Elderly Care Service Platform" is online, the resources for elderly care services can be "obtained at one stop" ["上海市养老服务平台" 开通上线 养老服务资源可 "一站获取"]. *China Central Government*, 1 June, http://www.gov.cn/xinwen/2019-06/01/content_5396549.htm.

Being at the forefront of AI and digital innovation in the public sector, Shanghai offers the view of a possible future where AI is deeply integrated in public service provision and public sector activities. Its experience gives researchers and practitioners the occasion to ponder what can be learnt, what can be improved, and what should be avoided when deploying AI and advanced technologies in this area. By looking ahead from the top of China's AI highland, we can see the opportunities and challenges of using artificial intelligence to improve public service provision and citizens' life, drawing important insights into how AI and advanced technologies can help us to shape the future we want.

References

Acharya, A. and Arnold, Z., 2019. *Chinese Public AI R&D Spending: Provisional Findings*. Center for Security and Emerging Technology, CSET Issue Brief, https://cset.georgetown.edu/publication/chinese-public-ai-rd-spending-provisional-findings/.

Arcesati, R., 2021. *Lofty principles, conflicting incentives: AI ethics and governance in China*. Mercator Institute for China Studies, https://merics.org/en/report/lofty-principles-conflicting-incentives-ai-ethics-and-governance-china.

Berryhill, J., Kok Heang, K., Clogher, R. and McBride, K., 2019. *Hello, World: Artificial Intelligence and its Use in the Public Sector*. OECD Working Papers on Public Governance, No. 36, https://doi.org/10.1787/726fd39d-en.

Calo, R., 2017. Artificial Intelligence Policy: A Primer and Roadmap, https://doi.org/10.2139/ssrn.3015350.

Campion, A., Gasco-Hernandez, M., Mikhaylov, S. and Esteve, M., 2020. Managing Artificial Intelligence Deployment in the Public Sector. *Computer*, 53, pp. 28–37, https://www.computer.org/csdl/magazine/co/2020/10/09206418/1npxF00DQru.

Castro, D. and McLaughlin, M., 2021. *Who Is Winning the AI Race: China, the EU or the United States?—2021 Update*. Center for Data Innovation, https://datainnovation.org/2021/01/who-is-winning-the-ai-race-china-the-eu-or-the-united-states-2021-update/.

Chen, P., 2019. Governance in the Era of Artificial Intelligence: Adaptation and Transformation [人工智能时代的政府治理: 适应与转变]. *E-Government* [电子政务], 3(195), pp. 27–34.

Chen, T., Ran, L. and Gao, X., 2019. AI innovation for advancing public service: The case of China's first Administrative Approval Bureau. *Proceedings of dg.o 2019: 20th Annual International Conference on Digital Government Research*, June 18–20, Dubai, United Arab Emirates. ACM, New York: USA, https://doi.org/10.1145/3325112.3325243.

Crawford, K. and Whittaker, M., 2016. *The AI Now Report 2016: The Social and Economic Implications of Artificial Intelligence Technologies in the Near-Term.* New York: New York University, https://ainowinstitute.org/AI_Now_2016_Report.pdf.

Chui, M., Harryson, M., Manyika, J., Roberts, R., Chung, R., van Heteren, A. and Nel, P., 2018. *Notes from the AI frontier: Applying AI for Social Good.* McKinsey Global Institute, https://www.mckinsey.com/featured-insights/artificialintelligence/applying-artificial-intelligence-for-social-good.

Chun, A. 2020. Breaking the Iron Triangle: AI in China's healthcare system. In: Elliot, H. ed., 2020. *The AI Powered State: China's approach to public sector innovation.* Nesta, May 2020, pp. 19–25, https://www.nesta.org.uk/feature/ai-powered-state/.

Creemers, R., 2020. The Ideology Behind China's AI Strategy. In: Elliott, H. ed., 2020. *The AI Powered State: China's approach to public sector innovation.* Nesta, May 2020, pp. 63–69, https://www.nesta.org.uk/feature/ai-powered-state/.

Cristianini, N. and Scantamburlo, T., 2019. On Social Machines for Algorithmic Regulation. *AI & Society*, 35, pp. 645–662, https://link.springer.com/article/10.1007/s00146-019-00917-8.

Desouza, K., 2021. Artificial Intelligence in the Public Sector: A Maturity Model. *IBM Center for the Business of Government*, Washington D.C.: USA, https://www.businessofgovernment.org/report/artificial-intelligence-public-sector-maturity-model.

Desouza, K., Dawson, G. and Chenok, D., 2020. Designing, developing, and deploying artificial intelligence systems: Lessons from and for the public sector. *Business Horizons*, 63(2), pp. 205–213. https://doi.org/10.1016/j.bushor.2019.11.004.

Ding, J., 2018. *Deciphering China's AI Dream.* Oxford: University of Oxford, https://www.fhi.ox.ac.uk/deciphering-chinas-ai-dream.

Dwivedi, Y.K., Hughes, L., Ismagilova, E., Aarts, G., Coombs, C., Crick, T., Duan, Y., Dwivedi, R., Edwards, J., Eirug, A., Galanos, V., Ilavarasan, P.V., Janssen, M., Jones, P., Kar, A.K., Kizgin, H., Kronemann, B., Lal, B., Lucini, B., Medaglia, R., Le Meunier-FitzHugh, K., Le Meunier-FitzHugh, L.C., Misra, S., Mogaji, E., Sharma, S.K., Singh, J.B., Raghavan, V., Raman, R., Rana, N.P., Samothrakis, S., Spencer, J., Tamilmani, K., Tubadji, A., Walton, P. and Williams, M.D., 2021. Artificial Intelligence (AI): Multidisciplinary perspectives on emerging challenges, opportunities, and agenda for research, practice and policy. *International Journal of Information Management*, 57, https://doi.org/10.1016/j.ijinfomgt.2019.08.002.

Eggers, W., Schatsky, D. and Viechnicki, P., 2017. *AI Augmented Government: Using Cognitive Technologies to Redesign Public Sector Work*. Deloitte Center for Government Insights, https://scholar.google.com/scholar_lookup?title=AI%20augmented%20government%3A%20using%20cognitive%20technologies%20to%20redesign%20public%20sector%20work&author=W.D.%20Eggers&publication_year=2017.

Elliott, H. ed., 2020. *The AI Powered State: China's Approach to Public Sector Innovation*. Nesta, May 2020, https://www.nesta.org.uk/feature/ai-powered-state/.

Engstrom, F., Ho, D., Sharkey, C., and Cuéllar, M., 2020. *Government by Algorithm: Artificial Intelligence in Federal Administrative Agencies*. Report Submitted to the Administrative Conference of the United States, https://ssrn.com/abstract=3551505.

Fatima, S., Desouza, K. and Dawson, G., 2020. National Strategic Artificial Intelligence Plans: A Multi-Dimensional Analysis. *Economic Analysis and Policy*, 67, pp. 178–194, https://doi.org/10.1016/j.eap.2020.07.008.

Fatima, S., Desouza, K., Denford, J. and Dawson, G., 2021. What explains governments interest in artificial intelligence? A signaling theory approach. *Economic Analysis and Policy*, 71, pp. 238–254, https://doi.org/10.1016/j.eap.2021.05.001.

Gal, D., 2020. China's Approach to AI Ethics. In: Elliot, H. ed., 2020. *The AI Powered State: China's Approach to Public Sector Innovation*. Nesta, May 2020, pp. 53–61, https://www.nesta.org.uk/feature/ai-powered-state/.

Hager, G., Drobnis, A., Fang, F., Ghani, R., Greenwald, A., Lyons, T., Parkes, D., Schultz, J., Saria, S., Smith, S. and Tambe, M., 2017. *Artificial Intelligence for Social Good*. Computing Community Consortium, https://cra.org/ccc/events/ai-social-good/.

Han, E., 2020. From Traffic Management to Smart Courts: China's Approach to Smart Cities. In: Elliott, H. ed., 2020. *The AI Powered State: China's Approach to Public Sector Innovation*. Nesta, May 2020, pp. 35–41, https://www.nesta.org.uk/feature/ai-powered-state/.

Heilmann, S., 2008. From Local Experiments to National Policy: The Origins of China's Distinctive Policy Process. *The China Journal*, 59, pp. 1–30, https://www.jstor.org/stable/20066378.

Henman, P., 2020. Improving public services using artificial intelligence: possibilities, pitfalls, governance. *Asia Pacific Journal of Public Administration*, 42(4), pp. 209–221, https://doi.org/10.1080/23276665.2020.1816188.

Howlett, M. and Ramesh, M., 2003. *Studying Public Policy: Policy Cycles and Policy Subsystems*. Oxford: Oxford University Press.

Kang, L. and Tang, Q., 2021. Innovation of Municipal Social Governance in the Era of Artificial Intelligence: Power, Challenges and Approaches [人工智能

时代的市域社会治理创新: 动力、挑战及进路]. *Jiangnan Forum* [江南论坛], 2021 (1), pp. 27–29.

Kankanhalli, A., Charalabidis, Y. and Mellouli, S., 2019. IoT and AI for Smart Government: A Research Agenda. Government Information Quarterly, 36(2), pp. 304– 309, https://doi.org/10.1016/j.giq.2019.02.003.

Knill, C. and Tosun, J., 2008. *Policy Making*. Chair of Comparative Public Policy and Administration, Department of Politics and Management, University of Konstanz, Working Paper 01/2008, http://kops.uni-konstanz.de/handle/123456789/3885.

Lee, C., 2022. *Artificial Intelligence in China: Players, Regulations, Prospects*. Webinar for the EU Delegation to China, 25 March 2022.

Li, L. and Li, Y., 2021. Risks in AI-embedded government governance and their avoidance [人工智能嵌入政府治理的风险及其规避]. *Journal of South China University of Technology (Social Science Edition)* [华南理工大学学报(社会科学版)], 23(5), pp. 1–13.

Li, X., 2019. A Redefinition of the Concept of AI and the Government's Governance: An Analysis from the Perspectives of Technology, Market and Politics [人工智能概念的再界定与政府的治理回应: 基于技术、市场和政治视角的分析]. *E-Government* [电子政务], 3(195), pp. 2–8.

Liu, Y. 2020. The Future of the Classroom? China's Experience of AI in Education. In: Elliot, H. ed., 2020. *The AI Powered State: China's Approach to Public Sector Innovation*. Nesta, May 2020, pp. 27–33, https://www.nesta.org.uk/feature/ai-powered-state/.

Mehr, H., 2017. Artificial Intelligence for Citizen Services and Government. *Harvard Kennedy School Ash Center for Democratic Governance and Innovation*, August 2017, https://ash.harvard.edu/files/ash/files/artificial_intelligence_for_citizen_services.pdf.

Mei, L., 2018. How AI Affects National Governance: A Predictive Analysis [人工智能如何影响国家治理: 一项预判性分析]. *Hubei Social Sciences* [湖北社会科学], 2018 (8), pp. 20–28.

Meng, Q. and Jun, J., 2021. AI-enabled Platform Government: A Technical Framework and A Practical Path [人工智能支撑的平台型政府: 技术框架与实践路径]. *E-Government* [电子政务], 09(225), pp. 37–46.

Mikalef, P. and Gupta, M., 2021. Artificial Intelligence Capability: Conceptualization, Measurement Calibration, and Empirical Study on its Impact on Organizational Creativity and Firm Performance. *Information & Management*, 58(3), pp. 1–20, https://doi.org/10.1016/j.im.2021.103434.

Mikhaylov, S., Esteve, M. and Campion, A., 2018. Artificial Intelligence for the Public Sector: Opportunities and Challenges of Cross-Sector Collaboration. *Philosophical Transactions of the Royal Society A: Mathematical, Physical and Engineering Sciences*, 376 (2128), https://doi.org/10.1098/rsta.2017.0357.

Mishra, S., Clark, J. and Perrault, C., 2020. *Measurement in AI Policy: Opportunities and Challenges*, 22 September, https://arxiv.org/abs/2009.09071.

Misuraca, G. and van Noordt, C., 2020. *Overview of the Use and Impact of AI in Public Services in the EU*. Luxembourg: Publications Office of the European Union, https://doi.org/10.2760/039619.

Molinari, F., van Noordt, C., Vaccari, L., Pignatelli, F. and Tangi, L., 2021. *AI Watch. Beyond Pilots: Sustainable Implementation of AI in Public Services*. Luxembourg: Publications Office of the European Union, https://publications.jrc.ec.europa.eu/repository/handle/JRC126665.

OECD (Organisation for Economic Co-operation and Development), 2019a. *Artificial Intelligence in Society*. Revised version, August 2019. Paris: OECD Publishing, https://doi.org/10.1787/eedfee77-en.

Oxford Insights and IDRC (International Research Development Centre), 2020. *Government AI Readiness Index 2020*. Oxford Insights and IDRC, on file with the author.

Reis, J., Santo, P. and Melão, N., 2019. Artificial Intelligence in Government Services: A Systematic Literature Review. In: Rocha Á., Adeli H., Reis L., Costanzo S. eds., 2019. New Knowledge in Information Systems and Technologies. *WorldCIST'19 2019. Advances in Intelligent Systems and Computing*, 930, pp. 241–252, https://doi.org/10.1007/978-3-030-16181-1_23.

Roberts, H., Cowls, J., Morley, J., Taddeo, M., Wang, V. and Floridi, L., 2020. The Chinese Approach to Artificial Intelligence: An Analysis of Policy, Ethics, and Regulation. *AI & Society*, 36, pp. 59–77, https://doi.org/10.1007/s00146-020-00992-2.

Scantamburlo, T., Charlesworth, A. and Cristianini, N., 2018. *Machine decisions and human consequences*. On file with the author.

Selbst, A., Boyd, D., Friedler, S., Venkatasubramanian, S. and Vertesi, J., 2019. Fairness and Abstraction in Sociotechnical Systems. *FAT* '19: Proceedings of the Conference on Fairness, Accountability, and Transparency*, pp. 59–68, https://doi.org/10.1145/3287560.3287598.

Stanford University, 2019. *The AI Index 2019 Annual Report*. AI Index Steering Committee, Human-Centered AI Institute, Stanford: Stanford University, December 2019, https://hai.stanford.edu/sites/default/files/ai_index_2019_report.pdf.

Stanford University, 2021a. *The AI Index 2021 Annual Report*. AI Index Steering Committee, Human-Centered AI Institute, Stanford: Stanford University, March 2021, https://aiindex.stanford.edu/report/.

Stanford University, 2021b. *Gathering Strength, Gathering Storms: The One Hundred Year Study on Artificial Intelligence (AI100) 2021 Study Panel Report*. Stanford: Stanford University, September 2021, http://ai100.stanford.edu/2021-report.

Sun, T. and Medaglia, R., 2019. Mapping the challenges of artificial intelligence in the public sector: Evidence from public healthcare. *Government Information Quarterly*, 36 (2), pp. 368–383, https://www.sciencedirect.com/science/article/abs/pii/S0740624X17304781.

Tao, Y., 2020. The Modernization of Public Management in the Era of Artificial Intelligence [人工智能时代公共管理现代化发展之路]. *Audit Observation* [审计观察], 2020 (8), pp. 64-67.

Tinholt, D., Carrara, W. and van der Linden, N., 2017. *Unleashing the potential of Artificial Intelligence in the Public Sector. Capgemini Consulting*, pp. 1–10, https://www.capgemini.com/consulting/wp-content/uploads/sites/30/2017/10/ai-in-public-sector.pdf.

Wang, X. and Wang, X., 2019. "Technological Leviathan": Potential Risks of Artificial Intelligence Embedded in Social Governance and Government Response ["技术利维坦": 人工智能嵌入社会治理的潜在风险与政府应对]. E-*Government* [电子政务], 5(197), pp. 86–93.

Wirtz B., Weyerer J. and Geyer, C., 2019. Artificial Intelligence in the Public Sector – Applications and Challenges. *International Journal of Public Administration*, 42(7), pp. 596–615, https://www.tandfonline.com/doi/abs/10.1080/01900692.2018.1498103?journalCode=lpad20.

Wu, X., 2021. Application Dilemmas and Policy Suggestions for AI in Government Governance [人工智能在政府治理中的应用困境与政策建议]. *China National Conditions and Strength* [中国国情国力], 8(343), pp. 51–53.

Yu, W., 2020. AI and Public Management: Opportunities and Challenges [人工智能与公共管理: 机遇与挑战]. *Journal of Beijing University of Aeronautics and Astronautics (Social Sciences Edition)* [北京航空航天大学学报 (社会科学版)], 33(4), pp. 50–54.

Zhang, L., Feng, X. and Tang, Z., 2019. The Realistic Basis and Path Choice of Building a Smart Society in China—An Analytical Dimension Based on Technology and System [中国建设智慧社会的现实基础与路径选择 — 基于技术与制度的分析维度]. *E-Government* [电子政务], 04(196), pp. 18–26.

Zhang, Q., 2019. Artificial Intelligence and the Normative Prospects of Public Services [人工智能与公共服务的规范前景]. *Administrative Tribune* [行政论坛], 2019 (6), pp. 115–120.

Glossary

Basic Concepts of Artificial Intelligence (Main Sources: Marcus and Davis, 2019; OECD, 2019a; Stanford, 2019; Brooks, 2017; Russell and Norvig, 1995)

Algorithm: A precisely defined sequence of instructions for performing a calculation or solving a problem from given input information in a finite number of steps. Algorithms form the basis for everything a computer can do, and therefore they are a fundamental aspect of all AI systems.

Artificial Neural Networks (ANNs, or neural networks): A subset of machine learning loosely inspired by the structure of the human brain. A neural network is composed of simple processing nodes, or "artificial neurons", which are connected to one another in layers. ANNs have three main components: an input layer, a hidden layer, and an output layer. Each layer is made up of several neurons or nodes. Each node receives data from several nodes "above" it, and gives data to several nodes "below" it through the use of various mathematical functions. Nodes attach a "weight" to the data they receive, and attribute a value to that data. If the data does not pass a certain threshold, it is not passed on to another node. Algorithms are trained until similar data input results in consistent outputs.

D. Todaro, *The Use of Artificial Intelligence in the Public Sector in Shanghai*, https://doi.org/10.1007/978-981-97-0597-9

Black box: It refers to situations when it is not possible to explain the reasons behind the predictions made by the AI system (i.e., the process of using data to complete missing information), but only to assess its input-output.

Computer vision: It indicates the capacity of machines to analyze, understand, and manipulate images and video. This capacity is expressed in different tasks, including: image classification, semantic segmentation, facial recognition and identification, and activity recognition in videos.

Deep learning (DL): It is a subset of machine learning based on artificial neural networks. It uses many layers of artificial neurons to solve problems that other AI techniques find difficult to address. DL has become one of the most used machine learning techniques. Its popularity increased significantly from the mid-2000s onwards, and it is behind much of the wider interest in AI today. Deep learning excels at dealing with unstructured information in vision and language, among others.

Machine learning (ML): An area of AI research that gives machines the ability to learn in an automated manner through patterns and inferences by leveraging big amounts of data, rather than through explicit hand-coded instructions from humans. When provided with sufficient data, a machine learning algorithm can learn to make predictions or solve problems, such as identifying objects in pictures or winning at particular games, for example.

Natural Language Processing (NLP): It indicates the capacity of machines to interpret, classify, manipulate, and generate language. It is expressed in tasks such as language understanding, reading comprehension, machine translation, text generation, and a combination of these tasks or speech recognition.

Reinforcement learning: It is an ML method that trains the machine by using goal-oriented algorithms. Such algorithms learn how to attain a complex objective, or maximize along a particular dimension, by performing actions that are rewarded or not rewarded. The machine learns through trial and error, where error is penalized and success rewarded. It then automatically adjusts its behavior over time, producing more refined actions.

Statistical AI: Indicates research approaches by which machines induce a trend from a set of patterns. Machine learning is usually considered a technique belonging to statistical AI.

Supervised learning: It is an ML method that trains the machine by using well-labeled data, meaning that some data are already tagged with the correct answer (e.g., pictures of cats that are labeled as "cat"). After that, the machine is provided with a new set of data, and supervised learning algorithms have to produce a correct outcome by examining such data. The basic aim is to approximate the mapping function so well that when there is a new input data (e.g., a new picture of cat), the corresponding output variable can be predicted (the machine recognizes the picture as a cat picture).

Symbolic AI (or classical AI, rule-based AI, Good Old-Fashioned AI): Indicates research approaches that use logical representations to deduce a conclusion from a set of constraints. It requires that researchers build detailed, human-understandable decision structures to translate real-world complexity and help machines arrive at human-like decisions.

Unsupervised learning: It is an ML method that trains the machine by grouping unsorted information according to similarities, patterns, and differences, without any prior training of data. The goal of the machine is to infer the structure within a dataset and automatically identify structure and trends in data by looking at the commonalities between different data points.

Bibliography

Acharya, A. and Arnold, Z., 2019. *Chinese Public AI R&D Spending: Provisional Findings*. Center for Security and Emerging Technology, CSET Issue Brief, https://cset.georgetown.edu/publication/chinese-public-ai-rd-spending-provisional-findings/.

Androutsopoulou, A., Karacapilidis, N., Loukis, E. and Charalabidis, Y., 2019. Transforming the Communication Between Citizens and Government Through AI-guided Chatbots. *Government Information Quarterly*, 36(2), pp. 358–367, https://doi.org/10.1016/j.giq.2018.10.001.

Arcesati, R., 2021. *Lofty Principles, Conflicting Incentives: AI Ethics and Governance in China*. Mercator Institute for China Studies, https://merics.org/en/report/lofty-principles-conflicting-incentives-ai-ethics-and-governance-china.

Baer, T. and Kamalnath, V., 2017. *Controlling Machine-Learning Algorithms and Their Biases*. McKinsey & Company, https://www.mckinsey.com/business-functions/risk/our-insights/controlling-machine-learning-algorithms-and-their-biases.

Balakrishnan, T., Chui, M., Hall, B. and Henke, N., 2020. *The State of AI in 2020*. McKinsey and Company, https://www.mckinsey.com/Business-Functions/McKinsey-Analytics/Our-Insights/Global-survey-The-state-of-AI-in-2020.

Barth, T. and Arnold, E., 1999. Artificial Intelligence and Administrative Discretion: Implications for Public Administration. *The American Review of Public Administration*, 29(4), pp. 332–351, https://doi.org/10.1177/02750749922064463.

D. Todaro, *The Use of Artificial Intelligence in the Public Sector in Shanghai*, https://doi.org/10.1007/978-981-97-0597-9

Barton, D., Woetzel, J., Seong, J. and Tian, Q., 2017. *Artificial Intelligence: Implications for China*. McKinsey & Company, https://www.mckinsey.com/featured-insights/china/artificial-intelligenceimplications-for-china.

Baxter, G. and Sommerville, I., 2011. Socio-technical Systems: From Design Methods to Systems Engineering. *Interacting with Computers*, 23(1), pp. 4–17, https://doi.org/10.1016/j.intcom.2010.07.003.

Bazavan, A., 2019. Chinese Government's Shifting Role in the National Innovation System. *Technological Forecasting & Social Change*, 148, pp. 1–11, https://doi.org/10.1016/j.techfore.2019.119738.

Behymer, K. and Flach, J., 2016. From Autonomous Systems to Sociotechnical Systems: Designing Effective Collaborations. *She Ji: The Journal of Design, Economics, and Innovation*, 2(2), pp. 105–114, https://doi.org/10.1016/j.sheji.2016.09.001.

Benington, J., 2005. From Private Choice to Public Value. Institute of Governance and Public Management (IGPM), Warwick Business School, pp. 1–36, https://www.researchgate.net/publication/252055942.

Benington, J. and Moore, M. eds., 2011. *Public Value Theory and Practice*. Basingstoke: Palgrave Macmillan.

Berryhill, J., Kok Heang, K., Clogher, R. and McBride, K., 2019. *Hello, World: Artificial Intelligence and its Use in the Public Sector*. OECD Working Papers on Public Governance, No. 36, https://doi.org/10.1787/726fd39d-en.

Bibel, W., 2018. On a Scientific Discipline (Once) Named AI. *Proceedings of the Twenty-Seventh International Joint Conference on Artificial Intelligence* (IJCAI-18), pp. 5143–5149, https://www.ijcai.org/proceedings/2018/0713.pdf.

Bijker, W., 1987. The Social Construction of Bakelite: Toward a Theory of Invention. In: Bijker, W., Hughes, T. and Pinch, T. eds., 1987. *The Social Construction of Technological Systems: New Directions in the Sociology and History of Technology*. Cambridge: MIT Press, pp. 159–187.

Bijker, W., Hughes, T. and Pinch, T. eds., 1987. *The Social Construction of Technological Systems: New Directions in the Sociology and History of Technology*. Cambridge: MIT Press.

Brenton, S., Baekkeskov, E. and Hannah, A., 2022. Policy Capacity: Evolving Theory and Missing Links. *Policy Studies*, pp. 1–19, https://doi.org/10.1080/01442872.2022.2043266.

Brooks, R., 2017. Machine Learning Explained. *The Future of Robotics and Artificial Intelligence*, http://rodneybrooks.com/forai-machine-learning-explained/.

Bryman, A., 2012. *Social Research Methods*. 4th ed. New York: Oxford University Press.

Burns, J. and Zhou, Z., 2010. Performance Management in the Government of the People's Republic of China: Accountability and Control in the Implementation of Public Policy. *OECD Journal on Budgeting*, Volume 2010/2, https://doi.org/10.1787/16812336.

Cai, Z., 2016. Forty Years of Chinese AI [中国人工智能40年]. *Science & Technology Review* [科技导报], 34(15), pp. 12–32, http://www.kjdb.org/CN/abstract/abstract13768.shtml.

CAICT (China Academy of Information and Communications Technology), 2021. *White Paper on China's Computing Power Development Index* [中国算力发展指数白皮书]. CAICT [中国信息通信研究院], No. 202110, September 2021, http://www.caict.ac.cn/kxyj/qwfb/bps/202109/t20210918_390058.htm. English translation excerpts by Jeffrey Ding: https://docs.google.com/document/d/1Mq5vpZQe7nrKgkYJA2-yZNV1Eo8swh_w36TUEzFWIWs/edit#heading=h.yx06um9bhugh.

CAICT, 2023. *White Paper on China's Computing Power Development Index* [中国算力发展指数白皮书]. CAICT, No. 202306, September 2023, http://www.caict.ac.cn/kxyj/qwfb/bps/202309/t20230914_461823.htm.

CAICT and AIIA (China Artificial Intelligence Industry Alliance), 2021. *White Paper on Artificial Intelligence Core Technologies Industry: the Era of AI Under the Drive of Deep Learning* [人工智能核心技术产业白皮书 – 深度学习技术驱动下的人工智能时代], CAICT, April 2021, http://www.caict.ac.cn/kxyj/qwfb/bps/202104/t20210419_374019.htm.

CAICT and BDA (Broadband Development Alliance), 2020. *Shanghai "Double Gigabit Broadband City" Development White Paper* [上海 "双千兆宽带城市" 发展白皮书], CAICT, November 2020, http://www.caict.ac.cn/kxyj/qwfb/bps/202011/P020201111484158729811.pdf.

CAICT and CMG (China Media Group), 2020. *China Regional and Urban Digital Economy Development Report* (2020) [中国区域与城市数字经济发展报告 (2020年)], CAICT, December 2020, http://www.caict.ac.cn/kxyj/qwfb/ztbg/202101/P020210104510830262645.pdf.

Calo, R., 2017. Artificial Intelligence Policy: A Primer and Roadmap, https://doi.org/10.2139/ssrn.3015350

Campion, A., Gasco-Hernandez, M., Mikhaylov, S. and Esteve, M., 2020. Managing Artificial Intelligence Deployment in the Public Sector. *Computer*, 53, pp. 28–37, https://www.computer.org/csdl/magazine/co/2020/10/09206418/1npxF00DQru.

Castro, D. and McLaughlin, M., 2021. *Who Is Winning the AI Race: China, the EU or the United States?—2021 Update*. Center for Data Innovation, https://datainnovation.org/2021/01/who-is-winning-the-ai-race-china-the-eu-or-the-united-states-2021-update/.

Castro, D., McLaughlin, M. and Chivot, E., 2019. *Who Is Winning the AI Race: China, the EU or the United States?* Center for Data

Innovation, https://www.datainnovation.org/2019/08/who-is-winning-the-ai-race-china-the-eu-or-the-united-states/.

Cath, C., 2018. Governing Artificial Intelligence: Ethical, Legal and Technical Opportunities and Challenges. *Philosophical Transactions of the Royal Society A: Mathematical, Physical and Engineering Sciences*, 376(2133), https://doi.org/10.1098/rsta.2018.0080.

Cave, S., Dihal, K. and Singler, B., 2018. *Portrayals and perceptions of AI and why they matter*. London: The Royal Society, https://royalsociety.org/-/media/policy/projects/ai-narratives/AI-narratives-workshop-findings.pdf.

CESI (China Electronics Standardization Institute), 2021. *Big Data Development Index Report of Key Cities (2021)* [重点城市大数据发展指数报告 (2021年)]. CESI [中国电子技术标准化研究院], http://www.cesi.cn/images/editor/20210719/20210719104506217.pdf.

CESI, 2022. *White Paper on City Brain Development (2022 edition)* [城市大脑发展白皮书 (2022 版)]. *China Electronics Standardization Institute* [中国电子技术标准化研究院], 5 January, https://www.cesi.cn/202201/8200.html.

Chen, P., 2019. Governance in the Era of Artificial Intelligence: Adaptation and Transformation [人工智能时代的政府治理: 适应与转变]. *E-Government* [电子政务], 3(195), pp. 27–34.

Chen, T., Ran, L. and Gao, X., 2019. AI Innovation for Advancing Public Service: The Case of China's first Administrative Approval Bureau. *Proceedings of dg.o 2019: 20th Annual International Conference on Digital Government Research*, June 18–20, Dubai, United Arab Emirates. ACM, New York: USA, https://doi.org/10.1145/3325112.3325243.

Chesterman, S., 2021. *We, the Robots? Regulating Artificial Intelligence and the Limits of the Law*. Cambridge: Cambridge University Press.

Chui, M., Harryson, M., Manyika, J., Roberts, R., Chung, R., van Heteren, A. and Nel, P., 2018. *Notes from the AI frontier: Applying AI for Social Good*. McKinsey Global Institute, https://www.mckinsey.com/featured-insights/artificialintelligence/applying-artificial-intelligence-for-social-good.

Chun, A. 2020. Breaking the Iron Triangle: AI in China's Healthcare System. In: Elliot, H. ed., 2020. *The AI Powered State: China's Approach to Public Sector Innovation*. Nesta, May 2020, pp. 19–25, https://www.nesta.org.uk/feature/ai-powered-state/.

Colvin, T., Liu, I., Babou, T. and Wong, G., 2020. *A Brief Examination of Chinese Government Expenditures on Artificial Intelligence R&D*. Institute for Defense Analysis, IDA Document D-12068, https://www.jstor.org/stable/resrep22826.1.

Crawford, K. and Whittaker, M., 2016. *The AI Now Report 2016: The Social and Economic Implications of Artificial Intelligence Technologies in the Near-Term*. New York: New York University, https://ainowinstitute.org/AI_Now_2016_Report.pdf.

Creemers, R., 2018. China's Social Credit System: An Evolving Practice of Control, https://doi.org/10.2139/ssrn.3175792.

Creemers, R., 2020. The Ideology Behind China's AI Strategy. In: Elliott, H. ed., 2020. *The AI Powered State: China's approach to public sector innovation*. Nesta, May 2020, pp. 63–69, https://www.nesta.org.uk/feature/ai-powered-state/.

Cristianini, N. and Scantamburlo, T., 2019. On social Machines for Algorithmic Regulation. *AI & Society*, 35, pp. 645–662, https://link.springer.com/article/10.1007/s00146-019-00917-8.

Dafoe, A., 2015. On Technological Determinism: A Typology, Scope Conditions, and a Mechanism. *Science, Technology, & Human Values*, 40(6), pp. 1047–1076, https://doi.org/10.1177/0162243915579283.

Deloitte China, 2019. *Scenarios and Potentials of AI's Commercial Applications in China*. Deloitte Digital Difference, https://www2.deloitte.com/cn/en/pages/innovation/articles/china-ai-industry-whitepaper-intelligence-driven-by-innovation.html.

Desouza, K., 2018. Delivering Artificial Intelligence in Government: Challenges and Opportunities. *IBM Center for the Business of Government*, Washington D.C.: USA, http://www.businessofgovernment.org/report/delivering-artificial-intelligence-government-challenges-and-opportunities.

Desouza, K., 2021. Artificial Intelligence in the Public Sector: A Maturity Model. *IBM Center for the Business of Government*, Washington D.C.: USA, https://www.businessofgovernment.org/report/artificial-intelligence-public-sector-maturity-model.

Desouza, K., Dawson, G. and Chenok, D., 2020. Designing, Developing, and Deploying Artificial Intelligence Systems: Lessons from and for the Public Sector. *Business Horizons*, 63(2), pp. 205–213. https://doi.org/10.1016/j.bushor.2019.11.004.

Ding, J., 2018. *Deciphering China's AI Dream*. Oxford: University of Oxford, https://www.fhi.ox.ac.uk/deciphering-chinas-ai-dream.

Ding, J., 2019. *China's Current Capabilities, Policies, and Industrial Ecosystem in AI*. Testimony before the U.S.-China Economic and Security Review Commission Hearing on Technology, Trade, and Military-Civil Fusion: China's Pursuit of Artificial Intelligence, New Materials, and New Energy, 7 June, https://www.uscc.gov/sites/default/files/June%207%20Hearing_Panel%201_Jeffrey%20Ding_China%27s%20Current%20Capabilities%2C%20Policies%2C%20and%20Indu.

Ding, J., 2020. Promoting Nationally, Acting Locally: China's Next Generation AI Approach. In: Elliott, H. ed., 2020. *The AI Powered State: China's approach to public sector innovation*. Nesta, May 2020, pp. 11–16, https://www.nesta.org.uk/feature/ai-powered-state/.

Dobbe, R., Krendl Gilbert, T. and Mintz, Y., 2021. Hard Choices in Artificial Intelligence. *Artificial Intelligence*, 300 (2021) 103555, pp. 1–17, https://doi.org/10.1016/j.artint.2021.103555.

Duan, Y., Edwards, J. and Dwivedi, Y., 2019. Artificial Intelligence for Decision Making in the Era of Big Data—Evolution, Challenges and Research Agenda. *International Journal of Information Management*, 48, pp. 63–71, https://www.sciencedirect.com/science/article/abs/pii/S0268401219300581.

Dwivedi, Y.K., Hughes, L., Ismagilova, E., Aarts, G., Coombs, C., Crick, T., Duan, Y., Dwivedi, R., Edwards, J., Eirug, A., Galanos, V., Ilavarasan, P.V., Janssen, M., Jones, P., Kar, A.K., Kizgin, H., Kronemann, B., Lal, B., Lucini, B., Medaglia, R., Le Meunier-FitzHugh, K., Le Meunier-FitzHugh, L.C., Misra, S., Mogaji, E., Sharma, S.K., Singh, J.B., Raghavan, V., Raman, R., Rana, N.P., Samothrakis, S., Spencer, J., Tamilmani, K., Tubadji, A., Walton, P. and Williams, M.D., 2021. Artificial Intelligence (AI): Multidisciplinary Perspectives on Emerging Challenges, Opportunities, and Agenda for Research, Practice and Policy. *International Journal of Information Management*, 57, https://doi.org/10.1016/j.ijinfomgt.2019.08.002.

Eggers, W., Schatsky, D. and Viechnicki, P., 2017. *AI Augmented Government: Using Cognitive Technologies to Redesign Public Sector Work*. Deloitte Center for Government Insights, https://scholar.google.com/scholar_lookup?title=AI%20augmented%20government%3A%20using%20cognitive%20technologies%20to%20redesign%20public%20sector%20work&author=W.D.%20Eggers&publication_year=2017.

Elliott, H. ed., 2020. *The AI Powered State: China's Approach to Public Sector Innovation*. Nesta, May 2020, https://www.nesta.org.uk/feature/ai-powered-state/.

Engin, Z. and Treleaven, P., 2019. Algorithmic Government: Automating Public Services and Supporting Civil Servants in using Data Science Technologies. *The Computer Journal*, 62(3), pp. 448–460, https://doi.org/10.1093/comjnl/bxy082.

Engstrom, F., Ho, D., Sharkey, C., and Cuéllar, M., 2020. *Government by Algorithm: Artificial Intelligence in Federal Administrative Agencies*. Report Submitted to the Administrative Conference of the United States, https://ssrn.com/abstract=3551505.

Ernst, D., 2020. *Competing in Artificial Intelligence Chips: China's Challenge amid Technology War*. Waterloo: Centre for International Governance Innovation, https://www.cigionline.org/publications/competing-artificial-intelligence-chips-chinas-challenge-amid-technology-war.

ETAPAS (Ethical Technology Adoption in Public Administration Services), 2021. *The Social Impacts of Disruptive Technologies in the Public Sector*. ETAPAS, 8 July, https://www.etapasproject.eu/news/?slug=the-social-impacts-of-disruptive-technologies-in-the-public-sector.

Fatima, S., Desouza, K. and Dawson, G., 2020. National Strategic Artificial Intelligence Plans: A Multi-Dimensional Analysis. *Economic Analysis and Policy*, 67, pp. 178–194, https://doi.org/10.1016/j.eap.2020.07.008.

Fatima, S., Desouza, K., Denford, J. and Dawson, G., 2021. What Explains Governments Interest in Artificial Intelligence? A Signaling Theory Approach. *Economic Analysis and Policy*, 71, pp. 238–254, https://doi.org/10.1016/j.eap.2021.05.001.

Franssen, M., 2015. Design for Values and Operator Roles in Sociotechnical Systems. In: van den Hoven, J., Vermaas, P. and van de Poel, I. eds., 2015. *Handbook of Ethics, Values, and Technological Design. Sources, Theory, Values and Application Domains*. Dordrecht: Springer, pp. 117–149.

Fu, X., Woo, W. and Hou, J., 2016. Technological Innovation Policy in China: the Lessons, and the Necessary Changes Ahead. *Economic Change and Restructuring*, 49, pp. 139–157, https://doi.org/10.1007/s10644-016-9186-x.

Fukuyama, F., 2013. What Is Governance? *Governance*, 26(3), pp. 347-368, https://doi.org/10.1111/gove.12035.

Gal, D., 2019. Perspectives and Approaches in AI Ethics: East Asia. In: Dubber, M., Pasquale, F. and Das, S. eds., 2019. *Oxford Handbook of Ethics of Artificial Intelligence*. Oxford University Press.

Gal, D., 2020. China's Approach to AI Ethics. In: Elliot, H. ed., 2020. *The AI Powered State: China's Approach to Public Sector Innovation*. Nesta, May 2020, pp. 53–61, https://www.nesta.org.uk/feature/ai-powered-state/.

Galanos, V., 2021. Science and technology studies. In: Dwivedi, Y.K., Hughes, L., Ismagilova, E., Aarts, G., Coombs, C., Crick, T., Duan, Y., Dwivedi, R., Edwards, J., Eirug, A., Galanos, V., Ilavarasan, P.V., Janssen, M., Jones, P., Kar, A.K., Kizgin, H., Kronemann, B., Lal, B., Lucini, B., Medaglia, R., Le Meunier-FitzHugh, K., Le Meunier-FitzHugh, L.C., Misra, S., Mogaji, E., Sharma, S.K., Singh, J.B., Raghavan, V., Raman, R., Rana, N.P., Samothrakis, S., Spencer, J., Tamilmani, K., Tubadji, A., Walton, P. and Williams, M.D., 2021. Artificial Intelligence (AI): Multidisciplinary Perspectives on Emerging Challenges, Opportunities, and Agenda for Research, Practice and Policy. *International Journal of Information Management*, 57, pp. 23–26, https://doi.org/10.1016/j.ijinfomgt.2019.08.002.

Gleeson, D., Legge, D. and O'Neill, D., 2009. Evaluating Health Policy Capacity: Learning from International and Australian Experience. *Australia and New Zealand Health Policy*, 6(3), pp. 1–15, https://doi.org/10.1186/1743-8462-6-3.

Grobelnik, M., 2021. There won't be Any Perfect Definition of AI, but We Urgently Needed a 'Good Enough' One Yesterday. Presentation at the Online Seminar *Regulation: What We Need to Talk about When We Talk About AI*, Humane AI Net, 3 June, https://www.humane-ai.eu/event/regulation/.

Haenlein, M. and Kaplan, A., 2019. A Brief History of Artificial Intelligence: On the Past, Present, and Future of Artificial Intelligence. *California Management Review*, 61(4), pp. 5–14, https://journals.sagepub.com/doi/10.1177/0008125619864925.

Hager, G., Drobnis, A., Fang, F., Ghani, R., Greenwald, A., Lyons, T., Parkes, D., Schultz, J., Saria, S., Smith, S. and Tambe, M., 2017. *Artificial Intelligence for Social Good*. Computing Community Consortium, https://cra.org/ccc/events/ai-social-good/.

Han, E., 2020. From Traffic Management to Smart Courts: China's Approach to Smart Cities. In: Elliott, H. ed., 2020. *The AI Powered State: China's Approach to Public Sector Innovation*. Nesta, May 2020, pp. 35–41, https://www.nesta.org.uk/feature/ai-powered-state/.

Hasmath, R., Teets, J. and Lewis, O., 2019. The Innovative Personality? Policy Making and Experimentation in an Authoritarian Bureaucracy. *Public Administration and Development*, 39(2), pp. 514–562, https://doi.org/10.1002/pad.1854.

Heilmann, S., 2008. From Local Experiments to National Policy: The Origins of China's Distinctive Policy Process. *The China Journal*, 59, pp. 1–30, https://www.jstor.org/stable/20066378.

Heilmann, S., Shih, L. and Hofem, A., 2013. National Planning and Local Technology Zones: Experimental Governance in China's Torch Programme. *The China Quarterly*, 216, pp. 896–919, https://doi.org/10.1017/S0305741013001057.

Henman, P., 2020. Improving Public Services using Artificial Intelligence: Possibilities, Pitfalls, Governance. *Asia Pacific Journal of Public Administration*, 42(4), pp. 209–221, https://doi.org/10.1080/23276665.2020.1816188.

House of Lords, 2018. *AI in the UK: Ready, Willing and Able?* House of Lords Select Committee on Artificial Intelligence, Report of Session 2017–19, HL Paper 100. London: Authority of the House of Lords, https://publications.parliament.uk/pa/ld201719/ldselect/ldai/100/100.pdf.

Howlett, M. and Ramesh, M., 2003. *Studying Public Policy: Policy Cycles and Policy Subsystems*. Oxford: Oxford University Press.

Howlett, M. and Ramesh, M., 2014. The Two Orders of Governance Failure: Design Mismatches and Policy Capacity Issues in Modern Governance. *Policy and Society*, 33, pp. 317–327, https://doi.org/10.1016/j.polsoc.2014.10.002.

Howlett, M. and Ramesh, M., 2015. Achilles' Heels of Governance: Critical Capacity Deficits and Their Role in Governance Failures, *Regulation & Governance*, 10(4), pp. 301–313, https://doi.org/10.1111/rego.12091.

Hughes, T., 1987. The Evolution of Large Technological Systems. In: Bijker, W., Hughes, T. and Pinch, T. eds., 1987. *The Social Construction of Technological*

Systems: New Directions in the Sociology and History of Technology. Cambridge: MIT Press, pp. 51–82.

Jia, K. and Jiang, Y., 2017. Three Fundamental Issues of Artificial Intelligence Governance: Technological Logic, Risks and Challenges, and Public Policy Decisions [人工智能治理的三个基本问题: 技术逻辑、风险挑战与公共政策选择]. *Chinese Public Administration* [中国行政管理], 10(388), pp. 40–45.

Johnson, D. and Verdicchio, M., 2017. Reframing AI Discourse. *Minds & Machines*, 27, pp. 575–590, https://doi.org/10.1007/s11023-017-9417-6.

Jones, A., Artikis, A. and Pitt, J., 2013. The Design of Intelligent Socio-Technical Systems. *Artificial Intelligence Review*, 39, pp. 5–20, https://doi.org/10.1007/s10462-012-9387-2.

Kang, L. and Tang, Q., 2021. Innovation of Municipal Social Governance in the Era of Artificial Intelligence: Power, Challenges and Approaches [人工智能时代的市域社会治理创新: 动力、挑战及进路]. *Jiangnan Forum* [江南论坛], 2021 (1), pp. 27–29.

Kankanhalli, A., Charalabidis, Y. and Mellouli, S., 2019. IoT and AI for Smart Government: A Research Agenda. *Government Information Quarterly*, 36(2), pp. 304–309, https://doi.org/10.1016/j.giq.2019.02.003.

Kipnis, A., Tomba, L. and Unger, J., 2009. *Contemporary Chinese Society and Politics*. London and New York: Routledge.

Kirk, H., Lee, K. and Micallef, C., 2020. The Nuances of Confucianism in Technology Policy: An Inquiry into the Interaction Between Cultural and Political Systems in Chinese Digital Ethics. *International Journal of Politics, Culture, and Society*, 35, pp. 129–152, https://doi.org/10.1007/s10767-020-09370-8.

Klein, H. and Kleinman, D., 2002. The Social Construction of Technology: Structural Considerations. *Science, Technology, & Human Values*, 27(1), pp. 28–52, https://doi.org/10.1177/016224390202700102.

Knill, C. and Tosun, J., 2008. *Policy Making*. Chair of Comparative Public Policy and Administration, Department of Politics and Management, University of Konstanz, Working Paper 01/2008, http://kops.uni-konstanz.de/handle/123456789/3885.

Knight, J., 2014. China as a Developmental State. *The World Economy*, 37(10), pp. 1335–1347, https://doi.org/10.1111/twec.12215.

Kostka, G., 2019. China's Social Credit Systems and Public Opinion: Explaining High Levels of Approval. *New Media & Society*, 21(7), pp. 1565–1593, https://doi.org/10.1177/1461444819826402.

Krafft, P., Young, M., Katell, M., Huang, K. and Bugingo, G., 2020. Defining AI in Policy Versus Practice. *Proceedings of the 2020 AAAI/ACM Conference on AI, Ethics, and Society (AIES '20)*, February 7–8, 2020, New York: USA, pp. 72–78, https://doi.org/10.1145/3375627.3375835.

Kroes, P., Franssen, M., van de Poel, I. and Ottens, M., 2006. Treating Socio-technical Systems as Engineering Systems: Some Conceptual Problems. *Systems Research and Behavioral Science*, 23, pp. 803–814, https://doi.org/10.1002/sres.703.

Kroes, P. and Mejiers, A., 2002. The Dual Nature of Technical Artifacts—Presentation of a New Research Programme. *Techné*, 6(2), https://scholar.lib.vt.edu/ejournals/SPT/v6n2/pdf/kroes_meijers.pdf.

Larsen, C., 2019. China's National AI Team. The role of National AI Open Innovation Platform. In: Webster, G. ed., 2019. *AI Policy and China: Realities of State-Led Development*. Stanford-New America DigiChina Project, 29 October, pp. 16–20, https://www.newamerica.org/cybersecurity-initiative/digichina/blog/special-report-ai-policy-and-china-realities-of-state-led-development/.

Lee, C., 2022. *Artificial Intelligence in China: Players, Regulations, Prospects*. Webinar for the EU Delegation to China, 25 March 2022.

Lee, K., 2018. *AI Superpowers: China, Silicon Valley, and the New World Order*. New York: Houghton Mifflin.

Lee, K. and Sheehan, M., 2018. *China's Rise in Artificial Intelligence: Ingredients and Economic Implications*. China in an Emerging World, Hoover Institution, Fall Series, Issue 218, https://www.hoover.org/research/chinas-rise-artificial-intelligence-ingredients-and-economic-implications.

Lee, K. and Triolo, P., 2017. *China Embraces AI: A Close Look and a Long View*. Eurasia Group, https://www.eurasiagroup.net/live-post/ai-in-china-cutting-through-the-hype.

Lewis, D., 2019. China's Techno-Utilitarian Experiments with Artificial Intelligence. *Digital Asia Hub*, 16 March, https://www.digitalasiahub.org/2019/03/16/chinas-techno-utilitarian-experiments-with-artificial-intelligence/.

Li, L. and Li, Y., 2021. Risks in AI-embedded Government Governance and Their Avoidance [人工智能嵌入政府治理的风险及其规避]. *Journal of South China University of Technology (Social Science Edition)* [华南理工大学学报(社会科学版)], 23(5), pp. 1–13.

Li, X., 2019. A Redefinition of the Concept of AI and the Government Governance: An Analysis from the Perspectives of Technology, Market and Politics [人工智能概念的再界定与政府的治理回应: 基于技术、市场和政治视角的分析]. *E-Government* [电子政务], 3(195), pp. 2–8.

Liu, Y. 2020. The Future of the Classroom? China's Experience of AI in Education. In: Elliot, H. ed., 2020. *The AI Powered State: China's Approach to Public Sector Innovation*. Nesta, May 2020, pp. 27–33, https://www.nesta.org.uk/feature/ai-powered-state/.

Luong, N. and Arnold, Z., 2021. *China's Artificial Intelligence Industry Alliance. Understanding China's AI Strategy Through Industry Alliances*. Center for Security and Emerging Technology, CSET Data Brief, https://cset.georgetown.edu/publication/chinas-artificial-intelligence-industry-alliance/.

Luong, N., Arnold, Z. and Murphy, B., 2021. *Understanding Chinese Government Guidance Funds. An Analysis of Chinese-Language Sources*. Center for Security and Emerging Technology, CSET Issue Brief, https://cset.georgetown.edu/publication/understanding-chinese-government-guidance-funds/.

Ma, L., Christensen, T. and Zheng, Y., 2023. Government Technological Capacity and Public-Private Partnerships Regarding Digital Service Delivery: Evidence from Chinese Cities. *International Review of Administrative Sciences*, Vol. 89(1), pp. 95–111. https://doi.org/10.1177/00208523211018849.

Makasi, T., Tate, M., Desouza, K. and Nili, A., 2021. Value-Based Guiding Principles for Managing Cognitive Computing Systems in the Public Sector. *Public Performance & Management Review*, 44(4), pp. 929–959, https://doi.org/10.1080/15309576.2021.1879883.

Mao, Y. and Shi-Kupfer, K., 2021. Online Public Discourse on Artificial Intelligence and Ethics in China: Context, Content, and Implications. *AI & Society*, 16 November, https://doi.org/10.1007/s00146-021-01309-7.

Marcus, G. and Davis, E., 2019. *Rebooting AI: Building Artificial Intelligence We Can Trust*. New York: Pantheon Books.

Mehr, H., 2017. Artificial Intelligence for Citizen Services and Government. *Harvard Kennedy School Ash Center for Democratic Governance and Innovation*, August 2017, https://ash.harvard.edu/files/ash/files/artificial_intelligence_for_citizen_services.pdf.

Mei, L., 2018. How AI Affects National Governance: A Predictive Analysis [人工智能如何影响国家治理: 一项预判性分析]. *Hubei Social Sciences* [湖北社会科学], 2018 (8), pp. 20–28.

Meng, Q. and Jun, J., 2021. AI-Enabled Platform Government: A Technical Framework and a Practical Path [人工智能支撑的平台型政府: 技术框架与实践路径]. *E-Government* [电子政务], 09(225), pp. 37–46.

Mikalef, P., Fjørtoft, S. and Torvatn, H., 2019. Artificial Intelligence in the Public Sector: A Study of Challenges and Opportunities for Norwegian Municipalities. *Proceedings of the 18th IFIP WG 6.11 Conference on e-Business, e-Services and e-Society,* 18–20 September, 2019, Trondheim: Norway, pp. 267–277, https://doi.org/10.1007/978-3-030-29374-1.

Mikalef, P. and Gupta, M., 2021. Artificial Intelligence Capability: Conceptualization, Measurement Calibration, and Empirical Study on its Impact on Organizational Creativity and Firm Performance. *Information & Management*, 58(3), pp. 1–20, https://doi.org/10.1016/j.im.2021.103434.

Mikhaylov, S., Esteve, M. and Campion, A., 2018. Artificial Intelligence for the Public Sector: Opportunities and Challenges of Cross-Sector Collaboration. *Philosophical Transactions of the Royal Society A: Mathematical, Physical and Engineering Sciences*, 376 (2128), https://doi.org/10.1098/rsta.2017.0357.

Mishra, S., Clark, J. and Perrault, C., 2020. *Measurement in AI policy: Opportunities and Challenges*, 22 September, https://arxiv.org/abs/2009.09071.

Misuraca, G. and van Noordt, C., 2020. *Overview of the Use and Impact of AI in Public Services in the EU*. Luxembourg: Publications Office of the European Union, https://doi.org/10.2760/039619.

Misuraca, G., van Noordt, C. and Boukli, A., 2020. The Use of AI in Public Services: Results from a Preliminary Mapping Across the EU. *Proceedings of the 13th International Conference on Theory and Practice of Electronic Governance (ICEGOV 2020)*, 23–25 September 2020, Athens: Greece, pp. 90–99, https://doi.org/10.1145/3428502.3428513.

Misuraca, G. and Viscusi, G., 2015. Shaping Public Sector Innovation Theory: An Interpretative Framework for ICT-Enabled Governance Innovation. *Electronic Commerce Research*, 15, pp. 303–322, https://doi.org/10.1007/s10660-015-9184-5.

Mittelstadt, B., Allo, P., Taddeo, M., Wachter, S. and Floridi, L., 2016. The Ethics of Algorithms: Mapping the Debate. *Big Data & Society*, pp. 1–21, https://journals.sagepub.com/doi/10.1177/2053951716679679.

Modaxia, 2021. How to Manage the "Single Platform for Urban Management" ["一网统管" 怎么管]. *Zhihu* [知乎专栏], 21 September, https://zhuanlan.zhihu.com/p/412455354.

Molinari, F., van Noordt, C., Vaccari, L., Pignatelli, F. and Tangi, L., 2021. *AI Watch. Beyond Pilots: Sustainable Implementation of AI in Public Services*. Luxembourg: Publications Office of the European Union, https://publications.jrc.ec.europa.eu/repository/handle/JRC126665.

Moore, M., 1995. *Creating Public Value: Strategic Management in Government*. Cambridge: Harvard University Press.

Moore, M., 2013. *Recognizing Public Value*. Cambridge: Harvard University Press.

Mukherjee, I. and Bali, A., 2019. Policy Effectiveness and Capacity: Two Sides of the Design Coin. *Policy Design and Practice*, 2(2), pp. 103–114, https://ink.library.smu.edu.sg/soss_research/3036.

Murdick, D., Dunham, J. and Melot, J., 2020. *AI Definitions Affect Policymaking*. Center for Security and Emerging Technology, https://cset.georgetown.edu/research/ai-definitions-affect-policymaking/.

Nature Machine Intelligence, 2020. Materializing Artificial Intelligence. *Nature Machine Intelligence*, 2(653), November 2020, https://doi.org/10.1038/s42256-020-00262-2.

OECD (Organisation for Economic Co-operation and Development), 2018. *AI: Intelligent Machines, Smart Policies*. Conference Summary, Paris, France, 26–27 October 2017. OECD Digital Economy Papers, August 2018, No. 270, https://www.oecdilibrary.org/science-and-technology/ai-intelligent-machines-smart-policies_f1a650d9-en.

OECD, 2019a. *Artificial Intelligence in Society*. Revised version, August 2019. Paris: OECD Publishing, https://doi.org/10.1787/eedfee77-en.

OECD, 2019b. *Scoping the OECD AI Principles: Deliberations of the Expert Group on Artificial Intelligence at the OECD (AIGO)*. OECD Digital Economy Papers, November 2019, No. 291, https://www.oecd-ilibrary.org/science-and-technology/scoping-the-oecd-ai-principles_d62f618a-en.

Ojo, A., Mellouli, S. and Ahmadi Zeleti, F., 2019. A Realist Perspective on AI-Era Public Management. *dg.o 2019: Proceedings of the 20th Annual International Conference on Digital Government Research*, pp. 159–170, https://doi.org/10.1145/3325112.3325261.

Oxford Insights and IDRC (International Research Development Centre), 2020. *Government AI Readiness Index 2020*. Oxford Insights and IDRC, on file with the author.

Painter, M. and Pierre, J., 2005. Unpacking Policy Capacity: Issues and Themes. In: Painter M. and Pierre, J. eds., 2005. *Challenges to State Policy Capacity: Global Trends and Comparative Perspectives*. Basingstoke: Palgrave Macmillan, pp. 1–18.

Paleyes, A., Urma, R. and Lawrence, N., 2020. Challenges in Deploying Machine Learning: a Survey of Case Studies. *NeurIPS 2020 Workshop: ML Retrospectives, Surveys & Meta-Analyses (ML-RSA)*, https://doi.org/10.48550/arXiv.2011.09926.

Pan, Y., Tian, Y., Liu, X., Gu, D. and Hua, G., 2016. Urban Big Data and the Development of City Intelligence. *Engineering*, 2(2), pp. 171–178, https://doi.org/10.1016/J.ENG.2016.02.003.

Panagiotopoulos, P., Klievink, B. and Cordella, A., 2019. Public Value Creation in Digital Government. *Government Information Quarterly*, 36(4), pp. 1–8, https://doi.org/10.1016/j.giq.2019.101421.

Partnership for Public Service and IBM (IBM Center for the Business of Government), 2018. *The Future Has Begun: Using Artificial Intelligence to Transform Government*. IBM Center for the Business of Government, 8 January, http://www.businessofgovernment.org/sites/default/files/Using%20Artificial%20Intelligence%20to%20Transform%20Government.pdf.

Pencheva, I., Esteve, M. and Mikhaylov, S., 2020. Big Data and AI—A Transformational Shift for Government: So, What's Next for Research? *Public Policy and Administration*, 35(1), pp. 24–44, https://doi.org/10.1177/0952076718780537.

Pinch, T. and Bijker, W., 1987. The Social Construction of Facts and Artifacts: Or How the Sociology of Science and the Sociology of Technology Might Benefit Each Other. In: Bijker, W., Hughes, T. and Pinch, T. eds., 1987. *The Social Construction of Technological Systems: New Directions in the Sociology and History of Technology*, Cambridge: MIT Press, pp. 17–50.

Reis, J., Santo, P. and Melão, N., 2019. Artificial Intelligence in Government Services: A Systematic Literature Review. In: Rocha Á., Adeli H., Reis L., Costanzo S. eds., 2019. New Knowledge in Information Systems and Technologies. *WorldCIST'19 2019. Advances in Intelligent Systems and Computing*, 930, pp. 241–252, https://doi.org/10.1007/978-3-030-16181-1_23.

Roberts, H., Cowls, J., Morley, J., Taddeo, M., Wang, V. and Floridi, L., 2020. The Chinese Approach to Artificial Intelligence: An Analysis of Policy, Ethics, and Regulation. *AI & Society*, 36, pp. 59–77, https://doi.org/10.1007/s00146-020-00992-2.

Rossi, F., 2021. Can We Really Define AI? Presentation at the Online Seminar *Regulation: What We Need to Talk About When We Talk About AI*, Humane AI Net, 3 June, https://www.humane-ai.eu/event/regulation/.

Russell, S. and Norvig, P., 1995. *Artificial Intelligence: A Modern Approach.* Englewood Cliffs: Prentice Hall.

Saich, T., 2008. *Providing Public Goods in Transitional China.* New York: Palgrave Macmillan.

Scantamburlo, T., Charlesworth, A. and Cristianini, N., 2018. Machine Decisions and Human Consequences. On file with the author.

Schaefer, C., Lemmer, K., Kret, K., Ylinen, M., Mikalef, P. and Niehaves, B., 2021. Truth or Dare?—How can we Influence the Adoption of Artificial Intelligence in Municipalities? *Proceedings of the 54th Hawaii International Conference on System Sciences*, pp. 2347–2356, http://hdl.handle.net/10125/70899.

Schmid, J. and Wang, F., 2016. Beyond National Innovation Systems: Incentives and China's Innovation Performance. *Journal of Contemporary China*, 26(104), pp. 280–296, https://doi.org/10.1080/10670564.2016.1223108.

Selbst, A., Boyd, D., Friedler, S., Venkatasubramanian, S. and Vertesi, J., 2019. Fairness and Abstraction in Sociotechnical Systems. *FAT* '19: Proceedings of the Conference on Fairness, Accountability, and Transparency*, pp. 59–68, https://doi.org/10.1145/3287560.3287598.

Sheehan, M., 2018. How China's Massive AI Plan Actually Works. *MacroPolo*, 13 February, https://macropolo.org/chinas-massive-ai-plan-actually-works/.

Sheehan, M., 2019. *The Transpacific Experiment: How China and California Collaborate and Compete for Our Future.* Counter Point Press.

SHFDI (Shanghai Foreign Investment Development Board), 2020. *Shanghai Foreign Investment Guide 2020* [2020上海外商投资指南], https://www.investsh.org.cn/upload/index/2020%20Shanghai%20Foreign%20Investment%20Guide.pdf.

SHFDI, 2021. *Shanghai Foreign Investment Guide 2021* [2021上海外商投资指南], https://www.investsh.org.cn/upload/upload/channel/file/2021_2/4_30/04koko3pi67s.pdf.

SJTU, CAICT and SEIDC (Shanghai Jiatong University AI Institute, China Academy of Information and Communications Technology Easter China Institute and Shanghai Economic and Information Development Research Center), ed. 2019. *AI@SH Action Report. Exploration and Practice of Building An Artificial Intelligence Development Highland in Shanghai* [AI@SH 行动报告—上海打造人工智能发展高地的探索与实践]. SJTU, CAICT and SHEITC [上海交通大学人工智能研究院, 中国信息通信研究院华东分院, 上海市经济和信息化发展研究中心], on file with the author.

Snyder, H., 2019. Literature Review as a Research Methodology: An Overview and Guidelines. *Journal of Business Research*, 104, pp. 333–339, https://doi.org/10.1016/j.jbusres.2019.07.039.

Sousa, W., Melo, E., Bermejo, P., Farias, R. and Gomes, A., 2019. How and Where is Artificial Intelligence in the Public Sector Going? A Literature Review and Research Agenda (Review). *Government Information Quarterly*, 36(4), pp. 1–14, https://doi.org/10.1016/j.giq.2019.07.004.

Stanford University, 2016. *Artificial Intelligence and Life in 2030: One Hundred Year Study on Artificial Intelligence*, Stanford: Stanford University, https://ai100.stanford.edu/2016-report.

Stanford University, 2019. *The AI Index 2019 Annual Report*. AI Index Steering Committee, Institute for Human-Centered AI, Stanford: Stanford University, December 2019, https://hai.stanford.edu/sites/default/files/ai_index_2019_report.pdf.

Stanford University, 2021a. *The AI Index 2021 Annual Report*. AI Index Steering Committee, Institute for Human-Centered AI, Stanford: Stanford University, March 2021, https://aiindex.stanford.edu/report/.

Stanford University, 2021b. *Gathering Strength, Gathering Storms: The One Hundred Year Study on Artificial Intelligence (AI100) 2021 Study Panel Report*. Stanford: Stanford University, September 2021, http://ai100.stanford.edu/2021-report.

Stanford University, 2023. *The AI Index 2023 Annual Report*. AI Index Steering Committee, Institute for Human-Centered AI, Stanford: Stanford University, April 2023, https://aiindex.stanford.edu/wp-content/uploads/2023/04/HAI_AI-Index-Report_2023.pdf.

Stanton, C., Lung, V., Zhang, N., Ito, M., Weber, S. and Charlet, K., 2019. What the Machine Learning Value Chain Means for Geopolitics. *Communications of the Association for Computing Machinery*, https://cacm.acm.org/news/238651-what-the-machine-learning-value-chain-means-for-geopolitics/fulltext.

Stepan, M. and Duckett, J. eds., 2018. *Serve the People: Innovation and IT in China's Social Development Agenda*. Mercator Institute for China Studies, https://merics.org/en/report/serve-people.

Sun, T. and Medaglia, R., 2019. Mapping the Challenges of Artificial Intelligence in the Public Sector: Evidence from Public Healthcare. *Government Information Quarterly*, 36 (2), pp. 368–383, https://www.sciencedirect.com/science/article/abs/pii/S0740624X17304781.

Sun, Y. and Cao, C., 2014. Demystifying Central Government R&D Spending in China. *Science*, 345(6200), pp. 1006–1008, https://www.science.org/doi/10.1126/science.1253479?cookieSet=1.

Tao, Y., 2020. The Modernization of Public Management in the Era of Artificial Intelligence [人工智能时代公共管理现代化发展之路]. *Audit Observation* [审计观察], 2020 (8), pp. 64-67.

Teets, J. and Hasmath, R., 2020. The Evolution of Policy Experimentation in China. *Journal of Asian Public Policy*, 13(1), pp. 49–59, https://doi.org/10.1080/17516234.2020.1711491.

Teets, J., Hasmath, R. and Lewis, O., 2017. The Incentive to Innovate? The Behavior of Local Policymakers in China. *Journal of Chinese Political Science*, 22, pp. 505–517, https://doi.org/10.1007/s11366-017-9512-9.

Tencent and CAICT (Tencent Research Institute, Tencent AI Lab and China Academy of Information and Communications Technology), 2017. *Artificial Intelligence: A National Strategic Initiative for Artificial Intelligence* [人工智能: 国家人工智能战略行动抓手]. Beijing: China Renmin University Press.

Tinholt, D., Carrara, W. and van der Linden, N., 2017. Unleashing the Potential of Artificial Intelligence in the Public Sector. *Capgemini Consulting*, https://www.capgemini.com/consulting/wp-content/uploads/sites/30/2017/10/ai-in-public-sector.pdf.

Toll, D., Lindgren, I., Melin, U. and Madsen, C., 2020. Values, Benefits, Considerations and Risks of AI in Government: A Study of AI Policy Documents in Sweden. *JeDEM—EJournal of EDemocracy and Open Government*, 12(1), pp. 40–60, https://doi.org/10.29379/jedem.v12i1.593.

Triolo, P. and Goodrich, J. 2018. From Riding a Wave to Full Steam Ahead: As China's Government Mobilizes for AI Leadership, Some Challenges Will Be Tougher Than Others. *New America DigiChina Project*, 28 February, https://www.newamerica.org/cybersecurity-initiative/digichina/blog/riding-wave-full-steam-ahead/.

Tsinghua University, 2018. *China AI Development Report 2018*. Beijing: China Institute for Science and Technology Policy at Tsinghua University, on file with the author.

Turner, J., 2019. *Robot Rules. Regulating Artificial Intelligence*. London: Palgrave Macmillan.

Twizeyimana, J. and Andersson, A., 2019. The Public Value of E-Government—A Literature Review. *Government Information Quarterly*, 36(2), pp. 167–178, https://doi.org/10.1016/j.giq.2019.01.001.

UNESCAP (United Nations Economic and Social Commission for Asia and the Pacific), 2018. *Evolution of Science, Technology and Innovation Policies for Sustainable Development: The Experiences of China, Japan, the Republic of Korea and Singapore*, UNESCAP, https://www.unescap.org/sites/default/files/publications/UN_STI_Policy_Report_2018.pdf.

United Nations, 2020. *E-Government Survey 2020. Digital Government in the Decade of Action for Sustainable Development*. New York: United Nations, https://publicadministration.un.org/en/Research/UN-e-Government-Surveys.

Valle-Cruz, D., Criado, J., Sandoval-Almazán, R. and Ruvalcaba-Gomez, E., 2020. Assessing the Public Policy-Cycle Framework in the Age of Artificial Intelligence: From Agenda-Setting to Policy Evaluation. *Government Information Quarterly*, 37(4), pp. 1–12, https://doi.org/10.1016/j.giq.2020.101509.

Van de Poel, I., 2020. Embedding Values in Artificial Intelligence (AI) Systems. *Minds and Machines*, 30, pp. 385–409, https://doi.org/10.1007/s11023-020-09537-4.

Van Noordt, C. and Misuraca, G., 2020. Evaluating the Impact of Artificial Intelligence Technologies in Public Services: Towards an Assessment Framework. *Proceedings of the 13th International Conference on Theory and Practice of Electronic Governance* (ICEGOV 2020), 23–25 September 2020, Athens: Greece, pp. 8–16, https://doi.org/10.1145/3428502.3428504.

Wang, X. and Wang, X., 2019. "Technological Leviathan": Potential Risks of Artificial Intelligence Embedded in Social Governance and Government Response ["技术利维坦": 人工智能嵌入社会治理的潜在风险与政府应对]. *E-Government* [电子政务], 5(197), pp. 86–93.

Webster, G. ed., 2019. AI Policy and China. Realities of State-Led Development. *Stanford-New America DigiChina Project*, Special Report No. 1, 29 October, https://d1y8sb8igg2f8e.cloudfront.net/documents/DigiChina-AI-report-20191029.pdf.

Wirtz, B. and Müller, W., 2019. An Integrated Artificial Intelligence Framework for Public Management. *Public Management Review*, 21(7), pp. 1076–1100, https://doi.org/10.1080/14719037.2018.1549268.

Wirtz B., Weyerer J. and Geyer, C., 2019. Artificial Intelligence in the Public Sector—Applications and Challenges. *International Journal of Public Administration*, 42(7), pp. 596–615, https://www.tandfonline.com/doi/abs/10.1080/01900692.2018.1498103?journalCode=lpad20.

Woo, J., 2021. *Capacity-building and Pandemics. Singapore's Response to Covid-19*. Singapore: Palgrave Macmillan.

Wu, X., 2021. Application Dilemmas and Policy Suggestions for AI in Government Governance [人工智能在政府治理中的应用困境与政策建议]. *China National Conditions and Strength* [中国国情国力], 8(343), pp. 51–53.

Wu, X., Howlett, M. and Ramesh, M. eds., 2018. *Policy Capacity and Governance: Assessing Governmental Competences and Capabilities in Theory and Practice*. Cham: Palgrave Macmillan.

Wu, X., Ramesh, M. and Howlett, M., 2015. Policy Capacity: A Conceptual Framework for Understanding Policy Competences and Capabilities. *Policy and Society*, 34, pp. 165–171, https://www.tandfonline.com/doi/full/10.1016/j.polsoc.2015.09.001.

Xu, C., 2011. The Fundamental Institutions of China's Reforms and Development. *Journal of Economic Literature*, 49(4), pp. 1076–1151, https://www.jstor.org/stable/23071664?seq=1.

Xu, L. and Xu, C., 2020. Double Orientations of Political Power in the Era of AI [人工智能时代政治权力的双重面相]. *Journal of Lanzhou University (Social Sciences)* [兰州大学学报 (社会科学版)], 48(221), pp. 56–63.

Xue, L., 1997. A historical perspective of China's innovation system reform: a case study. *Journal of Engineering and Technology Management*, 14(1), pp. 67–81, https://doi.org/10.1016/S0923-4748(97)00002-7.

Yang, K., 2021. Innovative Thinking and Analysis of Social Risk Governance in the Era of Artificial Intelligence [人工智能时代的社会风险治理创新思考分析]. *Digital Technology & Application* [数字技术与应用], 39(9), pp. 162–164.

Young, M., Katell, M. and Krafft, P., 2019. Municipal Surveillance Regulation and Algorithmic Accountability. *Big Data & Society*, 6(2), pp. 1–14, https://doi.org/10.1177/2053951719868492.

Yu, W., 2020. Artificial Intelligence and Public Management: Opportunities and Challenges [人工智能与公共管理: 机遇与挑战]. *Journal of Beijing University of Aeronautics and Astronautics (Social Sciences Edition)* [北京航空航天大学学报 (社会科学版)], 33(4), pp. 50–54.

Yu, X. and Cui, Z., 2020. Research on Artificial Intelligence and Public Management: Technological Possibility, Issue Reconstruction and Governance Innovation [人工智能与公共管理研究: 技术可能性、议题重构和治理创新]. *Chinese Public Administration* [国行政管理], 2020 (3), pp. 6–11.

Zeng, J., 2021. China's Artificial Intelligence Innovation: A Top-Down National Command Approach? *Global Policy*, 12(3), pp. 399–409, https://doi.org/10.1111/1758-5899.12914.

Zeng, Y., Lu, E. and Huangfu, C., 2019. Linking Artificial Intelligence Principles. *Proceedings of the AAAI Workshop on Artificial Intelligence Safety*, https://arxiv.org/abs/1812.04814.

Zhang, L., Feng, X. and Tang, Z., 2019. The Realistic Basis and Path Choice of Building a Smart Society in China—An Analytical Dimension Based on Technology and System [中国建设智慧社会的现实基础与路径选择 — 基于技术与制度的分析维度]. *E-Government* [电子政务], 4(196), pp. 18–26.

Zhang, Q., 2019. Artificial Intelligence and the Normative Prospects of Public Services [人工智能与公共服务的规范前景]. *Administrative Tribune* [行政论坛], 2019 (6), pp. 115–120.

Zhang, Y. and Zhu, X., 2019. Multiple Mechanisms of Policy Diffusion in China. *Public Management Review*, 21(4), pp. 495–514, https://doi.org/10.1080/14719037.2018.1497695.

Zhang, W., Zuo, N., He, W., Li, S. and Yu, L., 2021. Factors Influencing the Use of Artificial Intelligence in Government: Evidence from China. *Technology in Society*, 66, pp. 1–16, https://doi.org/10.1016/j.techsoc.2021.101675.

Zheng, Y., Yu, H., Cui, L., Miao, C., Leung, C. and Yang, Q., 2018. SmartHS: An AI Platform for Improving Government Service Provision. *Proceedings of the AAAI Conference on Artificial Intelligence*, 32(1), pp. 7704–7711, https://doi.org/10.1609/aaai.v32i1.11382.

Zhou, X., 2020. Organizational Response to COVID-19 Crisis: Reflections on the Chinese Bureaucracy and Its Resilience. *Management and Organization Review*, 16(3), pp. 473–484, https://doi.org/10.1017/mor.2020.29.

Zhou, X. and Lian, H., 2011. Modes of Governance of Chinese Bureaucracy: A "Control-Rights" Theory. On file with the author.

Zhou, X., Lian, H., Ortolano, L. and Ye, Y., 2013. A Behavioral Model of "Muddling-Through" in the Chinese Bureaucracy: The Case of Environmental Protection. *The China Journal*, 70, pp. 120-147, https://doi.org/10.1086/671335.

Zhu, X., 2014. Mandate vs. Championship: Vertical Government Intervention and Diffusion of Innovation in Public Services in Authoritarian China. *Public Management Review*, 16(1), pp. 117–139, https://www.tandfonline.com/doi/abs/10.1080/14719037.2013.798028.

Zuiderwijk, A., Chen, Y. and Salem, F., 2021. Implications of the Use of Artificial Intelligence in Public Governance: A Systematic Literature Review and a Research Agenda. *Government Information Quarterly*, 38(3), pp. 1–19, https://doi.org/10.1016/j.giq.2021.101577.

Main Policy Documents on AI Development in China and Shanghai

Ministry of Education, 2018. *Artificial Intelligence Action Plan for Institutions of Higher Education* [高等学校人工智能创新行动计划]. Jiaoji (2018) 3, 2 April, http://www.moe.gov.cn/srcsite/A16/s7062/201804/t20180410_332722.html.

Ministry of Education, National Development and Reform Commission, and Ministry of Finance, 2020. *Certain Opinions on Promoting Curricula Merging at "Double World-Class" Institutes of Higher Education, and on Accelerating the Cultivation of Graduate Students in the AI Field* [关于 "双一流" 建设高校促进学科融合 加快人工智能领域研究生培养的若干意见]. Jiao Yan (2020), 4, 21 January, https://web.archive.org/web/20201217173647/http:/www.gov.cn/zhengce/zhengceku/2020-03/03/content_5486326.htm.

Ministry of Industry and Information Technology, 2017. *Three-Year Action Plan for Promoting the Development of a New Generation Artificial Intelligence Industry (2018–2020)* [促进新一代人工智能产业发展三年行动计划 (2018–2020年)]. Gongxinbuke (2017) 315, 13 December, http://www.cac.gov.cn/2017-12/15/c_1122114520.htm.

Ministry of Industry and Information Technology, 2018. *Work Plan for Unveiling the Focus Tasks of the New Generation Artificial Intelligence Industry Innovation* [新一代人工智能产业创新重点任务揭榜工作方案]. Gongxin Tingke (2018) 80, 8 November, http://www.gov.cn/zhengce/zhengceku/2018-12/31/content_5443931.htm.

Ministry of Science and Technology, 2021. *Science and Technology Innovation 2030—"New Generation Artificial Intelligence" Major Project 2021 Project Application Guidelines* [科技创新2030—"新一代人工智能" 重大项目2021年度项目申报指南]. Guoke Fazi (2021) 191, 1 July, http://www.ncsti.gov.cn/kjdt/tzgg/202107/t20210707_36198.html.

Ministry of Science and Technology, 2018. *Science and Technology Innovation 2030—"New Generation Artificial Intelligence" Major Project 2018 Project Application Guidelines* [科技创新2030—"新一代人工智能" 重大项目2018年度项目申报指南]. Guoke Fazi (2018) 208, 12 October, http://www.gov.cn/zhengce/zhengceku/2018-12/31/content_5446330.htm.

National Development and Reform Commission, 2017. *The National Development and Reform Commission organization and implementation of the major projects of "Internet +", Artificial Intelligence Innovation Development, and digital economy pilot projects in 2018* [发展改革委组织实施2018年 "互联网+" 、人工智能创新发展和数字经济试点重大工程]. Fagaiban Gaoji (2017) 1668, 11 October, http://www.gov.cn/xinwen/2017-10/29/content_5235181.htm.

National and Development Reform Commission, Ministry of Science and Technology, Ministry of Industry and Information Technology and the Cybersecurity Administration of China, 2016. *Notice on the Release of the "Internet Plus" AI Three-Year Implementation Plan* [关于印发《"互联网+" 人工智能三年行动实施方案》的通]. Fagai Gaoji (2016) 1078, 18 May, http://www.gov.cn/xinwen/2016-05/23/content_5075944.htm.

Shanghai Municipal Commission of Economy and Informatization, 2019. *Action Plan on Building Shanghai into an AI Highland and Creating a First-Class Innovation Ecosystem (2019–2021)* [关于建设人工智能上海高地构建一流创新生态的行动方案 (2019–2021年)]. Hujingxinzhi (2019) 707, 13 September, http://www.sheitc.sh.gov.cn/xxfw/20190923/0020-683713.html.

Shanghai Municipal Commission of Economy and Informatization, Shanghai Development and Reform Commission, Shanghai Science and Technology Commission, Shanghai Human Resources and Social Security Bureau, 2018. *Implementation Measures for Accelerating the high-Quality Development of Artificial Intelligence in Shanghai* [加快推进上海人工智能高质量发展的实施办法]. Hujingxinji (2018) 569, 17 September, http://app.sheitc.sh.gov.cn/sswgh/679122.htm.

Shanghai Municipal Commission of Economy and Informatization, Shanghai Financial Affairs Bureau, 2017. *Shanghai Artificial Intelligence Innovation and Development Special Support Implementation Detailed Rules* [上海市人工智能创新发展专项支持实施细则]. Hujingxinfa (2017) 896, 12 December, http://app.sheitc.sh.gov.cn/zxzjzcwj/685847.htm.

Shanghai Municipal Government, 2017. *Implementation Opinions on Promoting the Development of a New Generation Artificial Intelligence in Shanghai* [关于本市推动新一代人工智能发展的实施意见]. Hufu Banfa (2017) 66, 26 October, http://www.sheitc.sh.gov.cn/cyfz/20171113/0020-675566.html.

State Council, 2017. *New Generation Artificial Intelligence Development Plan* [新一代人工智能发展规划]. Guo Fa (2017) 35, 8 July, http://www.gov.cn/zhengce/content/2017-07/20/content_5211996.htm.

Policy Documents of the Main Initiatives that Foster the Use of AI in the Public Sector in Shanghai

AI Pilot Application Scenarios

SHEITC (Shanghai Municipal Commission of Economy and Informatization) Notice, 2018. *Notice on the Collection of Solutions for the First Batch of AI Application Scenarios in Shanghai* [关于开展本市首批人工智能应用场景解决方案征集工作的通知]. Hujingxintui (2018), no. 963, 14 December, http://www.shpt.gov.cn/kw/tongzhi/20181214/365807.html.

SHEITC Notice, 2019a. *Notice of the Shanghai Municipal Commission of Economy and Informatization on the Announcement of the First Batch of AI Pilot Application Scenarios in Shanghai* [上海市经济信息化委关于公布本市首批人工智能试点应用场景的通知]. Hujingxintui (2019), no. 238, 19 April, http://app.sheitc.sh.gov.cn/xxfw/682323.htm.

SHEITC Notice, 2019b. *Notice on the Collection of Solutions for the Second Batch AI Application Scenarios in Shanghai* [关于征集本市第二批人工智能应用场景解决方案的通知]. Hujingxintui (2019), no. 402, 12 June, http://sheitc.sh.gov.cn/xxfw/20190612/0020-682748.html.

SHEITC Notice, 2019c. *Notice of the Shanghai Municipal Commission of Economy and Informatization on the Announcement of the Second Batch of AI Pilot Application Scenarios in Shanghai* [上海市经济信息化委关于公布本市第二批人工智能试点应用场景的通知]. Hujingxintui (2019), no. 663, 26 August, http://www.sheitc.sh.gov.cn/xxfw/20190902/0020-683526.html.

SHEITC Notice, 2020a. *Notice on the Collection of Solutions for the Third Batch of AI Application Scenarios in Shanghai* [关于征集本市第三批人工智能应用场景解决方案的通知]. Hujingxintui (2020), no. 506, 16 July, http://www.sheitc.sh.gov.cn/xxfw/20200717/aeec0bd27b7742518c4be5e4a55df642.html.

SHEITC Notice, 2020b. *Notice of the Shanghai Municipal Commission of Economy and Informatization on the Announcement of the Third Batch of AI Pilot Application Scenarios in Shanghai* [上海市经济信息化委关于公布本市第三批人工智能试点应用场景的通知]. Hujingxinwei (2020) 1084, 16 December, http://www.sheitc.sh.gov.cn/xxfw/20201216/5f61e1fa133a42408d51a98cda582fa3.html.

Government Online-Offline Shanghai

General Office of the CPC Shanghai Municipal Committee, Shanghai Municipal Government, 2018. *Work Plan for Comprehensively Promoting the "Government Online-Offline Shanghai" to Accelerate the Construction of Smart Government* [全面推进 "一网通办" 加快建设智慧政府工作方案]. Huweibanfa (2018) 14, 30 March, https://www.shanghai.gov.cn/newshanghai/xxgkfj/yiwangtongban.pdf.

Shanghai Municipal Government, 2019. *Working Points for Promoting the "Government Online-Offline Shanghai" in Shanghai in 2019* [2019年上海市推进 "一网通办" 工作要点]. Hufubanfa (2019) 8, 26 March, https://www.shanghai.gov.cn/nw44388/20200824/0001-44388_58587.html.

Shanghai Municipal Government, 2020. *Working points for deepening the reform of the "Government Online-Offline Shanghai" in Shanghai in 2020* [2020年上海市深化 "一网通办" 改革工作要点], 24 February, https://www.shanghai.gov.cn/nw12344/20200813/0001-12344_64071.html.

Shanghai Municipal Government, 2021. *Working points for comprehensively deepening the reform of the "Government Online-Offline Shanghai" in Shanghai in 2021* [2021年上海市全面深化 "一网通办" 改革工作要点], 12 March, https://www.shanghai.gov.cn/nw12344/20210312/4652749fb81d4e9c9ab4029322ff58c4.html.

Shanghai Municipal People's Congress, 2021. *Decision of the Standing Committee of the Shanghai Municipal People's Congress on Further Promoting and Ensuring the Reform of the Government Online-Offline Shanghai* [上海市人民代表大会常务委员会关于进一步促进和保障"一网通办"改革的决定], 23 June, http://www.spcsc.sh.cn/n8347/n8467/u1ai236289.html#:~:text=%E3%80%8A%E4%B8%8A%E6%B5%B7%E5%B8%82%E4%BA%BA%E6%B0%91%E4%BB%A3%E8%A1%A8,7%E6%9C%881%E6%97%A5%E8%B5%B7%E6%96%BD%E8%A1%8C%E3%80%82.

Single Platform for Urban Management

CPC Shanghai Committee, Shanghai Government General Office, 2020. *Three-Year Action Plan for the Construction of the "Single Platform for Urban Management" for Urban Operations in Shanghai (2020–2022)* [上海市城市运行 "一网统管" 建设三年行动计划 (2020–2022)]. Huwei Banfa (2020) 19, 8 May, https://www.digitalelite.cn/h-pd-1136.html.

Shanghai Municipal Government, 2020. *Several Opinions on Further Accelerating the Construction of Smart Cities* [关于进一步加快智慧城市建设的若干意见], 10 February, https://www.shanghai.gov.cn/nw44142/20200824/0001-44142_63566.html.

Shanghai Municipal People's Congress, 2022. *Decision of the Standing Committee of the Shanghai Municipal People's Congress on Further Promoting and Guaranteeing the Construction of the "Single Platform for Urban Management" for Urban Operations* [上海市人民代表大会常务委员会关于进一步促进和保障城市运行 "一网统管" 建设的决定], (XV) 109, 24 May, art. 11, http://www.spcsc.sh.cn/n8347/n8467/u1ai246617.html.

Index

D. Todaro, *The Use of Artificial Intelligence in the Public Sector in Shanghai*, https://doi.org/10.1007/978-981-97-0597-9

Q

R

S

SPRINGER NATURE

GPSR Compliance

The European Union's (EU) General Product Safety Regulation (GPSR) is a set of rules that requires consumer products to be safe and our obligations to ensure this.

If you have any concerns about our products, you can contact us on ProductSafety@springernature.com

In case Publisher is established outside the EU, the EU authorized representative is:

Springer Nature Customer Service Center GmbH
Europaplatz 3
69115 Heidelberg, Germany

FSC
www.fsc.org
MIX
Papier | Fördert gute Waldnutzung
FSC® C083411

Kolibri 360 GmbH
Ferdinand-Jühlke-Straße 7
99095 Erfurt, Deutschland
produktsicherheit@kolibri360.de